AF531378

Air Travel
Ticketing and Fare Construction

AIR TRAVEL TICKETING AND FARE CONSTRUCTION

(With Examination Questions)

Prof. (Dr.) JAGMOHAN NEGI
Ph.D., FHCIMA (London)
Professional Advance Tourism Courses, WTO (Switzerland)
Research Professor, Amity Institute of Travel and Tourism &
Amity School of Hospitality, New Delhi
Formerly Professor Institute of Hotel Management
Director, National Council for Hotel Management, New Delhi
and
Gaurav Manoher
Himalayan Tourism and Recreation in Mountains, New Delhi

KANISHKA PUBLISHERS, DISTRIBUTORS
NEW DELHI 110002

KANISHKA PUBLISHERS, DISTRIBUTORS
4697/5-21A, Ansari Road, Daryaganj
New Delhi -110 002
Phones : 2327 0497, 2328 8285
Fax : 011-2328 8285
E-mail : kanishka_publishing@yahoo.co.in

Air Travel Ticketing and fare Construction

First Published-2004
Second Edition-2019

ISBN: 978-81-7391-628-4

PRINTED IN INDIA

Published by Madan Sachdeva for Kanishka Publishers, Distributors, 4697/5-21A, Ansari Road, Daryaganj, New Delhi-110 002, Typeset by Sunshine Graphics, Delhi, and Printed at Rajdhani Printers, Delhi.

Acknowledgements

We gratefully acknowledge the contributions and cooperation rendered by various individuals, agencies, organisations, companies and universities, educational institutions, whose considerable efforts, suggestions, ideas and insights helped to make this text a valuable and viable learning instrument. Special acknowledgement is due to the staff of the following organisations: Air India, Indian Airlines, Transworld Airlines, British Airways, Modiluft, NEPC Airlines, SITA World Travel, Murcury Travels, Ashok Tour and Travels, Taj Tour and Travel, Travel House (ITC), India Tourism Development Corporation, Taj Group of Hotels, Oberoi Group of Hotels, Welcomgroup, New Delhi, Hilton, Hyatt Regency, Le Meridien, Park Hotel, Hertz, Budget, Rent-a-Car, Airlines Reporting Corporation, American Society of Travel Agents, Air Transport Association of America, Institute of Certified Travel Agents, International Air Transport Association, International Travel Academy, ITT Sheraton, Travel Agents Association of India, Association of Tour Operators, Indian Institute of Travel and Tourism, Department of Tourism (Government of India), Himalayan Tourism and Recreation in Mountains, International Culinary Foundation and a number of educators, consultants, government employees and travel industry executives who have contributed to the preparation of this book at various points in its development. Special thanks are to Shri Madan Sachdeva, Director, Kanishka Publishers, Distributors, New Delhi and his team of staff for putting extra efforts in bringing out this publication in the present form.

JAGMOHAN NEGI
GAURAV MANOHER

Preface

Increase in leisure time, cheaper travel and rising curiosity about land, people and their ways of life promises a bright future for tourism and travel industry. For developing countries the possession of attractive climate, scenery and other tourist resources offer the shape of economic stability and better future for their citizens. Being one of the biggest and dynamic industry, tourism and travel requires all the commitments of any profession being with good education and proper training. While it is partly a glamorous job, it entails much hard work. Properly executed it is emotionally and financially rewarding.

Last few years have seen a dramatic improvement in the way the travel business is conducted. Travel planning time has been reduced from days to minutes. Most reservations networks connect travel agents with hotels and airlines. Others have facilities like car rental reservation and railway reservation. With the connecting facility, all tourist has to do is to visit a travel agent who is a member of a network. Then sitting at a terminal the tourist can plan and reserve his/her entire tour in minutes. With the help of CRS he/she can reserve room after glancing through the fare charts/airline tickets and the seat he/she would prefer on the plane and book a car.

At international level we have reservation systems such as Amadeus, Galileo and SABRE, and many others owned by different groups of airlines. The need for having one system which would connect all their destinations gave birth to these networks. Data and booking facilities on hotels, car rentals and other travel related activities were added as an extension of services to the travellers.

There is an increasing demand for travel industry professionals and the need for specialized training for travel professionals. Many colleges/universities, privately managed institutions are continuously expanding their programmes to include courses on various aspects of travel and tourism.

The book deals extensively and highlights the air travel and role of world airlines in travel business. The book deals in detail the passenger aircraft and airlines, different types of airlines.

Preparation of this book has been challenging because of recent far reaching changes in collegiate education of travel and tourism. Changes that reflect new and different approaches, designed to improve both the policy and practices of managers of today's tourism and travel industry. The work is based on the searching analysis and worldwide findings. Latest thoughts and techniques on airfare construction and ticketing has been incorporated and explained thoroughly in their proper perspective. The book is desired to facilitate the developments and challenges taking place in this worldwide industry. Throughout this book emphasis is laid on basic areas of interest and concern of all students and readers of travel and tourism management not merely for those who contemplate careers as travel and tourism managers. The text is basically prepared and presented for use with or without supplementary readings and cases. The book is organised around the concept that tourism and travel is an integrated part of world developing economy. The aim is to provide a useful introduction for such important topics such as air travel and world airlines, passenger aircraft and different types of aeroplanes, airlines policies and practices, basic elements of airfares, airfare construction, air ticketing techniques, analysis of an airline ticket.

The topics seem complicated and technical in nature, particularly for those persons with a meagre background in travel and tourism profession. The book includes numerous innovations. Many additions resulted from the helpful and practical suggestions from students, professors and professionals who are directly or indirectly connected with this growing industry. The text is supported with figures, tables, diagrams, charts index, containing valuable information for students and readers to get desired information for study and solution of problems and questions.

AUTHORS

Contents

List of Tables

List of Figures

1

Air Travel and World Airlines

After learning this Chapter you shall be able to:

- *explain the term air travel: domestic and international;*
- *understand transport regulations;*
- *know the airlines of the world;*
- *discuss the main requirements of international travel;*
- *get familiar with carrier and airline codes of international carriers;*
- *explain the shared airlines designated codes;*
- *discuss airline classifications and provide examples of various types of carriers;*
- *give the correct carrier code for major airlines;*
- *know the rules and regulations of airlines; co-sharing agreements and fixing the price of the seat;*
- *read and study the time tables of various airlines;*
- *discuss passenger services rules and classes of service;*
- *understand the use of city and airport codes;*
- *identify the locations of major business destinations and tourism attractions.*

AIR TRAVEL

The air transportation industry is also known as commercial aviation industry. It generates a large amount of revenues and employs thousands of people. The airlines may be classified into two broad categories—Commercial Airlines and Major Airlines. Small carriers that operate aircraft with more than 30-seats are defined as commercial airlines and large carriers that fly direct routes between major cities are considered major airlines.

INTERNATIONAL CARRIERS

International Airlines or 'Flag Carriers' represent their country and normally have the country to flag painted on the airplane. The majority of the international carriers are owned and sponsored by the government of that country. The India's Flag Carrier is Air India. The international airlines and routes require agreements between the various governments based on socio-economic considerations as well as the frequency of flights from one nation to another. The IATA attempts to resolve policies and fares applicable to the participating international air carriers.

DOMESTIC CARRIERS

Several hundred airlines serve the world today. There are many airlines providing air transportation. No one air carrier serves every city in one country. These airlines have permanent operating rights within the region. These airlines are hired by the public and operate on a fixed schedule. The domestic carrier operating between the large cities include Sahara, Jet airways, Indian Airlines, etc.

As a travel agent, it is frequently necessary to use several airlines to complete a trip and since no one airline services every city, it becomes essential to know the major route structure and remember the general geographical regions served.

Air transport operation could be conveniently grouped under three broad headings:

(*i*) Scheduled air services,
(*ii*) Non-scheduled air services or chartered services, and
(*iii*) Air taxi services.

Scheduled Air Services

Air services in this category may be international or domestic. They operate on definite routes. They require government licence for their operation. These airlines operate on the basis of published time tables regardless of passenger load factors. These air services can also be categorised in two:

(*i*) State owned or public, and
(*ii*) Private owned.

In India, the public airline is the national flag carrier such as Air India and Indian Airlines Corporation. In USA all the airlines are operated by the private sector. Similarly in India we have Sahara, Jet Airways, etc. which have been operating in private sector. According to their network and relative importance within the air transport business air service carriers other than IA and IAC, may be identified as either second or third force airlines.

Second Force Airlines

The idea of a major force airline in the private sector to complement and compete with the public airline was proposed from time to time. There was also a suggestion that a more liberal policy be adopted towards the licensing of private airlines.

Leading airlines such as Jet Airways, and Sahara which provide competitive or complementary services to the Indian Airlines Corporation fall under this category.

Third Force Airlines or Feeder Services

Airlines which provide a network of regional or local services are included in this category.

Airlines require some assurance of traffic demand before they are prepared to commit their aircraft to regular services on a new route, while air-travellers in their turn require regular and frequent services in order to patronise a new route. Seat prices are high to compensate for low load factor and high overhead before traffic builds up. As soon as the route is popular, the pioneer airline is faced with increasing competition unless it is restricted or protected by the State. This in turn results in lower load factors and either higher price or reduced profit margins.

These aircrafts are designed and build to operate efficiently on either short-medium or long to haul routes. They are not easily interchangeable between routes. Aircraft earn money only while they are on the air. Therefore, they are scheduled for maximum number of hours flying each day.

Non-Scheduled Air Services/Chartered Services

Chartered air services grew on the expense of scheduled services. They reduce their price dramatically by setting a very high break-even load factor and by keeping overhead law. These airlines do not advertise their routes to the public and save on marketing costs, an operation cost, and on head office cost. These airlines are not obliged to operate to a time table. They can choose to withdraw their less fully booked flights. They have freedom to transfer their passengers to other chartered airlines or consolidate their flights with others.

Air Taxis

Air taxies are privately owned aircraft. They accommodate small groups comprising four to eighteen persons. Mostly these aircrafts are used by business travellers. They are very convenient and flexible. Routings can be tailor made for passengers. Small airfield close to destination could be used. Flights can be arranged or routings amended at short notice.

Air Brokers

These are the middlemen who act as intermediaries between aircraft owners and their potential charter market. They act both in an advisory and a sales capacity. Their main task is to find suitable aircraft at the right place both for ad-hoc and series charters. They maintain close contact both with airlines and with the chartered market. They play an important role in securing aircraft seats at times of shortage. They are active intermediaries in tour operator's flight consolidations.

Cabotage Routes

Carriage on routes within the national territory of one country is known as Cabotage routes. This is normally restricted to the national carriers of the country concerned. It has nothing to do with international agreements.

ROLE OF STATE IN AIR TRANSPORT

Air transport plays an important role in the modern society. It has affected the economic, social, political and environmental aspects of development. Some important factors are:

Economic Factors

Air transport has a profound impact on the economy of a region. The state will have to take steps to encourage the development of routes which appear to offer prospects of economic benefits and discourage services on those routes suffering from over capacity.

Competition

The state may have to encourage competition or to intervene where a route monopoly is forcing prices up. Similarly, the state may direct to rationalise excessive competition in order to save energy waste or to ensure profitability for the national flag carrier.

Passenger Safety

This is the first and foremost factor which requires that airlines be licensed and supervised.

Environmental Factors

State controls are also required to reduce noise and pollution.

Public Utility

In some areas air transport is an essential public utility, specially the distance places, deserts, islands and mountainous regions. It may not be commercially viable but be socially desirable to provide communication within a region where geographical terrain may make other form of transport difficult or impossible. The state provides necessary financial support or subsidy to maintain the service.

These factors, require the regulations of air transport both at national as well as international level.

AIR TRANSPORT REGULATIONS

The state regulates the air services in various ways. Three important methods of regulations are:

1. Regulation of Airports
2. Regulation of airfares
3. Approval and licensing.

Airports

At international level, scheduled air routes are assigned on the basis of agreement between the governments of the concerned countries.

Air Fares

At the international level, schedule airfares are established by the mutual agreement of the airline concerned and through the mediation of traffic conferences of IATA. Agreed tariffs are then subject to rectification by the appropriate governments.

Approval and Licence

At national level, the national government approves and licenses the carriers which are to operate on schedule routes, whether domestically or internationally. In India DGCA is assigned this responsibility and is made responsible for the licensing of charter and of tour operations organising package holidays abroad.

International Agreements

Air transport regulations are the result of number of international agreements between countries. The two important agreements are:

1. The Warshaw Convention, 1929.
2. Chicago Convention on Civil Aviation, 1944.

The Warshaw Convention, 1929 is the first common agreement on the extent of liability of the airlines in the event of death or injury of passengers or loss of passenger luggage.

In Chicago Convention on Civil Aviation 1944, eighty government designed to promote world air services and reached on agreement on standard operating procedures for air service between countries. The outcome of this meeting was the foundation of International Civil Aviation Organisation (ICAO), (which is now a specialised body of UNO) and the establishment of five freedoms of the air.

FIVE FREEDOMS OF AIR

As per the Chicago Convention, there are five privileges of the air at international level:

1. Flying across a country without landing.
2. Landing in a country for purposes other than the carriage of passengers or freight, *i.e.,* in order to refuel aircraft.
3. Off loading passengers, mail or freight from an aircraft of the country from which those passengers, mail or freight originated.
4. Loading passengers mail or freight on an aircraft of the country to which those passengers, mail or freight are destined.
5. Loading passenger's mail or freight on an aircraft not belonging to a country to which those passengers mail or freight are destined and off loading passengers, mail or freight from an aircraft not of the country from which those originated.

These five freedoms of the air privileges were designed to provide the framework for bilateral agreements between countries and to ensure that carriage of passengers, mail and freight between two countries would normally be restricted to the carriers of those countries.

In airline schedules and tariffs, each carrier or airline is referred to by a two-letter carrier code. For example AI is the code for Air India, DL is the carrier code for Delta and UA is the code for United Airlines. A 'tariff' is a rate book of air fares offered by IATA carriers. Carrier codes are designated by the International Air Transport Association (IATA), which represents more than 200 of the world's principal airlines. Each carrier also has a three digit airline code designated by IATA.

Commuter airlines, operate on short routes to enable passengers in smaller towns and cities to connect to cities with major airports. The commuter airlines, generally entered into special partnership agreement with major airlines. Such agreements entitle a commuter carrier to use the name of major airline. This type of arrangement is called code-sharing agreement.

Chartered airlines are airlines that have limited schedules and lease, or charter, aircraft to large groups or to other airlines. For example, an athletic club might charter an aircraft to travel to a competition. Flight are also chartered by major airlines to handle passengers over-loads. An over-load exists when the number of confirmed reservations on a particular flight, it might charter an aircraft to handle the over-load. An airline that is in financial trouble may use chartered planes to avoid the cost of purchasing new aircrafts.

AIRLINES OF THE WORLD

This listing in Table 1.2 gives the head office address of same of the scheduled airlines included in OAG Airlines. The two character code (*e.g.*, AM) immediately following the airline name is the airline designator. The three-figure number (*e.g.*, 139) is the IATA Form Number, used on tickets and air waybills.

The 2-character airline designators, assigned by IATA, are for use in reservations, timetables, ticketing, legal, tariffs, air waybills, schedule publications and in airline interline telecommunications as well as for other airline industry applications.

Table 1.1: Airline Features

EXPLANATION OF SIGNS AND SYMBOLS

①	Monday	Ex	Exceptions to daily service
②	Tuesday	★	Following day
③	Wednesday	▭	Free baggage allowance
④	Thursday	Σ	Meal served on board
⑤	Friday	Σ	Light refreshments served on board
⑥	Saturday	**P**	First Class Premium
⑦	Sunday	**F**	First Class
ρ	Daily	**J**	Business Class Premium
C	Business Class	**L**	Economy/Coach Discounted
S	Economy/Coach	**N**	Off-peak Fares applicable
Y	Economy/Coach	★	Cargo/Mail service only
B	Economy/Coach Discounted	♦	No local traffic accepted or traffic restricted as shown between points indicated
M	Economy/Coach Discounted		
Q	Economy/Coach Discounted		
T	Economy/Coach Discounted	✧	Stopover traffic only permitted between points indicated
K	Economy/Coach Discounted		

Table 1.2: Airlines of the World

▲ Active member of IATA.
Δ Associate member of IATA.
★ Cargo carrier only

AB Airlines

—See Air Briston

Aero Asia International (PVT) E1 532

43-J Block 6, P.E.C.H.S., Karachi 75400, Pakistan Tel: (21) 435980/ 446462 Fax: (21) 455 8344

AHK Air Hong Kong Ltd. LD ★ 288

201, Block 1, Tien Chu Center, 72 Pak Tai Street, Kowloon, Hong Kong Tel: 761 3632 Tlx: 37625 HX Fax: 761 3869

Air Bristol (d/b/a AB Airlines) 7L 698

Enterprise House, London Stansted Airport, Stansted, Essex CM241QW, England, U.K. Tel: (01279) 680909 (reservations 0345 46473)

Air Fiji PC 677

185 Victoria Parade, P.O. Box 1259, Suva, Fiji Tel. 314666 Tlx: 2258 FJ Fax: 30077

(*Contd.*)

(Contd.)

Air France AF ▲ 057

45 Rue de Paris, Roissy C.D.G. Cedex, 95747 France Tel: 43 23 81 81 Cable: AIRFRANS Tlx: 200666 Fax: 43 23 97 11

Air Kazakstan 9Y 452

111 Zhibek Zholy, Almaty, Kazakstan 480 004 Fax: (3272) 33 11 92

Air Lanka Ltd. UL ▲ 603

Grindlays Bank Building, 37 York Street, Colombo 1, Sri Lanka Tel: (1) 73 5555 Tlx: 21401 LANKAIR CE Fax: (1) 73 5122

Air Maldives L6 ▲ 900

Ameeru Ahmed Magu, Male 20-25, Republic of Maldives Tel: 32 24 38 Tlx: 77058 AIRMALE MF Fax: 32 50 56

Air Mauritius Ltd. MK ▲ 239

5 President John Kennedy Street, P.O. Box 441, Port Louis, Mauritius Tel: 208 7700 Cable: AIRMAU Tlx: 4414 IW Airmau Fax: 208 8331

Air Pacific Ltd. FJ ▲ 260

Private Mail Bag, Nadi Airport, Fiji Tel: 72 07 77 Tlx: 5131 FI Fax: 72 06 86

Air Philippines Corporation 3G

7/F Ramon Magsyasay Center, Roxas Boulevard, Manila, Philippines Tel: (2) 843 7001/25 Fax: (2) 845 1980

Air South Airlines Inc. WV 399

P.O. Box 280457, Columbia, South Carolina 29228, U.S.A. Tel: (803) 771 0038 Fax: (803) 771 9067

Air Tran Airways Inc. FL 332

6280 Hazeltine National Drive, Orlando, Florida 32822, U.S.A.

Air UK Ltd. UK ▲ 130

Stansted House, Stansted Airport, Essex CM24 1QT, England, U.K. Tel: (01279) 680 146 Tlx: 817052 Fax: (01279) 680 012

Air Zimbabwe Corp. UM ▲ 168

P.O. Box AP 1, Harare Airport, Harare, Zimbabwe Tel: (4) 575111 Tlx: 24383 ZW Fax: (4) 575068

American International Airways CB ★ 571

10054, Postal Road, Los Angeles, California 90045, U.S.A. Tel: (310) 641-5121

Avia Company Turkmenistan T5 542

Ashkhabad Airport, Ashkhabad, Turkmenistan

(Contd.)

(*Contd.*)

Bangkok Airways Co. PG 829

60 Queen Sirikit National Convention Center, New Rajadapisek Road, Klongioey, Bangkok, Thailand 10110 Tel: (2) 253 40 04 Tlx: 82654 BKPTH Fax: (2) 253 40 05

Biman Bangladesh Airlines BG ▲ 997

Motijheel C/A, Dhaka 1000, Bangladesh Tel: (2) 24 01 51 Cable: AIRBANGLA Tlx: 642649 Fax: (2) 86 30 05

British Airways BA ▲ 125

P.O. Box 10, Speedbird House, Heathrow Airport (London), Hounslow, Midx TW6 2JA, England, U.K. Tel: (0181) 759-5511 Cable: BRITISHAIR Tlx: 8813983 BAWYSC Fax: (0181) 562 9930

Canadian Airlines International Ltd. CP ▲ 018

700 2nd Street SW, Suite 2800, Calgary, Alberta, T2P 2W2 Canada Tel: (403) 294-2000 Cable: CANPACAIR Tlx: 03821124 Fax: (403) 294-2066

China Airlines Ltd. CI 297

131 Nanking East Road, Sec. 3 Taipei 104, Taiwan, Republic of China Tel: (2) 715-2626 Tlx: 11346 CHINAIR Fax: (2)-717-5120

Commercial Airways (Pty.) Ltd. MN ▲ 161

P.O. Box 7015, Bonaero Park, Gauteng 1622, South Africa Tel: (11) 921 01 11 Tlx: 7-46738 SA Fax: (11) 973 39 13

Cyprus Airways Ltd. CY ▲ 048

21 Alkeou Street, P.O. Box 1903, Nicosia, Cyprus Tel: (2) 443054 Tlx: 3855 Fax: (2) 443167

Delta Air Lines Inc. DL ▲ 006

1030 Delta Boulevard, Atlanta, Georgia 30320, U.S.A. Tel: (404) 715-2600 Tlx: 542316 Fax: (404) 767-8499

Deutsche BA Luftfahrtgesellschaft GmbH DI ▲ 944

Wartungsallee 13, Munchen-Flughafen 85356, Germany Tel: (89) 97 1500 Fax: (89) 975 91503

Eagle Aviation Y4 ▲ 067

P.O. Box 93926, Mombasa, Kenya Tel: (11) 227268 Tlx: (11) 432636

Egyptair MS ▲ 077

Cairo International Airport, Cairo, Egypt Tel: (2) 390 24 44 Tlx: 92116 EGYOP UN Fax: (2) 390 15 57

(*Contd.*)

(*Contd.*)

Emirates EK ▲ 176

P.O. Box 686, Dubai, United Arab Emirates Tel: (4) 82 2511 Tlx: 49262 EKENG EM Fax: (4) 82 2357

Ethiopian Airlines Enterprise ET ▲ 071

P.O. Box 1755, Bole Airport, Addis Ababa, Ethiopia Tel: (1) 61 22 22 Tlx: 21012 ETHAIR Fax: (1) 61 14 74

Everest Air E2

P.O. Box 482, Durbar Marg, Kathmandu, Nepal Tel: (1) 229412 Fax: (1) 226795

Florida Gulf (Division of US Airways Express) US

c/o US Airways

Garuda Indonesia GA ▲ 126

Jalan Merdeka Selatan No. 13, P.O. Box 1164, Jakarta 10110, Indonesia Tel: 3801901 Cable: GARUDAIR Tlx: 49113 GIA JKT Fax: 21-363595

Gujarat Airways G8

Vanijya Bhavan, Race Course Road, Vadodara 390007, India Tel: (265) 330664/322926 Fax: (265) 339628

Hawaiian Airlines HA 173

Honolulu International Airport, P.O. Box 30008, Honolulu, Hawaii 96820, U.S.A. Tel: (808) 537-5100 Cable: HAWAIR Tlx: 70483707

Hong Kong Dragon Airlines Ltd. (d/b/a Dragonair) KA ▲ 043

22nd Floor, Devon House, Taikoo Place, 979 Kings Road, Quarry Bay, Hong Kong Tel: 25 90 13 28 Tlx: 45936 DRAGH HX Fax: 25 90 13 33

Indian Airlines IC ▲ 058

Airlines House, 113 Gurdwara Rakabganj Road, New Delhi 110 001, India Tel: 388951 (8 lines) Cable: INDAIRCOR Tlx: 031-66110 ICHQ Fax: 381730/381410

Istanbul Airlines IL

Firuzkoy Yolu, No. 26, Avcilar, Istanbul, 34850, Turkey Tel: (212) 509 2121 Tlx: 21022/2102 Fax: (212) 593 6035

Japan Airlines Co. Ltd. JL ▲ 131

2-4-11 Higashi Shinagawa, Shinagawa-ku, Tokyo 140, Japan Tel: 5460-3756 Cable: JAPANAIR Fax: 5460-5973

Jet Airways Inc. QJ ★ 508

100 Everett Avenue, Suite 15, Chelsea, Massachusetts 02150, U.S.A. Tel: (617) 887 3300 Fax: (617) 887 3310

(*Contd.*)

(*Contd.*)

Jet Airways (India) Private Ltd. 9W ▲ 589

41/42 Maker Chambers III, Nariman Point, Mumbai 400 021, India Tel: (22) 821-5080 Fax: (22) 821-5079

Kazakhstan Airlines K4 ▲ 736

Zheltoksan Street 59, Almaty 480004, Rep. of Kazakhstan Tel: 32 72 336349 Fax: 32 72 335506

KLM-Royal Dutch Airlines KL ▲ 074

Amsterdamsweg 55, Amstelveen, 1182 GP, Netherlands Tel: 020-6499123 Cable: TRANSAERA Tlx: 11252 Fax: 020-6488391

Kuwait Airways Corporation KU ▲ 229

P.O. Box 394, Kuwait International Airport, Safat 13004, Kuwait Tel: 434-5555/6666/7777 Tlx: 23036/23067 KT Fax: 431-9912

Kyrghyzstan Airlines K2 758

Manas Airport Bishkek 720062, Kyrghyzstan Tel: (331) 2 313084 Tlx: 245166 PORT SU Fax: (331) 2 313084

Lufthansa Cargo AG LH ★ 020

Frachthof 3, Frankfurt Am Main, 6000 Germany Tlx: 4189 142 GCS D

Lufthansa German Airlines AG (Deutsche Lufthansa AG) LH 220

Von-Gablenz-Strasse 2-6, Cologne 50664, Germany Tel: (0221) 8260 Cable: LUFTHANSA KOLN Tlx: 8873531 Fax: (0221) 826 3818

Malaysia Airline System Berhad MH ▲ 232

33rd Floor, Bangunan MAS, Jalan Sultan Ismail, Kuala Lumpur 50250, Malaysia Tel: 2610555 Fax: 60-3-7462581

National Airlines Chile S.A. N4 ▲ 813

Huerfanos 725, Piso 3-B, Santiago, Chile

Nepal Airways 7E

Hattisar, P.O. Box 11, Kathmandu, Nepal Tel: (1) 410786 Fax: (1) 416574

Nigeria Airways Ltd. WT ▲ 087

Airways House, Murtala Mohammed Airport, P.O. Box 136, Lagos, Nigeria Tel: 900476 Cable: AIRNIGERIA Tlx: 22646

Northwest Airlines Inc. NW ▲ 012

501, Northwest Drive, M.S.B4940, St. Paul, Minnesota 55111-3034, U.S.A. Tel: (612) 726-2111 Cable: NWAIR St. PAUL 297024

Orient-Avia Airlines V6 931

29 Aya Khutorskaya Str. 29, Moscow, Russia 103287 Tel: (096) 211 3047 Fax: (095) 211 3047

(*Contd.*)

(Contd.)

Orient Thai Airlines OX

101-199 Kungkloonchonprthan Road, Baan Nai Fan, Chiang Mai 50100, Thailand Tel: (53) 291 567 Fax: (53) 201 565

Pacific Air GX ▲

3110 Domestic Airport Road, Pasay City, Metro Manila 1300, Philippines Tel: (2) 832 2731 Fax: (2) 833 7692

Pakistan International Airlines PK ▲ 214

PIA Building, Karachi Civil Airport, Karachi 11, Pakistan Tel: 412811 Tlx: 2832 PAC Fax: 92-21-727727

Philippine Airlines PR ▲ 079

10th Floor, Allied Bank Centre, 6754 Ayala Avenue, Makati City, Philippines 0750 Tel: 818-0111 Cable: FILAIRLINE Fax: (13) 818-3298

Qantas Airways Ltd. QF ▲ 081

Qantas International Centre, G.P.O. Box 489, Sydney, South Wales 2001, Australia Tel: (2) 691 3636 Cable: QANTAS Fax: (2) 691 3277

Royal Air Force RR

Movements Resources, HQ 38 GP, RAF High Wycombe, Buckinghamshire HP14 4UE, England, U.K. Tel: (017) 222-2542

Royal Jordanian RJ ▲ 512

P.O. Box 302, Amman, Jordan Tel: (6) 607300 Tlx: 21501 AUAJO Fax: (6) 672527

Royal Nepal Airlines Corporation RA 285

R.N.A.C. Building, Kanti Path, P.O. Box No. 401, Kathmandu, Nepal Tel: 214511 Cable: AARENACEE Tlx: NP2212

Royal Swazi National Airways Corp. Ltd. ZC ▲ 141

P.O. Box 939, Manzini Swaziland Tel: 53151 Tlx: 2149 WD Fax: 84420

Sabena SN ▲ 082

Avenue E, Mounierlaan 2, Brussels 1200, Belgium Tel: (02) 723 23 23 Cable: AIRSABENA Tlx: 2132

Sahara India Airlines S2 ▲ 705

7th Floor, 14 K.G. Marg, New Delhi-110 001, India

SAS (Scandinavian Airlines) SK ▲ 117

STOQX, Froesundaviks Alle 1, Stockholm S-195 87, Sweden Tel: 08-797-0000 Cable: SASYSTEM Tlx: 22263

(Contd.)

(Contd.)

Singapore Airlines Ltd. SQ ▲ 618

P.O. Box 501, Airmail Transit Centre, Singapore 918 101, Singapore, Rep. of Tel: 542 3333 Tlx: RS 21241 Fax: 65-5455749

Skyways AB JZ ▲ 752

Box 1537, Linkoping, S-581 15, Sweden

South African Airways SA ▲ 083

Airways Towers, Cnr Rissilk & Wolmarans St., Braamfontein, Johannesburg 2001, South Africa Tel: (011)28-1728 Cable: SARAIR Tlx: 424210 Fax: (011) 773-8988

Spanair JK ▲ 680

Aeropuerto Palma Mallorca, P.O. Box 50086, Palma de Mallorca, 07000, Spain

Swiftair W3 491

Gran Via 86, Grupo 1-Planta 14, 28013 Madrid, Spain Tel: (91) 542-5775 Fax: (91) 541-7654

Tashkent Aircraft Production Corporation PQ ★

61 Rubek Street, Tashkent, Uzebekistan Fax: 37 12 360183

Thai Air Cargo 2Y ★

CTI Tower, 191/1 Ratchadapisek Road, Khwaeng Khong Toey, Khel Klong Toey, Bangkok 10110, Thailand Tel: (2) 611000-7 Fax: (2) 611008

Trans World Airlines Inc. TW ▲ 015

One City Centre, 515 N 6th Street, St. Louis, Missouri 63101, U.S.A. Tel: (314) 895 5553 Fax: (314) 895 5428

UP Air UZ

Roopali House, A-2, Defence Colony, New Delhi 110 024, India Tel: (11) 463 8201 Fax: (11) 463 6584

Uzbekistan Airways HY 250

41 Movaronnakhr, Tashkent 700060, Uzbekistan Tel: (3712) 33 73 57 Fax: (3712) 33 18 85

Vanguard Airlines NJ 311

80 North West Rome Circle, Kansas City Missouri 64153, U.S.A. Tel: (816) 243-2106 Fax: (816) 243-2188

Vietnam Airlines VN 738

Gia Lam Airport, Ha Noi, Viet Nam

(Contd.)

(*Contd.*)

Volga Dnepr Airlines VI ★ 412

12 Karbysheva Street, 432062 Ulyanovsk, Russian Federation Tel: 8422 202675

West Air Sweden PT

P.O. Box 82, S-65103 Karlstad, Sweden Tel: (54) 18 00 10 Fax: (54) 18 44 10

World Airways WO 468

Washington Dulles International Airport, 13873 Park Center Road, Suite 490, Herndon, Virginia 22071, U.S.A. Tel: (703) 834 9200

Xiamen Airlines MF 731

Gaoql International Airport, Xiamen City, Fujjan Province 361009, China

Xinjiang Airways XO 651

Diwopu Airport, Uramai City, Xinjiang, P.R. China

Yugoslav Airlines JU

—See JAT

Yute Air Alaska Inc. 4Y

P.O. Box 180, Dillingham, Alaska 99576, U.S.A. Tel: (907) 842-5333

Zambia Express Airways (1995) Ltd. OQ 876

Private Bag E811, Lusaka, Zambia Tel: (1) 227 965 Fax: (1) 227 964

Zimbabwe Express Airlines Z7 247

P.O. Box 5130, Harare, Zimbabwe

AIRLINE CODE NUMBERS

The airline code number forms the first three digits of the document number shown on the passenger ticket, MCO, excess baggage ticket and air waybill. Table 1.3 indicates the code numbers of various airlines.

Table 1.3: Airline Code Numbers

Code	*Airlines*	*Code*	*Airlines*
001	American Airlines	018	Canadian Airlines International
005	Continental Airlines	027	Alaska Airlines
006	Delta Air Lines	034	Millon Air
012	Northwest Airlines	037	US Airways
014	Air Canada	042	VARIG
015	TWA	043	Dragonair
016	United Airlines		

(*Contd.*)

(Contd.)

Code	*Airlines*	*Code*	*Airlines*
044	Aerolineas Argentinas	094	Air Sask Aviation 1991
045	LAN-Chile	095	AVIACSA
047	TAP Air Portugal	096	Iran Air
048	Cyprus Airways	097	Kaliningrad Air Enterprise
050	Olympic Airways	098	Air India
051	LAB	099	Hamburg Airlines
052	Heli Inter	100	Air Jamaica Express
053	Aer Lingus	101	Air Dolomiti
054	Pelangi Air	102	LAl
055	Alitalia	104	Eurowings
058	Indian Airlines	105	Rnnair
059	Skyline NEPC1	106	BWIA International
060	Flight West Airlines	107	Crimea Air
061	Air Seychelles	108	Icelandair
063	Air Catedonie International	109	Air Mali
064	Czech Airlines	110	AVIACO
065	Saudia	113	Air Lines of Kuban
067	Eagle Aviation	114	El Al Israel Airlines
068	LAM-Linhas Aereas de Mocambique	115	JAT
		116	Bright Air
069	LAPA	117	SAS
070	Syrian Arab Airlines	118	TAAG-Angola Airlines
071	Ethiopian Airlines	119	ALM
072	Gulf Air	120	Air Koryo
073	Iraqi Airways	121	Ada-Air
074	KLM-Royal Dutch Airlines	122	Loganair Ltd.
075	IBERIA	123	Air Nauru
076	MEA	124	Air Algerie
077	Egyptair	125	British Airways
078	Aero California	126	Garuda Indonesia
079	Philippine Airlines	128	AVENSA
080	LOT-Polish Airlines	129	Martinair Holland
081	Qantas Airways	130	Air UK
082	SA6ENA	131	Japan Airlines
083	South African Airways	132	MEXICANA
085	SWISSAIR	133	LACSA
086	Air New Zealand	134	AVIANCA
087	Nigeria Airways	135	Air Tahiti
090	Ansett Australia	136	CUBANA
091	Air 2000	137	ACES
092	Air Afrique	139	Aeromexico
093	Wasaya Airways	140	LIAT

(Contd.)

(Contd.)

Code	Airlines	Code	Airlines
141	Royal Swazi National Airways Corporation	190	Air Caledonie
142	Air Botnia	191	Mericiana
143	Austral	192	Surinam Airways
145	Ladeco	193	Solomon Airlines
146	Compagnie Aerienne Corse Mediterranee	194	Sterling Airways
147	Royal Air Maroc	196	Balkan
148	Jamahiriya Libyan Arab Airlines	197	Air Tanzania Corporation
149	Luxair	199	Tunis Air
150	Tuninter	200	Sudan Airways
152	Aeropostal	201	Air Jamaica (1968) Ltd.
153	Helisul jjnhas Aereas	202	Taca International Airlines
154	Braathens SAFE	203	Cebu Pacific Air
156	SAETA	204	Tavrey Aircompany
157	Qatar Airways	205	All Nippon Airways Co. Ltd.
159	Airlink	206	Guyana Airways Corporation
160	Cathay Pacific Airways	207	Air Zaire
161	Commercial Airways	208	Bellview Airlines
162	Polynesian Airlines	209	Myanmar Airways int'l
163	Compania de Aviacion Faucett	210	Aeroperu
164	VIASA	214	Pakistan International Airlines
165	Adria Airways	215	Joint Stock Company East Line
166	Imair	216	Palair Macedonian Airlines
167	Air Malawi	217	Thai Airways International
168	Air Zimbabwe	218	Air Vanuatu
170	Trans Asia Airways	219	Air Creebec
171	GB Airways	220	Lufthansa
173	Hawaiian Airlines	222	West Coast Air
174	Air Mauritanie	223	Air Senegal
176	Emirates	224	Ryanair
178	Air Rwanda	227	Transwede Airways Services
180	Korean Air	228	BASE Regional Airlines
181	Dneproavia Avtn,	229	Kuwait Airways
182	MALEV	230	COPA
183	Air Ostrava	231	Lauda Air
185	Aic Gabon	232	Malaysia Airlines
186	Air Namibia	234	Japan Air System
188	Air Alliance	235	Turkish Airlines
189	Air Caribbean	236	British Midland
		237	Ghana Airways
		238	Arkia Israeli Airlines
		239	Air Mauritius

(Contd.)

(Contd.)

Code	*Airlines*	*Code*	*Airlines*
240	AVIATECA	302	Skywest Airlines
245	First Air	304	Downeast Express
246	Avant Airlines	305	Tower Air
247	Zimbabwe Express Airlines	306	Cape Air
248	Riga Airlines	307	Ot allenge Air Cargo
250	Uzbekistan Airways	309	Aerolineas Santo Domingo
251	Ryan Air	310	Corporate Express Airlines
252	Sunflower Airlines	311	Vanguard Airlines
253	Impulse Airlines	315	Air St. Thomas
255	Ariana Afghan Airlines	317	Alliance Airlines
257	Austrian Airlines	318	Western Pacific Airlines
258	Air Madagascar	321	Pacific Island Aviation
260	Air Pacific	322	Diamond Int'l Airlines
265	Far Eastern Air Transport	323	Larrys Flying Service
266	L.T.U International Airways	326	Airrnax
267	Jersey European Airways	327	Aloha Airlines
269	Tame	328	Eagle Canyon Airlines
270	TMA	329	Pern Air
273	Shorouk Air	330	Florida West
274	Go One Airways	332	Air Tran Airways
275	Aerosur	334	SAM
276	Air Aruba	336	TIE Aviation
277	Vladivostok Air	337	Sun Country Airlines
278	Servicios de Transportes	338	Reeve Aleutian Airways
279	Air Inter Europe	339	Penair
281	TAROM	340	Fine Air
282	Islena Airlines	341	ECUATORIANA
283	Air Moldoya International	343	VASP
285	Royal Nepal Airlines	344	Loken Aviation
286	PIONA	345	Northern Air Cargo
287	Air North	347	Aloha Islandair
288	AHK Air Hong Kong	349	MaerskAIr
289	MIAT-Monqolian Airlines	350	Maverick Airways
291	State Orenburg Ava.	351	Southern Air Transport
292	Affretair	352	Kitty Hawk Airways
293	Rio-Sul Services Aereos	353	Japan Transocean Air
	Regionais	354	CC Air
295	Windward Islands	355	Conquest Airlines
	Airways International	356	Trans Air
296	Alliance Air	359	Turan Air
297	China Airlines	363	Chautauqua Airlines
301	Souttr Central Air	365	Pine State Airlines

(Contd.)

(*Contd.*)

Code	*Airlines*	*Code*	*Airlines*
366	American Trans Air	449	Gulfstream International
367	New England Airlines	451	Camai Air
371	Mahalo Air	452	Air Kazakstan
373	Island Airlines	453	Mid West Express Airlines
375	Sunworld International	456	Aeroejecutivo
376	Rover Airways	457	Coastal Air Transport
378	Cayman Airways	458	Harbour Air
379	Caribair	460	West Air Commuter Airlines
381	Vieques Air Link	464	Empire Airlines
384	Reno Air	468	World Airways
385	Laker Airways	469	Ketchikan Air Service
386	Air Aurora	470	Skyward Aviation
387	Big Sky Airlines	471	Air Midwest
388	Pan American World Airways	472	Landair Int'l Airlines
389	Air Vegas	477	Salair
391	Cargolift International	480	Atlantic Coast Airlines
395	Allegheney Commuter Airlines	481	Horizon Air
397	Wings of Alaska	484	Airlines of Carriacou
398	Scenic Airlines	487	Spirit Airlines
399	Air South Airlines	488	Chicago Express Airlines
401	America West Airlines	490	Tradewinds Airlines
403	Polar Air Cargo	493	Skagway Air Service
404	Arrow Air	494	Evergreen Int'l Airlines
406	United Parcel Service	495	Harbor Airlines Inc.
407	Nordic European Airlines	497	Domodedovo Airlines
410	Action Airlines	499	Krasnoyarsk Airlines
412	Volga Dnepr Airlines	500	Air Georgia
414	Trans States Airlines	501	Crown Airways
421	Siberia Airlines	503	SANSA
422	Frontier Airlines	504	Aspen Mountain Air
423	DHL Airways	507	Air Truck
426	Colgan Air	508	Jet Airways
427	Societe Nouvelle Air Guadeloupe	509	Aero Zambia
		510	LAB Flying Service
428	Magadan Airlines	511	Alpine Aviation
429	Dinar Lineas Areas	512	Royal Jordanian
430	Express Airlines	514	International Flying Services
434	Airvantage	517	Frontier Flying Service
436	British Mediterranean Airways	519	40-Mile Air
445	Mount Cook Airlines	520	Estonian Aviation
448	NEPC Airlines	521	Carnival Air lines

(*Contd.*)

(*Contd.*)

Code	*Airlines*	*Code*	*Airlines*
522	Paradise Island Airlines •	600	Andesmar Lineas Aereas
525	UNI Airways	603	Air Lanka
526	Southwest Airlines (U.S.A.)	604	Cameroon Airlines
528	Eagle Airlines	609	Transeast Airlines
531	Piedmont Airlines	613	Helijet Airways
532	Aero Asia	614	Augsburg Airways
533	Mesa Airlines	615	European Air Transport
534	Romavia	616	Air Greece
536	Blackhawk Airways	617	Hapag Lloyd
538	Kiwi International Airlines	618	Singapore Airlines
540	Las Vegas Airlines	621	Merpati Nusantara Airlines
542	Avia Comp Turk	622	Calm Air International
548	Modiluft	625	Inter Air
550	Pacific Airlines	626	MBA Pty Ltd.
553	Falcon Express	627	Lao Aviation
555	Aeroflot	628	Belavia
557	Korsar	629	Silk Air
562	Pan Air	632	Bearskin Airlines
563	Papillon Airways	633	Aero Lloyd
566	Ukraine International Airlines	634	Central Mountain Air
568	Air Nevada	635	Yemenia Yemen Airways
569	L.B. Limited	636	Air Botswana
571	American International Airways	637	Chita Avia
		638	Air St. Pierre
572	Air Moldova	639	Albanian Airlines
573	Kiwi Travel Int'l	640	Safair
574	Air Atlantic	643	Air Malta
575	Coyne Aviation	646	AOM French Airlines
576	Jaro International •	647	Cimber Air
577	ADI Domestic Airlines	651	Xinjiang Airways
579	Island Express	653	Transbrasil
580	Flamenco Airways	656	Air Niugini
582	Mesaba Aviation ♦	657	Air Baltic
583	Cosmos Air	658	Royal Air Cambodge
589	Jet Airways	659	Air Littoral
590	West Isle Air	660	Itapemirim Transportes Aereos
591	Emery Worldwide		
592	China Yunnan Airlines	665	Virgin Express
593	Business Air	666	Bouraq Indonesia
594	Redwing Airways	668	Northwest Territorial Airways
595	Cirrusair	670	Transaero Airlines
596	Continental Micronesia	672	Royal Brunei Airlines

(*Contd.*)

(Contd.)

Code	Airlines	Code	Airlines
673	Uganda Airlines	734	Tyrolean Airways
674	Skywest Airlines	736	Kazakhstan Airlines
675	Air Macau	737	SATA Air Acores
677	Air Fiji	738	Vietnam Airlines
678	Kendell Airlines	739	SAN
679	Archana Airways	740	Shaheen Air Int'l
680	Spanair	741	Necon Air
684	Georgian Airlines	742	Air B.C.
685	Portugalia	743	Interimpex-Aviompex
687	Helenair Corporation	744	Air Tindi
688	Japan Asia Airways	746	Air Urga
689	Cityjet	746	Hemus Air
690	Sierra National Airlines	747	Heli Air Monaco
691	Tyumen Airlines	448	Hemus Air
692	Transportes Aereos del Mercosur	749	S.A. Airlink
		750	Brit Air
693	Alliance Airlines	752	Skyways
694	Air Nostrum	755	Air Rarotonga
695	EVA Airways	758	Kyrghyzstan Airlines
696	Transports Aereos de Cabo Verde	759	Falcon Aviation
		760	Air Austral
698	AB Airlines	761	DAS Air
701	Wideroe's Flyveselskap	763	Wairarapa Airlines
702	Maersk Air Ltd.	767	Atlantic Airways, Faroe Islands
704	OLT-Ostfriesische Luftransport	768	Air Nippon
705	Sahara India Airlines	771	Azerbaijan Hava Yollary
706	Kenya Airways	774	Shanghai Airlines
707	Air Saint Martin	778	Air Marshall Islands
709	Aklak Air	779	DAC Air
711	Perimeter Airlines	781	China Eastern Airlines
715	Air Tungaru Corp.	782	China Northern Airlines
718	Air Liberte	783	China Northwest Airlines
721	Lesotho Airways	784	China Southern Airlines
722	LASER	785	China Southwest
723	Aerocaribe	786	Gill Airways
724	Crossair	789	ALPI Eagles
725	Dominair	791	Fujian Airlines
726	Fast Air Carrier	796	Muk Air
728	Viva Air	798	Great China Airlines
731	Xiamen Airlines	802	Aero Costa Rica Acori
733	Donavia	803	Mandarin Airlines

(Contd.)

(*Contd.*)

Code	*Airlines*	*Code*	*Airlines*
806	Air Sunshine	878	Midway Airlines
807	Airasia	879	Cape Smythe Air Service Inc.
808	Era Aviation	881	Condor Flugdienst
810	Amerijet International	886	Comair
811	Americana de Aviacion	887	Air Toulouse
813	National Airlines	891	Air Ukraine
814	New York Helicopters	893	Southern Independent Air
819	Orbi Georgian Airways	896	Bhoja Air
821	Sempati Air	899	Hazelton Airlines
822	Zuliana de Aviacion	900	Air Maldives
824	Air Exel Netherlands	902	Lineas Aereas Allegro
828	Aeroperlas	903	Air Sinai
831	Croatia Airlines	904	Tatra Air
832	ABX Air	905	Pacific Coastal Airlines
834	Air Engiadina	906	Samara Airlines•
837	Passaredo Transportes	908	Voyageur Airways
838	TAESA	909	Athabaska Airways
842	Sibaviatrans	910	Oman Air
843	Air Lithuania	912	Hunting Cargo Airlines
844	Cityflyer Express	915	Rheintalflug Seewald
845	Aerorepublica	916	Manx Airlines
846	Great Lakes Aviation	917	APA International Air
848	Hexair	918	Air Caribbean
849	Air Atlantic Dominicana	924	Aurigny Air Services
851	Halisa Air	926	Aeromar
852	Khors Aircompany	927	Labrador Airways
855	Cardinal Airlines	928	Sun Air
856	Airpac Airlines	929	Aero Continente •
857	USAir Shuttle	930	Nicaraguenses de Aviacion
859	TAL Thuringia Airlines	931	Orient-Avia Airlines
860	Moldavian Airlines	932	Virgin Atlantic
861	Four Star Aviation	933	Nippon Cargo Airlines
864	Azzurrair	935	Airnorth Regional
865	Aerotransportes Mas de Carga	936	T.A.T. European Airlines
867	Air One	937	Latpass Airlines
870	Aerosweet Airlines	938	Emerald Airways
871	Air Martinique	940	Bashkir Airlines
872	Bemidji Airlines	941	Ansett New Zealand
874	Lithuanian Airlines	942	Transportes Aeromar
876	Zambia Express	944	Deutsche BA
877	Transportes Aereos Regionais (TAM)	947	DHL de Guatemala •

(*Contd.*)

(Contd.)

Code	*Airlines*	*Code*	*Airlines*
951	Arax Airways	979	Transavia Airlines
956	Armenian Airlines	981	Air St. Barthelemy
957	TAM ♦	982	Regional Airlines
959	Laparkan Airways	983	Air Nova
960	Estonian Air	984	Malmo Aviation
967	Interprovincial Airlines •	985	Servivensa
968	Prima Air/Flyair	986	Formosa Airlines
969	Suckling Airways	987	Mayan World Airlines•
970	Coast Air	988	Asiana Airlines
971	Royal Tongan Airlines	990	Highland Air
972	Flandre Air	991	Daallo Airlines
974	Monarch Airlines	992	DHL Aero Expreso S.A.
976	Aeromexpress	996	Air Europa
977	Proteus	997	Biman Bangladesh Airlines
978	VLM	999	Air China

Table 1.4: Airline Designator Codes

Code	*Airlines*	*Code*	*Airlines*
	A	AQ	Aloha Airlines
		AR	Aerolineas Argentinas
AA	American Airlines	AS	Alaska Airlines
AB	Superior Aviation (Cargo)	AT	Royal Air Maroc
AC	Air Canada	AU	Austral
AD*	Aspen Mountain Air (Passenger)	AV	AVIANCA
		AW	Dirgantara Air
AD*	Avialeasing Aviation (Cargo)	AX	Air Aurora (Cargo)
AE	Mandarin Airlines	AY	Finnair
AF	Air France	AZ	Alitalia
AG*	Hunting Cargo Airlines (Cargo)		**B**
AG*	Interprovincial Airlines (Passenger)	BA	British Airways
		BB	Seaborne Aviation
AH	Air Algerie	BD	British Midland
AI	Air India	BG	Biman Bangladesh Airlines
AJ	Air Belgium	BH	Transtate Airlines
AK	Airasia	BI	Royal Brunei Airlines
AM	Aeromexico	BK	Paradise Island Airlines
AN	Ansett Australia	BL	Pacific Airlines
AO	AVIACO	BM	Air Sicilia
AP	Air One	BN	Landair Int'l Airlines (Cargo)

(Contd.)

(Contd.)

Code	Airlines	Code	Airlines
BO	Bouraq Indonesia	CT	Northwestern Air Lease
BP	Air Botswana	CU	CUBANA
BQ*	Virgin Express (Passenger)	CV	Air Chathams (Passenger)
BQ*	Aeromar (Cargo)	CV*	Cargolux Airlines (Cargo)
BR	EVA Airways	CW	Air Marshall Islands
BS	British International	CX	Cathay Pacific Airways
BT	Air Baltic	CY	Cyprus Airways
BU	Braathens S.A.F.E.	CZ	China Southern Airlines
BV	Sun Air	C2	Air Caribbean
BW	BWIA International	C3	Icar
BX	Coast Air	C4	Airlines of Carriacou
BZ	Keystone Air Service	C6	Bright Air
B2	Belavia	C7	Bonaire Airways
B3	Bellview Airlines	C8	Chicago Express Airlines
B4	Bhoja Air		**D**
B5	Florida Cargo Express (Cargo)	DA	Air Georgia
B6	Top Air	DB	Brit Air
B7	UNI Airways	DC	Golden Air Flyg
B9	Caribair	DE	Condor Flugdienst
	C	DF	Aviosarda
CA	Air China	DG*	Island Airlines (Passenger)
CB*	Suckling Airways (Passenger)	DG*	Custom Air Transport (Cargo)
CB*	American International Airways (Cargo)	DI	Deutsche BA
CC*	Macair (Passenger)	DJ	Nordic European Airlines
CC*	Air Atlanta Icelandic (Cargo)	DK	Eastland Air
CD	Alliance Air	DL	Delta Air Lines
CE	Nationwide Air	DM	Maersk Air
CF	Compania de Aviacion Faucett	DP	Air 2000
CG	MBA Pty Ltd.	DQ	Coastal Air Transport
CH*	Bemidji Airlines (Passenger)	DR	Air Link
CH*	Ukraine Air Service (Cargo)	DS*	Air Senegal (Passenger)
CI	China Airlines	DS*	DHL Aero Expreso S.A. (Cargo)
CJ	China Northern Airlines	DT	TAAG-Angola Airlines
CK	Andesmar Lineas Aereas	DU	Hemus Air
CM	COPA	DV	Gordo Aero Service
CN	Islands Nationair	DW	Rottnest Airlines
CO	Continental Airlines	DX	Danish Air Transport
CP	Canadian Airlines International	D3	Daallo Airlines
CS	Continental Micronesia	D4	Aries Del Sur (Cargo)
		D6	Inter Air

(Contd.)

(Contd.)

Code	Airlines	Code	Airlines
D7	Dinar Lineas Areas	FG	Ariana Afghan Airlines
D9	Donavia	FH	Futura International
	E	FI	Icelandair
EB	Emery Worldwide (Cargo)	FJ	Air Pacific
EC	Heli Inter	FK	Flamenco Airways
ED*	CC Air (Passenger)	FL	AirTran Airways
ED*	Andes Airlines (Cargo)	FO	Expedition Airways
EF	Far Eastern Air Transport	FQ	Air Aruba
EG	Japan Asia Airways	FR	Ryanair
EH	SAETA	FS*	Missionary Aviation Fellowship (Passenger)
EI	New England Airlines	FS*	Servicios de Transportes (Cargo)
EK	Emirates	FU	Air Littoral
EL	Air Nippon	FX	Fedex (Cargo)
EM	Empire Airlines (Cargo)	FZ	Air Facilities
EN	Air Dolomiti	F2	Southern Independent Air
EO	Congo Airlines	F3	Flying Enterprise
EQ	Tame	F4	International Flying Services
ER	DHL Airways (Cargo)	F5	Archana Airways
ES	Helicusco	F8	Western Airlines
ET	Ethiopian Airlines	F9	Frontier Airlines
EU	ECUATORIANA		**G**
EW	Eurowings	GA	Garuda Indonesia
EX	Aerolineas Santo Domingo	GB	Air Glaciers (Passenger)
EY	Mayan World Airlines	GB*	ABX Air (Cargo)
EZ	Evergreen Int'l Airlines (Cargo)	GD	TAESA
E2	Everest Air	GE	Trans Asia Airways
E3	Domodedovo Airlines	GF	Gulf Air
E4	Aero Asia	GG	Tamair
E5	Samara Airlines	GH	Ghana Airways
E7	Downeast Express	GK	Go One Airways
E8	ALPI Eagles	GL	Greenlandair
E9	Compagine Africaine d'Aviation	GM	Air Slovakia
	F	GN	Air Gabon
FB	Fine Air (Cargo)	GO	Air Stord
FC*	TAL Thuringia Airlines (Passenger)	GQ	Big Sky Airlines
FC*	Falcon Express (Cargo)	GR*	Aurigny Air Services (Passenger)
FD	CityFlyer Express	GR*	Gemini Air Cargo (Cargo)
FE	Eagle Canyon Airlines	GS	Grant Aviation
FF	Tower Air		

(Contd.)

(Contd.)

Code	*Airlines*	*Code*	*Airlines*
GU	AVIATECA	II*	ADI Domestic Airlines (Cargo)
GV	Riga Airlines	IJ	T.A.T. European Airlines
GW*	Air Line of Kuban (Passenger)	IK	Imair
GW*	Golden West Airlines (Cargo)	IL	Istanbul Airlines
GX	Pacfic Air	IN	Macedonian Airlines
GY	Guyana Airways Corporation	IQ	Augsburg Airways
GZ	Air Rarotonga	IR	Iran Air
G3	Emerald Airways	IS	Island Airlines
G7	Guinee Airlines	IT	Air Inter Europe
G8	Gujarat Airways	IV	Fujian Airlines
	H	IW	AOM French Airlines
HA	Hawaiian Airlines	IX	Flandre Air
HB	Augusta Airways	IY	Yemenia Yemen Airways
HC	Naske Air	IZ	Arkia Israeli Airlines
HD	New York Helicopters		**J**
HE	LGW Walter	JA	Air Bosna
HF	Hapag Lloyd	JB	Helijet Airways
HG	Harbor Airlines Inc.	JD	Japan Air System
HI	Papillon Airways	JE	Manx Airlines
HJ	Holmstroem Air	JF	L.A.B. Flying Service
HK*	Swan Airlines (Passenger)	JG	Air Greece
HK*	Four Star Aviation (Cargo)	JH*	Nordeste (Passenger)
HX	Hamburg Airlines	JH*	Amerijet International (Cargo)
HY	Uzbekistan Airways	JI	Midway Airlines
H2	City Bird	JJ	TAM
H3	Harbour Air	JK	Spanair
H4	Hainan Airlines	JL	Japan AirLines
H5	Magadan Airlines	JM	Air Jamaica (1968) Ltd.
H6	Hageland Aviation Services	JP	Adria Airways
H7	Taquan Air Service	JR	Aero California
H8	Khabarovsk Aviation	JS	Air Koryo
	I	JT	Jaro International
		JU	JAT
IB	IBERIA	JV	Bearskin Airlines
IC	Indian Airlines	JW	Arrow Air (Cargo)
ID	Air Normandie	JX	Skybus
IE	Solomon Airlines	JY	Jersey European Airways
IF	Great China Airlines	JZ	Skyways
IG	Mendiana	J2	Azerbaijan Hava Yollary
IH	Falcon Aviation	J4	Buffalo Airways
II*	Business Air (Passenger)	J5	Sochi Airlines–Aviaprima

(Contd.)

(Contd.)

Code	Airlines	Code	Airlines
J6	Larrys Flying Service	LB	LAB
J7	Valujet Airline	LD	AHK Air Hong Kong (Cargo)
J8	Berjaya Air	LE	Helgoland Airlines
	K	LF*	Lufthansa Cargo India (Cargo)
KA	Dragonair	LG	Luxair
KB	Druk-Air	LH	Lufthansa
KD	Kendell Airlines	LI	LIAT
KE	Korean Air	LJ	Sierra National Airlines
KF	Air Botnia	LL	Lineas Aereas Allegro
KG	LAI	LM	ALM
KH	Kyrnair	LO	LOT-Polish Airlines
KI	Air Atlantique	LQ	Airpac Airlines (Cargo)
KJ	British Mediterranean Airways	LR	LACSA
KK	Transportes Aereos Regionais (TAM)	LS*	Iliamna Air Taxi (Passenger)
		LS*	Channel Express (Cargo)
KL	KLM-Royal Dutch Airlines	LT	L.T.U. International Airways
KM	Air Malta	LU	Air Atlantic Dominicana
KN	Coral Int'l Airlines	LV	Albanian Airlines
KO	Alaska Central Express	LW	Air Nevada
KP	Kiwi International Airlines	LX	Crossair
KQ	Kenya Airways	LY	El Al Israel Airlines
KR	Kitty Hawk Air Cargo (Cargo)	LZ	Balkan
KS	Penair	L2	Loken Aviation
KT	Kampuchea Airlines	L3	Kaiken Lineas Aereas
KU	Kuwait Airways	L4	Atlant-SV
KW	Carnival Air lines	L6	Air Maldives
KX	Cayman Airways	L7	Lviv Airlines
KZ*	LASER (Passenger)	L8	Laparkan Airways (Cargo)
KZ*	Nippon Cargo Airlines (Cargo)	L9	Air Mali
K2	Kyrghyzstan Airlines		**M**
K3	Ketchikan Air Service		
K4	Kazakhstan Airlines	MA	MALEV
K5*	Wings of Alaska (Passenger)	MD	Air Madagascar
K5*	Air East Africa (Cargo)	ME	MEA
K7	Sakha Avia	MF	Xiamen Airlines
K8	Kaliningrad Air Enterprise	MG	Djibouti Airlines
K9*	Skyward Aviation (Passenger)	MH	Malaysia Airlines
K9*	Itapemirim Transportes Aereos (Cargo)	MI	Silk Air
		MJ	LAPA
		MK	Air Mauritius
	L	ML	Aero Costa Rica Acori
LA	LAN-Chile	MM	SAM

(Contd.)

(Contd.)

Code	Airlines	Code	Airlines
MN	Commercial Airways	N4	National Airlines
MO	Calm Air International	N5	Sardairline
MP	Martinair Holland	N6	Aero Continente
MQ	Simmons Airlines	N8	Expresso Aereo
MR	Air Mauritanie	N9	North Coast Aviation
MS	Egyptair		**O**
MU	China Eastern Airlines		
MW	Maya Airways	OA	Olympic Airways
MX	MEXICANA	OB	Shepparton Airlines
MY*	Euroscott Express (Passenger)	OE	WestAir Commuter Airlines
MY*	Aerotransportes Mas de Carga (Cargo)	OF	Travaux Aeriens de Madagascar
MZ	Merpati Nusantara Airlines	OH	Comair
M3	Westjet Airlines	OI	Aspiring Air
M4	Interimpex-Aviompex	OJ	Air St. Barthelemy
M5	Kenmore Air	OK	Czech Airlines
M6	Chalair	OL	OLT-Ostfriesische Luftransport
	N	OM	MIAT-Mongolian Airlines
NA	Executive Airlines	ON	Air Nauru
NC*	National Jet (Passenger)	OO	Skywest Airlines
NC*	Northern Air Cargo (Cargo)	OQ	Zambia Express
ND	Airlink	OR	Crimea Air
NF	Air Vanuatu	OS	Austrian Airlines
NG	Lauda Air	OT	Avant Airlines
NH	All Nippon Airways Co. Ltd.	OU	Croatia Airlines
NI	Portugalia	OV	Estonian Air
NJ	Vanguard Airlines	OW	Metavia Airlines
NK	Spirit Airlines	OX	Orient Thai Airlines
NL	Shaheen Air Int'l	OZ	Asiana Airlines
NM	Mount Cook Airlines		**P**
NN	Cardinal Airlines		
NO	Aus Air	PA	Pan American World Airways
NP	Skytrans	PB	Air Burundi
NQ	Orbi Georgian Airways	PC	Air Fiji
NT	Binter Canarias	PD	Pem-Air
NU	Japan Transocean Air	PE	Helisul Linhas Aereas
NV	Northwest Territorial Airways	PG	Bangkok Airways
NW	Northwest Airlines	PH	Polynesian Airlines
NX	Air Macau	PI	Sunflower Airlines
NY	Norlandair	PJ	Air St Pierre
NZ	Air New Zealand	PK	Pakistan International Airlines
N2	Aerolineas Internacionales	PL	Aeroperu

(Contd.)

(Contd.)

Code	Airlines
PN	Air Martinique
PO	Polar Air Cargo (Cargo)
PQ	Tashkent Acft. Prod. (Cargo)
PR	Philippine Airlines
PS	Ukraine International Airlines
PT	West Air Sweden
PU	PLUNA
PV	Pan Air
PW	Pine State Airlines
PX	Air Niugini
PY	Surinam Airways
PZ	Transportes Aereos del Mercosur
P3	Air Provence
P4*	Aero Lineas Sosa (Passenger)
P4*	Pacific International (Cargo)
P5	Aerorepublica
P6	Trans Air
P7	Joint Stock Company East Line
P8	Pantanal Linhas Aereas
P9	Pro Air
	Q
QA	Aerocaribe
QF	Qantas Airways
QI	Cimber Air
QJ*	Latpass Airlines (Passenger)
QJ*	Jet Airways (Cargo)
QK	Air Nova
QL	Lesotho Airways
QM	Air Malawi
QN	Ord Air Charter
QO	Aeromexpress (Cargo)
QP	Airkenya Aviation
QQ	Reno Air
QR	Qatar Airways
QS	Tatra Air
QU	Uganda Airlines
QV	Lao Aviation
QW	Turks & Caicos Airways
QX	Horizon Air
QY	European Air Transport (Cargo)
Q2	Minerva Airlines
Q4	Mustique Airways
Q5	40-Mile Air
Q9	Sayakhat Air Co. (Cargo)
	R
RA	Royal Nepal Airlines
RB	Syrian Arab Airlines
RC	Atlantic Airways, Faroe Islands
RD	Avianova
RF	Florida West (Cargo)
RG	VARIG
RI	Mandala Airlines
RJ	Royal Jordanian
RK	Air Afrique
RO	TAROM
RQ	Air Engiadina
RR	Royal Air Force
RT	Lincoln Airlines
RU	TCI Skyking
RV	Reeve Aleutian Airways
RX	Redwing Airways
RY	Air Rwanda
RZ	SANSA
R2	State Orenburg Ava.
R3	Armenian Airlines
R5	Malta Air Charter
R7	Aeroservicios Carabobo
R8*	Regulijair (Passenger)
R8*	Corporate Charter Service (Cargo)
R9*	Carnai Air (Passenger)
R9*	Air Charter (Cargo)
	S
SA	South African Airways
SB	Air Caledonie International
SC	Shandong Airlines
SD	Sudan Airways
SE	DAS Air (Cargo)
SF	Shanghai Airlines
SG	Sempati Air

(Contd.)

(Contd.)

Code	Airlines	Code	Airlines
SH	Air Toulouse	TW	TWA
SJ	Southern Air Transport (Cargo)	TX	Societe Nouvelle Air Guadeloupe
SK	SAS	TY	Air Caledonie
SL	Rio-Sul Servicos Aereos Regionais	TZ	American Trans Air
SM	Sunworld International	T4*	Transeast Airlines (Passenger)
SN	SABENA	T4*	TIE Aviation (Cargo)
SP	SATA Air Acores	T5	Avia Comp Turk
SQ	Singapore Airlines	T6	Tavrey Aircompany
SR	SWISSAIR	T8	Transportes Aereos Neuquen del Estado
ST	Yanda Airlines	T9	Master Aviation
SU	Aeroflot		**U**
SV	Saudia	UA	United Airlines
SW	Air Namibia	UB	Myanmar Airways Int'l
SX	Aeroejecutivo	UC	Ladeco
SY*	Sun Country Airlines (Passenger)	UD*	Hex'Air (Passenger)
SY*	Southend Cargo Airlines (Cargo)	UD*	Fast Air Carrier (Cargo)
SZ	China Southwest	UE	Transeuropean Airlines
S2	Sahara India Airlines	UF	Turkestan Airlines
S6	Air Saint Martin	UG	Tuninter
S7	Siberia Airlines	UI	Alaska Seaplane Service
S8	Estonian Aviation	UJ	Aerosanta Airlines
S9	SK Air	UK	Air UK
	T	UL	Air Lanka
TA	Taca International Airlines	UM	Air Zimbabwe
TC	Air Tanzania Corporation	UN	Transaero Airlines
TE	Lithuanian Airlines	UP	Bahamasair
TG	Thai Airways International	UQ	O'Connor-Mount Gambiers Airline
TK	Turkish Airlines	US	US Airways
TL*	Airnorth Regional (Passenger)	UU	Air Austral
TL*	TMA (Cargo)	UV	Helicopteros del Sureste
TM	LAM-Linhas Aereas de Mocambique	UW	Perimeter Airlines
TP	TAP Air Portugal	UX	Air Europa
TQ	Transwede Airways	UY	Cameroon Airlines
TR	Transbrasil	UZ	UP Air
TS	Samoa Aviation	U2	Easyjet
TT	Air Lithuania	U3*	Travelair (Passenger)
TU	Tunis Air	U3*	Uralinteravia (Cargo)
		U5	International Business Air

(Contd.)

(Cont...)

Code	Airlines	Code	Airlines
U7	United Aviation	WE*	Challenge Air Cargo (Cargo)
	V	WF	Wideroe's Flyveselskap
VA	VIASA	WG	Wasaya Airways
VC	Servivensa	WH	China Northwest Airlines
VD	Air Liberte	WI*	U-Land Airlines (Passenger)
VE	AVENSA	WI*	Tradewinds Airlines (Cargo)
VF	Tropical Airlines	WJ	Labrador Airways
VG	VLM	WL	Aeŕoperlas
VH	Aeropostal	WM	Windward Islands Airways International
VI*	Vieques Air Link (Passenger)	WN	Southwest Airlines (U.S.A.)
VI*	Volga Dnepr Airlines (Cargo)	WO	World Airways
VJ	Royal Air Cambodge	WP	Aloha Islandair
VL	North Vancouver Air	WQ	Romavia
VM	Regional Airlines	WR	Royal Tongan Airlines
VN	Vietnam Airlines	WS	Air Caraibes Exploitation
VO	Tyrolean Airways	WT	Nigeria Airways
VP	VASA	WW	Whyalla Airlines
VQ	Impulse Airlines	WX	Cityjet
VR	Transportes Aereos de Cabo Verde	WY	Oman Air
VS	Virgin Atlantic	WZ	Acvila Air
VT	Air Tahiti	W3	Swiftair
VU	Air Ivoire	W7	Western Pacific Airlines
VV	Aerosweet Airlines	W8	La Costena
VW	Transportes Aeromar	W9	Eastwind Airlines
VX	ACES		**X**
VY	Formosa Airlines	XC*	K.D. Air Corp. (Passenger)
V2	Associated Airlines	XC*	Air Caribbean (Cargo)
V5	Vnukovo Airlines	XE	South Central Air (Cargo)
V6	Orient-Avia Airlines	XF	Vladivostok Air
V8	Contact Air	XG	Regional Lineas Aereas
V9	Bashkir Airlines	XJ	Mesaba Aviation
	W	XK	Compagnie Aerienne Corse Mediterranee
WA*	Newair (Passenger)	XL	Country Connection Airlines
WA*	Vensecar International (Cargo)	XO	Xinjiang Airways
WB	SAN	XQ	Action Airlines
WC	Islena Airlines	XT	Air Exel Netherlands
WD	Halisa Air	XV	Air Express
WE*	Rheintalflug Seewald (Passenger)	X5	Trans Pacific Air
		X7	Chita Avia

(Contd.)

(Contd.)

Code	Airlines
	Y
YC	Flight West Airlines
YD	Gomelavia
YH	Air Nunavut
YI	Air Sunshine
YJ	National Airlines
YM	Blue Sky Carrier
YN	Air Creebec
YO	Heli Air Monaco
YP	Aero Lloyd
YQ	Helikopterservice
YR	Scenic Airlines
YS	Proteus
YT	Skywest Airlines
YU	Dominair
YV	Mesa Airlines
YW	Air Nostrum
YX	MidWest Express Airlines
YZ	Transportes Aereos da Guine-Bissau
Y2	Alliance Airlines
Y4	Eagle Aviation
Y5	Arax Airways
Y7	F.S.Air Service
Y8	Passaredo Transportes
Y9	Trans Air Congo
	Z
ZB	Monarch Airlines
ZC	Royal Swazi National Airways Corporation
ZE	Cosmos Air
ZF	Airborne of Sweden
ZH	Air Truck
ZJ	Teddy Air
ZK	Great Lakes Aviation
ZL*	Hazelton Airlines (Passenger)
ZL*	Affretair (Cargo)
ZN	Eagle Airlines
ZP	Air St. Thomas
ZQ	Ansett New Zealand
ZR	Muk Air
ZS	Azzurrair
ZU*	Freedom Air (Passenger)
ZU*	Aerovias Colombianas (Cargo)
ZV	Air Midwest
ZY	Ada-Air
Z3	Promech Air
Z4	Tayfunair (Cargo)
Z6	Dneproavia Avtn.
Z7	Zimbabwe Express Airlines
Z8	DHL de Guatemala (Cargo)
Z9	Aero Zambia
	2
2E	Ireland Airways
2F	Frontier Flying Service
2G	Debonair
2J	Majestic Airlines (Cargo)
2K	Kitty Hawk Airways (Cargo)
2M	Moldavian Airlines
2P	Air Philippines
2S	Island Express
2Y*	Helenair Corporation (Passenger)
2Y*	Thai Air Cargo (Cargo)
2Z	Changan Airlines
	3
3A	Alliance Airlines (Cargo)
3B	AVIOR
3C	Corporate Express Airlines
3J	Air Alliance
3K	Tatonduk Flying Service
3M	Gulfstream International
3N*	Air Urga (Passenger)
3N*	Airvantage (Cargo)
3P	Georgian Airlines
3Q	China Yunnan Airlines
3R	Air Moldova International
3S	Shuswap Flight Center
3T	Turan Air
3U	Sichuan Airlines
3X	Japan Air Commuter
3Z	Necon Air

(Contd.)

(Contd.)

Code	Airlines
	4
4B	Olson Air Service
4D	Air Sinai
4E	Tanana Air Services
4G	Shenzhen Airlines.
4J	Love Air/Montserrat Airways
4K	Kenn Borek Air
4M	Minskavia
4N	Air North
4T	Tch of Russian Airlines
4V	Voyageur Airways
4W	Warbelow's Air Ventures
4X	Flairlines
4Y	Yute Air Alaska
	5
5A	Alpine Aviation
5D	Donbass Airlines
5E	BASE Regional Airlines
5F	Arctic Circle Air Service
5J	Cebu Pacific Air
5L	Aerosur
5M	Sibaviatrans
5Q	Skargardsflyg
5R*	Aero Service (Passenger)
5R*	Rover Airways (Cargo)
5V	Vistajet
5W	Interline
5X	United Parcel Service (Cargo)
5Y*	Isles of Scilly Skybus (Passenger)
5Y*	Atlas Air (Cargo)
	6
6A	AVIACSA
6B	Baxter Aviation
6C	Cape Smythe Air Service Inc.
6E	Malrmo Aviation
6F	Laker Airways
6G	Las Vegas Airlines
6K	Korsar
6L	Aklak Air
6M	Maverick Airways
6N*	Trans Travel Airlines (Passenger)
6N*	Aerosucre (Cargo)
6P*	DAC Air (Passenger)
6P*	Aeropuma (Cargo)
6R	Air Affaires Afrique
6S	Proteus Helicopteres
6T	Air Mandalay
6U	Air Ukraine
6V	Air Vegas
6W	Wilderness Airlines
6Y	Nicaraguenses de Aviacion
6Z	Corgolift International (Cargo)
	7
7A	Haines Airways
7B	Krasnoyarsk Airlines
7C*	Columbia Pacific Airlines (Passenger)
7C*	Coyne Aviation Cargo
7E	Nepal Airways
7F	First Air
7G	Bellair
7H	Era Aviation
7J	Skagway Air Service
7L	AB Airlines
7M	Tyumen Airlines
7P	APA International Air
7S	Ryan Air
7T	Trans Cote
7W	Air Sask Aviation 1991
7Y	West Isle Air
7Z	L.B. Limited
	8
8A	Americana de Aviacion
8C	Transeuropean Airlines
8D	Awood Air
8E	Bering Air
8H	Air South West
8J	Jetall (Cargo)
8K	Air Ostrava

(Contd.)

(Contd.)

Code	Airlines	Code	Airlines
8L	Grandair	9C	Gill Airways
8M	Mahalo Air	9E	Express Airlines
8O	West Coast Air	9F	Haiti Air Freight (Cargo)
8P	Pacific Coastal Airlines	9G	Caribbean Air
8Q	Baker Aviation	9J	Pacific Island Aviation
8R	Avia Air	9K	Cape Air
8S	Salair (Cargo)	9L	Colgan Air
8T	Air Tindi	9N	Trans States Airlines
8V	Wright Air Service	9P	Pelangi Air
8W	Burlington Air Express (Cargo)	9S	Sabourin Lake Airways
		9T	Athabaska Airways
8Y	Ecuato Guineana de Aviacion	9U	Air Moldova
8Z	Alaska Island Air	9W	Jet Airways
	9	9X*	Tasawi Air Services (Passenger)
9A	Air Atlantic	9X*	Diamond Int'l Airlines (Cargo)
9B	Intourtrans		

Table 1.5: Carrier and Airline Codes of International Carriers

Carrier Code	Airline	Airline Code	Headquarters Location
AF	Air France	057	Paris, France
AI	Air India	098	Bombay, India
AR	Aerolineas Argentinas	044	Buenos Aires, Argentina
AV	Avianca	134	Bogotá, Columbia
AY	Finnair	105	Helsinki, Finland
AZ	Alitalia	055	Rome, Italy
BA	British Airways	125	London, UK
CA	CAAC	999	Beijing, China
CX	Cathy Pacific Airways	160	Hong Kong, Hong Kong
EI	AER Lingu	053	Dublin, Ireland
FI	Icelandair-Flugleidir	108	Reykjavik, Iceland
IB	Iberia Airlines	075	Madrid, Spain
JL	Japan Airlines	131	Tokyo, Japan
KL	KLM Royaldutch Airlines	074	The Hague, Netherlands
LA	LAN-CHILE	045	Santiago, Chile
LH	Lufthansa German Airlines	220	Cologne, Germany

(Contd.)

(*Contd.*)

LY	EL AI Israel Airlines	114	Tel Aviv, Israel
NZ	Air New Zealand	286	Auckland, New Zealand
OA	Olympic Airways	050	Athens, Greece
OS	Austrian Airlines	257	Vienna, Austria
PR	Philippine Airlines	079	Makati, Philippines
QF	Quantas Airways	081	Sydney, Australia
RK	Air Afrique	092	Cote d'Ivoire, West Africa
SA	South African Airways	083	Johannesburg, South Africa
SH	SAHSA	274	Tegucigalpa, Honduras
SK	Scandinavian Airlines	117	Stockholm, Sweden
SN	Sabena Belgian World Airlines	082	Brussels, Belgium
SR	Swiss Air	085	Zurich, Switzerland
SU	Aeroflot	555	Moscow, Russia
TP	TAP Air Portugal	047	Lisbon, Portugal
UT	UTA French Airlines	142	Puteaux, France
WT	Nigeria Airways	087	Lagos, Nigeria

SHARED AIRLINE DESIGNATOR CODE

By agreement some airlines integrate their schedules and operations with other airlines, and sometimes share their airline codes. In a typical case some or all the flights operated by a commuter airline are identified with the code of the airline with which it has a special agreement.

In the *Worldwide-city-to-city schedules a* ♦ is shown in the Class column to identify flights where the airline code displayed is different from the code of the airline actually providing the service. The Table 1.6 below shows which airline actually provides the service for flights marked ♦.

Table 1.6: Shared Airline Designator Codes

Codes		*Shared Designation Airlines*
	AA American Airlines	
AA	3201-5838	American Eagle
AA	6001-6004	South African Airways
AA	6100-6101	Qantas Airways
AA	6102-6103	LOT-Polish Airlines

(*Contd.*)

(*Contd.*)

Codes		Shared Designation Airlines
AA	6106-6107	LOT-Polish Airlines
AA	6111-6112	Qantas
AA	6113-6116	LOT-Polish Airlines
AA	6117-6118	Qantas
AA	6350-6449	Aspen Mt / Lone Star Airlines
AA	6500-6998	Canadian Airlines/Canadian Regional
		AC Air Canada
AC	1003-1004	Royal Jordanian
AC	1021-1022	Finnair
AC	1041-1042	Swissair
AC	1071-1084	Korean Air
AC	1153-1166	Lufthansa
AC	1200-1499	Air Ontario
AC	1500-1718	Air B.C.
AC	1721-1809	Central Mountain Air
AC	1812-1886	Air B.C.
AC	1900-1934	Alberta Citylink
AC	1940-1999	Air B.C.
AC	5100-5431	United Airlines
AC	8101-8197	Air Alliance
AC	8203-8216	Aviation Quebec LAB
AC	8231-8299	Air Alliance
AC	8709-8899	Air Nova
AC	8951-8985	Northwest Territorial Airways
AC	9009-9014	Continental Airlines
AC	9207-8248	Lufthansa
AC	9300-9351	SAS Scandinavian Airlines
		AE Mandarin Airlines
AE	067-068	China Airlines
AE	821-822	Air New Zealand
		AF Air France
AF	230-237	Aeromexico
AF	293-294	Japan Air Lines
AF	990-992	City Jet
AF	994-997	City Jet

(*Contd.*)

(Contd.)

Codes		Shared Designation Airlines
AF	1503-1578	Eurowings
AF	1646-1647	LOT Polish Airlines
AF	1659-1660	City Jet
AF	1716-1717	Alitalia
AF	1720-1721	Eurowings
AF	1726-1727	Alitalia
AF	1820-1821	Eurowings
AF	1846-1847	LOT Polish Airlines
AF	1920-1921	Eurowings
AF	1933-1948	LOT Polish Airlines
AF	2020-2021	Eurowings
AF	2051-2054	Malev
AF	2055-2076	Czech Airlines
AF	2126-2127	Alitalia
AF	2460-2461	City Jet
AF	2528-2529	Alitalia
AF	2752-2753	Alitalia
AF	2760-2961	City Jet
AF	3201-3206	Regional Airlines
AF	3345-3347	LOT Polish Airlines
AF	3602-3607	Brit Air
AF	3862-3863	Air Seychelles
AF	5438-5439	Alitalia
AF	5512-5537	Alitalia
AF	5526-5527	Eurowings
AF	5536-5537	Alitalia
AF	5626-5627	Eurowings
AF	5636-5637	Alitalia
AF	5666-5667	Alitalia
AF	5712-5713	Alitalia
AF	5726-5727	Eurowings
AF	5738-5739	Alitalia
AF	5826-5827	Eurowings
AF	5912-5913	Alitalia
AF	5936-5939	Alitalia
AF	7604-7605	Air Gabon
AF	8300-8401	Air Inter Europe
AF	8477-8699	Air Inter Europe

(Contd.)

(Contd.)

Codes		Shared Designation Airlines
	AI Air India	
AI	365-366	Kuwait Airways
AI	967-968	SAS Scandinavian Airlines
AI	1365-1366	Kuwait Airways
AI	1541-1542	Austrian Airlines
AI	2744-2759	Air Mauritius
AI	3001-3002	United Airlines
	AM Aero Mexico	
AM	2154-2839	Servicios Aereos Litoral
AM	3080-3970	Mexicana
AM	4300-4637	Aeromar Airlines
AM	5020-5975	Delta Air Lines
AM	7102-7926	Aerocaribe / Aerocozumel
AM	8038-8039	Air France
AM	9618-9619	Aeroperu
AM	9701-9738	Delta Air lines (US Domestic Sectors)
	AN Ansett Australia	
AN	5351-5363	Kendell Airlines
AN	5551-5552	Skywest Airlines
AN	5633-5653	Aeropelican
AN	5920-6209	Kendell Airlines
AN	6301-6457	Kendell Airlines
AN	6501-6598	Skywest Airlines
AN	6620-6661	Aeropelican
AN	7000-7099	Flight West Airlines
AN	7101-7477	Impulse Airlines
AN	7501-7582	Hazelton Airlines
AN	8031-8208	Air New Zealand
AN	8311-8312	EVA Airways
AN	8811-8813	Korean Air
AN	8820-8833	Malaysian Airlines
	AQ Aloha Airways	
AQ	1126-1943	Aloha Islandair

(Contd.)

(*Contd.*)

Codes		*Shared Designation Airlines*
	AR Aerolineas Argentinas	
AR	201-202	Malaysia Airlines
AR	1100-1181	Iberia (European legs only)
AR	1236-1237	LAPSA Lineas Aereas
	AS Alaska Airlines	
AS	2001-2901	Horizon Airlines
AS	3201-3409	American Eagle
AS	4201-4274	Penair
AS	4325-4390	Reeve Aleutian Airways
AS	4500-4589	Harbor Air
AS	4700-4799	US Airways
AS	4800-4989	ERA Aviation
AS	5007-5988	Northwest Airlines
	AY Finnair	
AY	6502-6502	Lufthansa
AY	6512-6521	European Air Transport
AY	6601-6601	Lufthansa
AY	6701-6703	Austrian Airlines
AY	6712-6715	El Al Israel Airlines
AY	6722-6739	Estonian Air
AY	6741-6744	Alitalia
AY	6755-6758	Maersk Air
AY	6762-6792	SABENA
AY	6841-6855	Maersk Air
AY	6866-6867	Swissair
AY	6903-6924	Braathens S.A.F.E.
	AZ Alitalia	
AZ	522-531	Malev
AZ	600-601	Continental Airlines (MIL-NYC, NYC-MIL)
AZ	640-643	Continental Airlines
AZ	650-657	Canadian Airlines
AZ	1210-1211	Minerva Airlines
AZ	1300-1309	Minerva Airlines
AZ	1514-1515	Minerva Airlines

(*Contd.*)

(*Contd.*)

Codes		Shared Designation Airlines
AZ	1687-1693	Minerva Airlines
AZ	1801-1802	Minerva Airlines
AZ	1827-1828	Minerva Airlines
AZ	1860-1882	ALPI Eagles
AZ	3101-3101	Minerva Airlines
AZ	7022-7026	Gulf Air
AZ	7140-7145	Finnair
AZ	7330-7395	Air France
AZ	7510-7515	Czech Airlines
AZ	7540-7547	Croatia Airlines
AZ	7550-7559	LOT Polish Airlines
AZ	7640-7657	Continental Airlines
AZ	7688-7689	Korean Air
AZ	7700-7701	Cyprus Airways
AZ	7800-7897	British Midland
AZ	7900-7903	Meridiana
AZ	7910-7913	Minerva Airlines
	BA British Airways	
BA	025-026	British Asia Airways (HKG-TPE, TPE-HKG)
BA	998-999	Qantas Airways
BA	3142-3265	TAT European Airways
BA	4640-4731	Deutsche BA
BA	6200-6441	Commercial Airways
BA	6701-6712	British Mediterranean Airways
BA	6861-6993	GB Airways
BA	7410-7429	Qantas Airways
BA	7491-7496	Eastern Australia
BA	7501-7536	Canadian Airlines/Canadian Regional
BA	7540-7572	America West Airlines
BA	7600-7914	Manx Airlines
BA	7951-7997	Canadian Airlines/Canadian Regional
BA	8011-8192	CityFlyer Express
BA	8201-8292	Sun Air of Scandinavia
BA	8300-8397	Maersk Air

(*Contd.*)

(Contd.)

Codes		Shared Designation Airlines
BA	8701-8837	Manx Airlines
BA	8845-8899	Loganair
	BR EVA Airways	
BR	235-236	Garuda Indonesia
BR	301-302	Ansett Australia
BR	661-662	Air Macau
BR	901-908	Uni Airways
BR	2101-2102	Air Nippon
	BT Air Baltic	
BT	5101-5172	SAS-Scandinavian Airlines
BT	7243-7244	Lufthansa
	CA Air China	
CA	121-122	Finnair
CA	195-196	SAS Scandinavian Airlines
CA	965-966	Austrian Airlines
	Cl China Airlines	
Cl	254-288	Formosa Airlines
Cl	924-927	Vietnam Airlines
Cl	980-981	Garuda Indonesia
Cl	7101-7936	Formosa Airlines
	CO Continental Airlines	
CO	4-5	Transavia Airlines (LON-AMS, AMS-LON)
CO	19-35	Transavia Airlines (AMS-LON)
CO	52-53	Czech Airlines
CO	831-834	Continental Micronesia
CO	861-868	Air Micronesia
CO	900-993	Continental Micronesia
CO	2102-2993	America West Airlines
CO	3001-4237	Continental Express
CO	4400-4879	Skywest Airlines
CO	7003-7090	America West Airlines
CO	7119-7557	Gulfstream International

(Contd.)

(*Contd.*)

Codes		*Shared Designation Airlines*
CO	7670-7786	Colgan Air
CO	8024-8169	Air Canada
CO	8185-8198	Air Nova
CO	8370-8391	Business Air
	CP Canadian Airlines International	
CP	1021-1023	Air New Zealand (NAN-HNL, HNL-NAN)
CP	1025-1026	Qantas Airways (HNL-SYD, SYD-HNL)
CP	1027-1031	Air New Zealand (AKL-HNL, HNL-AKL)
CP	1035-1036	Qantas Airways (HNL-SYD, SYD-HNL)
CP	1037-1040	Air New Zealand (AKL-HNL, HNL-AKL)
CP	1091-1098	Air St. Pierre
CP	1100-1399	Canadian Regional
CP	1401-1498	Air Atlantic
CP	1555-1598	Calm Air
CP	1617-1722	Canadian Regional
CP	1731-1738	Air Alma
CP	1750-1997	Canadian Regional
CP	4700-4803	American Airlines/American Eagle
CP	5001-5103	British Airways
CP	5300-5999	American Airlines/American Eagle
CP	6017-6018	Mandarin Airways
CP	6024-6039	British Airways
CP	6040-6041	Alitalia
CP	6060-6069	Air New Zealand
CP	6080-6083	Qantas Airways
CP	6097-6098	Malaysia Airlines
CP	6112-6113	Philippine Airlines
CP	6150-6949	American Airlines/American Eagle

(*Contd.*)

(*Contd.*)

Codes		*Shared Designation Airlines*
	CU CUBANA	
CU	8623-8672	Spanair
	CX Cathay Pacific	
CX	762-765	Vietnam Airlines
CX	766-769	Cathay Pacific
CX	790-793	Vietnam Airlines
CX	1117-1118	Ansett Australia
CX	1222-1253	British Midland
	CY Cyprus Airways	
CY	597-598	Aeroflot
CY	1816-1817	Alitalia
	CZ China Southern Airlines	
CZ	381-382	Xiamen Airlines
	DB Brit Air	
DB	5581-5584	Flandre Air (CFR-RNS, RNS-CFR)
DB	8740-8745	Flandre Air (CFR-RNS, RNS-CFR)
	DE Condor Flugdienst	
DE	1422-1489	Germania
DE	1552-1555	Germania
DE	2422-2467	Germania
DE	2626-2627	Germania
DE	2790-2791	Germania
DE	2828-2829	Germania
DE	3446-3463	Germania
DE	3546-3547	Germania
DE	3600-3601	Germania
DE	3712-3713	Germania
DE	3822-3823	Germania
DE	3868-3869	Germania
DE	3966-3967	Germania
DE	4422-4485	Germania
DE	4526-4527	Germania
DE	4566-4573	Germania
DE	4682-4683	Germania

(*Contd.*)

(*Contd.*)

Codes		Shared Designation Airlines
DE	4938-5005	Germania
DE	5034-5035	Germania
DE	5444-5497	Germania
DE	5536-5585	Germania
DE	5702-5715	Germania
DE	5786-5787	Germania
DE	5816-5817	Germania
DE	5846-5847	Germania
DE	5888-5889	Germania
DE	5964-5989	Germania
DE	6238-6239	Lufthansa
DE	6320-6353	Lufthansa
DE	6406-6407	Germania
DE	6416-6475	Lufthansa
DE	6508-6527	Lufthansa
DE	6534-6539	Germania
DE	6556-6557	Lufthansa
DE	6560-6561	Germania
DE	6574-6575	Lufthansa
DE	6602-6617	Lufthansa
DE	6624-6625	Germania
DE	6628-6689	Lufthansa
DE	6706-6719	Lufthansa
DE	6728-6735	Germania
DE	6744-6791	Lufthansa
DE	6806-6875	Lufthansa
DE	6906-6907	Lufthansa
DE	6930-6931	Germania
DE	6946-6973	Lufthansa
DE	6982-6983	Germania
DE	7004-7005	Germania
DE	7154-7155	Lufthansa
DE	7402-7403	Germania
DE	7408-7411	Lufthansa
DE	7412-7413	Germania
DE	7434-7435	Germania
DE	7438-7439	Lufthansa
DE	7442-7443	Germania
DE	7466-7467	Lufthansa

(*Contd.*)

(Contd.)

Codes		*Shared Designation Airlines*
DE	7486-7487	Germania
DE	7496-7517	Lufthansa
DE	7538-7539	Germania
DE	7542-7553	Lufthansa
DE	7600-7643	Lufthansa
DE	7644-7659	Germania
DE	7662-7849	Lufthansa
DE	7868-7869	Germania
DE	7876-7933	Lufthansa
	DL Delta Air Lines	
DL	25-26	Singapore Airlines
DL	90-91	Malev
DL	100-121	Swissair
DL	2400-2574	Delta Express
DL	2600-2619	Aeromexico
DL	2620-2625	Aer Lingus
DL	2631-2637	Korean Airlines
DL	2641-2692	Swissair
DL	2693-2698	Aeromexico
DL	2700-2769	SABENA
DL	2770-2791	Austrian Airlines
DL	2792-2793	Malev
DL	2794-2799	Austrian Airlines
DL	2801-2820	Virgin Atlantic
DL	2822-2829	Aeromexico
DL	2846-2850	Swissair
DL	2856-2856	SABENA
DL	2862-2863	Austrian Airlines
DL	2870-2875	Finnair
DL	2876-2890	Austrian Airlines
DL	2892-2893	Swissair
DL	2896-2899	TAP Air Portugal
DL	2900-2949	Aeromexico
DL	2974-2983	SABENA
DL	2992-2995	Swissair
	The Delta Connection	
DL	3001-3999	Comair

(Contd.)

(Contd.)

Codes		Shared Designation Airlines
DL	4200-4964	Business Express
DL	5208-5997	Skywest Airlines
DL	7000-7998	Atlantic Southeast Airlines
	DM Maersk Air	
DM	140-157	Finnair
	DV Gorda Aero Service	
DV	200-303	North Sound Express
	EH SAETA	
EH	800-831	SANSA-Servicios Aereas Naccionales
	EI Aer Lingus	
EI	400-401	Hamburg Airlines
EI	449-449	British World Airlines
EI	634-639	SABENA
EI	860-861	Air Engiadina
EI	885-886	Finnair
	EK Emirates	
EK	467-468	South African Airways
	EW Eurowings	
EW	241-287	Gill Airways
EW	380-387	Air France
EW	491-498	Tyrolean Airways
	FI Icelandair	
FI	7436-7455	British Midland
	FJ Air Pacific	
FJ	500-503	Solomon Airlines
FJ	520-521	Qantas Airways
FJ	560-561	Polynesian Airlines
FJ	570-571	Air Vanuatu
FJ	580-581	Royal Tongan Airlines
FJ	590-591	Air Caledonie International

(Contd.)

(Contd.)

Codes		*Shared Designation Airlines*
	FL AirTran Airways	
FL	3300-3873	Comair
	FQ Air Aruba	
FQ	504-511	SAM
	F9 Frontier Airlines	
F9	12-498	Western Pacific Airlines
F9	1001-1992	Mountain Air Express
F9	5350-5361	Aspen Mountain/Lone Star
	GA Garuda	
GA	625-628	Korean Air
GA	693-694	Korean Air
GA	1833-1834	KLM
GA	1930-1931	EVA Airways
	GF Gulf Air	
GF	1852-1857	Air Malta
	GN Air Gabon	
GN	104-105	Air France
	GU AVIATECA	
GU	110-511	Taca International
GU	690-691	LACSA
GU	710-711	Taca International
	HA Hawaiian Airlines	
HA	1600-1671	Mahalo Air
HA	1700-1764	Reno Air
HA	3201-3497	American Eagle
	HP America West	
HP	70-79	Continental Airlines
HP	1408-1999	Continental Airlines
HP	3151-3990	Continental Express
HP	5000-5406	Mesa Airlines
	HX Hamburg Airlines	
HX	1586-1589	TAP Air Portugal

(Contd.)

(*Contd.*)

Codes		*Shared Designation Airlines*
	IB Iberia	
IB	4212-4212	AVIACO (ALC-BCN)
IB	4217-4217	AVIACO (BCN-ALC)
IB	4305-4306	AVIACO
IB	4522-4522	AVIACO
IB	6122-6123	Carnival Airlines (LAX-MIA, MIA-LAX)
IB	6621-6621	Macair
IB	6850-6850	Aerolineas Argentinas (MVD-BUE)
IB	6852-6895	Aerolineas Argentinas (ASU-BUE, BUE-ASU)
IB	7030-7031	Malaysia Airlines
IB	7101-7102	Korean Air
IB	7300-7301	Syrian Arab Airlines
IB	7372-7373	Croatia Airlines
IB	7576-7577	Tyrolean Airways
IB	7595-7596	Ukraine International
IB	7824-7825	Aerolineas Argentinas
IB	8201-8212	Air Nostrum
IB	8382-8717	Air Nostrum
IB	8768-8799	Air Nostrum
IB	8813-8999	Air Nostrum
	IE Solomon Airlines	
IE	706-707	Air Niugini
	IG Meridiana	
IG	303-306	Air Littoral
	IR Iran Air	
IR	773-774	Austrian Airlines
	IT Air Inter Europe	
IT	1024-2125	Air France
IT	3497-3498	Regional Airlines
IT	3693-3694	Regional Airlines
IT	3995-3996	Regional Airlines
IT	4308-4308	Tunis Air

(*Contd.*)

(Contd.)

Codes		Shared Designation Airlines
IT	4798-4798	Tunis Air
IT	5007-6193	Air France
IT	7300-8405	Air France
	JI Midway Airlines	
JI	1690-1831	Corporate Express
	JL Japan Air Lines	
JL	023-024	VARIG
JL	050-059	Japan Air Charter
JL	067-068	VARIG
JL	075-088	Japan Air Charter
JL	090-099	Air New Zealand
JL	411-414	KLM (AMS-ZRH, ZRH-AMS, AMS-MAD, MAD-AMS)
JL	435-436	Air France
JL	727-728	Japan Air Charter
	JM Air Jamaica	
JM	300-340	Air Jamaica
JM	982-985	Air Canada
	KE Korean Airlines	
KE	005-006	Delta Air Lines
KE	075-078	Air Canada
KE	692-693	Garuda Indonesia
KE	837-838	Air New Zealand
	KL KLM—Royal Dutch Airlines	
KL	002-496	KLM Cityhopper
KL	537-538	Cyprus Airways
KL	555-562	Kenya Airways
KL	720-770	Air Exel
KL	901-902	Aeroflot
KL	1046-1995	KLM Cityhopper
KL	2002-2099	Eurowings
KL	2148-2158	Air UK
KL	2271-2280	Maersk Air
KL	2320-2325	Air Engiadina

(Contd.)

(*Contd.*)

Codes		Shared Designation Airlines
KL	2406-2415	Air UK
KL	2441-2446	Regional Airlines
KL	2601-2617	Aer Lingus
KL	2701-2923	Air UK
KL	3001-3002	Transavia Airlines
KL	3420-3503	Kenya Airways
KL	3709-3782	Sun Air
KL	3800-3801	Oman Air
KL	4032-4975	Ansett Australia
KL	5002-6996	Northwest Airlines
KL	8008-8998	Northwest Airlines
	KM Air Malta	
KM	314-315	Tuninter
KM	900-923	Malta Air Charter
	KQ Kenya Airways	
KQ	1565-1566	KLM
	KS Penair	
KS	830-835	Katmai Air Taxi
	KW Carnival Airlines	
KW	6201-6783	Paradise Island Airlines
	LA LAN—Chile	
LA	5033-5134	Air New Zealand (PPT-AKL, AKL-PPT)
	LG Luxair	
LG	133-134	Conseta-Cirrus
	LH Lufthansa	
LH	175-190	Lufthansa Cityline
LH	801-804	Lufthansa Cityline
LH	833-833	Cimber Air
LH	884-971	Lufthansa Cityline
LH	1004-1004	Eurowings
LH	1012-1013	Cimber Air
LH	1016-1016	Air Atlantique

(*Contd.*)

(*Contd.*)

Codes		*Shared Designation Airlines*
LH	1017-1017	Cimber Air
LH	1019-1021	Air Atlantique
LH	1025-1025	Cimber Air
LH	1027-1027	Air Atlantique
LH	1050-1080	Deustche Bahn
LH	1304-1309	Lufthansa Cityline
LH	1500-1587	Cimber Air
LH	1590-1600	Eurowings
LH	1601-1601	Cimber Air
LH	1602-1602	Eurowings
LH	1620-1839	Air Atlantique
LH	2502-2637	Lufthansa Cityline
LH	3212-3248	Air Atlantique
LH	3376-3377	Lufthansa Cityline
LH	3612-3613	Lufthansa Cityline
LH	3638-3888	Air Atlantique
LH	4052-4057	Lufthansa Cityline
LH	4061-4061	Air Littoral
LH	4063-4102	Air Atlantique
LH	4110-4116	Air Littoral
LH	4123-4125	Air Atlantique
LH	4127-4127	Air Littoral
LH	4128-4158	Air Atlantique
LH	4201-4226	Lufthansa Cityline
LH	4412-4415	Air Atlantique
LH	4416-4416	Lufthansa Cityline
LH	4418-4502	Air Atlantique
LH	4545-4545	Lufthansa Cityline
LH	4693-4693	Business Air
LH	4720-4724	Business Air
LH	4738-4739	Lufthansa Cityline
LH	5052-5057	Air Atlantique
LH	506-5691	Crossair
LH	5749-5801	Air Littoral
LH	5838-5839	Crossair
LH	5892-5897	Air Littoral
LH	6000-6199	SAS-Scandinavian Airlines
LH	6200-6269	Lauda Air (until 25 Oct)

(*Contd.*)

(*Contd.*)

Codes		*Shared Designation Airlines*
LH	6200-6269	SAS-Scandinavian Airlines (from 26 Oct)
LH	6290-6297	Adria Airways (until 25 Oct)
LH	6292-6299	SAS-Scandinavian Airlines (from 26 Oct)
LH	6301-6326	Luxair (until 25 Oct)
LH	6300-6321	Thai Airways (from 26 Oct)
LH	6330-6337	Hamburg Airlines (until 25 Oct)
LH	6332-6367	Thai Airways (from 26 Oct)
LH	6350-6361	Business Air (until 25 Oct)
LH	6362-6365	Air Baltic Corporation (until 25 Oct)
LH	6370-6397	Business Air
LH	6400-6629	United Airlines
LH	6630-6653	South African Airways
LH	6658-6679	United Airlines
LH	6680-6685	VARIG
LH	6686-6699	United Airlines
LH	6710-6717	Thai Airways International
LH	6718-6721	Air Canada
LH	6743-6787	Thai Airways International
LH	6800-6807	Finnair
LH	6816-6819	LOT-Polish Airlines
LH	6820-6833	Air Dolomiti
LH	6840-6841	Air Canada (from 26 Oct)
LH	6840-6849	Air Dolomiti (until 25 Oct)
LH	6850-6851	Air Canada
LH	6860-6865	Varig
LH	6868-6869	Lauda Air
LH	6900-6999	SAS-Scandinavian Airlines
LH	9020-9025	British Midland
LH	9060-9099	Air Dolomiti
LH	9102-9107	Business Air
LH	9160-9167	Adria Airways
LK	9170-9171	Czech Airlines
LH	9180-9183	LOT Polish Airlines
LH	9190-9199	Hamburg Airlines
LH	9220-9221	Lauda Air

(*Contd.*)

(*Contd.*)

Codes		*Shared Designation Airlines*
LH	9244-9249	Rheintalflug
LH	9280-9287	Lauda Air
LH	9301-9326	Luxair
LH	9350-9353	Air Baltic Corporation
LH	9370-9373	VLM
LH	9382-9395	Augsburg Airways
LH	9400-9447	VLM (until 25 Oct)
LH	9430-9449	Rheintalflug (from 26 Oct)
LH	9450-9480	Deutsche Bahn
LH	9502-9567	Augsburg Airways
LH	9584-9598	Deutsche Bahn
LH	9600-9669	Augsburg Airways
LH	9690-9699	VLM
	LI LIAT	
LI	180-193	Airlines of Carriacou
LI	851-854	Dominair
	LM ALM	
LM	4101-4101	Air Aruba
	LO LOT—Polish Airlines	
LO	5219-5222	Austrian Airlines
LO	5307-5310	Alitalia
LO	5321-5324	Air France
LO	5515-5518	Czech Airlines
LO	5801-5837	American Airlines
	LR LACSA	
LR	215-216	TACA International
LR	230-231	Nicaraguense
LR	405-406	TACA International
LR	730-731	TACA International
LR	960-961	AVIATECA
LR	1610-1651	SANSA
	LT LT.U. International Airways	
LT	1518-1519	Air New Zealand

(*Contd.*)

(Contd.)

Codes		Shared Designation Airlines
	LX Crossair	
LX	471-498	Regional Airlines
LX	721-726	Regional Airlines
	LZ Balkan	
LZ	303-304	Czech Airlines
LZ	353-354	LOT Polish Airlines
LZ	405-406	Armenian Airlines
LZ	853-654	SIAC
LZ	865-872	Air Moldova
LZ	8307-6308	Olympic Airways
	MA MALEV	
MA	096-097	Delta Air Lines
MA	510-511	Delta Air Lines
MA	552-559	Air France
MA	828-829	Czech Airlines
MA	7234-7235	Olympic Airways
	MD Air Madagascar	
MD	282-282	Air Mauritius
	MH Malaysia Airlines	
MH	7-8	Lauda Air
MH	122-123	Ansett Australia
MH	140-141	Ansett Australia
MH	162-163	Air Maldives
MH	9001-9041	Ansett Australia
MH	9052-9059	Ansett New Zealand
MH	9069-9128	Ansett Australia
MH	9271-9347	British Midland
	MK Air Mauritius	
MK	492-497	Air Austral
	MX Compania Mexicana	
MX	1304-1477	Aeromexico
MX	1613-1631	Aeromexico
MX	1695-1696	Aeroperu

(Contd.)

(*Contd.*)

Codes		*Shared Designation Airlines*
MX	3003-3018	United Airlines
MX	4300-4762	Aeromar Airlines
MX	7100-7529	Aerocaribe / Aerocozumel
MX	7801-7975	Aerocaribe / Aerocozumel
MX	8154-8839	Servicios Aereos Utoral
	NC National Jet System	
NC	87-87	Norfolk Express
NC	97-97	Norfolk Express
	NF Air Vanuatu	
NF	210-211	Air Pacific
NF	704-711	Solomon Airlines
	NG Lauda Air	
NG	8001-8002	Malaysia Airlines
	NI Portugalia	
NI	200-200	TAP Air Portugal
	NV Northwest Territorial Airways	
NV	168-172	Buffalo Airways
NV	200-209	Air Tindi
NV	507-519	Northwestern Air Lease
	NW Northwest Airlines	
NW	3702-3799	Eurowings
NW	3800-3809	Pacific Island Aviation
NW	3901-3952	Asiana Airlines
NW	4095-4564	Hawaiian Airlines
NW	4600-4671	Mahalo Air Inc.
NW	4801-4898	America West Airlines
NW	4900-5039	Air UK
NW	7020-7722	Alaska Airlines
NW	8002-8995	KLM
	Northwest Airlink	
NW	2001-2829	Horizon Airlines
NW	2900-3690	Mesaba Airlines
NW	4700-4799	Trans States Airlines

(*Contd.*)

(*Contd.*)

Codes		Shared Designation Airlines
NW	5091-5854	Express Airlines
NW	6200-6421	Business Express
		NX Air Macau
NX	885-886	TAP Air Portugal
		NZ Air New Zealand
NZ	301-302	Royal Tongan Airlines
NZ	312-315	Polynesian Airlines
NZ	316-317	LAN-Chile (PPT-IPC/SCL, SCL/IPC-PPT)
NZ	323-334	Canadian Airlines International (HNL-YYZ/YVR, YYZ/YVR-HNL)
NZ	340-343	Air Pacific
NZ	377-378	Korean Air
NZ	2001-2968	Air New Zealand Link
NZ	3010-3976	Ansett Australia
NZ	4285-4380	Singapore Airlines
NZ	4404-4487	British Midland
NZ	4815-4941	United Airlines
NZ	5000-5995	Air New Zealand Link
NZ	8040-6857	Air New Zealand Link
		N4 National Airlines
N4	250-251	Aerosur
		OA Olympic Airways
OA	8229-8230	Aerosweet
OA	8308-6309	Swissair
OA	8330-8333	Malev
OA	8443-8444	Balkan
OA	8750-6751	VASP
		OK Czech Airlines
OK	4000-4007	Air Ostrava
OK	4030-4195	Continental Airlines
OK	4472-4473	Luxair
OK	4514-4517	Air Ostrava

(*Contd.*)

(Contd.)

Codes		Shared Designation Airlines
OK	4584-4589	Swissair
OK	4608-4615	Tyrolean Airways
OK	4616-4619	KLM
OK	4722-4729	Alitalia
OK	4760-4763	Air France
OK	4780-4783	LOT-Polish Airlines
OK	4786-4791	MALEV
OK	4954-4955	Air Ostrava
	OS Austrian Airlines	
OS	102-109	Lufthansa
OS	152-157	Lufthansa
OS	172-177	Lufthansa
OS	251-256	Iberia
OS	271-288	Lauda Air
OS	425-426	Lauda Air
OS	431-446	SABENA
OS	488-499	SABENA
OS	511-526	Delta Air Lines
OS	527-528	Swissair
OS	529-538	Delta Air Lines
OS	539-540	Air Mauritius
OS	544-544	Delta Air Lines
OS	545-546	Singapore Airlines
OS	555-555	All Nippon Airways (day 2 only)
OS	556-556	All Nippon Airways (day 3 only)
OS	559-580	Delta Air Lines
OS	589-589	Delta Air Lines
OS	623-628	LOT-Polish Airlines
OS	629-630	Tyrolean Airways
OS	631-632	LOT-Polish Airlines
OS	639-639	Tyrolean Airways
OS	640-641	Czech Airlines
OS	642-647	Tyrolean Airways
OS	648-649	Czech Airlines
OS	650-650	Tyrolean Airways
OS	681-688	Finnair
OS	802-848	Tyrolean Airways

(Contd.)

(*Contd.*)

Codes		*Shared Designation Airlines*
OS	941-952	SABENA
OS	8106-8187	Delta Air Lines
OS	8251-8256	Iberia
OS	8431-8446	SABENA
OS	8511-8512	Delta Air Lines
OS	8527-8528	Swissair
OS	8539-8540	Air Mauritius
OS	8545-8546	Singapore Airlines
OS	8623-8632	LOT-Polish Airlines
OS	8640-8649	Czech Airlines
OS	8681-8687	Finnair
OS	8902-8937	Lufthansa
OS	8941-8951	SABENA
OS	8952-8952	Lufthansa
OS	8954-8954	SABENA
OS	8957-8957	Lufthansa
OS	8963-8963	Finnair
	OV Estonian Air	
OV	7212-7221	Finnair
	OZ Asiana Airways	
OZ	241-242	Northwest Airlines
OZ	605-606	Qantas Airways
OZ	615-615	Qantas Airways
	PA Pan American World Airways	
PA	30-33	Carnival Air Lines
PA	76-77	Carnival Air Lines
PA	90-93	Carnival Air Lines
PA	3031-3308	Pan Am Airbridge
PA	5001-5611	Carnival Air Lines
	PH Polynesian Airlines	
PH	356-357	Air New Zealand
PH	565-566	Air Pacific
	PL Aeroperu	
PL	691-692	Pan American World Airways (NYC-MIA, MIA-NYC)

(*Contd.*)

(*Contd.*)

Codes		*Shared Designation Airlines*
PL	712-713	Transport Mercosur
PL	1695-1696	Mexicana
PL	9618-9619	Aeromexico
	PR Philippine Airlines	
PR	864-865	Egyptair
PR	933-934	Vietnam Airlines
	PS Ukraine International Airlines	
PS	104-105	KLM
PS	470-471	Swissair
PS	615-620	Austrian Airlines
	PU PLUNA	
PU	224-227	VARIG
	PY Surinam Airways	
PY	4973-4977	ALM (CUR/PAP-MIA, MIA-PAP/CUR)
	QF Qantas Airways	
QF	251-252	British Airways
QF	360-360	Japan Airlines
QF	361-366	Air Caledonie International
QF	367-368	Asiana Airlines
QF	369-369	Japan Airlines
QF	371-372	Solomon Airlines
QF	375-378	Air Vanuatu
QF	381-384	Air Niugini
QF	387-398	Air Pacific
QF	817-847	Eastern Australian Airlines
QF	850-960	Australian Airlink
QF	961-997	Southern Australian Airlines
QF	1950-1955	Australian Airlink
QF	2004-2294	Eastern Australian Airlines
QF	2300-2557	Sunstate Airlines
QF	2621-2766	Southern Australian Airlines
QF	3001-3008	American Airlines
QF	3009-3010	Canadian Airlines International

(*Contd.*)

(*Contd.*)

Codes		Shared Designation Airlines
QF	3017-3018	US Airways
QF	3021-3052	American Airlines
QF	3053-3054	Canadian Airlines International
QF	3304-3915	British Airways
	QQ Reno Air	
QQ	3201-3497	American Eagle
	RG VARIG Brazilian Airlines	
RG	328-329	Transbrasil
RG	378-379	Transbrasil
RG	400-401	Transbrasil
RG	470-471	Transbrasil
RG	704-704	TAP Air Portugal
RG	770-773	Lufthansa
RG	784-787	PLUNA
RG	918-949	PLUNA
	RJ Royal Jordanian	
RJ	9267-9849	Trans World Airlines
	RQ Air Engiadina	
RQ	414-417	SK Air
	SA South African Airways	
SA	158-159	Emirates
SA	186-187	Alliance Airlines
SA	1001-1728	South African Express
SA	7010-7326	American Airlines/American Eagle
SA	7500-7575	Lufthansa
SA	8002-8491	South African Airlink
	SB Air Caledonic International	
SB	148-165	Qantas Airways
	SK SAS Scandinavian Airlines	
SK	3023-3044	Falcon Airways
SK	3102-3112	Skyways
SK	3201-3346	Lufthansa

(*Contd.*)

(Contd.)

Codes		*Shared Designation Airlines*
SK	3383-3384	Regional Airlines
SK	3400-3407	Cimber Air
SK	3544-3545	Spanair
SK	3561-3568	Lufthansa
SK	3571-3572	Spanair
SK	3573-3580	Lufthansa
SK	3581-3584	Spanair
SK.	3585-3730	Lufthansa
SK	3738-3750	Air Baltic Corporation
SK	3761-3790	Lufthansa
SK	3851-3868	Icelandair
SK	3905-3952	United Airlines
SK	3954-3958	VARIG
SK	3960-3968	United Airlines
SK	3970-3978	Thai Airways International
SK	3980-3983	South African Airways
	SN SABENA	
SN	124-125	Delta Air Lines
SN	289-290	Sobelair
SN	330-333	Tyrolean Airways
SN	341-350	Austrian Airlines
SN	507-508	Sobelair
SN	541-548	Delta Air Lines
SN	597-614	Virgin Express
SN	630-637	Aer Lingus
SN	651-660	VLM
SN	661-668	Virgin Express
SN	769-770	Finnair (days 1-5)
SN	769-770	Sabena (day 7)
SN	793-798	Maersk Air
SN	811-820	Virgin Express
SN	871-880	Virgin Express
SN	4227-4228	Austrian Airlines
SN	4265-4266	Crossair
SN	4281-4282	Swissair
SN	4307-4320	Austrian Airlines
SN	4575-4594	Nationwide Air

(Contd.)

(*Contd.*)

Codes		Shared Designation Airlines
SN	8112-8242	Delta Air Lines
SN	9351-9362	Swissair
SN	9383-9399	Crossair
	SQ Singapore Airlines	
SQ	287-288	Air New Zealand
SO	1005-1016	American Airlines
	SR Swissair	
SR	1-1	Swissair
SR	1-5	Austrian Airlines
SR	3-3	Swissair
SR	5-5	Swissair
SR	6-6	Austrian Airlines
SR	7-15	Swissair
SR	22-31	Austrian Airlines
SR	33-96	Tyrolean Airways
SR	112-113	Delta Air Lines
SR	114-115	Austrian Airlines
SR	122-123	Delta Air Lines
SR	130-137	Air Canada
SR	144-145	LADECO (BUE-SCL, SCL-BUE)
SR	308-309	Crossair
SR	434-945	Crossair
SR	1568-1569	Crossair
SR	1966-1972	Crossair
SR	3238-3977	Crossair
SR	4023-4023	Delta Airlines
SR	4037-4037	Air Canada
SR	6438-6973	Crossair
SR	8012-8013	Delta Air Lines
SR	8014-8015	Austrian Airlines
SR	8022-8023	Delta Air Lines
SR	8036-8037	Air Canada
SR	8104-8148	Delta Air Lines
SR	8178-8179	Aeromexico
SR	8204-8225	Delta Air Lines
SR	8250-8251	Ladeco

(*Contd.*)

(Contd.)

Codes		Shared Designation Airlines
SR	8300-8391	Austrian Airlines
SR	8396-8399	Lauda Air
SR	8501-8556	Tyrolean Airlines
SR	8590-8593	Finnair
SR	8600-8641	Maersk Air
SR	8811-8841	Transwede
SR	8850-8851	Czech Airlines
SR	8860-8863	Malev
SR	8870-8873	Tatra Air
SR	9351-9362	Crossair
SR	9369-9426	SABENA
	SU Aeroflot	
SU	001-026	Domodedovo Airlines
SU	027-028	Bashkir Airlines
SU	035-036	Khabarovsk Aviation
SU	051-062	Domodedovo Airlines
SU	085-086	Bashkir Airlines
SU	091-092	Bashkir Airlines (MOW-YKS, YKS-MOW)
SU	091-092	Domodedovo Airlines (UFA-URJ, URJ-UFA)
SU	107-110	Chitaavia
SU	253-254	Tyumen Airlines
SU	335-342	Bashkir Airlines
SU	411-412	Tyumen Airlines
SU	651-652	Domodedovo Airlines
SU	730-738	State Orenburg AVA
SU	871-872	Domodedovo Airlines
SU	1171-1196	Donavia
SU	2207-2212	Domodedovo Airlines
SU	2411-2438	Air Pulkovo
SU	3835-3970	Khabarovsk Aviation
SU	3981-4032	Sakha Avia
SU	5719-5784	Bashkir Airlines
SU	5881-5910	State Orenburg AVA
SU	6111-6112	Donavia
SU	8467-8753	Air Pulkovo

(Contd.)

(*Contd.*)

Codes		Shared Designation Airlines
		SV Saudia
SV	2000-2001	United Airlines
		TA TACA International Airlines
TA	680-691	LACSA
TA	950-961	AVIATECA
		TG Thai Airways International
TG	7500-7503	South African Airways
TG	7826-7971	Lufthansa
TG	7972-7977	SAS Scandinavian Airlines
		TK Turkish Airlines
TK	701-704	Swissair
TK	1004-1005	Asiana Airlines
		TM LAM
TM	205-206	Air Malawi
TM	344-345	Air Zimbabwe
TM	420-423	Air Malawi
		TP TAP Air Portugal
TP	187-188	SATA Air Acores
TP	227-228	LAM
TP	302-303	Air Macau
TP	582-583	Hamburg Airlines
TP	801-851	Portugalia
TP	862-895	Aerocondor
TP	3201-3211	Delta Air Lines
		TR Transbrasil
TR	120-127	Interbrasil Star
TR	170-173	VARIG
TR	180-197	Interbrasil Star
TR	420-425	VARIG
TR	570-572	VARIG
TR	800-811	Pantanal Linhas Aereos
		TW Trans World Airlines
TW	7003-7799	Trans State Airlines

(*Contd.*)

(Contd.)

Codes		*Shared Designation Airlines*
		TZ American Trans Air
TZ	3101-3363	Chicago Express
		UA United Airlines
UA	3000-3211	Air Canada
UA	3300-3303	Air Nova
UA	3320-3355	Air B.C.
UA	3375-3495	CO Connection
UA	3496-3497	Saudia
UA	3500-3825	Lufthansa
UA	4026-4297	Aloha Airlines
UA	4300-4301	Emirates
UA	4351-4376	Air New Zealand
UA	4420-4485	Mexicana
UA	4498-4499	Aeromexico
UA	4500-4519	Cayman Airways
UA	4520-4565	SAS Scandinavian Airlines
UA	4571-4594	ALM
UA	4600-4649	Aeromar Airlines
UA	4650-4799	Trans States Airlines
UA	4900-4969	Ansett Australia
UA	4970-4989	Ansett New Zealand
UA	4990-4998	Ansett/Kendell
UA	5000-5495	United Express-Skywest
UA	5501-5699	United Express-AWAC
UA	5700-5763	United Express
UA	5803-6148	United Express-Great Lakes
UA	6150-6599	United Express-Atlantic Coast
UA	6970-7399	United Express-Westair
UA	7450-7999	United Express-Mesa
		UK Air UK
UK	588-597	Gill Airways
UK	950-965	Gill Airways
UK	984-989	Suckling Airways
UK	2046-2461	KLM
UK	2600-2605	Malmo Aviation
UK	2802-2821	City Jet
UK	2844-2855	Air Engiadina

(Contd.)

(Contd.)

Codes		Shared Designation Airlines
UK	3140-3145	Air Exel
UK	3681-3694	Jersey European
	UL Air Lanka	
UL	194-195	Royal Jordanian
	UM Air Zimbabwe	
UM	023-064	Qantas Airways
UM	542-543	LAM
	UP Bahamsair	
UP	118-120	Congo Air
UP	800-809	Sky Unlimited
	US US Airways	
US	2076-2087	Deutsche BA
US	3001-5999	US Airways Express
US	6001-6541	US Airways Shuttle
	VC Servivensa	
VC	500-501	Mexicana
	VN Vietnam Airlines	
VN	017-018	Lauda Air
VN	184-185	Swissair
VN	591-592	Philippine Airlines
VN	750-751	Malaysia Airlines
VN	766-769	Cathay Pacific
VN	946-947	Japan Air Lines
VN	1457-1596	Air France
	VP VASP	
VP	900-903	Ecuatoriana
	VS Virgin Atlanta Airways	
VS	501-529	Malaysia Airlines
VS	7445-7790	Sun Air

(Contd.)

(*Contd.*)

Codes		Shared Designation Airlines
VW Transportes Aeromar		
VW	2550-2557	Compania Mexicana
VW	3122-3135	Aeromexico
VY Formosa Airlines		
VY	251-290	China Airlines
WR Royal Tongan Airlines		
WR	210-211	Ansett Australia (AKL-SYD, SYD-AKL)
WR	300-305	Air Pacific
WR	351-359	Air New Zealand
WX CityJet		
WX	600-605	Malmo Aviation (LON-MMA, MMA-LON)
WX	921-928	Air UK
WY Oman Air		
WY	392-399	Swissair
W7 Western Pacific Airlines		
W7	504-941	Frontier Airlines
W7	1003-1992	Mountain Air Express
YV Mesa Airlines		
YV	1801-1831	Air Midwest
YX Midwest Express Airlines		
YX	1000-1908	Skyway Airlines
ZK Great Lakes Aviation		
ZK	141-144	Scenic Airlines
3J Air Alliance		
3J	228-229	Aviation Quebec
3R Air Moldova		
3R	203-204	Dneproavia Aviation

(*Contd.*)

(Contd.)

Codes	*Shared Designation Airlines*	
	4T Tch of Russia Airlines	
4T	469-1582	Aircompany Karat
	4Y Yute Air Alaska	
4Y	182-448	Merlin Express
4Y	550-560	Merlin Express
4Y	802-804	Merlin Express
	5E BASE Regional Airlines	
5E	159-162	TTA
	6Y Nicaraguenses de Aviacion	
6Y	260-261	AVIATECA
6Y	628-629	LACSA
	7F First Air	
7F	410-453	Air Inuit
7F	958-959	Greenlandair
	9C Gill Aviation	
9C	101-204	European Airways
9C	775-776	European Airways
	9K Cape Air	
9K	98-125	Nantucket Airlines

RULES AND REGULATIONS: EXAMPLE: ALASKA AIRLINES

DISCOVER AMERICA ZONE FARES

Rules and Conditions

Fare Basis Codes

MZONE — One-way adult
MCHZONE — One-way accompanying children

Booking Code: M

Area of Application

These fares apply to/from points between/within the zones published *in combination* with travel to/from any point from outside the area comprised of the 50 United States/District of Columbia/ Canada/Mexico.

Eligibility

Fares governed by this rule apply to residents of, or, U.S. Dept. of Defence/U.S. Embassy/active duty U.S. Military personnel and their dependents stationed in, a country/commonwealth/territory other than the 50 United States/District of Columbia/Canada/Mexico.

Documents Required

Proof of travel consisting of a round trip/circle trip/open jaw international ticket by commercial air/sea transportation or military transportation request showing carriage to/from U.S.A./Canada/ Mexico. Other documents required are proof of permanent residence or stationing in the form of passport, visa, government issued tourist card, driver's license or similar document.

The above documents are required to be shown to the ticketing agent and to Alaska Airlines upon check-in.

Maximum Stay

60 Days after beginning travel at these fares. All travel must be completed within 120 days after arrival in the U.S.A./Canada/ Mexico.

Reservations

Reservations for originating flights on Alaska Airlines/Horizon Air/participating AS codeshare carriers must be made at least seven (7) days prior to departure from the point of origin at this fare. Reservations for all other flights may be made any time before departure of each flight, however, seats are limited.

Ticketing

Tickets must be purchased and issued outside of the U.S.A./ Canada/Mexico, and before arrival in, the U.S.A./Canada/Mexico. The ticketing agent is required to enter the international ticket number in the Form of Payment box on tickets issued for these fares. Only one ticket at these fares may be issued in connection with each trip originating/terminating outside the U.S.A./Canada/Mexico. More than one zone of travel may be included on one ticket. Open tickets are allowed provided that the complete routing is specified. A Government Transportation Request can not be accepted as a form of payment. PTA's/MCO's are not permitted. Tickets must show the following endorsements: (1) Non-endorsable (2) Must show identification.

Stopovers

One free stopover only is permitted in either Anchorage, Seattle or Portland. Additional stopovers are allowed per the applicable routing for U.S. $40 each. Travel to Zone 11 from another zone includes free stopovers in both Nome and Kotzebue. Enroute transit stops for change of airplanes are not considered as stopovers.

Combinations

All travel must be entirely via Alaska Airlines/Horizon Air or participating Alaska Airlines code share carriers. These fares may not be combined with other fares to construct round trip/circle trip fares.

Children's Fares

Children 2 through 11 may travel at 90 per cent of the Adult Zone Fare when accompanied by an adult passenger paying a fare governed by this rule. Only one child per fare paying adult is permitted.

Changes/Cancellations/Refunds

The value of unused transportation will be refunded subject to a U.S. $35 refund processing fee. A U.S. $35 service charge applies for changes which require a ticket to be reissued after arrival in North America. For tickets that have already been issued, changes that require only a revalidation sticker can be made free of charge.

Routings

Travel is permitted only between city pairs where AS publishes a local fare. Fares are only valid via normal routings published in DRG1, CRG1, AS1. Backhaul routings are not allowed except upon payment of point to point local fares.

Involuntary Rerouting/Flight Changes

Passengers will not be rerouted via other carriers, but will be permitted to take the next available AS flight.

Additional Information

Complete rules governing Alaska Airlines DISCOVER AMERICA

ZONE FARES may be found in Airline Tariff Publishing Company's tariffs, including DFR3/AS1/EF2, and in ABC World Airways Guide (Red N-Z book, Airline Features Section).

Special Conditions

Senior Discounts/Coupons and Tour Conductor Discounts do not apply to these fares.

Fares effective for travel from April 1, 20..... through March 31, 20......

These fares do not include applicable transportation/departure taxes.

CO-SHARING AGREEMENT

Besides commuter carriers and chartered airlines, some larger airlines also have code-sharing agreements, primarily on international routes.

FIXING THE PRICE OF AIR SEATS

A number of factors are taken into account while fixing the price of airline seats. The main points considered are:

1. The size and type of aircraft to be operated on the route.
2. The route traffic density and level of competition.
3. The regularity of demand flow and the extent to which demand is balanced in both directions on the route.
4. The type of demand an air services on the route.
5. Determining the sales mix between first class, economy class, inclusive tour-basing fares and other discounted ticket sales.
6. The estimated break-even load factor, usually a scheduled airline must achieve 50% to 60% of seat occupancy.

The demand for air travel can change at short notice. It is inelastic in nature and depend on factors such as state of the economy of the generating country or the political stability of the destination, which in turn vitally affects the economic viability of the airlines.

Familiarity with the major air carriers, their backgrounds, and their influence in the aviation industry is beneficial to an understanding of the development and current status of the commercial aviation industry.

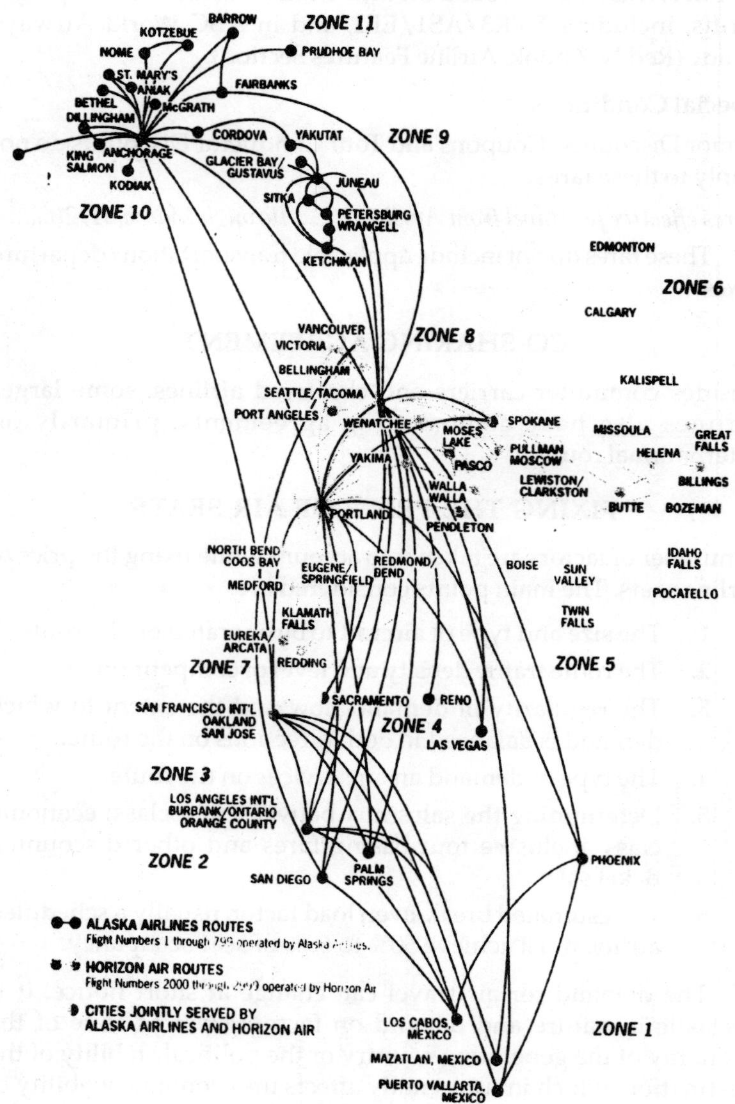

Fig. 1.1: Specimen of Alaska Airlines Routes.

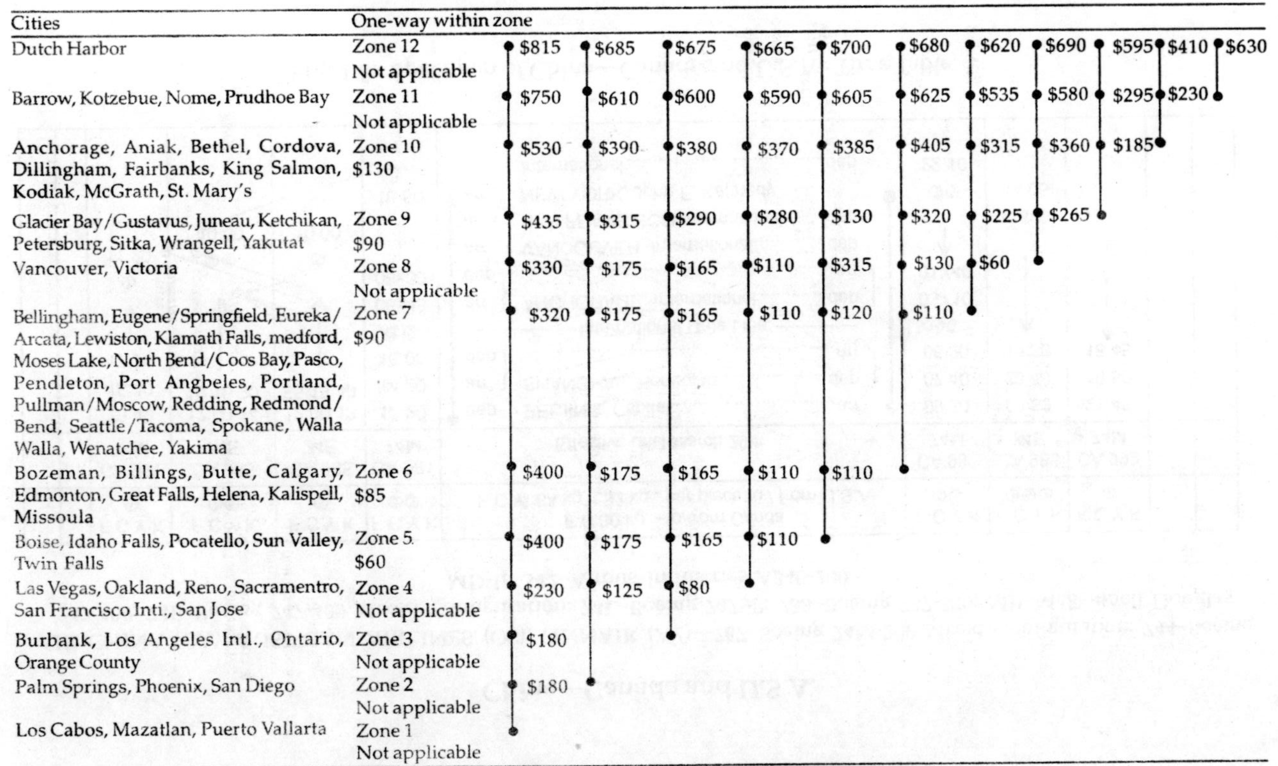

Alaska Airlines/Horizon Air Fares By Zone — All Fares in U.S. Dollars

Cities	One-way within zone											
Dutch Harbor	Zone 12 Not applicable	$815	$685	$675	$665	$700	$680	$620	$690	$595	$410	$630
Barrow, Kotzebue, Nome, Prudhoe Bay	Zone 11 Not applicable	$750	$610	$600	$590	$605	$625	$535	$580	$295	$230	
Anchorage, Aniak, Bethel, Cordova, Dillingham, Fairbanks, King Salmon, Kodiak, McGrath, St. Mary's	Zone 10 $130	$530	$390	$380	$370	$385	$405	$315	$360	$185		
Glacier Bay/Gustavus, Juneau, Ketchikan, Petersburg, Sitka, Wrangell, Yakutat	Zone 9 $90	$435	$315	$290	$280	$130	$320	$225	$265			
Vancouver, Victoria	Zone 8 Not applicable	$330	$175	$165	$110	$315	$130	$60				
Bellingham, Eugene/Springfield, Eureka/Arcata, Lewiston, Klamath Falls, medford, Moses Lake, North Bend/Coos Bay, Pasco, Pendleton, Port Angbeles, Portland, Pullman/Moscow, Redding, Redmond/Bend, Seattle/Tacoma, Spokane, Walla Walla, Wenatchee, Yakima	Zone 7 $90	$320	$175	$165	$110	$120	$110					
Bozeman, Billings, Butte, Calgary, Edmonton, Great Falls, Helena, Kalispell, Missoula	Zone 6 $85	$400	$175	$165	$110	$110						
Boise, Idaho Falls, Pocatello, Sun Valley, Twin Falls	Zone 5 $60	$400	$175	$165	$110							
Las Vegas, Oakland, Reno, Sacramentro, San Francisco Intl., San Jose	Zone 4 Not applicable	$230	$125	$80								
Burbank, Los Angeles Intl., Ontario, Orange County	Zone 3 Not applicable	$180										
Palm Springs, Phoenix, San Diego	Zone 2 Not applicable	$180										
Los Cabos, Mazatlan, Puerto Vallarta	Zone 1 Not applicable											

Fig. 1.2: Specimen of Alaska Airlines/Horizon Air Fares by Zone.

China—Canada and U.S.A.

AIR CHINA (CA), **AUSTRIAN AIRLINES** (OS), **FINNAIR** (AY)—**767**–Boeing **74M**-200 Mixed Configuration: **744**–Boeing 747-400: **74E**–Boeing 747-400 Mixed Configuration: **74L**–Boeing 747SP: **733**–Boeing 737-300: **MII**–McDonnell Douglas MD-II: **342**–Airbus Industries A340-200

		F C Y K ①	F C Y K ②⑥	F C Y K ⑤	F C Y K ③⑤	F C 30 kg. –to/from Canda F C Y 64 kg . :32 kg . per piece to / from U.S.A	F C Y K ⑤⑦	F C Y K ③⑥⑦	F C Y K ②		
....	....	CA 991 74M	CA 985 74E	CA 985 74E	CA 981 74M	Effective until March 29th ✈	CA 982 74M	CA 986 74E	CA 992 74M		
....	....	13 40	12 00 14	12 00 13	12 20	dep BELJING, Capital.............................arr	09 30	22 30	21 45	...	...
		15 40	10 15 20	55 15 40	14 20	arr SHANGHAL, Hongqiao.................... dep	07 40	20 40	19 50	...	...
		17 30	↓	↓	16 00	dep ....arr	06 20	19 30	18 45	...	...
		↓			③⑤	——International Date Line——	④⑥	↑	↑		
					06x45	arr ANCHORAGE, International .... dep	03X10				
		①			08x30	dep ....arr	01X40				
		11 20	②⑥	⑤	↓	arr VANCOUVER, International............ dep	↑		①	...	...
		....	10 00	10 00		arr SAN FRANCISCO International....... dep		②⑤⑥	13 50	...	...
		....	....	....	18 50	arr NEW YORK, John F. Kennedy International.................................. dep	③⑤ 22 10	14 05	...	...	...
								...	...	...	...

Fig. 1.3: Specimen of China—Canada and U.S.A.: Time Table.

China—Mongolia, Pakistan, Kuwait and Europe: Time Table

FC 30 kg. :Y MK20 kg.	FC YK ④	FC YK ⑦	FC YK ⑤	FC YK ①	FC YK ③	FC YK ②⑤	M ③	CM ①⑤	FC YK ⑤	FC YK ①④	FC YK ②	FC YK ⑥	FC YK ⑦	FC YK ④	FC YK ⑦	Y ①③	FC YK ③⑥	CYK ④	YK ②⑤
								(A)								(B)			
✈ CA Effective until March 29 th	937 74L	937 74M	933 744	933 74E	949 74E	911 74M	195 767	121 M11	907 767	909 767	931 74L	931 744	935 74E	931 74E	959 74L	965 342	939 74M	945 767	901 733
SHANGHAL, Hongqiqodep	....	....	08 40	....	....	....	....	....	....	....	09 25	09 25	....	....	....	....	....	....	....
BEIJING,Capital........ arr	....	....	10 35	....	....	....	....	....	....	....	11 30	11 30	....	....	....	....	....	....	....
..............................dep	11 50	11 50	12 25	12 25	08 00	08 35	10 00	11 55	09 15	15 25	13 20	13 20	08 10	13 20	09 00	12 40	09 20	10 35	09 25
SHANGHAI,					09 55								10 10						
Hongqial.................... arr					11 05								12 00						
................................Dep																			
ULAN BATOR Buyant-																			
Ukha .... arr																			
KARACHI.................. arr																			
................................Dep																			11 35
KUWAIT, Internationalarr																		15 20	....
MILAN, Malpensa ..... arr																		16 30	....
................................Dep																		17 55	....
ROME, Leonardo da Vinci-																	14 00	....	....
Fiumicino .... arr																	16 00	....	....
VIENNA .... arr																	17 00	....	....
ZURICH .... arr																16 15	....	....	....
FRANKFURT, International															13 20	....	....	....	....
.... arr											17 30	17 30	17 30	17 30	....	....	....	....	....
MOSCOW,................ arr										19 10	....	....	....	....	....	....	....	....	....
Sheremetyevo									13 00	....	....	....	....	....	....	....	....	....	....
BERLIN, Schonefeld. arr								14 45	....	....	....	....	....	....	....	....	....	....	....
HELSINKI, Vantaa .... arr						11 00		....	....	....	....	....	....	....	....	....	....	....	....
STOCKHOLM,						13 00		....	....	....	....	....	....	....	....	....	....	....	....
Arianda .... arr						14 00	13 00	....	....	....	....	....	....	....	....	....	....	....	....
................................dep			17 00	17 00	17 00	....	....	....	....	....	....	....	....	....	....	....	....	....	....
COPENHAGEN .... arr	15 30	15 30	....	....	....	....	....	....	....	....	....	....	....	....	....	....	....	....	....
PARIS, Charies......... arr																			
de Gaulle																			
LONDON, Heathrow . arr																			

(Contd.)

(*Contd.*)

FC 30 kg. :Y MK20 kg.	FC YK ④	FC YK ⑦	FC YK ⑤	FC YK ①	FC YK ③	FC YK ②⑤	M ③	CM ①⑤	FC YK ⑤	FC YK ①④	FC YK ②	FC YK ⑥	FC YK ⑦	FC YK ④	FC YK ⑦	Y ①③	FC YK ③⑥	CYK ④	YK ②⑤
								(A)								(B)			
✈ CA Effective until March 29th	937 74L	937 74M	933 744	933 74E	949 74E	911 74M	195 767	121 M11	907 767	909 767	931 74L	931 744	935 74E	931 74E	959 74L	965 342	939 74M	945 767	901 733
SHANGHAI, Hongqiqo dep	....	....	08 40	....	....	....	....	....	....	....	09 25	09 25	....	....	....	....	....	....	....
BEIJING, Capital .... arr	....	....	10 35	....	....	....	....	....	....	....	11 30	11 30	....	....	....	....	....	....	....
.... dep	11 50	11 50	12 25	12 25	08 00	08 35	10 00	11 55	09 15	15 25	13 20	13 20	08 10	13 20	09 00	12 40	09 20	10 35	09 25
SHANGHAI,					09 55								10 10						
Hongqial .... arr					11 05								12 00						
.... Dep																			
ULAN BATOR Buyant-																			
Ukha .... arr																			
KARACHI .... arr																			
.... Dep																			11 35
KUWAIT, International arr																		15 20	....
MILAN, Malpensa ..... arr																		16 30	....
.... Dep																		17 55	....
ROME, Leonardo da Vinci-																	14 00	....	....
Fiumicino .... arr																	16 00	....	....
VIENNA .... arr																	17 00	....	....
ZURICH .... arr																16 15	....	....	....
FRANKFURT, International															13 20	....	....	....	....
.... arr											17 30	17 30	17 30	17 30	....	....	....	....	....
MOSCOW, ... arr										19 10	....	....	....	....	....	....	....	....	....
Sheremetyevo									13 00	....	....	....	....	....	....	....	....	....	....
BERLIN, Schonefeld. arr								14 45	....	....	....	....	....	....	....	....	....	....	....
HELSINKI, Vantaa .... arr						11 00		....	....	....	....	....	....	....	....	....	....	....	....
STOCKHOLM,						13 00		....	....	....	....	....	....	....	....	....	....	....	....
Arianda .... arr						14 00	13 00	....	....	....	....	....	....	....	....	....	....	....	....
.... dep			17 00	17 00	17 00	....	....	....	....	....	....	....	....	....	....	....	....	....	....
COPENHAGEN .... arr	15 30	15 30	....	....	....	....	....	....	....	....	....	....	....	....	....	....	....	....	....
PARIS, Charies .... arr																			
de Gaulle																			
LONDON, Heathrow . arr																			

Fig. 1.4: Specimen of China—Mongolia, Pakistan, Kuwait and Europe: Time Table.

China—Myanmar, Thailand, Singapore and Indonesia

	FYK	FC YK	FC YK	CYK	CYK	CYK	CYK	CYK		CYK	CYK	CYK	CYK	CYK	CYK	FC YK	FC YK	FYK	
	3	④	⑦	①	②③	①③⑥	⑦	②④	FC 30 kh. : Y K 20 kg	⑤	①	③	②④⑦	③⑥	2	④	⑦	③	
	905	979	979	179	975	957	973	971	CA CA →	972	974	972	958	976	180	980	980	906	
	733	74L	767	767	767	767	767	767	Effective until March 29th	767	767	767	767	767	767	74L	767	733	
....	08 05	09 25	09 25	16 25	12 30	12 35	09 10	09 25	dep BEIJING Capital.............. arr	18 35	18 30	18 35	17 20	16 00	14 25	19 35	19 50	20 40	....
....						15 10		11 55	arr XIAMEN .... dep	15 55		16 05	14 35						....
						16 00		13 00	dep .... arr	14 55		15 00	13 40						
....							12 15		arr SHEZHEN .... dep		15 40								....
							13 15		dep .... arr		14 30								
....	11 35								arr KUNMING .... dep									17 40	....
	12 25								dep .... arr									17 00	
....	13 00								arr YANGON, International.... dep									13 40	....
									arr .... dep										
....		13 00	13 00	20 00					arr BANGKOK, International.. dep						09 00	14 20	14 20		....
									arr .... dep										
....					19 00	20 30			arr SINGAPORE, Changi ...... dep				09 30	09 55					....
....							16 45	16 45	arr JAKARTA, Soeakarno...... dep Hatta International	08 55	08 55	08 55							....

Fig. 1.5: Specimen of China—Myanmar, Thailand, Singapore and Indonesia: Time Table.

China—Australia, Japan and Rep of Korea

AIR CHINA (CA), **QANTAS AIRWAYS** (QF)—**767**-Boeing 767 : **74M**—Boeing 747-200 Mixed Configuration: **744**–Boeing 747-400: **74E**–Boeing 747-400 Mixed Configuration: **74L**–Boeing 747SP: **733**–Boeing 737-300: **M11**–McDonnell Douglas, MD-11

FC 30 kg. :Y K 20 kg.		FC YK	FYK	FYK	FY	FC YK	FC YK	FC YK	FC YK	FC YK	FC YK	FC YK Ex	FC YK	CYK
		Dly	①③⑤⑥	Dly	①②④⑥	②⑤	②	①④	②	③	⑤	④	④	③④
Effective until March 29th	✈ CA	123	125	127	129	923	919	929	929	929	929	925	925	951
		767	733	733	733	733	74M	767	74M	74M	767	767	74E	74M
BEIJING, Capital ◆	dep	0940	1510		1000	0845	0710	0830	0830	0830	0830	0920	0920	0930
QINGDAO (A)	dep			1030										
SHANGHAI, Hongqiac ◆	arr						0915	1025	1025	1025	1025			
	dep						1050	1125	1125	1125	1125			
DALIAN	arr					0955								1040
	dep					1045								1200
GUANGZHOU, Baiyun	arr													
	dep													
MELBOURNE, Tullamarine ◆	arr							Eff.						
	dep							3/3						
SYDNEY, Kingsford-Smith ◆	arr													
FUKUOK	arr													
OSAKA, Kansai	arr													
TOKYO, Narita	arr						1455	1455	1455	1455	1455	1350	1350	1540
SENDAI	arr					1430	...	...	...	...	...	...	...	...
PUSAN, Kimhae	arr				1320	...	...	...	...	...	...	...	...	...
SEOUL, Kimpo	arr	1220	1810	1250	...	...	...	...	...	...	...	...	...	...

FC 30 kg. :Y K 20 kg.		CYK	FC YK	FC YK	FC YK	FC YK	FC YK	FC YK	FC YK	FC YK	FC YK	FC YK	FC YK	FC YK
		⑦	①②	④	⑤	⑥	③⑥	⑦	③⑦	③⑥	④⑦	⑤ (C)	①	③
Effective until March 29th	✈ CA	951	921	921	921	921	151	921	927	953	915	174	175	177
		74M	740	767	74L	767	767	767	767	74L	767	74L	74L	74L
BEIJING, Capital ◆	dep	...	0800	0800	0800	0800	0935	1025	1340	0855	0935	1500	1510	...
QINGDAO (A)	dep	...												...
SHANGHAI, Hongqiac ◆	arr	...	0955	0955	0955	0950			1535		1130		1735	...
	dep	0900	1105	1105	1105	1050			1630		1225		1845	1720
DALIAN	arr	1040					1050			1005				
	dep	1200					1150			1145				
GUANGZHOU, Baiyun	arr											1800		
	dep											1920		
MELBOURNE, Tullamarine ◆	arr											⑥ 0615	② 0615	
	dep											0800	0800	
SYDNEY, Kingsford-Smith ◆	arr											0930	0930	0800
FUKUOK	arr									1420	1445	...	...	...
OSAKA, Kansai	arr		1405	1405	1405	1405	1500	1405	1930	...	...	...	...	...
TOKYO, Narita	arr	1540	...	...	...	...	...	...	...	...	...	...	...	...
SENDAI	arr	...	...	...	...	...	...	...	...	...	...	...	...	...
PUSAN, Kimhae	arr	...	...	...	...	...	...	...	...	...	...	...	...	...
SEOUL, Kimpo	arr	...	...	...	...	...	...	...	...	...	...	...	...	...

		FC YK	FYK	FYK	FY	FC YK	FC YK Ex	FC YK	FC YK	FC YK	FC YK	FC YK	FC YK	FC YK
		Dly	①③⑤⑥	Dly	①②④⑥	②⑤	④	④	②	③	①④	⑤	①④	⑦
Effective until March 29th	✈ CA	123	125	127	129	923	919	929	929	929	925	925	951	951
		767	733	733	733	733	74M	767	74M	767	767	74E	74M	74M
SEOUL, Kimpo	dep	1350	1910	1400	...	...	...	...	...	...	...	...	...	...
PUSAN, Kimhae	dep				1410	...	...	...	...	Eff.	...	...	...	...
SENDAI	dep					1550	...	...	...	3/3	...	...	...	...
TOKYO, Narita	dep						1455	1455	1555	1555	1600	1600	1700	1700
OSAKA, Kansai	dep													
FUKUOKA	dep													
MELBOURNE, Tullamarine ◆	dep													
SYDNEY, Kingsford-Smith ◆	arr													
	dep													
MELBOURNE, Tullamarine ◆ (B)	arr													
	dep													
GUANGZHOU, Baiyun	arr													
	dep													
SHANGHAI, Hongqiac ◆	arr								1825	1825	1825	1825		
	dep								1935	1935	1935	1935		
DALIAN (A)	arr					1830							1910	1910
	dep					1920							2010	2010
QINGDAO	arr			1420										
BEIJING, Capital ◆	arr	1440	2010	...	1530	2030	1810	1810	2135	2135	2135	2135	2120	2140

		FC YK	FC YK	FC YK	FC YK	FC YK	FC YK	FC YK	FC YK	FC YK	FC YK	FC YK	FC YK	FC YK
		①	④	②	⑤	④	⑥	⑦	③⑥	③⑥	①④⑦	⑥ (C)	②	④
Effective until March 29th	✈ CA	921	921	921	921	151	921	927	953	915	915	174	175	177
		740	767	74L	767	767	767	767	74L	767	767	74L	74L	74L
SEOUL, Kimpo	dep	...	...	...	...	...	...	...	...	...	...	...	...	...
PUSAN, Kimhae	dep	...	...	...	...	...	...	...	...	...	...	...	...	...
SENDAI	dep	...	...	...	...	...	...	...	...	...	...	...	...	...
TOKYO, Narita	dep	...	...	...	...	...	...	...	...	...	...	...	...	...
OSAKA, Kansai	dep	0930	0930	1535	1535	1535	1535	1535	1700	...	...	...	...	...
FUKUOKA	dep									1530	1555	...	...	...
MELBOURNE, Tullamarine ◆	dep											0800	...	...
SYDNEY, Kingsford-Smith ◆	arr											090	...	...
	dep											1050	1050	0920
MELBOURNE, Tullamarine ◆ (B)	arr													1050
	dep													1210
GUANGZHOU, Baiyun	arr											1755		
	dep											1905		
SHANGHAI, Hongqiac ◆	arr	1110	1045	1715	1715		1705	1715			1640		1850	2005
	dep	1205	1235	1820	1820		1830	1820			1740		2020	...
DALIAN (A)	arr								1850	1630				...
	dep								1950	1740				...
QINGDAO	arr													...
BEIJING, Capital ◆	arr	1405	1435	2015	2015	1810	2015	2015	2100	1900	1930	2200	2200	...

A – International online stopover traffic only on CA 921/922. B – No local traffic on CA 928. C – Operators in conjunction with QF.

Fig. 1.6: Specimen of Air Services: China—Australia, Japan and Rep of Korea: Time Table.

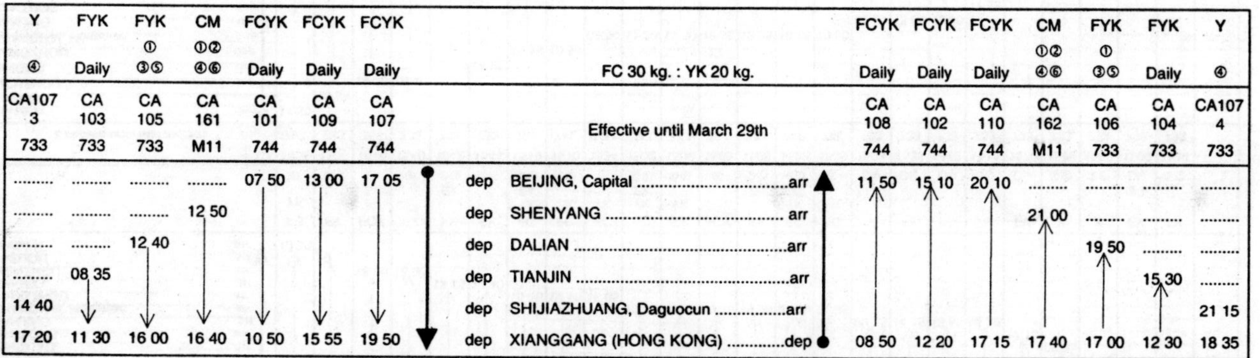

REGIONAL AIR SERVICES

Beijing, Shenyang, Dalian, Tianjin, Shijiazhuang—Xianggang (HONG KONG)

Y	FYK	FYK	CM	FCYK	FCYK	FCYK		FCYK	FCYK	FCYK	CM	FYK	FYK	Y
		①	①②								①②	①		
④	Daily	③⑤	④⑥	Daily	Daily	Daily	FC 30 kg. : YK 20 kg.	Daily	Daily	Daily	④⑥	③⑤	Daily	④
CA107 3	CA 103	CA 105	CA 161	CA 101	CA 109	CA 107	Effective until March 29th	CA 108	CA 102	CA 110	CA 162	CA 106	CA 104	CA107 4
733	733	733	M11	744	744	744		744	744	744	M11	733	733	733
....	....	....	....	07 50	13 00	17 05	dep BEIJING, Capital .... arr	11 50	15 10	20 10	....	....	....	....
....	....	....	12 50				dep SHENYANG .... arr				21 00	....	....	....
....	....	12 40					dep DALIAN .... arr					19 50	....	....
....	08 35						dep TIANJIN .... arr						15 30	....
14 40							dep SHIJIAZHUANG, Daguocun .... arr							21 15
17 20	11 30	16 00	16 40	10 50	15 55	19 50	dep XIANGGANG (HONG KONG) .... dep	08 50	12 20	17 15	17 40	17 00	12 30	18 35

Fig. 1.7: Specimen of Regional Air Services: Time Table.

DOMESTIC AIR SERVICES

Beijing—Huanghua, Yantai, Weihai, Qingdao, Nantong, Nanjing, Shanghai, Hangzhou, Ningbo, Wenzhou, Fuzhou & Xiamen

FC 30 kg. :Y K 20 kg.	FC YK ⑥	FY Dly	FCY Ex ④	FY ④	FY Ex ②⑤	FY ②⑤	FC YK Ex ④⑥	FC YK ④⑥	FY ② ④⑥	FC YK Ex ⑥⑦	FC YK ④	FC YK ⑥	FC YK ⑤	FC YK ①⑥	FC YK ④	Y Dly	FY Dly	FY ①⑤	Y Dly	FY Dly	FY Dly	Y ④⑦	Y ②⑤	FY Dly	Y ②④ ⑤⑦
✈ CA	1801	1505	1539	1539	1541	1543	1509	1509	1535	1501	1501	1501	1591	1521	1521	1507	1537	1563	1561	1513	1569	1587	1587	1585	1343
Effective until March 29th	767	733	767	733	733	733	767	74L	733	744	767	74L	744	74L	767	733	733	733	733	733	733	733	733	733	733
BEIJING, Capital ..... dep	08 10	07 40	15 40	15 40	09 05	15 10	08 20	08 20	14 20	08 40	08 40	08 40	17 55	19 35	19 35	07 30	12 25	14 10	16 50	15 20	08 15	16 05	17 00	08 35	09 00
HUANGHUA ..... arr																									11 20
YANTAI ..... arr																								09 55	
WEIHAI ..... arr																						17 10	18 10		
QINGDAO ..... arr																					09 35				
NANTONG ..... arr																				17 10					
NANJING ..... arr																09 15	14 15	15 55	18 20						
SHANGHAI, Hongqiao ..... arr										10 35	10 35	10 35	19 50	21 35	21 35										
HANGZHOU ..... arr							10 10	10 10	16 05																
NINGBO ..... arr					11 25	17 40																			
WENZHOU ..... arr			18 00	18 00																					
FUZHOU ..... arr		10 15																							
XIAMEN ..... arr	10 40																								

	FC YK ⑥	FY Dly	FCY Ex ④	FY ④	FY Ex ②⑤	FY ②⑤	FC YK Ex ④⑥	FC YK ④⑥	FC YK ①	FC YK Ex ④⑥	FC YK ④⑥	FCY ④	FY ③ ⑤⑦	FC YK ②⑤ ⑥⑦	FC YK ⑤	Y Dly	FY Dly	Y Dly	FY Dly	FY Dly	Y ④⑦	Y ②⑤	FY ②④ Dly	FY ⑤⑦	
✈ CA	1802	1506	1540	1540	1542	1544	1510	1510	1534	1502	1502	1568	1568	1522	1536	1508	1538	1562	1514	1570	1588	1588	1586	1344	
Effective until March 29th	767	733	767	733	733	733	767	74L	74M	744	767	767	733	74E	74L	733	733	733	733	733	733	733	733	733	
XIAMEN ..... dep	11 30																								
FUZHOU ..... dep		10 55																							
WENZHOU ..... dep			18 40	18 40																					
NINGBO ..... dep					12 05	18 20																			
HANGZHOU ..... dep							10 55	10 55																	
SHANGHAI, Hongqiao ..... dep									09 00	11 30	11 30	12 35	12 35	16 15	19 50										
NANJING ..... dep																09 55	15 05	19 00							
NANTONG ..... dep																			17 55						
QINGDAO ..... dep																				14 55					
WEIHAI ..... dep																					18 00	19 00			
YANTAI ..... dep																							10,35		
HUANGHUA ..... dep																								12 00	
BEIJING, Capital ..... arr	14 05	13 30	21 00	21 00	14 35	20 25	12 50	12 50	10 50	13 30	13 30	14 45	14 45	18 10	21 50	11 45	16 55	20 50	19 50	16 05	19 10	20 10	11 55	14 10	

Fig. 1.8: Specimen of Domestic Air Services: Time Table.

Hohhot, Baotou, Beijing, Shijiazhuang, Wuhan—Shanghai, Nanchang, Shantou, Shenzhen, Zguhai and Guangzhou

F C 30 kg.: Y K 20 kg.	Y ①③	FCYK Daily	FCYK Daily	Y ②	Y Daily	FY ②⑥	FY ④	FCYK Daily	FCYK Daily	FY Daily	FY Daily	FY ①③	FY Daily	Y ④		
✈	CA 1309	CA 1321	CA 1301	CA 1309	CA 1323	CA 1307	CA 1307	CA 1303	CA 1305	CA 1347	CA 1511	CA 1505	CA 1333	CA 1183		
Effective until 29 th	733	EQV	EQV	733	733	733	767	EQV	EQV	733	733	733	733	733	....	....
HOHHOT .... dep	08 00	....	....	....	....	....	....	....	....	....	....	....	....	13 00	....	....
BEIJING, Capital .... dep	↓	09 15	14 50	....	....	13 55	14 25	13 45	18 00	12 55	15 30	....	07 55	↓	....	....
SHIJIAZHUANG, Haguocun .... arr	09 00			....	....							....	↓	13 40	....	....
.... dep	09 40			09 40	....							17 00		....		
WUHAN, Hsu Kiaeng .... arr					....							↓	09 45	....	....	....
.... dep					10 40									....		
SANGHAI, Hongqiao .... arr													....	....	....	....
.... dep												19 05	....	....		
NANCHANG .... arr											17 40	....	....	....	....	....
SHANTOU .... arr										15 50	....	....	....	....	....	....
SHNZHEN .... arr								16 45	20 45	....	....	....	....	....	....	....
ZHUHAI .... arr						17 00	17 30	....	....	....	....	....	....	....	....	....
GUANGZHOU, BAIYUN .... arr	12 10	12 05	17 45	12 10	12 20	....	....	....	....	....	....	....	....	....	....	....

(*Contd.*)

(*Contd.*)

	Y ②	FC YK Daily	FCYK Daily	Y ①③	Y Daily	FY ②⑥	FY ④	FCYK Daily	FCYK Daily	FY Daily	FY Daily	Y ③⑦	FY ①	FY Daily	Y ④	FY ③
✈	CA 1310	CA 1322	CA 1302	CA 1310	CA 1324	CA 1308	CA 1308	CA 1306	CA 1304	CA 1348	CA 1512	CA 1582	CA 1516	CA 1334	CA 1184	CA 516
Effective until 29 th	733	EQV	EQV	733	733	733	767	EQV	EQV	733	733	733	733	733	733	733
GUANGZHOU, Baiyun dep	13 15	13 05	18 45	13 15	12 55	....	....	....	....	....	....	....	....	....	....	....
ZHUHAI.................. dep						17 50	18 10	....	....	....	....	....	....	....	....	....
SHENZHEN .... dep								09 30	17 40	....	....	....	....	....	....	....
SHANTOU................ dep										16 25	....	....	....	....	....	....
NANCHANG.............. dep											18 20	....	....	....	....	....
SHANGHAI, Hongqiao dep												17 45	19 50	....	....	....
WUHAN, Hsu Kiapeng . arr					14 35									....	....	....
.... dep					....									15 15	....	....
SHIJIAZHUANG, Daguocun .... arr	15 45			15 45	....								21 50		....	....
.... dep	16 20			....	....								....		22 05	22 30
BEIJING , Capital .... arr		16 10	21 25	....	....	21 10	21 30	12 25	20 35	19 15	20 30		....	17 00		
BAOTOU.................... arr		....	....	....	....	....	....	....	....	....	....	20 15	....	....		
HOHHOT .... arr	17 20	....	....	....	....	....	....	....	....	....	....	....	....	....	22 50	23 10

Fig. 1.9: Specimen of Hohhot, Baotou, Beijing, Shijiazhuang, Wuhan—Shanghai, Nanchang, Shantou, Shenzhen, Zguhai and Guangzhou: Time Table.

Beijing, Nanjing, Hangzhou—Zhengzhou, XI An, Chengdu, Chongqing, Guilin, Kunming, Nanning and Haikou

F C 30 kg.: Y K 20 kg.	FY ①③ ⑤⑦	FY ① ③⑥	FY ④ ⑥⑦	FY ①⑤	FY ③⑦	FY ② ④⑥	FY ①③ ⑥⑦	FY Daily	FY ②⑥	FC YK ⑤	FYK Daily	FC YK ②	FY ②⑥	FY ①④
✈ CA Effective until March 29th	1356 733	1316 733	1404 733	1366 733	1376 733	1336 733	1410 733	1406 733	1408 733	1206 767	1202 767	1206 767	1314 733	1314 733
BEIJING, Capital ... arr	2145	1520	1525	2155	2155	2150	1420	1440	2030	1540	1815	1950	1955	2010
NANJING ... arr	↑	↑	↑	↑	↑	↑	↑	↑	↑	↑	↑	↑	↑	↑
HANGZHOU ... arr														
ZHENGZHOU ... dep													1830	1850
XI AN, Xianyang ... dep										1350	1615	1800	....	....
arr										....	....	....	....	....
CHENGDU ... dep								1205	1745	....	....	....	....	....
CHONGQING ... dep							1145	....	....	....	....	....	....	....
GUILIN ... dep				1920	1920	1930	....	....	....	....	....	....	....	....
KUNMING ... dep			1225	....	....	....	....	....	....	....	....	....	....	....
NANNING ... dep		1210	....	....	....	....	....	....	....	....	....	....	....	....
HAIKOU ... dep	1810	....	....	....	....	....	....	....	....	....	....	....	....	....

(Contd.)

(Contd.)

F C 30 kg.: Y K 20 kg.	FY	FYK	FYK	FC YK	FC YK	FYK	FC YK	FY	FY	FY	FY	FY	FY	FY	FY	FY
	①④	①	③ ⑤⑦	⑤	Daily	③⑦	②	Daily	②⑥	①③ ⑥⑦	② ①⑤	④⑥	④ ③⑦	① ⑥⑦	①③ ③⑥	⑤⑦
✈ C	1313	1215	1215	1205	1201	1225	1205	1405	1407	1409	1365	1335	1375	1403	1315	1355
Effective until March 29th	733	767	733	767	767	733	767	733	733	733	733	733	733	733	733	733
BEIJING, Capital ... dep	1645	0735	0735	1110	1335	1410	1520	0845	1410	0825	...	...	...	0805	0805	1345
NANJING ... dep											1635	...	...			
HANGZHOU ... dep												1705	...			
ZHENGZHOU ... arr	1810												...			
XI AN, Xianyang ... arr	...	0910	0910	1300	1520	1600	1710						...			
dep	...	...	...	...	...	...	...						1630			
CHENGDU ... arr	...	...	...	...	...	...	...	1125	1705							
CHONGQING ... arr	...	...	...	...	...	...	...	...	...	1100						
GUILIN ... arr	...	...	...	...	...	...	...	...	...	...	1845	1850	1825			
KUNMING ... arr	...	...	...	...	...	...	...	...	...	...	...	...	...	1135		
NANNING ... arr	...	...	...	...	...	...	...	...	...	...	...	...	...	...	1140	
HAIKOU ... arr	...	...	...	...	...	...	...	...	...	...	...	...	...	...	...	1730

Fig. 1.10: Specimen of Beijing, Nanjing, Hangzhou—Zhengzhou, XI An, Chengdu, Chongqing, Guilin, Kunming, Nanning and Haikou: Time Table.

Hohhot—Beijing—Tianjin—Dalian, Dandong, Shenyang, Changchun, Jilin, Yanji, Mudanjiang & Harbin

F C 30 kg.: Y K 20 kg.	Y Ex ④	FCY Ex ③	FCY ③	FY ④⑦	FY ①⑤	FY ③⑦	Y ②⑥	Y ①④	FY Daily	Y Daily	FCY Daily	FCY ⑤	FY Daily	Y ⑦	FY ⑦	FYK Daily	FY ① ③⑤	FY Daily
✈ CA Effective until March 29th	1604 733	1622 767	1622 767	1632 733	1618 733	1616 733	1620 733	1620 733	1610 733	1630 733	1602 767	1626 767	1614 733	1636 733	1624 733	1608 733	1606 733	1102 733
HOHHOT .... arr	......	......	......	......	......	......	......	......	......	......	......	......	......	......	......	......	......	2200
BEIJING, Capital .... dep	......	......	......	......	......	......	......	......	......	......	......	......	......	......	......	......	......	2050
arr	1240	1920	2010	......	2040	2150	1300	2020	1210	2000	1125	1410	1950	2120	1320	1610	2155	......
TIANJIN .... arr				2045														......
DALIAN .... arr															1210	1450	2050	......
DANDONG .... arr														2020	......	......	......	......
SHENYANG .... arr											1005	1300	1850	......	......	......	......	......
CHANGCHUN .... arr									1035	1820	......	......	......	......	......	......	......	......
JILIN .... arr							1110	1830	......	......	733 on ④	......	......	......	......	......	......	......
YANJI .... arr						1940	......	......	......	......		......	......	......	......	......	......	......
MUDANJIANG .... arr					1845	......	......	......	......	......	......	......	......	......	......	......	......	......
HARBIN .... arr	1050	1750	1820	1900	......	......	......	......	......	......	......	......	......	......	......	......	......	......

(Contd.)

(*Contd.*)

F C 30 kg.: Y K 20 kg.	Y Daily	FY ⑦	FYK ① ③④	FYK Daily	FYK ⑦	FCY Daily	FCY ⑤	FY Daily	FY Ex ④	Y Daily	Y ②⑥	FY ①④	FY ③⑦	FY ①⑤	FY ④⑦	Y Ex ④	FCY Ex ③	FCY ③
✈ CA Effective until March 29th	1101 733	1623 733	1605 733	1607 733	1635 733	1601 767	1625 767	1613 733	1609 733	1629 733	1619 733	1619 733	1615 733	1617 733	1631 733	1603 733	1621 767	1621 767
HOHHOT ...... dep	0725	......	......	......	......	......	......	......	......	......	......	......	......	......	......	......	......	......
BEIJING, Capital ...... arr	0825	......	......	......	......	......	......	......	......	......	......	......	......	......	......	......	......	......
dep	......	1020	1040	1255	1800	0755	1100	1650	0810	1610	0830	1600	1710	1605	1320	0825	1500	1540
TIANJIN ...... dep	......																	
DALIAN ...... arr	......	1130	1150	1415														
DANDONG ...... arr	......	......	......	......	1920													
SHENYANG ...... arr	......	......	......	......	......	0915	1210	1750										
CHANGCHUN ...... arr	......	......	......	......	......	......	......	......	1000	1740								
JILIN ...... arr	......	......	......	......	......	733 on ⑦	......	......	......	......	1020	1750						
YANJI ...... arr	......	......	......	......	......		......	......	......	......	......		1900					
MUDANJIANG ...... arr	......	......	......	......	......	......	......	......	......	......	......	......	......	1305				
HARBIN ...... arr	......	......	......	......	......	......	......	......	......	......	......	......	......	......	1820	1010	1650	1730

Fig. 1.11: Specimen of Hohhot—Beijing—Tianjin—Dalian, Dandong, Shenyang, Changchun, Jilin, Yanji, Mudanjiang & Harbin: Time Table.

Tianjin—XI AN—Chengdu, Nanjing, Shanghai, Tunxi, Wenzhou, Fuzhou, Xiamen, Shantou, Shenzhen, Guangzhou & Haikou

F C 30 kg.: Y K 20 kg.	FY ③⑦	FY ③	FY Daily	FY ①③	FY ②④ ⑥⑦	FY ①④	FY ②⑥	FY ①⑦	FY ① ③⑤	FY Daily	FY ②⑥	FY ④	FY ① ④⑥
✈ CA Effective until March 29th	1372 733	1338 733	1318 733	1332 733	1320 733	1350 733	1530 733	1526 733	1528 733	1524 733	1532 733	1532 733	1422 733
TIANJIN .... arr	1500	1820	1440	2020	2025	2220	1305	1250	2155	1940	2035	2130	1545
XI AN, Xianyang .... dep													1355
arr													1310
CHENGDU .... dep													1135
NANJING .... dep											1850	1940	....
SHANGHAI, Hongqiao .... dep										1755	....	....	....
TUNXI .... dep		1610								....	....	....	....
arr		1530								....	....	....	....
WENZHOU .... dep									1935	....	....	....	....
FUZHOU .... dep								1025	....	....	....	....	....
XIAMEN .... dep							1035	....	....	....	....	....	....
SHANTOU .... dep						1935	....	....	....	....	....	....	....
SHENZHEN .... dep					1720	....	....	....	....	....	....	....	....
GUANGZHOU, Baiyun .... dep			1145	1725	....	....	....	....	....	....	....	....	....
HAIKOU .... dep	1140	1300	....	....	....	....	....	....	....	....	....	....	....

(Contd.)

(*Contd.*)

F C 30 kg.: Y K 20 kg.	FY ① ④⑥	FY ②⑥	FY ④	FY Daily	FCY ①	FY ③ ⑤⑦	FY ① ③⑤	FY ④⑦	FY ②⑥	FY ①④	FY ②④ ⑥⑦	FY Daily	FY ①⑤	FY ③	FY ③⑦
✈ CA Effective until March 29th	1421 733	1531 733	1531 733	1523 733	1567 767	1567 733	1527 733	1525 733	1529 733	1349 733	1319 733	1319 733	1331 733	1337 733	1371 733
TIANJIN .... dep	3715	1625	1710	1520	....	....	1625	0710	0710	1620	1340	0810	1330	0715	0715
XI AN, Xianyang .... arr	0900				....	....									
dep	0945				0950	0950									
CHENGDU .... arr	1055														
NANJING .... arr	....	1815	1900												
SHANGHAI, Hongqiao .... arr	....	....	....	1710	1150	1150									
TUNXI .... arr	....	....	....	....	....	....									
dep	....	....	....	....	....	....									
WENZHOU .... arr	....	....	....	....	....	....	1855								
FUZHOU .... arr	....	....	....	....	....	....	....	0945							
XIAMEN .... arr	....	....	....	....	....	....	....	....	0945						
SHANTOU .... arr	....	....	....	....	....	....	....	....	....	1905					
SHENZHEN .... arr	....	....	....	....	....	....	....	....	....	....	1640				
GUANGZHOU, Baiyun .... arr	....	....	....	....	....	....	....	....	....	....	....	1105	1625		
HAIKOU .... arr	....	....	....	....	....	....	....	....	....	....	....	....	....	1230	1100

Fig. 1.12: Specimen of Tianjin—XI AN—Chengdu, Nanjing, Shanghai, Tunxi, Wenzhou, Fuzhou, Xiamen, Shantou, Shenzhen, Guangzhou & Haikou: Time Table.

QUESTIONS AND DISCUSSIONS

Objective Type

Q. 1. *In each of the following sentences, write the correct word or phrase that belong to each blank:*

1. A .... is imposed by an airport authority fund an improvement project, such as the construction of a new runway or the expansion of airline terminal.
2. The longer the advance purchase requirements, the .... the fare.
3. Special promotion fares are often available on .... routes or during periods of ....
4. Tickets purchased in India for travel within India are subject to ....
5. Most excursion fares must be purchased in advance of the departure date and require travel to originate and terminate ....
6. On most international carriers, first class is referred to as ....
7. .... is the quality of the product that customers are willing to purchase at a particular price.
8. The price of a travel product must also be high enough to compensate for ....

Q. 2. *Identify the person word/phrase from each the following concepts:*

1. An airline that has a limited schedule and leases aircraft to large groups or to other airlines.
2. An agreement entitling a carrier to use the name of another airline on its flights.
3. A three digit numerical code assigned to each airline.
4. A two letter code designated by IATA to identify an airline in schedules and tariffs.
5. An intermediate point used by an airline to route passengers to multiple destination.
6. A letter in an aircraft code that indicates that the airplane has been configured to transport both passengers and cargo.
7. A letter in an aircraft code that indicates that the airplane has been configured for additional passenger seating.

8. The term for a kitchenette used by the flight crew to heat or prepare passenger meals on an aircraft.
9. A single point to point fare for a connection operated by different carriers.
10. A cooperative contract between two airlines that enables passengers to travel on a connection operated by both carriers.
11. A flight that requires passengers to change planes at an intermediate point between the original boarding point and the final destination, with no stop-overs.
12. A charge for baggage that exceeds the airlines present limit.
13. A limit on the amount of baggage that may be transported by a passenger free of charge.
14. The percentage of airline flights that leave the departure gate within 15 minutes of the scheduled departure time and arrive at the destination gate within 15 minutes of the scheduled arrived time.
15. A passenger who books a confirmed reservation but does not actually board the flight.
16. A list of people who would like a seat on a flight for which all the seats have already been sold.
17. A passenger who is stranded in a connecting city as a result of a delay or cancellation.
18. The pressurized cargo compartment of an aircraft where a pet can sometimes be transported.
19. A certificate issued by government agency authorizing an airline to operate passenger service in the country.
20. The largest Indian passenger carrier.

Q. 3. *Following is the list of terms. You are required to write the letter of the word, phrase or name next to the concept/definition that best matches it:*

A Itinerary
B ARNK Segment
C Leg
D Off Point
E Stop-over point
F Circle trip
G OAG
H Open Jaw
I Daylight serving
J Direct flight
K Departure point
L Outbound segment
M Time table

1. .... Any itinerary that originates and terminates at the same point, regardless of the number of stop-overs.
2. .... A flight that does not make any stops between the origin and destination.
3. .... Any point that is not a connecting point in an itinerary.
4. .... A list of points used to complete a trip, including both connecting and stopover points.
5. .... The practice of advancing standard time by one hair in the spring of each year, and sitting it back by one hair in the fall.
6. .... A circle trip in which an ARNK segment occurs just after the outbound segment or just before the return segment.
7. .... The second city or airport in an air segment.
8. .... Any flight segment of a connection.
9. .... The first city or airport in a connection.
10. .... A surface segment placed in an itinerary to maintain continuity between air segments.
11. .... The main guide to flight schedules, containing listing for all carriers.
12. .... A list of arrivals and departures of regularly schedule flights published by an airline.
13. .... The first segment in an itinerary.

Q. 4. *In each of the following sentences, write the correct word or phrase that belongs in each blank:*

1. The air transport industry, is called ....
2. Special meals could be requested due to .... preferences as well as .... requirements.
3. To transport a pet in the passenger cabin, the pet must be small enough to travel in a container that can be placed ....
4. By government regulations, the minimum liability of an airline for lost or damaged luggage is .... per passenger on domestic flights.
5. The process of reserving an airline seat is referred to as ....
6. Small carriers that operate aircraft with fewer than 30 seats are defined as ....

7. The formation of a large company that is capable of controlling an entire industry is called a ....
8. A flight that requires passengers to change plane at an intermediate point between the original boarding point and the final destination, with no stop-over allowed, is called as ....
9. Under the .... system passengers from different cities are transported to a central intermediate point to board plans to their final destinations
10. In an equipment code, the letter 'S' indicates that an airplane has been configured for .... and the letter 'M' indicates a 'multiple' configuration, designed to transport both .... and ....
11. On most 747 aircraft used, the seating is set up to handle .... passengers. The seating of a DC-10 is usually set up for about .... passengers.
12. For longer flights up to 3000 miles, the Boeing 727 and 737 the McDonnell Douglas DC-8, DC-9 and MD-80, and the European made .... are widely used.
13. An agreement that permits an airline to use the same name and carrier code as another airline is called a ....
14. In airline schedule and tariffs each airline is referred to by a ....

Q. 5. *In each of the following sentences, write the correct word or phrase that belongs in each blank:*

1 Each airline has its own free luggage allowance, based on the .... and the ....

2. Under .... of the airline industry regulations, if a flight is delayed or cancelled, the airline is required to provide passengers with alternative transportation at no additional cost, on request.

3. A .... flight may case a chain reaction, of flight delays throughout the air traffic network.

4. On time performance refers to the percentage of airline flights that leave the departure gate within .... of the schedule departure time and arrive at the destination gate within .... of the schedule arrival time.

5. .... Occurs when an airline books more reservation than the seating capacity of a flight.

6. When a travel agent becomes aware of a schedule change or cancellation, it is that agent's responsibility to ....
7. When a travel agent books a reservation for an unaccompanied minor, a .... must be sent to each carrier involved in the itinerary.
8. A list of people desiring reservations on a flight that has been sold out in a particular class of service is called a ....
9. Domestic and international airlines prohibit the booking of .... on the same carrier over the same itinerary.

Q. 6. *Scheduled appearing in the Airline Guide represent flights between cities adjacent Islands. For example, the North American Edition lists flights schedules to Chicago from such cities as Acapulco, Mexico; Denver, Colorado; Fairbanks, Alaska; Honolulu, Hawaii; Ottawa, Ontario; and Kingston, Jamaica. It does not list flight schedules to Chicago from such cities as Buenos Aires, Argentina; London, England; or Manila, Republic of the Philippines because these cities are not located in North America. Which of the following flight schedules would not appear in the North American Edition of Official Airline Guide (NAOAG)?*

A. Honolulu, Hawaii to Sydney, Australia
B. Toronto, Ontario to Montreal, Quebec
C. Cleveland, Ohio to Dallas, Texas
D. San Juan, Puerto Rico to Washington, D.C.

Ans. *(A) Honolulu, Hawaii to Sydney*

Q. 7. *It's easy to locate flight schedules in the Airline Guide. Simply look for the name of your destination city across the top of the columns. For example you will find it printed in large bold face type like this:*

TO SALT LAKE CITY, UTAH

At times, a "To" city listing will begin in the middle of a column instead of the top, but it will always be in correct alphabetical order. It schedules to Phoenix are found on Page 615, where would you expect to find schedules to San Francisco?

A. **Page 567**
B. **Page 819**

Ans. ***(B) Page 819***

Q. 8. *If you were planning a trip from New York to Detroit, Mich (a) you would first look for the heading "To ...." Having located it (b) you would then look down the listing beneath it until you found your "From" city, in this case ....*

A. To : Detroit, Mich
B. From : New York, N.Y.

Ans. *A. To : DETROIT, MICH.*
B. From : NEW YORK, N.Y.

Q. 9. *To be able to present all the necessary information for a flight schedule, it is necessary to condense this information into codes. Example: United Airlines is coded "UA". These codes can be found under "Abbreviations and Reference Marks" in the front pages of the Airline Guide. Locate them now in your sample Airline Guide and use them to answer the following questions: (a) the Carrier (Airline) Code "NC" stands for .... Airlines; (b) the Jet Aircraft "DIO" represents a .... aircraft; and (c) the Frequency Code "4" means ....*

Ans. *(a) North Central;*
(b) Douglas DC-10;
(c) Thursday

Q. 10. *All origin or destination cities are spelled out for easy reference, but each is given a three-letter code to standardize this information. These three-letter codes can be found in the "City/Airport Codes" in the front pages of the Airline Guide. Now locate this section in your Sample (back pages) Airline Guide and answer the following questions: (a) "CHA" stands for what city? .... ? (b) "KOA" stands for what city? .... ?*

Ans. *(a) Chattanooga, Tenn.;*
(b) Kona, Hawaii

Q. 11. *Your sample Airline Guide also contains a "Flight Itineraries" section. Each carrier's flights are listed here in numeric order with their origin, destination and enroute cities, if any. Please turn to these pages in your sample Airline Guide and locate Eastern Airlines Flight 569 listed under the Carrier Code EA. Note the flight itinerary is expressed in three-letter codes. Eastern's Flight 569 flies from BOS (Boston, Mass) to IAH (Houston, Texas) with a stop enroute in MSY (New Orleans, La.). (a) Where does Frontier*

Airlines (FL) Flight 61 originate? (Just jot down the three-letter code.) .... (b) What is its final stop? .... (c) Where else does it stop? ....

Ans. (*a*) *DFW (Dallas/Ft. Worth);*

(*b*) *SLC (Salt Lake City);*

(*c*) *DEN (Denver)*

Q. 12. Answer the questions in the space(s) provided; use the sample materials and exhibits, when necessary, at the end of the exercise.

1. Which of the following flight schedules would not appear in the World Wide Airline Guide?
   - A. Honolulu, Hawaii to Osaka, Japan
   - B. Montreal, Canada to Miami, Florida
   - C. Detroit, Michigan to Stockholm, Sweden
   - D. San Juan, Puerto Rico to London, England

Ans. (B) *Montreal, Canada to Miami, Florida. (While travel from Montreal to Miami is across an international border* (*Canada to the United States*) *both cities are located in North America. For flight schedules wholly within North America, consult the North American Edition of the OFFICIAL AIRLINE GUIDE*).

Short Answer Type

Q. 13. Explain the following:

(*a*) Airline codes
(*b*) Carrier codes
(*c*) Share airlines designator codes.

Q. 14. Define the following:

(*a*) Co-sharing agreements
(*b*) Aircraft
(*c*) International carriers
(*d*) Schedule air services.

Q. 15. Write notes on:

(*a*) Types of carriers
(*b*) Five freedom of Airtravel
(*c*) Fixing the price of a seat.

Q. 16. Differentiate between (with examples):

(*a*) Domestic and International Travel
(*b*) City Codes and Airport Codes.

Essay Type

Q. 17. Explain the term air travel. What are the main requirements for international travel?

Q. 18. Discuss passenger services rules and classes of service.

Q. 19. Explain the rules and regulations of airlines.

2

Passenger Aircrafts and Aeroplanes

After learning this Chapter you shall be able to:

- *understand the term passenger aircraft and designated flight ranges;*
- *explain the passenger aircraft capacity and seating arrangements and plans;*
- *identify the shape and designs of various models of aeroplanes by equipment code, flight range, and passenger capacity;*
- *get acquainted with executive class, hospitality class, supersonic class, smoking class, non-smoking class;*
- *identify rows in an aeroplane;*
- *explain the arrangement of food and beverages and services;*
- *describe the equipment codes and aircraft codes type (coding and decoding), type of aircrafts;*
- *understand the 'hub and spoke' system;*
- *describe the airport terminals—domestic and international.*

Several types of aircraft are used for international and domestic passenger service. Among other factors, the type of aircraft determines the maximum flight distance, passenger capacity, seating arrangements and availability of meal service.

FLIGHT DISTANCE

For short segments, medium flights and transactional (coast to coast) flights, different type of aircraft used. Table 2.1 indicates the flight ranges of various passenger aircraft.

Table 2.1: Passenger Aircraft and Designated Flight Ranges

Aircraft	*Range (in miles)*
CESSNA-402	239
PIPERT 1040	250
DeHAVILLAND TWIN OTTER	745
SHORTS 360	1151
AIRBUS INDUSTRIE A-300B	2100
McDONNELL-DOUGLAS DC-9	2200
BOEING 737	1300-2500
BRITISH AEROSPACE VANGUARD	2910
BOEING 727	2400-3000
McDONNELL-DOUGLAS MD-80	3060
BRITISH AEROSPACE HERALD	3150
LOCKHEED L-1011 TRISTAR	5998
McDONNELL-DOUGLAS DC-10	6350
BOEING 474	5500-6500

PASSENGER CAPACITY AND SEATING

Small aircraft are used on routes that have reduced traffic and larger aircraft such as Boeing 737, Boeing 727, Boeing 747 etc. are used on routes having larger traffic.

The seating arrangement on a passenger aircraft is determined partly by the aircraft's size and design. On most 727s and 737s, seats are arranged on two sides of a single aisle, with 5 to 6 seats in each row. On a wide-body aircraft, such as 747, DC-10, or L-1011, seats are arranged with two aisles and 8 to 10 seats per row.

Table 2.2 indicates the seating capacity of passenger aircraft.

Table 2.2: Aircrafts and their Seating Capacity

Aircraft	*Passenger capacity*
CESSNA-402	4-8
PIPER T-1040	9
DeHAVILLAND TWIN OTTER	20
BOEING 727	70-131
McDONNELL-DOUGLAS DC-9	90-139
LOCKHEED L-1011 TRISTAR	246-330
McDONNELL-DOUGLAS DC-10	250-380
AIRBUS INDUSRIE A-300B	201-345
BOEING 747	430-452

AIRCRAFT SEATING PLANS

The seating plan show represents standard congigurations and are subject to change without notice.

Key ▱ = Centre Table ■ = Video Δ = Exit/Emergency exit

747 Boeing 747-100/200 *(Air Canada Concorde)*

Executive Class: Rows 1-10; 39 seats
Hospitality Class: Rows 19-59, 61-66; 378 seats

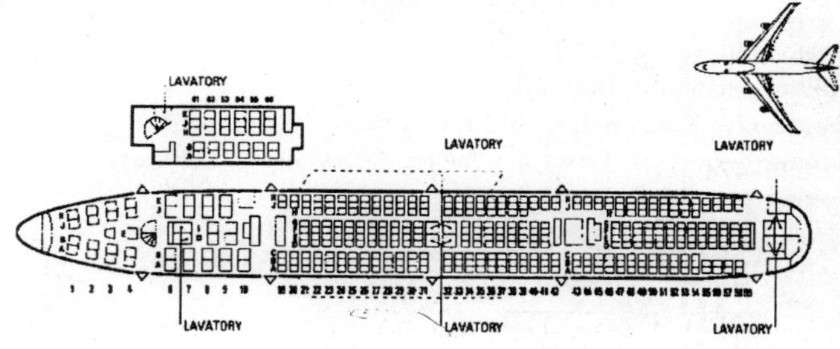

SSC *(Air France Concorde)*

Supersonic Class: Rows 1-28, 100 seats
Smoking permitted: Rows 8-10; Rows 26-28

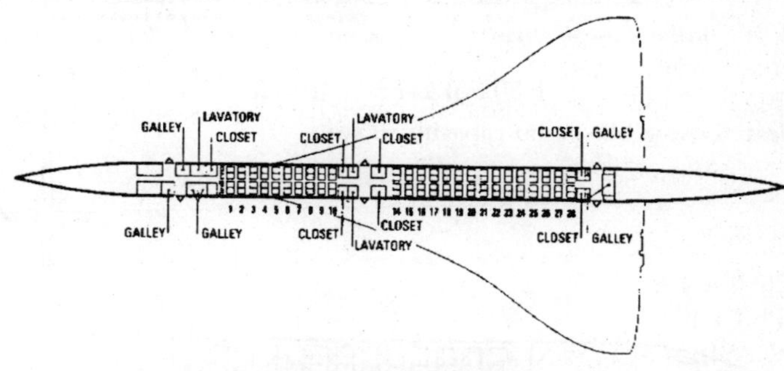

744 Boeing 747-400 (390 seats)

L'Espace 180: Rows 1-3; 13 seats
Smoking permitted: Row 3F,K,L
L'Espace 127: Rows 5-8; 60-66; 156 seats
Smoking permitted: Rows 7-8 *Tempo:* Rows 10-56; 321 seats
Smoking permitted: Rows 30-35

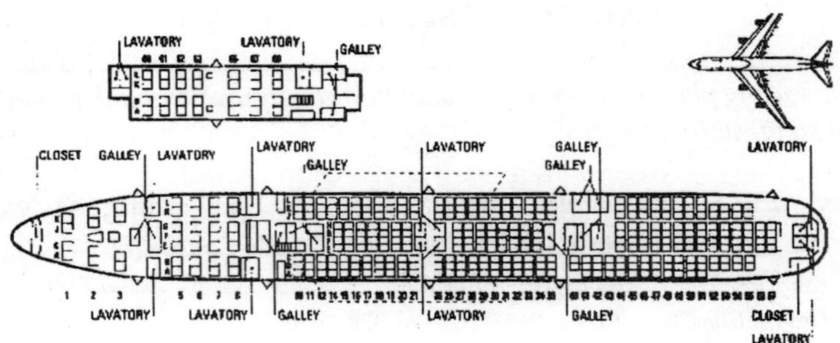

744 Boeing 747-400 (391 seats)

L'Espace 180: Rows 1-3; 13 seats
Smoking permitted: Row 3 F,K,L
L'Espace 127: Rows 5-8; 60-66; 156 seats
Smoking permitted: Rows 7-8 *Tempo:* Rows 10-56; 322 seats
Smoking permitted: Rows 31-36

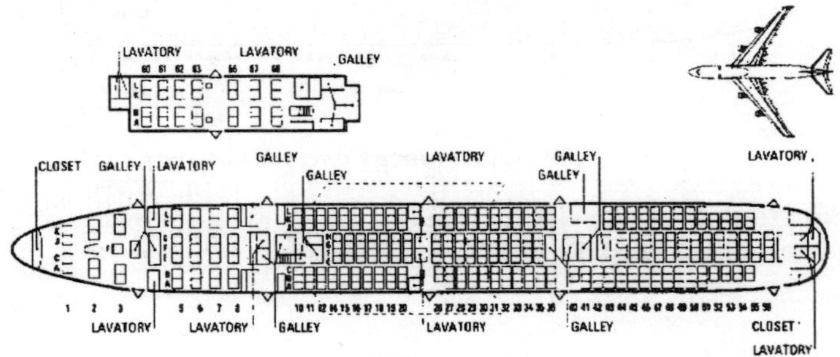

F 50 Fokker 50 *(Air UK)*

Class: Sterling Maximum capacity 50 seats

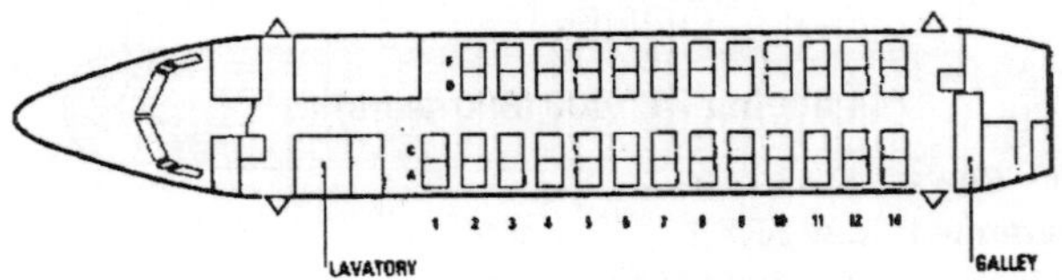

100 Fokker 100

Class: Sterling Maximum capacity 101 seats

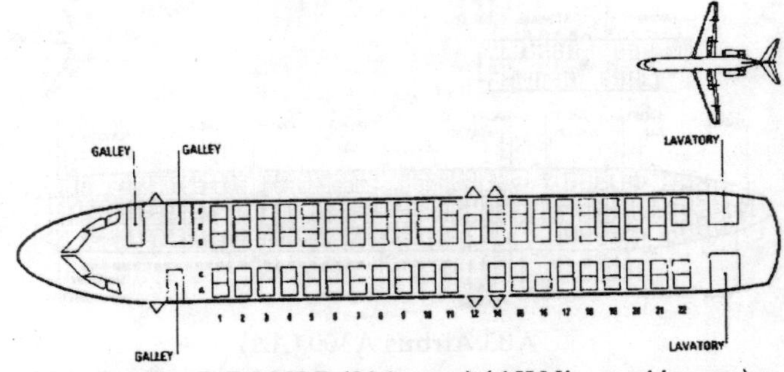

747 Boeing 747-200LR (306 seats) *(All Nippon Airways)*

First Class: Rows 1-12; 24 seats
Smoking permitted: 5H, K; Rows 11-12 *Club ANA:* Rows 18-30, 71-75; 88 seats
Smoking permitted: Rows 26-30 *Economy Class:* Rows 34-63; 214 seats
Smoking permitted: Rows 47-63

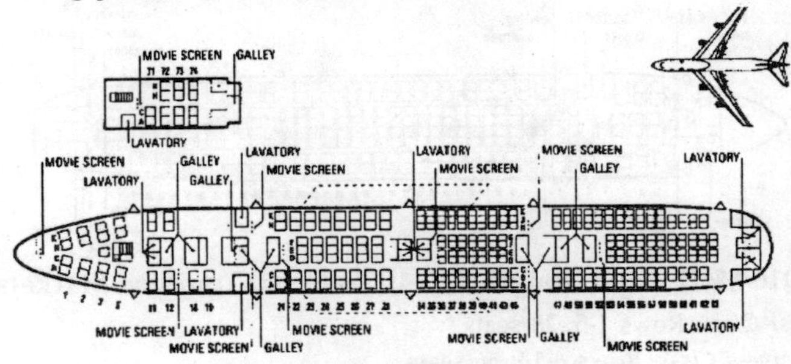

744 Boeing 747-400 (322 seats)

First Class: Rows 1-5; 19 seats
Club ANA: Rows 16-28, 71-84; 83 seats
Economy Class: Rows 34-63; 220 seats

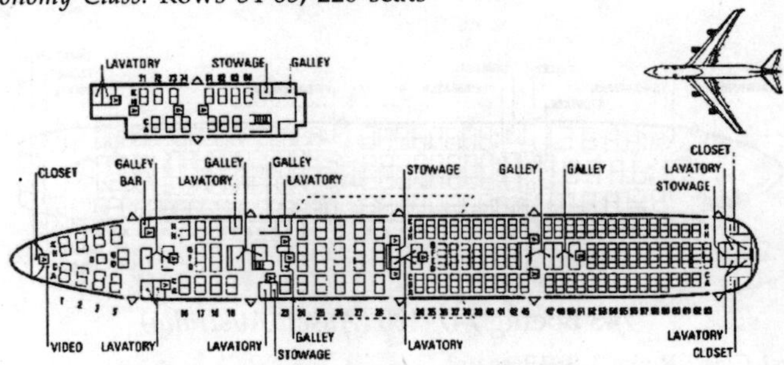

744 Boeing 747-400 (341 seats)

First Class: Rows 1-5; 19 seats
Club ANA: Rows 16-25, 71-84; 62 seats
Economy Class: Rows 29-63; 260 seats

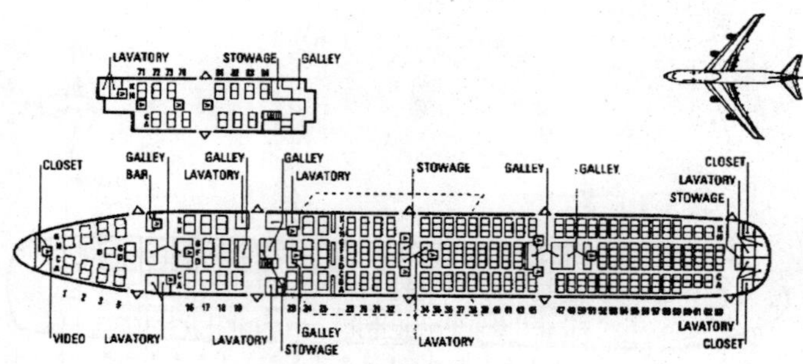

AB3 Airbus A300 (*AA*)

First Class: Rows 1-3; 16 seats
Coach/Economy Class: Rows 4-37; 251 seats

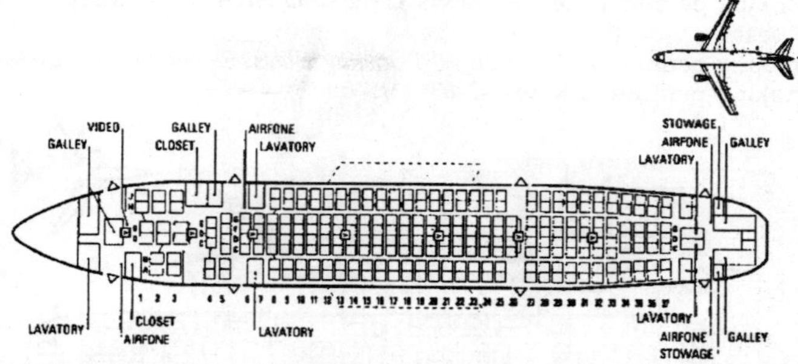

D10 McDonnell Douglas DC-10 (Selected Transcon Markets)

First Class: Rows 1-5; 28 seats
Business Class: Rows 6-13; 56 seats
Coach/Economy Class: Rows 24-41; 152 seats

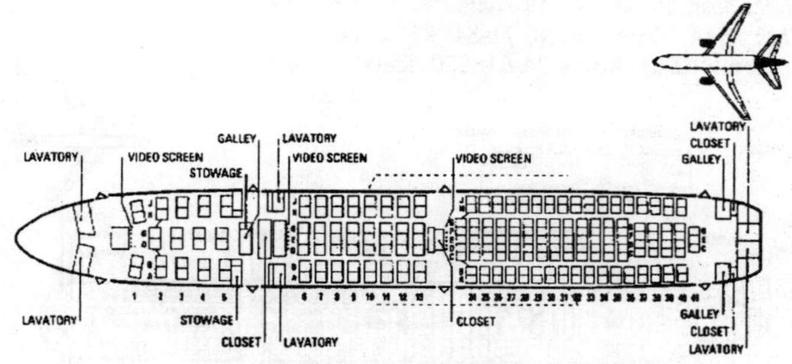

743 Boeing 747-300 (*Ansett Australia*)

First Class: Rows 1-3; 12 seats
Business Class: Rows 6-9; 20 seats
Economy Class: Rows 16-26 and 31-68; 386 seats

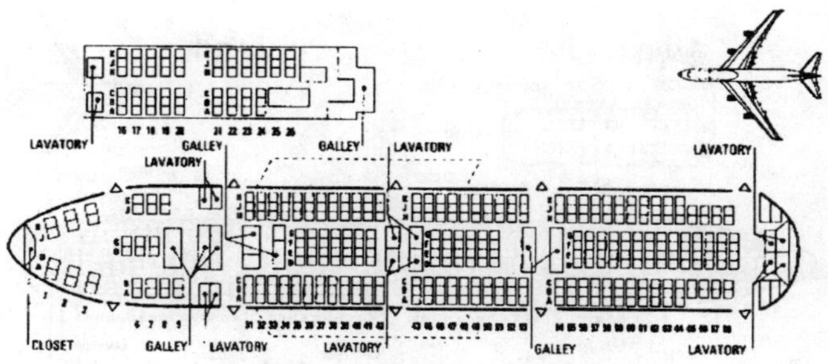

SSC *(British Airways Concorde)*

Supersonic Class: Rows 1-26; 100 seats
Smoking Permitted: Rows 8-10; Rows 22-26

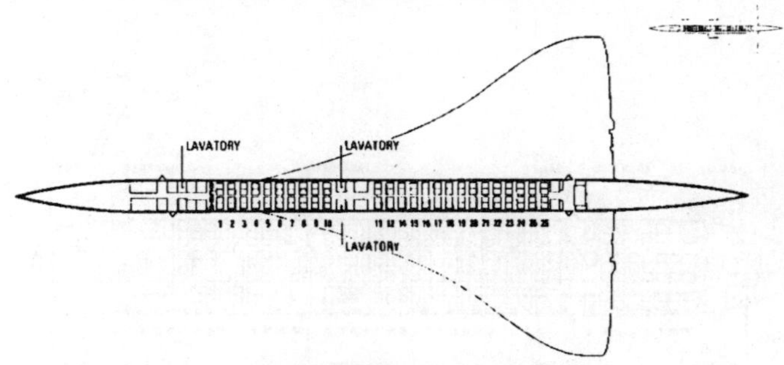

747 Boeing 747 (374 seats)

First Class: Rows 1-4; 18 seats
Club World: Rows 13-22, 56-60; 64 seats
World Traveller: Rows 26-60; 292 seats
Smoking will generally be permitted in seat rows at the rear of the aircraft. Please enquire at check-in

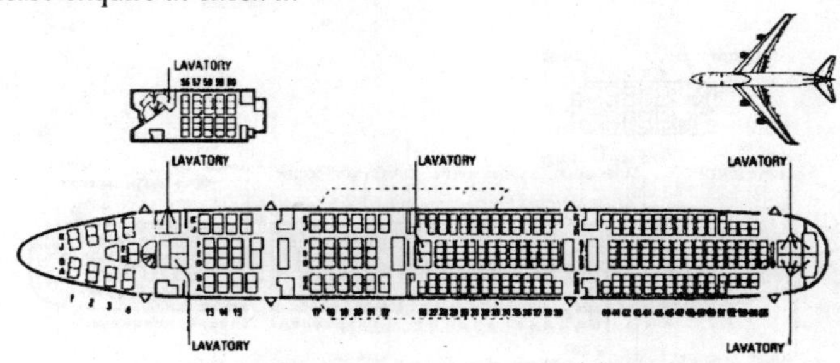

743 Boeing 747-300 (2 class) *(Cathay Pacific)*

Marco Polo Business Class: Rows 11-29; 73 seats
Economy Class: Rows 30-72; 361 seats

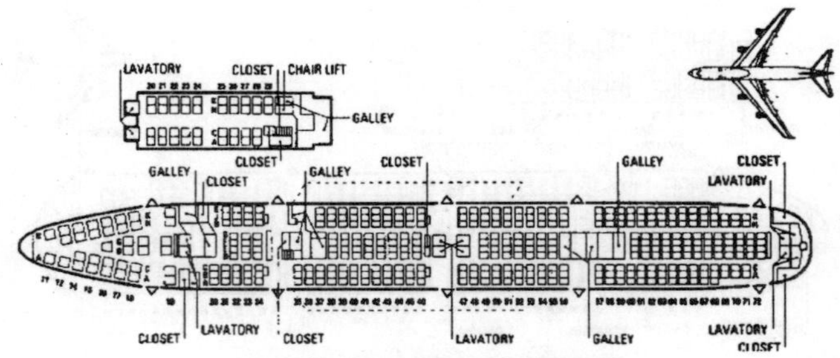

777 Boeing 777 *(Emirates)*

Business Class: Rows 1-7; 49 seats
Economy Class: Rows 8-41; 290 seats

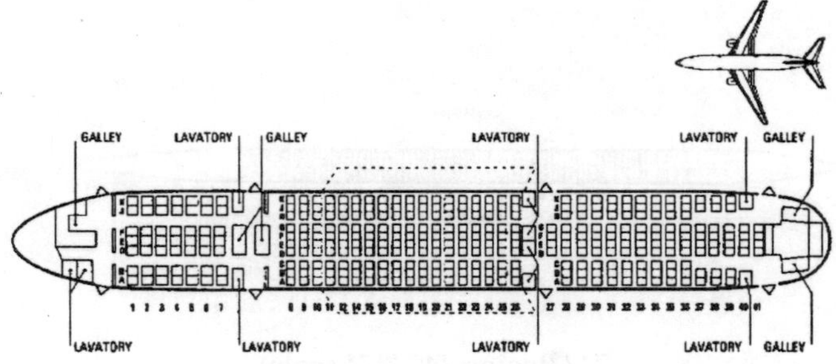

747 Boeing 747LR (336 seats) *(Jal)*

First Class: Rows 1-7; 22 seats
JAL Executive Class: Rows 10-13, 15-18 and 24-33; 92 seats
Economy Class: Rows 8-9 and 35-59; 222 seats

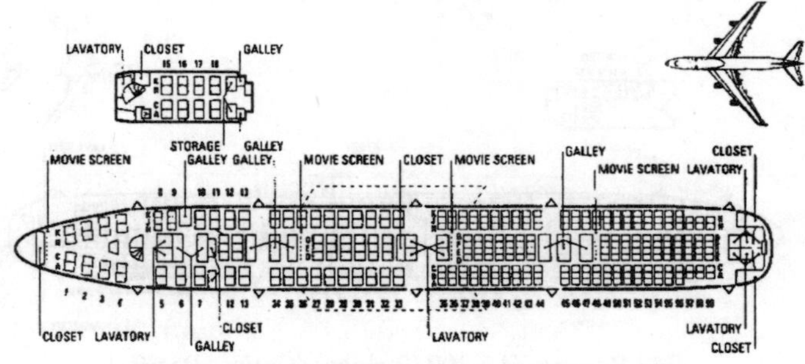

744 Boeing 747-400 (402 seats)

First Class: Rows 1-4; 19 seats
JAL Executive Class: Rows 9-13; 30 seats
Economy Class: Rows 27-60 and 61-71; 353 seats

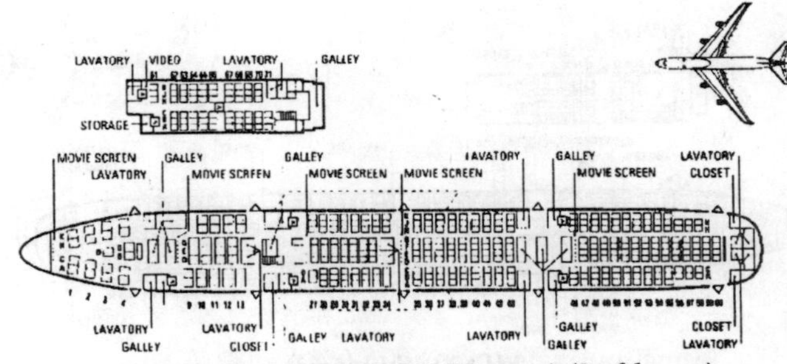

AB3 Airbus A300-600 (207 seats) (*Lufthansa*)

First Class: Rows 1-3; 18 seats
Business Class: Rows 18-26; 63 seats
Economy Class: Rows 28-44; 126 seats
Comment: The number of seats available for smoking varies.

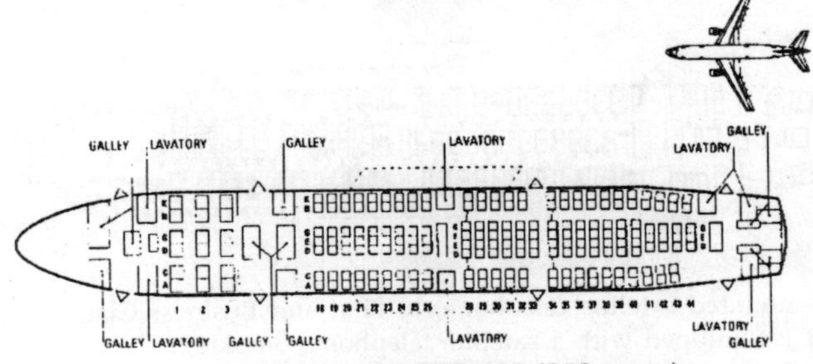

744 Boeing 747-400 (393 seats)

First Class: Rows 81-85; 20 seats
Business Class: Rows 1-12; 51 seats
Economy Class: Rows 14-56; 322 seats
Comment: The number of seats available for smoking varies.

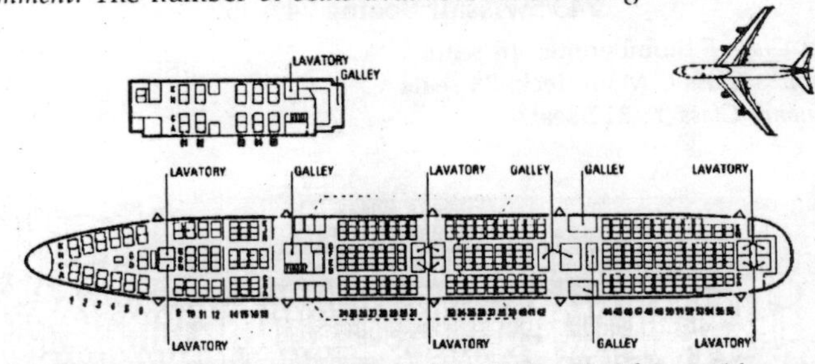

743 Boeing 747-300 (349 seats) [*SAA (South African Airways)*]

First Class: Rows 1-5; 18 seats
Smoking permitted: Rows 7-9
Business Class: Rows 21-33; 66 seats
Smoking permitted: Rows 21-25
Economy Class: Rows 7-18 and 35-60; 265 seats
Smoking permitted: Rows 39-44

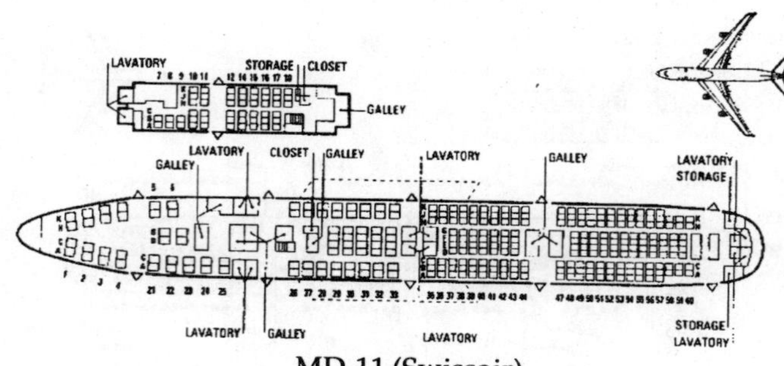

MD-11 (Swissair)

First Class F Slumberettes; 18 seats
Business Class C: 72 seats
Economy Class: Y: 153 seats

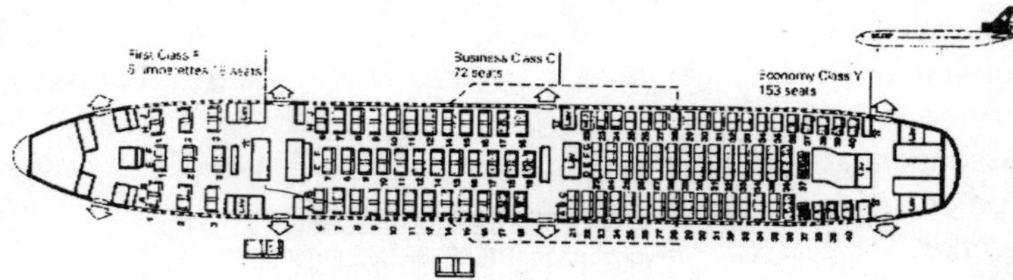

☎ Wall-mounted satellite telephone. In First and Business Class each seat pair is equipped with a satellite telephone; Smoking.
The proportion of non-smoking/smoking may occasionally be changed;
Seats with removable armrests for incapacitated passengers;
Movie screens are located near rows 1, 7, 10, 14, 22, 29, 34
First Class: Personal video LCD-Screen; Seats near lavatory: 20G, 40H

743 Swissair Boeing 747-357

First Class F Slumberettes 18 seats
Business Class C Main deck: 28 seats
Economy Class Y: 312 seats

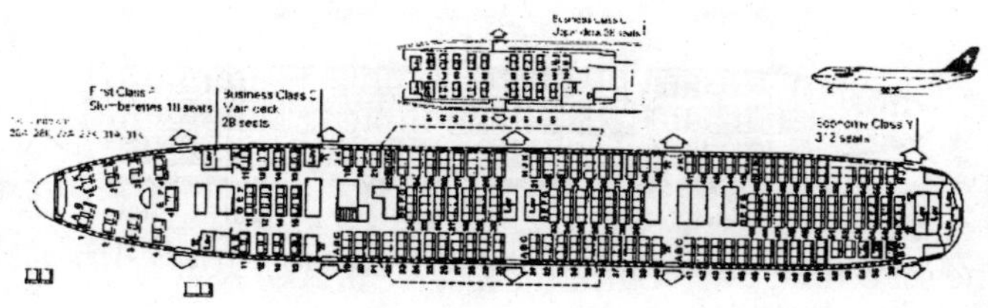

Smoking. The proportion of non-smoking/smoking may occasionally be changed;
Seats with removable armrests for incapacitated passengers;

Movie screens are located near rows 1, 11, 19, 23, 31, 32, 41, 45, 61, 66;
First Class: Personal Video LCD-Screen;
Seats near galley/lavatory: 19B, 19C, 19J, 19K, 20C, 20J, 21C, 21J, 61B, 61J.

☎ Wall-mounted satellite telephone.
In First and Business Class each seat pair is equipped with a satellite telephone.

Fig. 2.1: Seating Plans in Different Aircrafts.

FOOD AND BEVERAGE SERVICE

Hot meals are served only on airplanes equipped with galleys. A galley is a kitchenette used by the flight crew to heat or prepare passenger meals on an aircraft. Most small planes, such as Cessna, Convair, or DeHavilland, do not have galleys, so food and beverage service is unavailable. The type of meal service provided on passenger carriers varies from one airline to another. The standard type of meals served on major carriers along with their code are given in Table 2.3.

Table 2.3: Standard Meals and their Code

Meal Service	*Code*
Full breakfast	B
Continental breakfast	C
Lunch	L
Light meal or snacks	S
Dinner	D

Special meals can be requested due to religious preferences or special dietary restrictions.

EQUIPMENT CODE

Some passenger aircraft have more than one model. Each aircraft design or model has a three letter equipment code, which are used in airline schedules and computer reservation systems to indicate the type of aircraft used on each flight. For example, equipment code for the 727-200 is 72S. This represents special configuration of the 727. The S indicates that airplanes have been configured for additional passenger seating. Similarly 73M is used for MD-80, where M indicates a multiple configuration, designed to transport both passengers and cargo.

AIRCRAFT CODES

Encoding of Aircraft Types

The codes used in this chapter are Aircraft General Designators as specified in Appendix A of the Standard Schedules Information Manual issued by IATA.

Table 2.4: Aircraft Codes (Encoding)

J	Pure jet	*H*	Helicopter
P	Propeller	*T*	Prop jet
A	Amphibian/seaplane		

Aircraft Types	*Code*	*Number*
Aerospatiale AS 350/355 Exureuill Helicopter	*H*	NDE
Aerospatiale SE 210 Caravelle (all series)	*J*	CRV
Aerospatiale N262/Frakes Mohawk 298	*T*	ND2
Aerospatiale SA365 Dauphin-2 helicopter	*H*	NDH
Aerospatiale SN601 Corvette	*J*	NDC
Aerospatiale-British Aerospace (BAC) Concorde	*J*	SSC
Aerospatiale/Alenia ATR-42/72	*T*	ATR
Aerospatiale/Alenia ATR-72	*T*	AT7
Airbus Industrie A300-600C freighter	*J*	ABF
Airbus Industrie A300 (all series) passenger	*J*	AB3
Airbus Industrie A310 (all series) passenger	*J*	310
Airbus Industrie A319	*J*	319
Airbus Industrie A320-100/200	*J*	320
Airbus Industrie A321	*J*	321
Airbus Industrie A32S	*J*	32S
Airbus Industrie A330	*J*	330
Airbus Industrie A330-200	*J*	332
Airbus Industrie A330-300	*J*	333
Airbus Industrie 340	*J*	340
Airbus Industrie A340-200	*J*	342
Airbus Industrie A340-300	*J*	343
Antonov AN-12	*T*	ANF

(Contd.)

(*Contd.*)

Aircraft Types	*Code*	*Number*
Antonov AN-24	*T*	AN4
Antonov AN-26/32	*T*	AN6
Antonov AN-72/74	*J*	AN7
Avro International Aerospace Avroliner (all series)	*J*	ARJ
Beechcraft (all series prop and turboprop)		BEC
Beechcraft C99	*T*	BE9
Beechcraft 1900	*T*	BE1
Beli Helicopters	*H*	BH2
Boeing 707 freighter	*J*	70F
Boeing 707 passenger (all series)	*J*	707
Boeing 727 (mixed configuration)	*J*	72M
Boeing 727 freighter	*J*	72F
Boeing 727 passenger (all series)	*J*	727
Boeing 727-200 passenger	*J*	72S
Boeing 737 passenger (all series)	*J*	737
Boeing 737-200 freighter	*J*	73F
Boeing 737-200 (mixed configuration)	*J*	73M
Boeing 737-200 passenger	*J*	73S
Boeing 737-300	*J*	733
Boeing 737-400	*J*	734
Boeing 737-500	*J*	735
Boeing 737-600	*J*	736
Boeing 737-700	*J*	73G
Boeing 737-800	*J*	738
Boeing 747 (mixed configuration)	*J*	74M
Boeing 747 freighter (all series)	*J*	74F
Boeing 747 passenger (all series)	*J*	747
Boeing 747 SP	*J*	74L
Boeing 747-300 (mixed configuration)	*J*	74D
Boeing 747-300 passenger	*J*	743
Boeing 747-400 (mixed configuration)	*J*	74E
Boeing 747-400 passenger	*J*	744
Boeing 757-200	*J*	752
Boeing 757-300	*J*	753
Boeing 757 freighter	*J*	75F
Boeing 757 (all series) passenger	*J*	757

(*Contd.*)

(*Contd.*)

Aircraft Types	*Code*	*Number*
Boeing 767 (all series)	*J*	767
Boeing 767-300/300ER	*J*	763
Boeing 767 freighter	*J*	76F
Boeing 777-200	*J*	772
Boeing 777-300	*J*	773
Boeing 777 (all series)	*J*	777
British Aerospace ATP	*T*	ATP
British Aerospace (BAC) 111 (all series)	*J*	B11
British Aerospace (Hawker Siddeley) Heron	*P*	DHH
British Aerospace (Handley Page) Herald	*T*	HPH
British Aerospace (Hawker Siddeley) Argosy	*T*	HSF
British Aerospace (Hawker Siddeley) 748	*T*	HS7
British Aerospace (Hawker Siddeley) 125	*J*	H25
British Aerospace Jetstream 31	*T*	J31
British Aerospace Jetstream 41	*T*	J41
British Aerospace (BAC-Vickers) Viscount	*T*	VCV
British Aerospace (BAC-Vickers) Merchantman	*T*	VGF
British Aerospace 146 freighter	*J*	14F
British Aerospace 146 (all series) passenger	*J*	146
Canadair CL-44	*T*	CL4
Canadair Regional Jet	*J*	CRJ
Casa 212/Nusantara 212 Aviocar	*T*	CS2
Casa/Nusantara 235	*T*	CS5
Cessna (all series prop and turboprop)		CAN
Cessna Citation	*J*	CNJ
Convair (all series prop and turboprop)		CVR
Convair 440/580/600/640 freighter	*T*	CVF
Curtiss C-46 Commando	*P*	CWC
Dassault-Breguet Mystere-Falcon (all series)	*J*	DFL
de Havilland DHC2 Turbo Beaver	*T*	DHB
de Havilland DHC3 Otter	*P*	DHO
de Havilland DHC2 Beaver	*P*	DHP
de Havilland DHC6 Twin Otter	*T*	DHT
de Havilland DHC4 Caribou	*P*	DH4
de Havilland DHC7	*T*	DH7
de Havilland DHC8 Dash 8 (all series)	*T*	DH8
Douglas DC-3	*P*	DC3

(*Contd.*)

(Contd.)

Aircraft Types	*Code*	*Number*
Douglas DC-6 passenger	*P*	DC6
Douglas DC-6 freighter	*P*	D6F
Embraer EMB 110 Bandeirante	*T*	EMB
Embraer EMB 120 Brasilia	*T*	EM2
Embraer EMB 145	*J*	EM4
Fairchild Dornier 228	*T*	D28
Fairchild Dornier 328	*T*	D38
Fairchild Industries FH227	*T*	FK7
Fairchild Metroliner	*T*	SWM
Fokker F27 Friendship (all series)	*T*	F27
Fokker F28 Fellowship (all series)	*J*	F28
Fokker 50	*T*	F50
Fokker 70	*J*	F70
Fokker 100	*J*	100
GAF N22/N24 A Nomad	*T*	CD2
Gates Learjet	*J*	LRJ
Grumman Goose	*A*	GRG
Grumman Mallard	*A*	GRM
Gulfstream Aerospace Gulfstream 11/111/1V	*J*	GRJ
Gulfstream Aerospace (Grumman) Gulfstream 1/1-C	*T*	GRS
Helio Courier 725	*P*	HEC
Ilyushin IL-18	*T*	IL8
Ilyushin IL-62/62M	*J*	IL6
Ilyushin IL-76	*J*	IL7
Ilyushin IL-86	*J*	ILW
Ilyushin IL-96	*J*	IL9
Ilyushin IL-114	*T*	114
Israel Aircraft Industries Westwind	*J*	WWP
LET L410 Turbolet	*T*	L4T
Lockheed L100 Hercules freighter	*T*	LOH
Lockheed L1011 TriStar (all series)	*J*	L10
Lockheed L1011 TriStar (500 series)	*J*	L15
Lockheed L188 Electra	*T*	LOE
Lockheed L188 Electra (mixed configuration)	*T*	LOM
Lockheed L188 Electra freighter	*T*	LOF

(Contd.)

(*Contd.*)

Aircraft Types	*Code*	*Number*
Lockheed (Super) Constellation	*P*	L49
MBB-UL BO. 105 helicopter	*H*	MBH
McDonnell Douglas DC-3/C-47 freighter	*P*	D3F
McDonnell Douglas DC-8 (all series passenger)	*J*	DC8
McDonnell Douglas DC-9 (all series passenger)	*J*	DC9
McDonnell Douglas DC-10 freighter	*J*	D1F
McDonnell Douglas DC-10 (mixed configuration)	*J*	D1M
McDonnell Douglas DC-10 passenger (all series)	*J*	D10
McDonnell Douglas DC-8 freighter	*J*	D8F
McDonnell Douglas DC-8 (mixed configuration)	*J*	D8M
McDonnell Douglas DC-8 (all 60 and 70 series passenger)	*J*	D8S
McDonnell Douglas DC-9 freighter	*J*	D9F
McDonnell Douglas DC-9 (all 30, 40, 50 and 80 series passenger)	*J*	D9S
McDonnell Douglas MD-11 freighter	*J*	M1F
McDonnell Douglas MD-11 passenger	*J*	M11
McDonnell Douglas MD-11 (mixed configuration)	*J*	M1M
McDonnell Douglas MD-80 (all series)	*J*	M80
McDonnell Douglas MD-87	*J*	M87
McDonnell Douglas MD-90	*J*	M90
McDonnell Douglas MD-95	*J*	M95
Mil Mi-8 Helicopter	*H*	MIH
Mitsubishi MU-2	*T*	MU2
NAMC YS-11	*T*	YS1
Partenavia P68 Victor	*P*	PN6
Pilatus Britten Normal Trislander	*P*	BNT
Pilatus Britten Normal Islander	*P*	BNI
Pilatus PC6 Turbo-Porter	*T*	PL6
Piper (all series prop and turboprop)		PAG
Rockwell Commander	*P*	ACD
Saab SF 340	*T*	SF3
Saab 2000	*T*	S20
Shorts Skyvan	*T*	SHS
Shorts 330	*T*	SH3
Shorts 360	*T*	SH6
Shorts SC.5 Belfast	*T*	SHB

(*Contd.*)

(*Contd.*)

Aircraft Types	*Code*	*Number*
Sikorsky S-58 helicopter	*H*	S58
Sikorsky S-61 helicopter	*H*	S61
Sikorsky S-76 helicopter	*H*	S76
TriStar Freighter	*J*	L1F
Tupolev TU-134	*J*	TU3
Tupolev TU-154	*J*	TU5
Tupolev TU-204	*J*	T20
Yakovlev YAK 40	*J*	YK4
Yakovlev YAK 42	*J*	YK2
Yunshuji 7	*T*	YN7
Yunshuji 12	*T*	YN2
Bus		BUS
Equipment Varies		EQV
Hovercraft Launch/Boat		LCH
Limousine		LMO
Road Feeder Service (Truck)		RFS
Train a Grand Vitesse		TGV
Train		TRN

AIRCRAFT CODES

Decoding of Abbreviations

The codes used above are Aircraft General Designators as specified in Appendix A of the Standard Schedules Information Manual issued by IATA.

Table 2.5: Aircraft Codes (Decoding)

J	Pure jet	*H*	Helicopter
P	Propeller	*T*	Prop jet
A	Amphibian/seaplane		

Codes	*Number*	*Aircraft Type*
ABF	*J*	Airbus Industrie A300-600C freighter
AB3	*J*	Airbus Industrie A300 (all series passenger)
ACD	*P*	Rockwell Commander

(*Contd.*)

(Contd.)

Codes	*Number*	*Aircraft Type*
AN4	*T*	Antonov AN-24
AN6	*T*	Antonov AN-26
AN7	*J*	Antonov AN-72/74
ARJ	*J*	Avro International Aerospace Avroliner (all series)
ATP	*T*	British Aerospace ATP
ATR	*T*	Aerospatiale/Alenia ATR-42/72
AT7	*T*	Aerospatiale/Alenia ATR-72
A4F	*J*	Antonov AN-124 freighter
BEC		Beechcraft (all series prop and turboprop)
BE1	*T*	Beechcraft 1900
BE9	*T*	Beechcraft C99
BH2	*H*	Beli Helicopters
BNI	*P*	Pilatus Britten Normal Islander
BNT	*P*	Pilatus Britten Normal Trislander
B11	*J*	British Aerospace (BAC)111 (all series)
CD2	*T*	GAF N22/N24 A Nomad
CL4	*T*	Canadair CL-44
CNA		Cessna (all series prop and turboprop)
CNJ	*J*	Cessna Citation
CRJ	*J*	Canadair Regional Jet
CRV	*J*	Aerospatiale Caravelle (all series)
CS2	*T*	Casa 212/Nusantara 212 Aviocar
CS5	*T*	Casa/Nusantara 235
CVF	*T*	Convair 440/580/600/640 freighter
CVR		Convair (all series prop and turboprop)
CWC	*P*	Curtiss C-46 Commando
DC3	*P*	Douglas DC-3 passenger
DC6	*P*	Douglas DC-6 passenger
DC8	*J*	McDonnell Douglas DC-8 (all series passenger)
DC9	*J*	McDonnell Douglas DC-9 (all series passenger)
DFL	*J*	Dassault Breguet Mystere-Falcon (all series)
DHB	*T*	de Havilland DHC2 Turbo Beaver
DHH	*P*	British Aerospace (Hawker Siddeley) Heron
DHO	*P*	de Havilland DHC3 Otter
DHP	*P*	de Havilland DHC2 Beaver
DHT	*T*	de Havilland DHC6 Twin Otter

(Contd.)

(Contd.)

Codes	*Number*	*Aircraft Type*
DH4	*P*	de Havilland DHC4 Caribou
DH7	*T*	de Havilland DHC7
DH8	*T*	de Havilland DHC8 Dash 8 (all series)
D1F	*J*	McDonnell Douglas DC-10 freighter
D1M	*J*	McDonnell Douglas DC-10 (mixed configuration)
D10	*J*	McDonnell Douglas DC-10 passenger (all series)
D28	*T*	Fairchild Dornier 228
D3F	*P*	McDonnell Douglas DC-3/C-47 freighter
D38	*T*	Fairchild Dornier 328
D6F	*P*	Douglas DC-6 freighter
D8F	*J*	McDonnell Douglas DC-8
D8M	*J*	McDonnell Douglas DC-8 (mixed configuration)
D8S	*J*	McDonnell Douglas DC-8 (all 60 and 70 series passenger)
D9F	*J*	McDonnell Douglas DC-9 freighter
D9S	*J*	McDonnell Douglas DC-9 (all 30, 40, 50 & 80 series passenger)
EMB	*T*	Embraer EMB 110 Bandeirante
EM2	*T*	Embraer EMB 120 Brasilia
EM4	*J*	Embraer EMB 145
FK7	*T*	Fairchild Industries FH227
F27	*T*	Fokker F27 Friendship
F28	*J*	Fokker F28 Fellowship (all series)
F50	*T*	Fokker 50
F70	*J*	Fokker 70
GRG	*A*	Grumman Goose
GRJ	*J*	Gulfstream Aerospace Gulfstream 11/111/1V
GRM	*A*	Grumman Mallard
GRS	*T*	Gulfstream Aerospace (Grumman) Gulfstream 1/1-C
HEC	*P*	Helio Courier 725
HPH	*T*	British Aerospace (Handley Page) Herald
HSF	*T*	British Aerospace (Hawker Siddeley) Argosy
HS7	*T*	British Aerospace (Hawker Siddeley) 748
H25	*J*	British Aerospace (Hawker Siddeley) 125
ILW	*J*	Ilyushin IL-86
I14	*T*	Ilyushin IL-114

(Contd.)

(Contd.)

Codes	*Number*	*Aircraft Type*
IL6	*J*	Ilyushin IL-62/62M
IL7	*J*	Ilyushin IL-76
IL8	*T*	Ilyushin IL-18
IL9	*J*	Ilyushin IL-96
J31	*T*	British Aerospace Jetstream 31
J41	*T*	British Aerospace Jetstream 41
LOE	*T*	Lockheed L188 Electra
LOF	*T*	Lockheed L188 Electra freighter
LOH	*T*	Lockheed L100 Hercules freighter
LOM	*T*	Lockheed L188 Electra (mixed configuration)
LRJ	*J*	Gates Learjet
L1F	*J*	TriStar Freighter
L10	*J*	Lockheed L1011 TriStar (all series)
L15	*J*	Lockheed L1011 TriStar (500 series)
L4T	*T*	LET L410 Turbolet
L49	*P*	Lockheed (Super) Constellation
MBH	*H*	MBB-UL BO, 105 Helicopter
MIH	*H*	Mil Mi-8 Helicopter
MU2	*T*	Mitsubishi MU-2
M1F	*J*	McDonnell Douglas MD-11 freighter
M1M	*J*	McDonnell Douglas MD-11 (mixed configuration)
M11	*J*	McDonnell Douglas MD-11 passenger
M80	*J*	McDonnell Douglas MD-80 (all series)
M87	*J*	McDonnell Douglas MD-87
M90	*J*	McDonnell Douglas MD-90
M95	*J*	McDonnell Douglas MD-95
NDC	*J*	Aerospatiale SN 601 Corvette
NDE	*H*	Aerospatiale AS 350/355 Ecureuill Helicopter
NDH	*H*	Aerospatiale SA 365 Dauphin-2 Helicopter
ND2	*T*	Aerospatiale N 262/Frakes Mohawk 298
PAG		Piper (all series prop and turboprop)
PL6	*T*	Pilatus PC6 Turbo-Porter
PN6	*P*	Partenavia P68 Victor
SF3	*T*	Saab SF 340
SHB	*T*	Shorts SC.5 Belfast

(Contd.)

(Contd.)

Codes	*Number*	*Aircraft Type*
SHS	*T*	Shorts Skyvan
SH3	*T*	Shorts 330
SH6	*T*	Shorts 360
SSC	*J*	Aerospatiale-British Aerospaçe (BAC) Concorde
SWM	*T*	Fairchild Metroliner
S20	*T*	Saab 2000
S58	*H*	Sikorsky S-58 helicopter
S61	*H*	Sikorsky S-61 helicopter
S76	*H*	Sikorsky S-76 helicopter
TU3	*J*	Tupolev TU-134
TU5	*J*	Tupolev TU-154
T20	*J*	Tupolev TU-204
VCV	*T*	British Aerospace (BAC-Vickers) Viscount
VGF	*T*	British Aerospace (BAC-Vickers) Merchantman
WWP	*J*	Israel Aircraft Industries Westwind
YK2	*J*	Yakovlev YAK 42
YK4	*J*	Yakovlev YAK 40
YN2	*T*	Yunshuji 12
YN7	*T*	Yunshuji 7
YS1	*T*	NAMC YS-11
100	*J*	Fokker 100
14F	*J*	British Aerospace 146 freighter
146	*J*	British Aerospace 146 (all series) passenger
310	*J*	Airbus Industrie A310 passenger
319	*J*	Airbus Industrie A319
320	*J*	Airbus Industrie A320-100/200
321	*J*	Airbus Industrie A321
32S	*J*	Airbus Industrie A32S (all series)
330	*J*	Airbus Industrie A330
332	*J*	Airbus Industrie A330-200
333	*J*	Airbus Industrie A330-300
340	*J*	Airbus Industrie A340 (all series)
342	*J*	Airbus Industrie A340-200
343	*J*	Airbus Industrie A340-300
70F	*J*	Boeing 707 freighter

(Contd.)

(Contd.)

Codes	*Number*	*Aircraft Type*
707	J	Boeing 707 passenger (all series)
72F	J	Boeing 727 freighter
72M	J	Boeing 727 (mixed configuration)
72S	J	Boeing 727-200 passenger
727	J	Boeing 727 passenger (all series)
73F	J	Boeing 737-200 freighter
73G	J	Boeing 737-700
73M	J	Boeing 737-200 (mixed configuration)
73S	J	Boeing 737-200 passenger
733	J	Boeing 737-300
734	J	Boeing 737-400
735	J	Boeing 737-500
737	J	Boeing 737 passenger
738	J	Boeing 737-800
74D	J	Boeing 747-300 (mixed configuration)
74E	J	Boeing 747-400 (mixed configuration)
74F	J	Boeing 747 freighter (all series)
74L	J	Boeing 747 SP
74M	J	Boeing 747 (mixed configuration)
743	J	Boeing 747-300 passenger
744	J	Boeing 747-400 passenger
747	J	Boeing 747 passenger (all series)
75F	J	Boeing 757 freighter
752	J	Boeing 757-200
753	J	Boeing 757-300
757	J	Boeing 757 (all series) passenger
76F	J	Boeing 767 freighter
763	J	Boeing 767-300/300ER
767	J	Boeing 767 (all series)
772	J	Boeing 777-200
773	J	Boeing 777-300
777	J	Boeing 777 (all series)
BUS		Bus
EQV		Equipment Varies
HOV		Hovercraft
LCH		Launch/Boat
LMO		Limousine

(Contd.)

(Contd.)

Codes	*Number*	*Aircraft Type*
RFS		Road Feeder Service (Truck)
TGV		Train a Grand Vitesse
TRN		Train

THE HUB AND SPOKE SYSTEM

To add new point-to-point flights, an airline needed to invest substantial funds to purchase new aircraft. To solve this problem, the airline adopted a route system called the 'hub and spoke' system, under which passengers are transported to an intermediate point, called a hub to board plane to final destinations. To understand the hub and spoke system, imagine a bicycle wheel, with numerous spokes leading from the hub, or centre. The wheel's hub is a major city where passenger can board flights to various destinations. Each spoke is a route from the hub to one of these destination.

The hub and spoke system enables an airline to serve the maximum number of passengers, while still maintaining a competitive fare structure. A flight that requires passengers to change planes at an intermediate point between the original boarding point and the final destination, with no stop-over allowed, is called a connection. A point-to-point flight that does not require a change of aircraft is called a direct flight, regardless the number of stops.

One important benefit of the hub and spoke system is minimising the number of international connections. Before the hub and spoke system was developed, many carriers entered into cooperative contracts, called inter-line agreements which enabled passengers to travel on a connection involving different carriers while paying a single international point-to-point fare called a joint fare. On international routes, point fares are very common, especially between carriers that have code sharing agreements.

AIRPORT TERMINALS

A number of airports have more than one passenger terminal. Departing passengers, of persons meeting arrival passengers, at these airports can avoid considerably inconvenience by ensuring they go to the correct terminal.

In alphabetical sequence, this list highlights those airports where the different terminals are not in the same building, but in some cases are a considerably distance apart. For these airports, each terminal is named and followed by the designator codes of the airlines serving that terminal.

Designator codes followed by an * indicate that the airline serves more than one terminal at the same airport. (Contact the airline for details)

Table 2.6: Airport Terminals

	Bangkok Thailand BKK
International Terminal:	AF, AI, AY, AZ, BA, BG, BI, BR, CA, CI, CP, CX, CZ, DE, EK, ET, GA, GF, HY, IC, JL, JS, KB, KE, KL, KT, KU, LH*, LO, LT, LY, LZ, MA, MH, MS, MU, NG, NH, NW, NX, NZ, OA, OK, OX*, OZ, PK, PR, QF, QR, QV, RA, RG, RJ, RO, SA, SK, SN, SQ, SR, SU, SV, SZ, TG*, TK, TP, UA, UB, UL, UX, VJ, VN, 3Q, 6U
Domestic Terminal:	LH*, OX*, PG, TG*
	Chicago IL U.S.A. CHI
O'Hare International ORD	
Terminal 1:	LH*, MX*, NZ, SK*, UA*
Terminal 2:	AC, CO, HP, JM, KL*, NW*, OK, SK*, TK, TW, UA*, US
Terminal 3:	AA*, CP*, DL*, LO*, OS*, QF*, QQ, SA, SN, SQ, SY, XP
International Terminal 5:	AA*, AF, AI, AZ, BA, CP*, DL*, EI, GD, IB, JL, JM, KE, KL*, KU, LH*, LO*, LY, MX*, NW*, OS*, QF*, RJ, RO, SK*, SN*, SR, SU, TK, UA*
	Frankfurt Germany FRA
Terminal 1:	AA, AC, AH, AI*, AR, AT, AV, AY, AZ, BD, BG, BI, BT, BW*, CA, CI, CU, CY*, DA, DE, DL*, DM, EK, EN, ET, FI*, GA, GF, HF, HM, HY, IB, IG, IL, IR, IY, JP, JU, J2, J5, KE, KU, LA, LG, LH*, LN, LT*, LY, LZ, ME, MH, MK, MS, M4, NZ, OA, OS*, OU, OZ, PK, QF*, RA, RB, RG, RJ, RO, R3, SA*, SK, SQ, SR, SU, SV, SW, TG, TK, TP, TU, UA, UL, UM, UN, VO, VP, VR, YP, Z6, 3R
Terminal 2:	AF, AI*, AM, BA, B2, CO, CX, CY*, DL*, EI, EW, FI*,

(*Contd.*)

(Contd.)

	JL, KL, KM, LH*, LO, LT*, MA, NH, NW, NZ, OK, OS*, PR, PS, QF*, RQ, SA*, SN, TE, UK, US, VN
	Harare Zimbabwe HRE
International Terminal:	AF, BA, BP, DT, EK, ET, FO, GH, KL, LH, LZ, MK, MS, NW, QF, QM, QU, SA, SK, SR, SW, TC, TM, UM*, UY, ZC, 27*, Z9
Domestic Terminal:	UM*, 27*
	Helsinki Finland HEL
International Terminal:	AC, AF, AY*, BA, BT, CA, DL, FI, JT, JZ, KL, LH, LO, LY, LZ, MA, NW, OK, OS, OV, SK, SN, SR, SU, TE, UA
Domestic Terminal:	AY*, KF
	Kuala Lumpur Malaysia KUL
Terminal 1:	AI, AK*, AN, AR, AZ, BA, BG, BI, BR, CI, CP, CX, CZ, EK, GA, GF, HY, IB, IC, IR, JL, KE, KL, LH, L6, ME, MH*, MZ, NG, NH, NW, OX, PK, PR, QF, RJ, SG, SU, SV, TG, UB, UL, VJ, VS, 3Q
Terminal 2:	MH*, MK, NZ, SQ, VN, X5, 9P*
Terminal 3:	AK*, J8, MH*, 9P*
	Madrid Spain MAD
International Terminal:	AA, AF, AH, AI, AM, AR, AT, AV, AZ, BA, BQ, CO, CU, DL, EI, IB*, IR, IT, IY, JK*, JL, JU, KE, KL, KU, LA, LG, LH, LN, LO, LX, LY, LZ, MA, MH, MS, MU, NG, NI, OA, OK, OS, OU, PU, RB, RG, RJ, RO, SK, SN, SQ, SR, SU, TG, TK, TP, TW, US, UX*, VM, VO, 2G
Domestic Terminal:	AO, IB*, JK*, PV*, UX*, W3, ZH
Shuttle Terminal:	IB*
	Manchester United Kingdom MAN
Terminal 1:	AF, AY, BA, CB, CU, CY, DL*, EI, EK, IB, UI, JE, KL, LG, LH, LX, LY, NG, NI, NW, OK, QF, RQ, SK, SN, SR, TK, UA, UK, WA, 5E, 6F*, 9C
Terminal 2:	AA, AC, AI, CO, CP, CX, DL*, DP, FR, HY, IL, KM, LO, MK, PK, SQ, VS, 6F*

(Contd.)

(Contd.)

	Mumbai India BOM
Terminal 1 (Santa Cruz):	AI*, G8, IC*, S2, UZ, WY, 4S, 9W
Terminal 2 (Sahar):	AF, AI*, AZ, BA, BG, BE, CX, DL, EK, ET, GF, GK, IC*, IR, IY, KE, KL, KQ, KU, LH, LY, MK, MS, M9, NH, NW, PK QF, QR, RA, RB, RJ, SA, SQ, SR, SV, TC, UA, UL
	New York NY U.S.A. NYC
	John F. Kennedy International JFK
Terminal 1:	Under construction
Terminal 2:	AM*, AY*, CO, HP, LA, LR, RG*, SV*, TA*, TZ*, VS*
Terminal 3:	AM*, AV, AY*, CA, CI, CX, DL*, GH, LR, MA, OS, RG*, RO, SN, SQ, SR, SU, SV*, TA*, TP, UA*, VS*, 6U
Terminal 4W:	AF*, AI, AZ, BG, DL*, EI, FI*, GH, GY, HY, JM, KE, LY, MS, PK, SN, TK, TR*, VP, 7B, 70
Terminal 5:	RJ*, TW, UA*
Terminal 6:	KW, NJ, PA, PL, SY, TW*, TZ*, UA*
Terminal 7:	BA, EH, LA*, SK, SV, UA*, US
Terminal 8:	AA*, BW, LO*, UX
Terminal 9:	AA*, CP, LO*, QF, SA
Terminal FS:	FF*
	La Guardia LGA
Main Terminal:	AA, AC, CO, CP, HP, JI, QQ, SA, TW, UA, YX, 9L
Marine Air Terminal:	DL*
Delta Airlines Terminal:	AM, DL*, KL, NW
US Airways Terminal:	US*
	Newark EWR
Terminal A:	AA, CP, JI, KP, LO*, P9, SA, SK*, TW, UA*, US, 9L
Terminal B:	AC*, AF*, AM, AV, AZ, BA, BR, CO*, DL, EI, FQ, H2, JM, KE, KL, KW, LH, LO*, LY, MP, MX, NW, OK, PA, PR, SK*, SR, TP, UA*, VS, W7, YX*
Terminal C:	AF*, AC*, CO*, HP, YX*
	Singapore Singapore SIN
Terminal 1:	AA, AI, AZ, BA, BG, BO, BR, CA, CI, CX, CZ, EK*, GA, GF, HM, IC, JL, KE, KL, KU, LH, MK, MS, MU,

(Contd.)

(Contd.)

	MZ, NG, NH, NW, NZ*, OK, OX, OZ, PG, PK, PX, QF, QR, RA, RJ, SG, SK, SU, SV, SZ, TG, TK, UA, UL, VJ, VN, 3Q
Terminal 2:	AF, AY, BI, DL, EK*, MH, MI, NZ*, OS, PR, SQ, SR, UB
	Stockholm Sweden STO
Arianda ARN	
Terminal 2:	AY8, AZ, BU, DL, DM, EI, KM, OS, SN, SR, TQ
Terminal 3:	F3*, HJ, JZ*, PT, XV, ZF
Terminal 4:	IH, LH*, SK*
Terminal 5:	AA, AC, AF, AT, AY*, BA, BT, B2, CA, DL, FI, F3*, IB, IR, JU, JZ*, KL*, KQ, LH*, LO, LY, LZ, MA, MS, NW, OK, OU, OV, RB, RO, SK*, SU, TE, TG, TK, TP, UA, 4M, 5Q
	Tokyo Japan TYO
Narita NRT	
Terminal 1:	AA*, AF, AY, AZ, BA, CP, CX, JL*, KE, KL*, LH, NW, RG, SQ, UA, VS
Terminal 2:	AA*, AI, BG, CA, CO, DL, EG, FJ, GA, IB, IR, JD, JL*, KL*, MH, MS, MU, NH, NZ, OS, OZ, PK, PR, QF, SK, SN, SR, SU, TG, TK, UL
Haneda HND	
International Terminal:	CI
Domestic Terminal:	EL, JD, JL, NH, NU
	Toronto OT Canada YTO
Lester B. Pearson YYZ	
Terminal 1:	AR, BW, DL, KL*, LR, MX, NW, OA, TW, US, YX, 5V
Terminal 2:	AC, AF*, AI, AY, CO, CX, JM, JT, KE, LH, LY, OK, PK, RJ, SR, UA*
Terminal 3:	AA, AF*, AZ, BA, CP, KL*, NZ, PD, QF, UA*, VP
	Vancouver BC Canada YVR
Main Terminal:	AA, AC, AE, AS, BA, CA, CO, CP, CX, DL, HP, JB, JL, KE, KL, LH, MH, M3, NH, NW, NZ, PR, QF, QQ, SKL, SQ, SR, UA, XP, 7C*
South Terminal:	H3, VL, XC, 3S, 6W, 7C*, 8P

QUESTIONS AND DISCUSSIONS

Objective Type

Q. 1. In each of the following statements, write 'T' if the statement is true or 'F' if it is false:

1. To form a valid connection, each leg must arrive at the connecting point no more than two hours before the next leg departs.
2. The time table published by many carriers lists both direct flights and connection.
3. An ARNK segment is used to indicate surface travel in an air itinerary.
4. A point in an itinerary where a change of aircraft occurs is called a connecting point.
5. Routes flown by the flight of each carrier are listed in the flight itineraries section of OAG.
6. In an open jaw, an ARNK segment follows the outbound segment or precedes the return segment.
7. In airline tables, flights are listed by destination airport.
8. In 24 hour time, 5:55 PM is expressed as 1555.
9. In time tables, departure and arrivals times are always given in Greenwich Mean Time.
10. A frequency code indicates the days of the week on which a flight operates.

Q. 2. In each of the following sentences, write the correct word or phrase that belongs in each blank:

1. If a cancellation penalty applies, the penalty must be deducted from .... before the refund is made.
2. In a fare calculation, only .... codes are used.
3. If fares from different currencies, the amount must be converted to .... to determine the total fare.
4. Taxes included in the ticket price are shown in the tax box and are identified by ....
5. To determine the price of an international itinerary, the .... fares are added, and the total is then converted to the currency of the country where ....
6. On international itineraries, ... are referred to as sectors.
7. If the fare to an intermediate point is higher than the fare

to the turn around point, the .... must be used to construct the fare.

8. The basic passenger credential for international travel is a ....
9. Before a traveller is allowed to enter a country, he or she must declare to a .... any goods that were purchased in a foreign country.

Q. 3. *Read each of the following statement. Write 'T' if the statement is true or 'F' if the statement is false:*

1. Under the hub and spoke system, passengers are permitted a stop-over at an intermediate point between the original boarding point and the final destination.
2. The letter 'S' is an equipment code indicates that the aircraft has a meal service galley.
3. A Boeing 747 has a flight range of 5,500-6,500 miles.

Q. 4. *From the following list of terms, write the letter of the word, phrase, or name next to the concept/definition that best matches it below:*

A M
B Through fare
C Hub
D Galley
E Interline agreement
F Major airline
G Excess baggage allowance
H Carrier code
I Code sharing agreement
K Charter airline
L Airline code
M Certificate of public convenience and necessity
N Free baggage allowance
O No-show
P Distressed passenger
Q Hold
R Connection
S AI
T S
U Commuter carriers
V Indian Airline
W Waitlist
X Equipment Code

1. The largest Indian passenger carrier.
2. Small carriers that operate aircraft with fewer than 30 seats.
3. A three letter code identifying the type of aircraft used for a flight.
4. An airline that has a limited schedule and leases aircraft to large groups or to other airlines.

5. An agreement entitling a carrier to use the name of another airline on its flights.
6. A three digit numerical code assigned to each airline.
7. A two letter code designated by IATA to identify an airline in schedules and tariffs.
8. An intermediate point used by an airline to route passengers to multiple destination.
9. A letter in an aircraft code that indicates that the airplane has been configured to transport both passengers and cargo.
10. A letter in an aircraft code that indicates that the airplane has been configured for additional passenger seating.
11. The term for a kitchenette used by the flight crew to heat or prepare passenger meals on an aircraft.
12. A single point to point fare for a connection operated by different carriers.
13. A cooperative contract between two airlines that enables passengers to travel on a connection operated by both carriers.
14. A flight that requires passengers to change planes at an intermediate point between the original boarding point and the final destination, with no stop-overs.
15. A charge for baggage that exceeds the airlines present limit.
16. A limit on the amount of baggage that may be transported by a passenger free of charge.
17. The percentage of airline flights that leave the departure gate within 15 minutes of the scheduled departure time and arrive at the destination gate within 15 minutes of the scheduled arrived time.
18. A passenger who books a confirmed reservation but does not actually board the flight.
19. A list of people who would like a seat on a flight for which all the seats have already been sold.
20. A passenger who is stranded in a connecting city as a result of a delay or cancellation.
21. The pressurized cargo compartment of an aircraft where a pet can sometimes be transported.
22. A certificate issued by government agency authorizing an airline to operate passenger service in the country.

Short Answer Type

Q. 5. Define the following terms:

(*a*) Hospitality class
(*b*) Hub and spoke system
(*c*) Executive class.

Q. 6. Write short notes on:

(*a*) Equipment code
(*b*) Aircraft code
(*c*) Supersonic class
(*d*) Executive class.

Q. 7. Explain the following: (with examples)

(*a*) Food and Beverage Service in an aircraft
(*b*) International terminals
(*c*) Coding of Aircrafts
(*d*) Decoding of Aircrafts.

Essay Type

Q. 8. Draw a shape and design of an aircraft and explain its capacity and seating arrangements.

Q. 9. Explain the term 'equipment code' and aircraft codes. What is the significance of these codes in planning an itinerary?

Q. 10. What are the various classes of services available in a modern aeroplane? Explain by giving suitable examples.

3

Airlines Policies and Practices

After learning this Chapter you shall be able to:
❑ *understand various airlines policies and practices;*
❑ *know the policies regarding reservation, children and infants restricted and disabled passengers, changes, alteration schedule, stand by travel, check in cancellation and delays;*
❑ *explain baggage transportation policy, baggage allowances, checked baggage, excess baggage;*
❑ *discribe the pet transport policy, special meals;*
❑ *clarify minimum connecting times.*

The airline industry have regulations as regards to the treatment of passengers, which vary from carrier-to-carrier. The International Air Transport Association (IATA), a trade association of international carriers administers rules pertaining to reservations and ticketing. On other topics, each airline has its own set of rules. Many of these rules are printed on the back of the ticket or ticket jacket under the heading 'Terms and Conditions of Carriage'.

Topics are covered under air policies, practices and rules are discussed in detail:

RESERVATION POLICY

A reservation is an agreement to secure a seat on airline flight. The process of reserving an airline seat is referred to as booking airline space. When more than one airline carrier is involved in an itinerary, the travel agent should book the space through one carrier, usually the first carrier in the itinerary. However, travel agents may have their own discretion in this matter.

In case of domestic and international airlines the practice of booking of duplicate reservations on the same carrier over the same itinerary is prohibited. Take an example, a passenger travelling unaccompanied cannot book separate reservations at different fares from San Francisco to Honolulu on the same flight, intending to utilise only one seat. To rebook a reservation in different class or at different fare, the existing reservation must be cancelled. However, there is an exception to this policy. That is the wait-listed flight for which the passenger's reservation has not yet been confirmed. If all seats offered at a particular fare have been reserved, a passenger may be placed on a list of people desiring reservations. This list is referred to as a wait-list, and the action of placing a passenger on such a list is called wait-listing a reservation. If some one holding a confirmed reservation cancels it, a passenger on the wait-list will receive a confirmed reservation. To ensure that the passenger will receive a confirmed reservation, a wait-listed reservation and a confirmed reservation both may be booked on the same flight or on different flights, on the same itinerary.

POLICY REGARDING CHILDREN AND INFANTS

Some domestic airlines carriers offered discount of 25 per cent to 35 per cent to children between 2 to 11 years. They permit children under 2 years of age to accompany a fare-paying passenger at no additional charge on foreign carriers, an infant fare of 50 per cent to 75 per cent below the adult fare may be charged. Most carriers accept unaccompanied children, 5 years or older, for transport. Some carriers assess a charge for unaccompanied minors between 8 years to 11 years. Unaccompanied minors receive special handling. Personal assistance is provided by airline employees from the moment an unaccompanied child check into the time the child arrives at the final destination. When a travel agent books a reservation for an unaccompanied minor, a special service request may be sent to each carrier involved in the itinerary. The carriers must also be notified of the parties who are responsible for the child. The person who is responsible for the child prior to departure is called the 'sender' and the person who is responsible for the child on arrival is called the 'receiver'. The airline assumes responsibility for the child's comforts and security until the flight arrives at the destination.

POLICY REGARDING RESTRICTED AND DISABLED PASSENGERS

All carriers reserve the right to determine whether a passenger who is disabled can be safely transported by the air in view of the traveller, medical condition and needs. The criteria for acceptance are set-forth in the 'Medical Criteria for Passenger Flying'. Some carriers refuse to transport prisoners accompanied by law enforcement agents bearing sidearms. A reservation for a restricted passenger must be accompanied by complete and accurate information about the passenger, circumstances, and respectable parties.

CHANGES, ALTERATIONS IN SCHEDULES

The airlines revise their flight schedules at least twice annually to adjust to seasonal changes and fluctuation in passenger traffic. Sudden schedule changes may also occur, due to weather conditions, air traffic congestion, equipment problems, or other factors. In most cases, these airlines do not automatically notify passengers when a schedule change occurs. However, when a travel agent becomes aware of a schedule change or cancellation, it is that agent's responsibility to notify the passenger.

STAND BY TRAVEL

Some carriers permit passengers to 'stand by' for seats without a confirmed reservation. A stand by passenger is not assured of a seat until all the passengers who hold confirmed reservations have checked in at the departure gate, or, in some cases, have actually boarded the flight. If all the seats are occupied, stand by passengers are denied boarding on that flight. However, if the flight is not full, stand by passenger may be accommodated.

A discounted fare may be charged for stand by travel. A full fare passenger may also stand by for a seat on a different flight than the one on which reservations are confirmed. For example, Mr. Himanshu, has completed one-half of a round-trip itinerary and desires to return on an earlier flight. However, no seats are available at the fare that he paid originally. This passenger might pay the difference between the original fare and the higher fare to board the earlier flight, or, on an alternative, he might choose to stand by for a seat at no additional charge. The decision whether to permit a passenger to stand by in this type of situation is usually based on airline policy. Sometimes, the decision is left to the discretion of the ticket agent or boarding agent.

PASSENGER CHECK IN

It is to the passengers advantage to check in as early as possible. Domestic carriers reserve the right to deny boarding the passenger who fail to check in within ten minutes prior to the departure time. On international flights the time limit is one or two hours before the scheduled departure time.

Many flights are routinely over-booked by the airlines, based on past experience of 'no shows'. Over-booking occurs when an airline books more reservations than the seating capacity of a flight. A 'no-show' is a passenger who books a confirmed reservation but does not actually boards the flight. Industry-wise, the average no-show percentage is 12 per cent of the confirmed reservations. In many cases the no-show rate is as high as 50 per cent. To compensate for no shows, and in an effort to fill each flight, airlines will allow most flights to be over-booked.

Because of over-booking, more passengers may check in for departure than can be accommodated on a particular flight. In such instances, the airline may deny boarding to passengers who have confirmed reservations or tickets. The informal term for such an action is 'bumping' a passenger.

Voluntarily, an airline may compensate a passenger who was denied boarding on an over-booked flight. Most carriers provide 'bumped' passengers with some type of compensation, ranging from cash to a certificate for a free travel. Regardless of whether compensation is provided, the airline is obligated to transport a 'bumped' passenger on another flight to his or her destination or arrange for an alternative carrier. The airline may also offer to refund the unused ticket price. The unused price is the portion of the itinerary that the passenger has not yet travelled.

CANCELLATION AND DELAYS

Domestic airlines are required to maintain statistics regarding on time performance and to make this information available to the public on request. On time information refers to the percentage of airline flight that leave the departure gate within 15 minutes of the scheduled departure time and arrive at the destination gate within 15 minutes of the scheduled arrival time. The on-time performance of each flight now appears on the flight schedules of all airline computer reservation system. Cancellations or delays caused by mechanical problems are not included in on-time performance statistics.

A delayed or cancelled flight may cause a chain reaction throughout the air traffic network. For example, if a flight that is bound for a major hub is delayed, the airline may delay the connecting flights to accommodate the late arriving passengers. These delays in turn may cause other flights to be delayed. As per the airline regulations, if a flight is delayed or cancelled, the airline is required to provide passengers with alternative transportation at no additional cost, on request. In most cases, passengers are transported on another flight operated by the same carrier or by another airline. However, passengers may be routed to their final destination. For example, if a direct flight is cancelled, the passenger may be rerouted on two or three connecting flights, or if a connection is cancelled, passengers may be forced to connect in different city. However, alternative transportation must be requested by the passenger. Airlines are not obligated to provide this service except by request. If a passenger is required to stay overnight in a connecting city as a result of delay or cancelled flight, the airline may offer to pay for the passenger's lodging and meals. Passengers who come 'stranded' in a connecting city are referred to as 'distressed passengers'. Compensation to distressed passengers is voluntary, and, in most cases, must be specially requested by the passenger. However, airlines are not obligated to provide such a compensation and are unlikely to do so if the delay or cancellation results from a storm or some other natural cause.

BAGGAGE TRANSPORTATION

An airline ticket is basically a contract between the airline and the passenger. As per this contract the airline agrees to transport the passengers and his or her luggage to the same destination.

Baggage is defined as the personal effect transported by a passenger. The amount of baggage that may be transported by each passenger free of charge is subject to a limit, called the free baggage allowance. Excessive baggage beyond this limit is subject to an additional charge. Each airline has its own free baggage allowance, based on the number of pieces and the weight of each piece. For an example, passenger travelling on some airline are allowed three pieces of checked luggage or two pieces of checked luggage and one carry on item. The weight of each checked bags may not exceed 20 pounds. The combined dimension of each piece, calculated by adding the length, width, and depth may not exceed 62 inches. For bags that exceed the limits, an excess baggage charge varies from route-to-route and the type of aircraft. Most domestic airlines transport two checked bags up to 70 pounds each and one carry on bag free of charge. The carry-on item must be small enough to be stored on the aircraft under a passenger seat or in an overhead storage compartment provided for cabin baggage. On major foreign carriers, the free baggage allowance is usually 30 to 40 kgs. (66 to 88 pounds). Millions of piece baggage are transported by the airlines annually and thousands of passengers filed reports of lost, damaged, or mis-directed baggage. Each airline's liability for lost or damaged baggage varies and is stated on the terms and conditions of carriage on the back of the ticket or ticket jacket. However, by law, the maximum liability is fixed per passenger on domestic flights.

Baggage Allowances

This information provides a guide for passengers on flights operated by member airlines of IATA and most other international carriers.

It is important to note that some airlines may deviate significantly from these quoted standard allowances and excess baggage charges, either throughout their domestic/international network or on specific routes only. Therefore, to avoid unexpected charges, it is essential to check with the airline, or the travel agent, before travelling.

Key concepts

The Free Baggage Allowance comprises two elements:

Carry-on items

These are smaller items that passengers can take with them onto the aircraft. In addition to the checked baggage allowances, each passenger may carry, without additional charge, hand baggage suitable for placing in closed overhead rack, or under the passenger's seat. The maximum dimensions (the sum of the three dimensions of all such carry on items) shall not exceed 45 inches (115 cm.)

CHECKED BAGGAGE

This is baggage, up to a specified limit, to be carried in the hold of the aircraft.

There are two systems determining the amount of checked baggage allowed.

Table 3.1: Free Baggage Allowances

Item	*Applicable to*
1. 1 overcoat, wrap or blanket 2. 1 umbrella or walking stick 3. 1 small camera 4. 1 pair of binoculars 5. A reasonable amount of reading matter for the flight 6. 1 handbag, pocket book or purse, *i.e.* which is appropriate to normal travelling dress and is not being used as a container for the transportation of articles which would otherwise be regarded as baggage	All passengers except infants at 10% or no fare
Infant's food for consumption on flight 1. 1 infant's carrying basket 2. 1 fully collapsible stroller or pushchair (in cabin or cargo compartment of the aircraft)	Infants at 10% or no fare
1 fully collapsible wheel chair and/or 1 pair of crutches and/or braces or other prosthetic device for the passenger's use	Invalids who depend on such wheelchair, crutches, braces, prosthetic device
'Seeing eye/Hearing dog' (dogs trained to assist the blind or deaf).	1. Blind passengers who depend on such a dog 2. Deaf passengers who depend on such a dog.

Note: the dog, when properly harnessed, may be permitted to accompany such passenger in the cabin but shall not be permitted to occupy a seat.

1. the *Weight system* is based on the total weight of baggage, no matter how many different pieces there are.
2. the *Piece system* is based on the number of pieces of baggage.

Subject to space availability, airlines will carry amounts of baggage in excess of the free allowance at an *Excess Baggage Charge*. Passengers travelling together to the same destination by the same flight may, if they check-in together, pool their free, baggage allowances, perhaps avoiding excess baggage charges.

CHECKED BAGGAGE: THE WEIGHT SYSTEM

This system is used in all areas except where the 'piece' system is used.

The Free Baggage Allowance

The normal *Free Baggage Allowance* is:

First Class	40 kg (88 lb)
Economy Class	20 kg (44 lb)
Business Class	30 kg (66 lb)

Note: These are the normal allowances. Some carriers may have differing allowances, particularly on domestic routes. Please confirm with carriers.

Children are entitled to the same free baggage allowance as adult passengers. Infants not entitled to a seat are only allowed one fully collapsible stroller or pushchair.

An *Excess Baggage Charge* is levied on baggage in excess of the free allowance. The charge is 1.5% of the highest normal direct adult one way economy class (in local currency) for each kilogram in excess of the free allowance.

Exceptions:

1.	1%	From Austria, Bulgaria, Israel; from Australia, New Zealand (except 1.5% from Australia, New Zealand to South West Pacific); from Europe, Middle East to Australia, New Zealand
2.	1.35%	Within Europe (except 1% from Austria, Bulgaria, Finland).

Special Charges

Special charges apply for the carriage of:

1. Bulky or fragile items up to 75 kg (165 lb) as hand baggage warranting the use of one or more additional seats. Normal excess charges apply for the weight carried but will be not less than 75% of the full one-way adult fare for the class used by the passenger.

2. Accompanied pets. Normal excess charges apply but the weight of animal and container cannot be allowed in the passenger's free allowance.
3. Snow skiing equipment and golfing equipment. Special excess baggage charges apply for these items. The weight of these items can be included in the passenger's normal free allowance and only the overweight is charged at the special rate.

CHECKED BAGGAGE: THE PIECE SYSTEM

The Free Baggage Allowance

The normal Free Baggage Allowance is:

First and business class passengers

2 bags (pieces) where the total of the three dimensions does not exceed 158 cm (62 inches) for each bag.

Economy class passengers

2 bags (pieces) where the total of the three dimensions for any one bag does not exceed 158 cm (62 inches) and where the total for both bags does not exceed 273 cm (107 inches).

Maximum weight of any one bag is 32 kg (70 lb) except within North America where it is 23 kg (50 lb). (*Note:* domestic airlines within USA may apply a Free Baggage Allowance based on a weight or piece system).

Children are entitled to the same free baggage allowance as adult passengers. Infants not entitled to a seat are allowed one checked bag of which the total of the three dimensions should not exceed 115 cm (45 inches) plus one fully collapsible stroller or pushchair.

Articles considered as a single piece of baggage

The following articles, irrespective of their actual dimensions, may be considered as a piece of baggage at 135 cm (53 inches):

1. One sleeping bag or bedroll.
2. One rucksack/knapsack/backpack.
3. One pair of snow skis with one pair of ski poles and one pair of ski boots.
4. One golf bag, golf clubs and pair of golf shoes.

5. One duffle-type bag or B-4 type bag.
6. One suitably packed bicycle.
7. One pair of standard water skis or one slalom water ski.
8. Suitably packed fishing equipment comprising not more than two rods, one reel, one landing net, one pair of fishing boots and one fishing tackle box.
9. Certain sporting firearms (subject to each airlines conditions of carriage).
10. Any portable musical instrument not exceeding 100 cm (39 inches) in length.

EXCESS BAGGAGE CHARGE

The Excess Baggage Charge levied on baggage in excess of the free allowance is determined by a number of factors: the city or country of departure; city or country of arrival; and, in a number of instances, by the airlines of travel. Each combination of factors has a standard Excess Baggage Fee.

Each bag in excess of the number permitted which does not exceed the dimensions/weight limits is charged at the standard fee.

If within the baggage allowance a bag exceeds the dimensions limit for free carriage but does not exceed 203 cm (80 inches) and is within the weight limit, the standard fee is still applied. However, any bag both in excess of the number and dimensions, but where the sum of the three dimensions does not exceed 203 cm (80 inches) and is within the weight limit, twice the standard fee is charged.

Any piece of baggage in excess of 203 cm (80 inches) or in excess of the 32 kg (70 lb) or, within North America 23 kg (50 lb), weight limit will not be carried unless prior handling arrangements are made with the airline. If accepted for carriage, such bags are weighed and charged at three times the standard fee for any amount up to 45 kg (99 lb) and at the standard fee for each additional 10 kg (22 lb) or fraction thereof.

SPECIAL CHARGES

Special charges apply for the carriage of:

1. Bulky or fragile items as hand baggage warranting the use of one or more additional seats. To/from the USA the normal

piece system excess charges apply but the minimum charge will be 75% of the full one-way adult fare for the class used by the passenger. Elsewhere, a standard excess charge of 75% of the full one-way adult fare for the class used by the passenger applies.

2. Accompanied pets. The animal and container cannot be allowed in the passenger's free allowance. To/from USA the normal excess baggage fee is charged. Elsewhere, the charge is twice the standard fee.
3. Snow skiing and golf equipment. If in excess of the normal free allowance, one set of skis/ski poles/ski boots will be carried at 25% of the standard excess baggage fee and one golf bag/golf shoes at 50% of the standard fee. Additional sets are charged at the full standard fee.

Where the piece system applies

1. Between *USA/US Territories* and all countries.
2. Between *Canada* and Europe, Middle East, Southern Africa, South Asian Subcontinent, the Far East except Guam and South West Pacific, Argentina, Bolivia, Brazil, Chile, Mexico, Panama, Paraguay, Peru, Uruguay.
3. Between the *Far East* and Argentina, Bolivia, Brazil, Chile, Panama, Paraguay, Peru, Uruguay, Mexico, USA.
4. Between *Guam/Saipan* and Japan, Okinawa, Hong Kong, Korea Republic, China, Taiwan, Philippines, Thailand, Indonesia, Malaysia, Singapore, India.
5. Between *Pago Pago* and South West Pacific

Note: Some Governments have not approved the 'piece' system. The Free Baggage Allowance *from* such countries to USA/Canada is therefore based on the Weight System.

PET TRANSPORT POLICY

Pet transport policies regarding the transport of animals or passage aircraft vary depending upon the carrier and type of aircraft. Some passenger carriers accept small pets, such as dogs, cats or domesticated birds, if they are properly crated and transported in the cargo department. Portable pet kennels can be purchased from one carriers to transport a pet in the passenger cabin. Airlines that accept pets for transport permit only one pet in the cabin at a time. Approval for pet transport must be obtained from the airline when the owner's reservation is booked.

On some carriers, a passenger who is blind may be accompanied by his/her specially trained dog. In such cases, the dog must remain at the passenger's feet and the properly harnessed. Some carrier also require the dog to be muzzled. Some airlines, permit a pet to accompany a passenger free of charge in coach class, but not in first class. The pet must be small enough to travel in the container that can be placed under the passenger's aircraft seat. Other airlines charge fee for passenger transport. On international flights, in cabin pets are charged at the excess baggage rate. Travel agents do not receive commission on pet transportation fees. With advance notice, passengers can often arrange to have their pets transported as excess baggage in the pressurised cargo department, called the 'hold'. The total weight of the pet and its kennel a crate must not exceed 100 pounds. The combined length, width, and height of the container must not exceed 100 inches.

In many cases pet transported in the cargo compartment will not be checked enough to connecting flights. Thus, if passenger must change planes, the pet must be claimed by the passenger in the connecting city and rechecked to the final destination.

SPECIAL MEALS

On meal service flights, a passenger who has booked a confirmed reservation can request a special meal from the airline. Special meals can be requested for religious preferences as well as diet requirements. For example, most passengers low-cholestrol, or low-sodium meals for passengers with special dietary restrictions. The number and type of special meals on each flight are limited. To ensure that special meal will be available, the meal should be requested at least two weeks before the departure date. Special meals for children are available and meals for infants can be requested on some flights.

EXCESS MILEAGE PERCENTAGE

Indicates (a) published millage percentage from 1 to 19,900 is, (b) mileage permitted when published fare is increased by varyfing percentage such as 5%, 10%, 15%, 20%, and 25%.

Table 3.2: Excess Mileage Percentage

Published Mileage	*Mileage permitted when published Fare is increased by*				
	5%	*10%*	*15%*	*20%*	*25%*
(1)	*(2)*	*(3)*	*(4)*	*(5)*	*(6)*
1	1	1	1	1	1
2	2	2	2	2	2
3	3	3	3	3	3
4	4	4	4	4	5
5	5	5	5	6	6
6	6	6	6	7	7
8	8	8	9	9	10
9	9	9	10	10	11
10	10	11	11	12	12
11	11	12	12	13	13
12	12	13	13	14	15
13	13	14	14	15	16
14	14	15	16	16	17
15	15	16	17	18	18
16	16	17	18	19	20
17	17	18	19	20	21
18	18	19	20	21	22
19	19	20	21	22	23
20	21	22	23	24	25
21	22	23	24	25	26
22	23	24	25	26	27
23	24	25	26	27	28
24	25	26	27	28	30
25	26	27	28	30	31
26	27	28	29	31	32
27	28	29	31	32	33
28	29	30	32	33	35
29	30	31	33	34	36
30	31	33	34	36	37
31	32	34	35	37	38
32	33	35	36	38	40
33	34	36	37	39	41
34	35	37	39	40	42
35	36	38	40	42	43

(Contd.)

(Contd.)

(1)	(2)	(3)	(4)	(5)	(6)
36	37	39	41	43	45
37	38	40	42	44	46
38	39	41	43	45	47
39	40	42	44	46	48
40	42	44	46	48	50
41	43	45	47	49	51
42	44	46	48	50	52
43	45	47	49	51	53
44	46	48	50	52	55
45	47	49	51	54	56
46	48	50	52	55	57
47	49	51	54	56	58
48	50	52	55	57	60
49	51	53	56	58	61
50	52	55	57	60	62
51	53	56	58	61	63
52	54	57	59	62	65
53	55	58	60	63	66
54	56	59	62	64	67
55	57	60	63	66	68
56	58	61	64	67	70
57	59	62	65	68	71
58	60	63	66	69	72
59	61	64	67	70	73
60	63	66	69	72	75
61	64	67	70	73	76
62	65	68	71	74	77
63	66	69	72	75	78
64	67	70	73	76	80
65	68	71	74	78	81
66	69	72	75	79	82
67	70	73	77	80	83
68	71	74	78	81	85
69	72	75	79	82	86
70	73	77	80	84	87
71	74	78	81	85	88
72	75	79	82	86	90

(Contd.)

(Contd.)

(1)	(2)	(3)	(4)	(5)	(6)
73	76	80	83	87	91
74	77	81	85	88	92
75	78	82	86	90	93
76	79	83	87	91	95
77	80	84	88	92	96
78	81	85	89	93	97
79	82	86	90	94	98
80	84	88	92	96	100
81	85	89	93	97	101
82	86	90	94	98	102
83	87	91	95	99	103
84	88	92	96	100	105
85	89	93	97	102	106
86	90	94	98	103	107
87	91	95	100	104	108
88	92	96	101	105	110
89	93	97	102	106	111
90	94	99	103	108	112
91	95	100	104	109	113
92	96	101	105	110	115
93	97	102	106	111	116
94	98	103	108	112	117
95	99	104	109	114	118
96	100	105	110	115	120
97	101	106	111	116	121
98	102	107	112	117	122
99	103	108	113	118	123
100	105	110	115	120	125
200	210	220	230	240	250
300	315	330	345	360	375
400	420	440	460	480	500
500	525	550	575	600	625
600	630	660	690	720	750
700	735	770	805	840	875
800	840	880	920	960	1000
900	945	990	1035	1080	1125
1000	1050	1100	1150	1200	1250

(Contd.)

(Contd.)

(1)	(2)	(3)	(4)	(5)	(6)
1100	1155	1210	1265	1320	1375
1200	1260	1320	1380	1440	1500
1300	1365	1430	1495	1560	1625
1400	1470	1540	1610	1680	1750
1500	1575	1650	1725	1800	1875
1600	1680	1760	1840	1920	2000
1700	1785	1870	1955	2040	2125
1800	1890	1980	2070	2160	2250
1900	1995	2090	2185	2280	2375
2000	2100	2200	2300	2400	2500
2100	2205	2310	2415	2520	2625
2200	2310	2420	2530	2640	2750
2300	2415	2530	2645	2760	2875
2400	2520	2640	2760	2880	3000
2500	2625	2750	2875	3000	3125
2600	2730	2860	2990	3120	3250
2700	2835	2970	3105	3240	3375
2800	2940	3080	3220	3360	3500
2900	3045	3190	3335	3480	3625
3000	3150	3300	3450	3600	3750
3100	3255	3410	3565	3720	3875
3200	3360	3520	3680	3840	4000
3300	3465	3630	3795	3960	4125
3400	3570	3740	3910	4080	4250
3500	3675	3850	4025	4200	4375
3600	3780	3960	4140	4320	4500
3700	3885	4070	4255	4440	4625
3800	3990	4180	4370	4560	4750
3900	4095	4290	4485	4680	4875
4000	4200	4400	4600	4800	5000
4100	4305	4510	4715	4920	5125
4200	4410	4620	4830	5040	5250
4300	4515	4730	4945	5160	5375
4400	4620	4840	5060	5280	5500
4500	4725	4950	5175	5400	5625
4600	4830	5060	5290	5520	5750
4700	4935	5170	5405	5640	5875
4800	5040	5280	5520	5760	6000

(Contd.)

(Contd.)

(1)	(2)	(3)	(4)	(5)	(6)
4900	5145	5390	5635	5880	6125
5000	5250	5500	5750	6000	6250
5100	5355	5610	5865	6120	6375
5200	5460	5720	5980	6240	6500
5300	5565	5830	6095	6360	6625
5400	5670	5940	6210	6480	6750
5500	5775	6050	6325	6600	6875
5600	5880	6160	6440	6720	7000
5700	5985	6270	6555	6840	7125
5800	6090	6380	6670	6960	7250
5900	6195	6490	6785	7080	7375
6000	6300	6600	6900	7200	7500
6100	6405	6710	7015	7320	7625
6200	6510	6820	7130	7440	7750
6300	6615	6930	7245	7560	7875
6400	6720	7040	7360	7680	8000
6500	6825	7150	7475	7800	8125
6600	6930	7260	7590	7920	8250
6700	7035	7370	7705	8040	8375
6800	7140	7480	7820	8160	8500
6900	7245	7590	7935	8280	8625
7000	7350	7700	8050	8400	8750
7100	7455	7810	8165	8520	8875
7200	7560	7920	8280	8640	9000
7300	7665	8030	8395	8760	9125
7400	7770	8140	8510	8800	9250
7500	7875	8250	8625	9000	9375
7600	7980	8360	8740	9120	9500
7700	8085	8470	8855	9240	9625
7800	8190	8580	8970	9360	9750
7900	8295	8690	9085	9480	9875
8000	8400	8800	9200	9600	10000
8100	8505	8910	9315	9720	10125
8200	8610	9020	9430	9840	10250
8300	8715	9130	9545	9960	10375
8400	8820	9240	9660	10080	10500
8500	8925	9350	9775	10200	10625

(Contd.)

(Contd.)

(1)	*(2)*	*(3)*	*(4)*	*(5)*	*(6)*
8600	9030	9460	9890	10320	10750
8700	9135	9570	10005	10440	10875
8800	9240	9680	10120	10560	11000
8900	9345	9790	10235	10680	11125
9000	9450	9900	10350	10800	11250
9100	9555	10010	10465	10920	11375
9200	9660	10120	10580	11040	11500
9300	9765	10230	10695	11160	11625
9400	9870	10340	10810	11280	11750
9500	9975	10450	10925	11400	11875
9600	10080	10560	11040	11520	12000
9700	10185	10670	11155	11640	12125
9800	10290	10780	11270	11760	12250
9900	10395	10890	11385	11880	12375
10000	10600	11000	11500	12000	12500
10100	10605	11110	11615	12120	12625
10200	10710	11220	11730	12240	12750
10300	10815	11330	11845	12360	12875
10400	10920	11440	11960	12480	13000
10500	11025	11550	12075	12600	13125
10600	11130	11660	12190	12720	13250
10700	11235	11770	12305	12840	13375
10800	11340	11880	12420	12960	13500
10900	11445	11990	12535	13080	13625
11000	11550	12100	12650	13200	13750
11100	11655	12210	12765	13320	13875
11200	11760	12320	12880	13440	14000
11300	11865	12430	12995	13560	14125
11400	11970	12540	13110	13680	14250
11500	12075	12650	13225	13822	14375
11600	12180	12760	13340	13920	14500
11700	12285	12870	13455	14040	14625
11800	12390	12980	13570	14160	14750
11900	12495	13090	13685	14280	14875
12000	12600	13200	13800	14400	15000
12100	12705	13310	13915	14520	15145
12200	12810	13420	14030	14640	15250

(Contd.)

(Contd.)

(1)	(2)	(3)	(4)	(5)	(6)
12300	12915	13530	14145	14760	15375
12400	13020	13640	14260	14880	15500
12500	13125	13750	14375	15000	15625
12600	13230	13860	14490	15120	15750
12700	13335	13970	14605	15240	15875
12800	13440	14080	14720	15360	16000
12900	13545	14190	14835	15480	16125
13000	13650	14300	14950	15600	16250
13100	13755	14410	15065	15720	16375
13200	13860	14520	15180	15840	16500
13300	13965	14630	15295	15960	16625
13400	14070	14740	15410	16080	16750
13500	14175	14850	15525	16200	16875
13600	14280	14960	15640	16320	17000
13700	14385	15070	15755	16440	17125
13800	14490	15180	15870	16560	17250
13900	14595	15290	15985	16680	17375
14000	14700	15400	16100	16800	17500
14100	14805	15510	16215	16920	17625
14200	14910	15620	16330	17040	17750
14300	15015	15730	16445	17160	17875
14400	15120	15840	16560	17280	18000
14500	15225	15950	16675	17400	18125
14600	15330	16060	16790	17520	18250
14700	15435	16170	16905	17640	18375
14800	15540	16280	17020	17760	18500
14900	15645	16390	17135	17880	18625
15000	15750	16500	17250	18000	18750
15100	15855	16610	17365	18120	18875
15200	15960	16720	17480	18240	19000
15300	16065	16830	17595	18360	19125
15400	16170	16940	17710	18480	19250
15500	16275	17050	17825	18600	19375
15600	16380	17160	17940	18720	19500
15700	16485	17270	18055	18840	19625
15800	16590	17380	18170	18960	19750
15900	16695	17490	18285	19080	19875
16000	16800	17600	18400	19200	20000

(Contd.)

(Contd.)

(1)	*(2)*	*(3)*	*(4)*	*(5)*	*(6)*
16100	16905	17710	18515	19320	20125
16200	17010	17820	18630	19940	20250
16300	17115	17930	18745	19560	20375
16400	17220	18040	18860	19680	20500
16500	17325	18150	18975	19800	20625
16600	17430	18260	19090	19920	20750
16700	17535	18370	19205	20040	20875
16800	17640	18480	19320	20160	21000
16900	17745	18590	19435	20280	21125
17000	17850	18700	19550	20400	21250
17100	17955	18810	19665	20520	21375
17200	18060	18920	19780	20640	21500
17300	18165	19030	19895	20760	21625
17400	18270	19140	20010	20880	21750
17500	18375	19250	20125	21000	21875
17600	18480	19360	20240	21120	22000
17700	18585	19470	20355	21240	22125
17800	18690	19580	20470	21360	22250
17900	18795	19690	20585	21480	22375
18000	18900	19800	20700	21600	22500
18100	19005	19910	20815	21720	22625
18200	19110	20020	20930	21840	22750
18300	19215	20130	21045	21960	22875
18400	19320	20240	21160	22080	23000
18500	19425	20350	21275	22200	23125
18600	19530	20460	21390	22320	23250
18700	19635	20570	21505	22440	23375
18800	19740	20680	21620	22560	23500
18900	19845	20790	21735	22680	23625
19000	19950	20900	21850	22800	23750
19100	20055	21010	21965	22920	23875
19200	20160	21120	22080	23040	24000
19300	20265	21230	22195	23160	24125
19400	20370	21340	22310	23280	24250
19500	20475	21450	22425	23400	24375
19600	20580	21560	22540	23540	24500
19700	20685	21670	22655	23640	24625
19800	20790	21780	22770	23760	24750
19900	20895	21890	22885	23880	24875

CLASS OF SERVICE

The class of service in airline is determined by the fare and the cabin in which the passenger will sit. Two seating sections, or cabins, are widely found on flights operated by major carriers—(1) first class, and (2) coach.

In the first class cabin, seats are usually larger and more comfortable, and passengers receive the carrier's highest level of service. Passengers in the coach cabin receive the airline's standard level of service.

In many domestic and international flights you may find a third cabin, known as business, executive, ambassador, or cub-class depending on the carrier. Service in this cabin is superior to coach, but luxurious than first class. First class may also be called as 'premium class'.

There are many airlines which offer different classes for travel in the coach cabin, based on the fare. On flights operated by these carriers, a limited number of seats are available in the coach cabin for sale at discount. Different class codes are used for these discounted seats, so that carrier can control the seat inventory on each flight. The seat inventory is the quantity of seats available for sale at different fares on a flight.

Every passenger reservation must specify a class of service, so that the correct fare can be determined. Booking code are used to indicate the class of service as given in Table 3.3.

Table 3.3: Class of Service and the Booking Codes

Booking code	*Class*	*Description*
F, P	First Class	The carrier's highest level of service
C, J	Business Class	The carrier's superior service level
Y, S	Standard coach class	The carrier's standard level of service
B, Q, K, L, M, H, V	Discount coach class	Discounted fare for the carrier's standard level of service

Depending upon the restrictions, route, and carrier the first class fare is 35 per cent higher than the standard coach, fare for the same flight, the business class is 20-35 per cent higher than coach class fare and a discounted coach fare may be 20-75 per cent less than the standard coach fare.

SCHEDULE TEXTS

Some direct flight schedules published in the *Worldwide city-to-city* schedules section of OAG Airways Guide are qualified by schedule texts as given in Table 3.4. Any applicable schedule text is printed immediately after the direct flight which it qualifies.

Due to the limited space available some Schedule Texts have been abbreviated. Where this has been necessary, the abbreviations conform to the recommended practice defined in the Standard Schedules Information Manual (SSIM) issued by IATA.

Table 3.4: Schedule Texts Explained

Text	*Explanation*
C CLASS INTL CONX PAX	C Class tickets may only be purchased if travel on this flight is to be part of an International Transfer Connection
CM CLASS CONX/STPVR TFC	C and M class tickets may only be purchased if travel on this flight is to be part of a Transfer Connection, or part of a through journey within which a stopover is being made
CONDIT TFC	The carriage of passengers on this flight is subject to specific conditions. Apply to the airline for details.
CONEX/STPVR TFC ONLY	A passenger may only travel on this flight as part of a Transfer Connection, or if it forms part of a through journey within which a stopover is being made
CONEX TFC ONLY	A passenger may only travel on this flight as part of a Transfer Connection

(*Contd.*)

(*Contd.*)

Text	*Explanation*
CONEX TO OCCUR BOARD PT	The required stopover or connection must occur at the departure city
CONEX TO OCCUR OFF POINT	The required stopover or connection must occur at the arrival city
INTL CONX/STPVR TFC ONLY	A passenger may only travel on this flight as part of an International Transfer Connection or if it forms part of a through international journey within which a stopover is being made
INTL ONLN CNX/STPVR TFC	A passenger may only travel on this flight as part of an International Online Transfer Connection or if it forms part of a through international journey within which a stopover is being made and onward travel is on the same airline
INTL CONEX TFC ONLY	A passenger may only travel on this flight if it forms part of an International Transfer Connection
INTL ONLN CNX TFC ONLY	A passenger may only travel on this flight if it forms part of an International Online Transfer Connection
INTL STPVR TFC ONLY	A passenger may only travel on this flight if it forms part of a through international journey within which a stopover is being made
INTL ONLN STPVR TFC ONLY	A passenger may only travel on this flight if it forms part of a through international journey within which a stopover is being made and onward travel is on the same airline
ONLINE CONEX TFC ONLY	A passenger may only travel on this flight as part of an Online Transfer Connection
ONLINE STPVR TFC ONLY	A passenger may only travel on this flight as part of a through journey within which a stopover is being made and onward travel is on the same airline

(*Contd.*)

(*Contd.*)

Text	*Explanation*
ONLN CNX/STPVR TFC ONLY	A passenger may only travel on this flight as part of an Online Transfer Connection or as part of a through journey within which a stopover is being made and onward travel is on the same airline
OP SUBJ GOVT APPROVAL	The operation of this flight is subject to government approval. Apply to the airline for confirmation
OP SUBJ TO CONFIRMATION	The operation of this flight is subject to confirmation. Apply to the airline for confirmation
OPERATES ON DEMAND ONLY	This flight is only operated if there is sufficient passenger demand
PRIORITY FOR TRANS TFC	Priority is given to passengers using this flight as part of a Transfer Connection
REQ ALL RES	All requests for reservations should be confirmed with the operating airline
STPVR TFC ONLY	A passenger may only travel on this flight as part of a through journey within which a stopover is being made
STRICTLY LOCAL SALE ONLY	Only tickets issued by the operating airline will be accepted from passengers wishing to travel on this flight
TFC SUB GOVT APPROVAL	The operator's authority to carry passengers on this flight is subject to government approval. Apply to the airline for confirmation

Notes:

1. Transfer Connection means the physical transfer from one flight to another (online or interline) as part of a continuous journey within a reasonable time interval.
2. Stopover means a deliberate interruption of a through journey by the passenger, at an airport between the original city of departure and the ultimate destination which has been agreed to in advance by the airline.

MINIMUM CONNECTING TIMES

The shortest time interval needed to transfer from one flight to a connecting flight is the Minimum Connecting Time.

Standard minimum connecting times for each airport are, as far as practicable, administered by IATA and published on their behalf. The following pages list these standard times applicable at cities arranged alphabetically.

The display includes exceptions to the standard times applied by any specific carrier for online connections, or agreed between carriers on a bilateral basis.

Transfer connections displayed conform to the minimum connecting time requirements quoted on these pages.

How to use the Minimum Connecting Times

Terms Used in Minimum Connecting Times

Dom-Dom: transfers between domestic flights

Int-Int : transfers between international flights

Dom-Int : transfers from a domestic flight to an international flight

Int-Dom : transfers from an international flight to a domestic flight

Minimum Connecting Times are shown in hours and minutes. They apply to all connections except those listed under *except*.

Where one airline code is separated from another, or from a series of airline codes, by 'to' or 'to/from', the exception quoted is for connections involving different airlines (interline).

Anchorage ANC

Dom–Dom	**30**	
	except	**25** AS to BF; AS to/from TW
		25 AS; UA
		20 BF; DL
Dom–Int	**1.00**	
Int–Dom	**1.00**	
	except	1.20 AS to TW
		1.20 AS

Where one airline code, or a series of airline codes, follows the quoted exception time, this refers to connections between any two flights of the same airline (online) but NOT between different airlines.

In this example, the standard connecting time from international to domestic flights at Anchorage is one hour, except for those airlines specified: AS to TW is one hour and twenty minutes; AS to or from any other AS flight is also one hour and twenty minutes.

For any city/airport not listed, allow 20 minutes for transfers between domestic flights, and 1 hour for all other categories.

Fig. 3.1: Minimum Connecting Times.

HOW TO DETERMINE DOMESTIC INTERNATIONAL STATUS?

In order to identify the correct MCT it is necessary to establish whether a passenger will be treated as a Domestic or International traveller.

As a general rule flights wholly within one country are Domestic (DOM) and flights between two countries are International (INT). Exceptions are noted below.

When an international flight serves more than one city in the same country, use the following rule to decide whether to treat it as a Domestic or International flight for the purpose of determining Minimum Connecting Times.

Flights will be considered Domestic arrivals only if they have already made a landing within the same country and if full traffic rights exist for that carrier to carry local passengers between the two cities in that country. Otherwise, arrivals will be considered International. Flights will be considered Domestic departures only if they will make the next landing within the same country and if full traffic rights exist for that carrier to carry local passengers between the two cities in that country. Otherwise departures will be considered International.

It is important to read any text associated with the city as further exceptions to the International Domestic status will be shown here.

DEFINITION OF EUROPE

Europe means the area comprised the following countries:

Albania
Algeria
Andorra
Armenia
Austria
Azerbaijan
Belarus
Belgium
Bosnia Herzegovina
Bulgaria
Canary Island
Croatia
Cyprus
Czech Republic
Denmark
Estonia
Finland
France
Georgia
Germany
Gibraltar
Greece
Hungary
Iceland
Republic of Ireland
Italy
Kazakhstan (west of the Ural mountains)
Latvia
Liechtenstein

Lithuania
Luxembourg
Former Yugoslav Republic of Macedonia
Malta
Moldova
Monaco
Morocco
Netherlands
Norway
Poland
Portugal (including Azores and Madeira)
Romania
Russian Federation (west of the Ural mountains)
San Marino
Slovakia
Slovenia
Spain
Sweden
Switzerland
Tunisia
Turkey (in Europe and Asia)
Ukraine
United Kingdom
Yugoslavia.

ADMINISTRATION OF MINIMUM CONNECTING TIMES (MCTs)

MCTs are administered by the Manager, Passenger Services Development, IATA, Geneva in accordance with IATA resolution 765. Coordination of MCTs is undertaken by IATA Interline Services Assistant (YULTXXB).

Any airline having a passenger interline agreement with an IATA member airline, should have a designated MCT coordinator who will be the IATA contact on all MCT matters.

Airlines submitting new or revised MCTs should contact IATA via their MCT coordinator in accordance with the procedures specified in the IATA Airline Coding Directory.

Table 3.5: Minimum Connecting Times: Display of Transfer Connections

Abu Dhabi AUH		
International (AUH)		
Dom-Dom	1.00	
	except	40 GF
Dom-Int	1.00	
	except	1.30 All to AI
		40 GF
Int-Dom	1.00	
	except	1.30 All to AI
		40 GF
Int-Int	1.00	
	except	1.30 All to AI
		4.00 KL to GF, QR
		40 GF

(Contd.)

(*Contd.*)

	Ahmedabad AMD	
Dom-Dom	20	
	except	45 IC
		30 9W
Dom-Int	1.00	
	except	2.00 AI to All
Int-Dom	1.00	
	except	2.00 All to AI
	Bangkok BKK	
Dom-Dom	30	
	except	1.30 PG to/from All
Dom-Int	2.00	
	except	2.30 All to AI
		3.00 All to LY
		3.00 PG to All
		1.00 TG (from CNX, HDY, HKT) to JL, SK
		1.30 TG (ex from CNX, HDY, HKT) to SK
		1.15 TG to SR
		1.30 LH (exc to AKL, PNH, RGN)
		1.00 TG (from CNX, HKT, HDY)
		1.30 TG (other flights)

Birmingham U.K. BHX

Flights to the Rep. of Ireland and Channel Islands are domestic. Flights from these points are international

Dom	30	
	except	2.00 FR to/from All
		25 BA
		20 BD
Dom-Int	45	
	except	30 BA to SR
		2.00 FR to/from All
		35 JY (from BHD) to AF (to CDG)

(*Contd.*)

(*Contd.*)

		25 BA
		20 BD
Int-Dom	45	
	except	2.00 FR to/from All
		30 SR to BA
		25 BA
		20 BD
Int-Int	45	
	except	2.00 FR to/from All
		25 BA
		20 BD

Birmingham U.S.A. BHM

Interline connections involving WN are not permitted

Dom-Dom	30	
	except	25 DL
		15 OH, WN
		20 UA, US

Kolkata CCU

Dom-Dom	30	
	except	45 IC
Dom-Int	2.00	
	except	3.00 All to AI
		1.30 AI
		3.00 IC
Int-Dom	2.00	
	except	3.00 IC
Int-Int	1.30	
	except	2.00 All to AI

Chattanooga CHA

Dom-Dom	30	
	except	25 DL
		20 US

Chennai/(Madras) MAA

Dom-Dom	30	
	except	1.30 AI
		45 IC
Dom-Int	2.00	

(*Contd.*)

(*Contd.*)

	except	3.00 All to AI
		1.30 AI
Int-Dom	2.00	
	except	3.30 All to AI
		1.30 AI
Int-Int	1.00	
	except	2.00 All to AI
		1.30 AI
	Delhi DEL	
Dom-Dom	1.30	
	except	45 IC
		30 9W
Dom-Int	3.00	
	except	1.30 All to KL
		1.30 AI to SK
		1.30 AI
Int-Dom	3.00	
	except	4.00 Flights from AUH, BAH, BKK, DHA, DOH, HKG, KWI, MCT, RUH, SHJ, SIN
		1.30 AI
Int-Int	1.30	
	except	2.00 All to LY
	Dhaka DAC	
Dom-Dom	30	
Dom-Int	1.00	
Int-Dom	2.00	
Int-Int	1.00	
	Dubai DXB	
Int-Int	1.00	
	except	2.00 All to Al
		4.00 KL to GF, QR
		45 EK
		40 GF
	Dublin DUB	
Dom-Int	45	2.00 FR to/from All

(*Contd.*)

(*Contd.*)

	except	35 El (btwn acft F50) 40 El (other fits)
Int-Dom	45	
	except	2.00 FR to/from All 35 El (btwn acft F 50)
Int-Int	45	El (other fits)
	except	2.00 FR to/from All 35 El (btwn acft F 50) 40 El (other fits)

Ho Chi Minh City SGN

Dom-Dom	1.00	
Dom-Int	1.00	
Int-Dom	1.00	
Int-Int	1.00	

Hong Kong HKG

Int-Int	1.00	
	except	2.00 All connections between Taiwan and the Peoples' Republic of China 1.30 All to AI 2.00 All to LY 1.30 CI (from Taiwan) to All (to The Peoples' Rep. of China) 1.30 CA, CZ (from The Peoples' Rep. of China) to CI (to Taiwan) 1.30 CI to/from MU 1.30 CX(from Taiwan) to All (to The Peoples' Rep. of China) 50 CX to/from NZ 1.00 KA from PEK, SHA to/from CX to Taiwan 1.30 KA exc from PEK, SHA to/from CX to Taiwan 1.30 KE to/from All 45 UA to/from GA 1.30 VS to AN 50 CI, CX, JL

(*Contd.*)

(*Contd.*)

			1.00 KA (btwn Taiwan and The Peoples' Rep. of China)
			40 UA

Karachi KHI

Dom-Dom	30
Dom-Int	1.30
Int-Dom	1.30
Int-Int	1.30

Kathmandu KTM

Dom-Dom	30
Dom-Int	1.00
Int-Dom	1.00
Int-Int	45

Lahore LHE

Dom-Dom	15
Dom-Int	45
Int-Dom	45
Int-Int	45

London LON

Fights to the Rep. of Ireland and Channel Islands are Domestic. Flights from these points are international

Heathrow (LHR)

Terminal 1

AA, AC, AY, AZ, BA, B, D, BI, BQ, CP, CX, CY, EI, FI, GF, IB, IL, JE, LH, LY, MH, NZ, OS, QF, SA, SK, SN, TP, UA, UK, UL, Y2, VS

Dom-Dom	45		
Dom-Int	45		
		except	2.30 All to LY
			1.00 All to SA
			40 BD, JE to SN
			2.00 BA to TLV
			35 BD
Int-Dom	45		
		except	1.30 LY to All
			1.00 SA to All
			40 SN to BD, JE

(*Contd.*)

(*Contd.*)

Manila MNL		
Dom-Dom	45	
	except	1.00 PR to/from All
Dom-Int	2.00	
Int-Dom	2.00	
Int-Int	1.00	
	Mumbai BOM	
Dom-Dom	30	
	except	2.00 AI 45 IC
Dom-Int	2.00	
	except	3.00 To AUH, BAH, DHA, DOH, DXB, JED, KWI, MCT, RKT, RUH, SHJ 3.00 All to AI (exc to Gulf) 3.30 All to AI to Gulf 2.00 9W to All (except KU) 2.00 AI 3.00 IC
Int-Dom	3.00	
	except	4.00 From AUH, BAH, DHA, DOH, DXB (exc EK), JED, KWI, MCT, RKT, RUH, SHJ 3.30 All (except KU) to 9W 3.00 EK (from DXB) to All 2.00 AI 4.00 IC
Int-Int	1.30	
	except	2.00 All to AI

Paris PAR

Swissair flights (except to/from Nice) and all Air France and Crossair flights between Geneva and France are Domestic

Charles De Gaulle (CDG)

Terminal 1

AF, AH, AI, AR, AT, AV, AY, BA, BD, BR, CA, CB, CY, DM, EI, EK, EN,

(*Contd.*)

(*Contd.*)

FI, GA, GF, GN, GV, HN, IB, IG, IL, IW, KE, KL, KU, LH, LY, MH, MS, NH, NW, OA, PK, PR, PS, QF, RG, RK, RO, R3, SA, SH, SK, SQ, SU, SV, TE, TG, TP, TU, TW, UA, UK, UL, US, UX, UY, VD, VN, VR, ZS, 9U

Dom-Dom	1.00	
	except	1.15 UK
Dom-Int	1.00	
	except	2.00 All to AI
		2.00 All to LY
		1.15 All to NW
		1.15 UK
Int-Dom	1.00	
	except	3.30 LY to AI
		1.15 NW to All
		1.15 UK
Int-Int	1.00	
	except	2.00 All to AI
		2.00 All to LY
		3.00 LY to All
		1.15 NW to/from All
		30 BA (between BHX and MUC)
		45 BA (other flights), TW
		40 UA
		1.15 UK

Terminal 2

AC, AF, AM, AT, AZ, CO, CX, DL, EW, FI, HM, IT, JL, JP, JU, JY, LG, LO, LX, LZ, MA, MD, MK, NG, OK, OS, OU, RO, SN, SR, TU, UM, VN, VO, WX

Dom-Dom	45	
Dom-Int	45	
	except	1.00 All to JL
		1.00 IT to AF (to TLV)
		1.00 AF (to TLV)
		1.15 UK
Int-Dom	45	
	except	1.00 JL to All
Int-Int	45	
	except	1.30 All to TLV
		1.00 All to/from JL

(*Contd.*)

(*Contd.*)

		1.00 IT to AF (to TLV)
		1.00 AF (to TLV)
Train Terminal-TN		
AF		
Dom-Dom	45	
Dom-Int	1.15	
	except	1.00 AF train to IT
		1.00 AF train to AF
Int-Dom	1.30	
	except	1.15 IT to AF train
		1.15 AF to AF train

QUESTIONS AND DISCUSSIONS

Objective Type

Q. 1. *It's easy to locate flight schedules in the World Airline Guide. Simple look for the name of your destination city across the top of the columns. You will find it printed in large bold face type like this:*

> To, ROME, ITALY

At time, a "To" city listing will begin in the middle of a column instead of the top, but it will always be in proper alphabetical order. Schedules to Venice, Italy are found on Page 991. Where would you expect to find schedules to Sao Paulo, Brazil?

A. Page 1182

B. Page 789

Ans. *(B) Page 789*

Q. 2. *Having found your "To" or destination city look down the listing beneath it until you find your "From" or departure city in alphabetical order. (a) If, for example, you were planning a trip from New York to Copenhagen, Denmark, you would first look for the heading "To ...." (b) Having located it, you would then look down the listing beneath it until you found your "From" city, in this case ....*

Ans. (*a*) *to* **COPENHAGEN**, *DENMARK*

(*b*) *from* **NEW YORK**, *N.Y., USA*

Q. 3. *Due to the large number of flight schedules and the amount of information that must be displayed, codes were developed to conserve space. These codes may be found in the Worldwide Airline Guide under Abbreviations and Reference Marks. The page on which these codes are listed appears in the Index of the Airline Guide. Locate related Exhibits and use them to complete the following sentences:*

(*a*) the Carrier (Airline) code "AF" stands for ....;

(*b*) the Jet Aircraft Code "D10" represents a .... aircraft; and

(*c*) the Frequency code "4" means ....

Ans. (*a*) *Air France*

(*b*) *Douglas DC-10*

(*c*) *Thursday*

Q. 4. *Locate the "City/Airport Codes" which are listed alphabetically by code preceding the Quick Reference schedules section of the Worldwide Airline Guide.*

(*a*) The three-letter code "ASP" stands for ....

(*b*) "BEG" represents ....

Ans. (*a*) *Alice Springs, Australia*

(*b*) *Belgrade, Yugoslavia*

Q. 5. *Airline Guide at the end of the questions contains a "Flight Itineraries" section. Each carrier's flights making at least one stop between their origin and destination are listed in numerical order with their origin, cities en route, and destination. Answer the following:*

(a) Where does Swissair (SR) flight 336 originate? (Just jot down the three-letter code.) ....

(b) What is its final destination? ....

(c) Where else does it stop? ....

Ans. (*a*) *ZRH (Zurich, Switzerland)*

(*b*) *TLV (Tel Aviv, Israel)*

(*c*) *GVA (Geneva, Switzerland)*

Q. 6. *Many flights operate on only specific days of the week, thereby requiring extreme caution when quoting direct flights or constructing itineraries. The days of the week are given a number code and are referred to as "Frequency Codes". Their decodes can be found in the "Abbreviations and Reference Marks" section. Let us take an example:*

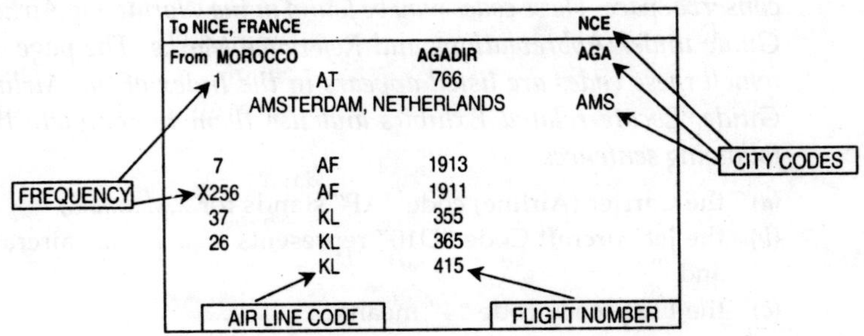

A flight will operate everyday of the week unless otherwise designated by frequency codes on the extreme left-hand side of the schedule.

In this example from Amsterdam, KL flight 355 operates only on Wednesday (3) and Sunday (7), while AF 1911 operates on Monday (1), Wednesday (3), Thursday (4), and Sunday (7) (the X256 indicates except Tuesday, Friday, and Saturday).

You are required to findout:

(*a*) What day(s) of the week does AF 1913 operate? ....

(*b*) What day(s) of the week does KL 415 operate? ....

Ans. (*a*) *Only on Sunday*

(*b*) *All week (Monday through Sunday)*

Q. 7. Two other important items in any schedule are the departure and arrival times. Examine the following:

Departure and arrival times are always printed in the local time (24-hour clock) of the departure and arrival city. In the sample schedule below from Seoul to Osaka, the first flight departs Seoul at 1100 and arrives in Osaka at 1230.

Freq.	Leave	Arrive	Flight	Class	Eq	S Eff./Dis.
To OSAKA, JAPAN						**OSA**
From SEOUL, REP. OF KOREA						**SEL**
25	1100	1230	KE	203		
	1220	1350	JL	962		
246	1330	1500	KE	503		
3	1330	1500	KE	505		
X347	1715	1845	KE	201		

DEPARTURE TIME   ARRIVAL TIME

You are required to findout:

(*a*) What day(s) of the week does KE flight 203 operate? ....

(*b*) If a passenger wishes to arrive in Osaka around 7:00 p.m. on Friday, what flight would you recommend? ....

(*c*) At what time does it depart from Seoul? ....

(*d*) If a passenger wishes to depart Seoul around 1: 00 p.m. on a Sunday, what flight would you recommend? ....

(*e*) At what time does this flight depart? ....

(*f*) When does it arrive in Osaka? ....

Ans. (*a*) *Tuesday and Friday* (*d*) *JL 962*
(*b*) *KE 201* (*e*) *1220 (12:20 p.m.)*
(*c*) *1715 (5:15 p.m.)* (*f*) *1350 (1:50 p.m.)*

Q. 8. Many cities have more than one airport serving the area. Whenever this is true, the three-letter code of the departure and/or arrival airport is shown immediately following the applicable departure or arrival time. To determine the name of the airport served, refer to the City/Airport decoding pages preceding the flight schedules section. Here is part of the London to Moscow schedule:

In this example,

(*a*) all the flights depart from .... (airport code) airport and

(*b*) arrive at .... (airport code) airport in Moscow.

DEPARTURE AIRPORT → LHR; ARRIVAL AIRPORT → SVO

2	0905	LHR	1535	SVO	SU	244
4	0905	LHR	1535	SVO	SU	312
156	0950	LHR	1620	SVO	BE	672
2	1005	LHR	1535	SVO	SU	244
4	1005	LHR	1535	SVO	SU	312

Ans. (*a*) *LHR (Heathrow)*
(*b*) *SVO (Sheremetyevo)*

Q. 9. Several items are presented in this sample Bombay to New York schedule as given below:

The three items introduced are:

1. the class/classes of service offered to a passenger on each particular flight;
2. the type of aircraft, and

3. the number of stops the aircraft makes between the two points. You will recall these items are decoded on the "Abbreviations and Reference Marks" pages in front of the Worldwide Airline Guide. The class(es) of service is denoted by capital letters. Night service is indicated by a small "n" after the general classification. *Example*:

Fn = Jet Night Coach in First Class Compartment
Yn = Jet Night Coach/Economy

To NEW YORK, N.Y., USA								NYC
From MUMBAY, INDIA								BOM
2	0100	1535	JFK	AI	103	FY	747	3
3	0100	1535	JFK	AI	105	FY	747	4
4	0100	1535	JFK	AI	107	FY	747	4
7	0100	1535	JFK	AI	115	FY	747	4
7	2115	1535+1	JFK	AI	101	FY	747	5
4	2115	1535+1	JFK	AI	109	FY	747	5
5	2115	1535+1	JFK	AI	111	FY	747	5

NUMBER OF STOPS
CLASS (ES OF SERVICE
TYPE OF AIRCRAFT

In the above schedule you are required to find out that

(*a*) AI 103 offers both .... and .... service.
(*b*) The airplane is a .... and makes .... stops between BOM and NYC.

Ans. (*a*) *Jet First Class; Jet Economy*
(*b*) *Boeing 747 Jet; 3 Stops*

Q. 10. The Paris (PAR) to New York (NYC) schedules is given below:

You are required to review:

(*a*) AF 015 leaves PAR at ...., arriving in NYC at .... The .... (type) aircraft offers .... (Class/es of service) service.
(*b*) A passenger wishes to arrive in New York around 3:30 p.m. on Wednesday, what flight would you recommend? .... How many stops does this flight make? ....
(*c*) If a passenger wishes to depart from Paris (Orly Field) on Tuesday) around 11:00 a.m., what flight would you recommend? .... Does this flight make any intermediate stops? .... What type of aircraft is used? ....

Freq.	Leave	Arrive		Flight		Class	Eq	S	Eff./Dis.
To NEW YORK, N.Y., USA									**NYC**
From PARIS, FRANCE									**PAR**
	1100 CDG	1225	JFK	AF	015	FY	707	0	
4	1140 ORY	1535	JFK	AI	107	FY	747	1	
7	1140 ORY	1535	JFK	AI	115	FY	747	1	
3	1145 ORY	1535	JFK	AI	105	FY	747	1	
2	1155 ORY	1535	JFK	AI	103	FY	747	1	
	1200 CDG	1255	JFK	TW	803	FY	747	0	
	1330 CDG	1515	JFK	AF	077	FY	747	0	
	1500 CDG	1715	JFK	TW	801	FY	83J	0	
14	1800 CDG	1945	JFK	AF	017	FY	747	0	
2	1800 ORY	1900	JFK	PK	703	FY	D10	0	
6	1800 ORY	1900	JFK	PK	711	FY	D10	0	

Ans. (*a*) *11:00 a.m.; 12:25 p.m.; Boeing 707; Jet First Class and Jet Economy*

(*b*) *AF 077 (Departs nearly 2 hours after AI 105)*

(*c*) *AI 103; One; Boeing 747*

Q. 11. Fares for international travel are published in the currency of the originating city/country. For this reason, a fare from London, England to Paris, France will be published in English Pounds. A three-letter code follows the fare indicating the currency used.

(a) Fares to London from Rome are published in (LIT) ....

(b) Fares from Mexico City to Zurich, Switzerland are published in (MEP) ....

Ans. (*a*) *Italian lira*

(*b*) *Mexican pesos*

Q. 12. One-way and round-trip fares are published in the currency of the origin (From) city for all destinations with direct service. In some cases, fares are published where only connecting service is shown. These fares are for your information and are dependent on the routing selected. All users should only use fares for direct service. Examine this exhibit which displays schedule and fare information from Cairo to Amsterdam.

The symbols F & Y located just under the "From" city name correspond to the classes of service available on the flights listed in the schedule. One-way and round-rip fares in Egyptian pounds are shown to the right of the symbols F and Y as indicated by the currency code EGL. In addition, excess baggage charges are shown immediately below the three-letter code of the "From" city, and are published in the currency of the "From" city. In most cases, the basis for excess baggage charges is Kilograms (the code "K" follows the excess baggage charge), but pounds are also used (an "L" is used to indicate pounds).

Freq.	Leave		Arrive	Flight		Class	Eq	S	Eff./Dis.
To AMSTERDAM, NETHERLANDS									**AMS**
From CAIRO, EGYPT									**CAI**
			F	EQ	189 950	379 900			1900K
			Y	EQ	130 350	260 700			
3	0600		1210	KL	548	Y	DC8	1	
5	1345		1745	KL	564	FY	D8S	0	
1	1345		1855	KL	566	FY	D8S	1	
			CONNECTIONS						
1	1435		1145 + 1	AT	251	FY	707	0	
		1740	GYA 1020	KL	332	Y	D9S	0	
4	1435		1145 + 1	AT	253	FY	727	0	
		1740	GYA 1020	KL	332	Y	D9S	0	

EXCESS BAGGAGE CHANGE

(*a*) In the above schedule, the First Class Jet fare from CAI to AMS is .... Egyptian pounds.

(*b*) The round-trip Jet Economy fare is .... Egyptian pounds.

(*c*) The excess baggage charge between CAI and AMS is .... Egyptian pounds per kilogram.

Ans. (*a*) *189.950*

(*b*) *260.700*

(*c*) *1.900*

Q. 13. Point-to-point maximum and non-stop mileages—separated by a/character—are published in the Worldwide Airline Guide following each "From" city name.*

To PANAMA CITY, PANAMA REP.									**PTY**
From GUAYAQUIL, EQUADOR 933/778									**GYE**
	F	189 00	378 00						189 K
	Y	127 00	254 00						
	GP S	109 00	218 00						
	EU Y	121 00	242 00						
		YE	30	DAY	226 00	EFF	ALL		
		OP SE	30	DAY	193 00	EFF	ALL		YEAR
6	0150	0330	BN	974	FY	DC8	0		E-FEB 2
7	0205	0345	BN	974	FY	D85	0		
6	0745	1220	EU	42	FY	720	0		
5	0815	1150	BN	906	FY	D85	0		
4	0915	1350	EU	46	FY	720	0		
3	1005	1145	BN	906	FY	D85	0		
36	1010	1200	OP	112	S	727	0		
7	1435	1615	BN	970	FY	D85	0		

These mileages are used for constructing unpublished fares. If no maximum or non-stop mileage is available, a zero (0) is shown on the appropriate side of the slash. Maximum mileages are shown on the left and non-stop mileages on the right.

(*a*) In the above schedule, the maximum mileage from Guayaquil to Panama City is .... miles.

(*b*) The nonstop mileage is .... miles.

*Maximum mileage is defined as the allowable mileage which can be travelled for a given fare. Nonstop mileage is defined as the non-stop or direct distance between a pair of cities.

Ans. (*a*) *933*

(*b*) *778*

Q. 14. (*a*) The round-trip Shoulder Economy fare from Los Angeles to Geneva is .... U.S. dollars approximately.

(*b*) A passenger flying First Class between London and Geneva one-way is charged .... U.K. pounds approximately.

(*c*) Fares in the Airline Guide are published in the currency of the .... (from/to) city.

Ans. (*a*) *1024.00*

(*b*) *77.00*

(*c*) *from*

Q. 15. A passenger wants to fly from Los Angeles to Geneva on Sunday afternoon March 21.

(*a*) To leave after 11:00 a.m., he must depart at .... on .... Airlines flight number ....

(*b*) He arrives at the connecting city, ... (city ode) at ....

(*c*) He then departs the connecting city at ....

(*d*) Airlines flight number .... which makes .... stop(s) and arrives in Geneva at .... on .... (day of week).

Ans. (*a*) *12:30 p.m.; TW 760; LHR*

(*b*) *7:40 a.m.; 9:45 a.m.*

(*c*) *BE 574: no (zero)*

(*d*) *11:10 a.m.; Monday*

Q. 16. Assume a passenger meets all conditions specified in the concerned Excursion Note from the Worldwide Airline Guide.

(*a*) What fare is he charged between Los Angeles and Geneva? ....

(*b*) Are there any direct flights between LAX and GVA? ....

Ans. (*a*) *$757.00*
(*b*) *Yes*

Q. 17. SN flight 211 originates in:

(*a*) .... (city name) stops in
(*b*) .... (city name) and terminates in
(*c*) ....

Ans. (*a*) *Brussels, Belgium*
(*b*) *Athens, Greece*
(*c*) *Beirut, Lebanon*

Q. 18. A passenger travelling from Manila, Philippines to Geneva, Switzerland on a Thursday would connect at

(*a*) .... (city name) and
(*b*) .... (city name) and arrive in Geneva on
(*c*) .... (day) at
(*d*) .... (time).

Ans. (*a*) *Bangkok, Thailand* (*c*) *Friday*
(*b*) *Rome, Italy* (*d*) *10:10 a.m.*

Objective Type 'True' and 'False'

Q. 19. Read each of the following statements. Write 'T' if it is true or 'F' if it is false:

1. LHR, STN and LGW are major London area airports.
2. DKR is the principal gateway to Western Africa.
3. ZIH, PVR and MEY are all Mexican gateways.
4. CDG and ORL are major Paris area airports.
5. FCO and CIA are major Rome area airports.
6. After Cuba and Hispaniola, Jamaica is the largest Caribbean island.
7. NAS is the code for the main airport in the Bahamas.
8. Airline geography is based on standards set by the International Air Transport Association.
9. OGG is the code for the main airport on Mani.
10. Any point represented by a city code or an airport code is a destination.
11. The Houston area is served by 2 major airports.

12. The Baltimore airport is considered a Washington DC area airport.
13. The city code for Detroit is the same as the airport code.
14. The city code for Orlando, Florida is the same as the airport code.
15. NAS is the code of the major airport in the Bahamas.

Q. 20. *In each of the following sentences, write the correct missing word or phrase that belongs to each blank:*

1. Visitors to Tokyo arrive at nearby .... Airport, which has the code ....
2. Visitors to the country of .... can cruise down the Nile River, relax at Mediterranean resorts, and/or go Scuba dicing in the Red Sea. The main gateway to the country has the code ....
3. Gambling casinos and world's most famous auto race are popular attractive in the country of ....
4. Milan, which has the code ...., is served by the Linate Airport.
5. The major airports in the Rome area are Fiumicino, which has the code .... and .... (CIA).
6. Paris, which has the code ...., is served by Charles DeGaulle Airport, which has the code .... and .... (ORY).
7. London is served by three major airports, ... (LHR), ... (LCW) and Stansted, which has the code ....
8. The ...., commonly called Great Britain, includes England, North Ireland, Scotland, and Wales.
9. The .... Mountain run the length of the western border of Argentina.
10. .... geography is concerned with the various cities, airports, and countries served by air carriers, and is based on the standards set by the ....

Q. 21. *In each of the following sentences, write the correct missing word or phrase that belongs to each blank:*

1. When a computer reservation is used to book airline reservations, the correct .... must be used.
2. A main entry point to a state or country is called a ....
3. New York is served by .... Airport (JFK), ... Airport (LGA) and the .... Airport (EWR).

4. .... is the major gateway to the New England region.
5. The America's capital is served by Dulles Airport, which has the code .... Washington National Airport, which has the code ...., and the .... Airport, which has the code BWI.
6. .... is the major gateway to the New England region.
7. The Disney World Epcot Centre Theme Park is the city of ...., which has the code ...., is one of the most popular fee based aviation in the world.
8. The city of Chicago, which has the code ...., is served by .... Airport (ORD) and .... Airport (MDW).

Q. 22. *Identify the person/word or phrase for each of the following concepts:*

1. The government agency that is currently responsible for authorizing airlines to operate a passenger service, approve air routes, and review passenger complaints.
2. Formation of a large company capable of controlling an entire industry.
3. Small carriers that operate aircraft with fewer than 30 seats.
4. A two-letter code designated by IATA to identify an airline in schedules and tariffs.
5. A three-digit numeric code assigned to each airline.
6. An agreement entitling a carrier to use the name of another airline on the flights.
7. An airline that has a limited schedule and leases aircraft to large groups or to other airlines.
8. A three-letter code identifying the type of aircraft used for a flight.
9. The term for a kitchenette used by the flight crew to heat or prepare passengers meals on an aircraft.
10. A letter is an aircraft code that indicates that the airplane has been configurated to transport both passengers and cargo.

Ans.:

1. Department of Civil Aviation
2. Monopoly
3. Commuter aircrafts
4. Carrier code
5. Airline code
6. Code sharing agreement
7. Charter airline
8. Equipment code
9. Galley
10. M.

4

Basic Elements of Air Fares

After learning this topic you should be able to:

- ❑ *understand the basic elements of air fares;*
- ❑ *get an idea of primary and secondary air codes;*
- ❑ *know the various taxes related to air force;*
- ❑ *understand the term minimum and maximum stay;*
- ❑ *it familiar with the city codes, and flight randy;*
- ❑ *explains the feers rules and their application;*
- ❑ *understand the produced validation of ticket.*

An understanding of air fares requires the familiarity with basic elements. There are three basic elements of air fares:

1. Class of service,
2. Fare basis, and
3. Rules and regulations.

CLASS OF SERVICE

Flights on most modern airlines offer two basic classes of service: (1) First class, and (2) Coach.

First Class Cabins

In this cabin, seats are relatively spacious and comfortable, alcoholic beverages are served free of charge, and superior meal service is provided. On international carriers, first class is often referred to as 'premium class'.

Coach/Economy Class or Cabin

The remainder of the aircraft is called as coach or economy cabin. In this class passengers receive the carrier's standard level of service. On some international carriers, coach class is also referred to as 'standard class'.

Many domestic and international carriers offer a premium coach class and is less expensive than first class but more expensive than coach class. Depending on the carrier, the third class of service may be called business, club, connoisseur, or ambassador class.

Some domestic airlines offer a variety of discounted fares of travel in the coach cabin. Passengers who purchase tickets at one of these fares generally enjoy the same level of service on other coach passengers. Best seats are generally reserved from passengers who pay the full fare. A certain number of seats on each flight are designated as 'undesirable' seats, for example, seats which do not decline or do not have a view of the movie screen. Depending on the carrier, these seats may be assigned to passengers travelling on low discount fares or to passengers who check in the late for boarding.

Excursion fares are the lowest and most restrictive type of fares. Most excursion fares must be purchased in advance of the departure date and require travel to originate and terminate at the same point. In most cases, the outbound and return segments must also be booked on the same carrier. Other restrictions, such as minimum stay, a Saturday stay-over, and penalties for cancellation or changes may also apply.

FARE BASIS

A fare basis is a price category determined by the class of service and factors such as the destination, season, day of the week, one-way or round trip travel advance purchase or length of stay. Each fare has a primary code and one or more secondary codes. For instance, take a code BAP 7. This applies to travel in B class and requires the ticket to be purchased at least seven days prior to departure, and the secondary codes AP 7 indicates the advance purchase requirement. The class is also called the booking code.

In some cases, the booking code is the same as the fare basis. For example, F is the fare basis for first-class fares, and Y is the fare basis for the full (undiscounted) coach fare. Different airlines use various primary codes for the same class. For example, 'C' class on same airlines is the same as 'J' class on some other airlines. Various primary codes are used for discounted coach travels including B, M, Q, V, H and soforth, as given in Table 4.1.

Table 4.1: Primary Fare Codes

Code	*Primary Fares*
P	Premium First Class
F	First Class
A	Discounted First Class
J	Premium Coach
C	Premium Coach
S	Standard Class
Y	Coach or Economy
K	Discount Coach
B	Discount Coach
M	Discount Coach
Q	Discount Coach
L	Discount Coach/Off-Pack Economy
V	Discount Coach/Off-Pack Economy
X	Free Travel (*e.g.* Mileage Club Members)

Secondary codes set each fare basis apart from other fare bases with the same primary code. For example, 'AP' is used to indicate an advance purchase requirement, and 'NR' denotes a non-refundable fare. Table 4.2 gives some Secondary Fare Codes.

Table 4.2: Secondary Fare Codes

Code	*Secondary Fares*
AP	Advance Purchase
CA	Discounted fare for government employees
CD	Senior Citizen Discovery
CH	Child's Fare (2-11 yrs)
CL	Clergy Fare
D	Discount Fare
DG	Discounted Government Fare
E	Excursion Fare
G	Group Fare
H	High (Day of Week, Time of Day, or Season)
IT	Inclusive Tour Fare
L	Low (Day of Week, Time of Day, or Season)
M	Military Discount
MR	Military recruit
N	Night off peak

(*Contd.*)

(Contd.)

Code	*Secondary Fares*
NR	Non-refundable
P	Family Plan
PE	Penalty for cancellation or change
PE	Round trip fare
R	Stand by fare
W	Weekend travel
X	Exception (May also mean weekday or midweek)
Z	Youth fare

Other Fare Basis Code

Numbers may be used to indicate days of the week. For instance, Y3 indicate a coach fare valid only for departure on Wednesday. Weekdays may also be indicative by one or two letters, such as W for Wednesday, TU for Tuesday. BTU fare is a discount coach fare valid only for departure on Tuesday. Numbers may also be used to indicate an advance purchase or maximum stay requirement. BAP 21 may indicate a discount coach fare that must be purchased 21 days prior to departure.

Fare Restructuring

When major changes are made in airlines pricing system, it is known as fare restructuring. In the past the restructuring plan created some basic fare type such as:

1. First Class
2. Full Coach
3. Discount Coach with short period advance purchase
4. Discount Coach with long period advance purchase.

AIR TRANSPORTATION TAXES

Fares for air travel at originating point are subjected to different types of taxes:

1. Air Transportation
2. International departure tax
3. Good and service tax
4. Sales Tax

5. Surcharges and fees:
   (*i*) Passenger fares
   (*ii*) Charges for airline security
   (*iii*) Passenger facilities
   (*iv*) Refuelling.

Ticket and Sales Taxes

In some countries these taxes are collected in addition to the fare when a ticket is issued. Other documents such as Excess Baggage Tickets and MCOs are also subject to tax in some countries.

Table 4.3 presents some example of ticket and sales taxes of some countries:

Table 4.3: Specimen Ticket and Sales Taxes

DOM = Domestic
INT = International
(A) = Taxes applicable to tickets irrespective of where purchased

Australia

Passenger Movement Charge AUD27 *Cairns Airport Authority Tax* for each INT departure and arrival AUD8 *Noise Levy Tax* INT arrivals at SYD AUD3.40

Bangladesh

Airport Tax (for each departure) Dep INT BDT300; Dep DOM BDT25

Pakistan

Foreign Travel Tax PKR1000 *Capital Value Tax* 3% on all International tickets issued in Pakistan

Singapore

Passenger Service Charge Dep from Changi SGD15 Dep from Seletar SGD10

Switzerland

Airport and Security Tax Charge will apply for each departure from a Swiss Airport Dep ZRH DOM CHF11.50; INT CHF14 Dep GVA DOM CHF11.50; INT CHF14.50 Dep BSL DOM CHF12.50; INT CHF15 Dep ACH INT CHF 13 Dep BRN DOM/INT CHF14 Dep LUG DOM CHF10; INT CHF13 Dep SIR DOM CHF7

United Kingdom

Air Passenger Duty Dep DOM and to European Union, Iceland/Norway and BSL/GVA GBP5; Dep INT GBP10. The tax does not apply to departure from Channel is, or to flights on aircraft with less than 20 seats

AIRPORT TAXES

These taxes are normally paid in local currency upon departure. In many countries diplomats, transit passengers, and Infants are exempt. Taxes for children vary.

Table 4.4 presents air fare taxes of some countries:

Table 4.4: Airport Taxes

DOM = Domestic
INT = International
A = Not applicable to transit passengers and infants under 2 years
B = Not applicable to transit passengers

Canada		
Vancouver Airport Improvement Fee (AIF) Dep Passengers departing from Vancouver International Airport are required to purchase an AIF at the airport before departure.		
Dep Vancouver to British Columbia and The Yukon	CAD	5
Dep Vancouver to North America (including Mexico and Hawaii)	CAD	10
Dep Vancouver to Outside North America Exceptions: *Same day connections*	CAD	15
India B		
Dep DOM, Myanmar and Subcontinent	INR	150
Dep INT, Rest	INR	300
Madagascar A		
Dep INT, To Africa: Non-Residents	FRF	80
Dep INT, To Rest: Non-Residents	FRF	100
Dep INT, To Africa: Residents	MGF	45000
Dep INT, To Rest: Residents	MGF	60000
Dep DOM, Residents	MGF	6000
Maldives		
Dep INT	USD	10
Mauritius A		
Dep INT	MUR	100
Pakistan A		
Dep DOM	PKR	20

(*Contd.*)

(*Contd.*)

Dep INT, 'F' Class	PKR	400
Dep INT, 'C' Class	PKR	300
Dep INT, 'Y' Class	PKR	200
Dep INT, Government Tax	PKR	280
Singapore A		
Dep Changi Airport	SGD	15
Dep Seletar Airport	SGD	10
Sri Lanka A		
Dep INT	LKR	500

When tax is excluded from the fare, the fare amount is referred to as the base fare. The air transportation tax is assessed on the total base fare for all segments in the itinerary. Let us take an example, assume an itinerary includes the following segments:

From	*To*	*Base Fare (Rs.)*
1. NEW DELHI	FRANKFURT	14,000
2. FRANKFURT	LONDON	6,000
3. LONDON	NEW DELHI	15,000

The total base in this example is Rs. 35,000. The total fare or ticket price is calculated as follows:

Total base fare	35,000
Tax (10 per cent)	3,500
Total fare	38,500

Passengers departing from any point in India to an international destination are subject to an international departure tax. This tax is assessed even if other taxes apply.

CUSTOMS USER FEES

Passengers arriving in some countries from a foreign destination by air or sea are subject to a certain percentage of charge assessed by their government. This charge is called a customs user fee. It is collected to defray the costs of custom operations. The fee applies to all passengers arriving into these countries from any foreign point. Assuming that a passenger will travel round-trip from New York to

London at a base fare of Rs. 9,500. Because the passenger will depart from US to a foreign country, the federal air transportation tax does not apply. However, the international departure tax is assessed. Because the return flight will arrive in New York from a foreign point of origin, the custom user free also applies. The total fare in this example is calculated as follows:

Base fare	Rs. 9,500
International departure tax	600
Custom user fee	Rs. 10,100

MISCELLANEOUS CHARGES

Other taxes, fees, and surcharges may also be added to a fare, depending on the itinerary. In USA a Passenger Facility Charge (PFC) is applied for flights that depart or arrive at various US points. A facility charge is imposed by an airport authority to fund an improvement project, such as the construction of a new run-away or the expansion of an airline terminal.

Other miscellaneous charges, such as surcharge for airport security or refuelling, may also be added to a fare depending on the itinerary. In some countries international passengers are subjected to an agricultural inspection fee.

FARE RULES

Discounted air fares are always subject to certain restrictions. Lower the fare, the more restrictions are applicable. These restrictions, commonly refer to as fare rules, fall into six main categories:

1. Minimum/Maximum Stay
2. Advance Purchase
3. Validity Dates
4. Combinability
5. Routing
6. Penalties
7. Other restrictions.

Minimum/Maximum Stay

With most discount fares, the length of time between outbound and return flights is restricted. For example, a fare may be valid only if the passenger is willing to stay over until the next Sunday before starting a return trip. This may be called a Saturday stay-over. A maximum stay may also apply. For example, passenger may be required to return no later than 21 days after arriving their destinations. In the example of fare rates given in Table 4.5, the minimum stay requirement is stated in the Min. stay field. In this case return travel may not commence before the first Sunday after the departure. In other words à Saturday stop-over is required.

Advance Purchase

In most of the discount fares, advance purchase prior to departure date is required, say 30 days in advance, which is commonly known as 'Super Saver'. Similarly, under ultra super-saver fares require 120 days advance purchase requirements. The range of the time period varies between 24 hours to three months depending upon the season and the carriers. Generally, the longer the advance purchase requirement, the lower the fare. In some cases advance purchase fares, require that the ticket may be purchased within 24 hours after the reservation is made.

In Table 4.5 the advance purchase requirement is stated in the RES/TKTG field. The reservation must be made no later than 7 days before the passenger departs from the origin point. The ticket must be purchased no later than 7 days before the departure date or within 14 days after making the reservation.

Validity Dates

The discount travel is generally valid only on certain dates. It has both an effective date and an expiration date. Certain dates may also be blacked out, meaning that the travel is not valid on those dates. Black out dates are periods of high demand, on the other hand, discount fares are designed to fill seats that would otherwise remain unoccupied during periods of law demand.

Combinability

Discount fares can be combined with other fare of types. For example, a traveller using an M-class fare on one segment may be able to use a V-class fare on another segment in the same trip. Usually, the lower the fare, the more restrictive the combinability. To obtain a QAP14R fare, the passenger may be required to travel round-trip in

Q class on all segments. In the example given in Table 4.5. the combinability rule is stated in the COMBINE field. The fare bases can be used in an open jaw, if the mileage between the open jaw points is equal to or less than the mileage of the shortest flight segment in the itinerary. A maximum of two stopovers is allowed on a circle trip at the fare basis.

Routing

Only permitted routings may be used in restrictive fare. The rating specifies the connecting and stopover points that can be used with a particular fare basis. As in example, the airline offered a restrictive air fare at the QSPCL fare basis, from Los Angeles to Sydney. Passengers at this fare are required to travel via Honolulu and Auckland. A stopover was permitted at Honolulu but not at Auckland. No other routings could be used with the QSPCL fare basis.

Penalties

Generally for cancellations or changes in itinerary under restrictive fares, penalties are imposed. In some cases restrictive fares are non-refundable. In the example given in Table 4.5, 10 per cent penalty applies. If after the ticket is purchased, the reservation is cancelled or any changes are made to the itinerary. In the event of death or illness of the passenger, the penalty is not assessed.

Other Restrictions

A number of other special conditions may also apply to discount fare. For example, a fare rule may require all segments of the itinerary to be confirmed at the time of ticketing, or may prohibit travel on certain dates of the week. The example (Table 3.5.) cannot be used for an itinerary with an open return. An open segment is a ticketed segment that is not booked on a specific flight. For example, if a client desires to hold a ticket for a return flight, but is uncertain of the exact date or time of the return departure, an open ticket may be issued. An open ticket is valid for travel in a specified class of service on any available flight. When the passenger decides on a departure date and time, a confirmed reservation must be made on a specific flight. If the flight is over-booked, a passenger with an open ticket may stand by for a flight without a reservation.

FARE RULES

Table 4.5: Some Fare Rules

QTE	F/B	BK	FARE	EFF	EXP	TKT	AP	MIN/MAX	RTG
10-ME70	M	R	Rs. 10,000	—	—	—	**	SUN/-	501

ORIGIN—DFW DESTINATION-NYC CXR-AA TRVL DATE: 8 JUL 97 RULES FOR FARE BASIS—ME TO RT FARE RULE 4165 ATP FEE ON CHG/REFUND

01. BK CODE -M-

02. Penalty: A 10 per cent penalty applies for TKTD* Itineraries or UNTKTD PTA. The SVC charge will be assessed on the applicable fare including tax. The penalty will only apply to the coupons where a change is applicable. For exceptions to penalties the following applies. In the event of death/illness of PSGR/IMMEDIATE family member—whether travelling or not/travelling companion, the penalty will be waved.

03. RES/TKTG: Reservation to be made not later than 7 days before departure from origin. TKT must be purchased no later than 7 days before departure from origin or 14 days after reservation is made, whichever comes first. Segment using this rule must be confirmed.

04. MIN STAY: Return travel is valid on the 1st Sunday after 12.01 A.M. Measured from departure from origin to departure from last stopover point.

14. DISCOUNT: Eighty per cent of the ADT fare is charged for a CHD PSGR 2 THRU 11 years of age. CHD passenger must be accompanied on all segments by an ADT PSGR travelling in the same compartment.

15. REROUTE: Prior to TKT issuance changes must be made 7 days before flight departure. After TKT issuance ticket must be made 7 days before FLT departure. After TKT issuance or on UTKID PTA, SVC charge may also apply—see penalty.

17. COMBINE: Open jaw is valid if the mileage between the open

(*Contd.*)

(Contd.)

jaw points is equal to/less than the mileage of the shortest flown sector. The inward point of arrival and the outward point of departure of an open jaw are considered to be the two stopovers. Circle trips are permitted with a maximum of 2 stopovers, including point of turn around.

18. OPEN RTN: Ticket may not be issued with open return.
19. REFUND: SVC charge may apply—see penalty.
22. CO-TERM: The following group of cities are considered to be the same point. WAS-BUA-MIA-FLL. LAX-ONT-LGB-SNA-BUR. NYC-EWR.

FARE CALCULATION

One Segment

In fare calculation, break-down the itinerary by fare to show how the total fare is calculated. Only base fare are used in calculation but airport surcharges may also be included. To illustrate, assume a passenger Mr. Manoher, will depart on April 18, travelling on way from New Delhi to London at the Y fare basis. Mr. Manoher will travel by Air India at a base fare of Rs. 8,000. The fare calculation for this itinerary will be written as follows:

18TH APL. ND AI LOND 8000Y TTL 8000

Methods

1. The departure date for the first segment in the itinerary is written first.
2. The carrier code is written between each board point and off point.
3. The base fare and fare basis are written after each off point.
4. The letters TTL indicate the total base fare for the itinerary. Since the itinerary consists of one segment, the total base fare is the same as the base fare for the air segment.

On the passenger ticket the tax is added to the total base fare to calculate the ticket price. In the example, above the total price is Rs. 8,000 + 10 per cent, *i.e.* Rs. 8,800.

MORE THAN ONE SEGMENT

There are two types of fare ladder used in calculation.

1. Horizontal Fare Calculation

Assume that Mr. Manoher will depart on the following itinerary:

Date	*CR/FLT*	*From*	*To*	*Fare Basis*	*Fare*
1. JULY 08	AI 330	NDL	LON	QAP14	Rs. 8,000
2. JULY 15	BA 740	HEATHROW	NEW YORK	MAP14	Rs. 5,000

In this example, the fare ladder may be written as follows:

1. Date (First Itinerary)
2. Origin Point (Board Point)—First Itinerary
3. Carrier/Flight—First Itinerary
4. Off Point—First Itinerary
5. Fare—First Itinerary
6. Fare Basis—First Itinerary
7. Carrier/Flight (Second Segment)
8. Off Point (Second Segment)
9. Fare (Second Itinerary)
10. Fare Basis
11. Total Fare (First + Second Itinerary).

In the above example, the horizontal fare ladder may be written as follows:

8 JUL = IA LOND 8000 QAP 14 BA NY 5000 MAP 14 TTL 13000

On hand written ticket, the information may be written on a vertical fare ladder Specimen of Vertical Fare as given in Table 4.6.

8 JUL ....
LON AI 8000 QAP14
NY BA 5000 MAP14
TTL 13000

Table 4.6: Fare Basis Code

Code	*Fares Basis*
F	First Class
FN	First class night
C	Business Class
Y	Coach

(Contd.)

(*Contd.*)

Code	*Fares Basis*
Y2	Coach, Tuesday departure required
YE7	Coach excursion, Sunday Departure required
KAP3	Economy, 3-day advance purchase
BXE30NR	Discount coach, 30-day advance purchase, non-refundable
BTUWETH	Discount coach, Tuesday, Wednesday, Thursday departure
BAP21 PE50	Discount coach, 21-days advance purchase, 50 per cent penalty
MLX12	Discount coach, Low season, not valid for Monday or Tuesday
MAP14	Discount coach, 14-days advance purchase
Q21RT	Discount coach, 21-days advance purchase, round trip
YCH	Child coach fare
YM	Military coach fare

2. Vertical Ladder Fare

In a vertical fare ladder, the date and origin points are written on the first line. The next line shows the off point, carrier fare and fare basis. The off point of this line is the board point of the next line, which shows the off point, carrier fare and fare basis of the next segment.

Table 4.6 represents only a small percentage of the fare basis that are used by domestic and international carriers. These fare and fare bases change frequently. As the rule become more complex, the fare basis codes go longer. The booking code indicates the class of service on the passenger ticket. For example, Y class denotes, a full coach fare, and B class indicates, discount coach fare. When a reservation is made at the YE30 fare basis, the booking code Y is used to book the flight. When the passenger's ticket is written, the class 'Y' and the fare basis 'YE30' appear on the ticket coupon.

SPECIAL AIR FARES

When an airline promotes a special discount fare, only a small number of seats are available on each flight at the advertised price. The difference between the lowest discount fare and the full fare amounts to several thousand rupees. In the past airlines offered special fares to attract certain travellers such as defence personnel, government employees, senior citizens or children accompanied by adult passengers. Special fares may be offered in different ways, such as:

1. Promotional fares
2. Group fares
3. Tour fares
4. Military fares
5. Senior citizen fares
6. Children fares.

Promotional Fares

Special promotional fares are often available on infrequently travel routes or during periods of slow demand.

Group Fares

Discounted of group fares are based on volume purchases by tour operators, conventions or the organisers of some other type of group.

Tour Fares

Tour fares are discounted fares offered to packages who guarantee to purchase a specified number of seats on particular routes.

Military Fares

Active members of the Indian armed forces including coast guard, may be eligible for discount fare when they travel on authorised leave or within certain number of days after discharge from service. The discount may vary from 50-60 per cent. The personnel may not be in uniform, but they must carry proper identification and their leave authorisation or discharge papers.

Senior Citizen Fares

Passengers 65 years or older may be eligible for a senior citizen fare. Advance purchase is not usually required, but most airlines require tickets to be issued at least one hour prior to departure. Proof of age must be presented and carried with the passenger during the trip.

Child Fares

On some carriers, children from 2 to 12 years of age may qualify for discount child fare from 60-75 per cent of the normal adult fare.

Children must be accompanied by an adult or another child 12 years or older. To travel free on domestic flight, infant under 2 years must be accompanied by a fare paying passenger and may not reserve a separate seat. Unaccompanied children are generally charged the adult fare.

To validate a ticket, the agency ID plate and the appropriate airline plate are inserted in the imprinter. Other traffic documents are also validated with the agency ID plate.

TICKET ISSUANCE

Separate tickets are used for each fare-paying passenger. Tickets are also issued to passengers flying free of charge as part of a mileage bonus programme or by special arrangement with the airline tickets identifying more than one passenger on the same ticket are issued for group travel only under special circumstances.

For domestic flights, a ticket is not issued for an infant who will not occupy a separate seat on the aircraft. More foreign carrier charge an infant fare and issue tickets for infants, even if they are not occupying a seat. The maximum of an infant varies with the carrier.

Supply and Security of Tickets

The ticket supply is obtained from the Ticket Division of IATA. The total stock on hand should be sufficient to cover the agency's needs for three months. The agency's agreement with IATA requires ticket stock to be kept in locked safe, or other steel container, at all times when the agency is unattended. Any ticket stock that is not required for daily use must be stored off-premises in a safety deposit box or other secure location.

Ticket Validation

An air ticket cannot be used for passage until it has been filled out and validated. A validated ticket is imprinted with the following items:

1. Airline Identification (Name, Code, Logo)
2. Place of Issue
3. Date of Issue.

1. Airline Identification

It includes the name and three-digit number of the issuing carrier. The first carrier in the itinerary is identified as the issuing carrier. In some cases, a carrier other than one in the itinerary may be used to validate a ticket. For instance, tickets can sometime be issued on IATA stock for travel on a foreign carrier, using a domestic carrier as the issuing airline.

2. The Place of Issue

It identifies the location where the ticket was written. If a ticket is written by a travel agent, the travel agency's name, location and IATA number must be imprinted on the face of the ticket.

3. The Date of Issue

The date of issue must also appear on the ticket.

The ticket validator, an imprinting machine, is used to validate the tickets. The validator imprints the airline identification, and agency identification in the proper place on the ticket. Each airline provides an identification or validation plate that can be used with a ticket validator. Machine tickets may be validated automatically. A ticket may be validated at the time it is printed, in this case, the machine validation is not required. When a ticket is validated by an agent, it has the same value as any ticket issued by the validating machine.

Validity Indicator for Special Fares

This information is to be used in conjunction with *Fare Notes*.

To determine the final date of validity of a ticket, find the date of the month on which travel starts Excess mileage percentage, and then read across to the date in the appropriate 21/30/45/90/120/180/270 day column.

Monthly Tickets

The final date of validity for a ticket valid one calendar month is the same date in the following month as the date of commencement of travel.

Exception

Where the commencement date is the last day of the month, the final date of validity is the last day of the next month.

Table 4.7 is an imaginary calendar indicating ticket validity for 21, 30, 45, 90, 120, 180 and 270 days.

Table 4.7: Validity Indicator for Special Fares

	January						
	Date of Expiry (Ticket Validity)						
	Number of days						
	21	30	45	90	120	180	270
1	22 Jan	31 Jan	15 Feb	1 Apr	1 May	30 Jun	28 Sep
2	23 Jan	1 Feb	16 Feb	2 Apr	2 May	1 Jul	29 Sep
3	24 Jan	2 Feb	17 Feb	3 Apr	3 May	2 Jul	30 Sep
4	25 Jan	3 Feb	18 Feb	4 Apr	4 May	3 Jul	1 Oct
5	26 Jan	4 Feb	19 Feb	5 Apr	5 May	4 Jul	2 Oct
6	27 Jan	5 Feb	20 Feb	6 Apr	6 May	5 Jul	3 Oct
7	28 Jan	6 Feb	21 Feb	7 Apr	7 May	6 Jul	4 Oct
8	29 Jan	7 Feb	22 Feb	8 Apr	8 May	7 Jul	5 Oct
9	30 Jan	8 Feb	23 Feb	9 Apr	9 May	8 Jul	6 Oct
10	31 Jan	9 Feb	24 Feb	10 Apr	10 May	9 Jul	7 Oct
11	1 Feb	10 Feb	25 Feb	11 Apr	11 May	10 Jul	8 Oct
12	2 Feb	11 Feb	26 Feb	12 Apr	12 May	11 Jul	9 Oct
13	3 Feb	12 Feb	27 Feb	13 Apr	13 May	12 Jul	10 Oct
14	4 Feb	13 Feb	28 Feb	14 Apr	14 May	13 Jul	11 Oct
15	5 Feb	14 Feb	1 Mar	15 Apr	15 May	14 Jul	12 Oct
16	6 Feb	15 Feb	2 Mar	16 Apr	16 May	15 Jul	13 Oct
17	7 Feb	16 Feb	3 Mar	17 Apr	17 May	16 Jul	14 Oct
18	8 Feb	17 Feb	4 Mar	18 Apr	18 May	17 Jul	15 Oct
19	9 Feb	18 Feb	5 Mar	19 Apr	19 May	18 Jul	16 Oct
20	10 Feb	19 Feb	6 Mar	20 Apr	20 May	19 Jul	17 Oct
21	11 Feb	20 Feb	7 Mar	21 Apr	21 May	20 Jul	18 Oct
22	12 Feb	21 Feb	8 Mar	22 Apr	22 May	21 Jul	19 Oct
23	13 Feb	22 Feb	9 Mar	23 Apr	23 May	22 Jul	20 Oct
24	14 Feb	23 Feb	10 Mar	24 Apr	24 May	23 Jul	21 Oct
25	15 Feb	24 Feb	11 Mar	25 Apr	25 May	24 Jul	22 Oct
26	16 Feb	25 Feb	12 Mar	26 Apr	26 May	25 Jul	23 Oct
27	17 Feb	26 Feb	13 Mar	27 Apr	27 May	26 Jul	24 Oct
28	18 Feb	27 Feb	14 Mar	28 Apr	28 May	27 Jul	25 Oct
29	19 Feb	28 Feb	15 Mar	29 Apr	29 May	28 Jul	26 Oct
30	20 Feb	1 Mar	16 Mar	30 Apr	30 May	29 Jul	27 Oct
31	21 Feb	2 Mar	17 Mar	1 May	31 May	30 Jul	28 Oct

(Contd.)

(Contd.)

Fabruary

Date of Expiry (Ticket Validity)

Number of days

	21	30	45	90	120	180	270
1	22 Feb	3 Mar	18 Mar	2 May	1 Jun	31 Jul	29 Oct
2	23 Feb	4 Mar	19 Mar	3 May	2 Jun	1 Aug	30 Oct
3	24 Feb	5 Mar	20 Mar	4 May	3 Jun	2 Aug	31 Oct
4	25 Feb	6 Mar	21 Mar	5 May	4 Jun	3 Aug	1 Nov
5	26 Feb	7 Mar	22 Mar	6 May	5 Jun	4 Aug	2 Nov
6	27 Feb	8 Mar	23 Mar	7 May	6 Jun	5 Aug	3 Nov
7	28 Feb	9 Mar	24 Mar	8 May	7 Jun	6 Aug	4 Nov
8	1 Mar	10 Mar	25 Mar	9 May	8 Jun	7 Aug	5 Nov
9	2 Mar	11 Mar	26 Mar	10 May	9 Jun	8 Aug	6 Nov
10	3 Mar	12 Mar	27 Mar	11 May	10 Jun	9 Aug	7 Nov
11	4 Mar	13 Mar	28 Mar	12 May	11 Jun	10 Aug	8 Nov
12	5 Mar	14 Mar	29 Mar	13 May	12 Jun	11 Aug	9 Nov
13	6 Mar	15 Mar	30 Mar	14 May	13 Jun	12 Aug	10 Nov
14	7 Mar	16 Mar	31 Mar	15 May	14 Jun	13 Aug	11 Nov
15	8 Mar	17 Mar	1 Apr	16 May	15 Jun	14 Aug	12 Nov
16	9 Mar	18 Mar	2 Apr	17 May	16 Jun	15 Aug	13 Nov
17	10 Mar	19 Mar	3 Apr	18 May	17 Jun	16 Aug	14 Nov
18	11 Mar	20 Mar	4 Apr	19 May	18 Jun	17 Aug	15 Nov
19	12 Mar	21 Mar	5 Apr	20 May	19 Jun	18 Aug	16 Nov
20	13 Mar	22 Mar	6 Apr	21 May	20 Jun	19 Aug	17 Nov
21	14 Mar	23 Mar	7 Apr	22 May	21 Jun	20 Aug	18 Nov
22	15 Mar	24 Mar	8 Apr	23 May	22 Jun	21 Aug	19 Nov
23	16 Mar	25 Mar	9 Apr	24 May	23 Jun	22 Aug	20 Nov
24	17 Mar	26 Mar	10 Apr	25 May	24 Jun	23 Aug	21 Nov
25	18 Mar	27 Mar	11 Apr	26 May	25 Jun	24 Aug	22 Nov
26	19 Mar	28 Mar	12 Apr	27 May	26 Jun	25 Aug	23 Nov
27	20 Mar	29 Mar	13 Apr	28 May	27 Jun	26 Aug	24 Nov
28	21 Mar	30 Mar	14 Apr	29 May	28 Jun	27 Aug	25 Nov

(Contd.)

(Contd.)

	March *Date of Expiry (Ticket Validity)* Number of days						
	21	30	45	90	120	180	270
1	22 Mar	31 Mar	15 Apr	30 May	29 Jun	28 Aug	26 Nov
2	23 Mar	1 Apr	16 Apr	31 May	30 Jun	29 Aug	27 Nov
3	24 Mar	2 Apr	17 Apr	1 Jun	1 Jul	30 Aug	28 Nov
4	25 Mar	3 Apr	18 Apr	2 Jun	2 Jul	31 Aug	29 Nov
5	26 Mar	4 Apr	19 Apr	3 Jun	3 Jul	1 Sep	30 Nov
6	27 Mar	5 Apr	20 Apr	4 Jun	4 Jul	2 Sep	1 Dec
7	28 Mar	6 Apr	21 Apr	5 Jun	5 Jul	3 Sep	2 Dec
8	29 Mar	7 Apr	22 Apr	6 Jun	6 Jul	4 Sep	3 Dec
9	30 Mar	8 Apr	23 Apr	7 Jun	7 Jul	5 Sep	4 Dec
10	31 Mar	9 Apr	24 Apr	8 Jun	8 Jul	6 Sep	5 Dec
11	1 Apr	10 Apr	25 Apr	9 Jun	9 Jul	7 Sep	6 Dec
12	2 Apr	11 Apr	26 Apr	10 Jun	10 Jul	8 Sep	7 Dec
13	3 Apr	12 Apr	27 Apr	11 Jun	11 Jul	9 Sep	8 Dec
14	4 Apr	13 Apr	28 Apr	12 Jun	12 Jul	10 Sep	9 Dec
15	5 Apr	14 Apr	29 Apr	13 Jun	13 Jul	11 Sep	10 Dec
16	6 Apr	15 Apr	30 Apr	14 Jun	14 Jul	12 Sep	11 Dec
17	7 Apr	16 Apr	1 May	15 Jun	15 Jul	13 Sep	12 Dec
18	8 Apr	17 Apr	2 May	16 Jun	16 Jul	14 Sep	13 Dec
19	9 Apr	18 Apr	3 May	17 Jun	17 Jul	15 Sep	14 Dec
20	10 Apr	19 Apr	4 May	18 Jun	18 Jul	16 Sep	15 Dec
21	11 Apr	20 Apr	5 May	19 Jun	19 Jul	17 Sep	16 Dec
22	12 Apr	21 Apr	6 May	20 Jun	20 Jul	18 Sep	17 Dec
23	13 Apr	22 Apr	7 May	21 Jun	21 Jul	19 Sep	18 Dec
24	14 Apr	23 Apr	8 May	22 Jun	22 Jul	20 Sep	19 Dec
25	15 Apr	24 Apr	9 May	23 Jun	23 Jul	21 Sep	20 Dec
26	16 Apr	25 Apr	10 May	24 Jun	24 Jul	22 Sep	21 Dec
27	17 Apr	26 Apr	11 May	25 Jun	25 Jul	23 Sep	22 Dec
28	18 Apr	27 Apr	12 May	26 Jun	26 Jul	24 Sep	23 Dec
29	19 Apr	28 Apr	13 May	27 Jun	27 Jul	25 Sep	24 Dec
30	20 Apr	29 Apr	14 May	28 Jun	28 Jul	26 Sep	25 Dec
31	21 Apr	30 Apr	15 May	29 Jun	29 Jul	27 Sep	26 Dec

(Contd.)

(Contd.)

April

Date of Expiry (Ticket Validity)

Number of days

	21	30	45	90	120	180	270
1	22 Apr	1 May	16 May	30 Jun	30 Jul	28 Sep	27 Dec
2	23 Apr	2 May	17 May	1 Jul	31 Jul	29 Sep	28 Dec
3	24 Apr	3 May	18 May	2 Jul	1 Aug	30 Sep	29 Dec
4	25 Apr	4 May	19 May	3 Jul	2 Aug	1 Oct	30 Dec
5	26 Apr	5 May	20 May	4 Jul	3 Aug	2 Oct	31 Dec
6	27 Apr	6 May	21 May	5 Jul	4 Aug	3 Oct	1 Jan
7	28 Apr	7 May	22 May	6 Jul	5 Aug	4 Oct	2 Jan
8	29 Apr	8 May	23 May	7 Jul	6 Aug	5 Oct	3 Jan
9	30 Apr	9 May	24 May	8 Jul	7 Aug	6 Oct	4 Jan
10	1 May	10 May	25 May	9 Jul	8 Aug	7 Oct	5 Jan
11	2 May	11 May	26 May	10 Jul	9 Aug	8 Oct	6 Jan
12	3 May	12 May	27 May	11 Jul	10 Aug	9 Oct	7 Jan
13	4 May	13 May	28 May	12 Jul	11 Aug	10 Oct	8 Jan
14	5 May	14 May	29 May	13 Jul	12 Aug	11 Oct	9 Jan
15	6 May	15 May	30 May	14 Jul	13 Aug	12 Oct	10 Jan
16	7 May	16 May	31 May	15 Jul	14 Aug	13 Oct	11 Jan
17	8 May	17 May	1 Jun	16 Jul	15 Aug	14 Oct	12 Jan
18	9 May	18 May	2 Jun	17 Jul	16 Aug	15 Oct	13 Jan
19	10 May	19 May	3 Jun	18 Jul	17 Aug	16 Oct	14 Jan
20	11 May	20 May	4 Jun	19 Jul	18 Aug	17 Oct	15 Jan
21	12 May	21 May	5 Jun	20 Jul	19 Aug	18 Oct	16 Jan
22	13 May	22 May	6 Jun	21 Jul	20 Aug	19 Oct	17 Jan
23	14 May	23 May	7 Jun	22 Jul	21 Aug	20 Oct	18 Jan
24	15 May	24 May	8 Jun	23 Jul	22 Aug	21 Oct	19 Jan
25	16 May	25 May	9 Jun	24 Jul	23 Aug	22 Oct	20 Jan
26	17 May	26 May	10 Jun	25 Jul	24 Aug	23 Oct	21 Jan
27	18 May	27 May	11 Jun	26 Jul	25 Aug	24 Oct	22 Jan
28	19 May	28 May	12 Jun	27 Jul	26 Aug	25 Oct	23 Jan
29	20 May	29 May	13 Jun	28 Jul	27 Aug	26 Oct	24 Jan
30	21 May	30 May	14 Jun	29 Jul	28 Aug	27 Oct	25 Jan

(Contd.)

(*Contd.*)

May

Date of Expiry (Ticket Validity)

Number of days

	21	30	45	90	120	180	270
1	22 May	31 May	15 Jun	30 Jul	29 Aug	28 Oct	26 Jan
2	23 May	1 Jun	16 Jun	31 Jul	30 Aug	29 Oct	27 Jan
3	24 May	2 Jun	17 Jun	1 Aug	31 Aug	30 Oct	28 Jan
4	25 May	3 Jun	18 Jun	2 Aug	1 Sep	31 Oct	29 Jan
5	26 May	4 Jun	19 Jun	3 Aug	2 Sep	1 Nov	30 Jan
6	27 May	5 Jun	20 Jun	4 Aug	3 Sep	2 Nov	31 Jan
7	28 May	6 Jun	21 Jun	5 Aug	4 Sep	3 Nov	1 Feb
8	29 May	7 Jun	22 Jun	6 Aug	5 Sep	4 Nov	2 Feb
9	30 May	8 Jun	23 Jun	7 Aug	6 Sep	5 Nov	3 Feb
10	31 May	9 Jun	24 Jun	8 Aug	7 Sep	6 Nov	4 Feb
11	1 Jun	10 Jun	25 Jun	9 Aug	8 Sep	7 Nov	5 Feb
12	2 Jun	11 Jun	26 Jun	10 Aug	9 Sep	8 Nov	6 Feb
13	3 Jun	12 Jun	27 Jun	11 Aug	10 Sep	9 Nov	7 Feb
14	4 Jun	13 Jun	28 Jun	12 Aug	11 Sep	10 Nov	8 Feb
15	5 Jun	14 Jun	29 Jun	13 Aug	12 Sep	11 Nov	9 Feb
16	6 Jun	15 Jun	30 Jun	14 Aug	13 Sep	12 Nov	10 Feb
17	7 Jun	16 Jun	1 Jul	15 Aug	14 Sep	13 Nov	11 Feb
18	8 Jun	17 Jun	2 Jul	16 Aug	15 Sep	14 Nov	12 Feb
19	9 Jun	18 Jun	3 Jul	17 Aug	16 Sep	15 Nov	13 Feb
20	10 Jun	19 Jun	4 Jul	18 Aug	17 Sep	16 Nov	14 Feb
21	11 Jun	20 Jun	5 Jul	19 Aug	18 Sep	17 Nov	15 Feb
22	12 Jun	21 Jun	6 Jul	20 Aug	19 Sep	18 Nov	16 Feb
23	13 Jun	22 Jun	7 Jul	21 Aug	20 Sep	19 Nov	17 Feb
24	14 Jun	23 Jun	8 Jul	22 Aug	21 Sep	20 Nov	18 Feb
25	15 Jun	24 Jun	9 Jul	23 Aug	22 Sep	21 Nov	19 Feb
26	16 Jun	25 Jun	10 Jul	24 Aug	23 Sep	22 Nov	20 Feb
27	17 Jun	26 Jun	11 Jul	25 Aug	24 Sep	23 Nov	21 Feb
28	18 Jun	27 Jun	12 Jul	26 Aug	25 Sep	24 Nov	22 Feb
29	19 Jun	28 Jun	13 Jul	27 Aug	26 Sep	25 Nov	23 Feb
30	20 Jun	29 Jun	14 Jul	28 Aug	27 Sep	26 Nov	24 Feb
31	21 Jun	30 Jun	15 Jul	29 Aug	28 Sep	27 Nov	25 Feb

(*Contd.*)

(*Contd.*)

	June *Date of Expiry (Ticket Validity)* Number of days						
	21	30	45	90	120	180	270
1	22 Jun	1 Jul	16 Jul	30 Aug	29 Sep	28 Nov	26 Feb
2	23 Jun	2 Jul	17 Jul	31 Aug	30 Sep	29 Nov	27 Feb
3	24 Jun	3 Jul	18 Jul	1 Sep	1 Oct	30 Nov	28 Feb
4	25 Jun	4 Jul	19 Jul	2 Sep	2 Oct	1 Dec	1 Mar
5	26 Jun	5 Jul	20 Jul	3 Sep	3 Oct	2 Dec	2 Mar
6	27 Jun	6 Jul	21 Jul	4 Sep	4 Oct	3 Dec	3 Mar
7	28 Jun	7 Jul	22 Jul	5 Sep	5 Oct	4 Dec	4 Mar
8	29 Jun	8 Jul	23 Jul	6 Sep	6 Oct	5 Dec	5 Mar
9	30 Jun	9 Jul	24 Jul	7 Sep	7 Oct	6 Dec	6 Mar
10	1 Jul	10 Jul	25 Jul	8 Sep	8 Oct	7 Dec	7 Mar
11	2 Jul	11 Jul	26 Jul	9 Sep	9 Oct	8 Dec	8 Mar
12	3 Jul	12 Jul	27 Jul	10 Sep	10 Oct	9 Dec	9 Mar
13	4 Jul	13 Jul	28 Jul	11 Sep	11 Oct	10 Dec	10 Mar
14	5 Jul	14 Jul	29 Jul	12 Sep	12 Oct	11 Dec	11 Mar
15	6 Jul	15 Jul	30 Jul	13 Sep	13 Oct	12 Dec	12 Mar
16	7 Jul	16 Jul	31 Jul	14 Sep	14 Oct	13 Dec	13 Mar
17	8 Jul	17 Jul	1 Aug	15 Sep	15 Oct	14 Dec	14 Mar
18	9 Jul	18 Jul	2 Aug	16 Sep	16 Oct	15 Dec	15 Mar
19	10 Jul	19 Jul	3 Aug	17 Sep	17 Oct	16 Dec	16 Mar
20	11 Jul	20 Jul	4 Aug	18 Sep	18 Oct	17 Dec	17 Mar
21	12 Jul	21 Jul	5 Aug	19 Sep	19 Oct	18 Dec	18 Mar
22	13 Jul	22 Jul	6 Aug	20 Sep	20 Oct	19 Dec	19 Mar
23	14 Jul	23 Jul	7 Aug	21 Sep	21 Oct	20 Dec	20 Mar
24	15 Jul	24 Jul	8 Aug	22 Sep	22 Oct	21 Dec	21 Mar
25	16 Jul	25 Jul	9 Aug	23 Sep	23 Oct	22 Dec	22 Mar
26	17 Jul	26 Jul	10 Aug	24 Sep	24 Oct	23 Dec	23 Mar
27	18 Jul	27 Jul	11 Aug	25 Sep	25 Oct	24 Dec	24 Mar
28	19 Jul	28 Jul	12 Aug	26 Sep	26 Oct	25 Dec	25 Mar
29	20 Jul	29 Jul	13 Aug	27 Sep	27 Oct	26 Dec	26 Mar
30	21 Jul	30 Jul	14 Aug	28 Sep	28 Oct	27 Dec	27 Mar

(*Contd.*)

(*Contd.*)

July

Date of Expiry (Ticket Validity)

Number of days

	21	30	45	90	120	180	270
1	22 Jul	31 Jul	15 Aug	29 Sep	29 Oct	28 Dec	28 Mar
2	23 Jul	1 Aug	16 Aug	30 Sep	30 Oct	29 Dec	29 Mar
3	24 Jul	2 Aug	17 Aug	1 Oct	31 Oct	30 Dec	30 Mar
4	25 Jul	3 Aug	18 Aug	2 Oct	1 Nov	31 Dec	31 Mar
5	26 Jul	4 Aug	19 Aug	3 Oct	2 Nov	1 Jan	1 Apr
6	27 Jul	5 Aug	20 Aug	4 Oct	3 Nov	2 Jan	2 Apr
7	28 Jul	6 Aug	21 Aug	5 Oct	4 Nov	3 Jan	3 Apr
8	29 Jul	7 Aug	22 Aug	6 Oct	5 Nov	4 Jan	4 Apr
9	30 Jul	8 Aug	23 Aug	7 Oct	6 Nov	5 Jan	5 Apr
10	31 Jul	9 Aug	24 Aug	8 Oct	7 Nov	6 Jan	6 Apr
11	1 Aug	10 Aug	25 Aug	9 Oct	8 Nov	7 Jan	7 Apr
12	2 Aug	11 Aug	26 Aug	10 Oct	9 Nov	8 Jan	8 Apr
13	3 Aug	12 Aug	27 Aug	11 Oct	10 Nov	9 Jan	9 Apr
14	4 Aug	13 Aug	28 Aug	12 Oct	11 Nov	10 Jan	10 Apr
15	5 Aug	14 Aug	29 Aug	13 Oct	12 Nov	11 Jan	11 Apr
16	6 Aug	15 Aug	30 Aug	14 Oct	13 Nov	12 Jan	12 Apr
17	7 Aug	16 Aug	31 Aug	15 Oct	14 Nov	13 Jan	13 Apr
18	8 Aug	17 Aug	1 Sep	16 Oct	15 Nov	14 Jan	14 Apr
19	9 Aug	18 Aug	2 Sep	17 Oct	16 Nov	15 Jan	15 Apr
20	10 Aug	19 Aug	3 Sep	18 Oct	17 Nov	16 Jan	16 Apr
21	11 Aug	20 Aug	4 Sep	19 Oct	18 Nov	17 Jan	17 Apr
22	12 Aug	21 Aug	5 Sep	20 Oct	19 Nov	18 Jan	18 Apr
23	13 Aug	22 Aug	6 Sep	21 Oct	20 Nov	19 Jan	19 Apr
24	14 Aug	23 Aug	7 Sep	22 Oct	21 Nov	20 Jan	20 Apr
25	15 Aug	24 Aug	8 Sep	23 Oct	22 Nov	21 Jan	21 Apr
26	16 Aug	25 Aug	9 Sep	24 Oct	23 Nov	22 Jan	22 Apr
27	17 Aug	26 Aug	10 Sep	25 Oct	24 Nov	23 Jan	23 Apr
28	18 Aug	27 Aug	11 Sep	26 Oct	25 Nov	24 Jan	24 Apr
29	19 Aug	28 Aug	12 Sep	27 Oct	26 Nov	25 Jan	25 Apr
30	20 Aug	29 Aug	13 Sep	28 Oct	27 Nov	26 Jan	26 Apr
31	21 Aug	30 Aug	14 Sep	29 Oct	28 Nov	27 Jan	27 Apr

(*Contd.*)

(Contd.)

	August						
	Date of Expiry (Ticket Validity)						
	Number of days						
	21	30	45	90	120	180	270
1	22 Aug	31 Aug	15 Sep	30 Oct	29 Nov	28 Jan	28 Apr
2	23 Aug	1 Sep	16 Sep	31 Oct	30 Nov	29 Jan	29 Apr
3	24 Aug	2 Sep	17 Sep	1 Nov	1 Dec	30 Jan	30 Apr
4	25 Aug	3 Sep	18 Sep	2 Nov	2 Dec	31 Jan	1 May
5	26 Aug	4 Sep	19 Sep	3 Nov	3 Dec	1 Feb	2 May
6	27 Aug	5 Sep	20 Sep	4 Nov	4 Dec	2 Feb	3 May
7	28 Aug	6 Sep	21 Sep	5 Nov	5 Dec	3 Feb	4 May
8	29 Aug	7 Sep	22 Sep	6 Nov	6 Dec	4 Feb	5 May
9	30 Aug	8 Sep	23 Sep	7 Nov	7 Dec	5 Feb	6 May
10	31 Aug	9 Sep	24 Sep	8 Nov	8 Dec	6 Feb	7 May
11	1 Sep	10 Sep	25 Sep	9 Nov	9 Dec	7 Feb	8 May
12	2 Sep	11 Sep	26 Sep	10 Nov	10 Dec	8 Feb	9 May
13	3 Sep	12 Sep	27 Sep	11 Nov	11 Dec	9 Feb	10 May
14	4 Sep	13 Sep	28 Sep	12 Nov	12 Dec	10 Feb	11 May
15	5 Sep	14 Sep	29 Sep	13 Nov	13 Dec	11 Feb	12 May
16	6 Sep	15 Sep	30 Sep	14 Nov	14 Dec	12 Feb	13 May
17	7 Sep	16 Sep	1 Oct	15 Nov	15 Dec	13 Feb	14 May
18	8 Sep	17 Sep	2 Oct	16 Nov	16 Dec	14 Feb	15 May
19	9 Sep	18 Sep	3 Oct	17 Nov	17 Dec	15 Feb	16 May
20	10 Sep	19 Sep	4 Oct	18 Nov	18 Dec	16 Feb	17 May
21	11 Sep	20 Sep	5 Oct	19 Nov	19 Dec	17 Feb	18 May
22	12 Sep	21 Sep	6 Oct	20 Nov	20 Dec	18 Feb	19 May
23	13 Sep	22 Sep	7 Oct	21 Nov	21 Dec	19 Feb	20 May
24	14 Sep	23 Sep	8 Oct	22 Nov	22 Dec	20 Feb	21 May
25	15 Sep	24 Sep	9 Oct	23 Nov	23 Dec	21 Feb	22 May
26	16 Sep	25 Sep	10 Oct	24 Nov	24 Dec	22 Feb	23 May
27	17 Sep	26 Sep	11 Oct	25 Nov	25 Dec	23 Feb	24 May
28	18 Sep	27 Sep	12 Oct	26 Nov	26 Dec	24 Feb	25 May
29	19 Sep	28 Sep	13 Oct	27 Nov	27 Dec	25 Feb	26 May
30	20 Sep	29 Sep	14 Oct	28 Nov	28 Dec	26 Feb	27 May
31	21 Sep	30 Sep	15 Oct	29 Nov	29 Dec	27 Feb	28 May

(Contd.)

(*Contd.*)

September

Date of Expiry (Ticket Validity)

Number of days

	21	30	45	90	120	180	270
1	22 Sep	1 Oct	16 Oct	30 Nov	30 Dec	28 Feb	29 May
2	23 Sep	2 Oct	17 Oct	1 Dec	31 Dec	1 Mar	30 May
3	24 Sep	3 Oct	18 Oct	2 Dec	1 Jan	2 Mar	31 May
4	25 Sep	4 Oct	19 Oct	3 Dec	2 Jan	3 Mar	1 Jun
5	26 Sep	5 Oct	20 Oct	4 Dec	3 Jan	4 Mar	2 Jun
6	27 Sep	6 Oct	21 Oct	5 Dec	4 Jan	5 Mar	3 Jun
7	28 Sep	7 Oct	22 Oct	6 Dec	5 Jan	6 Mar	4 Jun
8	29 Sep	8 Oct	23 Oct	7 Dec	6 Jan	7 Mar	5 Jun
9	30 Sep	9 Oct	24 Oct	8 Dec	7 Jan	8 Mar	6 Jun
10	1 Oct	10 Oct	25 Oct	9 Dec	8 Jan	9 Mar	7 Jun
11	2 Oct	11 Oct	26 Oct	10 Dec	9 Jan	10 Mar	8 Jun
12	3 Oct	12 Oct	27 Oct	11 Dec	10 Jan	11 Mar	9 Jun
13	4 Oct	13 Oct	28 Oct	12 Dec	11 Jan	12 Mar	10 Jun
14	5 Oct	14 Oct	29 Oct	13 Dec	12 Jan	13 Mar	11 Jun
15	6 Oct	15 Oct	30 Oct	14 Dec	13 Jan	14 Mar	12 Jun
16	7 Oct	16 Oct	31 Oct	15 Dec	14 Jan	15 Mar	13 Jun
17	8 Oct	17 Oct	1 Nov	16 Dec	15 Jan	16 Mar	14 Jun
18	9 Oct	18 Oct	2 Nov	17 Dec	16 Jan	17 Mar	15 Jun
19	10 Oct	19 Oct	3 Nov	18 Dec	17 Jan	18 Mar	16 Jun
20	11 Oct	20 Oct	4 Nov	19 Dec	18 Jan	19 Mar	17 Jun
21	12 Oct	21 Oct	5 Nov	20 Dec	19 Jan	20 Mar	18 Jun
22	13 Oct	22 Oct	6 Nov	21 Dec	20 Jan	21 Mar	19 Jun
23	14 Oct	23 Oct	7 Nov	22 Dec	21 Jan	22 Mar	20 Jun
24	15 Oct	24 Oct	8 Nov	23 Dec	22 Jan	23 Mar	21 Jun
25	16 Oct	25 Oct	9 Nov	24 Dec	23 Jan	24 Mar	22 Jun
26	17 Oct	26 Oct	10 Nov	25 Dec	24 Jan	25 Mar	23 Jun
27	18 Oct	27 Oct	11 Nov	26 Dec	25 Jan	26 Mar	24 Jun
28	19 Oct	28 Oct	12 Nov	27 Dec	26 Jan	27 Mar	25 Jun
29	20 Oct	29 Oct	13 Nov	28 Dec	27 Jan	28 Mar	26 Jun
30	21 Oct	30 Oct	14 Nov	29 Dec	28 Jan	29 Mar	27 Jun

(*Contd.*)

(Contd.)

	October *Date of Expiry (Ticket Validity)* Number of days						
	21	30	45	90	120	180	270
1	22 Oct	31 Oct	15 Nov	30 Dec	29 Jan	30 Mar	28 Jun
2	23 Oct	1 Nov	16 Nov	31 Dec	30 Jan	31 Mar	29 Jun
3	24 Oct	2 Nov	17 Nov	1 Jan	31 Jan	1 Apr	30 Jun
4	25 Oct	3 Nov	18 Nov	2 Jan	1 Feb	2 Apr	1 Jul
5	26 Oct	4 Nov	19 Nov	3 Jan	2 Feb	3 Apr	2 Jul
6	27 Oct	5 Nov	20 Nov	4 Jan	3 Feb	4 Apr	3 Jul
7	28 Oct	6 Nov	21 Nov	5 Jan	4 Feb	5 Apr	4 Jul
8	29 Oct	7 Nov	22 Nov	6 Jan	5 Feb	6 Apr	5 Jul
9	30 Oct	8 Nov	23 Nov	7 Jan	6 Feb	7 Apr	6 Jul
10	31 Oct	9 Nov	24 Nov	8 Jan	7 Feb	8 Apr	7 Jul
11	1 Nov	10 Nov	25 Nov	9 Jan	8 Feb	9 Apr	8 Jul
12	2 Nov	11 Nov	26 Nov	10 Jan	9 Feb	10 Apr	9 Jul
13	3 Nov	12 Nov	27 Nov	11 Jan	10 Feb	11 Apr	10 Jul
14	4 Nov	13 Nov	28 Nov	12 Jan	11 Feb	12 Apr	11 Jul
15	5 Nov	14 Nov	29 Nov	13 Jan	12 Feb	13 Apr	12 Jul
16	6 Nov	15 Nov	30 Nov	14 Jan	13 Feb	14 Apr	13 Jul
17	7 Nov	16 Nov	1 Dec	15 Jan	14 Feb	15 Apr	14 Jul
18	8 Nov	17 Nov	2 Dec	16 Jan	15 Feb	16 Apr	15 Jul
19	9 Nov	18 Nov	3 Dec	17 Jan	16 Feb	17 Apr	16 Jul
20	10 Nov	19 Nov	4 Dec	18 Jan	17 Feb	18 Apr	17 Jul
21	11 Nov	20 Nov	5 Dec	19 Jan	18 Feb	19 Apr	18 Jul
22	12 Nov	21 Nov	6 Dec	20 Jan	19 Feb	20 Apr	19 Jul
23	13 Nov	22 Nov	7 Dec	21 Jan	20 Feb	21 Apr	20 Jul
24	14 Nov	23 Nov	8 Dec	22 Jan	21 Feb	22 Apr	21 Jul
25	15 Nov	24 Nov	9 Dec	23 Jan	22 Feb	23 Apr	22 Jul
26	16 Nov	25 Nov	10 Dec	24 Jan	23 Feb	24 Apr	23 Jul
27	17 Nov	26 Nov	11 Dec	25 Jan	24 Feb	25 Apr	24 Jul
28	18 Nov	27 Nov	12 Dec	26 Jan	25 Feb	26 Apr	25 Jul
29	19 Nov	28 Nov	13 Dec	27 Jan	26 Feb	27 Apr	26 Jul
30	20 Nov	29 Nov	14 Dec	28 Jan	27 Feb	28 Apr	27 Jul
31	21 Nov	30 Nov	15 Dec	29 Jan	28 Feb	29 Apr	28 Jul

(Contd.)

(*Contd.*)

November *Date of Expiry (Ticket Validity)* Number of days	21	30	45	90	120	180	270
1	22 Nov	1 Dec	16 Dec	30 Jan	1 Mar	30 Apr	29 Jul
2	23 Nov	2 Dec	17 Dec	31 Jan	2 Mar	1 May	30 Jul
3	24 Nov	3 Dec	18 Dec	1 Feb	3 Mar	2 May	31 Jul
4	25 Nov	4 Dec	19 Dec	2 Feb	4 Mar	3 May	1 Aug
5	26 Nov	5 Dec	20 Dec	3 Feb	5 Mar	4 May	2 Aug
6	27 Nov	6 Dec	21 Dec	4 Feb	6 Mar	5 May	3 Aug
7	28 Nov	7 Dec	22 Dec	5 Feb	7 Mar	6 May	4 Aug
8	29 Nov	8 Dec	23 Dec	6 Feb	8 Mar	7 May	5 Aug
9	30 Nov	9 Dec	24 Dec	7 Feb	9 Mar	8 May	6 Aug
10	1 Dec	10 Dec	25 Dec	8 Feb	10 Mar	9 May	7 Aug
11	2 Dec	11 Dec	26 Dec	9 Feb	11 Mar	10 May	8 Aug
12	3 Dec	12 Dec	27 Dec	10 Feb	12 Mar	11 May	9 Aug
13	4 Dec	13 Dec	28 Dec	11 Feb	13 Mar	12 May	10 Aug
14	5 Dec	14 Dec	29 Dec	12 Feb	14 Mar	13 May	11 Aug
15	6 Dec	15 Dec	30 Dec	13 Feb	15 Mar	14 May	12 Aug
16	7 Dec	16 Dec	31 Dec	14 Feb	16 Mar	15 May	13 Aug
17	8 Dec	17 Dec	1 Jan	15 Feb	17 Mar	16 May	14 Aug
18	9 Dec	18 Dec	2 Jan	16 Feb	18 Mar	17 May	15 Aug
19	10 Dec	19 Dec	3 Jan	17 Feb	19 Mar	18 May	16 Aug
20	11 Dec	20 Dec	4 Jan	18 Feb	20 Mar	19 May	17 Aug
21	12 Dec	21 Dec	5 Jan	19 Feb	21 Mar	20 May	18 Aug
22	13 Dec	22 Dec	6 Jan	20 Feb	22 Mar	21 May	19 Aug
23	14 Dec	23 Dec	7 Jan	21 Feb	23 Mar	22 May	20 Aug
24	15 Dec	24 Dec	8 Jan	22 Feb	24 Mar	23 May	21 Aug
25	16 Dec	25 Dec	9 Jan	23 Feb	25 Mar	24 May	22 Aug
26	17 Dec	26 Dec	10 Jan	24 Feb	26 Mar	25 May	23 Aug
27	18 Dec	27 Dec	11 Jan	25 Feb	27 Mar	26 May	24 Aug
28	19 Dec	28 Dec	12 Jan	26 Feb	28 Mar	27 May	25 Aug
29	20 Dec	29 Dec	13 Jan	27 Feb	29 Mar	28 May	26 Aug
30	21 Dec	30 Dec	14 Jan	28 Feb	30 Mar	29 May	27 Aug

(*Contd.*)

(*Contd.*)

December

Date of Expiry (Ticket Validity)

Number of days

	21	30	45	90	120	180	270
1	22 Dec	31 Dec	15 Jan	1 Mar	31 Mar	30 May	28 Aug
2	23 Dec	1 Jan	16 Jan	2 Mar	1 Apr	31 May	29 Aug
3	24 Dec	2 Jan	17 Jan	3 Mar	2 Apr	1 Jun	30 Aug
4	25 Dec	3 Jan	18 Jan	4 Mar	3 Apr	2 Jun	31 Aug
5	26 Dec	4 Jan	19 Jan	5 Mar	4 Apr	3 Jun	1 Sep
6	27 Dec	5 Jan	20 Jan	6 Mar	5 Apr	4 Jun	2 Sep
7	28 Dec	6 Jan	21 Jan	7 Mar	6 Apr	5 Jun	3 Sep
8	29 Dec	7 Jan	22 Jan	8 Mar	7 Apr	6 Jun	4 Sep
9	30 Dec	8 Jan	23 Jan	9 Mar	8 Apr	7 Jun	5 Sep
10	31 Dec	9 Jan	24 Jan	10 Mar	9 Apr	8 Jun	6 Sep
11	1 Jan	10 Jan	25 Jan	11 Mar	10 Apr	9 Jun	7 Sep
12	2 Jan	11 Jan	26 Jan	12 Mar	11 Apr	10 Jun	8 Sep
13	3 Jan	12 Jan	27 Jan	13 Mar	12 Apr	11 Jun	9 Sep
14	4 Jan	13 Jan	28 Jan	14 Mar	13 Apr	12 Jun	10 Sep
15	5 Jan	14 Jan	29 Jan	15 Mar	14 Apr	13 Jun	11 Sep
16	6 Jan	15 Jan	30 Jan	16 Mar	15 Apr	14 Jun	12 Sep
17	7 Jan	16 Jan	31 Jan	17 Mar	16 Apr	15 Jun	13 Sep
18	8 Jan	17 Jan	1 Feb	18 Mar	17 Apr	16 Jun	14 Sep
19	9 Jan	18 Jan	2 Feb	19 Mar	18 Apr	17 Jun	15 Sep
20	10 Jan	19 Jan	3 Feb	20 Mar	19 Apr	18 Jun	16 Sep
21	11 Jan	20 Jan	4 Feb	21 Mar	20 Apr	19 Jun	17 Sep
22	12 Jan	21 Jan	5 Feb	22 Mar	21 Apr	20 Jun	18 Sep
23	13 Jan	22 Jan	6 Feb	23 Mar	22 Apr	21 Jun	19 Sep
24	14 Jan	23 Jan	7 Feb	24 Mar	23 Apr	22 Jun	20 Sep
25	15 Jan	24 Jan	8 Feb	25 Mar	24 Apr	23 Jun	21 Sep
26	16 Jan	25 Jan	9 Feb	26 Mar	25 Apr	24 Jun	22 Sep
27	17 Jan	26 Jan	10 Feb	27 Mar	26 Apr	25 Jun	23 Sep
28	18 Jan	27 Jan	11 Feb	28 Mar	27 Apr	26 Jun	24 Sep
29	19 Jan	28 Jan	12 Feb	29 Mar	28 Apr	27 Jun	25 Sep
30	20 Jan	29 Jan	13 Feb	30 Mar	29 Apr	28 Jun	26 Sep
31	21 Jan	30 Jan	14 Feb	31 Mar	30 Apr	29 Jun	27 Sep

CITY/AIRPORT CODES

The term 'Geography' is derived from the Greek word 'geos', for world, and means the study of the world. Airline geography is concerned with the various cities, airports, and countries served by air carriers. Domestic airline geography in India is concerned with India, Nepal, Bangladesh, Bhutan, Sri Lanka and other neighbouring countries, whereas international airline geography involves all other areas of the world. Airline geography is based on the standards set by the International Air Transport Association (IATA). The definitions, codes and spellings used by IATA are created by the International Standards Organisation (ISO), based on Geneva, Switzerland. You require a complete understanding of airline geography and a knowledge of IATA/ISO definitions and codes for a suitable job employment in the travel industry.

In airline geography, each city and airport is given a three-letter 'ISO' code. For example, DEL is the city code for NEW DELHI and 'CAL' is for Kolkata. The city code DEL refers to the New Delhi area, but not to a specific airport. The city code for London is LON, but the major airports are Heathrow (LHR), Gatwick (LGW) and Stansted (STN). The city code for Paris is PAR, and the major airports are Charles de Gaulle (CDG) and Orly (ORY). The city code for Rome is Rom, and the major airports are Fimuicino (FCO) and Ciampino (CIA).

To find the code for a city or airport to the departure cities arranged alphabetically in the *Worldwide city-to-city schedules.* Non-IATA codes assigned by Reed Travel Group are indicated by* in the Schedule.

Table 4.8: Important City/Airport Codes

Codes	*City: Airport*	*Codes*	*City: Airport*
	A	AAU	Asau, Samoa
AAA	Anaa, Tuamolu Islands	AAY	Al Ghaydah, Republic of Yemen
AAC	Al Arish, Egypt		
AAE	Annaba, Algeria	ABE	Allentown/Bethelehem, PA USA
AAL	Aalborg, Denmark		
AAN	Al Ain, United Arab Emirates	ABI	Abilene, TX USA
AAQ	Anapa, Russian Federation	ABI	Abilene Municipal Apt, TX USA
AAR	Aarhus, Denmark		
AAT	Altay, P R China	ABJ	Abidjan, Cote d'Ivoire

(*Contd.*)

(Contd.)

Codes	City: Airport	Codes	City: Airport
ABK	Kabri Dar, Ethiopia	AER	Adler/Sochi, Russian Federation
ABL	Ambler, AK USA	AES	Aalesund, Norway
ABM	Bamaga, QL Australia	AET	Allakaket, AK USA
ABQ	Albuquerque, NM USA	AEX	Alexandria, LA USA
ABR	Aberdeen, SD USA	AEX	Alexandria International Apt, LA USA
ABS	Abu Simbel, Egypt	AEY	Akureyri, Iceland
ABT	Al-Baha, Saudi Arabia	AFA	San Rafael, MD Argentina
ABV	Abuja, Nigeria	AFL	Alta Floresta, MT Brazil
ABX	Albury, NS Australia	AGA	Agadir, Morocco
ABY	Albany, GA USA	AGB	Munich Augsburg Apt, Germany
ABY	Albany Dougherty County Apt, GA USA	AGE	Wangerooge, Germany
ABZ	Aberdeen, UK	AGF	Agen, France
ACA	Acapulco, Mexico	AGH	Helsingborg, Sweden
ACC	Accra, Ghana	AGH	Helsingborg Angelholm Apt, Sweden
ACE	Lanzarote, Canary Is	AGJ	Aguni, Japan
ACH	Altenrhein, Switzerland	AGL	Wanigela, Papua New Guinea
ACI	Alderney, UK	AGN	Angoon, AK USA
ACK	Nantucket, MA USA	AGP	Malaga, Spain
ACT	Waco, TX USA	AGR	Agra, India
ACT	Waco Municipal Apt, TX USA	AGS	Augusta, GA USA
ACV	Arcata/Eureka, CA USA	AGS	Augusta Bush Field, GA USA
ACY	Atlantic City International, NJ USA	AGT	Ciudad del Este, Paraguay
ADA	Adana, Turkey	AGU	Aguascalientes, Mexico
ADB	Izmir Adnan Menderes Apt, Turkey	AHB	Abha, Saudi Arabia
ADD	Addis Ababa, Ethiopia	AHN	Athens, GA USA
ADE	Aden, Republic of Yemen	AHO	Alghero, Italy
ADH	Aldan, Russian Federation	AHS	Ahuas, Honduras
ADJ	Amman, Civil-Marka Airport, Jordan	AHU	Al Hoceima, Morocco
ADK	Adak Island, AK USA	AIA	Alliance, NE USA
ADL	Adelaide, SA Australia	AIC	Airok, Marshall Is
ADQ	Kodiak, AK USA	AIM	Ailuk Island, Marshall Is
ADQ	Kodiak Apt, AK USA	AIN	Wainwright, AK USA
ADU	Ardabil, Iran	AIT	Aitutaki, Cook Is
ADZ	San Andres Island, Colombia	AIU	Atiu Island, Cook Is
AEO	Aioun el Atrouss, Mauritania	AIY	Atlantic City, NJ USA
AEP	Buenos Aires Aeroparque J Newbery, BA Argentina		

(Contd.)

(Contd.)

Codes	*City: Airport*
AJA	Ajaccio, France
AJF	Jouf, Saudi Arabia
AJI	Agri, Turkey
AJR	Arvidsjaur, Sweden
AJU	Aracaju, SE Brazil
AJY	Agades, Niger
AKA	Ankang, P R China
AKB	Atka, AK USA
AKE	Akieni, Gabon
AKG	Anguganak, Papua New Guinea
AKI	Akiak, AK USA
AKJ	Asahikawa, Japan
AKK	Akhiok, AK USA
AKL	Auckland, New Zealand
AKL	Auckland International Apt, New Zealand
AKN	King Salmon, AK USA
AKP	Anaktuvuk Pass, AK USA
AKS	Auki, Solomon Is
AKU	Aksu, P R China
AKV	Akulivik, QU Canada
AKX	Aktybuinsk, Kazakstan
AKY	Sittwe, Myanmar
ALA	Almaty, Kazakstan
ALB	Albany, NY USA
ALB	Anbany County Airport, NY USA
ALC	Alicante, Spain
ALF	Alta, Norway
ALG	Algiers, Algeria
ALH	Albany, WA Australia
ALJ	Alexander Bay, S Africa
ALM	Alamogordo, NM USA
ALM	Alamogordo Municipal Apt, NM USA
ALO	Waterloo, IA USA
ALP	Aleppo, Syrian Arab Republic
ALS	Alamosa, CO USA
ALW	Walla Walla, WA USA
ALY	Alexandria, Egypt
ALZ	Alitak, AK USA
AMA	Amarillo, TX USA
AMA	Amarillo International Apt, TX USA
AMB	Ambilobe, Madagascar
AMD	Ahmedabad, India
AMH	Arba Mintch, Ethiopia
AMI	Mataram, Indonesia
AMM	Amman, Jordan
AMM	Amman Queen Alia International Apt, Jordan
AMQ	Ambon, Indonesia
AMS	Amsterdam, Netherlands
AMY	Ambatomainty, Madagascar
ANC	Anchorage, AK USA
ANC	Anchorage International Apt, AK USA
ANF	Antofagasta, Chile
ANG	Angouleme, France
ANI	Aniak, AK USA
ANJ	Zanaga, Congo
ANK	Ankara, Turkey
ANM	Antalaha, Madagascar
ANN	Annette Island, AK USA
ANR	Antwerp, Belgium
ANR	Antwerp Deurne Airport, Belgium
ANU	Antigua, Leeward Is
ANV	Anvik, K USA
ANX	Andenes, Norway
AOI	Ancona, Italy
AOJ	Aomori, Japan
AOK	Karpathos, Greece
AOO	Altoona, PA USA
AOR	Alor Setar, Malaysia
AOS	Amook, AK USA
AOU	Attopeu, Lao P D R
APF	Naples, FL USA
APL	Nampula, Mozambique

(Contd.)

(*Contd.*)

Codes	City: Airport	Codes	City: Airport
APN	Alpena, MI USA	ATL	Atlanta Hartsfield Intl Apt, GA USA
APO	Apartado, Colombia	ATM	Altamira, PA Brazil
APP	Asapa, Papua New Guinea	ATN	Namatanai, Papua New Guinea
APW	Apia, Samoa	ATP	Aitape, Papua New Guinea
PW	Apia Faleolo Apt. Samoa	ATQ	Amritsar, India
AQA	Araraquara, SP Brazil	ATR	Atar, Mauritania
AQG	Anqing, P R China	ATT	Atmautluak, AK USA
AQI	Qaisumah, Saudi Arabia	ATW	Appleton WI USA
AQJ	Aqaba, Jordan	ATY	Watertown, SD, USA
AQP	Arequipa, Peru	ATZ	Assiut, Egypt
ARC	Arctic Village, AK USA	AUA	Aruba
ARH	Arkhangelsk, Russian Federation	AUC	Arauca, Colombia
ARI	Arica, Chile	AUG	Augusta, ME USA
ARM	Armidale, NS Australia	AUH	Abu Dhabi, United Arab Emirates
ARN	Stockholm Arlanda Apt, Sweden	AUH	Abu Dhabi International Apt, United Arab Emirates
ARP	Aragip, Papua New Guinea	AUJ	Ambunti, Papua New Guinea
ART	Watertown, NY USA	AUK	Alakanuk, AK USA
ARU	Aracatuba, SP Brazil	AUL	Aur Island, Marshall Is
ARW	Arad, Romania	AUP	Agaun, Papua New Guinea
ARZ	N'Zeto, Angola	AUQ	Atuona, Marquesas Is
ASA	Assab, Eritrea	AUR	Aurillac, France
ASB	Ashkhabad, Turkmenistan	AUS	Austin, TX USA
ASD	Andros Town, Bahamas	AUS	Austin Robert Mueller Municipal Apt. TX USA
ASE	Aspen, CO USA	AUU	Aurukun Mission, QL Australia
ASF	Astrakhan, Russian Federation	AUV	AUMO, Papua New Guinea
ASJ	Amami O Shima, Japan	AUW	Wausau, WI USA
ASM	Asmara, Eritrea	AUX	Araguaina, TO Brazil
ASO	Asosa, Ethiopia	AUY	Aneityum, Vanuatu
ASP	Alice Springs, NT Australia	AVI	Ciego de Avila, Cuba
ASR	Kayseri, Turkey	AVL	Asheville, NC USA
AST	Astoria, OR USA	AVN	Avignon, France
ASU	Asuncion, Paraguay	AVP	Wilkes-Barre Scranton International Apt, PA USA
ASV	Amboseli, Kenya		
ASW	Aswan, Egypt		
ATC	Arthur's Town, Bahamas		
ATH	Athens, Greece		
ATK	Atqasuk, AK USA		

(*Contd.*)

(Contd.)

Codes	City: Airport
AVU	Avu Avu, Solomon Is
AWD	Aniwa, Vanuatu
AWZ	Ahwaz, Iran
AXA	Anguilla, Leeward Is
AXD	Alexandroupolis, Greece
AXK	Ataq, Republic of Yemen
AXM	Armenia, Colombia
AXP	Spring Point, Bahamas
AXT	Akita, Japan
AXU	Axum, Ethiopia
AYK	Arkalyk, Kazakstan
AYP	Ayacucho, Peru
AYQ	Ayers Rock, NT Australia
AYT	Antalya, Turkey
AZB	Amazon Bay, Papua New Guinea
AZD	Yazd, Iran
AZN	Andizhan, Uzbekistan
AZO	Kalamazoo, MI USA
AZR	Adrar, Algeria
	B
BAA	Bialla, Papua New Guinea
BAG	Baguio, Philippines
BAH	Bahrain
BAJ	Bali, Papua New Guinea
BAK	Baku, Azerbaijan
BAL	Batman, Turkey
BAQ	Barranquilla, Colombia
BAS	Balalae, Solomon Is
BAT	Barretos, SP Brazil
BAU	Bauru, SP Brazil
BAV	Baotou, P R China
BAX	Barnaul, Russian Federation
BAY	Baia Mare, Romania
BBA	Balmaceda, Chile
BBI	Bhubaneswar, India
BBK	Kasane, Botswana
BBM	Battambang, Combodia
BBN	Bario, Malaysia
BBO	Berbera, Somalia
BBR	Basse Terre, Guadeloupe
BBU	Bucharest Baneasa Apt, Romania
BCA	Baracoa, Cuba
BCD	Bacolod, Philippines
BCI	Barcaldine, QL Australia
BCL	Barra Colorado, Costa Rica
BCN	Barcelona, Spain
BCO	Jinka, Ethiopia
BCP	Bambu, Papua New Guinea
BCW	Benguera Island, Mozambique
BCX	Beloreck, Russian Federation
BDA	Bermuda
BDA	Bermuda International, Bermuda
BDB	Bundaberg, QL Australia
BDH	Bandar Lengeh, Iran
BDJ	Banjarmasin, Indonesia
BDL	Hartford Bradley International Apt, CT USA
BDO	Bandung, Indonesia
BDP	Bhadrapur, Nepal
BDQ	Vadodara, India
BDR	Bridgeport, CT USA
BDS	Brindisi, Italy
BDT	Gbadolite, DR of Congo
BDU	Bardufoss, Norway
BEB	Benbekula, UK
BEF	Bluefields, Nicaragua
BEG	Belgrade, Yugoslavia
BEH	Benton Harbor, MI USA
BEI	Beica, Ethiopia
BEJ	Berau, Indonesia
BEL	Belem, PA Brazil
BEO	Newcastle Belmont Apt, NS Australia
BER	Berlin, Germany
BES	Brest, France

(Contd.)

(Contd.)

Codes	City: Airport	Codes	City: Airport
BET	Bethel, AK USA	BHX	Birmingham, UK
BET	Bethel Municipal Apt, AK USA	BHX	Birmingham International Airport, UK
BEU	Bedourie, QL Australia	BHY	Beihai, P R China
BEW	Beira, Mozambique	BHZ	Belo Horizonte, MG Brazil
BEY	Beirut, Lebanon	BIA	Bastia, France
BFD	Bradford, PA USA	BID	Block Island, RI USA
BFF	Scottsbluff, NE USA	BII	Bikini Atoll, Marshall Is
BFH	Curitiba Bacacheri, PR Brazil	BIK	Biak, Indonesia
BFI	Seattle Boeing Field, WA USA	BIL	Billings, MT USA
BFL	Bakersfield, CA USA	BIM	Bimini, Bahamas
BFN	Bloemfontein, S Africa	BIM	Bimini International Apt, Bahamas
BFO	Buffalo Range, Zimbabwe	BIO	Bilbao, Spain
BFQ	Bahia Pinas, Panama	BIQ	Biarritz, France
BFS	Belfast, UK	BIR	Biratnagar, Nepal
BFS	Belfast International Apt, UK	BIS	Bismarck, ND USA
BFV	Buri Ram, Thailand	BIW	Billiluna, WA Australia
BGA	Bucaramanga Colombia	BJF	Batsfjord, Norway
BGF	Bangui, Cen Afr Rep	BJI	Bemidji, MN USA
BGI	Barbados	BJL	Banjul, Gambia
BGK	Big Creek, Belize	BJM	Bujumbura, Burundi
BGM	Binghamton, NY USA	BJR	Bahar Dar, Ethiopia
BGO	Bergen, Norway	BJS	Beijing, P R China
BGR	Bangor, ME USA	BJV	Bodrum Milas Airport, Turkey
BGY	Milan Orio al Serio, Italy	BJX	Leon/Guanajuato, Mexico
BHB	Bar Harbor, ME USA	BJZ	Badajoz, Spain
BHD	Belfast City Apt, UK	BKA	Moscow Bykovo Apt, Russian Federation
BHE	Blenheim, New Zealand	BKC	Buckland, AK USA
BHG	Brus Laguna, Honduras	BKI	Kota Kinabalu, Malaysia
BHH	Bisha, Saudi Arabia	BKK	Bangkok, Thailand
BHI	Bahia Blanca, BA Argentina	BKM	Bakalalan, Malaysia
BHJ	Bhuj, India	BKO	Bamako, Mali
BHK	Bukhara, Uzbekistan	BKQ	Blackall, QL Australia
BHM	Birmingham, AL USA	BKS	Bengkulu, Indonesia
BHO	Bhopal, India	BKW	Beckley, WV USA
BHQ	Broken Hill, NS Australia	BKX	Brookings, SD USA
BHR	Bharatpur, Nepal	BKY	Bukavu, DR of Congo
BHS	Bathurst, NS Australia		
BHU	Bhavnagar, India		
BHV	Bahawalpur, Pakistan		

(Contd.)

(Contd.)

Codes	City: Airport
BLA	Barcelona, Venezuela
BLE	Borlange, Sweden
BLF	Bluefield, WV USA
BLG	Belaga, Malaysia
BLI	Bellingham, WA USA
BLK	Blackpool, UK
BLL	Billund, Denmark
BLP	Bellavista, Peru
BLQ	Bologna, Italy
BLR	Bangalore, India
BLT	Blackwater, QL Australia
BLZ	Blantyre, Malawi
BMA	Stockholm Bromma Apt, Sweden
BMB	Bumba, DR of Congo
BMD	Belo, Madagascar
BME	Broome, WA Australia
BMI	Bloomington-Normal, IL USA
BMM	Bitam, Gabon
BMO	Bhamo, Myanmar
BMP	Brampton Island, QL Australia
BMV	Ban Me Thuot, Viet Nam
BMW	Bordj Badji Mokhtar, Algenia
BMY	Belep Island, New Caledonia
BNA	Nashville, TN USA
BNB	Boende, DR of Congo
BND	Bandar Abbas, Iran
BNE	Brisbane, QL Australia
BNJ	Bonn Main Rail Station, Germany
BNK	Ballina, NS Australia
BNN	Bronnoysund, Norway
BNP	Bannu, Pakistan
BNU	Blumenau, SC Brazil
BNY	Bellona, Solomon Is
BOB	Bora Bora, Society Is
BOC	Bocas Del Toro, Panama
BOD	Bordeaux, France
BOG	Bogota, Colombia
BOH	Boumemouth, UK
BOI	Boise, ID USA
BOJ	Bourgas, Bulgaria
BOM	Mumbai, India
BON	Bonaire, Netherlands Antilles
BOO	Bodo, Norway
BOS	Boston, MA USA
BOS	Boston Logan International Apt, MA USA
BOV	Boang, Papua New Guinea
BOX	Borroloola, NT Australia
BPE	Bagan, Myanmar
BPG	Barra Do Garcas, MT Brazil
BPN	Balikpapan, Indonesia
BPS	Porto Seguro, BA Brazil
BPT	Beaumont, TX USA
BPT	Beaumont Jefferson County Apt, TX USA
BPY	Besalampy, Madagascar
BQE	Bubaque, Guinea-Bosau
BQH	London Biggin Hill Apt, UK
BQK	Brunswick Glynco Jetport, GA USA
BQL	Boulia, QL Australia
BQN	Aguadilla, Puerto Rico
BQS	Blagoveschensk, Russian Federation
BQU	Port Elizabeth, Grenadine Is
BQW	Balgo Hills, WA Australia
BRA	Barreiras, BA Brazil
BRC	San Carlos de Bariloche, RN Argentina
BRD	Brainerd, MN USA
BRE	Bremen, Germany
BRI	Bari, Italy
BRK	Bourke, NS Australia
BRL	Burlington, IA USA
BRM	Barquisimeto, Venezuela
BRN	Berne, Switzerland
BRN	Berne Belp, Switzerland

(Contd.)

(*Contd.*)

Codes	*City: Airport*
BRO	Brownsville, TX USA
BRQ	Brno, Czecho Rep
BRQ	Brno Turany Apt, Czech Rep
BRR	Barra, UK
BRS	Bristol, UK
BRT	Bathurst Island, NT Australia
BRU	Brussels, Belgium
BRU	Brussels National Airport, Belgium
BRW	Barrow, AK USA
BRW	Barrow Willey Post/Will Rogers Memorial, AK USA
BRX	Barahona, Dominican Rep
BSA	Bossaso, Somalia
BSB	Brasilia, DF Brazil
BSC	Bahia Solano, Colombia
BSD	Baoshan, P R China
BSG	Bata, Equat Guinea
BSL	Basel, Switzerland
BSO	Basco, Philippines
BSU	Batam, Indonesia
BTI	Barter Island, AK USA
BTJ	Banda Aceh, Indonesia
BTK	Bratsk, Russian Federation
BTM	Buttle, MT USA
BTR	Baton Rouge, IA USA
BTR	Baton Rouge Ryan Apt, LA USA
BTS	Bratislava, Slovakia
BTS	Bratislva M R Stefanik Apt, Slovakia
BTT	Bettkesm, AK USA
BTU	Bintulu, Malaysia
BTV	Burlington, VT USA
BUA	Buka, Papua New Guinea
BUC	Burketown, QL Australia
BUD	Budapest, Hungary
BUE	Buenos Aires, BA Argentina
BUF	Buffalo, NY USA
BUG	Benguela, Angola
BUH	Bucharest, Romania
BUK	Albuq, Republic of Yemen
BUL	Bulolo, Papua New Guinea
BUO	Burao, Somalia
BUQ	Bulawayo, Zimbabwe
BUR	Burbank, CA USA
BUX	Bunia, DR of Congo
BUZ	Bushehr, Iran
BVA	Paris Tille Airport, France
BVB	Boa Vista, RR Brazil
BVC	Boa Vista, Cape Verde
BVE	Brive-La-Gaillarde, France
BVG	Berlevag, Norway
BVH	Bilhena, RO Brazil
BVI	Birdsville, QL Australia
BVR	Brava, Cape Verde
BWA	Bhairawa, Nepal
BWD	Brownwood, TX USA
BWI	Baltimore, MD USA
BWI	Baltimore Washington International Apt, MD, USA
BWK	Bol, Croatlia
BWN	Bandar Seri Begawan, Brunel Darussalam
BWQ	Brewarrina, NS Australia
BWT	Burnie, TS Australia
BXH	Balhash, Kazakstan
BXN	Bodrum, Turkey
BXU	Batuan, Phillippines
BXX	Borama, Somalia
BXZ	Bunsil, Papua New Guinea
BYA	Boundary, AK USA
BYB	Dibaa, Oman
BYK	Bouake, Cole d'Ivoire
BYM	Bayamo, Cuba
BYU	Bayreuth, Germany
BYW	Blakely Island, WA USA
BZA	Bonanzo, Nicaragua
BZB	Bazaruto Island, Mozambique

(*Contd.*)

(Contd.)

Codes	*City: Airport*	*Codes*	*City: Airport*
BZE	Belize City, Belize	CCI	Concordia, SC Brazil
BZE	Belize City Goldson Int'l Apt, Belize	CCJ	Calicut, India
BZK	Briansk, Russian Federation	CCK	Cocos Islands
BZL	Barisal, Bangladesh	CCM	Crisciuma, SC Brazil
BZN	Bozeman, MT USA	CCP	Concepcion, Chile
BZR	Beziers, France	CCS	Caracas, Venezuela
BZV	Brazzaville, Congo	CCU	Calcutta, India
BZZ	Brize Norton, UK	CCV	Craig Cove, Vanuatu
	C	CCZ	Chub Cay, Bahamas
CAB	Cabinda, Angola	CDB	Cold Bay, AK USA
CAC	Cascavel, PR Brazil	CDC	Cedar City, UT USA
CAE	Columbia, SC USA	CDG	Paris Charles de Gaulle Apt, France
CAE	Columbia Metropolitan Apt, SC USA	CDJ	Conceicao Do Araguaia, PA Brazil
CAG	Cagliari, Italy	CDL	Candle, AK USA
CAI	Cairo, Egypt	CDR	Chadron, NE USA
CAJ	Canaima, Venezuela	CDV	Cordova, AK USA
CAK	Akron/Canton, QH USA	CDV	Cordova Mile 13 Field, AK USA
CAK	Akron/Canton Ohio Regional, OH USA	CEB	Cebu, Philippines
CAL	Campbeltown, UK	CEC	Crescent City, CA USA
CAN	Guangzhou, P R China	CED	Ceduna, SA Australia
CAP	Cap Haitien, Haiti	CEI	Chiang Rai, Thailand
CAQ	Caucasia, Colombia	CEK	Chelyabinsk, Russian Federation
CAS	Casablanca, Morocco	CEM	Central, AK USA
CAW	Campos, RJ Brazil	CEN	Cudad Obregon, Mexico
CAY	Cayenne, Fr Gulana	CEO	Waco Kungo, Angola
CAZ	Cobar, NS Australia	CEQ	Cannes, France
CBB	Cochabamba, Bolivia	CER	Cherbourg, France
CBE	Cumberland, MD USA	CEZ	Cortez, CO USA
CBG	Cambridge, UK	CFE	Clermont-Ferrand, France
CBH	Bechar, Algeria	CFN	Donegal, Republic of Ireland
CBL	Ciudad Bolivar, Venezuela	CFR	Caen, France
CBO	Cotabato, Philippines	CFS	Coffs Harbour, NS Australia
CBQ	Calabar, Nigeria	CFU	Kerkyra, Greece
CBR	Canberra, AC Australia	CGA	Craig, AK USA
CCC	Cayo Coco, Cuba	CGB	Cuiaba, MT Brazil
CCF	Carcassonne, France	CGC	Cape Cloucester, Papua New Guinea

(Contd.)

(Contd.)

Codes	*City: Airport*	*Codes*	*City: Airport*
CGD	Changde, PR China	CIX	Chiclayo, Peru
CGH	Sao Paulo Congonhas Apt, SP Brazil	CJA	Cajamarca, Peru
CGI	Cape Girardeau, MO USA	CJB	Coimbatore, India
CGK	Jakarta Soekamo-Hatta Apt, Indonesia	CJC	Calama, Chile
CGN	Cologne, Germany	CJJ	Cheong Ju City, Rep of Korea
CGN	Cologne/Bonn K.A. Apt, Germany	CJL	Chitral, Pakistan
CGO	Zhengzhou, P R China	CJS	Ciudad Juarez, Mexico
CGP	Chittagong, Bangladesh	CJU	Cheju, Rep of Korea
CGQ	Changchun, P R China	CJU	Cheju Apt, Rep of Korea
CGR	Campo Grande, MS Brazil	CKB	Clarksburg, WV USA
CGX	Chicago Meigs Field, IL USA	CKD	Crooked Creek, AK USA
CGY	Cagayan de Oro, Philippines	CKG	Chongqing, P R China
CHA	Chattanooga,TN USA	CKS	Carajas, PA Brazil
CHC	Christchurch, New Zealand	CKX	Chicken, AK USA
CHG	Chaoyang, PR China	CKY	Conakry, Guinea
CHH	Chachapoyas, Peru	CLD	Carlsbad, CA USA
CHI	Chicago, IL USA	CLE	Cleveland, OH USA
CHM	Chimbole, Peru	CLE	Cleveland Hopkins International Apt, OH USA
CHO	Charlottesville, VA USA	CLJ	Cluj, Romania
CHP	Circle Hot Springs, AK USA	CLL	College Station, TX USA
CHQ	Chania, Greece	CLM	Port Angeles, WA USA
CHS	Charleston, SC USA	CLO	Cali, Colombia
CHT	Chatham Island, New Zealand	CLP	Clarks Point, AK USA
CHU	Chuathbaluk, AK USA	CLQ	Colima, Mexico
CHX	Changuinola, Panama	CLT	Charlotte, NC USA
CHY	Choiseul Bay, Solomon Is	CLY	Calvi, France
CIA	Rome Ciampino Apt, Italy	CMA	Cunnamulla, QL Australia
CIC	Chico, CA USA	CMB	Colombo, Sri Lanka
CID	Cedar Rapids, IA USA	CMB	Colombo Bandaranayike Apt, Sri Lanka
CIJ	Cobija, Bolivia	CMD	Cootamundra, NS Australlia
CIK	Chalkyitsik, AK USA	CME	Ciudad Del Carmen, Mexico
CIS	Canton Island, Kiribati	CMF	Chambery, France
CIT	Shimkent, Kazakstan	CMG	Corumba, MS Brazil
CIU	Sault Sainte Marie Chippewa County Apt, MI USA	CMH	Columba MS Brazil
CIW	Canouan Island, Grenadine Is	CMH	Columbus Port Columbus Intl Apt. OH USA
		CMI	Champaign IL USA
		CMH	Columbus, OH USA

(Contd.)

(*Contd.*)

Codes	*City: Airport*
CMH	Columbus, Port Columbus Intl Apt, OH USA
CMI	Champaign, IL USA
CMK	Club Makokola, Malawi
CMN	Casablanca Mohamed V Apt, Morocco
CMU	Kuniawa, Papua New Guinea
CMW	Camaguey, Cuba
CMX	Hancock, MI USA
CNB	Coonamble, NS Australia
CND	Constanta, Romania
CNF	Belo Horizonte Tancredo Neves Int Apt, MG Brazil
CNJ	Cloncurry, QL Australia
CND	Constanta, Romania
CNF	Belo Horizonte Tancredo Neven Int Apt, MG Brazil
CNJ	Cloncurry, QL Australia
CND	Constanta, Romania
CNF	Belo Horizonte Tancredo Neves Int Apt, MG Brazil
CNJ	Cloncurry, QL Australia
CNL	Sindal, Denmark
CNM	Carisbad, NM USA
CNP	Neerlerit Inaat Greenland
CNQ	Corrientes, CR Argentina
CNS	Cairns, QL Australia
CNX	Chiang Mai, Thailand
CNY	Moab, UT USA
COD	Cody, WY USA
COG	Condoto, Colombia
COJ	Connabarabran, NS Australia
COK	Cochin, India
COO	Contonou, Benin
COR	Cordoba, CD Argentina
COS	Colorado Springs, Co USA
COS	Colorado Springs Peterson Field, CO USA
COU	Columbia, MO USA
CPB	Capurgana, Colombia
CPC	San Martin de Los Andes, NE Argentina
CPD	Coober Pedy, Sa Australia
CPE	Campeche, Mexico
CPH	Copenhagen, Denmark
CPH	Copenhagen Apt, Denmark
CPI	Cape Orford, Papua New Guinea
CPO	Copiapo, Chile
CPQ	Campinas, SP Brazil
CPR	Casper, WY USA
CPT	Cape Town, S Africa
CPV	Campina Grande, PB Brazil
CPX	Culebra, Puerto Rico
CQA	Canarana, MT Brazil
CRD	Comodoro Rivadavia, CB Argentina
CRI	Crooked Island, Bahamas
CRK	Luzon Island Clark Field, Philippines
CRL	Brussels South Airport, Belgium
CRP	Corpus Christi, TX USA
CRP	Corpus Christi Inter-national Apt, TX USA
CRU	Carriacou, Grenada
CRV	Crotone, Italy
CRW	Charleston, WV USA
CSG	Columbus, GA USA
CSG	Columbus Metropolitan Apt, GA USA
CSI	Casino, NS Australia
CSK	Cap Skirring, Senegal
CSL	San Luis Obispo, CA USA
CSX	Changsha, P R China
CTA	Catania, Italy
CTC	Catamarca, CA Argentina
CTD	Chitre, Panama
CTG	Cartagena, Colombia
CTL	Charleville, QL Australia

(*Contd.*)

(Contd.)

Codes	City: Airport	Codes	City: Airport
CTM	Chetumal, Mexico	CWT	Cowra, NS Australia
CTN	Cooktown, QL Australia	CXB	Cox's Bazar, Bangladesh
CTS	Sapporo Chitose Apt, Japan	CXH	Vancouver Coal Harbour SPB, BC Canada
CTU	Chengdu, P R China	CXI	Christmas Island, Kirbati
CUC	Cucuta, Colombia	CXJ	Caxias Do Sul, RS Brazil
CUE	Cuenca, Ecuador	CYB	Cayman Brac, Cayman Is
CUG	Cudal, NS Australia	CYF	Chefornak, AK USA
CUJ	Gulion, Philippines	CYI	Chiayi, Taiwan R.O.C.
CUK	Caye Caulker, Belize	CYO	Cayo Largo del Sur, Cuba
CUL	Culiacan, Mexico	CYS	Cheyenne, WY USA
CUM	Cumana, Venezuela	CYS	Cheyenne Municipal Apt, WY USA
CUN	Cancun, Mexico	CYU	Cuyo, Philippines
CUQ	Coen, QL Australia	CZA	Chichen Itza, Mexico
CUR	Curacoa, Netherlands Antilles	CZE	Coro, Venezuela
CUU	Chihuahua, Mexico	CZH	Corozal, Belize
CUW	Cube Cove, AK USA	CZM	Cozumel, Mexico
CUZ	Cuzco, Peru	CZN	Chisana, AK USA
CVC	Cleve, SA Australia	CZS	Cruzeiro Do Sul, AC Brazil
CVG	Cincinnati, OH USA	CZX	Changzhow, P R China
CVG	Cincinnati Nothern Kentucky Intl Apt, OH USA		**D**
CVJ	Cuernavaca, Mexico	DAB	Daytona Beach, FL USA
CVL	Cape Vogel, Papua New Guinea	DAC	Dhaka, Bangladesh
CVM	Ciudad Victoria, Mexico	DAD	Da Nang, Viet Nam
CVN	Clovis, NM USA	DAL	Dallas/Fort Worth Love Field, TX USA
CVN	Clovis Municipal Apt, NM USA	DAM	Damascus, Syrian Arab Republic
CVO	Corvallis, OR USA	DAR	Dar Es Salaam, Tanzania
CVQ	Carnarvon, WA Australia	DAT	Datong, P R China
CVU	Corvo Island, Azores	DAU	Daru, Papua New Guinea
CWA	Wausa Central Wisconsin Apt, WI USA	DAV	David, Panama
CWB	Curitiba, PR Brazil	DAX	Daxian, P R China
CWB	Curtiba Afonso Pena, PR Brazil	DAY	Dayton, OH USA
CWC	Chernovtsy, Ukrine	DAY	Dayton Intl Apt, OH USA
CWL	Cardiff, UK	DBA	Dalbandin, Pakistan
CWS	Center Island, WA USA	DBM	Debra Marcos, Ethiopia
		DBO	Dubbo, NS Australia

(Contd.)

(Contd.)

Codes	City: Airport	Codes	City: Airport
DBQ	Dubuque, IA USA	DIR	Dire Dawa, Ethiopia
DBT	Debre Tabor, Ethiopia	DIS	Loubomo, Congo
DBV	Bubrovnik, Croatia	DIU	Diu, India
DCA	Washington National Apt, DC USA	DIY	Diyarbakir, Turkey
DCF	Dominica Cane Field, Dominica	DJB	Jambi, Indonesia
DCM	Castres, France	DJN	Delta Junction, AK USA
DDC	Dodge City, KS USA	DKI	Dunk Island, QL Australia
DDG	Dandong, P R China	DKR	Dakar, Senegal
DDI	Daydream Island, QL Australia	DLA	Douala, Cameroon
DDM	Dodoima, Papua New Guinea	DLC	Dalian, P R China
DEA	Dera Ghazi Khan, Pakistan	DLD	Geilo, Norway
DEC	Decatur, IL USA	DLG	Dillingham, AK USA
DEL	Delhi, India	DLH	Duluth/Superior, MN USA
DEM	Dembidollo, Ethiopia	DLH	Duluth International Apt, MN USA
DEN	Denver, CO USA	DLI	Dalat, Viet Nam
DEN	Denver, Intl Apt, CO USA	DLM	Dalaman, Turkey
DER	Derim, Papua New Guinea	DLO	Dolomi, AK USA
DET	Detroit City Apt, MI USA	DLU	Dali City, P R China
DEZ	Deirezzor, Syrian Arab Republic	DLY	Dillons Bay, Vanuatu
DFW	Dallas/Fort Worth, TX USA	DMB	Zhambyl, Kazakstan
DFW	Dallas/Fort Worth Intl Apt, TX USA	DMD	Dommadgee Mission, QL Australia
DGA	Dangriga, Belize	DME	Moscow Domodedovo Apt, Russian Federation
DGE	Mudgee, NS Australia	DMU	Dimapur, India
DGO	Durango, Mexico	DND	Dundee, UK
DGT	Dumaguete, Philippines	DNH	Dunhuang, P R China
DHA	Dhahran, Saudi Arabia	DNK	Dnepropetrovsk, Ukraine
DHI	Dhangarhi, Nepal	DNM	Denham, WA Australia
DHN	Dothan, AL USA	DNR	Dinard, France
DIB	Dibrugarh, India	DNZ	Denizil, Turkey
DIE	Antsiranana, Madagascar	DOF	Dora Bay, AK USA
DIJ	Dijon, France	DOG	Dongola, Sudan
DIK	Dickinson, ND USA	DOH	Doha, Qatar
DIL	Dili, Indonesia	DOK	Donetsk, Ukraine
DIN	Dien Bien Phi, Viet Nam	DOL	Deauville, France
		DOM	Dominica
		DOM	Dominica Melville Hall Apt, Dominica

(Contd.)

(*Contd.*)

Codes	City: Airport	Codes	City: Airport
DOO	Dorobisoro, Papua New Guinea	DXB	Dubai, United Arab Emirates
DOP	Dolpa, Nepal	DYG	Dayong, P R China
DOU	Dourados, MS Brazil	DYR	Anadyr, Russian Federation
DPL	Dipolog, Philippines	DYU	Dushanbe, Tajikistan
DPO	Devonport, TS Australia	DZA	Dzaoudzi, Mayotte
DPS	Denpasar Bali, Indonesia	DZN	Zhezkazgan, Kazakstan
DRB	Derby, WA Australia		**E**
DRG	Deering, AK USA	EAA	Eagle, AK USA
DRO	Durango, CO USA	EAE	Emae, Vanuatu
DRO	Durango La Plata Apt, CO USA	EAM	Nejran, Saudi Arabia
DRS	Dresden, Germany	EAR	Kearney, NE USA
DRT	Del Rio, TX USA	EAS	San Sebastian, Spain
DRT	Del Rio International Apt, TX USA	EAT	Wenatchee, WA USA
DRW	Darwin, NT Australia	EAU	Eau Claire, WI USA
DSD	La Desirade, Duadeloupe	EBA	Elba Island, Italy
DSE	Dessie, Ethiopla	EBB	Entebbe/Kampala, Uganda
DSK	Dera Ismail Khan, Pakistan	EBG	El Bagre, Colombia
DSM	Des Moines, IA USA	EBJ	Esbjerg, Denmark
DTD	Datadawai, Indonesia	EBO	Ebin, Marshall Is
DTM	Dortmund, Germany	EBU	St Etienne, France
DTR	Decatur Island, WA USA	ECN	Ercan, Cyprus
DTT	Detroit, MI USA	EDA	Edna Bay, AK USA
DTW	Detroit Wayne County, MI USA	EDI	Edinburgh, UK
DUB	Dubin, Republic of Ireland	EDO	Edremit/Korfez, Turkey
DUD	Dunedin, New Zealand	EDR	Edward River, QL Australia
DUE	Dundo, Angola	EEK	Eek, AK USA
DUJ	Dubois, PA USA	EEN	Keene, NH USA
DUR	Durban, S Africa	EFD	Houston Ellington Field, TX USA
DUR	Durban International Airport, S Africa	EFG	Efogi, Papua New Guinea
DUS	Dusseldorf, Germany	EFL	Kefallnia, Greece
DUS	Dusseldorf Apt, Germany	EGC	Bergerac, France
DUT	Dutch Harbor, AK USA	EGE	Vail, CO USA
DVL	Devis Lake, ND USA	EGL	Neghelli, Ethiopia
DVO	Davao, Philippines	EGM	Sege, Solomon Is
DWB	Soalala, Madagascar	EGS	Egilsstadir, Iceland
		EGX	Egegik, AK USA
		EHM	Cape Newenham, AK USA
		EIA	Eia, Papua New Guinea

(*Contd.*)

(Contd.)

Codes	City: Airport	Codes	City: Airport
EIN	Eindhoven, Netherlands	EPL	Epinal, France
EIS	Beef Island, Br Virgin Is	EPR	Esperance, WA Australia
EJA	Barrancabermeja, Colombia	EPS	EL Portillo/Samana, Dominican Rep
EJH	Wedjh, Saudi Arabia	EQS	Esquel, CB Argentina
EKB	Ekibastuz, Kazakstan	ERA	Erigavo, Somalia
EKO	Elko, NV USA	ERC	Erzincan, Turkey
ELC	Elcho Island, NT Australia	ERD	Berdyansk, Ukraine
		ERF	Erfut, Germany
ELD	El Dorado, AR USA	ERH	Errachidia, Morrocco
ELE	El Real, Panama	ERI	Erie, PA USA
ELG	El Golea, Algeria	ERM	Erechim, RS Brazil
ELH	North Eleuthera, Bahamas	ERS	Windhoek Eros Apt, Namibia
		ERZ	Erzurum, Turkey
ELI	Elim, AK USA	ESA	Esa'Ala, Papua New Guinea
ELM	Elmira/Corning, NY USA	ESB	Ankara Esenboga Apt, Turkey
ELP	El Paso, TX USA	ESC	Escanaba, MI USA
ELP	El Paso International Apt, TX USA	ESD	Eastsound, WA USA
		ESR	El Salvador, Chile
ELQ	Gassim, Saudi Arabia	ETH	Elat, Israel
ELS	East London, S Africa	ETZ	Metz/Nancy, France
ELV	Elfin Cove, AK USA	EUA	Eua, Tonga
ELY	Ely, NV USA	EUG	Eugene, OR USA
EMA	East Midlands, UK	EUN	Laayoune, Morocco
EMD	Emerald, QL Australia	EUX	ST Eustatius, Netherlands Antilles
EMI	Emirau, Papua New Guinea		
EMK	Emmonak, AK USA	EVE	Evenes, Norway
EMN	Nema, Mauritania	EVG	Sveg, Sweden
EMO	Emo, Papua New Guinea	EVN	Yerevan, Armenia
EMS	Embessa, Papua New Guinea	EVV	Evansville, IN USA
ENA	Kenai, AK USA	EWB	New Bedford, MA USA
ENF	Enontekio, Finland	EWN	New Bern, NC USA
ENS	Enschede, Netherlands	EWR	New York Newark International Apt, NJ USA
ENT	Enewetak Island, Marshall Is	EXI	Excursion Inlet, AK USA
ENU	Enugu, Nigeria	EXT	Exeter, UK
ENY	Yan'an, P R China	EYL	Yelimane, Mali
EOH	Medellin Enrique Olaya Herrerra Apt, Colombia	EYW	Key West, FL USA
		EYW	Key West International Apt, FL USA
EOI	Eday, UK		

(Contd.)

(Contd.)

Codes	*City: Airport*	*Codes*	*City: Airport*
EZE	Buenos Aires Ministro Pistarini, BA Argentina	FIE	Fair Isle, UK
EZS	Elazig, Turkey	FIH	Kinshasa, DR of Congo
		FIH	Kinshasa N'Djili Apt, DR of Congo
	F	FIN	Finschhafen, Papua New Guinea
FAE	Faroe Islands	FIZ	Fitzroy Crossing, WA Australia
FAI	Fairbanks, AK USA	FJR	Al-Fujarah, United Arab Emirates
FAI	Fairbanks International Apt, AK USA	FKI	Kisangani, DR of Congo
FAJ	Fajardo, Puerto Rico	FKL	Frankin, PA USA
FAK	Faise Island, AK USA	FLK	Franklin, PA USA
FAN	Farsund, Norway	FKL	Franklin Chess Lamberton Apt, PA USA
FAO	Faro, Portugal	FKS	Fukusima, Japan
Faq	Freida River, Papua New Guinea	FLG	Flagstaff, AZ USA
FAR	Fargo, ND USA	FLL	Fort Lauderdale FL USA
FAT	Fresno, CA USA	FLL	Fort Lauderdale/Hollywood Intl Apt, FL USA
FAT	Fresno Air Terminal, CA USA	FLN	Florianopolis, SC Brazil
FAV	Fakarava, Tuamotu Islands	FLO	Florence, SC USA
FAY	Fayetteville, NC USA	FLR	Florence, Italy
FAY	Fayetteville Municipal Apt, NC USA	FLR	Florence Peretola Apt, Italy
FBE	Francisco Beltrao, PR Brazil	FLS	Flinders Island, TS Australia
FBM	Lubumbashi, DR of Congo	FLT	Flat, AK USA
FBU	Oslo Fornebu Apt, Norway	FLW	Flores Island, Azores
FCA	Kalispell, MT USA	FMA	Formosa, FO Argentina
FCO	Rome leonardo da Vinci-Flumicino Apt, Italy	FMI	Kalemie, DR of Congo
FDE	Forde, Norway	FMN	Farmington, NM USA
FDF	Fort de France, Martinique	FMO	Munster, Germany
FDH	Friedrichshafen, Germany	FMY	Fort Myers, FL USA
FEG	Fergana, Uzbekistan	FNA	Freetown, Sierra Leone
FEN	Femando De Noronha, FN Brazil	FNA	Freetown Lungi Inter-national Apt, Sierra Leone
FEZ	Fez, Morocco	FNC	Funchal, Madeira Is
FGI	Apia Fagali'I Apt, Samoa	FNE	Fane, Papua New Guinea
FHU	Fort Huachuca/Sierra Vista, AZ USA	FNI	Nimes, France
FID	Fishers Island, NY USA	FNJ	Pyongyang, DPR of Korea
		FNL	Fort Collins/Loveland Municipal Apt, CO USA

(Contd.)

(*Contd.*)

Codes	City: Airport	Codes	City: Airport
FNT	Flint, MI USA		G
FOC	Fort Dodge, IA USA	GAJ	Yamagata Japan
FOE	Topeka Forbes AFB, KB USA	GAL	Galena, AK USA
FOR	Fortaleza, CE Brazil	GAM	Gambell, AK USA
FOU	Fougamou, Gabon	GAN	Gan Island, Maldives
FPO	Freeport, Bahamas	GAO	Guantanamo Los Canos Apt, Cuba
FRA	Frankfurt Germany	GAQ	Gao, Mali
FRA	Frankfurt International Apt, Germany	GAR	Garaina, Papua New Guinea
FRB	Forbes, NS Australia	GBD	Great Bend, KS USA
FRC	Franca, SP Brazil	GBE	Gaborone, Botswana
FRD	Friday Harbor, WA USA	GBJ	Marie Galante, Guadeloupe
FRE	Fera Island, Solomon Is	GCC	Gillette, WY USA
FRG	Farmingdale, NY USA	GCI	Guernsey, UK
FRM	Fairmont, MN USA	GCK	Garden City, KS USA
FRO	Floro, Norway	HCM	Grand Cayman Island, Cayman Is
FRS	Flores Guatemala	GCN	Grand Canyon, AZ USA
FRU	Bishkek, Kyrgyzstan	GCN	Grand Canyon National Apt, AZ USA
FRW	rancistown, Botswana	GDE	Gode, Ethiopia
FSC	Figari, France	GDL	Guadalajara, Mexico
FSD	Sioux Falls, SD USA	GDN	Gdansk, Poland
FSM	Fort Smith, AR USA	GDQ	Gondar, Ethiopia
FSP	St Pierre, Saint Pierre and Miqueion	GDT	Grand Turk, Turks and Caicos Islands
FTA	Futuna Island, Vanuatu	GDV	Glendive, MT USA
FTU	Fort Dauphin, Madagascar	GDX	Magadan, Russian Federation
FTW	Dallas/Fort Worth Meacham Field, TX USA	GEA	Noumea Magenta Apt, New Calendonia
FTX	Owando, Congo	GEG	Spokane, WA USA
FUE	Fuerteventura, Canary Is	GEG	Spokane International Apt, WA USA
FUJ	Fukue, Japan	GEL	Santo Angelo, RS Brazil
FUK	Fukuoka, Japan	GEO	Georgetown, Guyana
FUN	Funafuti Atol, Tuvalu	GER	Nueva Gerona, Cuba
FUT	Futuna, Wallis and Futuna Is	GES	General Santos, Phillippines
FVL	Flora Valley, WA Australia	GET	Geraldton, WA Australia
FWA	Fort Wayne, IN USA	GEV	Gallivare, Sweden
FWA	Fort Wayne Baer Field, IN USA	GEW	Gewoya, Papua New Guinea
FYU	Fort Yukon, AK USA		
FYV	Fayetteville, AR USA		

(*Contd.*)

(Contd.)

Codes	*City: Airport*
GFB	Togiak Fish, AK USA
GFF	Giffith, NS Australia
GFK	Grand Forks, ND USA
GEN	Grafton, NS Australia
GGG	Longview, TX USA
GHA	Ghardaia, Algeria
GHB	Governors Harbour, Bahamas
GHC	Great Harbour Cay, Bahamas
GHD	Ghimbi, Ethiopia
GHE	Garachine, Panama
GIB	Gibraltar
GIG	Rio de Janeiro International Apt, RJ Brazil
GIL	Gilgit, Pakistan
GIS	Gisbome, New Nealand
GIZ	Gizan, Saudi Arabia
GJA	Guanaja, Honduras
GJL	Jijel, Algeria
GJT	Grand Junction, CO USA
GKA	Goroka Papua New Guinea
GKL	Great Keppel Island, QL Australia
GLA	Glasgow, UK
GLA	Glasgow International Airport, UK
GLD	Goodland, KS USA
GLF	Golfito, Costa Rica
GLH	Greenville, MS USA
GLI	Glen Innes, NS Australia
GLT	Gladstone, QL Australia
GLV	Golovin, AK USA
GMA	Gemena, DR of Congo
GMB	Gambela, Ethiopia
GME	Gomel, Belarus
GMI	Gasmata, Papua New Guinea
GMR	Gambier Island
GNB	Grenoble, France
GND	Grenada, Grenada
GNR	General Roca, RN Argentina
GNU	Goodnews Bay, AK USA

Codes	*City: Airport*
GNV	Gainesville, FL USA
GOA	Genoa, Italy
GOB	Goba, Ethiopia
GOC	Gora, Papua New Guinea
GOE	Gonalia, Papua New Guinea
GOH	Nuuk, Greenland
GOI	Goa, India
GOJ	Nizhniy Novgorod, Russian Federation
GOM	Goma, DR of Congo
GON	New London/Groton, CT USA
GOQ	Golmud, P R China
GOR	Gore, Ethiopia
GOT	Gothenbury, Sweden
GOT	Gothenbury Landvetter Apt, Sweden
GOU	Garoua, Cameroon
GOV	Gove, NT Australia
GPA	Patras, Greece
GPB	Guarapuava, PR Brazil
GPI	Guapi, Colombia
GPN	Garden Point, NT Australia
GPT	Gulfport/Biloxi, MS USA
GPZ	Grand Rapids, MN USA
GRB	Green Bay, WI USA
GRI	Grand Island, NE USA
GRJ	George, S Africa
GRL	Garasa, Papua New Guinea
GRO	Gerona, Spain
GRP	Gurupi, GO Brazil
GRQ	Groningen, Netherlands
GRR	Grand Rapids, MI USA
GRU	Sao Paulo Guarulhos Int'l Apt, SP Brazil
GRW	Graciosa Island, Azores
GRX	Granada, Spain
GRY	Grimsey, Iceland
GRZ	Graz, Austria
GSA	Long Pasia, Malaysia

(Contd.)

(Contd.)

Codes	City: Airport	Codes	City: Airport
GSE	Gothenbury Saeve Apt, Sweden	GXF	Seiyun, Republic of Yemen
GSO	Greensporo/High point, NC USA	GYA	Guayaramerin, Bolivia
GSP	Greenville, SC USA	GYE	Guayaquil, Ecuador
GSP	Greenville/Spartanburg Apt, SC USA	GYL	Argyle, WA Australia
GST	Gustavus, AK USA	GYM	Guaymas, Mexico
GST	Gustavus Apt, AK USA	GYN	Goiania, Go Brazil
GTE	Groote Eylandt, NT Australia	GYY	Chicago Gary Regional Apt, IN USA
GTF	Greal Falls, MT USA	GZM	Gozo, Malta
GTF	Great Falls International Apt, MT USA	GZO	Gizo, Solomon Is
GTO	Gorontalo, Indonesia	GZT	Gaziantep, Turkey
GTR	Columbus Golden Triangle Regional Apt, MS USA		**H**
GUA	Guatemala City, Guatemala	HAA	Hasvik, Norway
GUB	Guerrero Negro, Mexico	HAC	Hachijo Jima, Japan
GUC	Gunnison, CO USA	HAD	Halmstad, Sweden
GUD	Goundam, Mali	HAE	Havasupai, AZ USA
GUG	Guari, Papua New Guinea	HAH	Moroni International Prince Said, Comoros
GUH	Gunnedah, NS Australia	HAJ	Hanover, Germany
GUM	Guam	HAK	Haikou, P R China
GUM	Guam Agana Field NAS, Guam	HAM	Hamburg, Germany
GUP	Gallup, NM USA	HAM	Hamburg Fuhlsbuffl Airport, Germany
GUR	Alotau, Papua New Guinea	HAN	Hanoi, Viet Nam
GUW	Atyrau, Kazakstan	HAP	Long Island, QL Australia
GUZ	Guarapari, ES Brazil	HAQ	Hanimaadhoo, Maldives
GVA	Geneva, Switzerland	HAR	Harrisburg, PA USA
GVI	Green River, Papua New Guinea	HAS	Hail, Saudi Arabia
GVR	Governador Valadares, MG Brazil	HAU	Haugesund, Norway
GVX	Gavle, Sweden	HAV	Havana, Cuba
GWD	Gwadar, Pakistan	HBA	Hobart, TS Australia
GWE	Gweru, Zimbabwe	HBH	Hobart Bay, AK USA
GWL	Gwalior, India	HBT	Hafr Albatin, Saudi Arabia
GWT	Westerland, Germany	HCQ	Halls Creek, WA Australia
GWY	Galway, Republic of Ireland	HCR	Holy Cross, AK USA
		HDD	Hyderabad, Germany
		HDN	Steamboat Springs Hayden Yampa Valley, CO USA
		HDS	Hoedspruit, S Africa

(Contd.)

(*Contd.*)

Codes	*City: Airport*	*Codes*	*City: Airport*
HDY	Hat Yai, Thailand	HKG	Hong Kong
HEH	Heho, Myanmar	HKG	Hong Kong Kai Tak Intl Apt, Hong Kong
HEK	Heihe, P R China	HKK	Hokitika, New Zealand
HEL	Helsinki, Finland	HKN	Hoskins, Papua New Guinea
HER	Heraklion, Greece	HKT	Phuket, Thailand
HET	Hohhot, P R China	HKY	Hickory, NC USA
HEX	Santo Domingo Herrera Apt, Dominican Rep	HLD	Hailar, P R China
HFA	Haifa, Israel	HLF	Hultsfred, Sweden
HFD	Hartford, CT USA	HLN	Helena, MT USA
HFE	Hefei, Israel	HLP	Jakarta Halim Perdana Kusuma Apt, Indonesia
HFD	Hartford, CT USA	HLZ	Hamilton, New Zealand
HFE	Hefei, P R China	HMA	Malmo City Hovercraft, Sweden
HFN	Homafjordur, Iceland	HME	Hassi Messaoud, Algeria
HFS	Hgfors, Sweden	HMO	Hermosillo, Mexico
HFT	Hammerfest, Norway	HNA	Morioka, Japan
HGA	Hargeisa, Somalia	HND	Tokyo Haneda Apt, Japan
HGD	Hughenden, QL Australia	HNH	Hoonah, AK USA
HGH	Hangzhou, P R China	HNL	Honolulu, HI USA
HGL	Helgoland, Germany	HNL	Honolulu International Apt, HI USA
HGN	Mae Hong Son, Thailand	HNM	Hana, HI USA
HGO	Korhogo, Cote d'Ivoire	HNS	Haines, AK USA
HGR	Hagerstown, MD USA	HOB	Hobbs, NM USA
HGU	Mount Hagen, Papua New Guinea	HOB	Hobbs Lea County Apt, NM USA
HHA	Huanghua, P R China	HOD	Hodeidah, Republic of Yemen
HHH	Hilton Head Island, SC USA	HOE	Houeisay, Lao P D R
HHN	Hahn, Germany	HOF	Hofuf, Saudi Arabia
HHQ	Hua Hin, Thailand	HOG	Holguin, Cuba
HIB	Hibbing/Chishoim, MN USA	HOI	Hao Island Tuamotu Islands
HID	Hom Island, QL Australia	HOK	Kooker Creek, NT Australia
HII	Lake Havasu City, AZ USA	HOM	Homer, AK USA
HIJ	Hiroshima, Japan	HON	Huron, SD USA
HIL	Shillavo, Ethiopia	HOQ	Hof, Germany
HIN	Chinu, Rep of Korea	HOR	Horta, Azores
HIR	Honjara, Solmon Is	HOS	Chos Malal, NE Argentina
HIS	Hayman Island, QL Australia	HOT	Hot Springs, AR USA
HJR	Khajuraho, India		
HKB	Healy Lake, AK USA		
HKD	Hakodate, Japan		

(*Contd.*)

(*Contd.*)

Codes	City: Airport
HOU	Houston, TX USA
HOU	Houston Hobby Apt, TX USA
HOV	Orsta-Volda, Norway
HPA	Ha'apai, Tonga
HPB	Hooper Bay, AK USA
HPH	Haiphong, Viet Nam
HPN	Westchester County, NY USA
HRB	Harbin, P R China
HRE	Harare, Zimbabwe
HRG	Hurghada, Egypt
HRK	Kharkov, Ukraine
HRL	Harlingen, TX USA
HSH	Las Vegas Henderson Sky Harbor Apt, NV USA
HSL	Huslia, AK USA
HSN	Zhoushan, P R China
HSV	Huntsville, AL USA
HSV	Huntsville Madison County Apt, AL USA
HTA	Chita, Russian Federation
HTI	Hamilton Island, QL Australia
HTN	Hotan, P R China
HTR	Hateruma, Japan
HTS	Huntington, WV USA
HUE	Hemera, Ethiopia
HUF	Terre Haute, In USA
HUH	Huahine Island, Society Is
HUI	Hue, Viet Nam
HUN	Hualien, Taiwan R.O.C.
HUS	Hughes, AK USA
HUU	Huanuco, Peru
HUV	Hudiksvall, Sweden
HUX	Huatulco, Mexico
HUY	Humberside, UK
HVA	Analalava, Madagascar
HVB	Hervey Bay, QL Australia
HVG	Honningsvag, Norway
HVN	New Haven, CT, USA
HVR	Havre, MT USA
HWN	Hwange National Park, Zimbabwe
HYA	Hyannis, MA USA
HYD	Hyderabad, India
HYF	Hayfields, Papua New Guinea
HYG	Hydaburg, AK USA
HYL	Hollis, AK USA
HYN	Huangyan, P R China
HYS	Hays, KS USA
HZG	Hanzhong, P R China
HZK	Husavik, Iceland
	I
IAD	Wasington Dulles International Apt, DC USA
IAH	Houston Intercontinental Apt, TX USA
IAN	Klana, AK USA
IAS	Iasi, Romania
IBI	Iboki, Papua New Guinea
IBZ	Ibiza, Spain
ICI	Cicla, Fiji
ICT	Wichita, KS USA
IDA	Idaho Falls, ID USA
IDB	Idre, Sweden
IDN	Indagen, Papua New Guinea
IDR	Indore, India
IEV	Klev, Ukraine
IEV	Kiev Zhulyany Apt, Ukraine
IFJ	Isafjordur, Iceland
IFN	Isfahan, Iran
IFO	Ivano-Frankovsk, Ukraine
IFP	Bullhead City, AZ USA
IGA	Inagua, Bahamas
IGG	Igiugig, AK USA
IGM	Kingman, AZ USA
IGO	Chigorodo, Colombia
IGR	Iguazu, Mi Argentina
IGU	Iguassu Falls, PR Brazil

(*Contd.*)

(Contd.)

Codes	City: Airport
IHU	Ihu, Papua New Guinea
IIS	Nissan Island, Papua New Guinea
IKI	Iki, Japan
IKO	Nikolski, AK USA
IKT	Irkutsk, Russian Federation
ILE	Killeen, TS USA
ILE	Killeen Municipal Apt, TX USA
ILI	Iliamna, AK USA
ILM	Wilmington, NC USA
ILO	Iloilo, Philippines
ILP	Ile Des Pins, New Caledonia
ILY	Islay, UK
ILZ	Zilina, Slovakia
IMF	Imphal, India
IMI	Ine Island, Marshal Is
IMK	Simikot, Nepal
IMP	Imperatriz, MA Brazil
IMT	Iron Mountain, MI USA
INC	Yinchuan, P R China
IND	Indianapolis, IN USA
INU	Nauru Island
INY	Invemess, UK
INZ	In Salah, Algeria
IOA	Ioannina, Greece
IOK	Iokea, Papua New Guinea
IOM	Isle of Man, UK
ION	Impfondo, Congo
IOP	Ioma, Papua New Guinea
IOS	Ilheus, BA Brazil
IPA	Ipota, Vanuatu
IPC	Easter Island, Chile
IPH	Ipoh, Malaysia
IPI	Ipiales, Colombia
IPL	Imperial, CA USA
IPL	Imperial County Apt, CA USA
IPN	Ipatinga, MG Brazil
IPT	Williamsport, PA USA

Codes	City: Airport
IQM	Iquique, Chile
IQT	Iquitos, Peru
IRA	Kirakira, Solomon Is
IRC	Circle, AK USA
IRG	Lockhart Rive, QL Australia
IRJ	La Rioja, LR Argentina
IRK	Kirksville, MO USA
IRP	Isiro, DR of Congo
ISA	Mount Isa, QL Australia
ISB	Islamabad, Pakistan
ISC	Isles of Scilly, UK
ISC	Isles of Scilly Saint Mary's Apt, UK
ISE	Isparta, Turkey
ISG	Ishigaki, Japan
ISJ	Isla Mujeres, Mexico
ISN	Williston, ND USA
ISO	Kinston, NC USA
ISP	Long Island Macarthur, NY USA
IST	Istanbul, Turkey
ITB	Itaituba, PA Brazil
ITH	Ithaca, NY USA
ITK	Itokama, Papua New Guinea
ITM	Osaka Itami Airport, Japan
IUE	Niue
IVA	Ambanja, Madagascar
IVC	Invercargill, New Zealand
IVL	Ivalo, Finland
IVR	Inverell, NS Australia
IVW	Inverway, NT Australia
IWD	Ironwood, MI USA
IWJ	Iwami, Japan
IXA	Agartala, India
IXB	Bagdogra, India
IXC	Chandigarh, India
IXE	Mangalore, India
IXJ	Jammu, India
IXK	Keshod, India
IXL	Leh, India

(Contd.)

(*Contd.*)

Codes	City: Airport
IXM	Madurai, India
IXR	Ranchi, India
IXS	Silchar, India
IXU	Aurangabad, India
IXZ	Port Blair, Andaman Is
IYK	Inyokern, CA USA
IZM	Izmir, Turkey
IZO	Izumo, Japan
	J
JAC	Jackson, WY USA
JAG	Jacobabad, Pakistan
JAI	Jaipur, India
JAN	Jackson, MS USA
JAN	Jackson Thompson Field, MS USA
JAQ	Jacquinot Bay, Papua New Guinea
JAT	Jabot, Marshall Is
JAV	Ilulissat, Greenland
JAX	Jacksonville, FL USA
JAX	Jacksonville International Apt, FL USA
JBR	Jonesboro, AR USA
JCA	Cannes Croisette H/P, France
JOB	Joacaba, SC Brazil
JCH	Qasigiannguit, Greenland
JCK	Julia Creek, QL Australia
JCU	Ceuta Heliport, Spain
JDF	Juiz De For a, MG Brazil
JDH	Jodhpur, India
JDO	Juazeiro Do Norte, CE Brazil
JDZ	Jingdezhen, P R China
JED	Jeddah, Saudi Arabia
JEG	Aasiaat, Greenland
JEJ	Jeh, Marshall Is
JER	Jersey, UK
JFK	New York J F Kennedy International Apt, NY USA
JFR	Paamiut, Greenland
JGA	Jamnagar, India
JGC	Grand Canyon H/P, AZ USA
JGN	Jiayuguan, P R China
JGO	Oeqertarsuaq, Greenland
JGR	Groennedal, Greenland
JHB	Johor Bahru, Malaysia
JHE	Helsingborg H/P, Sweden
JHG	Jinghong, P R China
JHM	Kapalua, HI USA
JHQ	Shule Harbour, QL Australia
JHS	Sisimiut, Greenland
JHW	Jamestown, NY USA
JIA	Juina, MT Brazil
JIB	Djibouti
JIK	Ikaria Island, Greece
JIL	Jilin, P R China
JIM	Jimma, Ethiopia
JIU	Jiujiang, P R China
JIW	Jiwani, Pakistan
JJI	Juanjui, Peru
JJN	Jinjiang, P R China
JJU	Qaqortoq, Greenland
JKG	Jonkoping, Sweden
JKH	Chios, Greece
JKR	Janakpur, Nepal
JKT	Jakarta, Indonesia
JLN	Joplin, MO USA
JMK	Mikonos, Greece
JMM	Malmo Harbour Heliport, Sweden
JMO	Jomsom, Nepal
JMS	Jamestown, ND USA
JMU	Jiamusi, P R China
JNB	Johannesburg, S Africa
JNB	Johannesburg International, S Africa
JNN	Nanortalik, Greenland
JNU	Juneau, AK USA
JNX	Naxos Is, Greece
JNZ	Jinzhou, P R China

(*Contd.*)

(Contd.)

Codes	*City: Airport*	*Codes*	*City: Airport*
JOE	Joensuu, Finland	KAQ	Kamulai, Papua New Guinea
JOG	Yogyakarta, Indonesia	KAT	Kaitaia, New Zealand
JOI	Joinville, SC Brazil	KAW	Kawthaung, Myanmar
JON	Johnston Island	KAX	Kalbarri, WA Australia
JOS	Jos, Nigeria	KBC	Birch Creek, AK USA
JPA	Joao Pessoa, PB Brazil	KBL	Kabul, Afghanistan
JPR	Ji-Parana, RO Brazil	KBM	Kabwum, Papua New Guinea
JQE	Jaque, Panama	KBP	Kiev Borispol Apt, Ukraine
JRH	Jorhat, India	KBR	Kota Bharu, Malaysia
JRO	Kilimanjaro, Tanzania	KBT	Kaben, Marshall Is
JRS	Jerusalem	KCA	Kuqa, P R China
JSH	Sitia, Greece	KCC	Coffman Cove, AK USA
JSI	Skiathos, Greece	KCG	Chignik Fisheries Apt, AK USA
JSR	Jessore, Bangladesh		
JST	Johnstown, PA USA	KCH	Kuching, Malaysia
JSU	Maniitsoq, Greenland	KCL	Chignik, AK USA
JSY	Syros Island, Greece	KCL	Chignik Lagoon Apt, AK USA
JTR	Thira, Greece		
JTY	Astypalaia Island, Greece	KCM	Kahramanmaras, Turkey
JUA	Juara, MT Brazil	KCO	Chignik Lake Apt, AK USA
JUJ	Jujuy, PJ Argentina	KCZ	Kochi, Japan
JUL	Juliaca, Peru	KDD	Khuzdar, Pakistan
JUM	Jumla, Nepal	KDI	Kendari, Indonesia
JUV	Upemavik, Greenland	KDM	Kaadedhdhoo, Maldives
JUZ	Juzhou, P R China	KDN	N'dende, Gabon
JVA	Ankavandra, Madagascar	KDO	Kadhodhoo, Maldives
JYV	Jyavaskyla, Finland	KDR	Kandrian, Papua New Guinea
	K	KDU	Skardu, Pakistan
KAB	Kariba, Zimbabwe	KDV	Kandavu, Fiji
KAC	Kameshli, Syrian Arab Republic	KEF	Reykjavik Kellavik Apt, Iceland
KAD	Kaduna, Nigeria	KEH	Kenmore Air Harbor, WA USA
KAE	Kake, AK USA		
KAG	Kangnung, Rep of Korea	KEJ	Kemerovo, Russian Federation
KAJ	Kajaani, Finland		
KAL	Kaltag, AK USA	KEK	Ekwok, AK USA
KAN	Kano, Nigeria	KEL	Kiel, Germany
KAO	Kuusamo, Finland	KEM	Kemi/Tomio, Finland

(Contd.)

(Contd.)

Codes	City: Airport
KEO	Odienne, Cote d'Ivoire
KEP	Nepalganj, Nepal
KER	Kkerman, Iran
KET	Kengtung, Myanmar
KEW	Keewaywin, OT Canada
KEX	Kanabea, Papua New Guinea
KFA	Kiffa, Mauritaria
KFG	Kalkurung, NT Australia
KFP	False Pass, AK USA
KGA	Kananga, DR of Congo
KGB	Konge, Papua New Guinea
KGC	Kingscote, SA Australia
KGD	Kaliningrad, Russian Federation
KGE	Kagau, Solomon Is
KGF	Karaganda, Kazakstan
KGI	Kalgoorlie, WA Australia
KGJ	Karonga, Malawi
KGK	Koliganek, AK USA
KGL	Kigali, Rwanda
KGO	Kirovograd, Ukraine
KGS	Koş, Greece
KGW	Kgi, Papua New Guinea
KGX	Grayling, AK USA
KHG	Kashi, P R China
KHH	Kaohsiung, Taiwan R.O.C.
KHI	Karachi, Pakistan
KHM	Khamti, Myanmar
KHN	Nanchang, P R China
KHS	Khasab, Oman
KHV	Khabarovsk, Russian Federation
KIB	Ivanof Bay, AK USA
KID	Kristianstad, Sweden
KIF	Kingfisher Lake, OT Canada
KIJ	Niigata, Japan
KIM	Kimberley, S Africa
KIN	Kingston, Jamaica
KIN	Kingston Norman Manley Intl Apt, Jamaica
KIO	Kili Island, Marshall Is
KIG	Kira, Papua New Guinea
KIR	Kerry County, Republic of Ireland
KIS	Kisumu, Kenya
KIT	Kithira, Greece
KIV	Kishinev, Moldova
KIX	Osaka Kansai International Airport
KJA	Krasnoyarsk, Russian Federation
KJP	Kerama, Japan
KKA	Koyuk, AK USA
KKB	Kitoi Bay, AK USA
KKC	Khon Kaen, Thailand
KKD	Kokoda, Papua New Guinea
KKE	Kerikeri, New Zealand
KKH	Kongiganak, AK USA
KKI	Akiachak, AK USA
KKJ	Kita Kyushu, Japan
KKN	Kirkenes, Norway
KKR	Kaukura Atoll, Tuamolu Islands
KKU	Ekuk, AK USA
KKX	Kikaiga Shima, Japan
KKZ	Koh Kong, Cambodia
KLG	Kalskag, AK USA
KLL	Levelock, AK USA
KLN	Larsen Bay, AK USA
KLO	Kalibo, Philippines
KLR	Kalmar, Sweden
KLU	Klagenfurt, Austria
KLW	Klawock, AK USA
KLX	Kalamata, Greece
KLZ	Kleinzee, S Africa
KMA	Kerema, Papua New Guinea

(Contd.)

(*Contd.*)

Codes	*City: Airport*	*Codes*	*City: Airport*
KME	Kamembe, Rwanda	KQA	Akutan, AK USA
KMF	Kamina, Papua New Guinea	KRB	Karumba, QL Australia
KMG	Kunming, P R China	KRF	Kramfors, Sweden
KMI	Miyazaki, Japan	KRI	Kikori, Papua New Guinea
KMJ	Kumamoto, Japan	KRJ	Karawari, Papua New Guinea
KMO	Manokotak, AK USA	KRK	Krakow, Poland
KMP	Keetmanshoop, Namibia	KRL	Korla, P R China
KMQ	Komatsu, Japan	KRN	Kiruna, Sweden
KMV	Kalemyo, Myanmar	KRP	Karup, Denmark
KMY	Moser Bay, AK USA	KRR	Krasnodar, Russian Federation
KNH	Kinmen, Taiwan R.O.C.	KRS	Kristiansand, Norway
KNK	Kakhonak, AK USA	KRT	Khartoum, Sudan
KNQ	Kone, New Caledonia	KRU	Kerau, Paua New Guinea
KNS	King Island, TS Australia	KRW	Turkmanbashi, Turkmenistan
KNZ	Kenieba, Mali	KRY	Karamay, P R China
KOA	Kona, HI USA	KSA	Kosrae, Caroline Is
KOC	Koumac, New Caledonia	KSC	Kosice, Slovakia
KOE	Kupang, Indonesia	KSD	Karlstad, Sweden
KOG	Khong, Lao P D R	KSH	Kermanshah, Iran
KOI	Kirkwall, UK	KSJ	Kasos Island, Greece
KOJ	Kagoshima, Japan	KSM	St Marys, AK USA
KOK	Kokkola/Pietarsaari, Finland	KSN	Kostanay, Kazakstan
KOP	Nakhon Phanom, Thailand	KSO	Kastoria, Greece
KOS	Sihanoukville, Cambodia	KSQ	Karshi, Uzbekistan
KOT	Kotlik, AK USA	KSU	Kristiansund, Norway
KOU	Koulamoutou, Gabon	KSW	Kiryat Shmona, Israel
KOV	Kokshetau, Kazakstan	KSY	Kars, Turkey
KOW	Ganzhou, P R China	KTA	Karratha, WA Australia
KOY	Olga Bay, AK USA	KTB	Thorne Bay, AK USA
KOZ	Ouzinkie, AK USA	KTD	Kitadaito, Japan
KPB	Point Baker, AK USA	KTE	Kerteh, Malaysia
KPC	Port Clarence, AK USA	KTG	Ketapang, Indonesia
KPI	Kapit, Malaysia	KTM	Kathmandu, Nepal
KPN	Kipnuk, AK USA	KTN	Ketchikan, AK USA
KPO	Pohang, Rep of Korea	KTN	Ketchikan International Apt, AK USA
KPR	Port Williams, AK USA		
KPS	Kempsey, NS Australia		
KPV	Perryville, AK USA		
KPY	Port Bailey, AK USA		

(*Contd.*)

(Contd.)

Codes	City: Airport
KTP	Kingston Tinson Apt, Jamaica
KTR	Katherine, NT Australia
KTS	Teller Mission, AK USA
KTT	Kittila, Finland
KTW	Katowice, Poland
KUA	Kuantan, Malaysia
KUD	Kudat, Malaysia
KUF	Samara, Russian Federation
KUH	Kushiro, Japan
KUK	Kasigluk, AK USA
KUL	Kuala Lumpur, Malaysia
KUM	Yakushima, Japan
KUN	Kaunas, Lithuania
KUO	Kuopio, Finland
KUQ	Kuri, Papua New Guinea
KUS	Kulusuk Island, Greenland
KUU	Kulu, India
KUV	Kunsan, Rep of Korea
KUY	Kanusi, Papua New Guinea
KVA	Kavala, Greece
KVB	Skovde, Sweden
KVC	King Cove, AK USA
KVD	Gyandzha, Azerbaijan
KVE	Kitava, Papua New Guinea
KVG	Kavieng, Papua New Guinia
KVL	Kivalina, AK USA
KWA	Kwajalein, Marshall Is
KWE	Guiyang, P R China
KWF	Waterfall, AK USA
KWG	Krivoy Rog, Ukraine
KWI	Kuwait
KWJ	Kwangju, Rep of Korea
KWK	Kwigillingok, AK USA
KWL	Guilin, P R China
KWM	Kowanyama, QL Australia
KWN	Quinhagak, AK USA
KWO	Kawito, Papua New Guinea
KWP	West Point, AK USA
KWT	Kwethluk, AK USA
KWY	Kiwayu, Kenya
KXA	Kasaan, AK USA
KXF	Koro Island, Fiji
KYA	Konya, Turkey
KYK	Karluk, AK USA
KYP	Kyaukpyu, Myamar
KYS	Kayes, Mali
KYU	Koyukuk, AK USA
KYX	Yalumet, Papua New Guinea
KZB	Zachar Bay, AK USA
KZF	Kaintiba, Papua New Guinea
KZI	Kozani, Greece
KZN	Kazan, Russian Federation
KZO	Kzyl Orda, Kazakstan
KZS	Kastelorizo, Greece
	L
LAA	Lamar, CO USA
LAB	Lablab, Papua New Guinea
LAD	Luanda, Angola
LAE	Lae, Papua New Guinea
LAF	Lafayette, IN USA
LAI	Lannion, France
LAJ	Lages, SC Brazil
LAN	Lansing, MI USA
LAO	Laoag, Philippines
LAP	La Paz, Mexico
LAR	Laramie, WY USA
LAS	Las Vegas, NV USA
LAS	Las Vegas Mc Carran International Apt, NV USA
LAU	Lamu, Kenya
LAW	Lawton, OK USA
LAX	Los Angeles, CA USA
LAX	Los Angeles International Apt, CA USA
LBA	Leeds Bradfor, UK
LBB	Lubbock, TX USA
LBB	Lubbock Municipal Apt, TX USA

(Contd.)

(Contd.)

Codes	*City: Airport*	*Codes*	*City: Airport*
LBE	Latrobe, PA USA	LFT	Lafayette, LA USA
LBF	North Platte, NE USA	LFT	Lafayette Regional Apt, LA USA
LBL	Liberal, KS USA	LFW	Lome, Togo
LBP	Long Banga, Malaysia	LGA	New York La Guardia Apt, NY USA
LBQ	Lambarene, Gabon	LGB	Long Beach, CA USA
LBS	Labasa, Fiji	LGB	Long Beach Apt, CA USA
LBU	Labuan, Malaysia	LGE	Lake Gregory, WA Australia
LBV	Libreville, Gabon	LGH	Leigh Creek, SA Australia
LBW	Long Bawan, Indonesia	LGI	Deadmans Cay, Bahamas
LBX	Lubang, Philippines	LGK	Langkawi, Malaysia
LCA	Larnaca, Cyprus	LGL	Long Lellang, Malaysia
LCE	La Ceiba, Honduras	LGP	Legaspi, Philippines
LCG	La Coruna, Spain	LGS	Malargue, MD Argentina
LCH	Lake Charles, LA USA	LGW	London Gatwick Apt, UK
LCP	Lonopue, NE Argentina	LHE	Lahore, Pakistan
LCY	London City Apt, UK	LHG	Lightning Ridge, NS Australia
LDB	Londrina, PR Brazil	LHR	London Heathrow Apt, UK
LDE	Lourdes/Tarbes, France	LHW	Lanzhou, P R China
LDH	Lord Howe Island, NS Australia	LHW	Lanzhou Apt, P R China
LDK	Lidkoping, Sweden	LIF	Lifou Loyalty is
LDN	Lamidanda, Nepal	LIG	Limoges, France
LDU	Lahad Datu, Malaysia	LIH	Kaual Island, HI USA
LDY	Londonderry, UK	LIH	Kauai Island Lihue Muncipal Apt, HI USA
LEA	Learmonth, WA Australia	LIJ	Long Island, AK USA
LEB	Lebanon, NH USA	LIK	Likiep Island, Marshall Is
LED	St Petersburg Pulkovo Apt, Russian Federation	LIL	Lille, France
LEH	Le Havre, France	LIL	Lille Lesquin Airport, France
LEI	Almeria, Spain	LIM	Lima, Peru
LEJ	Leipzig, Germany	LIN	Milan Linate Apt, Italy
LEL	Lake Evella, NT Australia	LIQ	Lisala, DR of Congo
LEQ	Lands End, UK	LIR	Liberia, Costa Rica
LER	Leinster, WA Australia	LIS	Lisbon, Portugal
LET	Leticia, Colombia	LIT	Little Rock, AR USA
LEV	Bureta, Fiji	LIW	Loikaw, Myanmar
LEX	Lexington, KY USA	LJA	Lodja, DR of Congo
LEX	Lexington Blue Grass Apt, KY USA		

(Contd.)

(*Contd.*)

Codes	*City: Airport*
LJG	Lijiang City, P R China
LJU	Ljubljana, Slovenia
LKB	Lakeba, Fiji
LKE	Seattle Lake Union SPB, WA USA
LKL	Lakselv, Norway
LKN	Leknes, Norway
LKO	Lucknow, India
LLA	Lulea, Sweden
LLI	Lalibela, Ethiopia
LLW	Lilongwe, Malawi
LMA	Lake Minchumina, AK USA
LMI	Lumi, Papua New Guinea
LML	Lae Island, Marshall is
LMM	Los Mochis, Mexico
LMN	Limbang, Malaysia
LMP	Lampedusa, Italy
LMT	Klamath Falls, OR USA
LNB	Lamen Bay, Vanuatu
LNE	Lonorore, Vanuatu
LNG	Lese, Papua New Guinea
LNK	Lincoln, NE USA
LNO	Leonora, WA Australia
LNS	Lancaster, PA USA
LNV	Lihir Island, Papua New Guinea
LNY	Lanai City, HI USA
LNZ	Linz, Austria
LOD	Longana, Vanuatu
LOF	Loen, Marshall Is
LON	London, UK
LOS	Lagos, Nigeria
LOV	Monclova, Mexico
LPA	Las Palmas, Canary Is
LPB	La Paz, Bolivia
LPI	Linkoping, Sweden
LPL	Liverpool, UK
LPM	Lamap, Vanuafu
LPP	Lappeenranta, Finland
LPQ	Luang Prabang, Lao P D R
LPS	Lopez Island, WA USA
LPT	Lampang, Thailand
LPU	Long Apung, Indonesia
LPY	Le Puy, France
LRD	Laredo, TX USA
LRE	Longreach, QL Australia
LRH	La Rochelle, France
LRM	La Romana, Dominican Rep
LRS	Leros, Greece
LRT	Lorient, France
LRU	Las Cruces, NM USA
LSA	Losuia, Papua New Guinea
LSC	La Serena, Chile
LSE	La Crosse, WI USA
LSH	Lashio, Myanmar
LSI	Shetland Islands Sumburgh Apt, UK
LSM	Long Semado, Malaysia
LSP	Las Piedras, Venezuela
LSQ	Los angeles, Chile
LSS	Terre-de-Haut, Guadeloupe
LST	Launceston, TS Australia
LSY	Lismore, NS Australia
LTK	Latakia, Syrian Arab Republic
LTL	Lastourville, Gabon
LTN	London Luton Apt, UK
LTO	Loreto, Mexico
LTQ	Le Touquet, France
LTT	St Tropez La Mole Airport, France
LUA	Lukia, Nepal
LUC	Laucala Island, Fiji
LUD	Luderitz, Namibia
LUG	Lugano, Switzerland
LUL	Laurel, MS USA
LUM	Luxi, P R China
LUN	Lusaka, Zambia
LUO	Luena, Angola

(*Contd.*)

(Contd.)

Codes	City: Airport	Codes	City: Airport
LUP	Kalaupapa, HI USA	MAF	Midland/Odessa, TX USA
LUQ	San Luis, SL Argentina	MAF	Midland Odessa Regional Apt, TX USA
LUR	Cape Lisburne, AK USA	MAG	Madang, Papua New Guinea
LUX	Luxembourg	MAH	Menorca, Spain
LVB	Livramento, RS Brazil	MAJ	Majuro, Marshall Is
LVD	Lime Village, AK USA	MAM	Matamoros, Mexico
LVI	Livingstone, Zambia	MAN	Manchester International Apt, UK
LVO	Laverton, WA Australia	MAO	Manaus, AM Brazil
LWB	Lewisburg, WV USA	MAQ	Mae Sot, Thailand
LWK	Shetland Islands Lerwick/Tingwall Apt, UK	MAR	Maracaibo, Venezuela
LWN	Gyoumri, Amenia	MAS	Manus Island, Papua New Guinea
LWO	Lvov, Ukraine	MAT	Matadi, DR of Congo
LWS	Lewiston, ID USA	MAU	Maupiti Island, Society Is
LWT	Lewistown, MT USA	MAV	Maloelap Island, Marshall Is
LWY	Lawas, Malaysia	MAY	Mangrove Cay, Bahamas
LXA	Lhasa, P R China	MAZ	Mayaguez, Puerto Rico
LXG	Luang Namtha Lao P D R	MBA	Mombasa, Kenya
LXR	Luxor, Egypt	MBC	M'bigou, Gabon
LXS	Lemnos, Greece	MBD	Mmabatho, S Africa
LYA	Luoyang, P R China	MBE	Monbetsu, Japan
LYC	Lycksele, Sweden	MBH	Marybrough, QL Australia
LYG	Lianungang, P R China	MBJ	Montego Bay, Jamaica
LYH	Lynchburg, VA USA	MBL	Manistee, MI USA
LYI	Linyi, P R China	MBP	Moyobamba, Peru
LYP	Faisalabad, Pakistan	MBS	Saginaw, MI USA
LYR	Longyearbyen, Norway	MBU	Mbambanakira, Solomon Is
LYS	Lyon, France	MBW	Moorabbin, VI Australia
LYS	Lyon Satolas Apt, France	MCE	Merced, CA USA
LZC	Lazaro Cardenas, Mexico	MCE	Merced Municipal Apt, CA USA
LZH	Liuzhou, P R China	MCG	McGrath, AK USA
LZO	Luzhou, P R China	MCI	Kansas City International Apt, MO USA
LZR	Lizard Island, QL Australia	MCK	McCook, NE USA
M		MCM	Monte Carlo, Monaco
MAA	Chennai/Madras, India	MCN	Macon Lewis B Wilson Apt, GA USA
MAB	Maraba, PA Brazil		
MAD	Madrid, Spain		
MAD	Madrid Barajas Apt, Spain		

(Contd.)

(*Contd.*)

Codes	*City: Airport*	*Codes*	*City: Airport*
MCO	Orlando International Apt, FL USA	MEM	Memphis International Apt, TN USA
MCP	Macapa, AP Brazil	MES	Medan, Indonesia
MCT	Muscat, Oman	MEU	Monte Dourado, PA Brazil
MCU	Montlucon, France	MEX	Mexico City, Mexico
MCV	McArthur River, NT Australia	MEX	Mexico City Benito Juarez Intl Apt, Mexico
MCW	Mason City, IA USA	MEY	Meghauli, Nepal
MCX	Makhachkala, Russian Federation	MFE	McAllen, TX USA
MCY	Sunshine Coast, QL Australia	MFF	Moanda, Gabon
MCZ	Maceio, AL Brazil	MFG	Muzaffarabad, Pakistan
MDC	Manado, Indonesia	MFJ	Moala, Fiji
MDE	Medellin, Colombia	MFM	Macau
MDE	Medellin Jose Maria Cordova Intl, Colombia	MFN	Milford Sound, New Zealand
MDG	Mudanjiang, P R China	MFO	Manguna, Papua New Guinea
MDI	Makurdi, Nigeria	MFR	Medford, OR USA
MDK	Mbandaka, DR of Congo	MFT	Machu Picchu, Peru
MDL	Mandalay, Myanmar	MFU	Mfuwe, Zambia
MDQ	Mar del Plata, BA Argentina	MFW	Magaruque, Mozambique
MDS	Middle Caicos, Turks and Caicos Islands	MFZ	Meselia, Papua New Guinea
MDT	Harrisburg International Apt, PA USA	MGA	Managua, Nicaragua
MDU	Mendi, Papua New Guinea	MGB	Mount Gambier, SA Australia
MDW	Chicago Midway Apt, IL USA	MGD	Magdalena, Bolivia
MDZ	Mendoza, MD Argentina	MGF	Maringa, PR Brazil
MEB	Melbourne Essendon Apt, VI Australia	MGH	Margate, S Africa
MED	Madinah, Saudi Arabia	MGL	Dusseldorf Moenchengladbach, Germany
MEE	Mare, Loyalty Is	MGM	Montgomery, AL USA
MEG	Malange, Angola	MGM	Montgomery Dannelly Field, AL USA
MEH	Mehamn, Norway	MGQ	Mogadishu, Somalia
MEI	Meridian, MS USA	MGS	Mangaia Island, Cook Is
MEL	Melbourne, VI Australia	MGT	Milingimbi, NT Australia
MEL	Melboume Airport, VI Australia	MGV	Margaret River, WA Australia
MEM	Mempis, TN USA	MGW	Morgantown, WV USA
		MGX	Moabi, Gabon
		MGZ	Myeik, Myanmar
		MHD	Mashad, Iran

(*Contd.*)

(Contd.)

Codes	*City: Airport*
MHG	Mannheim, Germany
MHH	Marsh Harbour, Bahamas
MHK	Manhattan, KS USA
MHP	Minsk International 1 Apt, Belarus
MHQ	Mariehamn, Finland
MHT	Manchester, NH USA
MHX	Manihiki Island, Cook is
MIA	Miami, FL USA
MIA	Miami International Apt, FL USA
MID	Merida, Mexico
MII	Marilia, SP Brazil
MIJ	Mili Island, Marshall Is
MIK	Mikkeli, Finland
MIL	Milan, Italy
MIM	Merimbula, NS Australia
MIR	Monastir, Tunisia New Guinea
MIU	Maiduguri, Nigeria
MJA	Manja, Madagascar
MJB	Mejit Island, Marshall Is
MJC	Man, Cote D'Ivoire
MJD	Mohenjodaro, Pakistan
MJE	Mosjoen, Norway
MJK	Monkey Mia, WA Australia
MJL	Mouila, Gabon
MJM	Mbuji-Mayi, DR of Congo
MJN	Majunga, Madagascar
MJT	Mytilene, Greece
MJV	Murcia, Spain
MKB	Mekambo, Gabon
MKC	Kansas City, MO USA
MKE	Milwaukee, WI USA
MKE	Milwaukee General Mitchll Field, WI USA
MKG	Muskegon, MI USA
MKJ	Makoua, Congo
MKK	Hoolehua, HI USA
MKL	Jackson, TN USA

Codes	*City: Airport*
MKM	Mukah, Malaysia
MKN	Malekolon, Papua New Guinea
MKP	Makemo, Tuamotu Islands
MKQ	Merauke, Indonesia
MKR	Meekatharra, WA Australia
MKS	Mekane Selam, Ethiopia
MKU	Makokou, Gabon
MKY	Mackay, QL Australia
MKZ	Malacca, Malaysia
MLA	Malta
MLB	Melbourne, FL USA
MLE	Male, Maldives
MLH	Mulhouse, France
MLI	Moline, IL USA
MLM	Morelia, Mexico
MLN	Melilla, Spain
MLO	Milos, Greece
MLQ	Malalaua, Papua New Guinea
MLS	Miles City, MT USA
MLU	Monroe, LA USA
MLW	Monrovia, Liberia
MLW	Monrovia Sprigg-Payne Apt, Liberia
MLX	Malatya, Turkey
MLY	Manley Hot Springs, AK USA
MMA	Malmo, Sweden
MMB	Memambetsu, Japan
MMD	Minami Daito, Japan
MME	Teesside, UK
MMJ	Matsumoto, Japan
MMK	Murmansk, Russian Federation
MMO	Maio, Cape Verde
MMX	Malmo Sturup Apt, Sweden
MMY	Miyako Jima, Japan
MNB	Moanda, DR of Congo
MNF	Mana Island, Fiji

(Contd.)

(*Contd.*)

Codes	*City: Airport*
MNG	Maningrida, NT Australia
MNJ	Mananjary, Madagascar
MNL	Manila, Philippines
MNL	Manila Ninoy Aquino International Apt, Philippines
MNT	Minto, AK USA
MNU	Maulmyine, Myanmar
MNY	Mono, Solomon Is
MOA	Moa, Cuba
MOB	Mobil, AL USA
MOB	Mobile Municipal Apt, AL USA
MOC	Montes Claros, MG Brazil
MOD	Modesto, CA USA
MOF	Maumere, Indonesia
MOG	Mong Hsat, Myanmar
MOI	Mitiaro Island, Cook Is
MOL	Molde, Norway
MON	Mount Cook, New Zealand
MON	Mount Cook Apt, New Zealand
MOQ	Morondava, Madagascar
MOT	Minot, ND USA
MOT	Minot International Apt, ND USA
MOU	Mountain Village, AK USA
MOW	Moscow, Russian Federa-tion
MOZ	Moorea, Society Is
MPA	Mpacha, Namibia
MPB	Miami SPB, FL USA
MPD	Mirpur Khas, Pakistan
MPH	Caticlan, Philippines
MPK	Mokpo, Rep Of Korea
MPL	Montpellier, France
MPM	Maputo, Mozambique
MPN	Mount Pleasant, Falkland Is
MPU	Mapua, Papua New Guinea
MPW	Mariupol, Ukraine
MQF	Magnitogorsk, Russian Federation
MQH	Minacu, GO Brazil
MQL	Mildura, VI Australia
MQN	Mo I Rana, Norway
MQT	Marquette, MI USA
MQT	Marquette County Apt, MI USA
MQX	Makale, Ethiopia
MRD	Merida, Venezuela
MRE	Mara Lodges, Kenya
MRM	Manare, Papua New Guinea
MRS	Marseille, France
MRU	Mauritius
MRV	Mineralnye Vody, Russian Federation
MRY	Monterey, CA USA
MRY	Monterey Peninsula Apt, CA USA
MRZ	Moree, NS Australia
MSA	Muskrat Dam, OT Canada
MSH	Musirah, Oman
MSJ	Misawa, Japan
MSL	Muscle Shoals, AL USA
MSN	Madison, WI USA
MSO	Missoula, MT USA
MSP	Minneapolis/St. Paul, MIN USA
MSP	Minneapolis International Apt, MN USA
MSQ	Minsk, Belarus
MSQ	Minsk International 2 Apt, Belarus
MSR	Mus, Turkey
MSS	Massena, NY USA
MST	Maastricht, Netherlands
MST	Maastricht Aachen DE Apt, Netherlands
MSU	Maseru, Lesotho
MSY	New Orleans International Apt, LA USA
MSZ	Namibe, Angola

(*Contd.*)

(*Contd.*)

Codes	*City: Airport*	*Codes*	*City: Airport*
MTF	Mizan Teferi, Ethiopia	MWU	Mussau, Papua New Guinea
MTH	Mizan Teferi, Ethiopia	MWV	Mundulkiri, Cambodia
MTI	Mosteiros, Cape Verde	MWZ	Mwanza, Tanzania
MTJ	Montrose, CO USA	MXH	Moro, Papua New Guinea
MTL	Maitland, NS Australia	MXL	Mexicali, Mexico
MTM	Metlakatla, AK USA	MXM	Morombe, Madagascar
MTO	Mattoon, IL USA	MXP	Milan Malpensa Apt, Italy
MTR	Monteria, Colombia	MXS	Maota Savail Is, Samoa
MTS	Manzini, Swaziland	MXT	Maintirano, Madagascar
MTT	Minatitlan, Mexico	MXX	Mora, Sweden
MTV	Mota Lava, Vanuatu	MXZ	Meixian, P R China
MTY	Monterrey, Mexico	MYA	Moruya, NS Australia
MTY	Monterrey General Mariano Escobedo Apt, Mexico	MYB	Mayoumba, Gabon
		MYD	Malindi, Kenya
		MYE	Miyake Jima, Japan
MUA	Munda, Solomon Is	MYG	Mayaguana, Bahamas
MUB	Maun, Botswana	MYJ	Matsuyama, Japan
MUC	Munich, Germany	MYG	Mayaguana, Bahamas
MUE	Kamuela, HI USA	MYJ	Matsuyama, Japan
MUK	Mauke Island, Cook Is	MYR	Myrtle Beach AFB, SC USA
MUN	Maturin, Venezuela	MYT	Myitkyina, Myanmar
MUR	Marudi, Malaysia	MYU	Mekoryuk, AK USA
MUW	Mascara, Algeria	MYW	Mtwara, Tanzania
MUX	Multan, Pakistan	MYX	Menyamya, Papua New Guinea
MVB	Franceville, Gabon		
MVD	Montevideo, Uruguay	MYY	Miri, Malaysia
MVN	Mt Vernon, IL USA	MZC	Mitzic, Gabon
MVR	Maroua, Cameroon	MZG	Makung, Taiwan R.O.C.
MVS	Mucuri, BA Brazil	MZI	Mopti, Mali
MVT	Mataiva, Tuamotu Islands	MZL	Manizales, Colombia
MVX	Minvoul, Gabon	MZO	Manzanilo, Cuba
MVY	Martha's Vineyard, MA USA	MZP	Motueka, New Zealand
MVZ	Masvingo, Zimbabwe	MZT	Mazatlan, Mexico
MWA	Marion, IL USA	MZV	Mulu, Malaysia
MWD	Mianwali, Pakistan		
MWF	Maewo, Vanuatu		**N**
MWH	Moses Lake Grant County Apt, WA USA	NAA	Narrabri, NS Australia
MWI	Maramuni, Papua New Guinea	NAG	Nagpur, India
		NAJ	Nakhichevan, Azerbaijan

(*Contd.*)

(Contd.)

Codes	City: Airport	Codes	City: Airport
NAK	Nakhon Ratchasima, Thailand	NER	Neryungri, Russian Federation
NAN	Nadi, Fiji	NEU	Sam Neua, Lao P D R
NAO	Nanchong, P R China	NEV	Nevis, St Kitts/Nevi
NAP	Naples, Italy	NFG	Nefteyugansk, Russian Federation
NAP	Naples Capodichino Apt, Italy	NFO	Niuafo'ou, Tonga
NAR	Nare, Colombia	NGA	Young, NS Australia
NAS	Nassau, Bahamas	NGB	Ningbo, P R China
NAS	Nassau International Apt, Bahamas	NGD	Anegada, Br Virgin Is
		NGE	Ngaoundere, Cameroon
NAT	Natal, RN Brazil	NGI	Ngau Island, Fiji
NAW	Narathiwat, Thailand	NGO	Nagoya, Japan
NBC	Naberevnye Cheiny, Russian Federation	NGS	Nagasaki, Japan
		NGX	Manang, Nepal
NBO	Nairobi, Kenya	NHA	Nha-Trang, Viet Nam
NBO	Nairobi Jomo Kenyatta International Apt, Kenya	NHV	Nuku Hiva, Marquesas Is
		NIB	Nikolai, AK USA
NCA	North Caicos Turks and Caicos Islands	NIM	Niamey, Niger
		NIX	Nioro, Mali
NCE	Nice, France	NJC	Nizhnevartovsk, Russian Federation
NCI	Necocli, Colombia		
NCL	Newcastle, UK	NKC	Nouakchott, Mauitania
NCP	Luzon Island, Phillppines	NKG	Nanjing, P R China
NCR	San Carlos, Nicaragua	NKI	Naukiti, AK USA
NCU	Nukus, Uzbekistan	NKN	Nankina, Papua New Guinea
NCY	Annecy, France	NKY	Nkayi, Congo
NDB	Nouadhibou, Mauritania	NLA	Ndola, Zambia
NDG	Qiqihar, P R China	NLD	Nuevo Laredo, Mexico
NDI	Namudi, Papua New Guinea	NLG	Nelson Lagoon, AK USA
NDJ	Ndjamena, Chad	NLK	Norfolk Island
NDK	Namdrik Island, Marshall Is	NLP	Nelspruit, S Africa
NDM	Mendi, Ethiopia	NLS	Nicholson, WA Australia
NDY	Sanday, UK	NLV	Nikolaev, Ukraine
NDZ	Nordhoiz-Spieka, Germany	NMA	Namangan, Uzbekistan
NEF	Neftekamsk, Russian Federation	NME	Nightmute, AK USE
		NMG	San Miguel, Panama
NEG	Negril, Jamaica	NNG	Nanning, P R China
NEJ	Nejjo, Ethiopia	NNK	Naknek, AK USA

(Contd.)

(*Contd.*)

Codes	City: Airport
NNL	Nondalton, AK USA
NNT	Nan, Thailand
NNX	Nunukan, Indonesia
NNY	Nanyang, P R China
NOB	Nosara Beach, Costa Rica
NOC	Knock, Republic of Ireland
NOJ	Nojabrxsk, Russian Federation
NOS	Nossi-Be, Madagascar
NOU	Noumea, New Caledonia
NOU	Noumea Tontouta Apt, New Caledonia
NOV	Huambo, Angola
NPE	Napier-Hastings, New Zealand
NPL	New Plymouth, New Zealand
NQL	Niquelandia, GO Brazil
NQN	Neuquen, NE Argentina
NQU	Nuqui, Colombia
NQY	Newquay, UK
NRA	Narrandera, NS Australia
NRK	Norrkoping, Sweden
NRL	North Ronaldsay, UK
NRT	Tokyo Narita Apt, Japan
NSB	Bimini North SPB, Bahamas
NSI	Yaounde Nsimalen Apt, Cameroon
NSK	Norilsk, Russian Federation
NSN	Nelson, New Zealand
NSO	Scone, NS Australia
NST	Nakhon Si Thammarat, Thailand
NSX	North Sound, Br Virgin Is
NTB	Notodden, Norway
NTE	Nantes, France
NTG	Nantong, P R China
NTL	Newcastle, NS Australia
NTL	Newcastle Williamtown Apt, NS Australia
NTN	Normanton, QL Australia
NTO	Santo Antao, Cape Verde
NTT	Niuatoputapu, Tonga
NTY	Sun City, S Africa
NUB	Numbulwar, NT Australia
NUE	Nuremberg, Germany
NUE	Nuremberg Apt, Germany
NUI	Nuiqsut, AK USA
NUL	Nulato, AK USA
NUP	Nunapitchuk, AK USA
NUS	Norsup, Vanuatu
NUX	Novyj Urengoj, Russian Federation
NVG	Nueva Guinea, Nicaragua
NVK	Narvik, Norway
NVR	Novgorod, Russian Federation
NVT	Navegantes, SC Brazil
NWI	Norwich, UK
NWT	Nowata, Papua New Guinea
NYC	New York, NY USA
NYK	Nanyuki, Kenya
NYM	Nadym, Russian Federation
NYN	Nyngan, NS Australia
NYO	Nykoping, Sweden
NYU	Nyaung-U, Myanmar
	O
OAG	Orange, NS Australia
OAJ	Jacksonville, NC USA
OAK	Oakland, CA USA
OAK	Oakland International Apt, CA USA
OAL	Cacoal, TO Brazil
OAX	Oaxaca, Mexico
OBO	Obihiro, Japan
OBU	Kobuk, AK USA
OCV	Ocana, Colombia
ODE	Odense, Denmark

(*Contd.*)

(*Contd.*)

Codes	City: Airport
ODN	Long Seridan, Malaysia
ODS	Odessa, Ukraine
ODW	Oak Harbor, WA USA
ODY	Oudomxay, Lao P D R
OER	Ornskldsvik, Sweden
OFK	Norfolk, NE USA
OFU	Ofu, American Samoa
OGG	Kahului, HI USA
OGN	Yonaguni Jima, Japan
OGS	Ogdensburg, NY USA
OGX	Ouargla, Algeria
OGZ	Vladikavkaz, Russian Federation
OHD	Ohrid, FYR Macedonia
OIM	Oshima, Japan
OIR	Okushiri, Japan
OIT	Oita, Japan
OKA	Okinawa, Japan
OKA	Okinawa Naha Apt, Japan
OKC	Oklahoma City, OK USA
OKC	Oklahoma City Will Rogers Apt, OK USA
OKD	Sapporo Okadama Apt, Japan
OKE	Okino Erabu, Japan
OKI	Oki Island, Japan
OKJ	Okayama, Japan
OKN	Okondja, Gabon
OKR	Yorke Island, QL Australia
OKU	Mokuti Lodge, Namibia
OLB	Olbia, Italy
OLF	Wolf Point, MT USA
OLH	Old Harbor, AK USA
OLJ	Olpoi, Vanuatu
OLP	Olympic Dam, SA Australia
OMA	Omaha, NE USA
OMA	Omaha Eppley Airfield, NE USA
OMB	Omboue, Gabon
OMD	Oranjemund, Namibia
OME	Nome, AK USA
OMH	Urmieh, Iran
OMR	Oradea, Romania
OMS	Omsk, Russian Federation
ONB	Ononge, Papua New Guinea
OND	Ondangwa, Namibia
ONG	Mornington Island, QL Australia
ONT	Ontario, CA USA
ONT	Ontario International Apt, CA USA
ONX	Colon, Panama
OOK	Toksook Bay, AK USA
OOL	Gold Coast, QL Australia
OOM	Cooma, NS Australia
OPB	Open Bay, Papua New Guinea
OPO	Porto, Portugal
OPS	Sinop, MT Brazil
OPU	Balimo, Papua New Giunea
ORB	Orebro, Sweden
ORD	Chicago O'Hare International Apt, IL USA
ORF	Norfolk, VA USA
ORF	Norfolk International Apt, VA USA
ORH	Worcester, MA USA
ORI	Port Lions, AK USA
ORK	Cork, Republic of Ireland
ORL	Orlando, FL USA
ORN	Oran, Algeria
ORN	Oran Es Senia Apt, Algeria
ORV	Noorvik, AK USA
ORW	Ormara, Pakistan
ORY	Paris Orly Apt France
OSA	Osaka, Japan
OSD	Ostersund, Sweden
OSH	Oshkosh, WI USA

(*Contd.*)

(*Contd.*)

Codes	*City: Airport*	*Codes*	*City: Airport*
OSK	Oskarshamn, Sweden	PAS	Paros, Greece
OSL	Oslo, Norway	PAT	Patna, India
OSR	Ostrava, Czech Rep	PAV	Paulo Afonso, BA Brazil
OSS	Osh, Kyrgyzstan	PAZ	Poza Rica, Mexico
OSW	Orsk, Russian Federation	PBC	Puebia, Mexico
OSY	Namsos, Norway	PBD	Porbandar, India
OSZ	Koszalin, Poland	PBE	Puerto Berrio, Colombia
OTD	Contadora, Panama	PBH	Paro, Bhutan
OTH	North Bend, OR USA	PBI	West Palm Beach, FL USA
OTM	Ottumwa, IA USA	PBI	Palm Beach International Apt, FL USA
OTP	Bucharest Otopeni Apt, Romania	PBJ	Paama, Vanuatu
OTR	Coto 47, Costa Rica	PBM	Paramaribo, Suriname
OTS	Anacortes, WA USA	PBM	Paramaribo John A Pengel Apt, Suriname
OTU	Otu, Colombia	PBO	Paraburdoo, WA Australia
OTZ	Kotzebue, AK USA	PBP	Punta Islita, Costa Rica
OUA	Ouagadougou, Burkina Faso	PBU	Putao, Myanmar
OUD	Oujda, Morocco	PBZ	Plettenberg Bay, S Africa
OUE	Ouesso, Congo	PCA	Portage Creek, AK USA
OUL	Oulu, Finland	PCL	Pucallpa, Peru
OUZ	Zouerate Mauritania	PCM	Playa del Carmen, Mexico
OVB	Novosibirsk, Russian Federation	PCP	Principe Island
OVD	Asturias, Spain	PCR	Puerto Carreno, Colombia
OWB	Owensboro, KY USA	PDA	Puerto Inirida, Colombia
OXB	Bissau, Guinea-Bissau	PDB	Pedro Bay, AK USA
OXR	Oxnard/Ventura, CA USA	PDG	Padang, Indonesia
OYE	Oyem, Gabon	PDL	Ponta Delgada, Azores
OZH	Zaporozhye, Ukraine	PDP	Punta Del Este, Uruguay
OZZ	Ouarzazate, Morocco	PDS	Piedras Negras, Mexico
		PDT	Pendleton, OR USA
	P	PDX	Portland, OR USA
PAC	Panama City Paitilla Apt, Panama	PEC	Pelican, AK USA
		PEE	Perm, Russian Federation
PAD	Paderborn, Germany	PEG	Perugia, Italy
PAH	Paducah, KY USA	PEI	Pereira, Colombia
PAJ	Para Chinar, Pakistan	PEK	Beijing Capital Apt, P R China
PAP	Port au Prince, Haiti	PEM	Puerto Maldonado, Peru
PAR	Paris, France	PEN	Penang, Malaysia

(*Contd.*)

(*Contd.*)

Codes	City: Airport
PEN	Penang International Apt, Malaysia
PER	Perth, WA Australia
PES	Petrozavodsk, Russian Federation
PET	Pelotas, RS Brazil
PEU	Puerto Lempira, Honduras
PEW	Peshawar, Pakistan
PFB	Passo Fundo, RS Brazil
PFN	Panama City Bay County Apt, FL USA
PFO	Paphos, Cyprus
PGF	Perpignan, France
PGK	Pangkalpinang, Indonesia
PGV	Greenville, NC USA
PGX	Perigueux, France
PGZ	Ponta Grossa, PR Brazil
PHB	Parnaiba, Pl Brazil
PHC	Port Harcourt, Nigeria
PHE	Port Hedland, WA Australia
PHF	Newport News, VA USA
PHL	Philadelphia, PA USA
PHL	Philadelphia International Apt, PA USA
PHO	Point Hope, AK USA
PHR	Pacific Harbour, Fiji
PHS	Phitsanulok, Thailand
PHW	Phalaborwe, S Africa
PHX	Phoenix, Sky Harbor Int'l Apt, AZ USA
PIA	Peoria, IL USA
PIB	Laurel Pine Belt Regional Apt, MS USA
PID	Nassau Paradise Island, Bahamas
PIE	St Petersburg, FL USA
PIE	St Petersburg/Clearwater Intl Apt, FL USA
PIF	Pingtung, Taiwan R.O.C.
PIH	Pocatello, ID USA
PIK	Glasgow Prestwick Apt, UK
PIP	Pilot Point, AK USA
PIP	Pilot Point Airport, AK USA
PIR	Pierre, SD USA
PIS	Politiers, France
PIT	Pittsburgh, PA USA
PIT	Pittsburgh International Apt, PA USA
PIU	Piura, Peru
PIX	Pico Island, Azores
PIZ	Point Lay, AK USA
PJC	Pedro Juan Caballero, Paraguay
PJG	Panjgur, Pakistan
PJM	Puerto Jimenez, Costa Rica
PKA	Napaskiak, AK USA
PKB	Parkersburg/Marietta, WV USA
PKC	Petropavlovsk-Kamchats, Russian Federation
PKE	Parkes, NS Australia
PKN	Pangkalanbun, Indonesia
PKR	Pokhara, Nepal
PKU	Pekanbaru, Indonesia
PKY	Palangkaraya, Indonesia
PKZ	Pakse, Lao P D R
PLB	Plattsburgh, NY USA
PLB	Plattsburgh Municipal Apt, NY USA
PLH	Plymouth, UK
PLJ	Placencia, Belize
PLM	Palembang, Indonesia
PLN	Pellston, MI USA
PLO	Port Lincoin, SA Australia
PLP	La Palma, Panama
PLQ	Palanga, Lithuania
PLS	Providenciales, Turks and Caicos Islands

(*Contd.*)

(*Contd.*)

Codes	City: Airport
PLU	Belo Horizonte Pamphula Apt, MG Brazil
PLW	Palu, Indonesia
PLX	Semipalatinsk, Kazakstan
PLZ	Port Elizabeth, S Africa
PMC	Puerto Montt, Chile
PMD	Palmdale AFB, CA USA
PMG	Ponta Pora, MS Brazil
PMI	Palma Mallorca, Spain
PML	Port Moller, AK USA
PMN	Pumani, Papua New Guinea
PMO	Palermo, Italy
PMR	Palmerston North, New Zealand
PMV	Porlamar, Venezuela
PMW	Palmas, TO Brazil
PMY	Puerto Madryn, CB Argentina
PMZ	Palmar, Costa Rica
PNA	Pamplona, Spain
PNB	Porto Nacionai, TO Brazil
PNC	Ponca City, OK USA
PND	Punta Gorda, Belize
PNH	Phnom Penh, Cambodia
PNI	Pohnpei, Caroline Is
PNK	Pontianak, Indonesia
PNL	Pantelleria, Italy
PNP	Popondetta, Papua New Guinea
PNQ	Poona, India
PNR	Pointe Noire, Congo
PNS	Pensacola, FL USA
PNS	Pensacola Municipal Apt, FL USA
PNZ	Petrolina, PE Brazil
POA	Porto Alegre, RS Brazil
POG	Port Gentil, Gabon
POI	Potosi, Bolivia
POJ	Patos De Minas, MG Brazil
POL	Pemba, Mozambique
POM	Port Moresby, Papua New Guinea
POP	Puerto Plata, Dominican Rep
POR	Pori, Finland
POS	Port of Spain, Trinidad/Toba
POT	Port Antonio, Jamaica
POU	Poughkeepsie, NY USA
POZ	Poznan, Poland
PPB	President Prudente, SP Brazil
PPG	Pago Pago, American Samoa
PPK	Petropavlovsk, Kazakstan
PPL	Phaplu, Nepal
PPN	Popayan, Colombia
PPP	Proserpine, QL Australia
PPQ	Paraparaumu, New Zealand
PPS	Puerto Princesa, Philippines
PPT	Papeete, Tahiti
PPV	Port Protection, AK USA
PPW	Papa Westray, UK
PQC	Phuquoc, Viet Nam
PQI	Presque, Mexico
PQQ	Port Macquarie, NS Australia
PQS	Pilot Station, AK USA
PRC	Prescolt, AZ USA
PRG	Prague, Czech Rep
PRH	Phrae, Thailand
PRI	Praslin Island, Seychelles
PRN	Pristina, Yugoslavia
PRS	Parasi, Solomon Is
PSA	Pisa, Italy
PSC	Pasco, WA USA
PSE	Ponce, Puerto Rico
PSG	Petersburg, AK USA
PSI	Pasni, Pakistan
PSO	Pasto, Colombia
PSP	Palm Springs, Ca USA
PSP	Palm Springs Muncipal Apt, CA USA
PSR	Pescara, Italy

(*Contd.*)

(*Contd.*)

Codes	*City: Airport*	*Codes*	*City: Airport*
PSS	Posadas, MI Argentina	PZB	Pietermaritzburg, S Africa
PSU	Putussibau, Indonesia	PZE	Penzance, UK
PSZ	Puerto Suarez, Bolivia	PZH	Zhob, Pakistan
PTA	Port Alsworth, AK USA	PZO	Puerto Ordaz, Venezuela
PTD	Port Alexander, AK USA	PZU	Port Sudan, Sudan
PTF	Malololailai, Fiji		
PTG	Pietersburg, S Africa		**Q**
PTH	Port Heiden, AK USA	QBC	Bella Coola, BC Canada
PTJ	Portland, VI Australia	QBF	Vail/Eagle Van Service, CO USA
PTO	Pato Branco, PR Brazil	QCE	Copper Mountain Van Service, CO USA
PTP	Pointe-a-Pitre, Guadeloupe	QDU	Dusseldorf Main Station, Germany
PTU	Platinum, AK USA	QFK	Selje Harbour, Norway
PTY	Panama City, Panama	QFQ	Maloy Harbour, Norway
PTY	Panama City Tocumen International, Panama	QJY	Kolobrzeg Bus Station, Poland
PUB	Pueblo, CO USA	QKB	Breckenridge Van Service, CO USA
PUF	Pau, France	QKL	Cologne Main Station, Germany
PUG	Port Augusta, SA Australia	QKS	Keystone Van Service, CO USA
PUJ	Punta Cana, Dominical Rep	QLE	Leeton Bus Station, NS Australia
PUQ	Punta Arenas, Chile	QRO	Queretaro, Mexico
PUS	Pusan, Rep of Korea		
PUT	Puttaparthi, India		**R**
PUV	Poum, New Caledonia	RAB	Rabaul, Papua New Guinea
PUW	Pullman, WA USA	RAE	Arar, Saudi Arabia
PUY	Pula, Croatia	RAH	Rafha, Saudi Arabia
PUZ	Puerto Cabezas Nicaragua	RAI	Praia, Cape Verde
PVA	Providencia, Colombia	RAJ	Rajkot, India
PVC	Provincetown, MA USA	RAK	Marrakech, Morocco
PVD	Providence, RI USA	RAM	Ramingining, NT Australia
PVH	Porto Velho, RO Brazil	RAO	Ribeirao Preto, SP Brazil
PVK	Preveza/Lefkas, Greece	RAP	Rapid City, SD USA
PVR	Puerto Vallarta, Mexico	RAP	Rapid City Municipal Apt, SD USA
PWM	Portland, ME USA		
PWQ	Pavlodar, Kazakstan		
PXM	Puerto Escondido, Mexico		
PXO	Porto Santo, Madeira Is		
PXU	Pleiku, Viet Nam		
PYE	Penrhyn Island, Cook Is		
PYH	Puerto Ayacucho, Venezuel		

(*Contd.*)

(*Contd.*)

Codes	*City: Airport*
RAR	Rarotonga, Cook Is
RAS	Rasht, Iran
RAT	Raduzhnyi, Russian Federation
RAW	Arawa, Papua New Guinea
RAZ	Rawala Kot, Pakistan
RBA	Rabat, Morocco
RBE	Ratanankiri, Cambodia
RBJ	Rebun, Japan
RBP	Rabaraba, Papua New Guinea
RBR	Rio Branco, AC Brazil
RBV	Ramata, Solomon Is
RBY	Ruby, AK USA
RCB	Richards Bay, S Africa
RCE	Roche Harbor, WA USA
RCH	Riohacha, Colombia
RCL	Redcliffe, Vanuatu
RCM	Richmond, QL Australia
RCU	Rio Cuarto, CD Argentina
RDC	Redencao, PA Brazil
RDD	Redding, CA USA
RDG	Reading, PA USA
RDM	Redmond, OR USA
RDS	Rincon de los Sauces, NE Argentina
RDU	Releigh/Durham, NC USA
RDV	Red Devil, AK USA
RDZ	Rodez, France
REC	Recife, PE Brazil
REG	Reggio Calabria, Italy
REK	Reykjavik, Iceland
REL	Trelew, CB Argentina
REN	Orenburg, Russian Federation
REP	Siem Reap, Cambodia
RES	Resistencia, CH Argentina
RET	Rost, Norway
REU	Reus, Spain
REX	Reynosa, Mexico
RFD	Rockford, IL USA
RFD	Rockford Greater Rockford Apt, IL USA
REP	Raiatea Island, Society Is
RFS	Rosita, Nicaragua
RGA	Rio Grande, TF Argentina
RGE	Porgera, Papua New Guinea
RGI	Rangiroa Island, Tuamotu Islands
RGL	Rio Gallegos, SC Argentina
RGN	Yangon, Myanmar
RHD	Rio Hondo, SE Argentina
RHE	Reims, France
RHI	Rhinelander, WI USA
RHO	Rhodes, Greece
RIA	Santa Maria, RS Brazil
RIB	Riberalta, Bolivia
RIC	Richmond, VA USA
RIG	Rio Grande, RS Brazil
RIJ	Rioja, Peru
RIK	Carrillo, Costa Rica
RIN	Ringi Cove, Solomon Is
RIO	Rio de Janeiro, RJ Brazil
RIS	Rishiri, Japan
RIW	Riverton, WY USA
RIX	Riga, Latvia
RIY	Riyan Mukalla, Republic of Yemen
RJH	Rajshahi, Bangladesh
RKD	Rockland, ME USA
RKS	Rock Springs, WY USA
RKT	Ras Al Khaimah, United Arab Emirates
RKU	Yule Island, Papua New Guinea
RKV	Reykjavik Apt, Iceland
RLG	Rostock-Laage, Germany
RMA	Roma, QL Australia
RMI	Rimini, Italy

(*Contd.*)

(Contd.)

Codes	*City: Airport*
RMK	Renmark, SA Australia
RMP	Rampart, AK USA
RNB	Ronneby, Sweden
RNE	Roanne, France
RNI	Com Island, Nicaragua
RNJ	Yoronjima, Japan
RNL	Rennell, Solomon Is
RNN	Bornholm, Denmark
RNO	Reno, NV USA
RNS	Rennes, France
ROA	Roanoke, VA USA
ROC	Rochester, NY USA
ROK	Rockhampton, QL Australia
ROM	Rome, Italy
ROO	Rendonopolis, MT Brazil
ROP	Rota, N. Mariana Is
ROR	Koror, Palau
ROS	Rosario, SF Argentina
ROT	Rotorua, New Zealand
ROV	Rostov, Russian Federation
ROW	Roswell, NM USA
RPM	Rome, Italy
RPN	Rosh Pina, Israel
RPR	Raipur, India
RRG	Rodrigues Island, Mauritius
RRS	Roros, Norway
RSA	Santa Rosa, LP Argentina
RSD	Rock Sound, Bahamas
RSH	Russian Mission, AK USA
RSJ	Rosario, WA USA
RST	Rochester, MN USA
RST	Rochester Municipal Apt, MN USA
RSU	Yosu, Rep of Korea
RSW	Fort Myers SW Florida Regional Apt, FL USA
RTA	Rotuma Island, Fiji
RTB	Roatan, Honduras
RTM	Rotterdam, Netherlands
RTM	Rotterdam Apt, Netherlands
RTS	Rottnest Island, WA Australia
RTW	Saratov, Russian Federation
RUH	Riyadh, Saudi Arabia
RUI	Ruidoso, NM USA
RUN	St Denis de la Reunion, Reunion Island
RUR	Rurutu, Tubual Is
RUS	Mmarau Island, Solomon Is
RUT	Rutland, VT USA
RVA	Farafangana, Madagascar
RVK	Roervik, Norway
RVN	Rovaniemi, Finland
RWI	Rocky Mount, NC USA
RXS	Roxas, Philippines
RYK	Rahim Yar Khan, Pakistan
	S
SAB	Saba, Netherlands Antilles
SAC	Sacramento, CA USA
SAF	Santa Fe, NM USA
SAH	Sanaa, Republic of Yemen
SAK	Saudarkrokur, Iceland
SAL	San Salvador, El Salvador
SAM	Salamo, Papua New Guinea
SAN	San Diego, CA USA
SAO	Sao Paulo, SP Brazil
SAP	San Pedro Sula, Honduras
SAQ	San Andros, Bahamas
SAT	San Antonio International Apt, TX USA
SAV	Savannah, GA USA
SAV	Savannah International Apt, GA USA
SAX	Sambu, Panama
SBA	Santa Barbara, CA USA
SBA	Santa Barbara Municipal Apt, CA USA
SBH	St Barthelemy, Guadeloupe

(Contd.)

(*Contd.*)

Codes	*City: Airport*
SBK	St Brieuc, France
SBN	South Bend, IN USA
SBP	San Luis Obispo County Apt, CA USA
SBS	Steamboat Springs, CO USA
SBS	Steamboat Springs Apt, CO USA
SBU	Springbok, S Africa
SBW	Sibu, Malaysia
SBY	Salisbury, MD USA
SBZ	Sibiu, Romania
SCC	Prudhoe Bay/Deadhorse, AK USA
SCE	State College, PA USA
SCJ	Smith Cove, AK USA
SCL	Santiago, Chile
SCL	Santiago Comodoro Arturo Merino Benitez, Chile
SCM	Scammon Bay, AK USA
SCN	Saarbrucken, Germany
SCN	Saarbrucken Ensheim, Airport, Germany
SCO	Aktau, Kazakstan
SCQ	Santiago de Compostela, Spain
SCT	Socotra, Republic of Yemen
SCU	Santiago, Cuba
SCV	Suceava, Romania
SCX	Salina Cruz, Mexico
SCY	San Cristobal, Ecuador
SCZ	Santa Cruz Island, Solomon Is
SDD	Lubango, Angola
SDE	Santiago Del Estero, SE Argentina
SDF	Louisville, KY USA
SDF	Louisville Standiford Field, KY USA
SDI	Saidor, Papua New Guinea
SDJ	Sendai, Japan
SDK	Sandakan, Malaysia
SDL	Sundsvall, Sweden
SDN	Sandane, Norway
SDP	Sand Point, AK USA
SDQ	Santo Domingo, Dominican Rep
SDQ	Santo Domingo Las Americas Apt, Dominican Rep
SDR	Santander, Spain
SDT	Saidu Sharif, Pakistan
SDU	Rio de Janeiro Santos Dumont Apt, RJ Brazil
SDV	Tel Aviv Yafo Sde Dov, Israel
SDY	Sidney, MT USA
SDZ	Shetland Islands, UK
SEA	Seattle, WA USA
SEA	Seattle-Tacoma Interna-tional Apt, WA USA
SEL	Seoul, Rep of Korea
SEL	Seoul Kimpo International Apt, Rep of Korea
SEY	Selibaby, Mauritania
SEZ	Mahe Island, Seychelles
SFA	Sfax, Tunisia
SFB	Orlando Sanford Apt, FL USA
SFD	San Fernando de Apure, Venezuela
SFG	St Martin, Guadeloupe
SFG	St Martin Esperance Apt, Guadeloupe
SFJ	Kangerlussuaq, Greenland
SFL	Sao Filipe, Cape Verde
SFN	Santa Fe, SF Argentina
SFO	San Francisco, CA USA
SFO	San Francisco International Apt, CA USA
SFQ	Sanliurfa, Turkey
SFS	Subic Bay, Philippines
SFT	Skelleftea, Sweden
SFU	Safia, Papua New Guinea

(*Contd.*)

(Contd.)

Codes	City: Airport
SGC	Surgut, Russian Federation
SGD	Sonderborg, Denmark
SGF	Springfield, MO USA
SGN	Ho Chi Minh City, Viet Nam
SGO	St George, OL Australia
SGU	St George, UT USA
SHA	Shanghai, P R China
SHG	Shungnak, AK USA
SHH	Shishmarel, AK USA
SHJ	Sharjah, United Arab Emirates
SHM	Nanki Shirahama, Japan
SHO	Sokcho, Rep of Korea
SHP	Qinhuangdao, P R China
SHR	Sheridan, WY USA
SHS	Shashi, P R China
SHT	Shepparton, VI Australia
SHV	Shreveport, LA USA
SHV	Shreveport Regional Apt, LA USA
SHW	Sharurah, Saudi Arabia
SHX	Shageluk, AK USA
SIA	Xi an, P R China
SIB	Sinop, Turkey
SIC	Sinop, Turkey
SID	Sal, Cape Verde
SIF	Simra, Nepal
SIG	San Juan Isla Grande Apt, Puerto Rico
SIL	Sila, Papua New Guinea
SIN	Singapore
SIN	Singapore Changi Apt, Singapore
SIP	Simferopol, Ukraine
SIR	Sion, Switzerland
SIT	Sitka, AK USA
SIU	Siuna, Nicaragua
SIX	Singleton, NS Australia
SJB	San Joaquin, Bolivia
SJC	San Jose, CA USA
SJC	San Jose International Apt, CA USA
SJD	San Jose Cabo, Mexico
SJI	San Jose, Philippines
SJJ	Sarajevo, Bosnia
SJK	Sao Jose Dos Campos, SP Brazil
SJO	San Jose, Costa Rica
SJO	San Jose Juan Santamaria Apt, Costa Rica
SJP	Sao Jose Do Rio Preto, SP Brazil
SJT	San Angelo, TX USA
SJT	San Angelo Mathis Field, TX USA
SJU	San Juan, Puerto Rico
SJU	San Juan Luis Munoz Marin Intl Apt, Puerto Rico
SJW	Shijazhuang, P R China
SJY	Seinajoki, Finland
SJZ	Sao Jorge Island, Azores
SKB	St Kitts, St Kitts/Nevi
SKD	Samarkand, Uzbekistan
SKE	Skien, Norway
SKG	Thessaloniki, Greece
SKH	Surkhet, Nepal
SKK	Shaktoolik, AK USA
SKN	Stokmarknes, Norway
SKO	Sokoto, Nigeria
SKP	Skopje, FYR Macedonia
SKS	Vojens, Denmark
SKU	Skiros, Greece
SKZ	Sukkur, Pakistan
SLA	Salta, SA Argentina
SLC	Salt Lake City, UT USA
SLE	Salem, OR USA
SLH	Sola, Vanuatu
SLK	Saranac Lake, NY USA
SLL	Salalah, Oman
SLM	Salamanca, Spain

(Contd.)

(*Contd.*)

Codes	*City: Airport*
SLN	Salina, KS USA
SLP	San Luis Potosi, Mexico
SLQ	Sleetmute, AK USA
SLU	St Lucia, St Lucia
SLU	St Lucia Vigie Apt, St Lucia
SLV	Simla, India
SLW	Saltillo, Mexico
SLX	Salt Cay, Turks and Caicos Islands
SLY	Salehard, Russian Federation
SLZ	Sao Luiz, MA Brazil
SMA	Santa Maria, Azores
SMF	Sacramento Metropolitan Apt, CA USA
SMI	Samos, Greece
SMK	St Michael, AK USA
SML	Stella Maris, Bahamas
SMM	Sempoma, Malaysia
SMQ	Sampit, Indonesia
SMR	Santa Marta, Colombia
SMS	Ste Marie, Madagascar
SMX	Santa Maria, CA USA
SNA	Santa Ana, CA USA
SNA	Santa An John Wayne Intl Apt, CA USA
SNB	Snake Bay, NT Australia
SNE	Sao Nicolau, Cape Verde
SNN	Shannon, Republic of Ireland
SNO	Sakon Nakhon, Thailand
SNP	St Paul Island, AK USA
SNV	Santa Elena, Venezuela
SNW	Thandwe, Myanmar
SOC	Solo City, Indonesia
SOD	Sorocaba, SP Brazil
SOF	Sofia, Bulgaria
SOG	Sogndal, Norway
SOI	South Molle Island, QL Australia
SOJ	Sorkjosen, Norway
SOM	San Tome, Venezuela
SON	Espiritu Santo, Vanuatu
SOO	Soderhamn, Sweden
SOP	Southern Pines, NC USA
SOQ	Sorong, Indonesia
SOU	Southampton, UK
SOY	Stronsay, UK
SPB	St Thomas SPB, VI US
SPC	Santa Cruz de la Palma, Canary Is
SPD	Saidpur, Bangladesh
SPH	Sopu, Papua New Guinea
SPI	Springfield, IL USA
SPK	Sapporo, Japan
SPN	Saipan, N. Mariana Is
SPP	Menongue, Angola
SPR	San Pedro, Belize
SPS	Wichita Falls, TX USA
SPS	Wichita Falls Sheppard AFB, TX USA
SPU	Split, Croatia
SPW	Spencer, IA USA
SQC	Southern Cross, WA Australia
SQG	Sintang, Indonesia
SQH	Son-La, Viet Nam
SQI	Strling, IL USA
SQJ	Shehdi, Ethiopia
SQO	Storuman, Sweden
SRA	Santa Rosa, RS Brazil
SRE	Sucre, Bolivia
SRG	Semarang, Indonesia
SRI	Samarinda, Indonesia
SRJ	San Borja, Bolivia
SRP	Stord, Norway
SRQ	Sarasota/Bradenton, FL USA
SRV	Stony River, AK USA
SRY	Sary, Iran
SRZ	Santa Cruz, Bolivia
SSA	Salvador, BA Brazil

(*Contd.*)

(Contd.)

Codes	City: Airport
SSB	St Croix SPB, VI US
SSG	Malabo, Equat Guinea
SSH	Sharm El Sheikh, Egypt
SSI	Brunswick, GA USA
SSJ	Sandnessjoen, Norway
SSM	Sault Sainte Marie, MI USA
SSR	Sara, Vanuatu
SSX	Samsun, Turkey
SSY	M'Banza Congo, Angola
STC	St Cloud, MN USA
STC	St Cloud Municipal At, MN USA
STD	Santo Domingo, Venezuela
STG	St George Island, AK USA
STI	Santiago, Dominican Rep
STL	St Louis, MO USA
STL	St Louis Lambert Intl Apt, MO USA
STM	Santarem, PA Brazil
STN	London Stansted Apt, UK
STO	Stockholm, Sweden
STR	Stuttgart, Germany
STR	Stuttgart Apt, Germany
STS	Santa Rosa, CA USA
STT	St Thomas Cyril E King Apt, VI US
STW	Stavropol, Russian Federation
STX	St Croix Island, VI US
STX	St Croix Island Alexander Hamilton Apt, VI US
SUB	Surabaya, Indonesia
SUF	Lamezia Teme, Italy
SUH	Sur, Oman
SUJ	Satu Mare, Romania
SUL	Sui, Pakistan
SUN	Sun Valey, ID USA
SUR	Summer Beaver, OT Canada
SUV	Suva, Fiji
SUX	Sioux City, IA USA
SVA	Savoonga, AK USA
SVB	Sambava, Madagascar
SVC	Silver City, NM USA
SVD	St Vincent
SVG	Stavanger, Norway
SVJ	Svolvaer, Norway
SVL	Savonlinna, Finland
SVO	Moscow Sheremetyevo Apt, Russian Federation
SVP	Kuito, Angola
SVQ	Seville, Spain
SVS	Stevens Village, AK USA
SVU	Savusavu, Fiji
SVX	Ekaterinburg, Russian Federation
SVZ	San Antonio, Venezuela
SWA	Shantou, P R China
SWD	Seward, AK USA
SWF	Newburgh, NY USA
SWG	Satwag, Papua New Guinea
SWJ	South West Bay, Vanuatu
SWP	Swakopmund, Namibia
SWR	Silur, Papua New Guinea
SWT	Strzhewoi, Russian Federation
SXB	Strasbourg, France
SXE	Sale, VI Australia
SXF	Berlin Schonefeld Apt, Germany
SXH	Sehulea, Papua New Guinea
SXL	Sligo, Republic of Ireland
SXM	St Maarten, Netherlands Antilles
SXO	Sao Felix Do Araguaia, MT Brazil
SXP	Sheldon Point, AK USA
SXR	Srinagar, India
SXS	Sahabat 16, Malaysia
SXW	Sauren, Papua New Guinea
SXZ	Siirt, Turkey

(Contd.)

(*Contd.*)

Codes	*City: Airport*	*Codes*	*City: Airport*
SYB	Seal Bay, AK USA	TBG	Tabubil, Papua New Guinea
SYD	Sydney, NS Australia	TBI	The Bight, Bahamas
SYD	Sydney Kingsford Smith Apt, NS Australia	TBJ	Tabarka, Tunisia
SYE	Sa Dah, Republic of Yemen	TBN	Frt Leonard Wood, MO USA
SYM	Simao, P R China	TBO	Tabora, Tanzania
SYO	Shonai, Japan	TBP	Tumbes, Peru
SYP	Santiago, Panama	TBS	Tbilisi, Georgia
SYQ	San Jose Tobias Bolanos Apt, Costa Rica	TBT	Tabatinga, AM Brazil
SYR	Syracuse, NY USA	TBU	Tongatapu, Tonga
SYW	Sehwen Sharif, Pakistan	TBZ	Tabriz, Iran
SYX	Sanya, P R China	TCA	Tennnant Creek, NT Australia
SYY	Stomoway, UK	TCB	Teasure Cay, Bahamas
SYZ	Shiraz, Iran	TCE	Tulcea, Romania
SZA	Soyo, Angola	TCG	Tacheng, P R China
SZG	Salzburg, Austria	TCH	Tohibanga, Gabon
SZK	Skukuza, S Africa	TCI	Tenerife, Canary Is
SZX	Shenzhen, P R China	TCO	Tumaco, Colombia
SZZ	Szczecin, Poland	TCP	TABA, Egypt
	T	TCQ	Tacna, Peru
TAB	Tobago, Trinidad/Toba	TCT	Tacotna, AK USA
TAC	Tacloban, Philippines	TDB	Tetabedi, Papua New Guinea
TAE	Taegu, Rep of Korea	TDD	Trinidad, Bolivia
TAG	Tagbilaran, Philippines	TEC	Telemaco Borba, P R Brazil
TAH	Tanna, Vanuatu	TED	Thisted, Denmark
TAI	Taiz, Republic of Yemen	THE	Tetlin, AK USA
TAJ	Tadji, Papua New Guinea	TEO	Terapo, Papua New Guinea
TAK	Takamatsu, Japan	TEP	Teptep, Papua New Guinea
TAL	Tanana, AK USA	TER	Terceira, Azores
TAM	Tampico, Mexico	TET	Tete, Mozambique
TAO	Qingdao, P R China	TET	Tete Matunda Apt, Mozambique
TAP	Tapachula, Mexico	TEU	Te Anau, New Zealand
TAS	Tashkent, Uzbekistan	TEX	Telluride, CO USA
TAT	Tatry/Poprad, Slovakia	TEZ	Tezpur, India
TAV	Tau, American Samoa	TFF	Tefe, AM Brazil
TBB	Tuyhoa, Viet Nam	TFI	Tufi, Papua New Guinea
TBE	Timbunke, Papua New Guinea	TFM	Telefomin, Papua New Guinea
		TFN	Tenerife Norte Apt, Canary Is

(*Contd.*)

(*Contd.*)

Codes	*City: Airport*
TFS	Tenerife Sur Reina Sofia Apt, Canary Is
TGD	Podgorica, Yugoslavia
TGG	Kuala Terengganu, Malaysia
TGH	Tongoa, Vanuatu
TGI	Tingo Maria, Peru
TGJ	Tiga, Loyalty Is
TGM	Tirgu Mures, Romania
TGN	Traralgon, VI Australia
TGR	Touggourt, Algeria
TGU	Tegucigalpa, Honduras
TGZ	Tuxtla Gutierrez, Mexico
THE	Teresina, PI Brazil
THF	Berlin Tempelhof Apt, Germany
THG	Thangool, QL Australia
THL	Tachilek, Myanmar
THN	Trollhattan, Sweden
THR	Tehran, Iran
THS	Sukhothai, Thailand
THU	Pituffik, Greenland
TIA	Tirana, Albania
TIC	Tinak Island, Marshall Is
TID	Tiaret, Algeria
TIE	Tippi, Ethiopia
TIF	Tippi, Ethiopia
TIF	Taif, Saudi Arabia
TIH	Tikehau Atoll, Tuamotu Islands
TIJ	Tijuana, Mexico
TIM	Tembagapura, Indonesia
TIQ	Tinian, N Mariana Is
TIR	Tirupati, India
TIS	Thursday Island, QL Australia
TIU	Timaru, New Zealand
TIV	Tivat, Yugoslavia
TIY	Tidjikja, Mauritania
TIZ	Tari, Papua New Guinea
TJA	Tarija, Bolivia
TJH	Toyooka, Japan
TJI	Trujillo, Honduras
TJK	Tokat, Turkey
TJM	Tyumen, Russian Federation
TJQ	Tanjung Pandan, Indonesia
TJS	Tanjung Selor, Indonesia
TKB	Tekadu, Papua New Guinea
TKE	Tenakee, AK USA
TKK	Truk, Caroline Is
TKN	Tokunoshima, Japan
TKU	Turku, Finland
TKX	Takaroa, Tuamotu Islands
TLA	Teller, AK USA
TLE	Tulear, Madagascar
TLH	Tallahassee, FL USA
TLJ	Tatalina, AK USA
TLL	Tallin, Estonia
TLN	Toulon, France
TLS	Toulouse Blagnac Apt, France
TLT	Tuluksak, AK USA
TLV	Tel Aviv, Israel
TLV	Tel Aviv Ben Gurion Int'l Apt, Israel
TMG	Tomanggong, Malaysia
TMI	Tumlingtar, Nepal
TMJ	Termez, Uzbekistan
TMM	Tamatave, Madagascar
TMP	Tampere, Finland
TMR	Tamanrasset, Algeria
TMS	Sao Tome Island, Sao Tome Is
TMT	Trombetas, PA Brazil
TMU	Tambor, Costa Rica
TMW	Tamworth, NS Australia
TMX	Timimoun, Algeria
TNA	Jinan, P R China
TNC	Tin City, AK USA
TNE	Tanegashima, Japan
TNG	Tangler, Morocco

(*Contd.*)

(Contd.)

Codes	City: Airport
TNK	Tununak, AK USA
TNN	Tainan, Taiwan R.O.C.
TNO	Tamarindo, Costa Rica
TNR	Antananarivo, Madagascar
TNX	Stung Treng, Cambodia
TOD	Toman, Malaysia
TOE	Tozeur, Tunisia
TOF	Tomsk, Russian
TOG	Toglak, AK USA
TOH	Torres, Vanuatu
TOL	Toledo, OH USA
TOL	Toledo Express Apt, OH USA
TOM	Tombouctou, Mali
TOP	Topeka, KS USA
TOS	Tromso, Norway
TOU	Touho, New Caledonia
TOW	Toledo, PR Brazil
TOY	Toyama, Japan
TPA	Tampa, FL USA
TPA	Tampa International Apt, FL USA
TPE	Taipel, Taiwan R.O.C.
TPE	Taipel Chiang Kai Shek Intl Apt, Taiwan R.O.C.
TPI	Tapini, Papua New Guinea
TPJ	Taplejung, Nepal
TPP	Tarapoto, Peru
TPQ	Tepic, Mexico
TRD	Trondheim, Norway
TRE	Tiree, UK
TRF	Sandefjord, Norway
TRG	Tauranga, New Zealand
TRI	Tri-Cities Regional, TN USA
TRK	Tarakan, Indonesia
TRN	Turin, Italy
TRO	Taree, NS Australia
TRS	Trieste, Italy
TRU	Trujillo, Peru
TRV	Trivandrum, India
TRW	Tarawa, Kiribati
TRZ	Tiruchirapally, India
TSA	Talpei Sung Shan Apt, Taiwan R.O.C.
TSB	Tsumeb, Namibia
TSE	Akmola, Kazakstan
TSF	Venice Treviso Apt, Italy
TSH	Tsushima, Japan
TSN	Tianjin, P R China
TSO	Isles of Scilly Tresco Apt, UK
TSR	Timisoara, Romania
TSS	New York East 34th Street H/P, NY USA
TST	Trang, Thailand
TSV	Townsville, QL Australia
TTB	Tortoli, Italy
TTE	Temale, Indonesia
TTJ	Tottori, Japan
TTN	Trendon, NJ USA
TTQ	Tortuquero, Costa Rica
TTS	Tsaratanana, Madagascar
TTT	Taitung, Taiwan R.O.C.
TTU	Tetuan, Morocco
TUB	Tubuai, Tubuai Is
TUC	Tucuman, TU Argentina
TUF	Tours, France
TUG	Tuguegarao, Philippines
TUI	Turaif, Saudi Arabia
TUJ	Tum, Ethiopia
TUK	Turbat, Pakistan
TUL	Tulsa, OK USA
TUL	Tulsa International Apt, OK USA
TUN	Tunis, Tunisia
TUO	Taupo, New Zealand
TUP	Tupelo, MS USA
TUR	Tucurui, PA Brazil
TUS	Tucson, International Apt, AZ USA

(Contd.)

(Contd.)

Codes	City: Airport
TUU	Tabuk, Saudi Arabia
TUZ	Tucuma, PA Brazil
TVA	Morafenobe, Madagascar
TVC	Traverse City, MI USA
TVF	Thief River Falls, MN USA
TVU	Taveuni, Fiji
TVY	Dawe, Myanmar
TWA	Twin Falls, ID USA
TWB	Toowoomba, QL Australia
TWF	Twin Falls, ID USA
TWU	Tawau, Malaysia
TXG	Taichung, Taiwan R.O.C.
TXK	Texarkana, AR USA
TXL	Berlin Tegel Apt, Germany
TXN	Tunxi, P R China
TYF	Torsby, Sweden
TYN	Taiyuan, P R China
TYO	Tokyo, Japan
TYR	Tyler, TX USA
TYS	Knoxville, T N USA
TZA	Belize City Municipal Apt, Belize
TZN	South Andros, Bahamas
TZX	Trabzon, Turkey
	U
UAK	Narsarsuaq, Greenland
UAQ	San Juan, SJ Argentina
UAS	Samburu, Kenya
UBA	Uberaba, MG Brazil
UBI	Buin, Papua New Guinea
UBJ	Ube, Japan
UBP	Ubon Ratchathani, Thailand
UBS	Colombus, MS USA
UCA	Utica, NY USA
UDI	Uberlandia, MG Brazil
UDJ	Uzhgorod, Ukraine
UDR	Udaipur, India
UEL	Quelimane, Mozambique
UEO	Kume Jima, Japan
UET	Quetta, Pakistan
UFA	Ufa, Russian Federation
UGB	Pilot Point Ugashik Bay Apt, AK USA
UGC	Urgench, Uzbekistan
UGI	Uganik, AK USA
UGO	Uige, Angola
UIB	Quibdo, Colombia
UIH	Quinhon, Viet Nam
UII	Utila, Honduras
UIK	Ust-Ilimsk, Russian Federation
UIN	Quincy, IL USA
UIO	Quito, Ecuador
UIP	Quimper, France
UIT	Jaluit Island, Marshall Is
UJE	Ujae Island, Marshal Is
UKA	Ukunda, Kenya
UKK	Ust-Kamenogorsk, Kazakshan
UKU	Nuku, Papua New Guinea
ULB	Ulei, Vanuatu
ULD	Ulundi, S. Africa
ULE	Sule, Papua New Guinea
ULG	Ulgit, Mongolia
ULN	Ulaanbaatar, Mongolia
ULP	Quilpie, QL Australia
UMD	Uummannaq, Greenland
UME	Umea, Sweden
UMR	Woomera, SA Australia
UNG	Kiunga Papua New Guinea
UNI	Union Island, Grenadine Is
UNK	Unalakleet, AK USA
UNN	Ranong, Thailand
UNT	Unst, UK
UPG	Ujung Pandang, Indonesia
UPN	Uruapan, Mexico
URA	Uralsk, Kazakshan

(Contd.)

(Contd.)

Codes	City: Airport	Codes	City: Airport
URC	Urumqi, P R China	VAW	Vardoe, Norway
URG	Uruguaiana, RS Brazil	VBV	Vanuabalavu, Fiji
URJ	Uraj, Russian Federation	VBY	Visby, Sweden
URO	Rouen, France	VCD	Victoria River Downs, NT Australia
URR	Urrao, Colombia	VCE	Venice, Italy
URT	Surat Thani, Thailand	VCE	Venice Marco Polo Apt, Italy
URY	Gurayat, Saudi Arabia	VCT	Victoria, TX USA
USH	Ushuaia, TF Argentina	VDA	Ovda, Israel
USL	Useless Loop, WA Australia	VDB	Fagemes, Norway
USM	Koh Samui, Thailand	VDC	Vitoria Da Conquista, BA Brazil
USN	Ulsan, Rep of Korea	VDE	Valverde, Canary Is
USU	Busuanga, Philippines	VDM	Viedma, RN Argentina
UTH	Udon Thani, Thailand	VDS	Vadso, Norway
UTK	Uttirik Island, Marshall Is	VDZ	Valdez, AK USA
UTN	Upington, S Africa	VEE	Venetle, AK USA
UTO	Utopia Creek, AK USA	VEL	Vemal, UT USA
UTP	Utapao, Thailand	VER	VeraCruz, Mexico
UTT	Umtata, S Africa	VEY	Vestmannaeyjar, Iceland
UUD	Ulan-Ude, Russian Federation	VFA	Victoria Falls, Zimbabwe
UUU	Manumu, Papua New Guinea	VGO	Vigo, Spain
UVE	Ouvea, Loyalty Is	VGT	Las Vegas North Air Terminal, NV USA
UVF	St Lucia Hewanorra Apt, St Lucia	VHC	Saurimo, Angola
UVL	New Valley, Egypt	VHM	Vilhelmina, Sweden
UVO	Uvol, Papua New Guinea	VIA	Videira, SC Brazil
UYN	Yulin, PR China	VIE	Vienna, Austria
	V	VII	Vinh City, Viet Nam
VAA	Vaasa, Finland	VIJ	Virgin Gorda, Br Virgin Is
VAG	Varginha, MG Brazil	VIL	Dakhla, Morocco
VAI	Vanimo, Papua New Guinea	VIS	Visalla, CA USA
VAK	Chevak, AK USA	VIT	Visalia, Spain
VAN	Chevak, Turkey	VIV	Vivigani, Papua New Guinea
VAO	Suavanao, Solomon Is	VIX	Vitoria, ES Brazil
VAR	Vama, Bulgaria	VKO	Moscow Vnukovo Apt, Russian Federation
VAS	Sivas, Turkey	VLC	Valencia, Spain
VAT	Vatomandry, Madagascar	VLD	Valdosta, GA USA
VAV	Vava'u, Tonga		

(Contd.)

(*Contd.*)

Codes	*City: Airport*
VLD	Valdosta Regional Apt, GA USA
VLI	Port Vila, Vanuatu
VLL	Valladolid, Spain
VLN	Valencia, Venezuela
VLP	Villa Rica, MT Brazil
VLS	Valesdir, Vanuatu
VME	Vila Mercedes, SL Argentina
VMU	Baimuru, Papua New Guinea
VNA	Saravane, Lao P D R
VNO	Vilnius, Lithuania
VNS	Varanasi, India
VOG	Volgograd, Russian Federation
VOH	Vohemar, Madagascar
VOZ	Voronezh, Russian Federation
VPS	Valparaiso, FL USA
VPS	Valparaiso Fort Walton Beach Apt, FL USA
VQS	Vieques, Puerto Rico
VRA	Varadero, Cuba
VRC	Virac, Philippines
VRK	Varkaus, Finland
VRN	Verona, Italy
VSA	Villahermosa, Mexico
VSG	Lugansk, Ukraine
VST	Vasteras, Sweden
VTE	Vientiane, Lao P D R
VTU	Las Tunas, Cuba
VTZ	Vishakhapatnam, India
VUP	Valledupar, Colombia
VVB	Mahanoro, Madagascar
VVI	Santa Cruz Viru Viru International Apt, Bolivia
VVO	Vladivostok, Russian Federation
VVZ	Illizi, Algeria
VXC	Lichinga, Mozambique
VXE	Sao Vicente, Cape Verde
VXO	Vaxjo, Sweden
	W
WAA	Wales, AK USA
WAD	Andriamena, Madagascar
WAE	Wadi Ad Dawasir, Saudi Arabia
WAG	Wanganui, New Zealand
WAI	Antsohihy, Madagascar
WAM	Ambatondrazaka, Madagascar
WAQ	Antsalova, Madagascar
WAS	Washington, DC USA
WAT	Waterford, Republic of Ireland
WAW	Warsaw, Poland
WBB	Stebbins, AK USA
WBC	Wapolu, Papua New Guinea
WBE	Bealanana, Madagascar
WBM	Wapenamanda, Papua
WBQ	Beaver, AK USA
WDG	Enid, OK USA
WDG	Enid Woodring Municipal Apt, OK USA
WDH	Windhoek, Namibia
WDH	Windhoek International, Namibia
WED	Wedau, Papua New Guinea
WEH	Weihai, P R China
WEI	Weipa, QL Australia
WFI	Fianarantsoa, Madagascar
WFK	Frenchville, ME USA
WGA	Wagga Wagga, NS Australia
WGE	Walgett, NS Australia
WGP	Waingapu, Indonesia
WHD	Hyder, AK USA
WHK	Whakatane, New Zealand
WIC	Wick, UK
WIL	Nairobi Wilson Apt, Kenya
WIN	Winton, QL Australia

(*Contd.*)

(Contd.)

Codes	City: Airport	Codes	City: Airport
WIR	Wairoa, New Zealand	WTL	Tuntutuliak, AK USA
WIU	Witu, Papua New Guinea	WTO	Wotho Island, Marshal Is
WJA	Woja, Marshall Is	WTP	Woitape, Papua New Guinea
WJU	Won-ju, Rep of Korea	WTS	Tsiroanomandidy, Madagascar
WKA	Wanaka, New Zealand	WUD	Wudinna, SA Austalia
WKJ	Wakkanai, Japan	WUG	Wau, aua New Guinea
WKK	Aleknagik, AK USA	WUH	Wuhan, P R China
WLG	Wellington, New Zealand	WUM	Wasum, Papua New Guinea
WLH	Walaha, Vanuatu	WUN	Wiluna, WA Australia
WLK	Selawik, AK USA	WUS	Wuyishan, P R China
WLS	Wallis Island	WVB	Walvis Bay, Namibia
WMA	Mandritsara, Madagascar	WVK	Manakara, Madagascar
WME	Mount Keith, WA Australia	WVN	Wilhelmshaven, Germany
WMH	Mountain Home, AR USA	WWK	Wewak, Papua New Guinea
WMK	Meyers Chuck, AK USA	WWP	Whale Pass, AK USA
WMN	Maroantsetra, Madagascar	WWT	Newtok, AK USA
WMO	White Mountain, AK USA	WWY	West Wyalong, NS Australia
WMR	Mananara, Madagascar	WXN	Wanxian, P R China
WNA	Napakiak, AK USA	WYA	Whyalla, SA Australia
WNN	Wunnummin Lake, OT Canada	WYN	Wyndham, WA Australia
WNP	Naga, Philippines		
WNR	Windorah, QL Australia		**X**
WNS	Nawabshah, Pakistan	XAP	Chapeco, SC Brazil
WNZ	Wenzhou, P R China	XBE	Bearskin Lake, OT Canada
WPB	Port Berge, Madagascar	XBN	Biniguni, Papua New Guinea
WRE	Whangarei, New Zealand	XCH	Christmas Island, Christmas Is
WRG	Wrangell, AK USA	XDB	Lille Europe Rail Station, France
WRL	Worland, WY USA	XFN	Xiangfan, P R China
WRO	Wroclaw, Poland	XGR	Kangiqsualujjuaq, QU Canada
WRY	Westray, UK	XIC	Xichang, P R China
WSN	South Naknek, AK USA	XIY	Xi an Xianyang Apt, P R China
WSP	Waspam, Nicaragua	XKH	Xieng Khouang, Lao P D R
WST	Westerly, RI USA	XKS	Kasabonika, OT Canada
WSU	Wasu, Papua New Guinea	XLB	Lac Brochet, MN Canada
WSX	Westsound, WA USA	XMG	Mahendranagar, Nepal
WSZ	Westport, New Zealand		
WTA	Tambohorano, Madagascar		
WTE	Wotje Island, Marshall Is		
WTK	Noatak, AK USA		

(Contd.)

(Contd.)

Codes	*City: Airport*	*Codes*	*City: Airport*
XMH	Manihi, Taumotu Islands	YBL	Campbell River, BC Canada
XMN	Xiamen, P R China	YBP	Yibin, P R China
XNN	Xining, P R China	YBR	Brandon, MN Canada
XPK	Pukatawagan, MN Canada	YBV	Berens River, MN Canada
XQP	Quepos, Costa Rica	YBX	Blanc Sabion, QU Canada
XQU	Qualicum, BC Canada	YCB	Cambridge Bay, NT Canada
XRY	Jerez de la Frontera, Spain	YCD	Nanaimo, BC Canada
XSC	South Caicos, Turks and Caicos Islands	YCD	Nanaimo Cassidy Apt, BC Canada
XSI	South Indian Lake, MN Canada	YCG	Castledger, BC Canada
		YCH	Chatham, NB Canada
XSP	Singapore Seletar Apt, Singapore	YCK	Colville Lake, NT Canada
		YCL	Charlo, NB Canada
XTG	Thargomindah, QL Australia	YCO	Kuglutuk Coppermine, NT Canada
XTL	Tadoule Lake, MN Canada		
XYA	Yandina, Solomon Is	YCR	Cross Lake, MN Canada
		YCS	Chesterfield Inlet, NT Canada
	Y	YCY	Cycle River, NT Canada
YAA	Anahim Lake, BC Canada	YDA	Dawson City, YT Canada
YAB	Arctic Bay, NT Canada	YDF	Deer Lake, NF Canada
YAC	Cat Lake, OT Canada	YDI	Davis Inlet, NF Canada
YAG	Fort Frances, OT Canada	YDL	Dease Inlet, NF Canada
YAI	Chillan, Chile	YDN	Dauphin, MN Canada
YAK	Yakutat, AK USA	YDP	Nain, NF Canada
YAM	Sault Sainte Marie, OT Canada	YEA	Edmonton International Apt, AL Canada
YAO	Yaounde, Cameroon	YEK	Arviat, NT Canada
YAP	YAP, Caroline Is	YEL	Elliot Lake, OT Canada
YAT	Attawapiskat, OT Canada	YER	Fort Sevem, OT Canada
YAX	Angling Lake, OT Canada	YEV	Inuvik, NT Canada
YAY	St. Anthony, NF Canada	YFA	Fort Albany, OT Canada
YAZ	Tofino, BC Canada	YFB	Iqaluit, NT Canada
YBA	Banff, AL Canada	YFC	Fredericton, NB Canada
YBB	Pelly Bay Townsite Apt, NT Canada	YFH	Fort Hope, OT Canada
		YFJ	Snare Lake, NT Canada
YBC	Bale Comeau, QU Canada	YFO	Flin Flon, MN Canada
YBE	Uranium City, SA Canada	YFR	Fort Resolution, NT Canada
YBG	Bagotville, QU Canada	YFS	Fort Simpson, NT Canada
YBI	Black Tickle, NF Canada	YFX	Fox Harbour, NF Canada
YBK	Baker Lake, NT Canada	YGB	Gillies Bay, BC Canada

(Contd.)

(Contd.)

Codes	*City: Airport*	*Codes*	*City: Airport*
YGH	Fort Good Hope, NT Canada	YKL	Schefferville, QU Canada
YGJ	Yonago, Japan	YKM	Yakima, Wa USA
YGK	Kingston Norman Rogers Apt, OT Canada	YKM	Ykima Air Terminal, WA USA
YGL	La Grande, QU Canada	YKN	Yankton, SD USA
YGO	Gods Narrows, MN Canada	YKQ	Waskaganish, QU Canada
YGR	Iles de la Madeleine, QU Canada	YKS	Ykutsk, Russian Federation
YGT	Igloolik, NT Canada	YKU	Chisasibi, QU Canada
YGV	Havre Saint Pierre, QU Canada	YKX	Kirkland Lake, OT Canada
YGW	Kuujurapik, QU Canada	YLC	Kimmirut/Lake Harbour, NT Canada
YGX	Gillan, MN Canada	YLD	Chapleau, OT Canada
YGZ	Grise Fiord, NT Canada	YLE	Wha Ti Lac ia Martre, NT Canada
YHA	Port Hope Simpson, NF Canada	YLH	Lansdowne House, OT Canada
YHD	Dryden, OT Canada	YLL	Lloydminster, AL Canada
YHF	Hearst, OT Canada	YLR	Leaf Rapids, MN Canada
YHG	Charlottetown, NF Canada	YLS	Lebel-Sur-Quevillon, QU Canada
YHI	Holman Island, NT Canada	YLW	Kelowna, BC Canada
YHK	Gjoa Haven, NT Canada	YMH	Mary's Harbour, NF Canada
YHM	Hamilton, OT Canada	YMM	Fort Mcmurray, AL Canada
YHN	Momepayne, OT Canada	YMN	Makkovik, NF Canada
YHO	Hopedale, NF Canada	YMO	Montreal, QU Canada
YHR	Chevery, QU Canada	YMS	Yurimaguas, Peru
YHY	Hay River, NT Canada	YMT	Chibougamau, QU Canada
YHZ	Halifax, NS Canada	YMX	Montreal Mirabel Intl Apt, QU Canada
YHZ	Halifax International Apt, NS Canada	YNA	Natashquan, QU Canada
YIF	Pakuashipi, QU Canada	YNB	Yanbu, Saudi Arabia
YIH	Yichang, P R China	YNC	Wemindji, QU Canada
YIK	Ivujvik, QU Canada	YND	Gatineau, QU Canada
YIN	Yining, P R China	YNE	Norway House, MN Canada
YIO	Fond Inlet, NT Canada	YNG	Youngslown, OH USA
YIV	Island Lake/Garden Hill, MN Canada	YNJ	Yanji, P R China
YIW	Yiwu, P R China	YNL	Points North Landing, Sa Canada
YJT	Stephenville, NF Canada	YNO	North Spirit Lake, OT Canada
YKA	Kamloops, BC Canada	YNS	Nemiscau, QU Canada
YKG	Kangirsuk, QU Canada		

(Contd.)

(Contd.)

Codes	City: Airport	Codes	City: Airport
YNT	Yantai, P R China	YRA	Rae Lakes, NT Canada
YOC	Old Crow, YT Canada	YRB	Resolute, NT Canada
YOH	Oxford House, MN Canada	YRD	Dean River, BC Canada
YOJ	High Level, AL Canada	YRF	Cartwright, NF Canada
YOL	Yola, Nigeria	YRG	Rigolet, NF Canada
YQP	Rainbow Lake, AL Canada	YRJ	Roberval, QU Canada
YOW	Ottawa, OT Canada	YRL	Red Lake, OT Canada
YOW	Ottawa McDonald Cartier Intl Apt, OT Canada	YRS	Red Sucker Lake, MN Canada
YPA	Prince Albert, SA Canada	YRT	Rankin Inlet, NT Canada
YPB	Port Albemi, BC Canada	YSB	Sudbury, OT Canada
YPC	Paulatuk, NT Canada	YSF	Stony Rapids, SA Canada
YPE	Peace River, AL Canada	YSG	Lutselke Snowdrift, NT Canada
YPH	Inukjuak, QU Canada	YSJ	St John, NB Canada
YPJ	Aupaluk, QU Canada	YSK	Saniklluaq, NT Canada
YPL	Pickle Lake, OT Canada	YSL	St Leonard, NB Canada
YPM	Pikangikum, OT Canada	YSM	Fort Smith, NT Canada
YPN	Port Menier, QU Canada	YSN	Salmon Arm, BC Canada
YPO	Peawanuck, OT Canada	YSO	Postville, NF Canada
YPR	Prince Rupert, BC Canada	YSR	Nanisivik, NT Canada
YPR	Prince Rupert, Digby Island Apt, BC Canada	YST	Ste Therese Point, MN Canada
YPW	Powell River, BC Canada	YSY	Sachs Harbour, NT Canada
YPX	Puvirnituq, QU Canada	YTA	Pembroke, OT Canada
XPY	Fort Chipewyan, AL Canada	YTE	Cape Dorset, NT Canada
YQB	Quebec, QU Canada	YTF	Alma, QU Canada
YQC	Quaqtaq, QU Canada	YTH	Thompson, MN Canada
YQD	The Pas, MN Canada	YTL	Big Trout Lake, OT Canada
YQG	Windsor, OT Canada	YTO	Toronto, OT Canada
YQH	Watson Lake, YT Canada	YTQ	Tasiujuaq, QU Canada
YQI	Yarmouth, NS Canada	YTS	Timmins, OT Canada
YQL	Lethbridge, AL Canada	YTZ	Toronto City Centre Apt, OT Canada
YQM	Moncton, NB Canada	YUB	Tuktoyaktuk, NT Canada
YQQ	Comox, BC Canada	YUD	Umiujaq, QU Canad
YQR	Regina, SA Canada	YUF	Pelly Bay, NT Canada
YQT	Thunder Bay, OT Canada	YUL	Montreal Dorval International Apt, QU Canada
YQU	Grande Prairie, AL Canada	YUM	Yuma, AZ USA
YQX	Gander, NF Canada	YUM	Yuma International Apt, AZ USA
YQY	Sydney, NS Canada		
YQZ	Quesnel, BC Canada		

(Contd.)

(*Contd.*)

Codes	*City: Airport*	*Codes*	*City: Airport*
YUT	Repulse Bay, NT Canada	YXZ	Wawa, OT Canada
YUX	Hall Beach, NT Canada	YYB	North Bay, OT Canada
YUY	Rouyn, QU Canada	YYC	Calgary, AL Canada
YVA	Moroni, Comoros	YYD	Smithers, BC Canada
YVC	La Ronge, SA Canada	YYE	Fort Nelson, BC Canada
YVM	Broughton Island, NT Canada	YYF	Penticton, BC Canada
YVO	Val D'Or, QU Canada	YYG	Charlottetown, PE Canada
YVP	Kuujjuaq, QU Canada	YYH	Taloyak, NT Canada
YVQ	Norman Wells, NT Canada	YYJ	Victoria, BC Canada
YVR	Vancouver, BC Canada	YYJ	Victoria International Apt, BC Canada
YVR	Varcouver International Apt, BC Canada	YYL	Lynn Lake, MN Canada
YVZ	Deer Lake, OT Canada	YYQ	Churchil, MN Canada
YWB	Kangiqsujuaq, QU Canada	YYR	Goose Bay, NF Canada
YWG	Winnipeg, MN Canada	YYU	Kapuskasing, OT Canada
YWG	Winnipeg International Apt, MN Canada	YYY	Mont Joli, OU Canada
YWH	Victoria Inner Harbour Apt, BC Canada	YYZ	Toronto Lester B Pearson Intl Apt, OT Canada
YWJ	Deline, NT Canada	YZE	Gore Bay, OT Canada
YWK	Wabush, NF Canada	YZF	Ywllowknife, NT Canada
YWL	Williams Lake, BC Canada	YZG	Salluit, QU Canada
YWP	Webequle, OT Canada	YZP	Sandspit, BC Canada
YXC	Cranbrook, BC Canada	YZR	Samia, OT Canada
YXD	Edmonton Municipal Apt, AL Canada	YZS	Coral Harbour, NT Canada
YXE	Saskatoon, SA Canada	YZT	Port Hardy, BC Canada
YXH	Medicine Hat, AL Canada	YZV	Sept-lles, QU Canada
YXJ	Fort Saint John, BC Canada		**Z**
YXL	Soux Lookout, OT Canada	ZAC	York Landing, MN Canada
YXN	Whale Cove, NT Canada	ZAD	Zadar, Croatia
YPP	Pangnirtung, NT Canada	ZAG	Zagreb, Croatia
PXR	Eartlon, OT Canada	ZAH	Zahedan, Iran
YXS	PrinceGeorge, BC Canada	ZAL	Valdivia, Chile
YXT	Terrace, BC Canada	ZAM	Zamboanga, Philippines
YXU	London, OT Canada	ZAQ	Nuremberg Main Station, Germany
YXU	London Municipal Apt, OT Canada	ZAT	Zhaotong, P R China
YXX	Abbotsford, BC Canada	ZAZ	Zaragoza, Spain
YXY	Whitehorse, YT Canada	ZBF	Bathurst, NB Canada
		ZBR	Chah-Bahar, Iran

(*Contd.*)

(*Contd.*)

Codes	*City: Airport*	*Codes*	*City: Airport*
ZBV	Beaver Creek Van Service, CO USA	ZNZ	Zanzibar, Tanzania
ZBY	Sayaboury, Lao PDR	ZOS	Osomo, Chile
ZCL	Zacatecas, Mexico	ZPB	Sachigo Lake, OT Canada
ZCO	Temuco, Chile	ZQN	Queenstown, New Zealand
ZDJ	Beme Hauptbahnhol, Switzerland	ZRF	Rockford Clock Tower Bus Station, IL USA
ZDN	Bmo Bus Station, Crech Rep	ZRH	Zurich, Switzerland
ZEL	Bella Bella, BC Canada	ZRJ	Round Lake, OT Canada
ZEM	East Main, QU Canada	ZRK	Rockford Van Galder Bus Stn, IL USA
ZFD	Fond du Lac, SA Canada	ZSA	San Salvador, Bahamas
ZFN	Tulta Fort Norman, NT Canada	ZSJ	Sandy Lake, OT Canada
ZGI	Gods River, MN Canada	ZSM	Santa Clara Bus Station, CA USA
ZGS	Gethsemani, QU Canada	ZTB	Tete-a-La Baleine, QU Canada
ZGU	Gaua, Vanuatu	ZTH	Zakinthos, Greece
ZHA	Zhanjang, P R China	ZTM	Shamattawa, MN Canada
ZIG	Ziguinchor, Senegal	ZUH	Zhuhai, P R China
ZIH	Bdapta/Zihuatanejo, Mexico	ZUM	Churchill Falls, NF Canada
ZJN	Swan River, MN Canada	ZVA	Mandrivazo, Madagascar
ZJO	San Jose Bus Station, CA USA	ZVK	Savannakhet, Lao P D R
ZKE	Kaschechewan, OT Canada	ZWL	Wollaston Lake, SA Canada
ZKG	Kegaska, QU Canada	ZYL	Sythet, Bangladesh
ZLO	Manzanillo, Mexico	ZYR	Brussels Midi Rail Station, Belgium
ZLT	La Tabatiere, QU Canada		
ZNA	Nanaimo Harbour Apt, BC Canada	ZYZ	Antwerp Berchem Rail Station, Belgium
ZNE	Newman, WA Australia	ZZU	Mzuzu, Malawi.

When a computer reservation system is used to book airline reservations, the correct city or airport code must be used. City and airport codes are also used on luggage tags to identify a passenger's destination.

Any point that is represented by a city or airport code is referred to as destination. The main entry points to a country are called gateways. Besides locations of countries, cities and airports, travel professional are also concerned with transportation routes, gateways, tourist attraction and social, cultural, economic and environmental aspects of destinations.

QUESTIONS AND DISCUSSIONS

Objective Type

Q. 1. In each of the following sentences, write the correct word or phrase that belong to each blank:

1. Fees imposed by an airport authority must be approved by ....
2. With most discount fares, the length of the time between .... and .... is restricted.
3. The customers user fee is collected to defray the cost of ....
4. In a Fare Basis Code, restrictions pertaining to days of the week may be indicated by .... or ....
5. An open segment is a ticketed segment that is not booked on.
6. Many domestic and international carriers offer a .... class that is less expensive than first class but higher price than coach class.
7. In a .... system airfare constantly change in proportion to demand.

Q. 2. The phrase 'MINIMUM CONNECTING TIME" means the minimum time required when making transfers from one aircraft to another. These charts are published for each city and can be located in the front pages of the Airline Guide. It must be remembered these are the minimum times *required for connections and they may* not *be reduced.*

"Off-line" connecting time must be used when a change of airlines is made. "On-line" connecting time is observed when the arriving and departing airlines are the same (connection is made on the same airline).

In the listings separate times are published for Midway (MDW) and for O'Hare (ORD) airports in Chicago. The minimum time is also published for surface transportation between the two airports if a passenger is arriving at one airport and departing from the other. Refer again to the minimum connecting lines for Chicago. If a passenger was scheduled to arrive at Midway Airport at 1:30 p.m. on United Air Lines, the minimum time required for a scheduled connection to an American Airlines flight is 25 minutes (Standard off-line time). Therefore, he may make a reservation

City	Off Line	On Line
BIG SPRING TAXES		
STANDARD	:20	
IT		:15
BILLINGS MONT.		
STANDARD	:30	
NW		:25
FL, WA		:20
BIMGHAMTON, N.Y.		
STANDARD	:25	
BIRMINGHAM, ALA.		
STANDARD	:30	
EA SO, UA		:20
BISMARCK, N.D		
STANDARD	:20	
NC		:10
BLOOMINGTON, IND.		
STANDARD	:25	
BOISE, IDAHO		
STANDARD	:30	
BETWEEN RW AND TJ	:25	
RW		:15
UA		:20
BOSTON, MASS.		
DOMESTIC		
STANDARD	:40	
DL TO/FROM DD/PM/PT/ QO/DE/NE/ZM/	:30	
AA. AL. EA		:30
DL		:25
TW, UA		:20
FLIGHTS TO/FROM BERMUDA. HAWAII MONTREAL. TORONTO. MASSA. AND PUERTO RICO ARE DOMESTIC		
INTERNATIONAL		
DOMESTIC TO INTL	1:00	
ALL TO AA	:40	
DL		:25
PA		:40
TW		:30
INTL TO DOMESTIC	1:00	
DL		:25
PA		1:05
INTL TO INTL	1:00	
BRADFORD, PA.		
STANDARD	:25	
BRAINERD MINN.		
STANDARD	:10	
BRIDGEPORT, CONM.		
STANDARD	:20	
AL		:25
BROOKINGS, S.D.		
STANDARD	:10	
BROWNSVILLE, TEXAS		
STANDARD	:20	
IF CONNECTION INVOLVES TRANSFER BETWEEN BROWNSVILLE AND MATAMORDS AIRPORTS	:5	
CHICAGO, ILL.		
ORD. DOMESTIC		
STANDARD	:50	
(FLIGHTS TO/FROM ALASKA, CANADA, HAWAII, BERMUDA, NASSAU, PUERTO RICO & U.S VIRGIN IS ARE DOMESTIC EXCEPTION AF AND BA FLIGHTS VIA CANADA AND JM FLIGHTS FROM NAS ARE CONSIDERED INTERNATIONAL)		
BETWEEN AA/DL/NC	:40	
BETWEEN AA/AL	:40	
AC TO TW	:40	
BETWEEN AL/NC	:40	
EA/NW TO/FROM CO	:30	
BETWEEN OZ/UA	:40	
AA. DL. EA		:30
UA		:40
NC. OZ		:20
NW. TW		:25
ORD. INTERNATIONAL		
DOMESTIC TO INTL	1:1:5	
ALL TO BN	:50	
ALL TO JM	:45	
ALL TO NW	1:00	
NW/UA TO DL	:50	
UA TO BA	1:00	
ALL TO TW	:50	:45
TW-DOMESTIC CONNECTING TIMES WILL APPLY TO ALL TW INTL FLIGHTS WHICH TRANSIT TO A POINT IN THE U.S PRIOR TO ARRIVAL/DEPARTURE		
ALL TO AA	:50	:30
EA, NW		:30
INTL TO DOMESTIC	1:30	
FROM BN (WITH STOP AT DFW. IAH. SAT)	:50	
FROM AA (WITH STOP AT DFW. HNL. SAT)	:50	:30
NW TO ALL	:50	
FROM ALL TO TW	1:00	1:00
MX TO UA	1:15	
AA (FROM ACA OR MEX NONSTOP)		1:00
EA		:30
NW		:25
INTL TO INTL	1:30	
MDW STANDARD	:25	
NC		:10
TW. UA		:20
INTER-AIRPORT SURFACE CONNECTIONS		
MDW TO/FROM ORD	2:40	
CINCINNATI, OHIO		
STANDARD	:40	
BETWEEN AL/NC/PI	:30	

on any American Airlines flight leaving at 1:55 p.m. or later. If the passenger arriving at MDW on United Air Lines at 1:30 p.m. were departing on another United Air Lines flight from MDW, he must be scheduled to leave at 1:50 p.m. or later because ....

Ans.: *The on-line connecting time (20 minutes) must be used.*

Q. 3. *Below is a specimen of a schedule.*

If a passenger was arriving at O'Hare on North Central from Milwaukee and was transferring to Pan American to London, the "DOMESTIC TO INT'L." off-line time of 75 minutes (1:15) must be used. What is the minimum time if the passenger was transferring to American Airlines for Mexico? ....

CITY		OFF LINE	ON LINE
CHICAGO, ILL			
ORD	DOMESTIC		
	STANDARD		:50
	(FLIGHTS TO/FROM ALASKA, CANADA, HAWAII, BERMUDA, NASSAU, PUERIO, RICO & U.S. VIRGIN IS ARE DOMESTIC EXCEPTION. AF AND BA FLIGHTS VIA CANADA AND JM FLIGHTS FROM NAS ARE CONSIDERED INTERNATIONAL)		
	BETWEEN AA/DL/NC		:40
	BETWEEN AA/AL		:40
	AC TO TW		:40
	BETWEEN AL/NC		:40
	#		
	BETWEEN OZ/UA		:40
	AA, DL, EA		:30
	UA		:40
	NC, OZ		:20
	NW, TW		:25
ORD	INTERNATIONAL		
	DOMESTIC TO INTL	1:15	
	ALL TO BN	:50	
	ALL TO JM	:45	
	ALL TO NW	1:00	
	NW/UA TO DL	:50	
	UA TO BA	1:00	
	ALL TO TW	:50	:45
	TW-DOMESTIC CONNECTING TIMES WILL APPLY TO ALL TW INTL FLIGHTS WHICH TRANSIT TO A POINT IN THE US PRIOR TO ARRIVAL/DEPARTURE		
	ALL TO AA	:50	:30
	EA NW		:30
	INTL TO DOMESTIC	1:30	
	FROM BN (WITH STOP AT DFW, IAH, SAT)	:50	
	FROM AA (WITH STOP AT DFW, HNL, SAT)	:50	:30
	NW TO ALL	:50	
	FROM ALL TO TW	1:00	1:00
	AA (FROM ACA OR MEX NONSTOP)		1:00
	EA		:30
	NW		:25
	INTL TO INTL	1:30	
MDW	STANDARD	:25	
	NC		:10
	TW UA		:20
INTER AIRPORT SURFACE CONNECTIONS			
	MDW TO/FROM ORD	2:40	

Ans.: *50 minutes (:50)*

Q. 4. *In cases where no logical connecting point is suggested, it is best to consult a map. Find a large city near the destination with the least deviation from a direct line between the origin and destination. Turn to the pages in the Airline Guide containing schedules to the final destination and determine if service is available from the selected connecting point to the final destination. If no schedules exist, select another city and check the concerned Airline Guide flight listings to the destination.*

NOTE: If several cities may be used as the connecting city, select the city with the most non-stop service in order to reduce flying time for the passenger. Assume a passenger wanted to fly from Buffalo, N.Y. to Grand Rapids, Mich. Using a map provided by the concerned Airline Guide, what city should be used as the connecting point?

Ans.: *Detroit*

Q. 5. *Minimum connecting times between airports in multiple-airport cities are also printed in the listings. This minimum connecting time includes travel times between airports, time for the passenger to claim baggage at the arrival airport, and check-in time at the departure airport. If a passenger arrived at O'Hare at 2:00 p.m., the earliest time he could be scheduled to depart on a flight from Midway Airport is ....*

Ans.. *4:40 P.M.*

Q. 5. *Examine the following schedule:*

To SEATTLE/TACOMA, WASH								**PDT**	**SEA**	
From HONOLULU, OAHU, HAWAII								**HST**	**HML**	
				TAX NOT INCL. SEE PGS 10-11						
	F			201.41				402.82		
	YL			123.41				246.82		
	YH			139.41				278.82		
	KL			116.41				232.82		
	KH			131.41				262.82		
	YM			104.41						
	11:00p	7:15p	S	PA	830	FYK		747	L	0
						EFFECTIVE				
	2:10p	9:28p	S	CO	982	FYK		D10	L	0
	2:15p	9:25p	S	NW	86	FYK		747	D	0
	2:30p	9:45p	S	PA	896	FYK		747	L	0
		PA 896			DISCOUNTED AFTER APR 24					
X14	9:20p	6:49p	S	NW	94	FYK		D10	S	1
						NW 94 EFFECTIVE APR 24				
X14	10:20p	6:49a	S	NW	94	FYK		D10	S	1
		NW	94		DISCOUNTED AFTER APR 23					

Occasionally, additional information pertinent to a flight must be shown on a second line. This line of information will always refer *only* to the flight listed directly *above* it.

The additional information shown in conjunction with PA 830 indicates the flight is "EFFECTIVE APR 25". This, of course, means PA 830 will not operate prior to April 25. Answer the following: (a) What is the additional information concerning PA 896? .... (b) What additional information is shown for NW 94? ....

Ans.: *PA 896 will discontinue service after April 24; NW 94 will terminate service departing 10:20 p.m. from Honolulu after April 23; On April 24 it will depart at 9:20 p.m.*

Q. 6. *The Airline Guide occasionally suggests such a logical connecting point or points with the words "CONEX VIA..." under the departure city. You can use the city or cities listed to determine a suitable schedule. Examine this Columbus to Wichita schedule.*

To WICHITA, KAM							CDT		ICT
6.0 MI SW 20 MIN L $ 2.65 RA									
From COLUMBUS, OHIO							EDT		CMH
CONEX VIA CHI. MCI/ S.T.L									
	Y	67.59	5.41	73.00		146.00			
TW	YM	55.00							
4:10p		8:01p	TW	547	Y		DC9	S	3

Answer the following:

This schedule lists one direct flight from Columbus to Wichita. The listing also suggests connections should be made at.................., ... or ....

Ans (a) *CHI (Chicago);*
(B) *MCI (Kansas City);*
(C) *STL (St. Louis)*

Q. 6. *Assume a passenger flying from Buffalo to Grand Rapids wanted to arrive in Grand Rapids as early on a Wednesday morning as possible. The arrival time at the destination is critical to the passenger. Examine the schedule below from Detroit to Grand Rapids. NC 971 is the earliest arrival, leaving at 7:10 a.m. and arriving at 7:44 a.m. Now examine the schedules from Buffalo Detroit. AA 23 is the earliest departure but it arrives in Detroit at 8:55 a.m., too late to connect to NC 971. Therefore, he must use a later DTW to CRR flight. Since the offline minimum connecting time at DTW is 45 minutes, his North Central flight to GRR must leave no earlier than 9:40 a.m. to be a valid connection. The passenger's itinerary should be AL421 BUF-DTW and ....(flight number) DTW-GRR.*

To DETROIT, MICH.							EST	DIT
From BUFFALO, N.Y.							EST	BUF
	F	50.00	4.00	54.00	108.00			
	S	35.19	2.81	38.00	76.00			
	Y	35.19	2.81	38.00	76.00			
	YW	29.00						
			AL EX/11 S WEEKEND			57.00		
	B		AL EX/5 SL 30 DAY			53.00		
	B		AA EX/5 YL 30 DAY			57.00		
			AA EX/11 Y WEEKEND					
8:00a	8:55a	M	AA	23	FYB	707	S	0
9:00a	10:35a	M	AL	421	SB	B11		0
3:35p	4:27p	M	AL	423	SB	D9S		0
7:55p	8:47p	M	AL	137	SB	D9S		0

To GRAND RAPIDS, MICH.								EST	GRR
From DETROIT, MICH. CONT.								EST	BUF
D-DET, M-DTW, R-YIP									
		A	23.15	1.85	25.00	50.00			
		S	28.70	2.30	31.00	62.00			
	NC	YW	23.00						
		B		NC EX/5 SL 30 DAY			43.00		
	7:10a	M	7:44a	NC	971	SB	CV5	S	0
	8:10a	M	9:10a	NC	343	SB	CV5		1
	12:35p	M	1:35p	NC	908	SB	CV5		1
	1:40p	M	2:14p	NC	345	SB	CV5		0
X6	2:10p	M	2:45p	NC	989	SB	CV5		0
X6	4:15p	M	4:49p	NC	979	SB	CV5		0
X6	5:25p	M	5:59p	NC	983	SB	CV5		0
	6:45p	M	7:45p	NC	347	SB	D9S		1
X6	9:00p	M	9:34p	NC	987	SB	CV5		0
			COMMUTER AIR CARRIERS						
X67	9:75a	M	10:10a	JB	202	A	B99		0
X67	10:45a	M	11:45a	JB	102	A	B99		1
X67	3:50p	M	4:35a	JB	206	A	B99		0
X6	6:00p	M	7:00p	JB	208	A	B99		1

Ans.: *NC 908*

Q. 7. A passenger wishes to fly from Peoria, Illinois to Harrisburg, Pennsylvania. He wishes to depart on a Friday, as late in the day as possible. Using the schedules that follow and Chicago as a connecting point, determine the most convenient schedule for this passenger.

To HARRISBURG, PA.								EDT	HAR
From CHICAGO, ILL.								CDT	CHI
M-MDW	O-ORD		C-CGX						
	F	69:44	5:56		75:00	150:00			
	S	53:70	4:30		58:00	116:00			
	Y	53:70	4:30		58:00	116:00			
	YM	43:00							
		AL EX 11 S WEEKENDING				87:00			
7:00a	O	10:31a	H	AL	876	SB	B		1
9:10a	O	12:27p	H	AL	878	SB			1
11:45a	O	3:41p	H	AL	908	FYB	S		1
1:10p	O	3:41p	H	AL	30	SB	L		0
1:45p	O	5:11p	H	TW	976	SB	S		1
3:45p	O	7:11p	H	AL	890	FYB			1
6:45p	O	10:21p	H	AL	884	SB	D		1
8:45p	O	12:16a	H	AL	944	SB			1

To Chicago, ILL							CDT	CHI
From PEORIA, ILL							CDT	PIA
		S	23.15	1.85	25.00	50.00		
		OZ	YM	19.00				
	7:02a	7:40a	O	OZ	920	SB	D95	0
X7	7:32a	8:20a	O	OZ	860	SB	FH7	0
X67	10:12a	11:00a	O	OZ	816	SB	FH7	0
	11:37a	12:15p	O	OZ	956	SB	D95	0
X6	1:45p	2:23p	O	OZ	928	SB	D95	0
67	2:57p	3:45p	O	OZ	890	SB	FH7	0
X67	3:42p	4:30p	O	OZ	826	SB	FH7	0
	4:37p	5:15p	O	OZ	976	SB	O95	0
X6	7:11p	7:59p	O	OZ	809	SB	FH7	0
X6	7:49p	9:14p	O	OZ	858	SB	FH7	1

Q. 8. Review the above schedules and answer the following:

A. The last flight from Peoria to Chicago is OZ 858, which arrives in Chicago at 9:15 p.m. Since the minimum off-line connecting time at O'Hare Airport is 50 minutes (determined from the Minimum Connecting Time Section in the front pages of the NAOAG), we must check the Chicago-Harrisburg listings for a flight departing O'Hare at 10:04 p.m. or later.

B. Example the Chicago-Harrisburg listings. The latest flight on a Friday is AL 944, which departs at 8:45 p.m. We must find an earlier PIA-CHI flight.

C. Now that you know the latest flight to Harrisburg leaves O'Hare at 8:45 p.m., simply look for a PIA-CHI flight which arrives at O'Hare earlier than 7:55 p.m. (minimum connecting time subtracted from the departure time).

D. OZ 809 does not satisfy the minimum connecting time requirements. Even though the difference is only 4 minutes, the minimum time may not be reduced.

E. OZ 976 is the next earlier PIA-CHI flight. It is the latest flight from PIA-CHI the passenger may take in order to make the connection to Harrisburg.

F. The passenger's itinerary, then, is OZ 976 PIA-CHI and AL 944 ORD-HAR. Or, is it? With this itinerary, the passenger has a 3 ½ hour wait at ORD. Perhaps there is another ORD-HAR flight a little earlier so we could reduce the waiting time. Please recheck the ORD-HAR schedule.

G. The next earlier ORD-HAR flight is AL 884 departing at 6:45 p.m. This flight satisfies the minimum connecting time requirement, and the passenger would only have to wait 1½ hours at O'Hare. The passenger's itinerary should be OZ 976 and .... ORD-HAR.

Assuming the passenger wanted to arrive in HAR as early on a Saturday as possible, answer the following:

H. The flight from the origin to the connecting city should be................. Airlines flight number ....

I. The flight from the connecting city to Harrisburg should be .... Airlines flight number ....

Ans. *(G) AL 884*
(H) Ozark; 860
(I) Allegheny; 878.

Q. 9. The NAOAG contains a complete Airline Index containing home office addresses of all airlines whose schedules appear in the North American Edition.

ATA/IATA Form Numbers Follow Two Letter Codes

AIRLINE AND HOME OFFICE		AIRLINE AND HOME OFFICE	
AEROLINE AS DEL PACIFICO S.A. (PN) Esqverro 40-B La Paz, Baja California, Mexico Tel.: 2-01-72		JAMAICA AIR TAXI, LTD. (JQ) P.O. Box 218 Montego Bay, Jamaica Tel.: 3205, 3416	
♣▲● AEROMEXICO (AM) Blvd. Aeropuerto Central 161 Mexico 9, D.F. Tel.: 903—571-3000	139	♣▲ JAPAN AIR LINES, LTD. (JL) Tokyo Bldg. 2-3-2 Marunouchi Tokyo, Japan Tel.: (03) 231-6211	131
AERONAVES ALIMENTADORAS Av. Revolucion No. 1608 Despacho 203 Mexico 20, D.F. Tel.: 903—71-20-11		♣▲ KLM—ROYAL DUTCH AIR LINES (KL) Schipol Int'l. Airport P.O. Box 7700 Netherlands Tel.: Amsterdam 020-499123	074
AERONAVES del CENTRO, S.A. (JZ) AERONAVES DEL MAYAB (JR) AERONAVES del OESTE, S.A. (JO) AERONAVES del SUR, S.A. (JS) AERONAVES DEL SURESTE (JH) C/o AERONAVES ALIMENTADORAS		KODIAK WESTERN ALASKA AIRLINES (KO) P.O. Box 2457 Kodiak, Alaska 99615 Tel.: 907—486-3271	366
AEROSERVICIOS DE CALIFORNIA (YM) APDO. Postal 299 Ensenada, B. Cfa., Mexico Tel.: 9-1844, 9-1825		♣ LACSA—LINES AEREAS COSTARRICENSES, S.A. (LR) P.O. Box 1531 San Jose, Costa Rica Tel.: 217315	133
♣ AEROVIAS QUISQUEYANA (QQ) El Conde 80 Santo Domingo, Dominican Republic Tel.: 689-7291/3	442	♣▲ LAN CHILE—LINEA AEREA NACIONAL DE CHILE (LA) Casilla (P.O. Box) 147-D Santiago, Chile Tel.: 572233	
AIR BVI, LTD. (BL) Box 85 Roadtown, Tortola, British Virgin Islands	644	♣ LEEWARD ISLAND AIR TRANSPORT SERVICES, LTD. (LI) Coolidge Airport Antigua, West Indies Tel.: 30140/30141	140

(Contd.)

(Contd.)

	AIRLINE AND HOME OFFICE			AIRLINE AND HOME OFFICE	
♣★▲●	AIR CANADA (AC) Place Ville Marie Montreal 113, Quebec, Canada	014		LIAT (See LEEWARD ISLANDS AIR TRANSPORT SERVICES LTD.)	
♣★▲	BRANIFF INTERNATIONAL AIRWAYS (BN) Braniff Airways Building, Exchange Park Dallas, Texas 75235 Tel.: 214—358-6011	002	♣▲	PHILLIPPINE AIRLINES (PR) 6780 Ayala Avenue, Pal Bldg. Makati, Rizal, Philippines Tel.: 88-10-61	079
♣▲	BRITISH AIRWAYS BRITISH OVERSEAS AIRWAYS CORP. (BA) London Airport Hounslow, Middlesex, England Tel.: 759-5511	161	♣★	PIEDMONT AVIATION, INC. (PI) Smith Reynolds airport Winston-Salem, N.C. 27102 Tel.: 919—767-5100	030
	BRITISH OVERSEAS AIRWAYS CORP. (See BRITISH AIRWAYS)		♣▲	QANTAS AIRWAYS, LTD. (QF) Qantas House, 70 Hunter St. P.O. Box 489 Sydney, N.S.W., Australia Tel.: 20369	081
♣▲	BRITISH WEST INDIAN AIRWAYS LTD. (BW) Kent House, Long Circular Rd. Maraval, Port of Spain, Trinidad Tel.: 21241	106	♣▲●	QUEBECAIR INC. (QB) P.O. Box 490 Montreal Int'l. Airport Dorval, Quebec, Hhy IBS, Canada Tel.: 418—631-9802	330
♣	CAYMAN AIRWAYS, LTD. (KX) P.O. Box 11 Grand Cayman, B.W.I. Tel.: 9-2311	378		REEVE ALEUTIAN AIRWAYS, INC. (RV) P.O. Box 559 Anchorage, Alaska 99510 Tel.: 272-9426	338
▲	CHICAGO HELICOPTER AIRWAYS, INC.(CH) 5313 W. 63rd St. Midway Airport, Chicago, Ill, 60638 Tel.: 312—735-0200	328		SFO HELICOPTER AIRLINES, INC. (OH) P.O. Box 2525 Metropolitan Oakland Int'l Airport Oakland, Calif, 94614 Tel.: 415—635-2222	352
♣	CHINA AIRLINES LTD. (CI) 26, Sec. III, Nanking East Rd. Taipei, Taiwan, Rep. of China Tel.: 571111	297	♣▲	SABENA BELGIAN WORLD AIRLINES (SN) (Societe Anonyme Belge D'Exploitation De La Navigation Aerienne) 35 Rue Cardinal Mercier Brussels, Belgium Tel.: 119060	082
♣★▲	CONTINENTAL AIR LINES, INC. International Airport Los Angeles, Calit, 90009 Tel.: 213—646-2810	005			

Note: ♣ Indicates carrier's participation to the agreement relating to liability limitations of the Warsaw Convention and The Hague Protocol, which carriers have signed and filled with the Civil Aeronautics Board counterparts of the Inter-carrier Agreement (CAB 18900—sometimes called the Montreal Agreement) providing for increase of liability limits to $75,000 and walver of defense under Article 20(1) of the Warsaw Convention of The Hague Protocol, with respect to passengers.

▲ Members and Associate Members of the International Air Transport Association (I.A.T.A.)

★ Members and Associate Members of the Air Transport Association of America (A.T.A.)

- Operator Members and Associate Members of the Air Transport Association of Canada (A.T.A.C.)

If, for example, you wished the address of the home office for Piedmont Aviation, locate Piedmont alphabetically. The address is printed immediately below the name of the airline.

A. Piedmont's home office is located in ....

B. Continental's home office is located in ....

Ans.: *(A) Winston–Salem, NC*

(B) Los Angeles, California.

5

Air Fare Construction

After learning this Chapter you shall be able to:

- *discuss the factors that influence pricing in the airline industry;*
- *understand the guidelines for international tariff rules;*
- *identify and explain the elements of fare bases code, and differences between various classes of service;*
- *calculate a total fare based on the base fare and the tax;*
- *explain and calculate a horizontal and vertical fare calculation;*
- *get familiar with the fare construction terminology;*
- *preparing flight itineraries for passenger travel;*
- *answer questions concerning flight frequencies, fares, number of stops, class of service, equipment types;*
- *describe the different types of air transport taxes, and fare rules, fare calculations, ticket validation, basic principles of international fares;*
- *explain the use of neutral unit of construction (NUC) and procedure of conversion;*
- *construct a fare using mileage system;*
- *explain higher intermediate points and the procedure of combining an excursion fare with local fare based on mileage;*
- *understand the difference between domestic and international ticket. Understand the currency codes, mileage system, class differentials etc.*
- *advise passengers of correct part of departure and/or arrival of the city in a multi-airport city;*
- *use the charts provided in the Airline Guide to determine minimum time required between flight in a connecting city;*
- *determine minimum connecting times between airports in multiple airport cities;*
- *convert pounds into kilograms for purposes of quoting excess baggage charges.*

International airlines or the 'flag carriers' represent their country and normally have their own country's flag painted on the airplane. The majority of the international carriers are owned and sponsored by the government of the country. The international airlines and routes require agreements between the various governments based on socio-economic consideration as well as the frequency of flight from one nation to another. Therefore, the International Air Transport Authority (IATA) attempts to resolve policies and fares applicable to the participating international air carriers.

As a travel agent it is necessary to use several airlines to complete a trip. Since no airlines services every city, it becomes essential to know the major route structure and remember the general geographical regions served. Airlines and travel agencies must have a complete copy of all tariffs at all offices where air tickets are being sold in order to obtain the correct fares. As soon as the latest revision are received it is essential to review and revise all tariffs promptly. To maintain a tariff properly, the agents should compare each revision transmittal number with the list on the cover sheet to be served that each revision is in sequence and complete. He should check the correct number on the pages published in the front of each tariff. He should know each effective date and any information on the transmittal that is specially important and then collate and insert in the tariff all effective pages.

AIRLINE REGULATIONS

India has a long history of airline regulations. Before 1952-53 there were no legal regulations in India for determine airline fares and each carrier charged whatever fares it believed necessary and treated passengers by whatever rule it thought necessary. In 1952-53 due to the nationalisation of airlines the Air India and Indian Airlines Act, were passed. The Civil Aviation Authority established that airlines should be regulated so that travellers should not be charged unreasonable rates and the methods of handling passenger be safe and uniform. All fares which an airline charges its travellers for transportation between any two points in the nation are approved by Civil Aviation Authority. The Civil Aviation Authority is responsible only to the President and has certain judicial powers delegated to it. The primary purpose of the Civil Aviation Authority has been as an economic regulatory agency for the airline industry. It would authorise reasonable competition to develop the quality of air service and would control the number of airlines allowed to operate over each available route.

Before a carrier could provide a centre state scheduled air service, it would have to obtain a certificate of public convenience and necessity. Each airline has to demonstrate to the Civil Aviation Authority that it is capable of performing the transportation properly and that the services would be a public convenience and necessity. After an airline has been certificated, it remains under the constant surveillance of the Civil Aviation Authority. While the airline must comply with a long list of service requirements, it is important to realise that a scheduled airline, Civil Aviation approved, must provide regular service to all points designated on its certificate according to a complete system flight scheduled filled with the agency. The carrier cannot suspend service at any uneconomic point without Civil Aviation Authority's authorisation. Airlines are required to file all fares with the Civil Aviation Authority, which can reject them if not justified in the public interest. Further regularly scheduled airlines must maintain records open to authority inspection at any time and file quarterly full service, traffic and financial reports. Air carriers cannot merge, consolidate or acquire another airline without Civil Aviation authority approved.

There is a provision for a 'Tariff' structure or guidelines to establish passenger rules and fares, and once a fare was approved between two cities, that became the only legal fare the airline could charge. Airline tariffs could include air costs for transportation and the rules covering such passages. Air tariffs are compendium of regulations and fares that public carriers are authorised to charge. All rules and fares are binding on both travellers and carriers. Travel agents are required to use two set of tariffs: domestic fares and rules and international regulations and fares.

All scheduled domestic airlines publish their fares in one official publication. Airline tariffs include the fares and route points in India and neighbouring countries.

The passenger tariff is generally divided into several categories which include:

1. The local and joint passenger rules tariffs,
2. The local passenger fares tariff, and
3. The joint passenger fares tariff.

The tariff is kept current through revisions which occur frequently and is used widely by travel agents and airline offices.

Airlines and travel agencies must have complete copy of all tariffs at all offices where air tickets are being sold in order to obtain the correct fares. Revisions are received at least monthly, sometimes weekly and it is essential to review and revise all tariffs promptly. To maintain a tariff properly, the agent should compare each revision transmittal numbers with the list on the cover sheet to be sure that each revision is in sequence and complete. It is important to check the correct numbers on the correction number pages published in the front of each tariff. The agent should note each effective date and any information in the transmittal that is specially important, and then collate and insert in the tariff all effective pages.

Be sure to keep all transmittal pages and any pages not yet effective in a separate three-ring binder. Keep this binder available at all times for future booking information.

The local and joint passenger rules tariff provides the individual and group airline policies governing the transportation of passengers and their baggage. There are airline rules for handicapped passengers, children under five years of age travelling alone, carrying fire arms abroad a commercial flight, food service abroad flight, excess baggage charges and hundreds of regulations in the Rule Tariff governing all aspects of airline and passenger relations. The Rule Tariffs are approved by the Civil Aviation Authority and became official guidelines for passenger handling. If a travel agent and an airline employee follow the rules published in the tariff, they will be correct, and to give advice or perform an act contrary to these rules would render the agent or the company liable.

The Local Passenger Fares Tariff contains hundreds of pages of the regular fares of each participating carrier. The Local Fare Tariff lists each participating airline's fares in alphabetical sequence. After some study, reading the fares is not a difficult task although this may not be so at first glance.

The joint one way and round tariff fares and rules are published to cover transportation on two different airlines, *i.e.*, a joint fare becomes one fare covering transportation over two different carriers with the stipulation that the passenger must change airplanes in a certain specified city.

Because the joint fare is available as a single amount to cover transportation over two different airlines, it becomes a lesser amount than the sum of the two one way fares would be over the same route.

GUIDELINES FOR FINDING AND READING INTERNATIONAL AIR TARIFF RULES

I. Make sure that the latest edition of Air Tariff is available, including the most recent supplements.

II. Check the airline tariff fare schedule for the applicable rule.

III. Consult the tariff index for the rate numbers; don't try to remember the rule numbers.

IV. Check the rule for the conditions governing normal and special fares. Analyse your questions and identify the section of the rules most applicable. Make sure there are no recent fare changes.

V. Know the subject headings and their general interpretation of the rules. Conditions governing normal and special fares are described under the subject heading listed below: These 'headings' always have the same sequence.

1. Application
   F/Y OW, RT or CT Fares
2. Period of application
   Fares apply all year
3. Fares
   The applicable fare is that quoted against the rule number
4. Validity
   (*a*) Maximum stay : one year
   (*b*) Minimum stay : No minimum stay requirement
   (*c*) Extension of Ticket validity
5. Group size
   The number stated in the rule is the minimum number of passenger required to make up a group. An entry under this heading will only found in a group fares rule.
6. Stop-overs:
   "Stop-over" means a stop at an intermediate point from which the passenger is not scheduled to depart on the day of arrival. If there is no scheduled connecting departure on the date of arrival, departure on the next day within 24 hours will not constitute a stop-over.
7. Advertising and sales

Advertising and sales (including but not limited to issuance of MCO's and XO's and PTS's) are permitted worldwide.

8. Affinity and own use provisions
9. Baggage
10. Cancellations and refunds

    Group Inclusive Tour Fares : See the Governing Rule X900.

    Affinity/Own Use Group Fares : See Governing Rule Z900. Other Fares: See General Rule R. 01
11. Combinations

    Combinations with international and domestic fares are permitted subject to Fares Construction Rules.
12. Commission

    Normal procedure apply
13. Discount

    Available for:
    - (*a*) Children, infants
    - (*b*) Tour conductors
    - (*c*) Sales Agents
14. Documentation

    Normal provisions apply—*e.g.*

    Passport

    Visas required, etc.
15. Eligibility:

    Unrestricted—*e.g.*, not restricted to a particular type of passenger such as military personnel
16. Minimum Tour Price:

    See Governing Rule X900
17. Modification of Inclusive Tours

    See Governing Rule X900
18. Name change and additions

    Rule Z900 will apply if the fare involved is governed by Rule Z900.

    Otherwise, no name changes and additions are permitted
19. Passenger Expenses
20. Payment
21. Reservations

    See General Rule T.03

22. Re-routing
    Inclusive Tour Fares : See Governing Rule X900
    Affinity Group Fares: See Governing Rule Z900
    Other Fares: See General Rule R.02
23. Routing
    Normal Fare Construction Rules apply, unless a routing map number is indicated opposite the fare shown in the yellow pages
24. Ticketing
25. Tour Features
26. Tour Literatures
27. Travel Together
    Group Inclusive Tour Fares: See Governing Rule X900.
    Affinity/Own Use Group Fares: See Governing Rule Z900.

VI. Find and read the rule very carefully. Read the entire rule in order to answer your question completely.

VII. Read carefully the first paragraph of the rule, which are applicable to all carriers.

VIII. Check the rules for the one carrier with which you are concerned.

IX. Study the paragraphs which begins,
"Not applicable to ...." and "Applicable to ...."
to see if the carrier is mentioned.

X. Look for NOTE or EXPLANATION statements to see if the carrier is mentioned.

GUIDELINES FOR FARE CONSTRUCTION

The term 'Itinerary' means all portions of the passenger's reservation to include surface transportation, if any, from original to final destination. In general, the types of itineraries include the following:

1. One way trips
2. Round trips (return journeys)
3. Circle trips
4. Around the world trips
5. Open jaw trips

One way trip: A one way trip is considered to be any journey which for fare calculation purposes, is not a complete round or circle trip entirely by air. Routing consists of carriers, class of service and cities served. Example,

DELHI
MADRAS/(CHENNAI) AIF

Round trip: The term 'round trip' means travel from one point to another and return to the point of origin by the same air route as that used for the outbound portion. This definition will still apply when the fares used for the outbound portion is different from that used for the inbound. Round trip means a point of origin to point of destination and return to point of origin. Example,

DELHI
MADRAS/(CHENNAI) AIF
DELHI AIF

The term 'round trip' also means travel from one point to another and return to the same point of origin by an air route different from that used for the outbound portion. This definition will only apply when the same one-way fare is applicable to both the outbound and inbound portion.

Circle trip: This means travel, other than a round rip, from one point and return to the same point by a continuous circuitous air route, including around the world trips. Circle trip can be to any number of cities using any routing and return to point of origin as long as all transportation is made by commercial scheduled airline.

NEW DELHI (DEL)
CHENNAI (MAD) AIF
MUMBAI (BOM) AIF
NEW DELHI (DEL) AIF

Around the world trip: Round the world trips are circle trips and apply to continuous eastbound or westbound travel commencing from and returning to the same point. The fare of an around the world trip is constructed in the same manner as a circle trip.

Open jaw: Open jaw is an itinerary which is essentially of a round trip or circle trip nature but has a segment not transmitted by air. Example,

NEW DELHI

CHENNAI OPEN JAW

MUMBAI

An open jaw trip consists of travel which is essentially of a round trip nature with the exception that either the outward point of arrival and inward point of departure are not the same.

LOWEST COMBINATION OF FARE METHOD

When a required fare between two points is not published, it may be constructed by the particular combination of two or more sectional fares along the desired routing which produces the lowest fare.

Example:

Given the itinerary, Mumbai-New York-San Francisco-Bangkok, you are required to calculate the fare construction by lowest combination of fare method.

Solution:

Possible combination of fares:

1.	Mumbai-New York	593
	New York-San Francisco-Bangkok	693
	Total Fare	1286
2.	Mumbai-New York-San Francisco	738
	San Francisco-Bangkok	520
	Total Fare	1258

In this particular case, the lowest combination of fare constructs over New York. A desired itinerary may be constructed over fictitious construction points to which the passenger is not, in reality travelling, if such a construction produces a lower fare.

MILEAGE SYSTEM

The mileage system should be used whenever a desired itinerary between two points is not included in an applicable diagrammatic or linear routing published in connection with a fare. There are three basic elements involved in the application of the mileage system. They are:

1. Maximum permitted mileage,
2. Non-stop sector mileages, and
3. Excess mileage surcharges.

In addition to these three basic elements, other factors must be taken into consideration when the mileage system is used. The most frequent consideration includes:

1. Extra mileage allowance and special mileage provisions,
2. Stop-overs,
3. Limitations on indirect travel,
4. Higher rated intermediate fares,
5. Special provisions for one way journeys (one way back haul rule),
6. Fictitious (Hidden) construction points, and
7. "More distant points" principle.

The maximum permitted mileage (MPM) published in connection with a fare governs the maximum distance a passenger is allowed to travel en-route between two particular points at the direct fare. When a thorough fare is constructed by combination of sector fares, thorough maximum mileage (if available) from the origin to the destination of such constructed fare may be used unless prohibited by rules applicable to use of the sector fares.

Non-stop sector mileages for all sectors of a routing are used to compute the total mileage of the journey flown. Only non-stop sector mileages published in the latest list of non-stop sector mileages, as amended may be used.

In order to determine whether a desired routing between two points is permissible at the thorough fare, the following basic steps should be taken:

1. Look up the applicable MPM between two particular points.
2. Add up the non-stop sector mileages between all the points of the routing. The computation must be made according to the actual route of travel, including scheduled stop-overs, intermediate transit points and connecting points.
3. Compare the total of the non-stop sector mileages to the applicable MPM permitted at the direct fare between the two points. If the total of the non-stop sector mileages is equal to or less than the MPM, the itinerary is allowed at the direct published fare, except as provided for in the rules.

Example:

From the itinerary given below prepare a suitable fare construction based on mileage system:

Itinerary: NYC-LON-AMS-MUC-ROME-NCE-LIS-TER-NYC

Solution:

Fare Construction Point : Rome

MPM New York- Rome 5136

New York-London	3456	Rome-NCE	294
London-Amsterdam	230	NCE-Lisbon	913
Amsterdam-MUC	420	Lisbon-TER	967
MUC-Rome	440	TER-BOS (Connecting point)	2293
		BOS-New York	191
Total	4546	Total	4658

Since the total sector mileage of each half of the itinerary is less than the MPM, the above routing is allowed at the thorough published fare.

Excess Mileage Surcharges

If the total sector mileage for a desired routing exceeds the MPM published in connection with a fare, a surcharge becomes necessary. The excess mileage percentage table must be used to determine the applicable amount.

The direct fare becomes subject to a surcharge in amounts varying from five to twenty five per cent depending upon the amount of mileage in excess of that published in connection with the fare. To use the Excess Mileage Percentage Table, you should refer to the first column of the table headed 'Published Mileage' and the figures in the column which cover every number up to 100 (after which the series progress in groups of 100 up to 24,900) in order to obtain the exact mileage. These figures present the normal MPM published in connection with a fare.

Example:

From the information given below you are required to:

(1) Do the fare construction as per mileage system

(2) Calculate the surcharge for the itinerary.

Itinerary : BOS-LIS-MAD-LON-AMS-FRA-MIL-ROM

MPM : Boston-Rome 4950

Excess Mileage Surchages

(Contd.)

(*Contd.*)

Published Mileage	*Mileage permitted when published fare is increased by*				
	5%	10%	15%	20%	25%
90	93	97	101	105	112
91	95	98	102	106	114
92	96	100	105	107	115
93	97	101	106	109	117
94	98	102	106	110	118
95	99	102	106	110	118
96	100	104	108	112	120
97	101	105	109	113	121
98	102	106	110	114	123
99	103	107	112	116	124
6000	6250	6500	6750	7000	7500
6100	6355	6609	6863	7117	7626
6200	6458	6717	6975	7233	7750
6300	6562	6825	7087	7350	7875
6400	6667	6934	7200	7467	8001
6500	6771	7042	7312	7583	8125
6600	6875	7150	7425	7700	8250
6700	6980	7259	7538	7817	8376
6800	7083	7367	7650	7933	8500
6900	7187	7475	7762	8050	8625

Solution:

(1) Sector Mileage Computation

Boston-Lisbon	3185
Lisbon-Chennai	319
Chinnai-Lisbon	765
London-Amsterdam	230
Amsterdam-Frankfurt	228
Frankfurt-Milan	311
Milan-Rome	311
	5249

Since the sum total of sector mileages of 5249 for the above itinerary exceeds the MPM of 4950 allowed between Boston and Rome, a surcharge becomes necessary. This charge is calculated by using the Excess Mileage Percentage Table; when the MPM of surcharge is calculated by using the Excess Mileage Percentage Table; when the MPM of 4950 is increased to the 10% surcharge level, the figure arrived at is 5363. This figure of 5363 is the only figure which exceeds the sum total of sector mileages of 5249. Therefore, the appropriate exceeds mileage surcharge for the above itinerary is ten per cent of the direct fare.

(2) Surcharging a Fare

The surcharge for the itinerary is calculated as follows:

Direct Fare Boston-Rome	Rs. 15,000
10% Fare Surcharge	Rs. 1,500
Total Fare	Rs. 16,500

If the sum total of non-stop sector mileages exceeds the adjusted MPM shown in the 25% column of the Excess Mileage Percentage Table, the applicable fare will be the combination of two or more fares along the desired routing which produces the lowest fare (including, for example, the case of such fare construction methods as "The More Distant Point Principle'). In certain areas of the world, extra mileage allowance are permitted in addition to the MPM's published in connection with fares.

The IATA Basic Fare Construction principle states that when no through fare is specifically published for a desired itinerary, it must be constructed. Such a construction fare must not be less than the lowest amount obtained by any of the following principles:

1. Lowest combination of fares principles
2. Mileage system
3. More distant point principle.

Fare constructed by the use of add-one are considered thorough fares. A published direct fare always takes precedence over any combination of fares, of the same type, which may exist between the same points for the same class of service, *e.g.*, for the direct journey. New Delhi-Mumbai-Chennai, the published fare New Delhi-Chinnai must be used even in the sum of New Delhi-Mumbai plus Mumbai-Chennai is lower.

A published direct fare takes precedence when such a fare is used as a component part of a constructed fare for a further point, e.g., for the direct journey New Delhi-Bangalore-Chennai-Kolkata, when no through fare is published. The correct construction to be used is New Delhi-Chennai plus Chennai-Kolkata, even though the result is higher.

Special domestic fares (*e.g.*, super saver, IT_X, etc.) may be combined with international fares, even though such a combination undercuts a published through international fare. The applicable fare will be the published or constructed through fare in effect at the time travel be given on the first flight coupon.

As per the basic fare construction principles of IATA when no through fare is specifically published for a desired itinerary, it needs to be constructed. The main point to be taken into account is that the constructed fare must not be less than the lowest amount obtained by way of the other principles such as lowest combination of fair principle, mileage system, and more distance point principle. The fares constructed by the use of add-one are considered 'through fares'.

A published direct fare always takes precedence over any combination of fares of the same type, which may exist between the same points for the same class of service. Let us take an example. For the direct journey between New Delhi-New York, the published fare New Delhi-New York must be used even if the sum of New Delhi-London plus London-New York is lower. A published direct fare takes precedence when such a fare is used as a component part of a constructed fare to a further point. For example, for the direct journey, New Delhi-Frankfurt-London-New York, when no thorough fare is published, the correct construction to be used is New Delhi-Frankfurt-London plus London, New York, even though the result is higher.

The applicable fare will be the publish or constructed through fare in effect at the time the agency begins on the first flight coupon.

Table 5.1: Common Abbreviations and Symbols used in Airlines

Abbreviation	*Terms*
AAA	American Automobile Association or AAA Worldwide Travel
AAR	Against All Risks
AAR	Association of British Travel Agents
ABTB	Trade Association of U.S. Bank Operated Travel Agent

(*Contd.*)

(*Contd.*)

Abbreviation	*Terms*
A/C	Air conditioning in Rental Cars
ACTO	Association of Caribbean Tour Operators
ACTOA	Airline Charter Tour Operators Association
AFTA	Australian Federation of Travel Agent
AGT	Agent or Travel Agent
AGTE	Association of Group Travel Executive
AH&MA	American Hotel and Motel Association
ALPA	Airline Pilot Association
ALTA	Association of Local Transportation Airline
AMAV	Association Mexican a DE Agencies de Visage (Mexican Travel Agent Association)
AMHA	American Motor Hotel Association
ARNK	Arrival unknown
ARTA	Association of Retail Travel Agents (USA)
ASI	American Sightseeing International
ASTA	American Society of Travel Agents
ATA	Air Transport Association (USA)
ATAC	Air Transport Association of Canada
ATBEC	Association of Tourist Board of Eastern Caribbean
ATC	Air Traffic Conference (USA)
A3B	European Airbrush A 300B, jet crafts equipment
ATX	Air Taxi
AX	American Express (Credit Card)
BA	Visa (formerly Bank American Card)
BB	Barclay Card
BHA	Bhamas Hotel Association
BAB	British Airways Board
BTA	British Tourist Authority
BP	Bermuda Plan
CA	Master Charge
CAB	Civil Aeronautics Board
CATM	Consolidated Air Tour Manual
CB	Carte Blanche
CCA	Caribbean Cruise Association
CCR	Compact Bar
CERR	Conference of European Rail Road Representatives
CF	Car Ferry
CHA	Caribbean Hotel Association
CHTR	Charter

(*Contd.*)

(*Contd.*)

Abbreviation	*Terms*
CL	Flight Closed, Wait List open
CLIA	Cruise Lines International Association
CONV	Convertible Car
CP	Continental Breakfast
CTA	Caribbean Tourism Association
CTC	Certified Travel Councillor
CTC	Contract
CTO	City Ticket Office
CTOA	Creative Tour Operators of America
CTRC	Caribbean Tourism Research Centre
CWGN	Compact Station Wagon
DATO	Discover America Travel Organisation
DBLB	Double Room with Bath or Shower
DBLN	Double Room with Shower
DC	Diner's Club
DEP	Departure
DET	Domestic Escorted Tour
DIT	Domestic Independent Travel
DOT	Department of Transportation (USA)
DP	Demi-Pension
DSM	District Sales Manager (airline, steamship or tour operator)
E&OE	Errors and Omission Expected
EB	East Bound
EC	Euro Card
EP	European Plan
ETA	Estimated Time of Arrival
ETC	European Travel Commission
ETD	Estimated Time of Departure
FAA	Federal Aviation Administration
FCU	Fare Construction Unit
FET	Foreign Escorted Tour
FGTO	French Govt. Tourist Office
FHTL	First Class Hotel
FIT	Foreign Independent Travel
FP	Full Pension
FN	Deluxe Night Coach
GIT	Group Incentive Tour
GMT	Greenwich Mean Time

(*Contd.*)

(Contd.)

Abbreviation	*Terms*
GSA	General Sales Agent
HL	Have Wait Listed
HN	Requesting (have need)
HSMA	Hotel Sales Management Association
HTL	Hotel
IACA	International Air Carrier Association
IATA	International Air Transport Association
IATC	Inter American Travel Congress
IATM	International Association of Tour Managers
ICAO	International Civil Aviation Organisation
ICC	Interstate Commerce Commission
ICCA	International Congress and Convention Association
ICTA	Institute of Certified Travel Agents
IHA	International Hotel Association
IN	Check in date (it is followed by date)
INF	Infant
IPSA	International Passenger Ship Association
ISTA	International Sightseeing and Tour Association
IT	Inclusive Tour
ITC	Inclusive Tour Charter
ITX	Inclusive Tour Excursion
IUOTO	International Union of Official Travel Organisation (now World Tourism Organisation)
JET	Aircraft with Jet Engines
JTO	Joint Tour Operators
K	Thrift Class
KH	Peak Thrift
KK	Confirming
KL	Off peak Thrift or Confirming from Wait List
KN	Night Thrift
KSML	Kosher Meal Request
LCAR	Luxury Class Hotel
LWGN	Luxury Station Wagon
MAA	Motel Association of America
MAP	Modified American Plan
MAXR	Maximum Room Rate Desired
MCO	Miscellaneous Charge Order

(Contd.)

(*Contd.*)

Abbreviation	*Terms*
MINR	Minimum Room Rate Desired
MODR	Modified Room Rate Desired
MPM	Maximum Permitted Mileage
MV	Motor Vessel
NACA	National Air Carrier Association
NARP	National Association of Rail Road Passengers
NATO	National Association of Travel Organisation
NB	North Bound
NPTA	National Passenger Traffic Association
NTBA	National Tour Brokers Association
NTSB	National Transportation Safety Board
NV	Nuclear Vessel
OAG	Official Airline Guide
OHRG	Official Hotel and Resort Guide
OK	Reservation Confirmed
OMFG	Optical Meeting Facilities Guide
OTC	Non-Stop Inclusive Tour Charter
Orbits	Polish Natural Travel Bureau
OW	One Way
PATA	Pacific Area Travel Association
PATCO	Professional Air Traffic Controllers Organisations
PAX or PSGR	Passenger
PTA	Prepaid Ticket Advice
PTM	Passenger Traffic Manager
Q	Surcharge
RT	Round Trip
Routing	Route Structure
RPM	Revenue Passenger Mile
RSM	Regional Sales Manager
RTPA	Rail Travel Promotion Agency (AMTRAK)
SATW	Society of American Travel Writers
SFML	Sea Food Meal Request
SST	Supersonic Transport
Suite	Double Room with Bath and Sitting Room
SUR	Surface Travel

(*Contd.*)

(*Contd.*)

Abbreviation	*Terms*
SWB	Single with Bath
SWGN	Standard Station Wagon
TC	Travel Card or Tourist Class Accommodation as on a Ship
TGC	Travel Group Charter
THTL	Tourists Class Hotel
TPPC	Transpacific Passenger Conference
TRPB	Triple Room with Bath
TRPN	Triple Room with Bath or Shower
TRPS	Triple Room with Shower
TS	Turbine Electric Ship
TSS	Turbine Ship
TUR	Tour
TWIN	Hotel Room having two Single Beds
TWNB	Double Room with twin Beds and Bath
TWNN	Double Room with twin beds but without Shower or Bath
TWNS	Double Room with Twin Beds and Shower
TWU	Transport Workers Union of America
UATP	Universal Air Travel Plan (Credit Card and carrier-sponsored Change Plan)
U-DRIVE	Automobile rented without Driver
UFTAA	Universal Federation of Travel Agent Association
USTOA	United States Tour Operators' Association
USTS	United States Travel Service
VAL	Value
VES	Vessel
WATA	World Association of Travel Agencies
WB	West Bound
WL	Wait List
WTO	World Tourism Organisation
XO	Surcharge Order
XS	Access
XX	Cancel
Y	Coach

TARIFF TERMINOLOGY

In Table 5.2 are some elementary tariff definitions that will be useful in fare construction:

Table 5.2: Tariff Terminology

Surface:	Refers to a portion of the complete itinerary of the passenger not transported by air, *i.e.*
ARNK:	Arrival unknown, or VOID *i.e.,* No air provided on that segment.
Online Service:	Means the segments of different carrier, *i.e.,* AI to AI.
Offline Service:	Means the segments of differenting carriers, *i.e.,* IA to BA.
Interline Service:	Means the segments of two or more differing carriers.
Local Fare:	Means a fare for online transportation.
Joint Fare:	Means a fare for offline or interline transportation.
Connection:	Means a required aircraft change at an intermediate point between point of departure and the point of destination. In order for a passenger to connect, he must depart the connection city on a flight scheduled to depart within four (4) hours of arrival; or on the first flight on which space is available; or on a flight that will provide for an international arrival.
Stop-over:	Refers to a deliberate interruption of travel by the passenger in agreement with the carrier, at a point between the place of origin and the place of destination equal to a bleak in the trip.
Intermediate stop:	Means a point of landing between the passenger's original place of departure and final destination which does not require deplanning by the passenger.
Non-stop:	Means a boarding point to a deplanning point with 'NO' intermediate stop(s).
Direct:	Means a boarding point to a deplanning point with any number of intermediate stops.

FARE CONSTRUCTION TERMINOLOGY

There are some elementary terminology which are very useful in fare construction:

Routing

Routing means a geographical logical sequence of point to point destinations. It consists of carriers, class of service, and cities served. For example,

MUMBAI	
NEW DELHI	AA–F

Itinerary

Itinerary plays an important part in the fare construction. It may be defined as all portions of the passenger's reservation to include surface transportation, if any, from origin to final destination. The different types of itineraries are:

1. One way trips
2. Round trips (return journey)
3. Circle trips
4. Round the world trips
5. Open jaw trips

One Way Trip

It is considered to be any journey which, for fare construction purposes, is not a complete round or circle trip entirely by air. For example,

KOLKATA	
DELHI	AA–F

Round Trip

It is a travel from one point to another and return to the point of origin by the same air route as that used for the out bound portion. It means any flight or base based on travel in both directions between two directions. In other words, it means a point of origin to the point of destination and return to point of origin. It also means travel from one point to another and return to the same point of origin by an air route different from that used by the out bound portion. This definition will only apply when the same one way fare is applicable to both the out bound and in bound portion. Example of a round trip is:

DELHI	
CHENNAI	AA–F
DELHI	AA–F

Circle Trip

It means a journey with that return to the point of departure without retracing its route. It is a travel, other than round trip, from one point and return to the same point by a continuous, circuitous air route, including around the world trips. These trips can be to any number of cities using any routing and return to point of origin as long as all transportation is made by commercial schedule airlines. Circle fares for individual segments of a circle trip. Example of a circle trip is:

NEW DELHI	
KOLKATA	AA–F
MUMBAI	AA–F
NEW DELHI	AA–F

Round the World Trip

These are the circle trips and apply to continuous last bound or west bound travel commencing from and returning to the same point via both east and west. The fare for an around trip is constructed in the same manner as a circle trip.

Open Jaw

It is an itinerary which is essentially of a around trip or circle trip nature but has segment not transmitted by air. It means a round trip itinerary in which the arrival point is different from the departure point. Usually it has a surface segment. This trip consists of travel which is essentially of a round trip nature with the exception that either the outward point of arrival or inward point of departure are not the same. Example of an open jaw itinerary is:

	NEW DELHI	
MUMBAI		OPEN JAW
	CHENNAI	

Surface

It refers to a portion of the complete itinerary of the passenger not transmitted by air for example,

NEW DELHI-ARRIVAL unknown; or VOID

No air provided on that segment.

Online Service

It means the segment of same airline, for example,

AI to AI

Off in Service

It means segments of differing carriers. For example,

AI to PANAMA

Interline Service

Interline indicates a cooperative relationship and/or reciprocal acceptance of tickets between airlines. Interline service means the segments of two or more differing carriers.

Local Fare

It is fare for one-line transportation.

Joint Fare

It is a fare for off-line or interline transportation.

Connections

A required air craft change at an intermediate point between point of departure and the point of destination. In order to enable the passenger to connect, he must depart the connection city on flight scheduled to depart with in four hours of arrival on the first flight on which space is available or on a flight that will provide an earlier arrival.

Stop-over

It means a stop along the route of a journey. The period of stop may be usually 24 hours or more. It refers to a deliberate interruption of a travel by the passenger in agreement with the carrier, at point between place of origin and the place of destination equal to a break in the trip.

Intermediate Stop

It is a point of landing between the passenger's original place of departure and final destination which does not require deplanning by the passenger.

Non-Stop

It means a flight made from one city airport to another, with non-stop end route. In other words, it means a boarding point to a deplanning point with no intermediate stops.

Direct

It means a boarding point out a deplanning point with any number of intermediate stops.

LOWEST COMBINATION OF FARES METHOD

This method is applied in cases where fare between two points is not established. In such cases the fare is constructed by the combination of two or more sectional fares along the desired routing which produces the lowest fares. A desired itinerary may be constructed over fictitious points to which the passenger is not, in reality, travelling, if such a construction produces a lower fare.

For example take an itinerary: New York-San Francisco-Bangkok. In this case there are two possible combination fares:

First construction fare

	Rs.
Bombay-New York	21,000.00
New York-San Francisco-Bangkok	24,000.00
	45,000.00

Second combination fare

Bombay-New York-San Francisco	22,500.00
San Francisco-Bangkok	19,500.00
	42,000.00

Thus we find that the lowest combination of fares constructs over New York.

Table 5.3: International Airlines and their Codes

Name	*Airline Code*	*Carrier Code*	*Country/ Headquarters*
Are Lingus	053	EI	Ireland, Dublin
Aeroflot	555	SU	Russia, Moscow
Aeromexico	139	AM	Mexico, Maxicoury
Air Afrique	092	RK	Ivorycoast, West Africa
Air Canada		AC	Canada, Montrel, Quebec
Air France	057	AF	France, Paris
Air India	098	AI	India, Bombay
Air New Zealand	086	NZ	New Zealand, Auckland,
Aerolineas Argentines	044	AR	Argentina
Alitalia	055	AZ	Italy, Rome
American Airlines	001	AA	USA, Dallas, Texas
Australian	257	OS	Austria, Vienna
Avianca	134	AV	Columbia (South Africa), Bogota
British Airways	125	BA	United Kingdom, London
CAAC	999	CA	China, Beijing
Delta	006	DL	USA, Georgia, Atlanta
Elal Israel Airlines	114	LY	Israel, Telaviv
Ethiopian*		ET	Ethiopia
Finnair	105	AY	Finaland, Helsinki
Iberia	75	IB	Spain, Madrid
Japan Airlines	131	JL	Japan, Tokyo
Klm-Royal Dutch Airlines	074	KL	Netherlands, The Hague
Korean*		KE	Korea
Kuwait Airways*		KU	Kuwait
Lan-Chile	045	LA	Chile, Santiago
Lot*		LO	Poland
Lufthansa German Airlines	220	LH	Germany, Cologne
Maxicana de Avacione*	132	MH	US, Maxico City
Nigeria Airways	087	WT	Nigeria, Lagos
Northwest	012	NW	USA, Minneapolis-St. Paul
Olympic Airways	050	OA	Greece, Thens

(*Contd.*)

(*Contd.*)

Name	*Airline Code*	*Carrier Code*	*Country/ Headquarters*
Philippine Air lines	079	PR	Philippines, Makati
Qantas Airways	081	QF	Australia, Sydney
Sabena Belgium	082	SN	Belgium, Brussels Word Air liens
Sahsa	274	SH	Honduras, Tegucigalpa
Scandianavan	274	SK	Sweden; Stockholm
Singapore Air lines*		SQ	Singapore
South African Airways	083	SA	Republic of South Africa, Johnesburg
Swissair	085	SR	Switzerland, Zurich
TAP Portugal	047	TP	Portugal, Libson
THAI Airways* International		TG	Thailand
TWQ (Transworld Airline)	015	TW	USA, New York
UTA French Airliens	142	UT	France, Futeaux
Varig, S.A		RG	Brazil
VIASA*		VA	Venezuela

MILEAGE SYSTEM

This system is used whenever a desired itinerary between two points is not included in an applicable diagrammatic or linear routing published in connection with a fare. Following basic elements are involved in the application of the mileage system:

1. Maximum permitted mileage
2. Non-stop sector mileage
3. Excess mileage surcharges
4. Extra-mileage allowances and special mileage provisions
5. Stop-overs
6. Limitation on indirect travel
7. Higher rated intermediate fares
8. Special provisions for one way journey/or one way backhand rule
9. Fictitious hidden construction points
10 The more distant point principle.

The maximum permitted mileage (MPM) published in connection with a fare governs the maximum distance a passenger is allowed to travel in route between two particular points at the direct fare. When a through fare is constructed by combination of sector fares, through maximum mileage (if available) from the origin of the destination of such constructed fare may be used unless prohibited by rules applicable to one of the sector fares. Non-stop sector mileages for all sectors of routing are used to complete the total mileage of the journey flown. Only non-stop sector mileages published in the latest list of non-stop sector mileages, as amended may be used.

In order to determine whether a desired routing between two points is permissible at the through fare, the following steps should be followed:

Firstly : Check the applicable MPM between the two particular points.

Secondly: Add up the non-stop sector mileage between all the points of routing. The combination must be made according to actual route of travel, including all scheduled stopovers, intermediate transit points and connection points.

Thirdly : Compare the total of the non-stop sector mileages to the applicable MPM permitted at the direct fare between the two points. If the total of non-stop sector mileage in equal to or less than the MPM, the itinerary is allowed at the published direct fare.

Example:

Take an itinerary as New York-London-Amsterdam-MUC (Monica)-Rome-Nice-Lisbon-TER-New York City.

1. Fare construction point = Rome
2. MPM New York-Rome = 5136
3. Total sector mileage of each half of the itinerary is 4546 and 4658 respectively.

In this case the total sector mileage of each half of the itinerary is less than the MPM, the above touring is allowed at through published fare.

Excess Mileage Surcharge

In case the total sector mileage for a desired routing exceeds the MPM published in connection with a fare, a surcharge becomes necessary. For this purpose the excess mileage percentage table must be used in order to determine the applicable amount. These tables indicate the published image and the different limits of mileage permitted when published fare is increased by different percentage varying from 5 per cent to 25 per cent. Thus the direct fare becomes subject to a surcharge in amounts varying from 5 per cent to 25 per cent depending upon the amount of mileage in excess of that published in connection with the fare.

Example:

Let us take an itinerary as:

BOSTON-LISBON-MADRID
LONDON-AMSTERDAM-FRANKFURT-MILAN-ROME

1. MPM: Boston Rome = 4590
2. Sector Mileage computations = 5249

In this case the sum total of sector mileages of 5249 exceeds the MPM of 4950, therefore a surcharge become necessary. When the MPM of 4950 is increased to 10 per cent surcharge level, the figure arrived at is 5363. This figure exceeds the sum total of sector mileages. Therefore, the approximate excess mileage for the above itinerary is 10 per cent of the direct fare.

MORE DISTANT POINT PRINCIPLE

In case the sum total of non-stop sector mileage exceeds the adjusted MPM shown in the 25 per cent column of the excess mileage percentage table, the applicable fare will be the combination of two or more fares along the desired routing which produces the lowest rate by using the more distant point principle. In certain region of the world, extra mileage allowance are permitted in addition to the MPM's published in connection with fares.

AIRWAYS COMPETITION

In the past air fare to the same places were similar and expensive. However, since last few years due to deregulation of the airlines and liberalised air carriers agreements with other nations, there are new airlines, new routes and new promotion fares generating lot of competition. In the past there used to be first class fare and economy class fares. Now, at national and international level there are different types of fares such as:

1. 14-27 day excursion
2. 22-45 day excursion
3. Midweek
4. Weekend
5. Apex
6. Super apex
7. Standby
8. Budget
9. Youth and Group fare
10. Discover India
11. Super saver
12. Freedom
13. No Frills
14. Super Jackpot
15. Children Feed
16. Small potatoes
17. Peanuts fare
18. Senior Saver fare
19. Super coach fare
20. Night fare

The increasing competition among airlines at national and international level has produced special conditions and reading the fine print has become necessity for the passenger and the travel agents.

FARE CALCULATION ON A HAND TICKET

The fare calculation is not normally required on a hand ticket for a domestic itinerary, except in special circumstances. The fare calculation is to be entered for any of the following:

1. Conjunction tickets,
2. Tickets which are issued in exchange for portion of another tickets,
3. Ticket for which a surcharge, stop-over charge or mileage charge applies, or
4. Ticket for an international itinerary.

If none of the above situations apply, the fare calculation is not required.

Method of Entering Manual Fare Calculation

The following procedure is adopted:

1. *'From' and 'To' Boxes:*

   Enter the city code for each board. Enter only city codes and not the airport codes or names. To indicate surface segment, 'X' is entered in 'From' and 'To' Boxes.

2. *Fare Calculation Box:*

   The base fare for each segment is entered. Only fare box (*i.e.* without tax) should be entered.

3. *The 'Fare' Boxes:*

   Enter the total base fare. There are two fare boxes, one on the far right and one on the lower left corner.

4. *'Commission and Tax' Box:*

   Directly below the last entitlement line are two boxes labelled 'commission' and 'tax'. The travel agency commission rate is entered in the commission box. For most domestic carriers, the normal commission rate is 1 per cent. However, for special branch offices, called in-plant agencies, the commission rate is 3 per cent. An in-plant agency is a branch office of a travel agency that functions as a department of a client company, handling all the company's travel arrangements. In most cases, the company that the plant agency serves is the agency's only client.

5. *'Tax' Box:*

   The tax rate is entered in the 'tax box'. For most domestic itineraries, the 10 per cent transportation applies. If no tax applies, zero is entered in the tax box. If any other tax rate besides 10 per cent is applied, the actual amount is entered in the tax box, instead of the rate.

6. *Fare, Tax, and Total Boxes:*

   The total base fare, tax and total fare, a ticket price, are entered in the appropriate boxes in the lower left corner of the ticket. If any other tax besides air transportation tax is assessed, each tax is listed separately and identified by a code. Technically, a passenger facility charge (PFC) is not a tax, but rather a surcharge levied by an airport authority. However, for ticketing purposes, the tax code XT is used to identify a PFC. If four or more taxes apply, the code XT, for a combined tax amount, may be used to identify the total tax.

7. *Form of Payment 'Box':*

   (*a*) When a passenger pays by a cheque, the word cheque is entered in this box.

   (b) When a credit card is used to purchase the ticket, the

appropriate credit card code and account number are entered in the box. Major credit card codes are listed as under:

AX	=	American Express
BA, VI	=	Bank Americard / Visa
Ca, IK, MC	=	Master Card / Intercard
CB	=	Carte Blanche
DC	=	Diners Club
DS	=	Discover Card
TP	=	Universal Air Travel Plan

(*c*) When a passenger, purchases a ticket by credit card, a universal credit charge form must be filled out to record the sale transaction.

8. *'Not Valid Before' and 'Not Valid After'*:

These boxes are used to indicate the effective date and the expiration date for these type of fares.

9. *Endorsement/Restrictions 'Box'*:

These boxes may be used for any of the following purposes:

(*a*) To indicate if the ticket is non-refundable as if a penalty applies for cancellation or change.
(*b*) To charge the passenger, class of service.
(*c*) To permit the ticket to be used on a different carrier.

After a ticket has been validated, it can often be used to travel on different carrier than the one specified. To change the carrier, the passenger must first obtain authorization from the alternative carrier. A ticket agent for the validating carrier must often sign over, or endorse, the ticket, to the new carrier. Under rule 240 of the airline industry regulations, if a flight is delayed or cancelled, the airline that operates the delayed or cancelled flight is required to provide each passenger with alternative transportation at the additional cost. Often the airline will endorse the passenger's ticket to a different airline, rather than re-issue a new ticket.

10. *Preparing Conjunction Tickets:*

When you use two or more multipart ticket booklets to ticket one itinerary, the city code for the full board point and the final off point are entered in the origin / destination box.

In a round-trip itinerary, the origin and destination are the same city. For example, assume an itinerary includes a three leg connection from Bombay to New York, and two leg connection from New York to Bombay. You will require five-flight coupons to ticket this itinerary, and therefore, two ticket booklets would be used. In the origin/destination box on both tickets, Bom./Bom. would be entered, indicating that Bombay is both first board point and final off point in the itinerary.

11. *'Booking Reference' Box:*

    In this box the airline record locator is entered. The record locator will enable ticket a reservation agents to retrieve the reservation record on the airline's computer system.

Call the airline and book the flights. Assuming the flights are available, circle OK and make a note of the airline reservationist's name and the date the booking was made. Give the airline reservationist the passenger's name, home phone contact, and the travel agency's phone number. Check the fare with the airline. They should have the information in their computer. She gives us a fare of YL (coach, low season) $320.00 one way. Double the fare for round-trip and add the $3.00 international tax.

Re-verify the fare. Refer to the Air Tariff-Worldwide, Book 1. Look up the fare from Boston to Paris. Note the YL one way fare which is $320.00 in the headline city currency (USD) and $302.00 in FCU's. (See the example below). The fare given by the airline is correct and now this reservation would be ready for ticketing. The above itinerary we have used was a very simple, basic itinerary.

Example:

Now let's suppose Ms. Saroj has decided to stop-over in London for a day enroute to Paris. Her itinerary is now BOS-LON-PAR-BOS. We must now check the mileage on the one way BOS-LON-PAR. In the tariff listing the maximum permitted mileage for the YL Boston to Paris fare is 4124. We will now refer to the "Routing-non-stop sector mileages" section of the tariff to check the non-stop sector mileages.

Since the allowed mileage is 4124 we are well within the mileage and it is not necessary to increase the fare. More complicated fare itineraries should always be verified with the airline's rate desk. They will give you a rate number, and the rate number should be written on the fare construction portion of the ticket.

PASSENGER AIR TICKET

.... DESTINCTION (COUPON)	BOSTON	DESTINATION BOSTON
	CONNECTION TICKET(S)	

FROM/TO	CARRIER	FARE CALCULATION	8453:976:709
BOS TON PAR			
BOS	TW	M	PLACE OF ISSUE
	BA	320.00	
	TW	320.00	

NAME OF PASSENGER	NOT TRANSFERABLE	ISSUED IN EXCHANGE FOR	DATE OF ISSUE	AUDITOR'S COUPON
Ms. SAROJ			21 NOV 2004	

COUPONS NOT VALID BEFORE

1	2	3	4	ORIGINAL ISSUE	CARRIER	FORM & SERIAL NUMBER	PLACE	DATE	AGENT NUMBER CODE

COUPONS NOT VALID AFTER

1	2	3	4	TICKET DESTINATION	TOUR CODE

X/O	NOT GOOD FOR PASSAGE		FARE BASES	ALLOW	CARRIER	PAGMT	CLASS	DATE	TIME	STATUS
	FROM	BOSTON	YL		TW	754	Y	Dec.16	1900	OK
O	TO	LONDON/ HEATHROW	YL		BA	032	Y	Dec.18	1100	OK
O	TO	PARIS/CHARLES DE GAULLE	YL		TW	811	Y	Dec.20	1345	OK
	TO	BOSTON	VOID							
	TO	VOID	COMMISSION 9					TOTAL	3.00	

RATE # 34268

FORM OF PAYMENT	CODE NUMBER	FARE	USD
CHECK	IN-9		640.00

IT IS UNLAWFULL TO PURCHASE OR RESELL THIS TICKET FROM/TO ANY ENTITY OTHER THAN, TIME SECURE CARRIER OR ITS AUTHORIZED AGENTS

PASSENGER TICKET & BAGGAGE CHECK—ISSUED BY

SUBJECT TO CONDITIONS OF CONTRACT ON PASSENGERS COUPON

FARE	EQ TT & AMT. PD	FORM	SERIAL NUMBER	CK	AIRLINE CODE
640.00	USD				

TAX	TOTAL	
3.00	643.00	‖ "8453976709 3 ‖"

Fig. 5.1: Specimen of a Passenger Air Ticket.

HEADLINE CITY					MAP RTE REF	GI/MPM
FROM/TO	FARE TYPE	CURRENCY	FCU	RULES		VIA PT.
BOSTON (BOS) Mas., U.S.A.			U.S.$ (USD)			
PARIS	F	675.00	636.00			4124
	YL	320.00	302.00			4124
	YH	406.00	383.00			4124
	YLE21	580.00	547.00	N201		4124
	YHE21	674.00	635.00	N202		4124
	YLE45	482.00	454.00	N226		4124
	YHE45	596.00	562.00	N228		4124
	YLZ	477.00	449.00	N151		4124
	YHZ	533.00	502.00	N153		4124
	YLGA	482.00	454.00	N515		4124
	YHGA	596.00	562.00	N517		4124
	YGC	482.00	454.00	N530		4124
	YGV	390.00	368.00	G225		4124
	YLGV	451.00	425.00	G206		4124
	YHGV	561.00	529.00	G207		4124

SECTOR MILEAGES

LONDON	UK	LON
Birmingham	UK	100
Bombay	India	4477
Bordeaux	Fra	449
Boston Mas	USA	3265
Bremen	Ger	405
Brussels	Bel	211
Bucharest	Rom	1302
Budapest	Hung	917
Cairo	Egypt	2185
Newquay	UK	213
New York NY	USA	3456
Nice	Fra	635
Norwich	UK	117
Oporto	Port	801
Oslo	Nor	730
Palma Majorca	Spain	826
Paris	Fra	209
Perpignam	Fra	612

By looking up the mileage under London, we have the sector mileage listings for both BOS-LON and LON-PAR. We now compute the sector mileage as follows:

BOS	LON	3265
	PAR	, 209
		3474

BASIC PRINCIPLES OF INTERNATIONAL AIR FARES AND TICKETING

In today's increasingly global travel industry, there is a lot of foreign investment in airlines and worldwide expansion of computer reservation systems. The industry expects a large increase in industry overseas travel. Therefore, there is a need for familiarity and knowledge of international fares and ticketing.

CURRENCY CONVERSIONS

Table 5.4 indicates only the name of the country currency and the code.

D— International fares are published in US Dollars. This rate of exchange is to be used solely to convert local currency domestic fares to US dollars. This will allow combination of domestic fares, and international fares, from this country on the same ticket, and provide a common industry base.

ZZ—Round off to whole units: less than 0.5 round down, otherwise round up.

Table 5.4: Currency Codes

Country	*Currency*	*Code*
Australia	Dollar	AVD
Austria	Schilling	ATS
Bahamas	Dollar	BHD
Barbados	Dollar	BDD
Belgium	Franc	BEF
Bermuda	Dollar	BMD
Canada	Dollar	CAD
Denmark	Krone	DKK
France	Franc	FRF

(Contd.)

(Contd.)

Country	*Currency*	*Code*
French Polynesia	Franc	FRF
Germany	Mark	XFF
Hong Kong	Dollar	DEM
Ireland	Pound	HKD
Italy	Lira	IEP
Japan	Yen	ITL
Kenya	Schilling	JPY
Luxembourg	Franc	KES
Netherland	Guilder	LUF
New Zealand	Dollar	NIG
Norway	Krone	NZD
Spain	Peseta	NOK
Sweden	Krone	ESP
Switzerland	Franc	SEK
United Kingdom	Pound	CHF
United States	Dollar	GBP
Zaire	Zaire	LRZ

Table 5.5: Currency Conversions

(Rates given in the Table are not exact but as an example only)

			Assumed Bank Exchange Rate		*Assumed IATA Exchange Rates:*	
Country	*Currency*	*IATA Code*	*GBP equiva-lent*	*USD equiva-lent*	*One NUC equals*	*Round off units for local currency*
(1)	*(2)*	*(3)*	*(4)*	*(5)*	*(6)*	*(7)*
Afghanistan	Afghani = 100 Puls	AFA	7985	4750	16000.00 (D)	1
Albania	LEK = 100 Quindarka	ALL	170.973	101.70	(D)	1
Algeria	Algerian Dinar = 100 Centimes	DZD	94.985	56.50	55.3905	1

(Contd.)

(Contd.)

(1)	*(2)*	*(3)*	*(4)*	*(5)*	*(6)*	*(7)*
American Samoa	US Dollar = 100 Cents	USD	1.6812	1.00	1.00	1.00 ZZ
Angola	Kwanza Reajustado	AOR	359525	213857	201994.00 (D)	1.00
Anguilla	E.C. Dollar	XCD	4.5391	2.70	(D)	1.00
Antigua and Barbuda	E.C. Dollar	XCD	4.5391	2.70	2.70 (D)	1.00
Argentina	Argentinian Peso	ARS	1.6804	0.9995	1.00 (D)	1
Armenia	Dram = 100 Luma	AMD	707.798	421.02	421.02 (D)	1
Aruba	Aruban Guilder	AWG	3.0093	1.79	1.79	1
Australia	Australian Dollar = 100 Cents	AUD	2.0703	1.2315	1.26759	1
Austria	Schilling = 100 Groschen	ATS	17.7736	10.5723	10.58458	10
Azerbaijan	Manat = 100 Gyapik	AZM	7111	4230	4230.00 (D)	1
Bahamas	Bahamian Dollar = 100 Cents	BSD	1.6812	1.00	1.00 (D)	1.00
Baharain	Bahraini Dinar = 1000 Fils	BHD	0.6343	0.3773	0.376	1
Bangladesh	Taka = 100 Poisha	BDT	71.3649	42.45	42.4499 (D)	1
Barbados	Barbados Dollar = 100 Cents	BBD	3.3813	2.0113	(D)	1.00
Belarus	Belarusian Rouble	BYB	38481	22890	22966.00 (D)	1
Belgium	Belgian Franc = 100 Centimes	BEF	52.0661	30.97	30.97302	10
Belize	Belize Dollar = 100 Cents	BZD	3.3623	2.00	2.00 (D)	1.00
Benin	CFA Franc = 100 Centimes	XOF	856.20	509.30	508.69825	100
Bermuda	Bermudian Dollar = 100 Cents	BMD	1.6812	1.00	(D)	1.00
Bhutan	Ngultrum	BTN	60.0171	35.70	35.635	1
Bolivia	Boliviano	BOB	8.7252	5.19	5.124 (D)	1
Bosnia and Herzegovina	Dinar	BAD	n/a	n/a	(D)	
Botswana	Pula = 100 Thebe	BWP	6.0153	3.5778	3.47514	1
Brazil	Real = 100 Centavos	BRL	1.7326	1.0306	(D)	1
Brunel Darussalam	Brunei Dollar = 100 Cents	BND	2.3541	1.4003	1.41296	1.00
Bulgaria	Lev = 100 Stotinki	BGL	527.041	313.50	(D)	1
Burkina Faso	CFA Franc = 100 Centimes	XOF	856.20	509.30	508.69825	100
Burundi	Burundi Franc = 100 Centimes	BIF	363.993	216.514	217.40738 (D)	10

(Contd.)

(Contd.)

(1)	(2)	(3)	(4)	(5)	(6)	(7)
Cambodia	New Riel = 100 Centimes	KHR	3866	2300	(D)	10
Cameroon	CFA Franc = 100 Centimes	XAF	856.20	509.30	508.69825	100
Canada	Canadian Dollar = 100 Cents	CAD	2.2514	1.3392	1.33485	1.00 ZZ
Cape Verde	C.V. Escudo = 100 Centavos	CVE	139.485	82.97	82.97 (D)	100
Cayman Is.	Cayman Islands Dollar = 100 Cents	KYD	1.3923	0.8282	0.8282 (D)	0.10
Central African Rep.	CFA Franc = 100 Centimes	XAF	856.20	509.30	508.698256	100
Chad	CFA Franc = 100 Centimes	XAF	856.20	509.30	508.69825	100
Chile	Chilean Peso = 10 Centavos	CLP	707.344	420.75	419.086 (D)	100
China	Ren Min Bi Yuan = 10 Jiao	CNY	13.9564	8.3017	8.30	1
Colombia	Colombian Peso = 100 Centavos	COP	1672	994.775	1000.39 (D)	100
Comoros	Comoro Franc = 100 Centimes	KMF	641.527	381.60	381.52369	100
Congo	CFA Franc = 100 Centimes	XAF	856.20	509.30	508.69825	100
Cook Is.	N.Z. Dollar = 100 Cents	NZD	2.3518	1.3989	1.40921	1
Costa Rica	C.R. Colon = 100 Centimos	CRC	365.566	217.45	(D)	10
Cote D'Ivoire	CFA Franc = 100 Centimes	XOF	856.20	509.30	508.69825	100
Croatia	Croatian Kuna	HRK	8.9853	5.3447	(D)	
Cuba	Cuban Peso = 100 Centavos	CUP	33.623	1.00	1.00 (D)	1
Cyprus	Cyprus Pound = 100 Cents	CYP	0.7681	0.4569	0.46012	1
Czech Republic	Koruna = 100 Hellers	CZK	44.7321	26.608	26.839	1
Denmark	Danish Krone = 100 Ore	DKK	9.6993	5.7694	5.77489	5
Djibouti	Djibouti Franc = 100 Centimes	DJF	268.984	160.00	162.00	100
Dominica	E.C. Dollar = 100 Cents	XCD	4.5391	2.70	(D)	1.00
Dominican Rep.	Dominican Peso = 100 Centavos	DOP	23.1663	13.78	(D)	1

(Contd.)

(Contd.)

(1)	*(2)*	*(3)*	*(4)*	*(5)*	*(6)*	*(7)*
Ecuador	Sucre = 100 Centavos	ECS	5726	3406	**(D)**	10
Egypt	Egyptian Pound = 100 Piastres	EGP	5.7138	3.3988	3.40052	1
El Salvador	El Salvador Colon = 100 Centavos	SVC	14.7101	8.75	**(D)**	1
Equatorial Guinea	CFA Franc = 100 Centimes	XAF	856.20	509.30	508.69825	100
Eritrea	Birr	ERB	10.4549	6.2189	6.40 **(D)**	1
Estonia	Kroon = 100 Cents	EEK	20.2054	12.0188	12.0276 **(D)**	1
Ethiopia	Birr	ETB	10.4549	6.2189	6.40 **(D)**	1
Falkland Is.	Falkland Islands Pound	FKP	1.00	0.5948	0.60417	1.00 **ZZ**
Faroe Is.	Danish Krone = 100 Ore	DKK	9.6993	5.7694	5.77489	5
Fiji	Fijjan Dollar = 100 Cents	FJD	2.2967	1.3661	1.38468	1
Finland	Markka = 100 Penni	FIM	7.6245	4.5353	4.53301	5
France	Franc = 100 Centimes	FRF	8.562	5.093	5.08698	5
French Guiana	Franch Franc = 100 Centimes	FRF	8.562	5.093	5.08698	5
French Polynesia	CFP Franc = 100 Centimes	XPF	155.522	92.509	92.4906	100
Gabon	CFP Franc = 100 Centimes	XAF	856.20	509.30	508.69825	100
Gambia	Dalasi = 100 Butut	GMD	16.6035	9.8763	**(D)**	1
Georgia	Georgian Lari	GEL	n/a	n/a	**(D)**	1
Germany	Deutsche Mark = 100 Plenning	DEM	2.5255	1.5023	1.50345	1
Ghana	Cedi = 100 Pesewas	GHC	2885	1716	1713.12 **(D)**	1
Gibraltar	Pound Sterling = 100 Pence	GIP	1.00	0.5948	0.60417	1.00 **ZZ**
Greece	Drachma = 100 Lepta	GRD	398.458	237.015	237.731	100
Greenland	Danish Krone = 100 Ore	DKK	9.6993	5.7694	5.77489	5
Grenada	E.C. Dollar	XCD	4.5391	2.70	**(D)**	1.00
Guadeloupe	French Franc	FRF	8.562	5.093	5.08698	5
Guam	U.S. Dollar = 100 Cents	USD	1.6812	1.00	1.00	1.00 **ZZ**
Guatemala	Quetzal = 100 Centavos	GTQ	10.0889	6.0012	**(D)**	1
Guinea	Guinean Franc	GNF	1681	1000	999.3976 **(D)**	100

(Contd.)

(Contd.)

(1)	(2)	(3)	(4)	(5)	(6)	(7)
Guinea Bissau	Guinea Bissau Pesco = 100 Centavos	GWP	39369	23418	(D)	100
Guyana	Guyana Dollar = 100 Cents	GYD	235.865	140.30	(D)	1
Halti	Gourde = 100 Centimes	HTG	25.6902	15.2813	(D)	1
Honduras	Lempira = 100 Centavos	HNL	21.1825	12.60	(D)	1
Hong Kong	H.K. Dollar = 100 Cents	HKD	12.9987	7.732	7.73208	10
Hungary	Forint = 100 Fillers	HUF	261.461	155.525	155.392	10
Iceland	Iceland Krone = 100 Aurar	ISK	110.805	65.91	66.10385	10
India	Indian Rupee = 100 Paise	INR	60.0171	35.70	35.675	1
Indonesia	Rupiah = 100 Sen	IDR	3942	2345	2347.99513 (D)	100
Iran	Rial = 100 Dinars	IRR	5043	3000	3000	10
Ireland	Irish Pound = 100 Pence	IEP	0.9984	0.5939	0.60285	1.00
Israel	New Shekel = 100 Agorot	ILS	5.4652	3.2509	(D)	1
Italy	Lira	ITL	2522	1500	1516.21615	1000
Jamaica	Jamaican Dollar = 100 Cents	JMD	57.1591	34.00	(D)	1
Japan	Yen	JPY	186.986	111.225	111.48581	100
Jordan	Jordanian Dinar = 1000 Fils	JOD	1.1932	0.7098	0.709	0.100
Kazakhstan	Tenge = 100 Tiyin	KZT	120.286	71.55	70.814 (D)	1
Kenya	Kenyan Shilling = 100 Cents	KES	93.2114	55.445	55.743 (D)	1
Kiribati	Australian Dollar = 100 Cents	AUD	2.0703	1.2315	1.26759	1
Korea D.P.R.	North Korean Won	KPW	3.6145	2.15	2.2126	1
Korea Rep.	Won = 100 Chon	KRW	1387	825.25	828.95869 (D)	100
Kuwait	Kuwait Dinar = 1000 Fils	KWD	0.5014	0.2983	0.29855	0.1
Kyrgyzstan	Som = 100 Tyn	KGS	n/a	n/a	(D)	1
Lao P.D.R.	New Kip = 100 Cents	LAK	1546	920.00	920.00 (D)	10
Latvia	Lat	LVL	0.9133	0.5433	0.5444 (D)	1

(Contd.)

(Contd.)

(1)	(2)	(3)	(4)	(5)	(6)	(7)
Lebanon	Lebanese Pound = 100 Piastres	LBP	2613	1554	(D)	100
Lesotho	Loti = 100 Lisente	LSL	7.7501	4.61	4.68685	1
Liberia	Liberian Dollar = 100 Cents	LRD	1.6812	1.00	1.00	1
Lithuania	Litas	LTL	6.7253	4.0004	4.00 (D)	1
Luxembourg	Luxembourg Franc = 100 Centimes	LUF	52.0661	30.9705	30.97302	10
Macau	Pataca	MOP	13.4277	7.9872	7.98738	1
Former Yugoslav Republic of Macedonia	Denar	MKD	67.1423	39.9383	40.18878 (D)	1
Madagascar	Malagasy Franc = 100 Centimes	MGF	6640	3950	4125.836 (D)	100
Malawi	Kwacha = 100 Tambala	MWK	25.7636	15.325	15.125 (D)	1
Malaysia	Ringgit = 100 Sen	MYR	4.234	2.5185	2.52296	1
Maldives	Rufiyaa	MVR	19.7871	11.77	(D)	1
Mall	CFA Franc = 100 Centimes	XOF	856.20	509.30	508.69825	100
Malta	Maltese Lira = 100 Cents	MTL	0.60	0.3569	0.35832	1.00 **ZZ**
Marshall Is.	U.S. Dollar = 100 Cents	USD	1.6812	1.00	1.00	1.00 **ZZ**
Martinique	French Franc	FRF	8.562	5.093	5.08698	5
Mauritania	Ouguiya = 5 Khoums	MRO	235.672	140.185	139.179	20
Mauritius	Mauritius Rupee = 100 Cents	MUR	33.5053	19.93	20.0897	5
Mayotte	French Franch	FRF	8.562	5.093	5.08698	5
Mexico	Mexican Peso	MXN	13.2315	7.8705	7.922 (D)	1000
Micronesia	U.S. Dollar = 100 Cents	USD	1.6812	1.00	1.00	1.00 **ZZ**
Moldova	Leu	MDL	7.8594	4.675	4.644 (D)	1
Monaco	French Franc = 100 Centimes	FRF	8.562	5.093	5.08698	5
Mongolia	Tugrik	MNT	784.542	466.67	(D)	
Montserrat	East Caribbean Dollar	XCD	4.5391	2.70	(D)	1.00
Morocco	Dirham = 100 Centimes	MAD	14.473	8.609	8.64074	5
Mozambique	Metical = 100 Centavos	MZM	18728	11140	11230.00	100
Myanmar	Kyat = 100 Pyas	MMK	9.8373	5.8515	5.91152	1

(Contd.)

(Contd.)

(1)	(2)	(3)	(4)	(5)	(6)	(7)
Namibia	Namibian Dollar	NAD	7.7501	4.61	4.68685	1
Nauru	Australian Dollar	AUD	2.0703	1.2315	1.26759	1
Nepal	Nepalese Rupee = 100 Paisa	NPR	94.4473	56.775	57.02988 (D)	1
Netherlands	Guilder = 100 Cents	NLG	2.834	1.6857	1.68732	1
Netherlands Antilles	Ant. Guilder = 100 Cents	ANG	3.0093	1.79	1.79	1
New Caledonia	Pacific Franc	XPF	155.522	92.509	92.4906	100
New Zealand	N.Z. Dollar = 100 Cents	NZD	2.3518	1.3989	1.40921	1
Nicaragua	Cordoba = 100 Centavos	NIC	14.8168	8.8135	8.78676 (D)	1
Niger	CFA Franc = 100 Centimes	XOF	856.20	509.30	508.69825	100
Nigeria	Naira = 100 Kobos	NGN	134.065	79.746	81.00 **(D)**	1
Niue	New Zealand Dollar = 100 Cents	NZD	2.3518	1.3989	1.40921	1
Norfolk Is.	Australian Dollar = 100 Cents	AUD	2.0703	1.2315	1.26759	1
Northern Mariana Is.	U.S. Dollar = 100 Cents	USD	1.6812	1.00	1.00	1.00 **ZZ**
Norway	Norwegian Krone = 100 One	NOK	10.6513	6.3357	6.30589	5
Oman	Omani Rial = 1000 Baizas	OMR	0.6472	0.385	0.385	1
Pakistan	Pakistani Rupee = 100 Paisa	PKR	57.3803	40.0799	40.22017	5
Palau	U.S. Dollar	USD	1.6812	1.00	1.00	1.00 **ZZ**
Panama	Balboa = 100 Cents	PAB	1.6812	1.00	1.00 **(D)**	1
Papua New Guinea	Kina = 100 Toea	PGK	2.2536	1.3405	1.33849	1
Paraguay	Guarani = 100 Centimes	PYG	3513	2090	(D)	1000
Peru	Nuevo Sol	PES	4.3239	2.572	(D)	0.10
Phillippines	Philippine Peso = 100 Centavos	PHP	44.1722	26.275	(D)	1
Poland	Zloty = 100 Groszy	PLN	4.7266	2.8115	2.8057 **(D)**	1
Portugal	Escudo = 100 Centavos	PTE	255.215	151.81	152.19875	100
Puerto Rico	U.S. Dollar	USD	1.6812	1.00	1.00	1
Qatar	Qatar Riyal = 100 Dirhams	QAR	6.1207	3.6408	3.63999	10

(Contd.)

(Contd.)

(1)	*(2)*	*(3)*	*(4)*	*(5)*	*(6)*	*(7)*
Reunion	French Franc = 100 Centimes	FRF	8.562	5.093	5.08698	5
Romania	Leu = 100 Bani	ROL	5997	3567	3459.00 (D)	1
Russian Federation	Russian Rouble	RUR	9244	5499	5476.80 (D)	1
Rwanda	Rwanda Franc	RWF	537.289	319.596	(D)	10
St. Kitts and Nevis	East Caribbean Dollar	XCD	4.5391	2.70	(D)	1.00
St. Lucia	East Caribbean Dollar	XCD	4.5391	2.70	(D)	1.00
St. Pierre and Miqueion	French Franc	FRF	8.562	5.093	5.08698	5
St. Vincent and Grenadines	East Caribbean Dollar	XCD	4.5391	2.70	(D)	1.00
Samoa	Tala = 100 Sene	WST	4.0652	2.4181	2.39589	1
Sao Tome and Principle	Sao Tome Dobra = 100 Centavos	STD	4009	2385	(D)	100
Saudi Arabia	Saudi Riyal = 100 Halalah	SAR	6.3052	3.7505	3.745	1
Senegal	CFA Franc = 100 Centimes	XOF	856.20	509.30	508.69825	100
Seychelles	Seychelles Rupee = 100 Cents	SCR	8.4007	4.997	5.0047	1
Sierra Leone	Leone = 100 Cents	SLL	1260	750.00	(D)	1
Singapore	Singapore Dollar = 100 Cents	SGD	2.3541	1.4003	1.40045	1
Slovakia	Koruna = 100 Halers	SKK	51.7038	30.755	30.88	1
Slovenia	Tolar	SIT	227.897	135.56	136.85466	1
Solomon Is.	Solomon Islands Dollar = 100 Cents	SBD	5.9515	3.5401	3.5401	1
Somalia	Somali Shilling = 100 Cents	SOS	4404	2620	(D)	1
South Africa	Rand = 100 Cents	ZAR	7.7501	4.61	4.68685	1
Spain	Peseta = 100 Centimos	ESP	212.539	126.425	126.66574	5
Sri Lanka	Sri Lanka Rupee = 100 Cents	LKR	95.1531	56.60	56.50288	1
Sudan	Sudanese Dinar	SDD	246.289	146.50	137.00	1
Suriname	Surinam Guilder = 100 Cents	SRG	689.271	410.00	410.00 (D)	1
Swaziland	Lilangeni	SZL	7.7501	4.61	4.68685	1
Sweden	Swedish Krona = 100 Ore	SEK	11.1255	6.6178	6.61333	5
Switzerland	Swiss Franc = 100 Centimes	CHF	2.1299	1.2669	1.26736	1

(Contd.)

(Contd.)

(1)	(2)	(3)	(4)	(5)	(6)	(7)
Syria	Syrian Pound = 100 Piastres	SYP	70.5242	41.95	42.00	1
Taiwan	New Taiwan Dollar = 100 Cents	TWD	46.2316	27.50	27.5068	1
Tajikistan	Tajik Ruble	TJR	n/a	n/a	(D)	1
Tanzania	Tanzanian Shilling = 100 Cents	TZS	991.878	590.00	590.60 (D)	10
Thailand	Baht = 100 Satang	THB	42.7265	25.415	25.41997	5
Togo	CFA Franc = 100 Centimes	XOF	856.20	509.30	508.69825	100
Tonga	Pa'anga	TOP	2.0703	1.2315	1.26759	1
Trinidad and Tobago	Trinidad & Tobago Dollar = 100 Cents	TTD	10.3184	6.1377	(D)	1
Tunisia	Tunisian Dinar = 1000 Milliemes	TND	1.6283	0.9686	0.97036	0.500
Turkey	Turkish Lira = 100 Kurus	TRL	168526	100245	98150.40 (D)	1000
Turkmenistan	Manat = 100 Tenge	TMM	n/a	n/a	(D)	1
Turks and Caicos Is.	U.S. Dollar	USD	1.6812	1.00	(D)	1
Tuvalu	Australian' Dollar	AUD	2.0703	1.2315	1.26759	1
Uganda	Ugandan Shilling = 100 Cents	UGX	1765	1050	1070.80 (D)	1
Ukraine	Hryvnia	UAH	2.9694	1.7663	1.8596 (D)	1
United Arab Emirates	Dirham = 100 Fils	AED	6.1746	3.6729	3.67099	10
United Kingdom	Pound Sterling = 100 Pence	GBP	1.00	0.5948	0.60417	1.00 **ZZ**
U.S.A.	U.S. Dollar = 100 Cents	USD	1.6812	1.00	1.00	1.00 **ZZ**
U.S. Minor Is.	U.S. Dollar = 100 Cents	USD	1.6812	1.00	1.00	1.00 **ZZ**
Uruguay	Peso Uruguayo = 100 Centimos	UYU	14.4075	8.57	8.534 (D)	100
Uzbekistan	Sum	UZS	n/a	n/a	(D)	1
Vanuatu	Vatu	VUV	186.524	110.95	110.954	100
Venezuela	Bolivar = 100 Centimos	VEB	791.830	471.005	471.352 (D)	10
Viet Nam	Dong	VND	18626	11079	11073.90 (D)	
Virgin Is.	U.S. Dollar	USD	1.6812	1.00	1.00	1.00 **ZZ**
Wallis and Futuna Is.	Pacific Franc	XPF	155.522	92.509	92.4906	100

(*Contd.*)

(Contd.)

(1)	(2)	(3)	(4)	(5)	(6)	(7)
Yemen	Riyal = 100 Fils	YER	218.55	130.00	100.00	1
Yugoslavia	New Dinar	YUM	8.361	4.9734	(D)	1
Zaire	New Zaire = 100 Makuta	ZRN	158055	94016	(D)	1
Zambia	Kwacha = 100 Ngwee	ZMK	2143	1275	(D)	5
Zimbabwe	Zimbabwe Dollar = 100 Cents	ZWD	18.0387	10.73	10.66798	1.00 **ZZ**

WORLD AIRWAYS GUIDE

OAG® has used its best efforts in collecting and preparing material for inclusion in OAG® World Airways Guide Fares Supplement but can not warrant that the information contained in this product is complete or accurate and does not assume and hereby disclaims, liability to any person for any loss or damage caused by. erros or omissions in the OAG® World Airways Guide Fares Supplement whether such errors or omissions result from negligence, accident or any other cause.

CURRENCY SYSTEM (FARE CONSTRUCTION UNIT)

The term currency refers to the system of monetary exchange established by the government of the country. In the early days of the traffic conference system only two currencies were used for airline fares—the US dollar for travel in the Western Hemisphere and the British pound sterling for travel in the Eastern Hemisphere. In 1973, a system called Fare Contruction Unit (FCU) was introduced. According to this system, fares were stated in the currency of the country where the flight originated, and then converted into fare construction units. The fare was then converted from FCU into the currency of the country in which the ticket was sold.

GUIDE TO FARE CONSTRUCTION

The Airline Industry introduced a new currency system on 1 July 1989. The system is based on local currency fares. To enable fares to be combined a unit for currency construction has been established, called the *Neutral Unit of Construction* (NUC).

NUC Conversion Factors are specified to convert local currency amounts to NUC amounts and to convert the total NUC amount back to the currency of sale. These conversion factors change four times a year (1 January, 1 April, 1 July, 1 October), or more frequently if a particular currency has a significant change in its value between these months. These factors are published in the ABC World Airways Guide Fares Supplement every month and it is important that users use the factors quoted in the current edition for all sales, *i.e.* for sales made in July, use the July edition of the Fares Supplement. This rule also applies to advance sales, so that for a journey commencing in September, but sold in July, use the conversion factors published in the July edition.

Where D is shown in the IATA exchange rate column, fares are sold in US Dollars. Refer to country U.S.A. for factors.

Local currency amounts will not be affected by changes in the NUC conversion factors, except where the fare is constructed, using an add-on which is specified in another currency. They will only be affected by normal periodic fare changes.

An example:

A fare from Vancouver to Paris, quoted in Canadian Dollars, is actually made up of an add-on from Vancouver to Montreal in Canadian Dollars, added to a fare from Montreal to Paris also in Canadian Dollars. As these amounts are both in the same local currency, they can be added together, and they are unaffected by conversion factor changes.

However a fare from Paris to Vancouver quoted in French Francs, is actually made up of a fare from Paris to Montreal in French Francs and an add-on from Montreal to Vancouver in Canadian Dollars. As these two amounts are in different local currencies, they are first converted to NUCs, and then the total NUC value is converted to French Francs and therefore the total in French Francs will be affected by changes in the relationship between the NUC and the Canadian Dollar/French Franc.

HOW TO USE NEUTRAL UNIT OF CONSTRUCTIONS (NUCs) TO CALCULATE FARES?

To combine fares which have different local currencies the following procedure must be followed:

Firstly take the fares in the relevant local currency, and convert the amount to NUCs, by dividing the conversion factors published and taking the answer to two decimal places with no rounding off. Add the NUC amounts together and multiply the total by the conversion factor from NUC to the currency of departure country.

For example:

A journey from London to Rome, Rome to Stockholm and Stockholm to London.

(1) *Find the quoted Fares:*

London to Rome	:	GBP 406.00
Rome to Stockholm	:	ITL 1335000
*Stockholm to London	:	GBP 444.00

(2) *Convert to NUCs:*

London to Rome	:	GBP 406.00	:	divided by NUC conversion 0.58 = NUC 700.00
Rome to Stockholm	:	ITL 1335000	:	divided by NUC conversion 1374 = NUC 971.61
*Stockholm to London	:	GBP 444.00	:	divided by NUC conversion 0.58 = NUC 765.51

Total NUC amounts

700.00
971.61
765.51
______
2437.12

(3) *Convert to currency of departure country:*

Currency of departure country GBP.

Multiply NUC 2437.12 by IATA exchange rate to GBP 0.58 = GBP 1413.52

The result is then rounded off to give a total of GBP 1414.00

Note: The figures quoted above are examples and they must not be taken as actual fares or conversion factors

* If the last sector leads back to the country of origin, use the local currency fare from the country of origin, use the local currency the last sector Stockholm to London takes you back to the United Kingdom, which is the country of commencement, therefore the fare in GBP from London is used.

In the year 1989, the FUC system was replaced with a system based on Neutral Units of Construction (NUC). In this system, international fares are published in NUC and in the currency of the departure country. To determine the price of an international itinerary, the NUC fares are added and the total is then converted to the currency of the country, where the ticket will be sold. The rate of exchange (ROE) for converting NUC to various currencies is published quarterly by IATA. These rates are changed periodically to reflect changes in foreign rates.

In a computer reservation system, international fares are usually given in the currency of the departure country. For example, if fares are displaced for travel from New Delhi to Tokyo, the fares are given in Indian rupees. However the fare display can be automatically converted to NUC on request. If fares from different departure points are quoted in different currencies, the amount must be converted to NUC to determine the total fare. For example, assume a client is planning a Mumbai-Paris, London-New York itinerary. The Mumbai-Paris fare is quoted in Indian rupees, and Paris-London-New York fare is quoted in French francs, and London-New York fare is quoted in pounds. To determine the total ticket price, all the three fares must be converted to NUC. All the NUC fares are added and the sum is converted from NUC to the currency of the country where the ticket would be sold.

The Air Tariff

International fares are published in a rate book, called 'air tariff'. International fare rules and regulations are published in a handbook provided to IATA-approved travel agencies.

Fare Construction

International fares are published by IATA in NUC and in the local currency of the departure city called the 'headline city'. To price an international itinerary involving multiple point-to-point fares, the total fare must be constructed, using NUCs. As an example, assume that a traveller is planning a London-Rome-Paris itinerary. Let us assume the air tariff gives the following fare for each segment:

From/To	*NUC*	*Local currency*
LON-ROM	362-44	GBP 21,500
ROM-PARIS	377.22	ITL 52,000.

You will observe that the fare for the segment that commences in London is given in British currency (GBP) whereas the fare for the segment that commences in Rome is given in Italian currency franc (ITL). In each case the currency code is written before the amount.

Based on the NUC fares, the total fare for the itinerary in above example is calculated. The next step is to convert the total fare from NUC to the currency of the country in which the ticket would be sold. Assume the ticket will be sold in UK and the ROE for British currency is 0.59320, the total price will be calculated as follows:

739.66 × 0.59320 = 438.77 Total Fare.

One NUC equals one US dollar. Thus, if the above itinerary is ticketed in the US, the total fare would be USS = 739.66.

THE MILEAGE SYSTEM

Minimum Permitted Mileage (MPM)

The total fare for a complex itinerary can be constructed using a technique called the mileage system under this system, a passenger is permitted to travel between two international points at the published fare, with any number of stopovers, as long as the minimum permitted mileage (MPM) is not exceeded. Let us take an example, Mr. G.M. Negi, a passenger is planning a round-trip itinerary from New Delhi (ND)-New York. He would like to stop-over in Zurich (ZRH), Paris (PAR) and Milan (MLN) en route. The outbound itinerary appears as follows:

ND — MILAN (MIL)
MIL — ZURICH (ZRH)
ZURICH — PARIS (PAR)
PARIS — NYC.

Ticketed Point Mileages

The sectors are shown half alphabetical sequence. Therefore, to find Amsterdam to London see from Amsterdam to London, but to find Zurich to London see from London to Zurich.

All mileages are statute miles, airport to airport, either non-stop or by the shortest operated route where there is no non-stop service Maximum permitted mileages (mpm) are shown with fares.

Mileages for routes between Japan, Korea Republic, Australia, New Zealand and Europe may vary according to the route flown.

The following route indicators are used:

AP: Atlantic/Pacific; EH: Eastern Hemisphere via India/Pakistan route; PC; via Pacific; PO: via Polar route; TS: via Siberia route.

Examples of Ticketed Point Mileages of some of the country are given in Table 5.6.

Table 5.6: Ticketed Point Mileages

	Agra, India		
Delhi	111		
Khajuraho	197		
Varansi	386		
	Amritsar, India		
Delhi	258		
Jammu	69		
Srinagar	158		
	Calicut, India		
Dubai	1650	Kuwait	2179
Chennai	322	Muscat	1420
Ras Al Khama	1638	Sharjah	1650
	Chinnai, India		
Madurai	261	Port Blair	853
Mangalore	356	Riyadh	2327
Muscat	1597	Singapore	1816
New York	8465	Tiruchirapaly	183
Paris France	4994	Toronto	8457
Penang	1469	Trivandrum	383
Poona	632	Vishakhapatna	386
	Colombo, Sri Lanka		
Delhi	1489	Denpasar Bali	2668
Shahran	2357	Doha	2247
Dubai	2045	Dusseldof	5105
Frankfurt	5012	Fukuoka	3700

(Contd.)

(*Contd.*)

Hamburg	5001	Hong Kong	2547
Jakarta	2256	Jeddah	2886
Karachi	1486	Kuala Lampur	1517
Kuwait	2573	London UK	5403
Chennai	402	Male	484
Moscow	eh 4138	Moscow	fe 4138
Munich	4848	Muscat	1816
Paris France	5274	Riyadh	2504
Rome	4732	Singapore	1709
Sofia	4203	Tiruchiapaly	260
Tokyo	4266	Trivandrum	222
Vienna	4631	Zurich	4985
Deirezzor, Syria			
Kuwait	619		
Kolkata, India			
Chittagong	218	Imphal	376
Delhi	816	Jorhat	458
Dhaka	146	Kathmandu	400
Dibrugarh	531	London UK	4985
Dimapur	448	Lucknow	555
Subai	2094	Madras	860
Gauahati	311	Moscow	eh 3433
Hyderabad Ind	740	Moscow	fe 3433
Mauritius			
Melbourne Aus	5220	Rodrigues Is	376
Moroni	1182	Rome	5182
Munich	5533	St. Denis	144
Nairobi	1928	Singapore	3476
Paris France	5867	Zurich	5593
Perth	3659		
Mirpur Khas, Pakistan			
Mohenjodaro	131		
Nawabshah	204		
Sukkur	159		

In fare calculation, city codes are used, not air codes. The mileage section of the tariff gives the non-stop mileage between ticketed points. Assuming that the maximum permitted mileage from ND to NYC is 10,000, the total on-way mileage is calculated as follows:

ND—MIL	5,500
MIL—ZRH	135
ZURICH—PAR	299
PARIS—NYC	299
Total	9,938

The total mileage based on the three intermediate points, Milan, Zurich and Paris is 9,938, which is less than the maximum permitted mileage of 10,000. In this case the published fare from New Delhi to NYC may be used for the entire outbound trip, without an additional charge for the stop-overs in Milan, Zurich and Paris. If the total mileage between the points exceeds the maximum permitted mileage, a surcharge is added to the published fare. The surcharge is determined from the Excess Mileage Table in the Tariff.

Higher Intermediate Point (HIP)

When the mileage system is used to construct a fare, the point-to-point fare cannot always be applied if the fare to an intermediate point is higher than the fare to the turn around point, the higher fare must be used to construct the fare. Assume Ms. Ritushka is planning a round-trip itinerary from Mumbai (India) to Milan (Italy). On the out-bound trip, Ms. Ritushka wishes to stayover in Athens (ATH) and Zurich (ZRH). Her outbound itinerary is as follows:

BOM—MIL
ATH—ZRH
ZRH—MIL.

Assume the published BOM-MIL fare is NUC 411.50, but the BOM-ZRH fare is NUC 469.80. In this example, ZRH is a higher intermediate point, or HIP. The higher fare, NUC 469.80 must be charged for the itinerary, even though the final destination is MIL.

Class Differentials

On international itineraries, flight segments are referred to as sectors. Passengers do not necessarily have to travel in the same class of service on all flight sectors. A selected sector in an itinerary can be booked at a higher class of service by adding a charge, called a class differentials to the total fare.

Assume a passenger, Mr. Ravi desires to travel from Kolkata to Tokyo via Bangkok, as follows:

KOL—BKK
BKK—TKO.

Mr. Ravi desires to travel in Y-class on the CAL-BKK sector and F-class on BKK-TKO sector. To construct this fare, the Y-class fare can be used for the entire itinerary, with a class differential added on the F-class sector. The difference is determined by subtracting the Y-class fare from the F-class fare for the applicable sector. Suppose the F-class from BKK-TKY sector is NUC 955.60, and Y-class fare is NUC 642.10, the class differential is calculated as follows:

955.60	BKK-THR	F-fare
–642.10	BKK-THR	Y-fare
313.50	F/Y differential	

In total fare in Y-class from Koikata to BKK is NUC 1189.90 based on the mileage system. The total fare, before converting to currency, is calculated as follows:

BKK—TKO fare	1189.80
+ F/Y differential	+313.50
Total fare	1503.30

Before the ticket is sold, the fare must be converted from NUC to local currency.

Advance Purchase Excursion Fares

A discounted fare that requires an advance purchase and a circle trip is called an advance purchase excursion (APEX). When excursion fares are used, the mileage system does not apply. Excursion fares have set effective dates and expiration dates. Often, no stopovers are allowed between the origin and destination. In most cases the entire itinerary must be booked and ticketed on the same carrier. However, some excursion fares can be used for an open jaw, allowing local fares to be used for intermediate sectors.

A passenger Mr. Ashok, desires to travel on the following itinerary:

ND—ROM
ROM—GVA
GVA—PAR
PAR—ND.

This itinerary can be handled as an open jaw with an ARNK segment from ROM to PAR. In this case, the ND-PAR excursion fare can be used for the ND-ROM and PAR-ND sectors. The remaining sectors can be ticketed separately, using local excursion fares on the mileage system.

Suppose the ND-ROM excursion fare is NUC 449.50, and the ROM-PAR fare is NUC 334.60 based on mileage, with a stopover allowed at GVA, the total fare is calculated as follows:

ND—PAR—ND

449.50	Round trip excursion fare
	ROM—GNV—PAR
+334.60	Local fare based on mileage
784.10	Total fare

The total fare can be ticketed at a price of NUC 784.10, enabling the passenger to take advantage of the excursion fare. The total fare based on mileage for the entire itinerary might be several hundred rupees higher.

International Tickets

Tickets for international travel may be issued on IATA ticket stock. The following additional items and differences may be noted on an international ticket.

Baggage Allowance

A separate box is used to indicate the baggage allowance on a foreign carrier. There are two methods used to calculate the international baggage allowance:

1. The piece method, and
2. The weight method.

In the piece method, the free baggage allowance is determined by the number of pieces and total dimensions.

In the weighted method, the free baggage allowance is based on the maximum weight of all the pieces, including carry on items as well as checked luggage.

If the weight method is used, the free luggage allowance is entered in the allowance box on the ticket in kilograms (kgs.) or pounds (lbs.). If the piece method is used, this box is usually left blank.

FARE

The total fare is shown in the fare box. The currency and the fare paid by the passenger are shown in the equivalent amount paid box. Any taxes included in the ticket price may be shown in the tax box. Each tax is identified by the two-letter ISO code of the country that imposes the tax, as given below in the example:

Tax Entry	Country
IND 100	India
GB 500	UNITED KINGDOM
US 200	UNITED STATES

Technically, a passenger facility charge (PFC) is not a tax, but rather a surcharge levied by an airport authority. However, for ticketing purposes, the tax code XF is used to identify a PFC.

If four or more taxes are included in the ticket price, the code XT is used to identify the combined tax amount.

HOW TO USE THE FARES INFORMATION?

The *World Airways Guide* fares supplement gives a world-wide coverage of normal and excursion fares in an easy-to-use format.

This description shows how to use the *Fares* section, but you may also need to refer to the *Fares Notes* section. It may also be necessary to use the *Ticketed Point Mileages* section and the *Maximum Permitted Mileages* to calculate if any excess fare is applicable.

Below is an example explaining the meaning of the information contained therein:

Departure city — [1]**TOKYO** Japan[2]

Country and city code — TYO

Arrival city and city code — [3]**Las Vegas** LAS

Type of fare — Y[4]

[1]TOKYO Japan[2]	TYO		JPY[5]
[3]**Las Vegas**	LAS		
F	6789		1116800
Y[4]	6789		708200[6]
Los Angles US LAX			
mpm: np 6541; at 15249[9]			
P	6814		535700[10]
P	6814		**957300**
F	6814[7]	np	576600
F		at	1138900
C2	6833	KE	**294000**
C2	6834	KE	168400
YLAP2M	6849	RG[8]	**249000**

Local currency. The three-letter IATA currency code is used; for example, JPY is Japanese Yen. To find out the meaning of the codes see *Currency Conversions*.
Some fares are shown with a $ symbol to show they are quoted in US Dollars instead of the departure city local currency.

One-way fares are shown in light type.

Round-trip normal fares are double the one-way fares, unless a round-trip fare is specifically quoted.

Round trip fares are shown in **bold type**.

Fare notes. These numbers refer to special conditions listed in the *Fares Notes* section. The notes list reductions for children, dates when the fares are applicable, any minimum or maximum stays, and conditions about stopovers, sales and reservations.

0317 Europe-M. East PEX

Children:	Child 50%, Infant 10%
Dates:	01 July-30 Sep
Minimum stay:	6 days
Maximum stay:	2 months
Sales:	Limited to country of origin
Stopovers:	None
Reservations:	To be completed at the same time as payment and ticketing. Must be booked for entire journey.

'Via' code. Where the 'via' code is in capital letters, it refers to a particular airline. See *Airline Codes*.

Where the 'via' code is in small letters it refers to geographical routing codes. Some journeys can be taken using alternative routes, which may have different fares.

The geographical routing codes are as follows:

ap	Atlantic/Pacific routing	np	North pacific routing
at	Atlantic routing	pa	Pacific routing
di	Direct routing	po	Polar routing
eh	Eastern Hemisphere routing	ts	Siberian routing.

Maximum permitted mileage

This is used to calculate if a passenger has to pay an excess fare due to the routing being flown.

As an example, the maximum mileage from Tokyo to Los Angeles, via the North Pacific route, is 6541.

If a passenger wishes to go via Honolulu and Vancouver, refer to the *Ticketed Point Mileages* section to find the mileage for each sector of the journey.

This would show that the mileage would be:

Tokyo-Honolulu	3831
Honolulu-Vancouver	2706
Vancouver-Los Angeles	1071
Total	7608

This is higher than the maximum permitted mileage of 6541, so the fare has to be increased. Reference to the *Excess Mileage Percentage Table* indicates that, in this case, the fare should be increased by 20%.

Fig. 5.2: Using the Fares Information for World Airways Guide.

Fare Notes

Special conditions apply to many fares. In the main fare section of OAG Airlines Guide these are indicated by four digit numerical codes. This numerical listing explains the applicable special conditions. Some examples of fare note are given in Table 5.7.

Additional qualifiers

A single numeric character following an alphabetic character at the end of a fare type code (eg. J2) indicates that additional restrictions apply as specified in the Fare Note.

Table 5.7: Fare Notes

	002 DS African Excursion
Children:	Child: 50% Infant: 10%
Dates:	All Year
Minimum Stay:	7 Days
Maximum Stay:	1 Month
Stopovers:	1 permitted
Routing:	Available on DS flights
Combinations:	Combinable with domestic fares
	0003 OQ African Normal
Children:	Child: 50% Infant: 10%
Dates:	All Year
Mamimum Stay:	1 Year
Routing:	Available on OQ flights
	0201 GF Middle East Excn
Children:	Child: 50% Infant: 10%
Dates:	All Year
Minimum Stay:	5 Days
Maximum Stary:	1 Month
Routing:	Available on GF flights
	0301 Europe-M. East Excn
Children:	Child: 67%, except from Iran and Yeamen: 50%; Infant: 10%
Dates:	All Year
Minimum Stay:	10 Days. Except. 6 Days: From BAH/MCT/DOH/ to ATH. From Egypt/Kuwait/Saudi Arabia (except to VIE/ZRH: 10 Days). From Italy to Iran/Iraq: 8 Day.
Maximum Stay:	1 Month/35 Days/2 Months/3 Months
Stopovers:	2 permitted Except: from Egypt: 1 additional permitted in Egypt except, to Greece

Table 5.8: Fare Types and Reservation Codes

Fare types		*Reservation booking codes*	
R	Supersonic	AP	Apex fares
P	First class premium	BB	Eurobudget
F	First class	AB	Super Apex
A	First class discounted	D	Economy discounted fare
J	Business class premium	EE	Excursion fares
C	Business class	FL	Domestic budget
D	Business class discounted	H	High season fares, *e.g.* YHE
Z	Business class discounted	HP	High season pex, *e.g.*, YHP
W	Economy/coach premium	IP	Ipex fares
S	Economy/coach	J	Intermediate level, *e.g.*, YJE
Y	Economy/coach	K	Shoulder Season fares, *e.g.*, YKE
B	Economy/coach discounted	L	Low Season fares, *e.g.*, YLE
M	Economy/coach discounted	LP	Low Season pex, *e.g.*, YLP
Q	Economy/coach discounted	N	Night fares, *e.g.*, YN, FN
T	Economy/coach discounted	O	Shoulder Season fares, *e.g.*, YOE
V	Economy/coach discounted	OX	One-way excursion
U	Air shuttle	P	Peak of Peak
	(no reservation needed)	PX	Pex fares
		UU	No reservations
		UG	Domestic: guaranteed standby
		IS	International: late booking fare
		W	Weekend
		X	Midweek
		Z	Intermediate level, *e.g.*, YZE

CITY-TO-CITY FARES

Imaginary City-to-City Fares are indicated in Table 5.9.

Table 5.9: City-to-City Fares

Type	*Note*	*Via*	*Local*
AGARTALA India **IXA**			INR
Calcutta CCU			
Y	4702	D5	1250
Y	4701	D5	$ 41.00
J	4701	IC	$ 61.00
Y	4701	IC	$ 42.00
AGRA India **AGR**			USD
Delhi DEL			
J	4701	IC	52.00
Y	4701	IC	35.00
Khajuraho HUR			
J	4701	IC	79.00
Y	4701	IC	53.00
Varanasi VNS			
J	4701	IC	113.00
Y	4701	IC	76.00

(*Contd.*)

(*Contd.*)

Type	*Note*	*Via*	*Local*
AHMEDABAD India **AMD**			INR
Bangalore BLR			
F	4701	D2	7980
F	4702	D2	$ 251.00
J	4701	D2	7980
J	4702	D2	$ 251.00
C	4701	D2	7980
C	4702	D2	$ 251.00
Y	4701	D2	5340
Y	4702	D2	$ 168.00
J	4701	IC	$ 251.00
Y	4701	IC	$ 168.00
Delhi DEL			
F	4701	AI	$ 183.00
FN	6003	AI	$ 137.00
J	4701	AI	$ 146.00
JN	6003	AI	$ 110.00
Y	4701	AI	$ 98.00
YN	6003	AI	$ 74.00
J	4701	IC	$ 146.00
Y	4701	IC	$ 98.00
J	4702	M9	4620
J	4701	M9	$ 157.00
Y	4702	M9	3100
Y	4701	M9	$ 98.00
C	4711	9W	4084
C1	4701	9W	$ 146.00
Y	4711	9W	2635
Y1	4701	9W	$ 98.00
Hyderabad Ind HYD			
J	4701	IC	$ 192.00
Y	4701	IC	$ 128.00
Jaipur JAI			
J	4702	M9	3640
J	4701	M9	$ 126.00
Y	4702	M9	2627
Y	4701	M9	$ 90.00
Madras/Chennai MAA			
F	4701	D2	8650
F	4702	D2	$ 273.00
J	4701	D2	8650
J	4702	D2	$ 273.00
C	4701	D2	8650
C	4702	D2	$ 273.00
Y	4701	D2	5790
Y	4702	D2	$ 183.00
J	4701	IC	$ 273.00
Y	4701	IC	$ 183.00

(*Contd.*)

(*Contd.*)

Type	*Note*	*Via*	*Local*
Mumbai/ Bombay BOM			
F	4701	AI	$ 115.00
FN	6003	AI	$ 86.00
J	4701	AI	$ 92.00
JN	6003	AI	$ 69.00
Y	4701	AI	$ 62.00
YN	6003	AI	$ 47.00
F	4701	D2	2920
F	4702	D2	$ 92.00
J	4701	D2	2920
J	4702	D2	$ 92.00
C	4701	D2	2920
C	4702	D2	$ 92.00
Y	4701	D2	1970
Y	4702	D2	$ 62.00
J	4701	IC	$ 92.00
Y	4701	IC	$ 62.00
C	4711	9W	2685
C1	4701	9W	$ 92.00
Y	4711	9W	1732
Y1	4701	9W	$ 62.00
Muscat MCT *mpm eh 1072*			
F	8220		13635
F	8220		**24785**
J	8220		10755
J	8220		**19560**
C	8220		10755
C	8220		**19560**
Y	8220		9355
Y	8220		**17005**
F		IC	13635
F		IC	**24785**
C		IC	10755
C		IC	**19560**
Y		IC	9355
Y		IC	**17005**

FLIGHT ROUTINGS

The complete routings of all multi-sector flights shown in the Worldwide City-to-City schedules. No routing is shown for single sector flights. Where two airline names appear separated by a '/', this indicates that IATA have allocated the code to two airlines operating in different parts of the world. Airlines with alpha/alpha designation are arranged alphabetically. These are followed by airlines with numeric/alpha designators in numeric/alpha sequence. Fights are shown in numerical order for each airline. Where routings vary, days and/or dates of departure from the origin airport are shown immediately after the routings to which they apply. Use the airline's code. Airport codes can be decoded.

Table 5.10: Some of Airlines Flight Routings

AIR INDIA	
101	BLR-BOM-LHR-JFK Day 2
101	MAA-BOM-LHK-JFK Until 23 Oct
101	BLR-BOM-LHR-JFK Days 56
101	BOM-LHR-JFK From 30 Oct
102	JFK-LHR-BOM-BLR
111	BOM-DEL-LHR-JFK
112	JFK-LHR-DEL-BOM
124	ORD-LHR-BOM-AMD
125	AMD-BOM-LHR-ORD
126	ORD-LHR-BOM-AMD
127	AMD-BOM-LHR-ORD
130	MAN-FCO-DEL-BOM
131	BOM-DEL-FCO-MAN Until 20 Oct
131	BOM-DEL-auh-FCO-MAN From 27 Oct
138	MAN-FCO-DEL-BOM
139	BOM-DEL-FCO-MAN Day 4
139	BOM-DEL-auh-FCO-MAN Day 5
140	CDG-FRA-DEL-BOM Until 26 Oct
140	CDG-DEL-BOM From 2 Nov
141	BOM-DEL-FRA-CDG Until 25 Oct
141	BOM-DEL-CDG From 1 Nov
142	CDG-FRA-DEL-BOM Until 21 Oct
142	CDG-DEL-BOM From 28 Oct
143	BOM-DEL-FRA-CDG Day 1
143	BOM-DEL-CDG Day 2
146	CDG-DEL-BOM
147	BOM-DEL-CDG
148	AMS-FRA-DEL-BOM
149	BOM-DEL-FRA-AMS
150	FRA-DEL-BOM
151	BOM-DEL-FRA
154	FRA-DFL-BOM
155	BOM-DEL-FRA
156	FRA-DEL-BOM
157	BOM-DEL-FRA
158	FRA-DEL-BOM
159	BOM-DEL-FRA
160	CDG-FRA-DEL-BOM
161	BOM-DEL-FRA-CDG
170	GVA-FCO-DEL-BOM
171	BOM-DEL-Auh-FCO-GVA Until 25 Oct
171	BOM-DEL-Auh-FCO-GVA From 1 Nov
172	GVA-FCO-DEL-BOM
173	BOM-DEL-FCO-GVA Until 22 Oct

(*Contd.*)

(*Contd.*)

173	BOM-DEL-Auh-FCO-GVA	**433**	SIN-MAA-BOM
	From 29 Oct	**434**	BOM-MAA-SIN
184	YYZ-LHR-DEL-BOM	**436**	BOM-MAA-SIN
185	BOM-DEL-LHR-YYZ	**437**	SIN-MAA-BOM
188	YYZ-LHR-DEL-BOM	**438**	BOM-MAA-SIN
189	BOM-DEL-LHR-YYZ	**439**	SIN-MAA-BOM
200	DAR-NBO-BOM	**440**	BOM-BLR-SIN
201	BOM-NBO-DAN	**441**	SIN-BLR-BOM
208	DAR-NBO-BOM	**442**	BOM-BLR-SIN
209	BOM-NBO-DAR	**443**	SIN-BLR-BOM
212	DUR-JNB-BOM	**446**	BOM-BLR-SIN
215	BOM-DUR-JNB	**447**	SIN-BLR-BOM
216	DUR-JNB-BOM	**457**	SIN-TRV-BOM
217	BOM-DUR-JNB	**458**	BOM-TRV-SIN
301	NRT-DEL-BOM	**475**	CGK-SIN-MAA-BOM
302	BOM-DEL-BKK-NRT	**476**	BOM-MAA-SIN-CGK
304	BOM-DEL-NRT	**477**	CGK-SIN-MAA-BOM
305	NRT-BKK-DEL-BOM	**478**	BOM-MAA-SIN-CGK
306	BOM-CCU-BKK-NRT	**482**	MAA-SIN-KUL
307	NRT-DEL-BOM	**483**	SIN-KUL-MAA
308	BOM-DEL-NRT	**488**	BOM-MAA-SIN-KUL
309	NRT-BKK-CCU-BOM,	**489**	SIN-KUL-MAA-BOM
	Until 25 Oct	**701**	MAA-TRV-MCT
309	NRT-BKK-DEL	**702**	UXB-MCT-BOM
	From 1 Nov	**717**	MAA-HYD-JED
310	BOM-DEL-HKG-SEL	**718**	JED-HYD-MAA-BOM
311	SEL-HKG-DEL-BOM	**720**	DXR-MCT-BOM
312	BOM-DEL-HKG-SEL	**721**	BOM-BLR-DXB-MCT
313	SEL-HKG-DEL-BOM	**722**	DXB-DUL-BOM
314	BOM-DEL-HKG-KIX	**723**	BOM-DEL-UXB
315	KIX-HKG-DEL-BOM	**726**	DXB-DEL-AMD
316	BOM-DEL-HKG	**727**	BOM-DEL-DXB
317	HKG-UFL-BOM	**728**	MCT-DXB-BLR-BOM
318	BOM-DEL-HKG-KIX	**729**	BOM-MCT-DXB
319	KIX-HKG-DEL-BOM	**735**	BOM-MAA-DXB
401	SIN-MAA-BOM	**738**	AUH-DXB-MAA
402	BOM-TRV-SIN	**739**	MAA-AUH-OXB
405	SIN-TRV-BOM	**740**	MCT-AUH-BOM
412	BOM-DEL-SIN	**765**	BOM-DEL-AUH
415	SIN-DEL-BOM	**802**	JED-DEL-BOM
419	SIN-DEL-BOM	**803**	HYD-BOM-DEL-JED
428	BOM-MAA-SIN	**806**	JED-KWI-BOM-HYD
430	BOM-MAA-SIN	**807**	HYD-BOM-KWI-JED
431	SIN-MAA-BOM	**808**	JED-KWI-UUM

(*Contd.*)

(Contd.)

809	HYD-BOM-KWI-JED
818	UHA-MCT-BOM
821	TRV-BOM-RUH
824	RUH-BOM-TRV
826	RUH-BOM-TRV
827	TRV-BOM-RUH
829	TRV-BOM-RUH
831	BOM-DXB-MCT
834	DXB-MCT-BOM
835	BOM-DXB-MCT
837	BOM-MCT-AUH
852	KWI-BOM-TRV
853	TRV-BOM-KWI
872	DOH-BAH-BOM
873	BOM-DOH-BAH
874	BAH-DOH-BOM
875	BOM-BAH-DOH
876	BAH-DOH-BOM
877	BOM-BAH-DOH
910	MCT-MAA-TRV
914	AUH-TRV-MAA
918	DXB-AUH-TRV
927	TRV-DXB-AUH
931	TRV-MAA-KWI
932	KWI-MAA-TRV
952	DOH-BAH-TRV
953	TRV-DOH-BAH
3001	DEL-LHR-IAD
3002	IAD-LHR-DEL

BRITISH AIRWAYS

009	LHR-BKK-SYD-MEL
	Until 24 Oct
009	LHR-BKK-SYD-BNE
	Until 25 Oct
009	LHR-BKK-SYD-MEL
	From 26 Oct
010	MEL-SYD-BKK-LHR
	Until 25 Oct
010	BNE-SYD-BKK-LHR
	Until 27 Oct
010	MEL-SYD-BKK-LHR
	From 26 Oct
011	LHR-SIN-PER
012	PER-SIN-LHR
015	LHR-SIN-BNE
016	BNE-SIN-LHR
025	LHR-HKG-TPE
026	TPF-HKG-LHR
031	LHR-HKG-MNL
032	MNL-HKG-LHR
033	LHR-KUL-CGK
034	CGK-KUL-LHR
054	DUR-JNB-LHR
	Until 24 Oct
054	GBE-JNB-LHR
054	DUR-JNB-LHR
	From 26 Oct
054	GBE-JNB-LHR
	From 28 Oct
055	LHR-JNB-DUR
	Until 25 Oct
055	LHR-JNB-GBE
	Until 24 Oct
055	LHR-JNB-DUR
055	LHR-JNB-GBE
	From 27 Oct
055	LHR-JNB-DUR
	From 1 Nov
094	PIT-YUL-LHR
095	LHR-YUL-PIT
102	THR-LCA-LHR
103	LHR-LCA-THR
122	MCT-DXB-LHR
123	LHR-DXB-MCT
124	AUH-BAH-LHR
125	LHR-BAH-AUH
126	CMB-DXB-LHR
127	LHR-DXB-CMB
142	CCU-DEL-LHR
143	LHR-DEL-CCU
144	DAC-DEL-LHR
145	LHR-DEL-DAC
922	LHR-STR-SKG
923	SKG-STR-LHR
976	LHR-HAJ-LEJ
979	LEJ-HAJ-LHR
1011	LHR-SIN-PER

(Contd.)

(*Contd.*)

1506	YYZ-JFK-BHX	**2066**	DAR-EBB-LGW
1507	BHX-JFK-YYZ	**2067**	LGW-EBB-DAR
1514	BOS-JFK-GLA	**2068**	EBB-NBO-LGW Until 26 Oct
1515	GLA-JFK-BOS	**2068**	DAR-NBO-LGW Until 24 Oct
1603	CDG-MAN-ABZ	**2068**	MRU-NBO-LGW From 27 Oct
1608	ABZ-MAN-CDG	**2068**	SEZ-NBO-LGW From 30 Oct
1616	MAN-BRU-FCO	**2069**	LGW-NBO-EBB Until 25 Oct
1617	BRU-MAN-GLA	**2069**	LGW-NBO-DAR 2 Oct-23 Oct
1619	FCO-BRU-MAN	**2069**	LGW-NBO-MRU From 26 Oct
1622	GLA-MAN-BRU	**2069**	LGW-NBO-SEZ From 29 Oct
1640	GLA-MAN-MAD	**2078**	ACC-KAN-LGW
1641	MAD-MAN-GLA	**2081**	LGW-ACC-KAN-LGW Until 19 Oct
1660	GLA-MAN-LIN	**2081**	LGW-KAN-ACC Until 24 Oct
1661	LIN-MAN-GLA	**2081**	KAN-ACC-LGW Until 24 Oct
1674	EDI-MAN-GVA	**2081**	LGW-KAN-ACC From 29 Oct
1675	GVA-MAN-EDI	**2128**	ISB-MAN-LGW
1705	FRA-MAN-EDI	**2129**	LGW-MAN-ISB
1714	EDI-MAN-FRA	**2136**	CMB-DXB-LGW
1752	GLA-BHX-HAJ	**2137**	LGW-DXB-CMB
1753	HAJ-HAM-BHX-GLA	**2244**	GIG-GRU-LGW Day 5
1758	GLA-BHX-FRA	**2244**	SCL-GIG-LGW Day 3
1759	FRA-BHX-GLA	**2244**	SCL-GRU-LGW Day 7
1768	EDI-BHX-MUC	**2244**	GRU-GIG-LGW Day 1
1769	MUC-BHX-EDI	**2244**	SCL-GRU-LGW Day 2
1777	DUS-BHX-EDI	**2245**	LGW-GRU-GIG Day 4
1780	EDI-BHX-DUS		
1781	DUS-BHX-EDI		
1782	GLA-BHX-DUS		
1783	DUS-BHX-GLA		
1784	EDI-BHX-DUS		
1801	CDG-BHX-GLA		
1802	EDI-BHX-CDG		
1803	CDG-BHX-EDI		
1806	GLA-BHX-CDG		
1807	CDG-BHX-GLA		
1808	EDI-BHX-CDG		
1809	CDG-BHX-EDI		
1810	GLA-BHX-CDG		
2044	LLW-LUN-LGW		
2045	LGW-LUN-LLW		
2052	LUN-HRE-LGW		
2053	LGW-HRE-LUN		
2062	MRU-SEZ-LGW		
2063	LGW-SEZ-MRU		

(*Contd.*)

(*Contd.*)

2245	LGW-GRU-SCL	**4033**	EDI-BRS-PLH-JER-CDG
	From 4 Oct	**4034**	CDG-JER-PLH-BRS
2245	LGW-GIG-GRU	**4035**	EDI-BRS-JER-GCI
	From 5 Oct	**4036**	CDG-JER-PLH-BRS
2245	LGW-GIG-SCL	**4038**	GCI-BRS-EDI
	From 7 Oct	**4040**	CDG-JER-PLH-BRS-EDI
2248	BOG-CCS-LGW	**4046**	BRS-EDI-GLA-BRS
2249	LGW-CCS-BOG	**4052**	BRS-NCL-ABZ
2252	GND-ANU-LGW	**4053**	ABZ-NCL-BRS-JER
	Until 25 Oct	**4056**	JER-BRS-NCL-ABZ
2252	BGI-ANU-LGW	**4057**	ABZ-NCL-BRS
	Until 21 Oct	**4068**	BRS-PLH-GCI-JER
2252	UVF-ANU-LGW	**4069**	JER-GCI-BRS-PLH
	From 26 Oct	**4086**	NCL-BRS-CDG
2252	GND-ANU-LGW	**4095**	CDG-SOU-NCL-ABZ
	From 28 Oct	**4098**	ABZ-NCL-SOU-CDG
2253	LGW-ANU-GND	**4108**	BRS-PLH-ORK
	Until 25 Oct		Day 6
2253	LGW-ANU-BGI	**4108**	PLH-BRS-ORK
	Until 21 Oct		Until 19 Oct
2253	LGW-ANU-UVF	**4108**	BRS-PLH-ORK
	From 26 Oct		From 26 Oct
2253	LGW-ANU-GND	**4109**	ORK-PLH-BRS
	From 28 Oct	**4504**	GCM-NAS-LGW
2254	UVF-BGI-LGW	**4505**	LGW-GCM-NAS-LGW
2255	LGW-BGI-UVF		Day 5
2264	MBJ-KIN-LGW	**4505**	LGW-NAS-GCM
2265	LGW-KIN-MBJ		Day 2
2276	SAN-PHX-LGW	**6333**	JNB-HDS-SZK-JNB
2277	LGW-PHX-SAN	**6701**	LHR-BEY-DAM
2770	LGW-ARN-HEL		26 Oct-17 Nov
2771	HEL-ARN-LGW	**6701**	LHR-BEY-AMM
2824	SVG-LGW-CDG		29 Oct-20 Nov
4002	PLH-NQY-LGW	**6702**	DAM-BEY-LHR
4003	LGW-PLH-NQY-LGW		27 Oct-18 Nov
4005	LGW-PLH-NQY-LGW	**6702**	AMM-BFY-LHR
4007	LGW-NQY-PLH-LGW		30 Oct-21 Nov
4009	LGW-NQY-PLH	**6707**	LHR-ALY-DAM
4010	BRS-PLH-LGW		2 Oct-23 Oct
4011	LGW-PLH-BRS	**6707**	LHR-DAM-AMM
4020	PLH-BRS-GLA		3 Oct-24 Oct
4029	GLA-BRS-PLH	**6707**	LHR-ALY-DAM
4031	EDI-BRS-PLH-JER-CDG		From 4 Oct

(*Contd.*)

(Contd.)

6708	DAM-ALY-LHR 3 Oct-24 Oct
6708	AMM-DAM-LHR 4 Oct-25 Oct
6708	DAM-ALY-LHR From 26 Oct
6711	LHR-TBS-FRU
6712	FRU-TBS-LHR
6873	FNC-PXO-LGW
6976	LGW-OPO-FNC
6877	FNC-OPO-LGW
6912	LGW-GIB-RAK
6913	RAK-GIB-LGW
6916	LGW-AGA-RAK-LGW
6917	CMN-GIB-LHR
6918	LHR-GIB-CMN
6924	LHR-TNG-CMN
6925	CMN-TNG-LHR
6927	CMN-GIB-LHR
6948	LGW-TUN-MLA-LGW
6966	LGW-MJV-VLC-LGW
6974	LGW-VLC-XRY
6975	XRY-VLC-LGW
6978	LGW-XRY-AGP-LGW
7702	SOU-LBA-ABZ
7703	ABZ-LBA-SOU
7704	SOU-LBA-ABZ
7745	EDI-BLK-JER
7746	JER-BLK-EDI
7760	MAN-JER-GCI-MAN
7768	MAN-GCI-JER-MAN
7783	SOU-MAN-BFS
7786	BFS-MAN-SOU
7802	CDG-CWL-BHD-ABZ
7805	ABZ-BHD-CWL-CDG
7833	CWL-BHD-ABZ
7834	ABZ-BHD-CWL
7836	EDI-NCL-CWL
7837	CWL-NCL-EDI
7838	EDI-NCL-CWL
7839	CWL-NCL-EDI
7859	SOU-EDI-GLA-SOU
7872	BRU-SOU-GCI
7873	GCI-SOU-BRU
7877	GCI-SOU-BRU
8014	ANR-LGW-JER
8022	GCI-LGW-NCL
8025	NCL-LGW-GCI

INDIAN AIRLINES

141	•BOM-VTZ-BBI-BOM
155	BOM-MAA-SIN
156	SIN-MAA-BOM
167	DEL-BOM-TRV
168	TRV-BOM-DEL
213	•CCU-IMF-JRH-CCU
215	•CCU-TEZ-DMU-CCU
219	•CCU-IXS-JRH-CCU
255	•CCU-IXS-IMF
256	•IMF-IXS-CCU
257	•CCU-JRH-DMU-CCU
407	•DEL-AGR-HJR-VNS
408	•VNS-HJR-AGR-DEL
411	•DEL-LKO-PAT-CCU
412	•CCU-PAT-LKO-DEL
421	•DEL-IXJ-SXR
422	•SXR-IXJ-DEL
433	•DEL-GWL-BHO-IDR-BOM Days 1246
433	•DEL-BHO-IDR-BOM Days 357
434	•BOM-IDR-BHO-GWL-DEL Days 1246
434	•BOM-IDR-BHO-DEL Days 357
467	•DEL-GOI-COK
468	•COK-GOI-DEL
469	•DEL-NAG-RPR
470	•RPR-NAG-DEL
473	•DEL-JAI-JDH
474	•JDH-JAI-DEL
485	•DEL-IXC-ATQ-AMD-BOM
486	•BOM-AMD-ATQ-IXC-DEL
491	•DEL-JAI-UDR-BOM
492	•BOM-UDR-JAI-DEL
493	•DEL-JAI-UDR-IXU-BOM

(Contd.)

(*Contd.*)

494	•BOM-IXU-UDR-JAI-DEL	**992**	FJR-SHJ-CCJ-BOM
537	•MAA-BLR-COK	**993**	BOM-CCJ-RKT-SHJ
538	•COK-BLR-MAA	**994**	RKT-SHJ-CCJ-BOM
542	•CCU-VTZ-MAA	**995**	CCJ-GOI-KWI
559	•MAA-BLR-IXE	**996**	KWI-GOI-CCJ
560	•IXE-BLR-MAA	**997**	CCJ-DOH-BAH
569	•MAA-HYD-BBI	**998**	BAH-DOH-CCJ
570	•BBI-HYD-MAA		**PAKISTAN INTERNATIONAL AIRLINES**
571	•HYD-VTZ-CCU		
663	BOM-AMD-SHJ		
664	SHJ-AMD-BOM	**106**	KHI-MJD-KDD
695	BOM-VNS-LKO-BOM	**107**	KDD-MJD-KHI
714	IMF-GAU-CCU	**108**	KHI-HDD-MJD
715	CCU-JAI-AMD-BOM	**113**	WNS-SYW-KHI
725	CCU-IXR-PAT-CCU	**114**	KHI-SYW-MJD-SKZ
769	CCU-BBI-NAG-HYD	**115**	SKZ-SYW-KHI
770	HYD-NAG-BBI-CCU	**121**	KHI-PSI-TUK
809	DEL-PAT-IXR-DEL	**122**	TUK-PSI-KHI
855	DEL-CCU-BKK	**123**	KHI-ORW-TUK
856	BKK-CCU-DEL	**124**	TUK-ORW-KHI
879	DEL-IXB-GAU-DEL	**125**	KHI-TUK-DBA-UET
885	DEL-AMD-MCT	**126**	UET-DBA-TUK-KHI
886	MCT-AMD-DEL	**127**	KHI-TUK-DBA-UET
889	DEL-GAU-IMF-DEL	**128**	UET-DBA-TUK-KHI
913	MAA-BLR-CCJ	**131**	KHI-ORW-PSI
914	CCJ-BLR-MAA	**132**	PSI-ORW-KHI
917	MAA-BLR-PNQ	**140**	KHI-RYK-MUX-LHE
918	PNQ-BLR-MAA	**141**	LHE-RYK-KHI
951	MAA-BLR-AMD	**142**	KHI-RYK-LHE
952	AMD-BLR-MAA	**143**	LHE-RYK-KHI
959	MAA-KUL-SIN	**144**	KHI-RYK-LHE
960	SIN-KUL-MAA	**145**	LHE-MUX-RYK-KHI
961	BLR-MCT-SHJ	**201**	LHE-AUH-DHA
962	SHJ-MCT-BLR	**205**	LHE-PEW-KWI
969	MAA-PUT-BOM	**206**	KWI-PEW-LHE
970	BOM-PUT-MAA	**207**	DXB-ISB-PEW
981	HYD-AMD-KWI		Days 27
982	KWI-AMD-HYD	**207**	DXB-PEW-ISB
985	MAA-CJB-CCJ		Day 3
986	CCJ-CJB-MAA	**208**	ISB-PEW-DXB
989	BOM-CCJ-SHJ	**212**	AUH-ISB-LHE
990	SHJ-CCJ-BOM	**220**	AAN-AUH-PEW
991	BOM-CCJ-FJR-SHJ	**223**	DXB-LHE-PEW

(*Contd.*)

(*Contd.*)

227	KHI-MCT-DXB	**352**	KHI-UET-PEW
228	DXB-MCT-KHI	**354**	KHI-MUX-LHE-PEW
230	DOH-AUH-KHI	**355**	PEW-UET-KHI
	Until 20 Oct	**376**	KHI-LYP-ISB
230	AUH-DOH-KHI	**385**	ISB-LHE-MUX
	From 27 Oct	**386**	MUX-LHE-ISB
231	DXB-PEW-LHE	**387**	ISB-LHE-MUX
232	LHE-PEW-DXB	**388**	MUX-LHE-ISB
238	AAN-AUH-PEW	**390**	KHI-SKZ-LHE-ISB
240	BAH-DOH-KHI	**391**	ISB-LHE-SKZ-KHI
242	DHA-DXB-KHI	**394**	KHI-MJD-SKZ
243	ISB-LHE-DHA	**397**	SKZ-MJD-KHI
244	DHA-LHE-ISB	**398**	DEA-LHE-ISB
247	ISB-LHE-DHA	**399**	ISB-LHE-DEA
248	DHA-LHE-ISB	**417**	ISB-MWD-LHE
253	KHI-AUH-AMM-DAM-IST	**418**	LHE-MWD-ISB
254	IST-DAM-AMM-AUH-KHI	**425**	ISB-MFG-RAZ
255	KHI-THR-BAK	**438**	ISB-PEW-PAJ
257	ISB-AUH-CAI-IST	**439**	PAJ-PEW-ISB
258	IST-CAI-AUH-KHI	**490**	KHI-PEW-ISB
259	KHI-LHE-TAS	**505**	KHI-TUK-JIW
260	TAS-ALA-LHE-KHI	**506**	JIW-GWD-KHI
279	ISB-LHE-AUH	**513**	KHI-GWD-JIW
280	AUH-LHE-ISB	**514**	JIW-TUK-KHI
282	BAH-DOH-KHI	**519**	KHI-PSI-TUK
284	DOH-AUH-KHI	**520**	TUK-PSI-KHI
285	KHI-AUH-DOH	**521**	KHI-TUK-PJG
288	DOH-BAH-KHI	**522**	PJG-TUK-KHI
293	KHI-ISB-ALA-TAS	**523**	KHI-TUK-UET
294	TAS-ISB-KHI	**524**	UET-TUK-KHI
314	KHI-LHE-PEW	**525**	KHI-TUK-GWD
315	PEW-LHE-KHI	**526**	GWD-PJG-KHI
324	KHI-UET-ISB	**527**	KHI-TUK-KDD
325	ISB-UET-KHI	**528**	KDD-TUK-KHI
328	KHI-RYK-LYP-ISB	**530**	KHI-SYW-MJD-SKZ
329	ISB-LYP-RYK-KHI	**532**	KHI-HDD-SKZ-SUL
335	DEA-UET-KHI	**533**	SUL-SKZ-KHI
338	KHI-MUX-LYP	**534**	KHI-WNS-MJD
344	KHI-LYP-ISB	**535**	MJD-HDD-KHI
345	ISB-LYP-KHI	**536**	KHI-WNS-JAG
346	KHI-RYK-MUX-LHE	**537**	JAG-WNS-KHI
347	LHE-MUX-RYK-KHI	**538**	KHI-WNS-MJD
348	KHI-UET-DEA	**540**	KHI-SKZ-SUL

(*Contd.*)

(*Contd.*)

541	SUL-SKZ-KHI	**632**	ISB-SDT-PEW
544	KHI-SKZ-UET	**633**	PEW-SDT-ISB
545	UET-SKZ-KHI	**682**	ISB-PEW-DSK-PZH-UET
546	KHI-WNS-JAG	**683**	UET-PZH-DSK-PEW-ISB
551	KHI-TUK-PJG	**684**	ISB-PEW-DSK-PZH-MUX
552	PJG-TUK-KHI	**685**	MUX-PZH-DSK-PEW-ISB
553	KHI-PJG-TUK	**688**	PEW-DSK-LHE
554	TUK-GWD-KHI	**689**	LHE-DSK-PEW-ISB
557	KHI-PSI-PJG	**703**	KHI-ISB-FRA-JFK
558	PJG-PSI-KHI	**704**	JFK-FRA-LHE-KHI
561	KHI-PJG-GWD	**706**	CPH-ISB-LHE
564	KHI-MJD-JAG	**707**	KHI-ISB-FCO
565	JAG-SKZ-WNS-KHI	**708**	FCO-ISB-KHI
566	KHI-WNS-MJD	**709**	LHE-KHI-MAN
567	MJD-HDD-KHI	**710**	MAN-KHI-LHE
569	KHI-TUK-UET	**711**	KHI-CDG-JFK
570	UET-TUK-KHI	**712**	JFK-FRA-LHE-KHI
571	KHI-PJG-UET	**713**	KHI-LHE-AMS-JFK
572	UET-PJG-KHI	**714**	JFK-AMS-ISB-KHI
573	KHI-PJG-UET	**715**	KHI-LHE-FRA-JFK
574	UET-PJG-KHI	**716**	JFK-FRA-ISB-KHI
576	GWD-TUK-KHI	**717**	KHI-ISB-FRA-JFK
580	KHI-WNS-JAG	**718**	JFK-CDG-ISB-KHI
581	JAG-WNS-KHI	**719**	KHI-ISB-Zrh-YYZ
582	KHI-MPD-MJD	**720**	YYZ-ZRH-LHE-KHI
583	MJD-WNS-KHI	**721**	LHE-KHI-COG-JFK
584	KHI-MJD-SKZ	**722**	JFK-CDG-LHE-KHI
584	KHI-PEW-LHE	**723**	KHI-ISB-AMS-JFK
585	SKZ-WNS-KHI	**724**	JFK-AMS-LHE-KHI
587	MJD-MPD-KHI	**727**	ISB-LHE-RUH
588	KHI-SKZ-BHV	**728**	RUH-LHE-ISB
589	BHV-SKZ-KHI	**734**	FRA-ZRH-KHI
594	KHI-SKZ-BHV	**736**	JED-LHE-PEW
596	KHI-MJD-JAG	**738**	CDG-ISB-KHI
597	JAG-WNS-KHI	**739**	KHI-LHE-CPH
598	KHI-SKZ-UET	**740**	CPH-LHE-KHI
599	UET-KDD-SKZ-KHI	**743**	KHI-DXB-NBO
601	ISB-LHE-HDD-KHI	**744**	NBO-DXB-KHI
602	KHI-HDD-LHE-ISB	**745**	KHI-DXB-NBO
603	ISB-LHE-BHV	**746**	NBO-DXB-KHI
604	BHV-LHE-ISB	**747**	ISB-LHE-JED
617	ISB-LHE-DEA	**748**	JED-ISB-LHE
618	DEA-LHE-ISB	**754**	RUH-PEW-ISB
			Day 2

(*Contd.*)

(*Contd.*)

754	RUH-PEW-LHE Day 7
783	ISB-KHI-LHR
787	KHI-DXB-LHR
788	LHR-DXB-KHI
789	ISB-KHI-MAN
792	ZRH-CDG-KHI
798	YYZ-ZRH-ISB-KHI
799	KHI-LHE-FRA-ZRH-YYZ
850	KHI-PEK-NRT
851	NRT-PEK-ISB-KHI
852	KHI-ISB-PEK-NRT
853	NRT-PEK-ISB-KHI
860	KHI-BKK-MNL-NRT
861	NRT-MNL-BKK-KHI
862	KHI-BKK-MNL-NRT
863	NRT-MNL-BKK-KHI
866	KHI-SIN-CGK
867	CGK-SIN-KHI
868	ISB-LHE-SIN
869	SIN-KUL-KHI
870	KHI-SIN-CGK
871	CGK-SIN-KHI
873	SIN-KUL-LHE-ISB
874	KHI-MLE-CMB
877	CMB-MLE-KHI
878	ISB-RGN-BKK Until 20 Oct
878	ISB-LHE-BKK From 27 Oct
892	ISB-LHE-BKK
893	BKK-RGN-KHI Until 24 Oct
893	BKK-KTM-KHI From 31 Oct
895	BKK-LHE-ISB
896	KHI-KTM-BKK
897	BKK-LHE-ISB

ROYAL NEPAL AIRLINES

167	KTM-SIF-PKR
177	KTM-DHI-XMG
178	XMG-DHI-KTM
179	KTM-SKH-KEP
180	KEP-SKH-KTM
229	KTM-DXB-FRA-LGW
230	LGW-FRA-DXB-KTM.
231	KTM-DXB-FRA-ORY
232	ORY-FRA-DXB-KTM
407	KTM-BKK-SIN
408	SIN-BKK-KTM
411	KTM-SHA-KIX
412	KIX-SHA-KTM

TICKET DESIGNATOR

A special category of travel may be indicated in the 'ticket designation' box. The passenger category is indicated by a two-letter code, as given in the following example:

AD = Agent's reduced transportation
BT = Bulk inclusive tour
GV = Group inclusive tour
GS = Ship's crew.

In some cases, other numbers or codes may appear with the category code, for example, GV 15 indicates a group inclusive tour fare and shows that a minimum of 15 passengers are required to travel at this fare.

ALTERATIONS, REISSUANCE AND REFUNDS

Alterations, reissuance and refunds of an international ticket is permitted under special circumstances only, because of various fare restrictions, and differing airline policies. Authorisation must be obtained from the validating carrier before a ticket may be altered or reissued.

Revalidation of ticket may be done by using an adhesive revalidation label, provided following conditions are fulfilled:

1. No change of carrier is involved.
2. No change in fare is required
3. The fare restriction do not change.
4. Authorisation is received from the validating carrier.

The procedures for refunding an international ticket are the same as those for domestic tickets. If no portion of ticket has been used, and if the ticket is refundable, a refund may be made using a standard IATA cash or credit card refund notice. If a cancellation penalty applies, the penalty must be deducted from the total ticket price before the refund is made.

If one or more copies have already been used, a partial refund can be made for the unused portion of the ticket, unless the ticket is non-refundable. The fare for the first segment that have already been flown must be deducted from the total ticket price, before the refund is made.

A ticket cannot be refunded or re-issued more than 12 months after the date of issue. To process a refund or reissue a ticket in this case, the ticket must be sent to the validating carrier. If the mileage system was used to determine any portion of the fare, the validating carrier should be contacted for instructions before a refund is made.

AGENCY COMMISSION

The foreign carriers pay retail travel agencies a commission of fixed per cent, which is indicated on the ticket by the code IN8. If a ticket is sold in conjunction with a prepaid package tour, an 11 per cent commission may apply. The tour rate is indicated by the code IT11.

Besides commission, incentives, called oversides or rebates are also offered by various carriers.

QUESTIONS AND DISCUSSIONS

Objective Type

Q.1. *Identify the person/word/phrase in each of the following concept:*

1. The process of determining the total fare for an international itinerary, using IATA rules.
2. A stopover point for which a higher fare is charged than for the turn-around point.
3. A publication listing the official fares and rules of major international carriers.
4. An additional amount charged for a stopover.
5. The method of determining the free baggage allowance based on the number of prices.
6. The unit of neutral value used to construct fares based on the currencies of different countries.
7. A document issued by a government entitling a citizen to travel abroad.
8. An endorsement placed in a passport or on a separate document by a consular representative or another official of the country to be visited.
9. Government fees assessed on the value of goods brought into the country.
10. The system of monetary exchange established by the government of the country.
11. A discounted fare that requires an advance purchase and circle trip.

Ans.:

1. *Fare Construction Unit*
2. *Higher intermediate point*
3. *Air traffic*
4. *Surcharge*
5. *Piece Method*
6. *Neutral Unit of Construction* (NUC)
7. *Passport*
8. *Visa*
9. *Custom Duties*
10. *Currency*
11. *Advance Purchase Excursion.*

Q. 2. *In each of the following sentences write the correct word or phrase that belongs to each blank:*

1. To form a valid connection, each leg must arrive at the

connecting point no more than .... hours before the next leg departs.

2. If the departure city is not found in the OAG, a .... must be constructed.
3. The term .... refers to the origin destination and all the stopping points on a traveller trip.
4. An ARNK segment is used to maintain .... in the itinerary, when air segments are interrupted by .... travel.
5. If a trip involves an airline connection, a separate .... must be included for each connecting flight.
6. An .... is a circle rip in which an ARNK segment occurs just after the outbound segment or just before the return segment.
7. A point in a connection where a .... access is called a connecting point.
8. In a time table ...., the departure and arrival times are given in ....
9. A circle trip is any itinerary that originates and terminate the same point, regardless of the member of ....
10. The abbreviation EFF followed by a date indicates the .... of a flight schedule.
11. To convert time from 1.00 PM to 12.00 AM to 24 hour time .... are added to the time.
12. In airline time tables, flights are listed first by .... city and then by .... city.
13. If a flight is travelling east bound, one hair is .... for each time zone crossed to calculate the actual elapsed time.
14. Whereas a time table lists only the flight schedules of one carrier, the OAG lists schedules of ....
15. A .... flight is one that does not make any stops between the origin and the passenger's intended destination.
16. The .... section is an index of the routes flown by the flight of each carrier.
17. A direct flight is one that does not require the passenger to ....
18. The .... section is an index of the routes flown by the flights of each carrier.
19. Collectively, all points used to complete a trip are called the ....
20. In the OAG, flight schedule are organised by ....
21. The .... section is an index of the routes flown by the flights of each carrier.

Q. 3. *Write the correct aircraft name for each of the following equipment codes:*

727	AB3
778	DC9
	L10.

Q. 4. *Rank each of the following aircraft in terms of maximum flight range. Write '1' next to the aircraft with the greatest flight range, '2' next to the aircraft with the second greatest range, etc.*

Airbus Industries A–300B
Boeing 727
Boeing 737
Boeing 747
Lockheed L-1011 Tri Star
McDonnell-Douglas – DC9
McDonnell-Douglas – DC10.

Q. 5. *Match the major carriers on the left with the hub cities on the right. (Some hubs are used by more than one carrier, and some carriers use more than one hub)*

(*a*) American	(*i*) Atlanta
(*b*) Continental	(*ii*) Chicago
(*c*) Delta	(*iii*) Dallas
(*d*) North West	(*iv*) Denver
(*e*) TWA	(*v*) Houston
(*f*) United	(*vi*) Indian Polis
	(*vii*) Kansas City
	(*viii*) Minneapolis–St. Paul
	(*ix*) St. Louis.

Q. 6. *Identify the equipment code for each of the following aircraft types:*

(*a*) Boeing 727	90
(*b*) Boeing 727-200	70-131
(*c*) Boeing 747	90-145
(*d*) McDonnel-Douglas DC9	250-380
(*e*) McDonnel-Douglas DC10	430-452.

Q. 7. *Give the correct carrier code for each of the following domestic and international airlines:*

(*a*) Air Canada	(*d*) British Airways
(*b*) Alaska Airlines	(*e*) Lufthansa German Airlines
(*c*) America West Airlines	(*f*) Qantas

(*g*) Air India
(*h*) Alitalia
(*i*) Austrian Airlines
(*j*) Continental Airlines
(*k*) North West Airlines
(*l*) United Airline.

Q. 8. *Identify the airport code for each of the following destinations:*

(*a*) Jakarta-Soekarno-Hatta
(*b*) London-Gatwick
(*c*) London-Heathrow
(*d*) London-Stansted
(*f*) Milan-Linate
(*g*) Paris-De Gaulle
(*h*) Paris-Orly
(*i*) Rome-Fiumicino
(*j*) Stockholm-Ariando
(*k*) Tokyo-Narita.

Q. 9. *Identify the city code for each of the destinations:*

(*a*) Amsterdam, Netherlands
(*b*) Bangkok, Thailand
(*c*) Cairo, Egypt
(*d*) Denpasar, Indonesia
(*e*) Frankfurt, Germany
(*f*) Lima, Peru
(*g*) London, United Kingdom
(*h*) Madrid, Spain
(*i*) Milan, Italy
(*j*) Nairobi, Kenya
(*k*) New Delhi, India
(*l*) Papeete, French
(*m*) Paris, France
(*n*) Rome, Italy
(*o*) Sao Paulo, Brazil
(*p*) Sydney, Ausralia
(*q*) Tokyo, Japan.

Q. 10. *Identify the airport code for each of the followings:*

(*a*) Battimore-Washington
(*b*) Chicago-Midway
(*c*) Chicago-O'Hare
(*d*) Detroit-Wayne Country
(*e*) Houston-Hobby
(*f*) New York-Kennedy
(*g*) New York-LaGuardia
(*h*) New York-Newark
(*i*) Washington-Dulles
(*j*) Washington-National.

Q. 11. *Identify the city code for each of the following destinations:*

(*a*) Atlanta, Georgia
(*b*) Chicago, Illinois
(*c*) Cincinnati, Ohio
(*d*) Claveland, Ohio
(*e*) Dallas Ft. Worth, Texas
(*f*) Divner, Colorado
(*g*) Fort Lauderdale, Florida
(*h*) Ixtapa-Zihuatanejo, Maxeco
(*i*) Memphis, Tennessee
(*j*) Miami, Florida
(*k*) Minneapolis-St.Paul, Minnesota
(*l*) New Orleans, Louisiana
(*m*) Pittsburgh, Pennsylvania
(*n*) Portland, Oregon
(*o*) San Antonio, Texas
(*p*) San Diego, California
(*q*) San Franciso, California
(*r*) St. Louis, Missouri
(*s*) Washington, D.C.

Q. 12. Read each of the following statements and write 'T' if the statement is true and 'F' it is false:

1. A typical senior citizen fare is equal to the normal coach or first class fare discounted 10%.
2. Excursion fares are usually the highest and least restriction type of fares.
3. Passengers departing from India to an international destination are subject to an international departure tax.
4. Passengers arriving in India from a foreign destination by air or sea are subject to an immigration fee.
5. A seat in the same cabin and class may be sold at many different rates, based on the number already sold.
6. A passenger facility charge may be imposed by an airport authority for refuelling aircrafts.
7. Price elasticity is the raising and lowering of prices to eliminate discount fares.
8. When a domestic fare is quoted by an airline, central transportation tax is not included.
9. An open segment is a ticketed segment that is not booked on a computer reservation system.
10. The booking code indicates the agency commission.

Q. 13. Answer all of the following questions about the Airline Guides:

1. In the Worldwide Airline Guide, schedules to Milan are presented .... schedules to Prague.
2. Schedules to Berlin are found toward the .... of the book.
3. The Carrier Code AZ stands for .... Airlines.
4. A CVL is a ....Jet.
5. The Frequency Code 2 represents ....
6. SK Flight 607 originates in .... After .... stops, it terminates in ....
7. The three-letter City Code STO represents .... SVO represents .... BNE represents ....
8. In the North American Edition, schedules to Phoenix are presented .... schedules to Rochester, N.Y.
9. Schedules to Boston (NAOAG) are found toward the .... of the book.
10. The Carrier Code SO stands for .... Airways.
11. A Bill is a .... Jet.
12. The Frequency Code 2 represents ....
13. FL Flight 27 originates in .... After .... stops, it terminates in ....

14. The three-letter City Code MRY stands for ....
YYZ stands for .... BFL represents ....

Ans.: 1. *before*
2. *front*
3. *Alitalia*
4. *Caravelle*
5. *Tuesday*
6. *ARN (Stockholm, Sweden-Arlanda Arpt.)*
GVA (Geneva, Switzerland)
7. *Stockholm, Sweden*
Moscow, U.S.S.R.
Brisbane, Australia
8. *before*
9. *front*
10. *Southern*
11. *BAC 111 (General Designator)*
12. *Tuesday*
13. *STL (St. Louis, Mo.)*
PHX (Phoenix, Ariz.)
14. *Monterey, Calif*
Toronto, Ontario, Canada
Bakersfield, Calif.

Q. 14. Examine the following schedule and fill in the gaps:

Freq.	Leave	Arrive		Flight		Class	Eq	Ml	S
To PITTSBURGH,P.A.									
A-AGC (ALLEGHENY COUNTY ARPT.)							EST	PIT	
P-PIT (GREATER PITTSBURGH)									
From ST. LOUIS. MC.							CST	STI	
X7	7:00a	9:20a	P	AL	172	SB	D95	B	0
	7:15a	9:38a	P	TW	76	FYB	707	B	0
X6	9:05a	12:14p	P	TW	546	YB	DC9		1
	11:35a	1:55p	P	AL	180	SB	D9S	S	0
	1:45p	4:08p	P	TW	876	FYB	707	S	0
	2:10p	4:30p	P	AL	242	SB	D9S		0
X6	4:55p	7:18p	P	TW	246	YB	DC9	D	0
X6	6:50p	10:35p	P	AL	230	SB	D9S	S	2
	7:00p	9:20p	P	AL	164	SB	D9S	D	0

MEAL SERVICE

NUMBER OF STOPS

The symbol "B" has been added to the listing for AL 172 just to the right of the equipment code.

(a) A look at the Abbreviations and Reference Marks—"Food Service" section of your Sample NAOAG shows the "B" representing ....

(b) The last column on the right indicates the number of stops the flight makes. How Many stops does TW 546 make?................

(c) What type of meal is served on TW 246? ....

(d) How many stops does AL 230 make between PIT and STL? ....

Ans.: (*a*) *Breakfast;*
(*b*) *One;*
(*c*) *Dinner;*
(*d*) *Two.*

Q. 15. To be able to present all the necessary information for a flight schedule, it is necessary to condense this information into codes. Example: United Airlines is coded "UA". These codes can be found under "Abbreviations and Reference Marks" in the front pages of the NAOAG.

Locate them now in your sample NAOG and use them to answer the following questions:

(*a*) The Carrier (Airline) Code "NC" stands for .... airlines;

(*b*) The Jet Aircraft Code "D10" represents a .... aircraft; and

(*c*) The Frequency Code "4" means ....

Ans.: (*a*) *North Central;*
(*b*) *Douglas DC-10;*
(*c*) *Thursday.*

Q. 16. All origin or destination cities are spelled out for easy reference, but each is given a three-letter code to standardize this information. These three-letter codes can be found in the "City/Airport Codes" in the front pages of the NAOAG.

Now locate this section in your Sample (back pages) NAOAG and answer the following questions:

(*a*) "CHA" stands for what city? ....?

(*b*) "KOA" stands for what city? .... ?

Ans.: (*a*) *Chattanooga, Tenn;*
(*b*) *Kona, Hawaii.*

Q. 17. Your Sample NAOAG also contains a "Flight Itineraries" section. Each carrier's flights are listed here in numeric order with their origin, destination and en route cities, if any. Please turn to these pages in your sample NAOAG and locate Eastern Air Lines Flight 569 listed under the Carrier Code EA. Note the flight itinerary is expressed in three-letter codes. Eastern's Flight 569 flies from BOS

(Boston, Mass) to IAH (Houston, Texas) with a stop en route in MSY (New Orleans, La.)

(*a*) Where does Frontier Airlines (FL) Flight 61 originate? (Just jot down the three-letter code.) ....

(*b*) What is its final stop? ....

(*c*) Where else does it stop? ....

Ans.: (*a*) *DFW (Dallas/Ft. Worth)*

(*b*) *SLC (Salt Lake City)*

(*c*) *DEN (Denver).*

Q. 18. To determine the fare for a connecting schedule, refer to the Fare Codes listed in alphabetical order directly above the connecting schedules. Next to each Fare Code is the one-way fare excluding tax, immediately followed by the tax amount and tha total one-way fare.

CONNECTIONS

A	116.37	9.31	125.68
B	105.56	8.44	114.00
C	98.15	7.85	106.00
D	96.30	7.70	104.00
E	92.59	7.41	100.00
F	90.74	7.26	98.00
G	89.52	7.16	96.68
H	86.74	6.95	93.68
I	75.93	6.07	82.00
J	73.15	5.85	79.00
K	70.37	5.63	76.00
L	69.44	5.56	75.00

(a) What is the one-way fare excluding tax for code B? ....

(b) What is the amount of tax for code B? ....

(c) The total one-way for code B? ....

(d) What is the total one-way fare for code D? ....

(e) What is the tax amount for code F? ....

(f) What is the one-way fare excluding tax for code H? ....

Ans.: (*a*) *$ 105.56* (*d*) *$ 104.00*

(*b*) *$ 8.44* (*e*) *$ 7.26*

(*c*) *$ 114.00* (*f*) *$ 86.74.*

Short Answer Type

Q. 19. Answer the following:

(*a*) Ms. Kokila wishes to transport her pet cockatoo on an airline flight. Another passenger on the same flight has already arranged to bring a parakeet in a small cage into the cabin. Will cockatoo be allowed on the plane? If so, in what section of the plane will the cockatoo be transported.

(*b*) Despite having a confirmed reservation and a ticket, Mr. Nautiyal was denied boarding on his flight, due to overbooking by the airline. What compensation is the airline legally required to offer Mr. Nautiyal.

(*c*) A small airline carrier is planning to purchase a new aircraft to fly business passengers from Mumbai to Jauli Grant (Dehradun). The company estimates that each flight will carry an average of 15 passengers. What type of aircraft would you recommend? Why?

(*d*) Mr. and Mrs. Thakur will be flying on an Indian Airlines flight from New Delhi to Kolkata. Their flight departs at 9.45 A.M. By what time must they check in at the boarding gate?

(*e*) Mr. JKS Sajwan will travel on British Airways from Hyderabad to Kolkata, where he will board an Air India flight to Australia. Through which airline should this reservations be placed? Why?

(*f*) Mr. Raju has a confirmed reservation in coach class on Air India flight. He has a coupon entitling him to a free upgrade to first class, subject to availability. To ensure that a first class seat will be available, he requests a duplicate reservation in first class. How could this situation be handled?

(*g*) Ms. Jayanti, who is blind, is dependent on her specially trained dog. If she travels by air, will she be allowed to take her dog on the plane? If so under what situations?

(*h*) Mrs. Devi's flight has been cancelled due to a schedule change. Who is responsible for notifying he passenger?

(*i*) Mrs. Jaya will be travel with her 18 month old infant Praful. If Mrs. Jaya's air fare is Rs.14,400, what is the approximate amount of Praful's fare.

(*j*) An Indian Airline is planning to acquire new year craft to fly various routes. The plane will travel not stop between points from 1200 miles to 2500 miles apart. Each plane will made two trips per day. The airline would like to be able to carry an average of 150 passengers per day per plane (including both trips). What type of aircraft would you recommend? Why?

Essay Type

Q. 20. *In what situation can rail service effectively compete with air service.*

Q. 21. *What are the important services provided to business travellers at airport?*

Q. 22. *How does the business class section of an airplane meet the needs of the business traveller?*

Q. 23. *List the advantage and disadvantages by travelling by chartered flights?*

Q. 24. *How did World War II influence the development of the commercial airline industry?*

Q. 25. *Who owns the airports in India? Explain the organisational structure of this authority.*

Q. 26. *Describe the main parts of an airport?*

Q. 27. *Give the Airlines Codes of the following:*

(*i*) Cathay Pacific
(*ii*) Lufthansa
(*iii*) Egypt Air
(*iv*) Air Lanka
(*v*) Aeroflot.

Q. 28. *Argue the case for and against deregulation in the airline industry.*

Q. 29. *Prepare a profile of Indian Airlines, setting out its:*

(*i*) Rate network
(*ii*) Aircraft Equipment
(*iii*) Company structure.

Q. 30. *Many people are appreciative about flying service. They cannot understand how an aircraft remain air horne. Explain how an aircraft flies by referring to the theory of flight.*

Q. 31. *How can an aircraft land in par visibilities?*

Q. 32. *A travel company wishes to operate packaging tours to Spain involving air traffic on chartered flights.*

(*i*) What licence or authority does the tour company need?
(*ii*) What licence or authority does the chartered airline need?

Q. 33. How does a pilot calculate the fuel requirement for a flight?

Q. 34. Trace the history of airlines industry.

Discuss the history of the commercial aviation industry in relation to modern air travel. In your discussion, answer the following questions:

(*i*) What role did the development of new technologies play in the development of travel industry.

(*ii*) Which individuals were instrumentation the development of the aviation industry? What were their contributions?

Q. 35. What is the airline's liability for lost or damaged baggage stoled.

Q. 36. What more than one airline carrier is involved in an itinerary, through which carrier should the reservation be booked?

Q. 37. Ms. Sundaram will travel round-trip from New Delhi to London. The base fare is Rs.13,500. What type of taxes apply? What are the applicable tax percentage? Calculate the total fare, including all applicable taxes and fees.

Q. 38. Mr. Bhardwaj will travel round trip from Calcutta to Chicago. The round trip airfare is Rs.35,000. Calculate the total fare, and itemize all applicable taxes and fees.

Q. 39. Mrs. Manjula will travel round trip from New York to Honolulu. The base fare is $415.00. Calculate the total fare, and itemize all applicable taxes and fees.

Q. 40. Ms. Paul will travel round trip from San Francisco to Tokyo. The base fare is $800.00. Calculate the total fare, including all applicable taxes and fees.

Q. 41. Mr. Raju will travel one-way from Bombay to Fort Yoken Alaska. The base fare is Rs.21,000. Calculate the total fare, including applicable taxes.

Q. 42. Mr. J. Mohan will travel round-trip from New York to Paris. The base fare is $850.00. Calculate the total fare, including all applicable taxes and fees.

Q. 43. Assume the base fare for the following itinerary is $585.00.

1. AC 787 Y 28 JANIAHYYZ
2. AC 793 Y 15 JUL Y YZIAH

Calculate the total fare, including all applicable taxes and fees.

Q. 44. *Assume the base fare for the following itinerary is $385.00.*

1. CO 811V 23 APR TUSONT
2. CO 833Q 25 APR ONTTUS

Calculate the total fare, including all applicable taxes and fees.

Q. 45. *Assume the base fare for the following itinerary is $1050.00*

1. CO 23Y 25 JAN LAXBUE
2. CO 25Y 31 JAN BUELAX

Calculate the total fare, including all applicable taxes and fees.

Q. 46. *Write a horizontal fare calculation for each of the following itineraries:*

	Ca/Ft/Cls	*Date*	*From/To*	*Fare*
(i)	1 AA 20 Y	NOV 15	LAXDCA	$377.27
(ii)	1 DL 176 M	JAN 26	BNAFLL	$159.00
(iii)	*(a)* 1 TW 195 B	APR 18	ORDLAS	$181.00
	(b) TW 297 B	APR 25	LASORD	$181.00

Q. 47. *Explain the meaning of the following fare basis codes:*

(a) YTU
(b) QLAP 14 NR
(c) BH X 67.

Q. 48. *Which fare bases in the following list is valid for travel in the high season?*

(i) QE 14 PE5O
(ii) MHAP7
(iii) BL 21 NR.

Q. 49. *Assume that in the following itinerary the base fare for each segment is $148.18.*

Write the horizontal fare calculation

(i) US 167 Y 12 FEBSFOLAX
(ii) US 174 Y 15 FEBLAXSFO.

Q. 50. *Assume that the base fare in the following segment is $366.60. Write the horizontal fare calculation in this segment*

UA 240Q 14 JUL JFKSFO.

Q. 51. *Assume that the total fare for a segment is Rs. 5,400 and the tax is Rs. 540. Determine the base fare.*

Q. 52. What tax(es) apply to each of the following itineraries.

(*i*) A passenger will depart from Calcutta and arrive in Bombay

(*ii*) A passenger will depart from New Delhi and arrive in London

(*iii*) A passenger will depart from Bombay and arrive in Toronto

(*iv*) A passenger will travel round-trip from Madras to Tokyo

(*v*) A passenger will travel from London to Honolulu.

Q. 53. Determine the current rate for each of the following taxes:

(*i*) Air transportation tax

(*ii*) International departure tax

(*iii*) General sales tax

(*iv*) Customs user fee.

Q. 54. What is the cancellation penalty for a fare purchased at the VAP14PE25 fare basis?

Q. 55. Under the mileage system, if the total mileage does not exceed the maximum permitted mileage had many stop-overs are permitted between the origin point and turn around point?

Q. 56. Assume a passenger will travel from LON to NBO, with a stop-over in ATH. Based on mileage, the fare from LON to NBO is NUC 627.72, and the fare from LON to ATH is NUC 648.25. Which fare would be used to ticket the passenger?

6

Air Ticketing Techniques

After learning this chapter, you should be able to:

- ❑ *understand the importance of air travel;*
- ❑ *fill up the Reservation Sheet;*
- ❑ *know the air reservation system;*
- ❑ *describe the fare system of air ticketing and document used for the purpose;*
- ❑ *improve your use of an Airline Guide to prepare passenger flight itineraries;*
- ❑ *correctly answer passenger's questions concerning flight frequencies, fares, numbers and location of stops, class of service, meals, equipment types and general transportation;*
- ❑ *advise passengers of correct airport of departure and of arrival if a city is a multiple-airport city;*
- ❑ *determine minimum time required between flights in a connecting city;*
- ❑ *determine minimum connecting times between airports in multiple-air port cities;*
- ❑ *answer the questions in the space(s) provided.*

Airline Ticketing is one of the most important activity of the travel agency business. The important point regarding the airline ticketing are as follows:

1. Preparation and completion of reservation sheet
2. Booking the desired tickets with the appropriate carrier(s)
3. Writing the airline tickets
4. Invoicing the sale.

RESERVATION SHEETS/CARDS

Basic airline ticketing begins with the proper completion of a reservation sheet, booking desired travel with the appropriate carrier(s); writing the airline ticket; and invoicing the sale. A travel agency must account (to ATC) weekly for all ticket stock and any funds received for ticket must be reported. An invoice system is usually employed to account for the ticket stock issued and payment (credit cards) received for sale.

The reservation sheet contains a shorthand of travel information, *i.e.*, Airline Codes, Airport Codes, flight numbers and types of service. All of the information on the reservation sheet is important, for example, the status designation of a flight means:

O.K. : in the status box means that this particular segment has been confirmed by the airline.

OK/F : in the status box means that this particular segment has been confirmed

WL/Y : FIRST CLASS and is WAIT LISTED on the Y/COACH CLASS.

RQ : in the status box means that this particular segment has been placed on request from another airline.

NO-OP : in the status box means that this particular leg (segment) does not operate as you have requested it.

UK : in the status box means that this particular leg is unable to confirm either class of service (often times, during peak travel periods, a flight can be waitlisted both classes of service).

Airline ticketing requires the completion of a Reservation Sheet for several reasons:

1. To prepare and organise the trip prior to telephoning the airlines for the actual reservation,
2. To establish permanent agency record of the customer's travel intentions, and
3. To make it possible for any individual agent in an office to complete the transactions in the absence of the original agent.

The basic step in airline ticketing is the preparation and completion of reservation sheet. These sheets may differ from one travel agency to another but all of them contain the travel information i.e. airline codes, airport, codes, flight member and type of service etc. The basic information included in these sheet is concerning the following:

1. Date
2. Name/s
3. Number in party
4. Home address(es) including zip code
5. Telephone (home and/on office)
6. Ages of children
7. Billing information-credit card, cash etc
8. Travel plan-from..... to, ...
9. Carrier
10. Flight number
11. Day of week
12. Date of arrival
13. Status (OK or standby)
14. The fare and taxes of each flight
15. Other information such as name of airline, representation making reservation, date of reservation, hotel, tour, rail, rental car bookings.

Thus it is clear that the Reservation Sheet (Ref. Fig. 6.1) contains all the relevant information necessary for the trip of the customer. Each head of information gives a clear picture about itself. Take an example of an item like 'STATUS'.

A Reservation Sheet or 'Res Cards' is a specially designed form on which the passenger itinerary is written by hand. The introduction of computer has eliminated the use of reservation sheets, the technique of taking an airline reservation has not changed significantly. Most travel sales are originated by a customer requesting a reservation. In most cases the request is for airline reservation. As soon as the request is received the travel responds by qualifying the customer—gathering the information required to fulfil the customer's request. Now-a-days, most reservations are made by computers. Airlines which do not participate in the computer reservation systems, require travel agents to book reservations directly with the carrier, by telephone.

The act of placing an airline reservation is called selling airline space. Regardless of whether the space is sold by computer or telephone, the following information is required:

RESERVATION SHEET/CARD

NAMES	NO. PARTY	TEL.HOME 345-9282	BILLING INFORMATION TRAVEL SERVICE
Mr. / Mrs. BHARDWAJ	2	OFFICE 345-2289	15 Industrial Drive, IA. 33466
MAHER GAON, LANSDOWNE, Uttaranchal		OTHER	

FROM	TO	AIR	FLT	CLASS	DATE	DEP	ARR	STATUS	TX & SKD CHANGE	FORM OF PAYMENT CASH......... CHECK......... CHARGE
New Delhi		NC 309 F			5/2	1100 AM	1207 PM	OK	NC 309 4/29 1110 AM – 1217 PM	CREDIT CARD VISA
Mumbai-New Delhi		NC 308 F			5/6	102 PM	220 PM	OK		OTHER
										OTHER INFO Confirmed by AI

FARE	200.00	DEPOSITS	AMOUNT 220.00	DATE 4/15	AUTO AJAY CAR RENTAL CAT.C $20.00 DAY – Unlimited Mileage		AMOUNT		
TAX	16.00		202.00	6/10	HOTEL HOLIDAY INN-DOWNTOWN $35.00 DAY DBL				
TOTAL-AIR	216.00	TOTAL-ALL			OTHER				
COMM.	14.00	60 8.40	40 5.60		PAID	DATE	AMOUNT	LESS COMM.	PAID TO ESTAB
NET REMIT	202.00				PAID	4/14	140.00	14.00	126.00-HOLIDAY INN
					PAID				

Fig. 6.1: Specimen of a Reservation Sheet.

1. The member in the party—name(s) of passenger(s), number of children, ... ages etc.
2. The name of the caller
3. The origin, destination, and any desired stop-overs
4. The departure and return dates
5. The preferred departure time
6. The preferred class of service or fare range
7. The preferred airline, if any
8. Business and residence telephone number
9. How the customer plans to pay for the tickets—cash, cheque, or credit card.

Now, the agent will check the flight schedules and fares and quotes a price. The most important concern of travel agency customers is obtaining the lowest fare. Therefore, the agent should discuss all possible ways of reducing fares and explain the restrictions that govern special discount fares.

Whenever an airline reservation is made an agent also inquires of the customer needs—hotel room and rental car. Leisure travellers are prospective buyers of sight-seeing tours, golf, tennis or other activities. It is also advisable to ask about the customer's future travel plans, especially vacation travel. On conclusion of travel sales, thank the customer for patronising the agency.

The specimens of a Reservation Card is given in Figs. 6.1 and 6.2. Although with the introduction of computers, these cards are obsolete; but the basic information required for reservation remains unchanged.

Besides air space, computer reservation system is also used to sell hotel space, car rentals, tours and cruises. Generally, these services are booked directly with the vendor, as the choice of vendors, price ranges and option is important for customers.

An agent evaluates the customer's needs and budgets as early as possible, to avoid over selling and under selling. Customers who repeatedly ask for price are either cost conscious or at a limited budget. Others who are unconcerned about price are most likely to acquire luxury accommodation.

He must learn exactly why each traveller is making the trip and where he or she needs to stay. An executive travelling on business need to stay near a particular company or office building, whereas a family on vacation may want to be near a particular tourist

RESERVATION CARD

ABC INTERNATIONAL NEW DELHI — **RESERVATION CARD**

Mail | P | UP | DEL

Name

Agent

Date...... No. ......

Address

H.No.

Acct./CC

Requested by:

B.No.

Name Exp.

X/O	From	To	Fare Basis	Carrier	FLT/CL	Date	Time LV	Time ARR	Day	Meal	Status	Contd. by	FARE From/To	FARE Break Down Carrier	FARE Break Down Fare
													Fare Rs.		
													Base Rs.		
													Tax Rs.		
													Total Rs.		

CAR RENTAL

Budget ☐ Hertz ☐

LOC

Avis ☐ National ☐

Date

Conf.

Other

Tkt

Hotel

Name/Address Nites Dates Room Rate Guar. Conf.#/Date

Fig. 6.2: Specimen of Reservation Card.

attraction. The business travellers tend to emphasize or promises facilities such as coffee shop, restaurant, cocktail lounge, laundry, and valet service. They prefer to be near the airport on a particular area where they are conducting business. Those with expense accounts paid by their employers often opt for luxury properties that enhance their image. Many desire a suite that allows business to be conducted in hotel room.

A family on vacation may want to be near a particular tourist attraction. These families prefer hotels that offer family plans which permit children of a particular age to stay free or on a reduced rates.

Leisure travellers prefer resort locations as out of town properties. Tourists are concerned with recreational facilities than on premises food and beverage service.

Pack your suitcases, book your ticket on your favourite airline, get hotel reservation...... all through the Internet. Using internet for travel purposes is fast catching up with the internet users in the country. By using this facility, the prospective traveller can bypass the travel agents. For once there is no need to lose one's sleep over getting hotel booking done, or chasing agents for airlines tickets.

Not only that ! They can also enjoy heavy discounts from the airlines and the hotels. By eliminating a travel agent, it will not only save some money, but the chance of undesired miscommunication during transit is also minimised.

The packages available on the net are very tempting and comprehensive indeed. They help you not only to decide the venue, but you can also browse in the lobby of a hotel and the rooms. And if that's not enough, you have the choice of colour of the car you would like to see on arrival at the airport to take you to your favourite hotel. Without parting with a single penny.

The Department of Tourism's address on the Web site is *http://www.tourIndia.com*. Designed by Infoware Solution Inc. New York, U.S.A, the package has all the basic related information of the country. Along with the details of tourist destinations, route options and rate cards, which will be updated regularly.

Tourism is the largest industry in the world, yet unfortunately it has not been tapped upto its full potential. The reason is lack of awareness on the international level. We need to publicise it in a more effective and in a pro-active manner. And internet is one good choice With a reach of 50 million surfers, the internet has also attracted the attention of Federation of Hotels and Restaurants of India (FHRAI).

Example:

This example illustrates the creation of PNR's (Passenger Name Record) and shows the necessary entries to establish an electronic reservation.

Solution:

"An agent at Welcome Abroad Travel in Chicago receives a telephone call from a customer Mr. Gosain……" I need a one way reservation to New York around 8.00 AM tomorrow morning, First Class.

The agent keys in the request for a display of available flight to the computer.

1. A27 NOVPORDNYC800A:

A	:	Availability Entry Code
27NOV	:	DATE OF ARRIVAL
ORDNYC	:	CITY OR AIRPORT CODES
800A	:	Approximate time of requested departure.

2. Depress the 'Enter' Key.

The computer responds immediately, displaying the seat availability of the morning flights on the date. (maximum of four flights shown)

27 NOV	F 70.00	Y56.00	EX. 89.00	
1. TW114F443	ORDEWR	830A	242P727	LL 03
2. AA332F2Y4	ORDEWR	835A	117P720	BS 02
3. AA 2F547	ORDJFK	845A	1246P720	BB 00

The computer displays, for example, on line 2:

AA	:	Airline Code
332	:	Flight Number
F2Y4	:	Number of seats available per class of service, 2 First Class and 4 Coach
ORDEWR	:	Airport Codes, *i.e.,* New York Airport
835A	:	Time of departure
117P	:	Time of arrival
720	:	Type of aircraft

BS : Meals
02 : Number of stops

"Yes", I can confirm a first class seat for you on a non-stop flight, departing at 8.45 AM". The agent then specifies the flight to the computer and the inventory is adjusted.

3. Inventory adjustment:

N1F3
N = Need
1 = Number of seats
F = Class
3 = Location of desired segment in availability display

The computer responds by displaying the confirmation instantly:

1 2F 27NOV ORDJKF SS1 845A 1246P

"Under what name may I hold this reservation?"
"Gosain, D.S."

The agent keys in the name and inserts it. It is preceded by an 'Entry Code' that instructs the computer as to what type of information is being entered.

—Gosain/D.S. (—Entry Code for Name)
"And your home phone number, Mr. Gosain?"
"New Delhi, 4610709

She/He keys in the number and enters it by "Entry Code, City, home phone"

ICHIND 4610709

"I will pick up my ticket at the travel agency"

"That will be fine, Mr. Gosain, we will have them ready for you".

"Mr. Gosain, you hold a first class Reservation on AA flight 2 departing O'Hare at 8.45 AM tomorrow morning, and arriving in JFK airport at 12.46 PM. Is there anything else we may help you with at this time such a rental of car, hotel return reservation?"

"No, thank you."

"Thank you for calling. Welcome Abroad Travel."

The computer edits all information sent to it. If any items of the programme of information are not entered by the agent, such as the Gosain's phone number, the computer could have immediately reminded the agent of the error or oversight (Need Phone).

A PNR (Passenger Name Record) has been created for Mr. Gosain's, now reservation has been completed. This PNR is filled in the computer. Any agent can request later retrieval and display of Mr. Gosain's or any other passenger's PNR. Changes can be made to a PNR and then it can be filled away again, *i.e.*, rental cars, hotels, additional flights, travelling with infant, special mean, or requires special attention.

A computer reservation system can be the travel agency's partner in providing passenger service. Any agent in the office has instant access to any Passenger Name Record in the computer even though the computer may be 3000 miles away. In seconds the computer can display any PNR requested on the agent's screen. Necessary changes in the PNR : cancellations, rebooking, passenger name changes, etc., can be made by any agent who later speaks with the passenger.

Through the computer's automatic teletype processing, messages are sent to other airlines or received from other airlines. Through computer terminals, a travel agency is able to select not only the best available flight on all airlines, but the most advantageous fares currently applicable on a carrier basis and to furnish full and accurate pricing information. Computer permit immediate selection, booking and confirmation of an airfare/flights, and confirm hotel reservations and car rentals all in one swift step.

To clients, this means instant confirmation of requests without wasted time on call backs.

Sales personnel no longer are required to work at convention desks. Instead, they are now seated at reservation sets that use video screens and typewriters like the boards and are linked directly to the airline's main computer centre. Client can receive immediate confirmation for flight operated by over hundreds of domestic and foreign airlines as well as hotels, and car rental companies throughout the world.

Computer reservation systems provide instant confirmation of hotel reservations, including the domestic and international properties of leading hotel companies (Holiday Inn, Hilton, Hyatt, Howard Johnson, Ranada, Western International, Sheraton, Quality

Inns and Americana) and car rental companies (Hertz, Aris, National, Budget, Econo Car and Dollar).

A computer reservation system enables travel agents to direct their attention and effort on knowing clients as individuals and providing that 'personal touch'. Automatic reservations help agents to immediately determine a customer's need wants, and preferences, and enables booking and ticketing to be accompanied quickly and accurately. Computers will enable travel agents to provide customers with the full courteous attention they expect and deserve.

AIRLINE RESERVATIONS

All scheduled airlines have established standard reservations procedures. It is important to realise that each airline has its own method of controlling seats on an airplane. Carriers operate on the principle of centralised space control on a first come, first served basis, and each system is designed to give the public an immediate 'yes' or 'no' answer in regard to available airplane seats. To deal with general public, travel agent, with another carrier, or between their own offices. Every airline must have certain basic information in order to make a reservation.

The first contact between travel agent, his client, and airline reservations agent, is the telephone call. (Some 2,000 travel agency reservations are using computer terminals). If the travel agent knows in advance what the client desires, he can prepare his information prior to the call and thereby efficiently relaying this information to the airline reservations agent. The travel agent should know the items needed by the reservations agent in order to conclude a reservations transaction so that the telephone conversation can be expedited.

The majority of airlines use similar procedures in their telephone handling with prospective passengers. The information that a reservations agent requires is generally the same regardless of the carrier contacted.

The reservations agent will need to know the following items (with example in parenthesis) for each flight segment with regard to a planned reservation:

1. The flight number : (e.g., AA 701)
2. Class of service : (e.g., F)

3. Date of departure : (e.g., 3-29)
4. The original point : (e.g., BOS)
5. The destination : (e.g., DCA)
6. The desired number of seats : (e.g., 1)
7. The passenger's family name and first initial(s), and residence and/or business telephones contact (e.g., Ms. Kusum, A: 603-784-0621, business telephone).
8. The time as given by which the passenger must secure the confirmed ticket or else suffer loss of reservation: (e.g., 3-21, 5.00 PM).
9. Travel agent's name and name of individual handling itinerary (e.g., Windson Travel; Dwight).

When issuing, reissuing or revalidating the passenger's ticket; it's necessary to check with the airline office that cleared the space in order to verify the reservations claimed for the passenger and to remove the time limit.

All space must be obtained by contacting the (nearest) reservations office of the originating airline. This will simplify the ticketing when more than one airline is involved, protect the passenger travelling via connecting flights by providing the receiving carrier with for other arrival information, and ensure proper execution of reconfirmation rules when applicable.

The airlines recognise that under usual circumstances the travel agent may be required by the passenger to obtain continuing space from the individual airlines concerned. If so, the travel agent must give originating airline the passenger's complete itinerary, including the current reservation status of each flight. The agent must give each other airline the passenger's means of arrival and originating flight at the time of the original request.

When the travel agent prepares itineraries for his customers, it is important, as a service to the passenger and a requirement of the airline, that sufficient time be allowed for the passenger and his baggage to move from one airline to the other. It is the travel agent's responsibility to determine and adhere to the minimum connecting of times published in the airline guides.

The airline reservation agents must know the passenger's telephone number, the travel agency's name, and telephone number and the name of the particular travel agents handling the reservation.

The reservations agent must have the passenger's contact in the event there are any operational difficulties and it is either too late or inconvenient to call the travel agent.

If the reservation is for more than one passenger and if names are different, each name should be given to the airline reservation agent. If the itinerary of the passenger begins at a point other than where the reservation is being made, the reservation agent will desire to know-how the passenger will be arriving at the first boarding point. If it is possible, the passenger's contact at the city where he will board his first flight should be given to the reservation agent. This will enable the reservation's office at the passenger's boarding point to be able to contact the passenger if the occasion arises.

As per the governing tariff rule, certain member airlines require ticketed passengers, under certain given circumstances, to reconfirm, *i.e.*, advise the airline at the boarding point of their intentions to use their reservations no later than the time set for the in the tariff rules. Upon failure to reconfirm, the concerned passenger's reservations are cancelled, including their complete remaining itineraries. When ticketing a passenger, the travel agent must inform the passenger of their responsibility to reconfirm each segment of his itinerary subject to the reconfirmation rule.

DOMESTIC AIRLINE TICKETING

Customers approach the travel agency office to purchase a trip. The travel agency must find out the following information:

From the Customer

1. Name of the client
2. Place to be visited
3. Date and time of departure
4. Other related information.

Thereafter

1. Refer the official airline guide and select the appropriate flights and time and date of departures.
2. Next step is to enter the flights you have chosen on your reservation sheet.
3. Call the airlines to book the flights.

4. After the airline reservation list has confirmed the flight, ask the air fare from the airline.
5. Double the one way fare to arrive at a round trip first class fare.
6. To complete the tax refer to arrive at a round trip first class fare.
7. To complete the tax refer to the concerned taxable.
8. Add international, tax if any.
9. Calculate the total of base fare, tax and international tax.
10. Complete the ticket.

Guidelines for Domestic Airline Ticket

Example:

On November 20, Mr. Hemant comes into your Boston office to purchase a trip to Honolulu. He would like to depart on November 23, but wants to stopover in Los Angeles for two nights. He prefers to travel first class. Based on the information given below you are required to collect the necessary information and write the airline ticket in the proper format. You would now refer to the *Airline Guide* and look up to Los Angeles from Boston. See Schedule-A.

Solution:

Mr. Hemant has asked for a mid-afternoon departure. You select TWA flight 65, which depart Boston at 3:00 PM and arrives Los Angeles at 5:45 PM. Your client wishes to proceed to Honolulu from Los Angeles on November 25. You again refer to concerned airline guide and look up to Honolulu from Los Angeles. See Schedule-B as given.

Your client wants a mid-day departure, so you choose Western #501 which departs from Los Angeles at 12:35 PM and arrives in Honolulu at 2:55 PM.

On his return from Honolulu, Mr. Hemant would like to stop over in San Francisco for three nights. He wants to leave Honolulu on December 14. In the Airline Guide to San Francisco from Honolulu, you select a late afternoon departure from Honolulu on Western Airlines flight #530 departing at 4:10 PM and arriving in San Francisco at 11:59 PM. See Schedule-C.

Schedule-A

Freq.	Leave	Arrive	Flight	Class	Eq	MI	S
To **LOS ANGELES CALIF.**						PDT	LAX
B-BUR (BURBAN(R) O-ONT (ONTARIO)							
L-LAX (INTERNATIONAL)							
V-VNY (VAN NUYS ARPT)							
ALSO SEE LONG BEACH, CALIF.							
BOSTAL MASS.						EDT	BOS
	F	276.85	22:15	299.00	598.00		
	Y	212.96	17:04	230.00	460.00		
	FN	212.96	17:04	230.00	460.00		
	YN	170.37	13:63	184.00	368.00		
	YM	172.00					
	H	AP/20	YN	WEEKEND	276.00		
	H	AP/20	YN	MIDWEEK	230.00		
	H	AP/20	TW	7:45 DAY	322.00		
	H	AP/20	YX	7:45 DAY	276.00		
7:45a	12:00n	O	UA 211	FY	72S	BL	1
9:30a	12.11p	L	AA 11	FY	D10	BS	0
9:45a	2:08p	L	TW 7	FY	L10	L	1
12:00n	5:37p	L	TW 265	FY	707	•	2
				TW 265 • MEALS LS/L			
12:30p	6:19p	L	TW 107	FY	72S	LD	3
3:00p	5:54p	L	TW 65	FY	L10	D	0
			•	TW 65 EFFECTIVE OCT 29			
5:25p	8:06p	L	AA 49	FY	D10	D	0
5:55p	8:35p	L	TW 65	FY	L10	D	0
				TW 65 DISCONTINUED AFTER OCT 28			
6:00p	11:50p	L	TW 245	FY	707	D	2
				TW 245 DISCONTINUED AFTER OCT 8			
6:00p	11:50p	L	TW 811	FY	707	D	2
				TW 811 EFFECTIVE OCT 9			
7:10p	11:37p	L	AA 29	FnYn	D10	S	1
9:00p	1:10a	L	TW 137	FnYn	L10	S	1
9:00p	1:49a	L	AA 457	FnYn	72S	S	2
		CONNECTIONS					
A	286.11	22:89	309.00	L	CC		
B	276.85	22:15	299.00	F	JT/THRU		
C	272.22	21:78	294.00		CC		
D	265.74	21:26	287.00		(PIA)		
E	222.22	17:78	240.00	L	CC		
F	212.96	17:04	230.00	FN/Y	JT/THRU		
G	212.96	17:04	230.00	Y	THRU		
G	212.96	17:04	230.00	Y	THRU		
H	208.34	16:67	225.01		(PIA)		
J	192.60	15:41	208.01	H	CC		
J	183.34	14:67	198.01	L	CC		
K	183.34	14:67	198.01	H/L	CC		
K	183.34	14:67	198.01	L/H	CC		
L	183.34	14:67	198.01		CC		
M	170.37	13:63	184.00	YN	THRU		
N	164.82	13:19	178.01		CC		

Schedule-B

Freq.	Leave		Arrive	Flight		Class	Eq	MI	S
To **HONOLULU, OAHU; HAWAII**								HST	HNL
LOSS ANGELES, CALIF.								PDT	LAX
		L-LAX	B-BUR	O-ONT		V-VNT			
				TAX NOT INCL-SEE PGS 10-11					
				FARE CLASS APPL-SEE PG 4					
		F	224.00			448.00			
		YH	156.00			312.00			
		YL	141.00			282.00			
	PA	YL	140.00			280.00			
		KH	148.00			296.00			
		KL	133.00			266.00			
		YM	125.00						
	CO	YM	126.00						
	PA	YM	127.00						
	WA	YM	127.00						
	8:05a								
		L	10:35a	UA	195	FYK	747	B	0
				UA 195 DISCONTINUED AFTER OCT 28					
SPEC	8:05a	L	11:40a	UA	195	FYK	747	B	0
						OP NOV 26			
X3	8:05a	L	11:40a	UA	195	FYK	747	B	0
				UA 195 EFFECTIVE DEC 21 – DEC 26					
	8:45a	L	11:10a	PA	1	FYK	747	B	0
				PA 1 DISCONTINUED AFTER OCT 1					
	8:50a	L	11:15a	CO	603	FYK	D10	L	0
X37	9:15a	L	11:35a	WA	511	FYK	D10	L	0
	9:30a	L	1:05p	UA	191	FYK	747	L	0
				UA 191 EFFECTIVE OCT 29					
367	10:00a	L	12:20p	KE	001	FY	747		0
				KE 001 CONDITIONAL STOPOVER TRAFFIC					
2	10:00a	L	12:20p	KE	001	FY	D10		0
				KE 001 CONDITIONAL STOPOVER TRAFFIC					
	10:00a	L	12:25p	UA	191	FYK	747	L	0
				UA 191 DISCONTINUED AFTER OCT 28					
	11:30a	L	3:10p	UA	1131	YK	DC8	L/	0
				UA 1131 EFFECTIVE DEC14 - JAN 8					
1	12:00n	L	3:42p	WA	567	YK	B72	L/	1
	12:05p	L	2:30p	CO	607	FYK	D10	L	0
	12:35p	L	2:55p	WA	501	FYK	D10	L	0
X1	1:10p	L	3:45p	WA	561	YK	B72	L/	0
	1:20p	L	3:40p	NW	21	FYK	747	D	0
	1:30p	L	3:55p	UA	193	FYK	747	L	0
				UA 193 DISCONTINUED AFTER OCT 28					
	1:30p	L	5:00p	UA	193	FYK	747	L	0
				UA 193 EFFECTIVE OCT 29					
5	2:15p	L	4:40p	CI	005	FY	74L		0
				CI 005 CONDITIONAL STOPOVER TRAFFIC					
246	3:00p	L	5:25p	JL	063	FY	747		0
				JL 063 CONDITIONAL STOPOVER TRAFFIC					
	3:15p	L	5:40p	CO	925	FYK	D10	D	0
	4:00p	L	6:25p	UA	5	FYK	747	D	0
				UA 5 DISCONTINUED AFTER OCT 28					
	4:00p	L	7:30p	UA	5	FYK	747	D	0
				UA 5 EFFECTIVE OCT 29					

(Contd.)

(Contd.)

Freq.	Leave		Arrive	Flight		Class	Eq	Ml	S
5	4:15p	L	6:40p	PA	809	FYK	747	D	0
				PA 809 DISCONTINUED AFTER OCT 28					
5	4:15	L	7:45p	PA	809	FYK	747	D	0
				PA 809 EFFECTIVE OCT 29					
	6:30p	L	8:50p	WA	610	FYK	D10	D	0
	7:30p	L	11:00p	UA	111	FYK	747	D	0
				UA 111 EFFECTIVE OCT 29					
X5	8:15p	L	10:40p	PA	811	FYK	747	D	0
				PA 811 DISCONTINUED AFTER OCT 28					
X5	8:15p	L	11:45p	PA	811	FYK	747	D	0
				PA 811 EFFECTIVE OCT 29					
	9:15p	L	11:55p	TE	505	FY	D10	D	0
				TE 505 DISCONTINUED AFTER OCT 27					
				TE 505 CONDITIONAL STOPOVER TRAFFIC					
SPEC	9:15p	L	11:55p	TE	505	FY	D10	D	0
				OP OCT 28					
				TE 505 CONDITIONAL STOPOVER TRAFFIC					
1234	9:30p	L	11:55p	CO	903	FYK	D10	D	0
146	11:50p	L	2:15a	CI	007	FY	747		0
				CI 007 CONDITIONAL STOPOVER TRAFFIC					
356	11:55p	L	2:15p	KE	005	FY	D10		0
				KE 005 CONDITIONAL STOPOVER TRAFFIC					
147	11:55p	L	2:15a	KE	005	FY	747		0
				KE 005 CONDITIONAL STOPOVER TRAFFIC					
				CONNECTIONS					
				TAX NOT INCL SEE PGS 10-11					
				FARE CLASS APPL SEE PG 4					
A	227.52		227.52		L	CC			
B	224.00		224.00		F	JT			
C	171.02		171.02		H	CC			
C	156.02		156.02		L	CC			
D	168.15		168.15		H	CC			
D	153.15		153.15		L	CC			
E	164.02		164.02		KH	CC			
E	148.02		148.02		KL	CC			
F	156.00		156.00		YH	JT			
F	141.00		141.00		YL	JT			
77	7:15a	O	11:05p	WA	328	YK	73S		0
(BBCE)	8:18p	SFO	9:00p	PA	841	FYK	747	D	0
				INTRA-STATE AIR CARRIER CONNECTIONS					
X7	7:10a	O	11:05a	PS	191	K	72S		0
(AFF)	8:10a	SFO	9:00a	UA	181	FYK	747	B	0
7	8:00a	O	11:45a	OC	707	SK	73S		0
(D•)	8:55a	SJC	9:30a	UA	1097	YK	DC8	L/	0
67	8:30p	O	9:20p	PS	595	K	72S		0
(AFF)	6:30p	SFO	7:15p	UA	189	FYK	747	D	0

Schedule-C

To **San Francisco / Oakland, Ca.**								PDT	SFO	
HONOLULU, OAHU HAWAII								HST	HNL	
TAX NOT INCL –SEE PGS 10-11										
FARE CLASS APPL-SEE PG 4										
		F	209.00				418.00			
		YH	145.00				290.00			
		YL	130.00				260.00			
		KH	138.00				276.00			
		KL	123.00				246.00			
	PA	KL	122.00				244.00			
		YM	116.00							
	PA	YM	117.00							
	WA	YM	117.00							
7	5:40 a	1:30p	S	OF	3	FY	747	B	0	
OF 3 DISCONTINUED AFTER OCT 22										
OF 3 CONDITIONAL STOPOVE TRAFFIC										
7	6.40a	1:30p	S	OF	3	FY	747	B	0	
OF 3 EFFECTIVE OCT 29										
OF 3 CONDITIONAL STOPOVER TRAFFIC										
	9:10a	5.00p	S	PA	842	FYK	747	L	0	
PA 842 DISCONTINUED AFTER OCT 28										
	9:30a	4:20p	S	U	180	FYK	747	B	0	
UA 180 EFFECTIVE OCT 29										
	9:30a	5:25p	S	U	180	FYK	747	B	0	
UA 180 DISCONTINUED AFTER OCT 28										
	10:10a	5.00p	S	PA	842	FYK	747	L	0	
PA 842 EFFECTIVE OCT 29										
	11:10a	7:05p	S	NW	10	FYK	747	L	0	
X37	11:15a	7:05p	S	QF	3	FY	747	L	0	
OF 3 DISCONTINUED AFTER OCT 28										
OF 3 CONDITIONAL STOPOVER TRAFFIC										
3	11:15a	7:05p	S	QF	3	FY	747	L	0	
OF 3 DISCONTINUED AFTER OCT 25										
OF 3 CONDITIONAL STOPOVER TRAFFIC										
	12:00n	7:50p	S	UA	96	FYK	747	L	0	
UA 96 DISCONTINUED AFTER OCT 28										
	12:30n	8:10p	S	PR	106	FY	D10		0	
PR 106 CONDITIONAL STOPOVER TRAFFIC										
	1:00p	7:50p	S	UA	96	FYK	747	L	0	
UA 96 EFFECTIVE OCT 29										
	1:30p	9:30p	O	UA	1094	YK	DC8	L	0	
UA 1094 DISCONTINUED AFTER OCT 28										
	2:30p	9:25p	O	UA	1094	FYK	DC8	D	0	
UA 1094 DISCONTINUED AFTER OCT 29-FAN 9										
345	2:30p	10:28p	O	WA	582	YK	707	L/	0	
X5	4:10p	11:59p	S	WA	530	FYK	D10	D	0	
	10:10p	6:03a	S	WA	574	FYK	D10	S	0	
124	10:45p	6:40a	S	UA	1184	YK	DC8	S/	0	

(Contd.)

(*Contd.*)

			UA 1184 DISCONTINUED AFTER OCT 28						
SPEC	10:45p	6:40a	S	UA	1184	YK	D8S	S/	0
			OP OCT 25						
	11:10p	7:00a	S	UA	22	FYK	747	S	0
			UA 22 DISCONTINUED AFTER OCT 28						
	11:45p	6:35a	S	UA	22	FYK	747	S	0
			UA 22 EFFECTIVE OCT 29						
124	11:59p	6:45a	S	UA	1184	YK	DC8	S/	0
			UA 1184 EFFECTIVE OCT 29 – DEC 13						
	11:59p	6:54a	S	UA	1184	YK	DC8	S/	0
			UA 1184 EFFECTIVE DEC 14 –JAN 8						
			CONNECTIONS						
			TAX NOT INCL –SEE PGS 10-11 FARE CLASS APPL-SEE PG 4						
A	253.00		253.00			(SMF)			
B	182.00		182.00		H	(SMF)			
B	166.00		166.00		L	(SMF)			
C	174.00		174.00		H	(SMF)			
C	159.00		159.00		L	(SMF)			
	3:15p	12:57a	S	WA	500	FYK	D10	D	S
(ABC)	11:25p	LAX	11:50p	WA		FnYn	725		0

Your client wants to return from San Francisco to Boston on December 17, first thing in the morning. You again refer to the NAOAG and look up to Boston from San Francisco. You select TWA flight 32 departing San Francisco at 8:30 AM and arriving at 4:40 PM. See Schedule-D.

Scheduled-D

Freq.	Leave	Arrive	Flight	Class	Eq.	MI	S	
To **BOSTON , MASS.**						**EST**	**BOS**	
SAN FRANCISCO / OAKLAND, CA.					**PDT**	**SFO**		
	S-SFO,	O-OAK						
		F	286.11	22.89	309.00	618.00		
		Y	220.37	17.63	238.00	476.00		
		FN	220.37	17.63	238.00	476.00		
		YN	175.93	14.07	190.00	380.00		
		YM	178.00					
		H	AP/20	YN	WEEKEND	286.00		
		H	AP/20	YN	MIDWEEK	238.00		
		H	AP/20	YW	7-45 DAY	333.00		
		H	AP/20	YX	7-45 DAY	286.00		
12:25a	S	11:40a	TW	266	FnYn	707	SB	2
12:35a	S	12:26p	DL	612		72S	SB	2
					DL 612 FnYn MSY–FY			
1:00a	S	1:49p	AA	84	FnYn	72S	SBL	3
8:30a	S	4:40p	TW	32	FY	L 10	LS	0
8:40a	S	7:46p	TW	149	FY	707	BLD	2
11:30a	S	7:45p	UA	94	FY	D10	L	0
9:10p	S	8:43a	TW	16	FnYn	L10	S	2
9:30p	S	7:29a	AA	18	FnYn	D10	S	1
10:00p	S	7:46a	TW	44	FnYn	L10	S	1
11:15p	S	11:40a	TW	266	FnYn	707	SB	3

Your next step is to enter the flights you have chosen on your reservation sheet and call the airlines to book the flights. After the airline reservationist has confirmed the flight, you should ask her for the air fare. She has current fare information in her computer. In the example we have your completed reservation sheet as given in Fig. 6.3.

At this time you are ready to compute the air fare. You should refer to the *Squire's Tariff Joint Fares* and look up between Boston and Honolulu. See example below:

Tariff Joint Fare For the Application of Fares, See Rule 3

MARKET	*FARE CLASS*	*FARE*	*ROUTING*	*ROUTING*	*ROUTING*
between BOSTON and Honolulu	F OW	449.00	AL CHI CO	AA/TW CHI CO/NW	UA CHI NW
			AA/DL/EA DFW BN	TW DEN CO/WA	UA DEN WA
			TW LAS WA	AA LAX CO/NW/PA/UA/WA	EA LAX CO/NW/PA/UA/WA
			TW LAX CO/NW/PA/UA/WA	UA LAX PA/WA	DL/EA NYC NW/UA
			NA/TW/UA NYC NW	AA/TW PHX WA	EA PDX CO/PA
			UA PDX NW/PA	AA SAN UA/WA	AA/TW SFO NW/PA/UA/WA
			UA SFO PA/WA	EA SEA CO/PA	UA SEA NW/PA
			UA YVR CP		

We first look under Honolulu. The client is travelling First Class and his outbound routing is via Los Angeles using Trans World Airlines from Boston to Los Angeles and Western from Los Angeles to Honolulu. The time which verifies that your routing is allowed at the joint one-way fare of $449.00 is as follows:

TW LAX CO/NW/PA/VA/WA

The line which verifies your return routing is as follows:

AA/TW SFO NW/PA/VA/WA

We now double the one-way fare of $449.00 to arrive at a round-trip first-class fare of $898.00. Hawaii fares are shown in the tariff without tax. To compute the tax you refer to the Hawaiian tax tables in the OAG. Note that for Boston we must figure the tax from Column 25 of Hawaiian Tax Table II.

RESERVATION SHEET

Name: Mr. Hemant Joshi SS 194 Lowell Street Manchester, New Hampshire	Home Phone 345-6789	Order Rec'd 11-20	Pick up Date 11-22	Fare	898.00
				Tax	
	Office Phone 345-5432	Call Client	Advised Client OK unless we call — X	Total	
				Passport	
				Small Pox	
				Option Date	
				Ticket No.	By

Date	Day	Itinerary	Fl. No.	Class	Status	Leave	Arrive
11 / 23	M T W TH F SA SU	BOS	TW 65	F A T Y K R	OK Req. List	AM 3:00 PM	5:45 AM PM
11 / 25	M T W TH F SA SU	LAX	WA 501	F A T Y K R	OK Req. List	AM 12:35 PM	AM 2:55 PM
12 / 14	M T W TH F SA SU	HNL	WA 530	F A T Y K R	OK Req. List	AM 4:10 PM	AM 11:59 PM
12 / 17	M T W TH F SA SU	SFO	TW 32	F A T Y K R	OK Req. List	8:30 AM PM	4:40 AM PM
	M T W TH F SA SU			F A T Y K R	OK Req. List	AM PM	AM PM
	M T W TH F SA SU			F A T Y K R	OK Req. List	AM PM	AM PM
	M T W TH F SA SU			F A T Y K R	OK Req. List	AM PM	AM PM
	M T W TH F SA SU			F A T Y K R	OK Req. List	AM PM	AM PM
	M T W TH F SA SU			F A T Y K R	OK Req. List	AM PM	AM PM

Fig. 6.3: Specimen of Reservation Sheet.

TAX TABLE I

When the city is: City	Code	Figure the Tax from Colum	When the city is: City	Code	Figure the Tax from Colum
Akron	CAK	18	Ely	ELY	7
Albany, GA	ABY	15	Erie	ERI	19
Albany, NY	ALB	24	Eugene	EUG	4
Albuquerque	ABQ	8	Eureka	ACV	3
Alexandria	E S F	11	Evansville	EVV	15
Allentown	ABE	23			
Amarillo	AMA	9	Fairbanks	FAI	6
Anchorage	ANC	6	Fairmont	FRM	14
Asheville	AVL	18	Fargo	FAR	14
Astoria	AST	4	Fayetteville, AR	FYV	14
Atlanta	ATL	15	Fayetteville, NC	FAY	18
Augusta	AGS	18	Flint	FNT	17
Austin	AUS	9	Florence, SC	FLO	18
			For Lauderdale	FLL	18
Bakersfield	BFL	2	Fort Leonard Wood	TBN	11
Baltimore	BAL	22	Fort Meyers	FMY	18
Bangor	BGR	25	Fort Polk	POE	11
Baton Rouge	BTR	13	Ft. Smith, AR	FSM	11
Beloit	JVL	16	Ft. Wayne	FWA	17
Benton Harbor, MI	BEH	16	Fresno	FAT	2
Billings	BIL	8			
Binghamton	BGM	23	Gainesville, Fia	GNV	15
Birmingham	BHM	15	Galveston	GLS	10
Mismarck	BIS	12	Garden City, Kan	GCK	12
Bloomington, IL	BMI	16	Goldsboro, NC	GSB	22
Boise	BOI	7	Goodland, Kan	GLD	12
Boston	BOS	25	Grand Canyon	GCN	7
Bozeman	BZN	8	Grand Forks	GFK	12
Bradford	BFD	22	Grand Junction	GJT	8
Bristol	TRI	19	Grand Rapids	GRR	17
Brownsville	BRO	9	Great Bend, Kan	GBD	12
Brownwood	BWD	9	Great Falls	GTF	8
Buffalo	BUF	21	Green Bay	GRB	16
Burlington, IA	BRL	16	Greensboro	GSO	20
Butte	BTM	8	Greenville, MS	GLH	11
			Greenville, SC	GSP	18
Calgary	YYC	7	Gulfport	GPT	13
Cape Girardeau	CGI	11			
Casper	CPR	8	Harlingen	HRL	9
Castiegar, BC	YCG	5	Harrisburg	HAR	23
Cedar Rapids	CID	16	Hartford	BDL	25
Champaign	CMI	16	Hays, Kan	HYS	12
Charleston, SC	CHS	18	Helena	HLN	8
Charleston, WV	CRW	18	Homer	HOM	6
Charlotte	CLT	18	Hot Springs	HOT	11
Chattanooga	CHA	15	Houston	IAH	10
Elmira	ELM	22	Lamar, Colo	LAA	12
El Paso	ELP	8	Lansing	LAN	17

(Contd.)

(Contd.)

When the city is: City	*Code*	*Figure the Tax from Colum*
Las Vegas	LAS	7
Laurel/Hattiesburg	PIB	13
Lawton	LAW	9
Lexington	LEX	15
Lincoln	LNK	12
Little Rock	LIT	11
London, ONT	YXU	20
Long Beach	LGB	2
Los Angeles	LAX	2
Louisville	SDF	15
Lubbock	LBB	9
Lynchburg	LYH	21
Macon	MCN	17
Madison	MSN	16
Manitowoc	MTW	17
Mankato	MKT	14
Marion	MWA	16
Mattoon	MTO	16
Medford	MFR	4
Melbourne	MLB	18
Memphis	MEM	15
Merced	MCE	2
Meridian	MEI	16
Miami	MIA	18
Midland, TX	MAF	9
Milwaukee	MKE	16
Minneapolis	MSP	14
Missoula	MSO	8
Mobile	MOB	15
Modesto	MOD	2
Moline	MLI	16
Monroe	MLU	11
Monterey	MRY	3
Montgomery	MGM	15
Montreal	YUL	25
Mt. Vernon	MVN	16
Muskegon	MKG	17
Muscle Shoals	MSL	20
Myrtle Beach	CRE	22
Nashville	BNA	15
Newark	EWR	24
New Bern	EWN	22
New Orleans	MSY	13
Newport News	PHF	23
Pueblo	PUB	9
Quebec, QUE	YQB	25
Quincy	UIN	11
Raleigh	RDU	22
Rapid City	RAP	9
Red Bluff	RBL	4
Redding	RDD	4
Regina, SASK	YQR	14
Reno	RNO	7
Rhinelander	RHI	16
Richmond	RIC	22
Roanoke	ROA	21
Rochester, MN	RST	14
Rochester, NY	ROC	22
Rockville, IL	RFD	16
Sacramento	SMF	2
Saginaw	MBS	17
St. Louis	STL	11
Salem	SLE	4
Salina	SLN	12
Salt Lake City	SLC	8
San Antonio	SAT	10
San Diego	SAN	2
San Francisco	SFO	3
San Jose	SJC	3
Santa Barbara	SBA	2
Santa Maria	SMX	2
Sarasota	SRO	18
Saskatoon, SASK	YXE	14
Savannah	SAV	18
Scotts Bluff	BFF	12
Scranton	AVP	23
Seattle	SEA	5
Shreveport	SHV	14
Sheridan	SHR	8
Sioux City	SUX	12
Sioux Falls	FSD	12
South Bend	SBN	17
Spokane	GEG	7
Springfield, IL	SPI	16
Springfield, MO	SGF	11
Stockton	SCK	2
Syracuse	SYR	23
Tallahassee	TLH	15
Tampa	TPA	18

Fig. 6.4: Specimen of Tax Table I.

Tax Table II

Amount \ Column	1	2	3	4	5	6	7	8	9	10	11	12	13
$ .50	.00	.00	.00	.00	.00	.00	.01	.01	.01	.01	.02	.02	.02
1.00	.00	.00	.00	.00	.00	.00	.01	.02	.03	.03	.03	.03	.03
2.00	.00	.00	.00	.00	.00	.01	.02	.05	.05	.06	.06	.06	.06
3.00	.00	.00	.00	.01	.01	.01	.03	.07	.08	.08	.09	.09	.09
4.00	.00	.00	.00	.01	.01	.02	.04	.09	.10	.11	.12	.12	.13
5.00	.00	.00	.00	.01	.02	.02	.05	.12	.13	.14	.15	.16	.16
6.00	.00	.00	.00	.01	.02	.02	.06	.14	.16	.17	.18	.18	.19
7.00	.00	.00	.00	.02	.02	.03	.07	.16	.18	.20	.21	.22	.22
8.00	.00	.00	.00	.02	.03	.03	.08	.19	.21	.22	.24	.25	.25
9.00	.00	.00	.00	.02	.03	.04	.09	.21	.23	.25	.28	.26	.28
10.00	.00	.00	.00	.02	.03	.04	.10	.23	.26	.28	.31	.31	.32
20.00	.00	.00	.01	.05	.06	.06	.20	.46	.52	.56	.62	.62	.64
30.00	.00	.01	.01	.07	.10	.12	.31	.70	.78	.84	.93	.94	.95
40.00	.00	.01	.02	.09	.13	.16	.41	.93	1.04	1.12	1.22	1.25	1.26
50.00	.01	.02	.02	.12	.16	.20	.51	1.16	1.30	1.41	1.53	1.56	1.58
60.00	.01	.02	.02	.14	.19	.23	.61	1.39	1.56	1.69	1.84	1.87	1.90
70.00	.01	.02	.03	.16	.22	.27	.71	1.82	1.82	2.07	2.14	2.18	2.21
80.00	.02	.02	.03	.19	.26	.31	.82	1.86	2.06	2.25	2.45	2.50	2.53
90.00	.02	.03	.04	.21	.29	.35	.92	2.09	2.34	2.53	2.75	2.81	2.84
100.00	.02	.03	.04	.23	.32	.39	1.02	2.32	2.60	2.81	3.06	3.12	3.16
200.00	.04	.06	.08	.46	.64	.78	2.04	4.64	5.20	5.62	6.12	6.24	6.32
300.00	.06	.09	.12	.69	.96	1.17	3.06	6.96	7.80	8.43	9.18	9.36	9.48
400.00	.08	.12	.18	.92	1.28	1.56	4.08	9.28	10.40	11.24	12.24	12.48	12.64
500.00	.10	.15	.20	1.15	1.60	1.95	5.10	11.60	13.00	14.05	15.30	15.60	15.80

(Contd.)

(*Contd.*)

Amount \ Column	14	15	16	17	18	19	20	21	22	23	24	25
.50	.02	.02	.02	.02	.02	.02	.02	.02	.02	.02	.02	.02
1.00	.03	.03	.04	.04	.04	.04	.04	.04	.04	.04	.04	.04
2.00	.06	.07	.07	.06	.08	.08	.08	.08	.06	.08	.08	.09
3.00	.10	.10	.11	.11	.11	.12	.12	.12	.12	.12	.13	.13
4.00	.13	.14	.14	.15	.15	.16	.16	.16	.17	.17	.17	.17
5.00	.16	.17	.18	.19	.19	.20	.20	.20	.21	.21	.21	.21
6.00	.19	.21	.21	.23	.23	.23	.23	.24	.25	.25	.25	.26
7.00	.23	.24	.25	.26	.27	.27	.27	.28	.29	.29	.29	.30
8.00	.26	.28	.28	.30	.31	.31	.31	.32	.33	.33	.33	.34
9.00	.29	.31	.32	.34	.34	.35	.35	.36	.37	.37	.38	.36
10.00	.32	.35	.35	.38	.38	.39	.39	.40	.41	.41	.42	.43
20.00	.64	.69	.70	.75	.76	.78	.78	.79	.83	.83	.84	.85
30.00	.97	1.04	1.05	1.13	1.15	1.17	1.17	1.19	1.24	1.24	1.25	1.29
40.00	1.29	1.38	1.40	1.50	1.53	1.56	1.56	1.58	1.65	1.65	1.67	1.71
50.00	1.61	1.73	1.76	1.88	1.91	1.95	1.96	1.98	2.07	2.07	2.09	2.14
60.00	1.93	2.07	2.11	2.25	2.29	2.34	2.35	2.37	2.48	2.48	2.51	2.56
70.00	2.25	2.42	2.46	2.63	2.67	2.73	2.74	2.77	2.89	2.89	2.93	2.99
80.00	2.58	2.76	2.81	3.00	3.06	3.12	3.13	3.16	3.30	3.30	3.34	3.42
90.00	2.90	3.11	3.16	3.38	3.44	3.51	3.52	3.56	3.72	3.72	3.76	3.84
100.00	3.22	3.45	3.51	3.75	3.82	3.90	3.91	3.95	4.13	4.13	4.18	4.27
200.00	6.44	6.90	7.02	7.50	7.64	7.80	7.82	7.90	8.26	8.26	8.36	8.54
300.00	9.66	10.35	10.53	11.25	11.46	11.70	11.73	11.85	12.39	12.39	12.54	12.81
400.00	12.88	13.80	14.04	15.00	15.28	15.60	15.64	15.80	16.52	16.52	16.72	17.08
500.00	16.10	17.25	17.55	18.75	19.10	19.50	19.55	19.75	20.65	20.65	20.90	21.35

Fig. 6.5: Specimen of Tax Table II.

THE AIR TICKET: DOMESTIC

ENDORSEMENTS/RESTRICTIONS (CARBON)

ORIGIN: **BOSTON** DESTINATION: **BOSTON**

CONJUNCTION TICKET(S)

AUDITOR'S COUPON

8453:976:709

FROM/TO	CARRIER	FARE CALCULATION
BOS		
LON	TW	
HNL	WA	449.00
SFO	WA	
BOS	TW	449.00

PLACE OF ISSUE – AGENCY

NAME OF PASSENGER: **Hemant / Mr.** NOT TRANSFERABLE ISSUED ON EXCHANGE FOR DATE OF ISSUE: **21 NOV 1919**

COUPONS NOT VALID BEFORE: 1 2 3 4

ORIGINAL ISSUE: CARRIER FORM & SERIAL NUMBER PLACE DATE AGENT NUMBER CODE

COUPONS NOT VALID AFTER: 1 2 3 4

TICKET DESTINATION TOUR CODE

X/O	NOT GOOD FOR PASSAGE	FARE BASES	ALLOW	CARRIER	FLIGHT/	CLASS	DATE	TIME	STATUS
	FROM BOSTON	F		TW	65	F	Nov.22	3:50	OK
O	TO LOS ANGELES	F		WA	501	F	Nov.25	12:00	OK
O	TO HONOLULU	F		WA	530	F	Dec.14	4:18	OK
O	TO SAN FRANCISCO	F		TW	35	F	Dec.17	8:30	OK
O	TO BOSTON	COMMISSION			TAX 44.34				

VOID

COMM. RATE: IN-7 FARE: 898.00

FORM OF PAYMENT

PASSENGER TICKET & BAGGAGE CHECK — ISSUED BY

SUBJECT TO CONDITIONS OF CONTRACT ON PASSENGERS COUPON

CK AIRLINE CODE

FORM SERIAL NUMBER

FARE: 898.00 EQUTV AMT. NO

TAX: 38.34 6.00 TOTAL: 942.34

ǁ "8453976630 1ǁ"

IT IS UNLAWFULL TO PURCHASE OR REDELL TINS TICKET FROM/TO ANY ENTITY OTHER THAN, TIME RESUME CARRIER OR ITS AUTHORITIES AGENTS

Fig. 6.6: Specimen of Air Ticket: Domestic.

First look at Hawaiian Tax Table I. Look up the Continental U.S. city of departure to determine which column of Hawaiian Tax Table II to use. Our total joint fare BOS-NHL is $898.00. In Tax Table II you look under the Column Amount. The amount goes up to only $500.00. So to compute the tax for $898.00, we will use the $400 column first and double the amount. Then use the $90.00 amount and the $8.00 amount.

Column Amount	Column 25
$400	$17.08
400	17.08
90	3.84
8	.34
$898	$38.34

We must now add International Tax of $3.00 for a one-way or $6.00 for round-trip to the tax we just computed. Our total fare is as follows:

Base Fare	$898.00
Tax from Column 25	38.34
International Tax	6.00
TOTAL	$942.34

We are now ready to write the ticket.

INTERNATIONAL AIRLINE TICKET

Example:

Tina Negi comes into the office. She wants to book a round-trip flight from Boston to Paris. She will depart Boston on December 16 and return on December 20. Express the full procedure of international airline ticket by using the necessary information and draw the filled in air ticket in the proper performa.

Solution:

Procedure for International Airline Ticket:

1. As an agent you will refer to the Worldwide Edition (December) of the Airline Guide, and look up to Paris from Boston. See sample page of the Airline Guide.

Freq.	Leave	Arrive		Flight			Class	Eq	S EN.	/Div.
To **PARIS, FRANCE**										**PAR**
BOSTON, MASS, USA 4124/3437										**BOS**
	F	745.00	1490.00							
	YL	320.00	640.00							
	EX/35		YOUTH		YL	501.00				
	EX/41		14-45 DAY		YE	539.00				
	2030		0910+1	CDG	TW	810	FYK	707	0	
				CONNECTIONS						
146	0926		2335	CDG	AA	427	FY	727	0	D-JAN 1
	DCA	1047	IAD	1330	AF	054	R	SSC	0	
26	0926		2335	CDG	AA	427	FY	727	0	E-JAN 2
	DCA	1047	IAD	1330	AF	054	R	SSC	0	
		AF	054	PENDING GOVT. APPROVAL						
14	0925		2335	CDG	AA	427	FY	727	0	E-JAN 2
	DCA	1047	IAD	1330	AF	054	R	SSC	0	
146	1034		2335	CDG	EA	375	FY	727	0	D-DEC 12
	DCA	1150	IAD	1330	AF	054	R	SSC	0	
6	1100		2335	CDG	AA	621	FYV	727	0	D-DEC 13
		1239	IAD	1330	AF	054	R	SSC	0	
15	1430		0730+1	ORY	AA	25	FY	72S	0	
	LGA	1521	JFK	1830	IR	778	FY	74L	0	
15	1430		0730+1	ORY	AA	187	FY	707	0	D-DEC 13
		1526	JFK	1830	IR	778	FY	74L	0	
1567	1600		0835+1	CDG	DL	324	FY	72S	0	
	YUL	1655	YMX	1940	AF	032	FY	747	0	
	2100		1130+1	CDG	BA	270	FYK	747	0	
		0810	LHR	0930	AF	809	FY	A83	0	
X56	2100		1230+1	CDG	BA	270	FYK	747	0	
		0810	LHR	1030	BA	308	FY	L10	0	
56	2100		1230+1	CDG	BA	270	FYK	747	0	
		0810	LHR	1030	BA	308	FY	TRD	0	

2. On a reservation pad write the data, client's name, and home telephone contact. Then write in the flight you have selected and date for customer's flight.
3. Once again refer to the Airline Guide to select her return flight. Look up to Boston from Paris. Her return date is December 20. Transfer this information to the itinerary pad.
4. Call the airline and book the flights. Assuming the flights are available, circle OK and make a note of the airline reservationist's name and the date the booking was made. Give the airline reservationist the passenger's name, home phone contact, and the travel agency's phone number. Check the fare with the airline. They should have the information in their computer. She gives us a fare of YL (coach, low season) $320.00 one way. Double the fare for round trip and add the $3.00 international tax. Review completed sample of itinerary sheet below:

ITINERARY SHEET

Name: Ms. Tina McCarthy 4 Dwight Lane Boston, Mass.	Home Phone (617) 343-0000	Order Rec'd 11-28	Pick up Date 11-30	Fare	640.00
				Tax	3.00
	Office Phone (603) 342-4121	Call Client	Advised Client OK unless we call —	Total	643.00
				Passport	

Date	Day	Itinerary	Fl. No.	Class	Status	Leave	Arrive		
								Small Pox	
								Option Date	
12 16	M T W TH F SA SU	BOS	TW 810	F A T Y K R	OK Req. List	20:30 AM PM	09:10 AM PM	Ticket No.	By
12 20	M T W TH F SA SU	PAR	TW 811	F A T Y K R	OK Req. List Maria	13:45 AM PM	15:35 AM PM	YL 320.00	O.W.
	M T W TH F SA SU	BOS		F A T Y K R	OK Req. 11-28 List	AM PM	AM PM		

Fig. 6.7: Specimen of Itinerary Sheet.

To **BOSTON, MASS, USA**										**BOS**
PARIS, FRANCE 4124/3437										**PAK**
	F			FFR	3775			7550		
	YL			FFR	1765			3530		
	EX/35		YOUTH	YL		FFR	2540			
	EX/41		14-45 DAY	YE		FFR	2735			
	1345	CDG	1535	TW		811	FYK	707	0	
				CONNECTIONS						
	1030	CDG	1405		AF	810	FY	A83	0	
		1030	LHR	1200	BA	271	FYK	747	0	
	1100	CDG	1146		AF	001	R	SSC	0	E-DEC 14
	JFK	0845	LGA	1055	AA	206	FY	72S	0	
	1100	CDG	1219		AF	001	R	SSC	0	D-DEC 13
	JFK	0845	LGA	1130	AA	244	FY	72S	0	
	1100	CDG	1315		AF	001	R	SSC	0	E-DEC 13
	JFK	0845	EWR	1225	EA	54	FY	727	0	
3457	1100	ORY	1405		IR	731	FY	74L	0	
		1100	LHR	1200	BA	271	FYK	747	0	
26	1100	ORY	1405		IR	733	FY	707	0	
		1100	LHR	1200	BA	271	FYK	747	0	
1	1100	ORY	1405		IR	731	FY	707	0	
		1100	LHR	1200	BA	271	FYK	747	0	
4	1200	CDG	1902		TW	803	FYK	747	0	
		1355	JFK	1800	TW	910	YKV	707	0	
1567	1230	CDG	1843		AF	033	FY	747	0	
	YMX	1400	YUL	1750	DL	409	FY	72S	0	
	1300	CDG	1750		AF	077	FYM	747	0	E-DEC 13
		1455	JFK	1645	EA	64	FY	L10	0	
15	1300	ORY	1750		IR	779	FY	741	0	E-DEC 13
		1500	JFK	1645	EA	64	FY	L10	0	
	1300	CDG	1811		AF	077	FYM	747	0	D-DEC 12
		1455	JFK	1720	EA	64	FY	L10	0	
15	1300	ORY	1811		IR	779	FY	74L	0	D-DEC 12
		1500	JFK	1720	EA	64	FY	L10	0	
467	1745	CDG	2328		AF	017	FYM	747	0	D-DEC 13
		1940	JFK	2235	AA	118	FY	707	0	
47	1745	CDG	0010+1		AF	017	FYM	747	0	E-DEC 14
	JFK	1940	LGA	2325	AA	288	FY	72S	0	
467	1745	CDG	0124+1		AF	017	FYM	747	0	
	JFY	1940	LGA	0040	DL	433	FnYn	72S	0	
357	2000	CDG	2120		AF	053	R	SSC	0	D-DEC 31
	IAD	1755	DCA	2013	DL	208	FY	72S	0	
15	2000	CDG	2120		AF	053	R	SSC	0	E-JAN 1
	IAD	1755	DCA	2013	DL	208	FY	72S	0	
		AF	053		PENDING GOVT. APPROVAL					
37	2000	CDG	2120		AF	053	FY	SSC	0	E-JAN 1
	IAD	1755	DCA	2013	DL	208	FY	77S	0	

5. **Re-verify the fare. Refer to the *Air Traffic Worldwide,* Book I. Look up the fare from Boston to Paris. Note the YL one way fare which is $320.00 in the headline city currency (USD) and $302.00 in FCU's.**

FROM/TO	FARE TYPE	HEADLINE CITY CURRENCY	FCU	RULES	MAP RTE REF	CI/MPM VIA PT.
BOSTON (BOS) MAS., U.S.A.		U.S. $ (USD)				
PARIS	F	675.00	636.00			4124
	YL	320.00	302.00			4124
	YH	406.00	383.00			4124
	YLE21	580.00	547.00	N201		4124
	YHE21	674.00	635.00	N202		4124
	YLE45	482.00	454.00	N226		4124
	YHE45	596.00	562.00	N228		4124
	YLZ	477.00	449.00	N151		4124
	YHZ	533.00	502.00	N153		4124
	YLGA	482.00	454.00	N515		4124
	YHGA	596.00	562.00	N517		4124
	YGC	482.00	454.00	N530		4124
	YGV	390.00	368.00	G225		4124
	YLGV	451.00	425.00	G206		4124
	YHGV	561.00	529.00	G207		4124

The fare given by the airline is correct and now this reservation would be ready for ticketing. The above itinerary we have used was a very simple, basic itinerary. Now let's suppose Ms. Negi has decided to stopover in London for a day enroute to Paris. Her itinerary is now BOS-LON-PAR-BOS. We must now check the mileage on the one way BOS-LON-PAR. In the tariff listing the maximum permitted mileage for the YL Boston to Paris fare is 4124. We will now refer to the "Routing-non-stop sector mileages" section of the tariff to check the non-stop sector mileages.

LONDON	UK	LON	Newquary	UK	213
Birmingham	UK	100	New York NY	USA	3456
Bombay	India	4477	Nice	Fra	635
Bordeaux	Fra	449	Norwich	UK	117
Boston Mas	USA	3265	Oporto	Port	801
Bremen	Ger	405	Oslo	Nor	730
Brussels	Bel	211	Palma Majorca	Spain	826
Bucharest	Rom	1302	Paris	Fra	209
Budapest	Hung	917	Perpignam	Fra	612
Cairo	Egypt	2185			

By looking up the mileage under London, we have the sector mileage listings for both BOS-LON and LON-PAR.

BOS	
LON	3265
PAR	209
	3474

Since the allowed mileage is 4124 we are well within the mileage and it is not necessary to increase the fare. More complicated fare itineraries should always be verified with the airline's rate desk. They will give you a rate number, and the rate number should be written on the fare construction portion of the ticket.

In case of international airline the procedure is slightly different from the domestic ticket. The step by step procedure is as follows:

When the client approaches the travel agency, the following information may be acquired.

(1) Name of client
(2) Type of flight
(3) Place of departure
(4) Place of destination
(5) Date of journey/departure
(6) Date of Return
(7) Refer the worldwide edition of and look up to the place of departure from the place of destination.
(8) Write the date, client's name and residential phone contact on reservation pad.
(9) Write the flight you have selected and date for customer's flight.
(10) Again refer the OAG to select return flight of the client. Look up to the place of destination from place of departure. See the date of return.
(11) Transfer all this information to the itinerary pad.
(12) Contact the concern airline and book the flights.
(13) If the flights are available circle 'OK'.
(14) Make a note of the airline reservation's name and date on which the booking was made.
(15) Convey the passenger's name, residential telephone contact and travel agency phase number to the airline reservationist.
(16) Check the fee with the airline.
(17) The fare for round-trip and add the international tax.
(18) Reverify the fare. Refer to the Air Traffic Worldwide Book I (latest edition, Yellow Pages). Check the fare from place of departure to the place of destination. Note the fare.
(19) If you find that the fare given by the airline is correct, the reservationist should be ready for ticketing.

AIRLINE TICKET

ENDORSEMENTS/RESTRICTIONS (CARBON)

ORIGIN	DESTINATION	FROM/TO	CARRIER	FARE CALCULATION
BOSTON	BOSTON	BOS		
		LON	TW	
		PAR	BA	M
		BOS	TW	320.00
				320.00

8453:976:709

PLACE OF ISSUE – AGENCY

CONJUNCTION TICKET(S)

AUDITOR'S COUPON

NAME OF PASSENGER	NOT TRANSFERABLE	ISSUED ON EXCHANGE FOR	DATE OF ISSUE
Negi / T. Ms.			21 NOV 2004

COUPONS NOT VALID BEFORE: 1 2 3 4

ORIGINAL ISSUE: CARRIER FORM & SERIAL NUMBER PLACE DATE AGENT NUMBER CODE

COUPONS NOT VALID AFTER: 1 2 3 4

TICKET DESTINATION

TOUR CODE

X/O	NOT GOOD FOR PASSAGE	FARE BASES	ALLOW	CARRIER	FLIGHT/	CLASS	DATE	TIME	STATUS
	FROM BOSTON	YL		TW	754	Y	Dec.16	1900	OK
O	TO LONDON/HEATHROW	YL		BA	032	Y	Dec.18	1100	OK
O	TO PARIS/CHARLES DeGaule	YL		TW	811	Y	Dec.20	1345	OK
	TO BOSTON	VOID							
	TO VOID								

RATE # 34268

USD

CODE NUMBER	FARE
IN-9	640.00

FORM OF PAYMENT: CHECK

IT IS THIS UNLAWFULL TO PURCHASE OR RESELL TICKET FROM/TO ANY ENTITY OTHER THAN, TIME ISSUING CARRIER OR ITS AUTHORITIES AGENTS

PASSENGER TICKET & BAGGAGE CHECK — ISSUED BY

COMMISSION: 9

TAX: 3.00

SUBJECT TO CONDITIONS OF CONTRACT ON PASSENGERS COUPON

FARE	EQTTV AMT. NO
640.00	USD

TAX	TOTAL
3.00	643.00

FORM SERIAL NUMBER

CK AIRLINE CODE

ıı "8453976709 3ıı"

Fig. 6.8: Specimen of Airline Ticket.

Similarly, in case of stop-over in some other city for a day in route to the place of destination there will be different itinerary. Check the mileage on the same way, in the tariff listing. Thereafter, refer to the 'Routing ... non-stop sector mileages section of the tariff to check the non-stop sector mileages. By looking up the mileage nude the stop-over place, we may get the sector mileage listings for both the segments. Now one can complete the sector mileage by adding. Compare both the mileages: the allowed mileage and the computed mileage. If the computed mileage is well within the allowed mileage, it is not necessary to increase the fare. In case of complicated fare itineraries, verification should be made with the airline rate desk. They will give the rate number. This rate number should be written on the fare construction portion of the ticket.

QUESTIONS AND DISCUSSIONS

Objective Type

Q. 1. From the following list of terms, write the letter of the word, phrase, or name next to the concept/definition that best matches it below:

A Auditor
B Passage
C Port of Call
D Travel Vendor
E Travel and Tourism Market
F Traffic
G Leisure travel
H Block
I Passenger mile
J Cruises
K Retail travel agency
L Ticket agents
M Full-service hotel
N Institutional travel
O Limited service hotel
P Special interest travel
Q Tour wholesaler
R Commercial group travel
S Consolidator
T Convention.

1. .... Travel conducted primarily for reservation, entertainment or sport.
2. ....The segment of the business market that consists of attendees of meetings and conferences.
3. ....A type of hotel that has food and beverage service and a bell staff in addition to guest rooms.
4. ....Airport employees who work at ticket counters, booking reservation, weighing and checking luggage, and issuing tickets.
5. ....Any business that sells as travel-related service.
6. ....Destination where a cruise-ship docks to allow passengers to go ashore.

7. ....A reservation to travel on cruise ship.
8. ....The segment of the travel industry that have the highest ground rate.
9. ....A set number of airline seats that can be sold by wholesalers.
10. ....A wholesaler that sells travel products such as airline space, without assembling them in package tours.
11. ....A business that assembles package vacations to be sold to the public by retail travel agencies.
12. ....A hotel employee responsible for book-keeping, billing and financial record keeping.
13. ....A type of hotel that does not offer full food and beverage service.
14. ....A unit of measurement determined when one passenger travels one mind on a transportation carrier.
15. ....The number of passengers carried by an airline, ship line, railway or bus line.
16. ....The fastest-growing segment of the leisure market.
17. ....The segment of the business market that includes employees of governments, schools and hospitals.
18. ....A gathering of people with a common interest or purpose.
19. ....All the end-users who, at one time or another, purchase a travel product.
20. ....A type of business that sells airline tickets, cruises, accommodation, and other travel arrangements directly to the public.

Q. 2. *Many flights operate on only specific days of the week, thereby requiring extreme caution when constructing itineraries. The days of the week are given a number code and are referred to as "Frequency Codes". Their decodes can be found in the "Abbreviations and Reference Marks" section. (Refer to the Sample Airline Guide).*

FREQUENCY CODES →

To **PEORIA, ILL.**		PIA
From **CHICAGO, ILL.**		**CHI**
	OZ	819
	OZ	955
X67	OZ	821
X6	OZ	859
X67	OZ	831
	OZ	977
	OZ	951
X6	OZ	969
6	OZ	933
X6	OZ	739

A flight will operate every day of the week unless otherwise designated by frequency codes on the extreme left hand side of the schedule. In the above example, OZ flight 859 operates every day *except* Saturday (shown by X6 in the frequency column). When frequency codes appear without an X preceding the day code, the flight will operate on that day (or those days) only. Referring to the above table, OZ 993 operates on day 6 (Saturday) only. (a) OZ 969 operates .... (b) Does OZ 831 operate on Sunday? .... (c) OZ 819 operates ....

Ans.: (*a*) *Every day except Saturday;*

(*b*) *No;*

(*c*) *Every day of the week*

Q. 3. Departure and arrival times are located between the frequency and carrier codes. (Note: Immediately to the left of the 3-letter city code is the time zone of the "To" city and the "From" city.) Examine the following:

	Departure Time	Arrival Time		Time Zone	City Code
To Pittsburg, PA				EDT	PIT
X7	7:03a	8:00a	AL	629	EDT WAS
X7	7:15a	8:06a	NW	323	
	8:15a	9:08a	UA	649	
X7	9:30a	11:30a	AL	633	
X67	10:00a	10:52a	NW	311	
X7	10:33a	11:30a	AL	620	
X6	12:35p	1:27p	NW	341	
X6	1:33p	2:30p	AL	619	
	2:25p	4:00p	AL	626	
	3:03p	4:00p	AL	626	
	3:55p	4:48p	NW	355	
X6	6:33p	7:30p	AL	625	
	6:55p	7:48p	UA	699	
X6	6:59p	9:02p	AL	739	
	8:07p	8:55p	AL	823	
	9:15p	10:00p	NW	389	
	10:00p	10:50p	AL	557	

Departure and arrival times are always printed in the local time of the departure and arrival cities. From the sample schedule above, answer the following:

(*a*) The first morning flight leaves Washington at 7:03 a.m. and arrives in Pittsburgh at 8:00 a.m. local time. AL 633 leaves Washington at .... and arrives in Pittsburgh at 8:00 a.m. local time. AL 633 leaves. **Washington at** .... and arrives in Pittsburgh at ....

(*b*) What day(s) of the week does it operate? ....

(*c*) If the passenger wants to arrive at the Pittsburgh airport near 10:00 a.m. on Sunday, what flight would you suggest to him? ....

(*d*) Does AL 619 operate on Sunday? ....

Ans. *(a) 9:30 a.m.;* *(c) Every day except Sunday;*
(b) 11:30 a.m.; *(d) UA 649;*
(e) Yes.

Q. 4. *Using the NYC to PHL schedules below, let's review the questions given below:*

Freq.	Leave		Arrive		Flight		Class	Eq	MI	S
To PHILADELPHIA Ps/#									**ESI**	**PHL**
P-PHL (INTERNATIONAL)										
N-PHE (NORTHEAST #)										
From **NEW YORK, N.Y.**									**EST**	**NYC**
X7	6:20a	E	7:02a	P	NW	515	FYB	D10		
	7:00a	J	7:48a	P	AA	159	FYB	707		
	7:25a	E	8:04a	P	AA	229	FYB	727		
	7:25a	E	8:10a	P	EA	35	FYB	L10		
7	8:45a	E	9:27a	P	TW	31	FYB	707		
	9:20a	E	9:52a	P	DL	455	FYB	725		
	10:30a	E	11:08a	P	NW	537	FYB	725		
7	11:30a	E	12:12p	P	TW	121	FYB	727		
	12:32a	J	11:10p	P	DL	317	FYB	725		
	1:00p	E	1:38p	P	NA	411	FY	725		
7	1:15p	E	1:55p	P	NW	51	FYB	D10		
	3:20p	J	4:02p	P	EA	810	FYB	L10		
	3:35p	E	4:14p	P	AA	465	FYB	707		
	3:35p	J	4:20p	P	NA	415	FY	725		
16	4:00p	E	4:40p	P	NW	223	FYB	725		
	4:22p	J	5:00p	P	DL	265	FYB	725		
	6:45p	E	7:23p	P	NA	417	FY	725		
	6:45p	J	7:40p	P	TW	573	FYB	725		
	9:00p	E	9:45p	P	AA	325	FnYnB	727		
	9:52p	E	10:33p	P	EA	481	FnYnB	727		

A. (*a*) DL Flight 455 leaves EWR at ...., arriving in PHL at ....

(*b*) The .... (type) aircraft offers .... (class(es) of service)

B. The earliest time on a Saturday one can depart JFK for PHL is at ....

C. A passenger wishes to leave from EWR on Saturday afternoon around 2:00 p.m.

(*a*) What flight could you offer to him? ....

(*b*) At what time will he leave Newark? ....

(*c*) At what time will he arrive in PHL? ....

Ans.: A. *(a) 9.20 a.m.;* *9.52 a.m.* *(b) Boeing 727-200; Jet First Class/ Jet Coach Service Controlled Inventory—Coach;*

B. *7.00 a.m.;*

C. (*a*) *NA 411 (EA 810 Departs JFK)*
(NW 51 operates Sunday only)
(*b*) *1.00 p.m.; 1.38 p.m.*

Q. 5. Here is an extract of part of the RST to CHI Schedule.

Freq.	Leave	Arrive			Flight	Class	Eq	MI	S
To CHICAGO ILL. C-CGX (# FIELD) O-ORD (O'HARE) M-MDW (MIDWAY)								CST	CHI
From **ROCHESTER. MINN.**								CST	RST
	8:10a	9:04a	O	NW	206	FYB	727		
	9:16a	10:20a	O	NC	700	SB	CV5		
	10:30a	11:19a	O	NW	740	FYB	72S		
	11:38a	12:30p	O	NC	295	SB	D9S		
	2:00p	2:50p	O	NW	352	FYB	727		
X6	3:35p	4:27p	O	NC	704	SB	D9S		
	5:45p	6:43p	O	NW	416	FYB	727		

Answer the following questions:

A. (*a*) A passenger wants to depart RST at approximately 9:00 A.M. on a Saturday. What flight closely meets his needs? ....

(*b*) The aircraft is a .... (type) leaving Rochester, Minn. at ...., arriving in CHI at ....

(*c*) The class(es) of service offered is/are ....

B. (*a*) Does the flight departure at 5:45 P.M. operate on Sunday? ....

(*b*) What is the latest flight on Saturday with Jet Custom or Standard Class Service? ....

(*c*) What type of plane is it? ....(code).

Ans.: A. (*a*) *NC 700;*
(*b*) *CV5 (Convair 580, 9:16 a.m.); 10:20 a.m.*
(*c*) *One class standard service.*

B. (*a*) *?*
(*b*) *?*
(*c*) *Controlled Inventory-Coach.*

Q. 6. Below is an extract of a schedule:

Freq.	Leave	Arrive			Flight	Class	Eq	MI	S
To **PITTSBURGH, PA**								EST	PIT
From **ST. LOUIS, MO**								CST	STR
X7	7:00a	9:20a	P	AL	172	SB	D9S	B	0
	7:15a	9:38a	P	TW	76	FYB	707	B	0
X6	9:05a	12:14p	P	TW	546	YB	DC9		1
	11:35a	1:55p	P	AL	180	SB	D9S	S	0
	1:45a	4:08p	P	TW	876	FYB	707	S	0
	2:10p	4:30p	P	AL	242	SB	D9S		0
X6	4:55p	7:18p	P	TW	246	YB	DC9	D	0
X6	6:50p	10:35p	P	AL	230	SB	D95	S	2
	7:00p	9;20p	P	AL	164	SB	D95	D	0

In the schedule above, the symbol "B" has been added to the listing for AL 172 just to the right of the equipment code. Answer the following:

(*a*) a look at the abbreviations and Reference marks—"Food Service" section of your Sample Airline Guide shows the "B" representing ....

(*b*) The last column on the right indicates the number of stops the flight makes.

(*c*) How many stops does TW 546 make? ....

(*d*) What type of meal is served on TW 246? ....

(*e*) How many stops does AL 230 make between PIT and STL? ....

Ans.: (*a*) *Breakfast;*

(*b*) *One;*

(*c*) *Dinner;*

(*e*) *Two.*

Q. 7. Examine the following RST to CHI schedule.

Freq.	Leave	Arrive		Flight		Class	Eq	MI	S
To **CHICAGO, ILL.** **C-CGX (MEIGS FIELD)** **M-MDW (MIDWAY)**								**CST**	**CHI**
From **NASHVILLE, TENN**								**CST**	**BNA**
	7:50a	9:04a	O	DL	760	FYB	D9S	B	O
	9:46a	10:58a	O	EA	258	FYB	727	S	O
	12:05a	1:19p	O	DL	568	FYB	D9S	L	O
	3:40p	4:54p	O	DL	668	FYB	D9S		O
	4:39p	6:00p	O	EA	894	FYB	DC9	S	O
X6	6:55p	8:09p	O	DL	566	FYB	D9S	D/S	O

Let us review the above schedule:

On some flights, only passengers in First Class receive complimentary meal service. On others, passengers in the Coach cabin do not receive the same type of meal service as passengers travelling in First Class. In the above schedule, when travelling First Class on DL 566, passengers receive a full dinner while Coach passengers are served a snack ("B" class passengers receive the same meals as Coach passengers). On EA 894, First Class passengers receive a snack; Coach passengers are not served a meal (no code follows the slash (/)—See Abbreviations and Reference Marks). When only one letter appears with no slash(/), passengers in all compartments (except K/J/L classes) receive the same type of meal service. Do passengers in Coach receive a meal when travelling on EA 258?

Ans.: *Yes.*

Q. 8. *When an aircraft makes stops enroute, some passengers may receive a meal on part of the trip and another meal on another part of the trip. Below is an extract of schedule:*

Freq.	Leave		Arrive		Flight		Class	Eq	Ml	S
To **HOUSTON, TEXAS**									**CST**	**IAH**
IAH (INTERNATIONAL ARPT)										
H-HOU (HOBBY ARPT)										
From **SEATTLE/TACOMA, WASH.**									**PST**	**SEA**
	12:25a	S	9:03a	I	CO	430	FnYnB	72S	B	3
	12:35a	S	7:50a	I	BN	96	FnYnB	727	S	1
	7:45a	S	3:02p	I	CO	984	FYKBL	D10	BL	1
	12:00n	S	7:22p	I	CO	988	FYKBL	D10	LD	1
	1:50p	S	10:32p	I	CO	452	FYKBL	72S	SD	3
	3:00p	S	10:12p	I	CO	724	FYKBL	72S	SD	1

In this schedule, passengers on CO 984 receive both a breakfast and lunch. This is shown by the symbols B and L, not separated by a "/" symbol. You are required to answer the following:

(*a*) What meal service is available on CO 452? ....

(*b*) Do passengers in both First Class and Coach receive the same type of meal? ....

(*c*) Do Coach passengers on BN 96 receive any meal service? ....

Ans.: (*a*) *Snack and Dinner;*

(*b*) *Yes;*

(*c*) *Yes (Snack).*

Q. 9. *Use the following schedule, and answer the question given below:*

A. (*a*) Does the 2:30 p.m. departure from IAH operate on Friday? ....

(*b*) What type of aircraft is it? ....

(*c*) How many stops does it make? ....

(*d*) What airline operates the flight? ....

(*e*) Do they offer Coach service on this flight? ....

B. At what airport does NA 474 arrive? ....

Freq.	Leave		Arrive		Flight		Class	Eq	Ml	S
To **NEWYORK, N.Y.** **E-EWR (NEW ARK) J-JFK (KENNEDY)** **F-LGA (LAG SUARDLA) W-JRB (WALL ST.)** **F-FLU (FLUSHING)**									**EST**	**NYC**
From **HOUSTON, TEXAS**									**CST**	**IAH**
#										
	6:45a	I	12:49p	J	DL	326	FYB	72S	BL	2
X6	7:00a	I	12:20p	E	BN	20	FYB	727	SB	1
	7:00a	I	1:44p	J	NA	64	FY	D10	BL	2
	8:30a	I	12:30p	L	DL	370	FYB	72S	BL	0
	8:40a	I	1:59P	E	DL	116	FYB	72S	BL	1
	9:00a	I	12:51p	L	EA	50	FYB	727	BL	0
	10:40a	I	3:28p	#	DL	122	FYB	72S	LS	1
	11:30a	I	5:54p	E	EA	380	FYB	72S	LS	2
	12:#	I	4:18p	#	EA	64	FYB	727	LS	0
	12:25p	I	4:25p	J	DL	224	FYB	72S	LS	0
	12:45p	I	8:20p	L	AA	26	FYB	727	LS	3
	1:30p	I	6:15p	J	NA	474	FY	727	SO	3
	2:00p	I	7:15p	L	BN	100	FYB	727	D	1
X6	2:30p	I	7:40p	L	AA	290	FYB	727	S	1
	3:00p	I	8:25p	E	SN	26	FYB	727	D	1
	4:00p	I	7:55p	L	EA	52	FYB	727	D	0
X6	4:20p	I	8:00p	L	DL	218	FYB	727	D	0
X6	5:50p	I	9:40p	E	EA	56	FYB	727	D	0
	6:31p	I	11:27p	L	EA	554	FYB	72S	D	1
	9:25p	I	1:23a	J	EA	494	FnYnB	727	S	0

C. A passenger has an engagement in New York at 1: 00 p.m.

(*a*) What flight would you offer him? ....

(*b*) What is the departure time? ....

D. What type of meal is served on NA 474? ....

Ans.: A. (*a*) *Yes;* (*c*) *One;*

(*b*) *Boeing 727 Jet;* (*d*) *American Airlines;*

(*e*) *Yes.*

B. (*a*) *JFIC (Kennedy)*

C. (*a*) *DL 370;* (*b*) *8.30 a.m.; (EA 50 arrives in New York at 12:51 p.m. which would not allow the passengers enough time to get into the city. B on 20 and DL 326 arrive around the same time on DL 370, but both leave much earlier—an in convenience to the passenger)*

D. *Snack and Dinner.*

Q. 10. *Assuming that the Standard off-line connecting time at O'Hare Airport is 50 minutes. Shorter connecting times are printed for those airlines who share the same area in the airport. At O'Hare, AA, Dl and NC share the same wing of the terminal. Only 40 minutes are required for transfer between these airlines. Answer the following:*

(*a*) What is the minimum connecting time at ORD for transfer from Air Canada (AC) to TWA? ....

(*b*) If a passenger arrived at O'Hare on Continental Airlines at 4:00 p.m., at what time could he leave if his transfer was to Eastern Air Lines? ....

(*c*) If a passenger arrived at O'Hare on Delta Air Lines at 4: 00 p.m., at what time could he leave on another Delta Air Lines Flight? ....

Ans.: (*a*) *40 minutes;*

(*b*) *4:30 p.m.;*

(*c*) *4:30 p.m.*

Q. 11. Here is a connecting schedule given below:

To POCATELLO, IDAHO									MST	PIN
From CHICAGO, ILL M-MDW, O-ORD C-CGX CONNECTIONS									CST	CHI
9:15a	O	2:15p	AA	563	FYB	727	B	0		
11.28a	SLC	1:40p	WA	406	YB	73S		0		

Review the schedule and answer the following:

(*a*) In this schedule, the passenger leaves Chicago's O'Hare Airport at ...., arriving at Pocatello at ....

(*b*) The flight number from ORD to the connecting city ...., (name of city) is .... (carrier code and number).

(*c*) The .... (type) aircraft arrives in the connecting city at ....

(*d*) There the passenger changes to .... (carrier name) Airlines flight number .... leaving at ....

(*e*) This flight makes .... Stop/s.

(*f*) What class/es of service is/are available on AA 563? ....

(*g*) Is there meal service on A 563? ....

Ans.: (*a*) *9.15 a.m.; 2.15 p.m.;*

(*b*) *Salt Lake City; AQA 563;*

(*c*) *Boeing 727; 11.28 a.m.;*

(*d*) *Western; 406; 1.40 p.m.;*

(*e*) *O;*

(*f*) *Jet First Class, Jet Coach and Controlled Inventory Coach*

(*g*) *Yes (Breakfast).*

Q. 12. In the Airline Guide, direct schedules are shown prior to the connecting schedules. If no direct schedules exist, only connections will be shown. Analyse the following schedule and answer the questions given below:

To **NASHVILLE, TENN**									**CST**	**BNA**
From **COLUMBUS, OHIO C-CMH. O-OSU**									**EST**	**CMN**
				CONNECTIONS						
X7	7.30a	C	8.55a	NC	421	SB	D9S			0
	7.55a	DAY	9.00a	AA	357	FYB	727		S	0
	8.40a	C	10.53a	AA	489	FYB	707		S	0
	9.26a	SDF	11.14a	AA	603	FYB	727			0
	10.15a	C	2.09p	AA	33	FYB	727			1
	11.36a	CVG	2.20p	AA	255	FYB	727			0
	5.48p	C	9.22p	AL	358	SB	B11			0
	6.25p	PIT	9.00p	AL	245	SB	D9S			0
X6	6.05p	C	9.24p	TW	159	FYB	B3J			0
	6.42p	CVG	9.35p	AA	35	FYB	727			0
	CAMPUS CHRISTI TEXAS								**CST**	**CRP**
				CONNECTIONS						
X6	9.45a		12.55p	BN	24	FYB	727			0
	10.45a	DFW	11.30a	BN	14	FYB	727		L	0
X6	1.50p		6.34p	BN	140	FYB	72S			0
	2.50p	DFW	5.05p	AA	568	FYB	727		S	0
	2.45p		8.00p	TI	870	SB	DC9			0
	3.27p	IAH	6.30p	AA	670	FYB	707		D	0
X6	4.45p		9.07p	BN	30	FYB	727			0
	5.45p	DFW	7.40p	AA	622	FYB	727			0
6	6.35p		12.57a	BN	282	FYB	72S			1
	8.30p	DFW	10.40p	AA	264	Fn/YnB	727			1

(*a*) If a passenger wishes to leave Columbus as late as possible on Saturday, wKat departure time would you suggest to him? ....

(*b*) At what time would he arrive in Nashville? ....

Ans.: (*a*) *5.48 p.m.;*

(*b*) *9.22 p.m.*

Q. 13. Schedules for Commuter and Intra-State carriers can be found directly after "CONNECTIONS" and use the same format as a direct flight of a Certified Air Carrier (if no connections are published, then Commuter and Intra-State carriers are located directly after "Certificated Direct Flights").

In the example, Midstate Airlines (IU) operates between Chicago and Stevens Point with one stop. What type of aircraft does Midstate Airlines use? .... ,

Freq.	Leave		Arrive		Flight		Class	Eq	MI	S
To	**CHICAGO, ILL** C-CGX (MEIGS-FIELD), O-ORD (O'HARE) M-MDW (MIDWAY)								CST	CHI
From	**STEVENS POINT,** S-STE C-CWA								CST	STE
	7:51a	C	9:20a	O	NC	450	SB		D9S	1
	12:57p	C	2:30p	O	NC	452	SB		D9S	1
	3:30p	C	5:35p	O	NC	454	SB		CV5	2
	4:32p	C	7:00p	O	NC	574	SB		CV5	2
	4:55p	C	5:39p	O	NC	576	SB		D9S	0
	6:25p	C	8:10p	O	NC	456	SB		D9S	1
					COMMUTER AIR CARRIERS					
	7:05a	S	8:30a	O	IU	10	A		B99	1
X67	12:50p	S	2:20p	O	IU	16	A		B99	1
	3:45p	S	5:10p	O	IU	12	A		B99	1

Ans.: *B 99 (Beach 99).*

Q. 14. One-way and round-trip fares for direct flight are published immediately preceding the direct flight schedules. These fares will only apply to direct flights. Connection fares will be discussed later.

To **MIAMI, FLA**							EST	MIA
From **DALLAS/FT. WORTH, TEXAS** D-DFW L-DAL							CST	DFW
	F	142.59	11.41	154.00	309.00			
	Y	95.37	7.63	103.00	206.00			
8:45a	D	12:05a	BN	79	FYB	72S	B	0
9:00a	D	12:20p	EA	977	FYB	727	B	0
12:05p	D	3:25p	BN	63	FYB	72S	L	0
2:30p	D	5:50p	BN	243	FYB	72S	S	0
5:20p	D	8:40p	BN	169	FYB	72S	D	0
6:00p	D	10:10p	BN	127	FYB	72S	D	1
7:15p	D	11:23p	BN	67	FYB	72S	D	1

Let us analyse and review the above schedule.

The first fare line contains the Jet First Class fares (designated by the letter F.) The one-way fare, shown as the first item immediately following the letter designating the type of service, is published without tax, followed by the amount of tax and then the *total one-way fare*. The last amount in the column is the round-trip fare, published *only* with tax included. In the above example, the First Class one-way jet fare from DFW to MIA is $142.59 U.S. dollars. The tax on this amount is shown as $11.41 and the total one-way First Class fare is published as $154.00. The round-trip Jet

First Class fare is $308.00 including tax. One-way Jet Coach is $95.37.

(*a*) The tax one-way is .... and the total one-way Jet Coach fare is ....

(*b*) The round-trip Jet Coach fare including tax is ....

Ans.: (*a*) *$7.63; $103.00;*

(*b*) *$206.00.*

Q. 15. Many times numerous fares will appear in the heading. The fare to be selected from the group is the one corresponding to the class of service the passenger is using.

In the schedule given below, if a passenger were flying on NC 450 "S" class one-way, his fare would be $39.81 (plus tax). However, if his reservation was on IU 10, which offers "A" (Propeller First Class) only, he must pay the "A" fare of $33.33 (plus tax). The "A" fare would be charged only if he were travelling on an "IU" (a Commuter Air Carrier) flight.

Freq.	Leave	Arrive	Flight	Class	Eq	MI	S
To **CHICAGO, ILL** **C-CGX (MEIGS FIELD) O-ORD (O'HARE)** **M-MDW (MIDWAY)**						**CST**	**CHI**
From **STEVENS POINT, WIS** **S-STE C-CWA**						**CST**	**STE**
	A	33.33 2.67	36.00	72.00			
	S	39.81 3.19	43.00	86.00			
	7:51a C	9:20a O	NC	SB		D9S	1
	12:57p C	2:30p O	NC	SB		D9S	1
	3:30p C	5:35p O	NC	SB		CVS	2
	4:32p C	7:00p O	NC	SB		CVS	2
	4:55p C	5:39p O	NC	SB		D9S	0
	6:25p C	8:10p O	NC	SB		D9S	1
		COMMUTER AIR CARRIERS					
	7:05a S	8:30a O	IU	A		B99	1
X67	12:50p S	2:20p O	IU	A		B99	1
	3:45p S	5:10p O	IU	A		B99	1

Answer the following questions:

A. (*a*) If a passenger had an "S" class reservation on NC 576, what fare would be pay for round-trip travel including tax? ....

(*b*) If another passenger travelled round-trip on "IU", what fare would apply? ....

B. If a passenger was flying to his destination on NC "S" and returning on IU, his total round-trip fare before tax would be $ .... (Just add NC's one-way S fare to IU's A fare).

Ans.: A. *(a) $86.00;*
(b) $72.00;
B. *$73.14.*

Q. 16. Coach and Economy Fares to or from Hawaii and Puerto Rico are based on the day of the week travel commences.

YH—Peak—applies 12:01 a.m. Friday thru midnight Sunday unless otherwise noted with fare.

YL—Off Peak—applies 12:01 a.m. Monday thru midnight Thursday unless otherwise noted with fare.

The fares are published without U.S. Transportation Taxes. Taxes on Hawaiian travel (other than $3.00 International Travel Tax) must be computed by using charts in the front of the NAOAG.

To **HONOLULU, OAHU; HAWAII**									**HST**	**HNL**
From **SEATTLE/TACOMA, WASH.**									**PST**	**SEA**
S-SEA B-BFI										
	TAX NOT INCL. SE PGS 10-11									
	F	201.41			402.82					
	YL	123.41			246.82					
	YH	139.41			278.82					
	KL	116.41			232.82					
	KH	131.41			262.82					
	YL	104.41								
8:45a	S	12:30p	NW	87	FYK	747		L	0	
9:00a	S	12:45p	CO	981	FYK	D10		SL	0	
9:15a	S	12:55p	PA	895	FYK	747		L	0	
1:05a	S	6:10p	NW	95	FYK	D10		D	1	
1:05p	S	7:35p	NW	95	FYK	D10		D	2	

Analyse and examine the schedule and answer the following question:

A passenger flying Jet Coach between Seattle and Honolulu on Thursday pays $123.41 one-way before tax. If travel was on Saturday, the round-trip Jet Coach fare before tax would be ....

Ans.: *$278.82.*

Q. 17. Many discounted fares are also published in the fares section of each listing. Below is a part of a schedule.

To **CHICAGO, ILL**							**CST**	**CHI**
From **DUBUQUE, IOWA**							**CST**	**DBQ**
	A	30.56	2.44	33.00	66.00			
	S	31.48	2.52	34.00	68.00			
	YM	25.00						
XV	YZ	25.00						
		XV EX/30		A 30 DAY	56.00			
		OZ EX/2		S 30 DAY	54.00			
		XV EX/33		A 30 DAY	43.00			
	B	OZ EX/5		SL 30 DAY	48.00			
	7:27a	8:05A	O	OZ	980	SB	D9S	0
	1:54p	2:59p	O	OZ	866	SB	FH7	1
X6	9:35p	10:38p	O	OZ	888	SB	FH7	1
		COMMUTER AIR CARRIERS						
X67	8:40a	9:48a	O	XV	22	A	899	1
	11:45a	12:53p	O	XV	24	A	899	1
X67	3:00p	4:08p	O	XV	26	A	899	1
	6:20p	7:28p	O	XV	28	A	899	1

Review the above schedule and answer the following questions given below:

The reduced fare for Military Reservation passengers is coded YM. Reduced fares are listed one-way, *including tax*. In the Dubuque to Chicago schedule above, the Military Reservation fare on OZ is $25.00, including tax. "XV" offers a "Youth Fare" (YZ); how much is it? ....

Ans.: *$25.00.*

Q.18. Published in the fares section of each listing are Excursion fares (if any) which are coded EX/(number), this number corresponds to a note number in the "Excursion Fare Note Explanation" pages in your NAOAG. All Excursion fares are published for round-trip travel and are always shown including tax.

(*a*) In the above schedule, from DBQ to CHI, an EX/33 Excursion fare is ....

(*b*) For what carrier does EX/33 apply? ....

Ans.: *(a) $ 43.00;*

(b) XV (Mississippi Valley Airways, Inc.)

Q. 19. Review the following schedule and answer the questions given below:

A. (*a*) If a passenger wishes to arrive in Washington (National Airport) around noon what flight/flights would you recommend? ....

(*b*) On what type of equipment would the passenger fly? ....

(*c*) How many stops would he make? ....

To **WASHINGTON, D.C.** **N-DCA (NATIONAL) D-1AD (DULLES)** **I-BAL (BALTIMORE) WASHINGTON INT'L**							**EST**	**WAS**
From **ELMIRA, N.Y.**							**EST**	**ELM**
		A	38.00	3.11	42.00	84.00		
	CB	A	46.30	3.70	50.00	100.00		
	AL	YM	32.00					
	CB	YM	46.01					
	B	AL EX/5		S 30	DAY	59.00		
	2.56p	4.55p	N	AL	318	AB	CV5	1
				CONNECTIONS				
X7	8.30a	11.48a	D	AL	458	SB	B11	1
	9.50a	LGA	10.50a	SO	713	SB	DC9	0
X7	8.30a	12.03p	N	AL	458	SB	B11	1
	9.50a	LGA	11.05a	AA	463	FYB	727	0
X67	1.19p	3.48p	N	AL	247	SB	D9S	0
	2.05p	PIT	3.00p	NW	338	FYB	727	0
6	4.11p	6.51p	N	AL	461	SB	B11	0
	5.00p	PIT	6.00p	#	960	FYB	737	0
X6	4.11p	8.55p	N	AL	461	SB	B11	0
	5.00p	PIT	8.05p	NW	354	FYB	727	0
	4.11p	9.00p	N	AL	461	SB	B11	0
	5.00p	PIT	8.15p	UA	658	FYB	727	0
				COMMUTER AIR CARRIERS				
X67	1.15p	3.00p	N	C8	300	A	SWM	1
X67	4.00p	5.45p	N	C8	500	A	SWM	1

B. (*a*) A passenger wishes to depart Elmira at 3: 00 p.m. What flight/flights would you recommend? ....

(*b*) What would be his "normal" one-way fare including tax? ....

(*c*) At what airport would he arrive? ....

C. (*a*) What would be the Military Reservation fare for an army captain flying to DCA on CB (Commuter Airlines)? ....

(*b*) On what days could the captain travel? ....

Ans.: A. (*a*) *AL 458 Connecting at LGA to AA 463;*

(*b*) *B 11 and 727;*

(*c*) *2 (LGA + 1);*

B. (*a*) *AL 318; $42.00; National;*

C. *$46.01; Monday thru Friday.*

Q. 20. Determining fares for connecting service in the concerned Airline Guide is a simple procedure. First, select the connection flight and class of service as before.

(*a*) If the passenger wishes to leave Houston some time before

9 : 00 a.m. using the schedule shown above you would suggest the flight departing at .... a.m.

To **AKRON/CANTON, OHIO**								**EST**	**CAK**
From **HOUSTON, TEXAS** **I-IAH H-HOU**								**CST**	**IAH**
			CONNECTIONS						
6.45a	I	12.26p	DL	326	FYB	72S	B	0	
9:18a ATL 10:55a			UA	600	FYB	737	S	0	
11:38a	I	6:27p	EA	380	FYB	72S	L	0	
2:20p ATL 5:00p			UA	570	FYB	727	D	0	
11:45a	I	6:43p	DL	156	FYB	72S	L	0	
1:50p ORD 3:45a			AL	222	SB	D9S		1	
3:00p	I	7:54p	AA	146	FYB	707	D	0	
6:22p PIT 7:26p			AL	187	SB	D9S		0	

(*b*) This flight arrives in the connecting city at .... a.m. . Akron at .... p.m. The clases of service offered on both flights are ....

Ans.: (*a*) *6.45 a.m.;*

(*b*) *9.18 a.m.;* *12.26 p.m.;*

Jet First Class/Jet Coach/Controlled Inventory Coach.

Q. 21. *When the connecting flights and classes of service have been selected, note the Fare Code Identifier located in the parentheses immediately to the left of the connecting city arrival time (on the second line of the connection). For the flight departing from Houston at 6:45 a.m. and arriving in the connecting city at 9:18 a.m., the Fare Identifier is BD@.*

FARE CODE IDENTIFIER

To **AKRON/CANTON, OHIO**								**EST**	**CAK**
From **HOUSTON, TEXAS** **I-IAH H-HOU**								**CST**	**IAH**
			CONNECTIONS						
			CONNECTION FARE LOCATION						
	6.45a I 12.26p	DL	326	FYB	72S	B	0		
(BD@)	9:18a ATL 10:55a	UA	600	FYB	737	S	0		
	11:38a I 6:27p	EA	380	FYB	72S	L	0		
(BD@)	2:20p ATL 5:00p	UA	570	FYB	727	D	0		
	11:45a I 6:43p	DL	156	FYB	72S	L	0		
(AC@)	1:50p ORD 3:45a	AL	222	SB	D9S		1		
	3:00p I 7:54p	AA	146	FYB	707	D	0		
(BD@)	6:22p PIT 7:26p	AL	187	SB	D9S		0		

Review the above schedute and answer the following question.

What is the Fare Code Identifier for the flight leaving Houston at 11:45 a.m. and arriving in the connecting city at 1:50 p.m.? ....

Ans.: *AC@.*

Q. 22. Many cities have more than one airport serving the area. Whenever this is true, a one-letter symbol representing the departure and/or arrival airport is shown immediately the applicable departure or arrival time. This symbol is decoded in the heading of the "To" and the "From" listings.

DEPARTURE AIRPORT CODE — ARRIVAL AIRPORT CODE

To **CHICAGO, ILL** — CDT — CHI
C-CGX (MEGIS FIELD) O'-ORD (O'HARE), M-MID (MIDWAY)

From **Washington, D.C.** — EDT — WAS

D-IAD	N-DCA		I-BAL			
	7:25a	D	9:20a	O	UA	659
	7:30a	N	8:19a	O	AA	563
X7	7:40a	N	9:25a	O	NW	39
X7	8:00a	N	8:49a	O	TW	237
	8:10a	I	9:00a	O	UA	253
	8:10a	N	9:02a	O	UA	271
X7	8:30a	I	9:14a	O	TW	117
	8:30a	N	9:24a	O	AA	285
X7	8:50a	N	11:29a	O	AA	429
	10:00a	N	11:46a	O	UA	285
	10:10a	N	11:02a	O	UA	327
	10:20a	N	11:09a	O	UA	183
	10:20a	D	11:15a	O	NW	3
	10:30a	N	11:17a	O	AA	223
	11:15a	N	12:03p	O	UA	277
	11:20a	I	12:10p	O	UA	171
	11:30a	N	12:21p	O	UA	423
	12:10p	N	12:59p	O	TW	377
	12:15p	I	12:59p	O	TW	445
	12:15p	N	1:57p	O	TW	493
X6	12:30p	N	1:16p	O	AA	525
X6	12:35p	N	2:57p	M	NW	341

From the example above answer the following:

(*a*) All AA flights depart from Airport.

(*b*) What airport does NW 341 arrive at? ....

(*c*) If a passenger wanted to make a reservation for a flight leaving Washington's National Airport on a Sunday around 8:00 a.m., what flight should he take? ....

(*d*) He would arrive at .... Airport at ....

Ans.: *(a) National Airport (see decode of DCA);*

(b) Midway;

(c) UA 271;

(d) O'Hare; 9:02 a.m.

Q. 23. Several more items are introduced in this sample SFO to MSY schedule as given below:

To **NEW ORLEANS, LA**										**CST**	**MSY**
From **SAN FRANCISCO CALIFPST SFO**										CLASS(ES) OF SERVICE	
	12:25a	S	8:07a	M	NA	28	FnYnB	725			
	7:44a	S	2:32p	M	DL	972	FYBJ	D85			
	10:35a	S	5:21p	M	DL	814	FYBJ	DC8		TYPE OF AIRCRAFT	
	1:23p	S	8:11p	M	DL	928	FYBJ	D85			
	1:25p	S	7:05p	M	NA	46	FYBJ	D10			
56	9:20p	S	4:12a	M	DL	984	FnYnB	D85			

The two items introduced are (1) the class(es) of service offered to a passenger on each particular flight, and (2) the type of aircraft. You will recall both of these items are decoded in the "Abbreviations and Reference Marks" section in the front of an airline guide. Using this section, answer the following:

(*a*) Determine flight number 972 is operated by .... (name of airline).

(*b*) Determine class(es) of service............... every "capital" letter represents a class of service on a given flight. To indicate "night" service, an "n" is used; *i.e.*, Fn–Night Coach Class in First Class Compartment and Yn–Night Coach Class Service.

(*c*) What classes of service are offered on National Airlines Flight 28? ....

(*d*) What type of equipment is used? ....

Ans. *(a) Delta Airlines;*

(b) Night Coach Class in First Class Compartment;

(c) Night Coach Class/Controlled Inventory–Coach;

(d) Boeing 727-200.

Q. 24. Below are given specimen Schedules Information:

To GRAND RAPIDS, MICH **EDT** **GRR**
13.0 MI SE 30 MIN T RA

From CHICAGO, ILL M-MDW **CDT** **CHI**
O-ORD C-CGX P-PIT A-AGC

		F	27.78	2.22	30.00	60.00		
		S	21.30	1.70	23.00	46.00		
		Y	21.30	1.70	23.00	46.00		
		YM	17.00					

Freq.	Leave		Arrive	Flight		Class	Eq	S
7	5:55a	O	7:38a	UA	572	FYB	737	0
X67	8:00a	O	10:09a	NC	911	SB	CV5	1
	8:44a	O	10:27a	UA	642	FYB	737	0
	12:00n	O	1:46p	UA	650	FYB	737	0
	12:30p	O	2:36p	NC	915	SB	CV5	1
	1:15p	O	3:00p	UA	770	FYB	737	0
	3:25p	O	5:10p	UA	628	FYB	737	0
	4:50p	O	6:56p	NC	919	SB	CV5	1
X6	7:20p	O	8:57p	NC	106	SB	D9S	0
	7:40p	O	9:28p	UA	626	FYB	737	0
	9:30p	O	11:07p	NC	927	SB	D9S	0

Freq. Leave Arrive Flight Class Eq MI S

To CHICAGO, ILL **CDT** **CHI**
C-CGX (MEIGS FIELD)
O-ORD (O'HARE) M-MDW (MIDWAY)

From SPRINGFIELD, ILL **CDT** **SPI**

		A	25.93	2.07	28.00	56.00
QX	1	A	25.93	2.07	28.00	56.00
		1	INTRASTATE			
		S	27.78	2.22	30.00	60.00
UX		YM	19.00			
OZ		YM	22.00			
UX		YZ	19.00			
			QX-YM 19.00			
		*	INTRASTATE			
		QX*YZ	19.00			
		*	INTRASTATE			

Freq.	Leave	Arrive		Flight		Class	Eq	S
	6:27a	7:40a	O	OZ	920	SB	D9S	1
X67	9:35a	11:00a	O	OZ	816	SB	FH7	1
	11:05a	12:15p	O	OZ	956	SB	D9S	1
X67	1:00p	2:00p	O	OZ	820	SB	FH7	0
67	2:20p	3:45p	O	OZ	890	SB	FH7	1
X67	3:05p	4:30p	O	OZ	826	SB	FH7	1
X6	4:47p	5:47p	O	OZ	842	SB	FH7	0
	5:25p	6:25p	O	OZ	848	SB	FH7	0
X6	7:03p	8:30p	O	OZ	854	SB	FH7	1
		INTRA – STATE						
X67	7:00a	7:45a	C	QX	701	A	748	0
X67	9:00a	9:45a	C	QX	703	A	748	0
X67	1:45p	2:30p	C	QX	705	A	748	0
X67	3:45p	4:30p	C	QX	707	A	748	0
X67	5:45p	6:30p	C	QX	709	A	748	0
		COMMUTER AIR CARRIERS						
X67	7:20a	8:20a	C	UX	212	A	DTO	0
67	1:30p	2:30p	C	UX	422	A	DTO	0
X67	4:30p	5:30p	C	UX	152	A	DTO	0

Freq.	Leave		Arrive	Flight		Class	Eq	Ml	S
To **MIAMI, FLA**								**EDT**	**MIA**
From **PITTSBURGH, P.A.**			**P-PIT A-AGC**					**EDT**	**PIT**
		F	108.33	8.67	117.00		234.00		
		Y	83.33	6.67	90.00		180.00		
		FN	83.33	6.67	90.00		180.00		
		YN	65.74	5.26	71.00		142.00		
		YM	68.00						
EX/4 Y7-21 DAY 139.00									
	9:00a	P	11:19a	EA	303	FYB	D9S	B	0
EA 303 DISCONTINUED AFTER DEC 2									
	9:00a	P	11:19a	EA	303	FYB	72S	B	0
EA 303 EFFECTIVE DEC 3									
	9:10a	P	2:04p	EA	731	FYB	D9S	L	3
	9:55a	P	12:15p	UA	563	FYB	727	L	0
	12:05p	P	3:26p	EA	305	FYB	727	L	1
	5:50p	P	9:37p	EA	327	FYB	727	D	1
	6:30p	P	8:50p	UA	315	FYB	727	D	0
	6:55p	P	10:07p	EA	309	FYB	72S	D	1
	10:35p	P	12:56a	EA	483	FnYnB	D9S	S	0
EA 483 EFFECTIVE DEC 16									

Freq.	Leave		Arrive	Flight		Class	Eq	Ml	S
To **GRAND JUNCTION, COLD**								**MDT**	**GJT**
From **SALT LAKE CITY, UTAH**								**MDT**	**SLC**
		A	27.78	2.22	30.00		60.00		
	FS	A	36.11	2.89	39.00		78.00		
		S	27.78	2.22	30.00		60.00		
	FL	YM	22.00						
6	1:50p		2:42p	FL	578	S	CV5	S	O
				FL	578 EFFECTIVE DEC 7				
	6:28p		7:20p	Fl	515	S	CV5	S	O
				CONNECTIONS					
A	77.78		6.22	84.00			CC		
B	73.15		5.85	79.00			CC		
C	62.67		5.01	67.68	S		CC-T		
D	60.82		4.87	65.69			CC-T		
E	42.59		3.41	46.00	S		(GUC)		
	7:25a		10:45a	TT	989	SB	DC9	B	0
(C@)	8:30a DEN		10:00a	FL	63	SB	73S		0
	7:35a		10:45a	FL	14	SB	73S	B	0
(E@)	8:40a DEN		10:00a	FL	63	SB	73S		0
	7:40a		10:45a	UA	166	FYB	727	B	0
(AC@)	8:45a DEN		10:00a	FL	63	SB	73S		0
	12:00n		2:39p	FL	62	SB	73S	L	0
(BD@)	1:03p DEN		1:55p	UA	303	FYB	727		0
X6	3:30p		6:47p	TT	987	SB	DC9		0
(C@)	4:35p DEN		5:50p	FL	677	SB	CV5	S	0
X6	5:00p		8:44p	FL	66	SB	73S	S	0
(E@)	6:03p DEN		7:47p	FL	675	SB	CV5		0
6	5:00p		9:04p	FL	66	SB	73S	S	0
(E@)	6:03p DEN		7:47p	FL	875	SB	CV5		1
X6	6:25p		9:27p	WA	492	Y	737	D	0
(C@)	7:30p DEN		8:30p	FL	671	SB	CV5		0
				COMMUTER AIR CARRIERS					
	5:30a		7:10a	FS	362	A	PNV		2
X7	12:15p		1:25p	WE	103	A	PRP		0
X7	5:30p		6:40p	WE	170	A	PRP		0
	6:00p		7:40p	FS	366	A	PNV		2

Freq.	Leave	Arrive	Flight		Class	Eq	MI	S
To **CINCINNATI, OHIO From EL PASO, TEXAS SALT LAKE CITY, UTAG**						**EDT MDT**		**CVG ELP**
A	132.41	10.59	143.00	F		JT/THRU		
B	126.85	10.15	137.00	F		((SDF))		
C	101.85	8.15	110.00	FnY		JT/THRU		
D	98.15	7.85	106.00	Y		((SDF))		
E	90.74	7.26	98.00	Y		((ABQ)) ((IND))		
F	81.48	6.52	88.00	YN		THRU		
6	3:15a	9:15a	AA	206	FnYnB	72S	S	0
(CF@)	5:40a DFW	6:15a	AA	70	FnYnB	707	B	0
X6	3:15a	9:15a	AA	206	FnYnB	72S	S	0
(CF@)	5:40a DFW	6:15a	AA	70	FnYnB	727	B	0
	3:15a	12:01p	AA	206	FnYnB	72S	SB	1
(BD@)	8:54a ORD	10:05a	DL	759	FYB	D9S		0
	7:00a	2:42p	AA	332	FYB	707	B	1
(AC@)	11:54a ORD	12:45p	AA	282	FYB	727	S	0
	7:00a	2:56p	AA	332	FYB	707	B	1
(AC@)	11:54a ORD	1:00p	DL	643	FYB	D9S	S	0
	8:40a	3:55p	CO	204	FYKB	72S	B	0
(ACE@)	11:04a DFW	12:55p	AA	342	FYB	707	L	0
	8:45a	3:55p	AA	98	FYB	72S	B	0
(AC@)	11:10a DFW	12:55p	AA	342	FYB	707	L	0
	12:3p	8:23p	AA	116	FYB	727	L	0
(AC@)	3:59p ORD	6:30p	DL	337	FYB	72S	S	0
6	2:20p	9:20p	AA	128	FYB	D10		0
(AC@)	4:45p DFW	6:20p	AA	394	FYB	727	D	0
X6	2:20p	9:20p	AA	128	FYB	D10		0
(AC@)	4:45p DFW	6:20p	AA	394	FYB	707	D	0
X6	2:50p	11:24p	AA	336	*	707	D	1
(*)	8:01p ORD	9:25p	AA	216	FYB	727		0
				AA 336 FYKB-SAT-FYB				

To **PHILADELPHIA, PA 13.0 MI SE 30 MIN T RA**							**EDT**	**PHL**	
From **NEW YORK, N.Y. J-JFK L-LGA S-WKW E-EWH**							**EDT**	**NYC**	
		F	21.30	1.70	23.00	46.00			
	NA	F	22.22	1.78	24.00	48.00			
	NW	F	22.22	1.78	24.00	48.00			
		A	19.44	1.56	21.00	42.00			
	DR	A	25.00	2.00	27.00	54.00			
		Y	16.67	1.33	18.00	36.00			
	NA	Y	17.59	1.41	19.00	38.00			
	NW	Y	17.59	1.41	19.00	38.00			
		FN	16.67	1.33	18.00	36.00			
		YN	12.96	1.04	14.00	28.00			
		YM	14.00						
	NA	YM	15.00						
	NW	YM	15.00						
	2:10a	E	2:44a	P	DL	689	FnYnB	D8S	0
	7:10a	L	7:55a	P	EA	519	FYB	727	0
	7:50a	E	8:30a	P	EA	507	FYB	727	0
	9:00a	E	9:32a	P	DL	257	FYB	72S	0
X6	10:30a	E	11:06a	P	NW	537	FYB	727	0
	1:45p	E	2:22p	P	NA	411	FYB	72S	0
	3:07p	J	3:53p	P	NA	415	FYB	72S	0
X6	4:15p	E	4:52p	P	NW	223	FYB	727	0
	6:55p	E	7:32p	P	NA	417	FYB	72S	0
	9:00p	E	9:40p	P	EA	481	FnYnB	D9S	0
			COMMUTER AIR CARRIERS						
X67	9:00a	S	9:30a	S	DR	9	A	DTO	0
X67	9:30a	J	10:15a	P	WQ	161	A	HRN	0
X67	11:00a	S	11:30a	S	DR	11	A	DTO	0
X67	1:00p	S	1:30p	S	DR	1	A	DTO	0
X67	2:15p	J	3:00p	P	WQ	163	A	HRN	0
X67	3:00p	S	3:30p	S	DR	3	A	DTO	0
	4:45p	J	5:30p	P	WQ	165	A	HRN	0
X67	5:00p	S	5:30p	S	DR	5	A	DTO	0
X67	6:15p	S	6:45p	S	DR	7	A	DTO	0
	7:15p	J	8:00p	P	WQ	167	A	HRN	0
	9:45p	J	10:30p	P	WQ	169	A	HRN	0

Review the above schedules and answer the following questions:

(*a*) The first morning non-stop flight from Pittsburgh to Miami on December 23 is .... Airlines flight number .... leaving at .... and arriving at .... The type of aircraft is a .... The class/es of service is/are .... Do both First Class and Coach passengers receive the same type of meal service? ....

Ans.: (*a*) *Eastern*

303, 9:00 a.m., 11:19 a.m.

Boeing 727-200

Jet First Class/Jet Coach/Controlled Inventory-Coach

Yes.

(*b*) What is the one-way fare, including tax, on a Sun Valley Key (Commuter Air Carrier) flight from Salt Lake City to Grand Junction? ....

Ans.: (*b*) *$39.00.*

(*c*) What is the 7-21 day excursion fare published between Pittsburgh and Miami? .... Does this include tax? ....

Ans.: (*c*) *$139.00*

Yes.

(*d*) The Military Reservation Fare one-way, including tax, between Grand Rapids and Chicago is ....

Ans.: (*d*) *$17.00.*

(*e*) From what airport does the 7:10 a.m. flight from New York to Philadelphia depart? ....

Ans.: (*e*) *LGA (La Guardia).*

(*f*) What is the latest time on Saturday a passenger could depart El Paso, Texas to fly to Cincinnati, Ohio? .... The connecting city for this flight is .... From ELP to the connecting city, the passenger would fly on .... Airlines flight number .... This flight arrives at .... Is there any meal service? .... From connecting city to CVG, the passenger uses .... Airlines flight number ...., departing at .... and arriving at .... How many stops does this flight make? .... Is there any meal service? .... What is the total fare (including tax) for a Jet Coach passenger on this connection? ....

Ans.: (*f*) *2:20 p.m.*
DFW (Dallas/Ft. Worth)
American
128
4:45 p.m.
No
American
394
6:20 p.m.
9:20 p.m.
0
Yes (Dinner)
$110.00.

(*g*) What is the latest time on a Saturday that a passenger could depart New York's JFK Airport to fly to Philadelphia? ....

Ans.: (*g*) *9:45 p.m.*

(*h*) A passenger wants to fly from Springfield, Ill. to Grand Rapids, Mich., leaving as early in the day as possible. Determine the best possible schedule.

Connecting city ....
Springfield to connecting city .... (Carrier and flight number)
Connecting city to Grand Rapids .... (Carrier and flight number)

Ans.: (*h*) *Chicago*
OZ 920
UA 643.

(The passenger could not use QX 701 which leaves SPI later than OZ 920, which seems to have enough Minimum Connecting Time, because QX 701 arrives at Meigs Field (C) and not O'Hare (O). Additional travelling time is required between airports at the connecting city.)

(*i*) How many miles and in what direction is the Grand Rapids airport from the city? .... What type of ground transportation is available? ....

Ans.: (*i*) *13.0 miles southeast*
taxi, rental car.

Essay Type

Q.25. What general information should travellers have concerning foreign currency?

Q. 26. Under what conditions an international ticket be revalidate?

Q. 27. Explain redifference between the piece method and the weight method of calculating the free baggage allowance?

Q. 28. What are the custom limits for Indian travellers returning with goods purchased overseas?

Q. 29. What is the purpose of a passport?

Q. 30. Where can a passport be obtained?

7

Analysis of an Airline Ticket

After learning this lesson you should be able to:

- *define an airline ticket and know its contents;*
- *draw an airline ticket;*
- *distinguish the part of an airline tickets;*
- *write an airline ticket;*
- *identify the coupons of a flight booklet and explain its purpose;*
- *understand the ticket reservation procedure;*
- *describe repreparation of manual ticketing and machine ticketing;*
- *explain refilling up the flight coupons;*
- *understand reprocedure for international airline ticketing;*
- *know retechnique of entering manual fare calculation;*
- *identify the credit cards and their uses;*
- *understand the purpose and objectives of Prepaid Ticket Advice (PTA), Refund Exchange Note (REN), Cash Refund Notice and Credit Refund Notice;*
- *explain repurpose of miscellaneous change voucher;*
- *describe reprocedure for processing traffic documents;*
- *understaind recontent of tour order and its uses;*
- *understand the importance of traffic documents and identify major ARC traffic documents;*
- *describe the full procedure for processing and safeguarding stock;*
- *understand the procedure of preparation, validation and issuance of an airline ticket to a pasenger;*
- *understand the procedure of manual ticketing;*
- *know the procedure of mechanical and computerized ticketing;*
- *get a good knowledge of airline ticket related documents.*

AIRLINE TICKETS

An air ticket is a legal contract between an air carrier and a passenger, entitling the bearer, at a stated fare, to travel on one or more specified flights. A passenger who misplaces ticket may be denied the right to board, and even worse, may be denied a refund. An airline ticket contains all the following:

1. Authorised passage between specified board points and all points.
2. Evidence that the passenger has paid the applicable fare for passage.
3. The departure date.
4. The flight number.
5. The class of service.
6. Any other information for accounting purposes.
7. Form number and serial number.

All airline tickets issued by the travel agencies are written in standard forms. A ticket may be written by hand, or by computer, using a ticket printer. A ticket written by hand is called a hand ticket and a ticket written by computer is called a machine ticket.

Most travel agencies approved by IATA issue tickets on special ticket forms provided by IATA. Tickets purchased from an air consolidator or tour wholesaler are sometimes written on wholesaler's own ticket forms. Different forms are used for hand tickets and machine tickets. Tickets forms issued by IATA are referred to as ticket stock. Each ticket has a form number and serial number. Together these numbers make up the ticket, or document, number. Blank ticket stock is provided to travel agencies by IATA, or in some cases, by airlines. The serial numbers are recorded, both for accounting purposes and also in the event of loss or theft. When the travel agency reports ticket sale to IATA through the area bank, each serial number must also be reported.Among the various activities of travel agency, writing the airline ticket is an exciting and interesting work. The interesting part of ticket writing is the very activity which represents the totality of a travel agent's work *i.e.* counselling, reservation works and customer satisfaction. All the tickets stock is accountable as unused, issued, voided or refunded. The travel agency is responsible for ticket stock received, collection of the correct amounts, written on the issued tickets and remittance of all funds collection in trust for the air carriers. Air passenger tickets are usually issued in sequence by several number and reported in the same way. The amount of ticket said is also reported on a foreign currency. The passenger's coupon form a standard airline ticket. It has five parts:

1. Front Cover
2. Passenger's Coupon/Receipt
3. Auditor's Coupon (green)
4. Agent's Coupon (pink)
5. First Flight Coupon (required for passenger boarding).

The various parts of an airline ticket are given in Figures 7.1 to 7.8.

The auditor's coupon contains such information as the passenger's name, all flight segments of the passages, fare calculation and form of payment collected. This coupon along with the sales report is mailed weekly to the Central Account Office. The fares calculated by travel agents is checked by Central Accounting. Any discrepancies are reported and adjusted.

THE PARTS OF AN AIRLINE TICKET

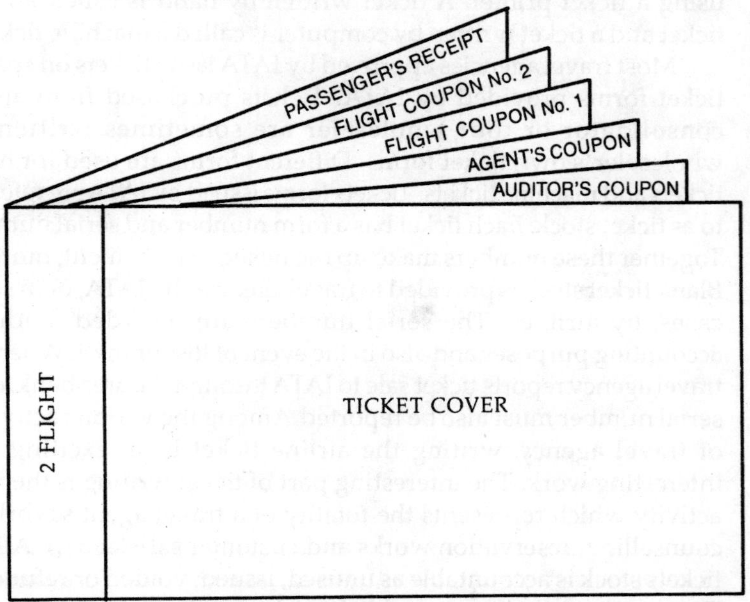

Fig. 7.1: Specimen of the Parts of an Airline Ticket.

The flight coupon authorises passage between the points shown on the light area of the coupon and serves as evidence that the fares shown on the coupon has been paid. The coupon is an agreement between the airline and the passenger for reserve seat on the specified flight. The coupon contains all necessary information for expeditious handling of the passenger and his luggage. It helps airline agent's, to guide the passenger on the correct flights. It indicates all conditions which must be known to a ticket agent in case he have to reissue or refund the coupon. It also contains information which enables the carrying airline to bill the issuing airline for the fare between the two permits indicated on it, if the issuing airline and carrying airline are not the same. These coupons cannot be honoured indivtdually. The passenger must present the coupon to the carrier to which it is made out in the order in which it is issued and copy of all unused coupons are presented together.

TICKET COUPONS

The airlines tickets consists of several parts (Ref. Figures 7.1, 7.2, 7.3, 7.4, 7.5, 7.6 and 7.7) called coupon, such as:

1. Cover
2. *Auditor's coupon:* Kept by the agency for accounting purpose.
3. *Agent's coupon:* Kept by the agency for accounting purpose.
4. *Flight coupon:* It is a portion that entitles the passenger to board a flight.
5. *Flight coupons*: A separate flight issued for each flight segment. In case of a connection, a separate flight coupon is required for each leg.
6. *Passenger receipt:* It is kept by the passenger, but is not valid for passage. This receipt lists all the flight segments for which flight coupons have been issued and serves as of proof that passenger has paid the fare.

Two basic types of ticket stock are issued:

1. Multipart stock
2. Card stock.

In a multipart, or paper ticket, all the coupons are attached, so information can be written in the appropriate spaces on all the coupons at the same time. Multipart paper tickets may be either handwritten or printed by a computer. These tickets are booklets

AUDITOR'S COUPON

ENDORSEMENT/RESTRICTIONS (CARBON) | ORIGIN | DESTINATION | FROM/TO | CARRIER | FARE CALCULATION | 1400:585:727

CONNECTION TICKET

AUDITOR'S COUPON

PLACE OF ISSUE–AGENCY

VOID

IT IS UNLAWFUL TO PURCHASE OR RESELL THIS TICKET FROM/TO ANY ENTITY OTHER THAN THE ISSUING CARRIER OR ITS AUTHORIZED AGENTS

NAME OF PASSENGER | NOT TRANSFERABLE | ISSUED IN EXCHANGE FOR | DATE OF ISSUE

COUPONS NOT VALID BEFORE: 1 | 2 | 3 | 4

ORIGINAL ISSUE | CARRIER | FORM AND SERIAL NO. | PLACE | DATE | AGENT'S NUMERICAL CODE

COUPONS NOT VALID AFTER: 1 | 2 | 3 | 4

TICKET DESIGNATOR | TOUR CODE

X/O	NOT GOOD FOR PASSAGE	FARE BASIS	ALLOW	CARRIER	FLIGHT/ CLASS	DATE	TIME	STATUS
	FROM							
	TO							
	TO							
	TO							
	TO							

COMML. RATE | FARE

FORM OF PAYMENT

COMMISSION | TAX

PASSENGER TICKET & BAGGAGE CHECK—ISSUED BY

SUBJECT TO CONDITION OF CONTRACT ON PASSENGERS COUPON

FARE | EQUIV. AMOUNT PD

TAX | TOTAL

FROM | SERIAL NUMBER | CK | AIRLINE CODE

O

||" 1400585727 2 ||"

Fig. 7.2: Specimen of Auditor's Coupon.

AGENT'S COUPON

ENDORSEMENT/RESTRICTIONS (CARBON)	ORIGIN	DESTINATION	FROM/TO	CARRIER	FARE CALCULATION	1400:585:727
	CONNECTION TICKET	AGENT'S COUPON				PLACE OF ISSUE–AGENCY VOID
NAME OF PASSENGER / NOT TRANSFERABLE	ISSUED IN EXCHANGE FOR	DATE OF ISSUE				IT IS UNLAWFUL TO PURCHASE OR RESELL THIS TICKET FROM/TO ANY ENTITY OTHER THAN THE ISSUING CARRIER OR ITS AUTHORIZED AGENTS

COUPONS NOT VALID BEFORE				ORIGINAL ISSUE	CARRIER	FORM AND SERIAL NO.	PLACE	DATE	AGENT'S NUMERICAL CODE
1	2	3	4						
COUPONS NOT VALID AFTER				TICKET DESIGNATOR			TOUR CODE		
1	2	3	4						

X/O	NOT GOOD FOR PASSAGE	FARE BASIS	ALLOW	CARRIER	FLIGHT/ CLASS	DATE	TIME	STATUS
	FROM							
	TO							
	TO							
	TO							
	TO							

COMML. RATE | FARE

FORM OF PAYMENT

	COMMISSION	TAX	PASSENGER TICKET & BAGGAGE CHECK—ISSUED BY SUBJECT TO CONDITION OF CONTRACT ON PASSENGERS COUPON

FARE	EQUIV. AMOUNT PD	ROUTE CODE	ENCODE	CPM	AIRLINE CODE	FROM	SERIAL NUMBER	CK
TAX	TOTAL							

O ||" 1400585727 2 ||"

Fig. 7.3: Specimen of Agent's Coupon.

FIRST FLIGHT COUPON (The Second, Third and Fourth Coupons are identical except for the coupon number)

ENDORSEMENT/RESTRICTIONS (CARBON) | ORIGIN | DESTINATION | FROM/TO | CARRIER | FARE CALCULATION | 1400:585:727

CONNECTION TICKET | FLIGHT COUPON 1

PLACE OF ISSUE–AGENCY

VOID

NAME OF PASSENGER | NOT TRANSFERABLE | ISSUED IN EXCHANGE FOR | DATE OF ISSUE

COUPONS NOT VALID BEFORE			
1	2	3	4

COUPONS NOT VALID AFTER			
1	2	3	4

ORIGINAL ISSUE | CARRIER | FORM AND SERIAL NO. | PLACE | DATE | AGENT'S NUMERICAL CODE

TICKET DESIGNATOR | TOUR CODE

X/O	NOT GOOD FOR PASSAGE	FARE BASIS	ALLOW	CARRIER	FLIGHT/ CLASS	DATE	TIME	STATUS
	FROM							
	TO							
	TO							
	TO							
	TO							

COMML. RATE | FARE

FORM OF PAYMENT

IT IS UNLAWFUL TO PURCHASE OR RESELL THIS TICKET FROM/TO ANY ENTITY OTHER THAN THE ISSUING CARRIER OR ITS AUTHORIZED AGENTS

BAGGAGE CHECKED UNCHECKED → | PCS / WT | UNCK. WT | PCS / WT | UNCK. WT | PCS / WT | UNCK. WT | PCS / WT | UNCK. WT

PASSENGER TICKET & BAGGAGE CHECK—ISSUED BY

SUBJECT TO CONDITION OF CONTRACT ON PASSENGERS COUPON

FARE | EQUIV. AMOUNT PD

TAX | TOTAL

ROUTE CODE | ENCODE | CPM 1 | AIRLINE CODE | FROM | SERIAL NUMBER | CK

||"1400585727 6||"

Fig. 7.4: Specimen of First Flight Coupon.

PASSENGER'S COUPON

ENDORSEMENT/RESTRICTIONS (CARBON)	ORIGIN	DESTINATION	FROM/TO	CARRIER	FARE CALCULATION	See below for Airline Form, Serial Number
	CONNECTION TICKET	PASSENGER'S COUPON				PLACE OF ISSUE—AGENCY

NAME OF PASSENGER	NOT TRANSFERABLE	ISSUED IN EXCHANGE FOR	DATE OF ISSUE

COUPONS NOT VALID BEFORE: 1 | 2 | 3 | 4

ORIGINAL ISSUE	CARRIER	FORM AND SERIAL NO.	PLACE	DATE	AGENT'S NUMERICAL CODE

COUPONS NOT VALID AFTER: 1 | 2 | 3 | 4

TICKET DESIGNATOR — TOUR CODE

X/O	NOT GOOD FOR PASSAGE	FARE BASIS	ALLOW	CARRIER	FLIGHT/ CLASS	DATE	TIME	STATUS
	FROM							
	TO							
	TO							
	TO							
	TO							

FARE

FORM OF PAYMENT

IT IS UNLAWFUL TO PURCHASE OR RESELL THIS TICKET FROM/TO ANY ENTITY OTHER THAN THE ISSUING CARRIER OR ITS AUTHORIZED AGENTS

BAGGAGE CHECKED UNCHECKED →	PCS / WT	UNCK. WT	PCS / WT	UNCK. WT	PCS / WT	UNCK. WT	PCS / WT	UNCK. WT

PASSENGER TICKET & BAGGAGE CHECK — ISSUED BY

SUBJECT TO CONDITION OF CONTRACT ON PASSENGERS COUPON

FARE	EQUIV. AMOUNT PD	ROUTE CODE	ENCODE	CPM	AIRLINE CODE	FORM	SERIAL NUMBER	CK
TAX	TOTAL			‖" 1400585727 2 ‖"				

Fig. 7.5: Specimen of Passenger's Coupon.

BACK COVER WITH CONDITION OF CONTRACT OF PASSENGER'S TRAVEL

NOTICE

If the passenger's journey involves an ultimate destination or stop in a country other than the country of departure the Warsaw Convention may be applicable and the Convention governs and in most cases limits the liability of carriers for death or personal injury and in respect of loss of or damage to baggage. See also notice headed "Advice to International Passengers on Limitation of Liability."

Conditions of Contract

1. As used in this contract "ticket" means this passenger ticket and baggage check, of which these conditions and the notices form part, "carriage" is equivalent to "transportation", "carrier" means all air carriers that carry or undertake to carry the passenger or his baggage hereunder or perform any other service incidental to such air carriage, "WARSAW CONVENTION" means the Convention for the Unification of Certain Rules Relating to International Carriage by Air signed at Warsaw, 12th October, 1929, or that Convention as amended at The Hague, 28th September, 1955, whichever may be applicable.

2. Carriages hereunder is subject to the rules and limitations relating to liability established by the Warsaw Convention unless such carriage is not "International Carriage" as defined by that Convention.

3. To the extent not in conflict with the foregoing carriage and other services performed by each carrier are subject to: (I) provisions contained in this ticket, (II) applicable tariffs, (III) carrier's conditions of carriage and related regulations which are made part hereof (and are available on application at the offices of carrier), except in transportation between a place in the United States or Canada and any place outside thereof to which tariffs in force in those countries apply.

4. Carrier's name may be abbreviated in the ticket, the full name and its abbreviation being set forth in carrier's tariff, conditions of carriage, regulations of timetables; carrier's address shall be the airport of departure shown opposite the first abbreviation of carrier's name in the ticket; the agreed stopping places are those places set forth in this ticket or as shown in carrier's timetables as scheduled stopping places on the passenger's route; carriage to be performed hereunder by several successive carriers is regarded as a single operation.

5. Any exclusion or limitation of liability of carrier shall apply to and be for the benefit of agents, servants and representatives of carrier and any person whose aircraft is used by carrier for carriage and its agents, servants and representatives.

6. Checked baggage will be delivered to bearer of the baggage check. In case of damage to baggage moving in international transportation complaint must be made in writing to carrier forthwith after discovery of damage and, at the latest, within 7 days from receipt; in case of delay, complaint must be made within 21 days from date the baggage was delivered. See tariffs or conditions of carriage regarding non-international transportation.

7. This ticket is good for carriage for one year from date of issue, except as otherwise provided in this ticket, in carrier's tariffs, conditions of carriage, or related regulations. The fare for carriage hereunder is subject to change prior to commencement of carriage. Carrier may refuse transportation if the applicable fare has not been paid.

8. Carrier undertakes to use its best efforts to carry the passenger and baggage with reasonable dispatch. Times shown in timetable or elsewhere are not guaranteed and form no part of this contract. Carrier may without notice substitute alternate carriers or aircraft, and may alter or omit stopping places shown on the ticket in case of necessity. Schedules are subject to change without notice. Carrier assumes no responsibility for making connections.

9. Passenger shall comply with Government travel requirements, present exit, entry and other required documents and arrive at airport by time fixed by carrier or, if no time is fixed, early enough to complete departure procedures.

10. No agent, servant or representative of carrier has authority to alter, modify or waive any provision of this contract.

CARRIER RESERVES THE RIGHT TO REFUSE CARRIAGE TO ANY PERSON WHO HAS ACQUIRED A TICKET IN VIOLATION OF APPLICABLE LAW OR CARRIER'S TARIFFS, RULES OR REGULATIONS

Issued by the Carrier whose name is in the "Issued By" section on the face of the Passenger Ticket and Baggage Check — SUBJECT TO TARIFF REGULATIONS

Fig. 7.6: Specimen of Back Cover with Condition of Contract of Passenger's Travel.

Supplemental Notice of overbooking of flights
Notice – Overbooking of Flights

Airline flights may be overbooked, and there is a slight change that a seat will not be available on a flight for which a person has a confirmed reservation. If the flight is overbooked, no one will be denied a seat until airline personnel first ask for volunteers willing to give up their reservation in exchange for a payment of the airline's choosing. If there are not enough volunteers the airline will deny boarding to other persons in accordance with its particular boarding priority. With few exceptions, persons denied boarding involuntarily are entitled to compensation. The complete rules for the payment of compensation and each airline's boarding priorities are available at all airport ticket counters and boarding locations.

Fig. 7.7: Specimen of Supplemental Notice of Overbooking of Flights.

containing either two or four flight coupons. If an itinerary has more than four segments, additional booklets may be used. The serial number of all the tickets used to complete one itinerary must be in consecutive order. Multiple ticket booklets issued for one itinerary are called conjunction tickets. Any coupons that are not used in multipart ticket booklet must be avoided. To void an unused coupon the agent removes the coupon from the booklet and writes the word 'void', across the face of the coupon in large upper case letters.

Let us take an example. Assume an itinerary having six segments. In this case, two four-flight booklets are required, supplying a total of eight coupons. Six-flight coupons would be used to ticket the air segments, and two coupons would be removed from the booklet and voided. A four-flight booklet may not be combined with a two-flight booklet, because the serial numbers of the conjunction tickets must be consecutive. Four-flight booklets and two-flight booklets are issued separately, and therefore, have different starting serial numbers. Thus if an itinerary requires five segments, two four-flight booklets must still be used. In this case, five-flight coupons would be used to ticket the itinerary, and three coupons would be voided.

When a ticket has been filled out and validated, the flight coupons and passenger receipts are given to the passenger. The auditor's coupon and agent's coupon are kept by the issuing agent. Eventually, the auditor's coupon will be sent back to the airline. The agents coupon is kept by the travel agency to its book-keeping records.

In a multipart ticket booklet, the auditor's coupon is green, and the agent's coupon is pink. These coupons are detached from the booklet, along with any unused flight coupons, before the ticket is given to the passenger.

On a card ticket, each coupon is printed separately by computer, the flight coupons are then stapled together by the issuing agent. When a card ticket is issued by computer, each coupon is printed separately. The issuing agent stamps the flight coupons together along with the passenger receipts and gives them to the passenger.

The passenger must present a flight coupon before boarding flight. Each coupon is valid for a specific departure date, flight and class of service. An airline ticket is valid only for the passenger whose name is written on the flight coupon. The ticket may not be hold on otherwise transferred by the passenger to someone else.

AIR TICKET INFORMATION

The tickets are of two types:

(*i*) Machine Tickets, and
(*ii*) Hand Tickets.

Machine Ticketing

A machine ticket may be written on either paper stock or card stock. Machine tickets and hand tickets differ in design but the same information is shown on both type of tickets.

It includes following basic information as given in Figures 7.8, 7.9 and 7.10.

1. *Name of the Issuing Carrier:* It appears on the upper left corner. The airline name is imprinted on the ticket by the ticket validator a ticket printer.
2. *The Endorsement/Restriction Box:* This box is located immediately beneath the validating carrier. Any important restrictions or cancellation penalties that apply to the ticket appear in this box.
3. *The Passenger's Name:* The Passenger's Surname appears first, followed by the first name or initial. A title, such as Mr., Mrs., Miss., Mstr., and so forth, may be written after the passenger name.
4. *The Itinerary:* The boxes labelled 'from' and 'to' are used for the itinerary. The following informations are written in these boxes:
   (*i*) The 'From' box shows the board point of each segment.
   (*ii*) The 'To' box shows the off point of each segment.
   (*iii*) The 'carrier' box shows the carrier code of the airline operating the flight.
   (*iv*) The 'Flight' and 'Class' boxes show the flight number and class of service.
   (*v*) The 'Date' box shows the departure date.
   (*vi*) The 'Time' box shows the departure time.
   (*vii*) The 'Status' box shows whether the reservation is confirmed; 'OK' indicates a confirmed reservation;

AIRLINE MACHINE TICKET

PASSENGER TICKET AND BAGGAGE CHECK

Subject to conditions contained in this ticket — 8888/000/227

Issued by **AIR INDIA** — Conjunction Ticket

Endorsement and Restrictions **NON-REFUNDABLE**

Passenger's Name	Date of Issue	Origin	VOID
	14 APL	Destination	For Training Purpose Only
	Not Transferable	**STS / STS**	
GORE LAAL	....	Issued in exchange for	

X/O	From	Carrier		Flight	Class	Date	Time	Status	Fare Basis/Ticket Designator	Not Valid before	Not Valid after	Allowance
O	To	SANTA ROSA	AI	3260	Y	21 APL	12.15P	OK	49			
O	To	SAN FRANCISCO	TW	240	K	21 APL	1.52 P	OK	KIA3NR01			
O	To	WASHINGTON NATL	CO	1281	B	24 APL	700 A	OK	BA3HP			
O	To	SAN FRANCISCO	AI	3255	Y	24 APL	130 P	OK	49			
	To	SANTA ROSA		–								

Fare — Fare Calculation **STS AI X/SP 090.00 TW WAS 221.82 CO X/SF 0221.82**

Rs. 62364.00 — **AI STS 90.00 62364 END**

Equivalent Fare Paid Rs. .... — Approval Code .... — Tour Code ....

Tax **Rs. 6236.00** — Airline .... — C.K. .... — Commission .... — Tax ..... — Comm. Rate

Tax ....

Total **8660.00** — Form of Payment **AX 37705503541005# 02/99**

A/L Agent Info ....

Control No.............. — 8888/000/227

Fig. 7.8: Specimen of an Airline Machine Ticket.

AUTOMATED AIR TICKET

PASSENGER TICKET AND BAGGAGE CHECK

Subject to conditions contained in this ticket 777/356/088

Issued by BRITISH AIRWAYS CONJUNCTION TICKET Origin ....

Endorsement CHANGE SUBJECT TO FEE Date of Issue .... Destination ....

Passenger's Name Not Transferable .... Issued in exchange for .... VOID

JOSHI DEV For Training Purpose

X/O		From	Carrier	Flight	Class	Date	Time	Status	Fare Basis/Ticket Designator	Not Valid before	Not Valid after	Allowance
	To	NEW YORK–KNNED	BA	45	V	15 FEB	10.00A	OK	VAP 14			
O	To	MIAMI, FLORIDA							VOID			
	To	VOID							VOID			
	To	VOID							VOID			
	To	VOID							VOID			

Fare Rs. 28,000.00 Fare Calculation 15 FEB NYC BA MIA 28,000 TL 28,000

Equivalent fare Paid Rs. 28,000.00

Tax Rs. 2800.00

Tax .... Form of Payment .... Approval Code .... Toúr Code ....

Total Rs. 30,800.00

A/L Agent Info .... Check .... Airline .... C.K. Commission ..... Tax ..... Comm. Rate ....

Control No. 777/356/088

Fig. 7.9: Specimen of Air Ticket (Printed on Agency Automation System).

COMPUTER GENERATED TICKET

Issued by ……..											8892/885/005
			Flight Coupon					INTERNATIONAL TRAVEL			
			Date								
NEGI/GAURAV											
X/O	From	Good for Passage	Carrier	Flight	CI	Date	Time	Status	Fare/Basis		
Rs……………………	……………………………………………………										
……………………	CK										
………… …………	8892/888/005										

Fig. 7.10: Specimen of a Computer Generated Ticket.

'RQ' indicates that the reservation has been requested, but not confirmed.

(*viii*) The 'Fare Basis' box shows the fare basis code.

5. The boxes in the lower left corner of the ticket, show the total base fare, tax and total fare.
6. The 'Fare Calculation' shows how the fare was calculated. On a machine ticket, such as one in the figure, the fare calculation is written in a horizontal format. On a hand-written ticket, the fare calculation would be written in a vertical format.
7. The 'Form of Payment' box, shows whether the ticket was paid for with cash, by cheque, or by credit card. If the form of payment is a credit card, the credit card account number is shown in this box.
8. *Accounting Information:* The airline number and ticket number, appear at the bottom of the ticket. The ticket number consists of a form number and a serial number. On a paper ticket, the ticket number also appears in the upper right corner. On card tickets, the ticket number is called the 'document number'.
9. 'Commission' box indicates the rate of commission of the travel agency.

WRITING AIRLINE TICKETS

Learning how to write an airline ticket is usually an on-the-job activity and can be both exciting and interesting work. Writing airline tickets can be likened to a child who learns for the first time about writing bank checks; the ticket you write can be for a Rs. 50/- or more, and only requires a validation stamp in order to be a negotiable instrument. All ticket stock is accountable as unused, issued, voided or refunded. The interesting part of ticket writing is the very activity represents the totality of a travel agent's work, i.e., counselling, reservations work and customer satisfaction.

Fig. 7.11 is an example of a passenger's coupon from a standard interline ticket. The first *two digits* of the form serial number indicate that it is an agency ticket (8) with four coupons (4), and the rest of the digits are the serial number. The *ticket examples start on the following page.*

1400:585:727

4 FLIGHT

PASSENGER TICKET and BAGGAGE CHECK

SUBJECT TO CONDITIONS OF CONTRACT ON PASSENGER'S COUPON

IT IS UNLAWFUL TO PURCHASE OR RESELL THIS TICKET FROM TO ANY ENTITY OTHER THAN THE ISSUING CARRIER OR ITS AUTHORIZED AGENTS

Fig. 7.11: Specimen of Passenger Ticket and Baggage Check (Front Cover).

INSIDE COVER WITH LIMITATION OF LIABILITY

Advice to International Passengers on Limitation of Liability

Passengers on a journey involving an ultimate destination or a stop in a country other than the country of origin are advised that the provisions of a treaty known as the Warsaw Convention may be applicable to the entire journey, including any portion entirely within the country of origin or destination. For such passengers on a journey to, from, or with an agreed stopping place, the Convention and special contracts of carriage embodied in applicable tariffs provide that the liability of certain carriers, parties to such special contracts, for death of or personal injury to passengers is limited in most cases to proven damages not to exceed (a fixed amount) per passenger, and that this liability up to such limit shall not depend on negligence on the part of the carrier. The limit of liability (the fixed amount) is inclusive of legal fees and costs except that in case of a claim brought in a state where provision is made for separate award of legal fees and costs, the limit shall be the sum of (a fixed amount) exclusive of legal fees and costs. For such passengers travelling by a carrier not a party to such special contracts or on a journey not to, from, or having an agreed stopping place, liability of the carrier for death or personal injury to passengers is limited in most cases Rs............. only.

The names of carriers, parties to such special contracts, are available at all ticket offices of such carriers and may be examined on request.

Additional protection can usually be obtained by purchasing insurance from a insurance company. Such insurance is not affected by any limitation of the carrier's liability under the Warsaw Convention or such special contracts of carriage. For further information please consult your airline or insurance company representative.

Notice of Baggage Liability Limitations

Liability for loss, delay, or damage to baggage is limited as follows unless a higher value is declared in advance and additional charges are paid:

(1) For most international travel (including domestic portions of international journeys) to approximately $9.07 per pound ($20.00 per kilo) for checked baggage and $400 per passenger for unchecked baggage;

(2) For travel wholly between U.S. points, to $750 per passenger on most carriers (a few have lower limits). Excess valuation may not be declared on certain types of valuable articles. Carriers assume no liability for fragile or perishable articles. Further information may be obtained from the carrier.

Fig. 7.12: Inside Cover with Limitation of Liability (Specimen).

IMPORTANT RECONFIRMATION NOTICES

International Journeys

If you break your journey for more than 72 hours at any point, please reconfirm your intention of using your continuing or return reservation. To do so, please inform the airline office at the point where you intend to resume your journey at least 72 hours before departure of your flight. Failure to reconfirm will result in the cancellation of your reservation.

If your journey is wholly within Europe, this notice does not apply to you.

Journeys within Canada / USA and to or from Mexico

Contact the carrying airline for the applicable requirements.

Insert with baggage liability limitations notice and reconfirmation requirements.

Fig. 7.13: Notice of Baggage Limitations and Important Reconfirmation Notices.

MANUAL TICKETING

Writing a hand ticket is referred to as a manual ticketing. Although most tickets are written by computer, a knowledge of manual ticketing is important to air ticket agents, travel agents, tour wholesalers, and other job position. In case airline computer reservation systems are out of service, the tickets must be written manually. Figures 7.14 and 7.15 are specimen of manual ticketing.

The procedure for writing a ticket is as follows:

1. Before writing a ticket, a travel agent must telephone each airline in the itinerary to secure a reservation for the passenger.
2. On acceptance of reservation on telephone, the airline furnishes the travel agent with a confirmation code, called a 'record locator'. This code identifies the passenger's reservation on the airline's computer system and can be used by an airline ticket or reservation agent to retrieve the reservation record.

In Figure 7.14, both segments are direct flights, whereas in Figure 7.15 two of the segments are connecting flights. In both these examples, the fare calculation is written in vertical format, to the right of the itinerary. On domestic itinerary, as the fare calculation entries are not normally required, except in special circumstances.

The board point, carrier, flight, class, date, status and fare basis are shown by each segment, as is in the case of a computer ticket. The lines where this information is written are called 'entitlement lines'. The world 'VOID' is written in any entitlement lines that are not used. The last point in the itinerary is written by itself in the 'To' box, and the rest of the entitlement line is voided.

Figure 7.15 is an example of an open jaw—a round trip itinerary with a surface segment just before the return. The out bound flights in this itinerary form a connection. The connecting point is Tokyo.

Stopover Indicators

A stopover indicator must be written before each off point from which another flight departs, to indicate whether a stopover is allowed.

Stop-over Allowed

Figure 7.14 is an example of a round-trip ticket from New Delhi to London. Both segments are direct flights. Each point on the hand

A HAND WRITTEN TICKET

ENDORSEMENT/RESTRICTIONS	ORIGIN/DESTINATION	BOOKING REFERENCE A1767	FROM/TO	CARRIER	FARE CALCULATION	8808/123/002
	CONJUNCTION TICKET		NEW DELHI	CO	Rs. 20,000	PLACE OF ISSUE—AGENCY
			LONDON	CO	Rs. 20,000	
			NEW DELHI	CO		NOT VALID OR PASSAGE 8808/125/005

NAME OF PASSENGER NEGI / GM	NOT TRANSFERABLE	ISSUED IN EXCHANGE FOR	DATE OF ISSUE

COUPONS NOT VALID BEFORE				CARIER	FORM AND SERIAL NO.	PLACE	DATE	AGENT'S NUMERICAL CODE
1	2	3	4					

COUPONS NOT VALID AFTER				TICKET DESIGNATOR	TOUR CODE
1	2	3	4		

X/O	NOT GOOD FOR PASSAGE		CARRIER	RLIGHT/CLASS	DATE	TIME	STATUS	FARE BASIS	ALLOW
	FROM	NEW DELHI	CO	721 Y	07 JUN	8.30 A	OK	Y	
	TO	LONDON	CO	755 Y	09 JUN	9.35 A	OK		
	TO	NEW DELHI		— VOID —					
	TO	— VOID —		— VOID —					
	TO	— VOID —		— VOID —					
	TO	— VOID —		— VOID —					
	TO		COMMISSION 10					TAX 10	

COMM. RATE	FARE
10	Rs. 40,000

FORM OF PAYMENT CHECK

FOR TRAINING PURPOSE ONLY

FARE	EQUIV. AMOUNT PD	ROUTE CODE	ENCODE	CPM	AIRLINE CODE	FORM	SERIAL NUMBER	CK
Rs. 40,000								
TAX Rs. 4,000	TOTAL Rs. 44,000						8808/125/005	0

Fig. 7.14: Specimen of a Hand Ticket Showing a Round Trip with Direct Flights.

ticket is indicated by name, not by the city or airport code. Passengers are more familiar with the name of the cities and airport than with codes. As the flight coupons are presented by the passenger at board point, therefore, the city or airport name are used to avoid confusion. In the case of a multi-airport city, the airport must be specified.

In Figure 7.14, the board point of the out bound flight is New Delhi, and the off point is London. However London is also the board point of the next segment. In this case, the stopover indication 'O' indicates that stopover is allowed before the next flight is boarded.

Stop-over Not Allowed

If a stopover is not allowed, as in the case of connection, the non-stop indicator 'X' is written before the board point. In Figure 7.15 Tokyo is the off point of the first segment and the board point of the second segment. The non-stop indicator 'X' indicates that a stopover is not allowed before the next flight is boarded.

A stopover occurs whenever the time between adjoining flights exceeds the maximum permitted connecting time, usually four hours. In a connection, no stopover is allowed at any of the connecting points. The first two segments are connecting flights, and therefore no stopover is allowed in the connecting point, Tokyo.

Note the void segment between New York and London. In this example, the passenger will arrive in Tokyo, but will depart from London in the return flight after a stopover. The void segment between New York and London is an ARNK segment, indicating surface travel.

Status Codes

OK—Confirmed	:	The status code 'OK' is entered in the status box to indicate a confirm reservation
RQ—Requested	:	It is entered if the reservation has been requested but has not yet been confirmed at the time of ticketing.
SA—Stand by	:	It indicates stand by travel.
NS—No Seat	:	It is entered on an infant ticket with an international itinerary, denoting 'no seat'.

A HAND WRITTEN TICKET

ENDORSEMENT/RESTRICTIONS	ORIGIN/DESTINATION	BOOKING REFERENCE ST1759	5555/123/450
	CONNECTION TICKET		PLACE OF ISSUE—AGENCY STOC
NAME OF PASSENGER JOSHI / J	NOT TRANSFERABLE	ISSUED IN EXCHANGE FOR	DATE OF ISSUE
			NOT VALID OR PASSAGE 01555/123/450

FROM/TO	CARRIER	FARE CALCULATION
DLI	AI	Rs. 75,000
TKY	AI	
NYK X	AI	Rs. 75,000
LON		
DLI	AI	

COUPONS NOT VALID BEFORE			
1	2	3	4
COUPONS NOT VALID AFTER			
1	2	3	4

CARRIER	FORM AND SERIAL NO.	PLACE	DATE	AGENT'S NUMERICAL CODE

TICKET DESIGNATOR	TOUR CODE

X/O	NOT GOOD FOR PASSAGE		CARRIER	FLIGHT/CLASS	DATE	TIME	STATUS	FARE BASIS	ALLOW
	FROM	NEW DELHI	AI	343 Y	06 JUN	10.20 A	OK	YCD	
X	TO	TOKYO	AI	329 Y	06 JUN	1.55 P	OK	YCD	
O	TO	NEW YORK		— VOID —					
O	TO	LONDON	NW	701 Y	15 JUL	8.40 A	OK	YCD	
	TO	NEW DELHI		— VOID —					

COMM. RATE	FARE
10	Rs. 1,50,000

FORM OF PAYMENT CASH

COMMISSION | TAX

FOR TRAINING PURPOSE ONLY

FARE Rs. 1,50,000	EQUIV. AMOUNT PD
TAX Rs. 15,000	TOTAL Rs. 1,65,000

ROUTE CODE	ENCODE	CPM	AIRLINE CODE	FORM	SERIAL NUMBER	CK
					5555/123/450	0

Fig. 7.15: Specimen of a Hand Ticket Showing an Open Jaw Connecting Flights.

Filling up the Flight Coupon

The flight coupon needs to be filled up very carefully. Figure 7.16 is an specimen of an Airflight Coupon with Boarding Pass and Figure 7.17 is a specimen of a Round Trip International Ticket.

The following is the general procedure adopted in airline ticketing.

Name

Enter the passenger's surname followed by a slash, first initial and then title. If the passenger has an unaccompanied minor, enter UM followed by the age in brackets. For example,

NAME	/	NOT TRANSFERABLE
NEGI	/	ANIRUDH MAJ
NEGI	/	HIMANSHU MASTER (UM 15)

Itinerary

Enter the passenger's complete itinerary using block letters. Start with the city of origin and list each connection, city, stop-over city, and destination. When a city is served by more than one airport, enter both the city name and the airport name. For example,

FROM: NEW DELHI/INDIRA GANDHI INTERNATIONAL AIRPORT
TO: NEW YORK KENNEDY

Carrier

Enter two letter code of the airline involved. For example, for Air India.

Carrier
AI

Flight/Class

Enter the passengers flight number followed by the class of service. The class of service determines in which compartment of the aircraft the passenger will be seated. For example,

Flight/Class
554 Y

AN AIR FLIGHT COUPON

Boarding Pass

Passenger Ticket

Issued by **AIR INDIA** | Place of Issue **NEW DELHI** | Agent's Code **88057756** | Name of Passenger **SINHA / JM**

Name of Issuing Agent **ABC TRAVEL** | Carrier Code **5ZIOD8/UA** | Fare Basis/ Ticket Designator **QAP 21** | Date of Issue **07 MAR** | From **SAN FRANCISCO**

Service Carrier ID **D** | To **LOS ANGELES**

Passenger **SINHA / JM** | Carrier Flight **US 5223** | Class Rate Time **Q 7 MAR /11.30 A** | Status **OK** | ....

....

X/O From **SAN FRANCISCO** | Not valid after **24 MAR** | Not valid before **06 FEB** | Carrier **AIR INDIA**

X/O To **LOS ANGELES**

PENALTY APPLIES TO CNC LN

FP CHEK FC 07 MAR SFOUS LAX 160.00 QAP 21

Issuing Agent No. **X7QZB** | Carrier **AI** | Flight **US 5223** | Class **Q** | Date **07 MAR** | Time **100 A**

Endorsement and Restrictions ....

Gate **45** | Seat **8A** | Smoke **N**

Fare **Rs. 16,000** | Equivalent fare Paid Rs..............

Tax **Rs. 1,600** | Stock Control No. **ISSUE** | CK | CPN | Document No. | OK

Total **Rs. 17,600**

....

0 088 81881279123 9 **0 088 81881279123 9**

Fig. 7.16: Specimen of an Air Flight Coupon with Boarding Pass.

INTERNATIONAL TICKET

Endorsement/Restriction (Coupon)	Origin/Destination **NEW DELHI/N. DELHI**	Booking Reference **RE 108L**	From /To	Carrier	Fare Calculation	**950:000:000**
	Connection Ticket **504/505**	**Agents Coupon**	**DL**	**AI**		Place of Issue–Agency
			PAR	**AI**	**M**	**Void**
			LON	**AF**	**Rs.**	
Name of Passenger **MALLICK/HM** / Non-Transferable	Issued in Exchange for	Date of issue void	**NYC**	**AF**	**50,000**	**For Training Purposes only**
			LON	**AI**	**M/Rs.**	
			DL	**AI**	**50,000**	

Coupon not valid before				Original Issue	Carrier	Form & Sl. No.	Place	Date	Agent Numerical Code
1	**2**	**3**	**4**						

Coupon not valid after				Ticket Designator	Tour Code
1	**2**	**3**	**4**		

IT IS UNLAWFUL TO PURCHASE OR RESELL THE TICKET FROM/TO ANY ENTITY OTHER THAN THE ISSUING CARRIER OR ITS AUTHORISED AGENTS

SB

X/O		Not good for passage	Carrier	Flight /class	Date	Time	Status	Fare Basis	Allowance
	From	New Delhi/IGIAP	**IA**		**18 Jul**	**13.15**	**OK**	**F**	
	To	**Paris/**	**—**		**Void**		**—**		
	To	**Lon/Heathrow**	**—**		**Void**		**—**		
	To	**NYC/JFK**	**—**		**Void**		**—**		
	To	**—Void—**							

Commission	Tax	Form of Payment **Cash**	Commission **Rate 10**	Fare **Rs. 1,000,000**
		Passenger Ticket & Baggage Check—Issued by Void for Training Purposes only Subject to Conditions of Contract on Passenger's Ticket		

Fare **Rs. 1,00,000**	Equiv. Fare Rs.	Route Code	Encode	CPN	AIRLINE CODE	FORM	SERIAL NO.	CK
Tax **Rs. 10,000**	Total **Rs. 1,10,000**						**950:000:000**	

Fig. 7.17: Specimen of A Round Trip International Ticket.

Date

Enter the date using a 3-letter abbreviation for the months and a 2-digit for the day. For example,

Date
08 JAN

Time

Enter the time that the flight departs on international tickets indicating the line in the 24 hour clock style. For example,

Time
2130

On domestic tickets use 'A' or 'AM', 'P' or 'PM' and 'N' for noon. For example,

Time
8.25 AM

Status

Enter the status of the reservation confirmed or wait listed or requested. For example,

Status				
OK	or	WL	or	RQ

Fare Basis

Enter the fare basis code. This code consists of three parts the prime code, secondary code and discount code. All ticket must have the prime code which indicate the class of service. If applicable use the secondary and discount codes. For example,

Fare Basis
YLE 42

In this case 'Y' is the prime code which indicates that this is for coach seating and 'L' is the secondary code which indicates the low season. E 42 is the discount code which indicates the passenger is travelling on a 42 day excursion.

Ticket Designator

Enter the type of discount if it applies to the entire ticket. For example, for Chile:

Ticket Designator
CH

Tour Code

Enter the official tour code number if issuing the ticket on an international journey. On a domestic ticket involving a tour, use a tour ticket.

Tour Code

Coupon Not Valid Before

If the passenger is travelling on an excursion or restricted fare, enter the earliest return date for each segment.

Coupon not valid before			
1	2	3	4

Coupon Not Valid After

Enter the date by which all travel must be completed.

Coupon not valid after			
1	2	3	4

Allowance

On international travel only enter the free luggage weight allowance when applicable. Domestic travel and most of the major international routes are now using a per-piece allowance.

Allowance

Fare Calculation

This box is required to be calculated in case of conjunction tickets, re-issued tickets, when a city not shown on the itinerary is used to construct the fare to show a surcharge, a differential, a stop-over charge, or mileage charge.

From/To	Carrier	Fare Calculation

Fare

In case of international ticket, enter the fare (without tax) and currency code.

Fare

Equivalent Amount Paid

The amount of currency collected from the passenger and the currency code should be entered.

Equivalent Amount Paid

Tax

Enter the amount of tax. In case a ticket involves both international and domestic tax these should be indicated separately.

Tax

Total

The sum of the fare and tax should be entered.

Total

Form of Payment

When the payment is made by other than the travellers cheque, enter the form of payment. When an exchange ticket is issued enter the form of payment as indicated on the original ticket. In case of credit sale enter the '2' letter code of the credit card company and the credit card.

Form of Payment

Origin and Destination

Enter the full name of the city showing where the transportation will commence and terminate.

Origin	Destination

Conjunction Tickets

In case conjunction tickets are issued to complete a passenger itinerary, enter the complete form and serial number of all other and tickets being issued to complete the passenger's itinerary.

Conjunction Tickets

Issued in Exchange For

This box is to be completed when a ticket is issued in exchange for another ticket. Complete form and serial number of the original ticket must be entered.

Issued in Exchange for

Original Issues, Carrier, Form and Serial Number, Place, Date, Agent's Numerical Code

Enter the number of the original tickets, the place and date of original issue and the agent's numerical code.

Original Issue	Carrier	Form and Serial No.	Agent's Numerical Code

Endorsement/Restriction

Any special restrictions or information or requested or wait listed flights are indicated in this column.

Endorsement / Restrictions

Place of Issue-Agency

This box is complete with the validator and shows the agency name, location and numerical code.

Place of Issue-Agency

Commission and Tax

Enter the appropriate commission and tax. Enter these as percentage or write in the actual dollar amount.

Commission	Tax

Commission Rate

Enter the commission codes applicable to the ticket. For example, to indicate an 8 per cent commission based on family travel.

Commission	Fare
FT-8	

Connection No., No Stop-Over (X) *Or Stop-Over* (O)

On domestic tickets use an 'X' to indicate a connection no stop-over permitted or a 'O' to indicate stop-over need to all cities except original and destination.

O/X	

AIR TICKET RELATED TRAFFIC DOCUMENTS

The act of issuing an airline ticket or booking an auxiliary product constitute a sale transaction. The documents that are used to process sales transactions are referred to as traffic documents. Modern day travellers who purchase the right to travel on an airline, occupy a hotel room, or rent an automobile also receive documents verifying the services to which they entitle. Airline tickets, rail tickets, hotel vouchers, car rental vouchers, and tour vouchers are examples of such documents. To sell airline tickets, a travel agency must be authorised by an airline or accredited by the IATA. IATA was formed by the airlines to coordinate the collection of revenues from ticket sales by retail travel agencies. Weekly, each agency submits a sales report and deposits all monies from ticket sales in a special bank account. IATA withdraws funds from the agency's account to pay the airlines. The bank that holds the travel agency's account is called an 'area bank'. Besides airline tickets, other types of transactions, such as prepaid hotel reservations, car rentals, and package tours, can also be processed through the area bank system.

Following is the list of traffic documents:

1. Airline Ticket
2. Prepaid Ticket Advice (PTA)
3. Refund Exchange Notice (REN)
4. Universal Credit Card Charge Form

5. Miscellaneous Charges Order (MCO)
6. Hotel Voucher
7. Car Rental Voucher
8. Tour Voucher
9. Transfer Voucher
10. Cash Card Refund Notice
11. Credit Card Refund Notice
12. Ticket Exchange Notice
13. Agent's Automated Deduction
14. Sales Report Settlement Authorization
15. Other documents:
    - (*a*) Debit Memos
    - (*b*) Credit Memos
    - (*c*) PTA Refund Authorities
    - (*d*) Recall Commission Form.

The travel agency is responsible for the ticket stock received, collection of the correct amounts written on the issued tickets and remittance of all funds collected in trust for the air carriers. Since 1964 travel agents have used the common ticket coupons for both ATC/IATA carriers, this standard ticket permits a uniform accounting and remittance procedure under the area settlement plan. Air passenger tickets are usually issued in sequence by serial number and reported in the same way; the tickets sold also are reported by dollar value (or monetary amount in a foreign currency). The auditor's coupon contains all information: the passenger's name, all flight segments of the passage, fare calculation, and form of payment collected. The auditor's coupon, included with sales report, is mailed weekly to the central accounting office. The fares calculated by travel agents is checked by central accounting; discrepancies are reported; and agents are liable for under collections of fares.

In review, it is essential that the travel agent knows the function of each flight coupon. The coupon authorises passage between the points shown on the light area of the coupon, and serves as evidence that the fare shown on the coupon has been paid. The coupon is an agreement between the airline and the passenger for reserved seat on the flight specified. The coupon contains all information necessary to insure expeditious handling of the passenger and his luggage. In other words, it helps airline agents to guide the passenger on the correct flights. The coupon establishes all the conditions which must be known to a ticket agent should be have to re-issue or refund the coupon. The coupon contains all the necessary information which enables the carrying airline to bill the issuing airline for the fare between the two points shown on it, if the issuing airline and carrying airline are not the same. Flight coupons cannot be honoured individually. The passenger must present the coupon to the carrier to which it is made out, in the order in which it is issued and only if all unused coupons are presented together.

HOW TO MAKE AN AIRLINE TICKET ?

IATA ticket stock is supplied in booklet form with carbon-backed pages. Ticket forms are supplied in either 2 or 4-coupon booklets. For itineraries with more than four air segments, multiple ticket forms, or conjunction tickets, are used. The serial number of conjunction tickets must be in consecutive order. An itinerary with five segments would require two 4-coupon booklets, supplying a total of eight coupons. Five-coupon would be used for flight segments, and there would be voided. Because serial numbers of conjunction tickets must be consecutive, 4-coupon booklets may not be mixed with 2-coupon booklets.

A separate passenger coupon is prepared for each air segment in the itinerary. Two coupons are removed and retained from the ticket by the travel agent. Each flight coupon is valid from one point to another. Thus in the case of a connection, a separate coupon must be issued for each leg of the trip.

Each blank ticket has a serial number imprinted in the upper right corner and repeat at the bottom. When blank ticket stock is issued to a retail travel agency, the serial numbers are recorded. As tickets are issued, the serial numbers must be reported to back to the IATA area home in consecutive order. The airline ID plate for the carrier with which the space was booked is used to validate the ticket. Tickets are always issued in consecutive order.

If the wrong carrier's plate is used in error to validate a ticket, the entire ticket must be avoided.

The full hand written procedure for filling is given in Figure 7.18, as per the following guidelines:

1 & 1A. *Place of Issue Agency, and Date of Issue:* Place proper airline identification plate and your agency identification plate in

HANDWRITTEN AIR TICKET

Endorsement/ Restrictions 25	Origin/Destination 18	Booking Reference	From/ To 21	Carrier 21	Fare calculation 21	3330:111:222
	Conjunction Ticket(s) 17					
Name of Passenger 2 / Not Transferable	Issued in Exchange for 19	Date of Issue VOID 1a				Place of Issue–Agency 1 VOID For training purposes only
Coupon Not Valid Before 14: 1 / 2 / 3 / 4	Original issue 20a / Carrier 20 20b / Form/ Serial No. 20c	Place 20d / Date 20e / Agent's Numberical code	24 Auditor's Coupon			KM 13
Coupon Not Valid After 14: 1 / 2 / 3 / 4	Ticket Destination 15	Tour Code 22				
X/O Not good for passage 4	Carrier 8 / Flight/ Class 9 / Date 10 / Time 11	Status 12 / Fare Basis 7 / Allowance 7a				23 Camm. Code Rate
From 3						
To			Form of Payment 16			It is unlawful to purchase of resell this ticket from/to any entity other than the issuing carrier or its authorised agents.
To						
To						
	Commission 24a	Tax	Passenger Ticket and Baggage Check: Issued by VOID For Training Purpose only Sujet to conditions of contract on passenger's coupon 1b			
Fare 5	Equivalent fare paid Rs. 6	Route Code / EN Code				
Tax	Total		CPN	Airline Code	Form	Serial No. / CK 3330:111:222

Fig. 7.18: Specimen of a Handwritten Ticket.

ticket writer and validate. The date of validation must be the date of the ticket entries are made.

Place of Issue Agency 1	Date of Issue 1a	Subject to Conditions of Contract on Passenger's Coupon 1b

2. *Name of Passenger:* Enter passenger last name, slash, initial, and title:

Name of Passenger Negi/Gaurav M./Mr.	Not Transferable 2

3. *From/To:* Enter passenger itinerary. Include state abbreviations and airport names if applicable.

	FROM
	TO ....
	....
	....
	3

4. *X/O:* Enter applicable stop-over, ..o stop-over code.

OX	FROM
X	TO
O	
X	4

5. *Fare, Tax and Total:* Enter applicable 'Fare', 'Tax' and 'Total' and, if applicable, ISO country or IATA currency codes.

FARE Rs............	
TAX Rs............	TOTAL Rs........... 5

6. *Equivalent Fare PD*: Enter amount in Rupees, if Ticket issued in foreign currency.

EQUIVALENT FARE Rs..............
6

7. *Fare Basis:* Enter primary, restrictive and other applicable alpha/tariff numeric code(s) representing fare construction.

FARE BASIS
Y
Y
Y
7

7a. *Allowance:* When the baggage weight allowance is other than the Indian free allowance, insert the free weight figure in the 'Allow' box opposite the segment to which it applies.

ALLOWANCE
7a

8. *Carrier:* Enter Carrier, official airline designator.

CARRIER
AI
AI
AI
AI
8

9. *Flight/Class:* Print flight number followed by aircraft compartment code reflect space reserved or requested.

FLIGHT/CLASS
....
....
....
9

10. *Date:* Enter two digit scheduled boarding date of departure and mark (3 letter abbreviation).

DATE
8 JUL
....
....
....
10

11. *Time:* Enter departure time using conventional clock (A or AM, P or PM, N-Noon, M-Midnight).

TIME
2.30 P
4.15 P
6.00 P
11.00 P
11

12. *Status:* Print code for reservation status.

STATUS
O.K.
O.K.
O.K.
12

13. *Sign:* Sign of reservation agent from whom ticketing information was obtained or to whom also given. Also, the agent writing the ticket may initial here.

		13

14. *Coupons not valid before and after*: If appropriate insert either expiration date of applicable tariff or date by which travel must be completed, also insert any minimum stay restrictions or other type restrictions imposed due to advance reservations/purchase requirements.

COUPONS NOT VALID BEFORE			
1	2	3	4
COUPONS NOT VALID AFTER			
1	2	3	4
			14

15. *Ticket Designator:* Enter alpha code (*e.g.* CD, CL) when the fare is calculated as a percentage of a full published fare. Follow with percentage of discount.

TICKET DESIGNATOR
....
15

16. *Form of Payment:* Enter appropriate form of payment. When issuing ticket issued in exchange for an another ticket enter form of payment shown on original ticket.

FORM OF PAYMENT
Cheque
16

17. *Conjunction Tickets:* Enter airline form and serial number, and last two digits of the serial number of all tickets being issued to provide flight coupons for the passenger's itinerary.

CONJUNCTION TICKET(S)
17

18. *Origin/Destination:* Enter city name(code) whenever tickets are issued in exchange or conjunction.

ORIGIN/DESTINATION
IND
18

19. *Issued in Exchange For:* Enter airline, form and serial number of ticket(s) or order being exchanged.

ISSUED IN EXCHANGE FOR
....
19

20. *Original Issue, Carrier, Form and Serial Number, Place, Date, Agent's Numeric Code:* Enter carrier, form and serial number, and place of issue, date and agent, numeric code of original ticket or order.

ORIGINAL ISSUE	CARRIER	FORM AND SERIAL NUMBER	PLACE	DATE	AGENT'S NUMERICAL CODE
					20

21. *From/To, Carrier and Fare Calculation:* Required only for conjunction tickets; re-issued tickets; of a city not shown in itinerary is used in constructing fare, surcharge, differential, stop-over charge, or mileage charge if applicable.

FROM/TO DEL	CARRIER	FARE CALCULATION
...	AI	Rs.............
...	AI	Rs.............
DEL	AI	Rs.............
		21

22. *Tour Code:* Enter IT numbers if required by carrier.

TOUR CODE
....
22

23. *Commission Code*: If using a code in the commission code box enter the same code in this box. If no commission code applies, leave this area blank.

23

24. *Commission: Auditor, and Agent's Coupons:* Enter commission and tax information for reporting purposes.

COMMISSION	TAX
....	 24

25. *Endorsement/Restriction (Carbon):* Show any special restriction.

ENDORSEMENT/RESTRICTION
....
25

After the ticket has been completed and validated, the green (auditor's) coupon and pink (agent's) coupon are detached, along with any voided coupons. The passenger receipt and flight coupons are given to the passenger.

AIRLINE TICKETING PROCEDURES

Example:

Below is given a specimen of an airline ticket with column 1 boxes numbered. You are required to explain the procedure to be followed for filling in this ticket:

STANDARD BANK SETTLEMENT PLANE TICKET

ENDORSEMENT/RESTRICTIONS (CARBON) 24	ORIGIN 20	DESTINATION 20	FROM/TO	CARRIER	FARE CALCULATION 14	8453:976:632
	CONNECTION TICKET 21	AGENT'S COUPON				PLACE OF ISSUE—AGENCY 25

NAME OF PASSENGER 1	NOT TRANSFERABLE	ISSUED IN EXCHANGE FOR 22	DATE OF ISSUE

COUPONS NOT VALID BEFORE				ORIGINAL ISSUE	CARRIER	FORM AND SERIAL NO. 23	PLACE	DATE	AGENT'S NUMERICAL CODE
11	2	3	4						
COUPONS NOT VALID AFTER				TICKET DESIGNATOR 9				TOUR CODE 10	
12	2	3	4						

X/O	NOT GOOD FOR PASSAGE	FARE BASIS	ALLOW	CARRIER	FLIGHT/ CLASS	DATE	TIME	STATUS
	FROM 2	8	13	3	4	5	6	7
23	TO							
	TO							
	TO							
	TO							

COMML. RATE 27 | FARE

FORM OF PAYMENT 19

IT IS UNLAWFUL TO PURCHASE OR RESELL THIS TICKET FROM/TO ANY ENTITY OTHER THAN THE ISSUING CARRIER OR ITS AUTHORIZED AGENTS

COMMISSION 26	TAX 26	PASSENGER TICKET & BAGGAGE CHECK—ISSUED BY SUBJECT TO CONDITION OF CONTRACT ON PASSENGERS COUPON

FARE 15	EQUIV. AMOUNT PD 16
TAX 17	TOTAL 18

ROUTE CODE ENCODE CPM AIRLINE CODE FROM SERIAL NUMBER CK

O ||" 8453976632 3 ||"

Fig. 7.19: Specimen of a Standard Bank Settlement Plane Ticket.

Example:

---

1. Enter the passengers surname followed by a slash, first initial and then title. EXAMPLE: Govind/T. Mr. If the passenger is an unaccompanied minor, enter UM followed by the age in brackets. EXAMPLE: ANIRUDH/A. Master (UM 8)
2. Enter the passengers complete itinerary using block letters starting with the city of origin and listing each connection, city, stopover city, and destination. When a city is served by more than one airport, enter both the city name and the airport name. EXAMPLE:

   From:

From:	NEW YORK/ KENNEDY
To:	LONDON/HEATHROW

3. Enter the two-letter code of the airline involved. EXAMPLE: AA
4. Enter the passengers flight number followed by the class of service. The class of service determines in which compartment of the aircraft the passenger will be seated. EXAMPLE: 501Y
5. Enter the date using a 3-letter abbreviation for the month and a 2-digit for the day. EXAMPLE: 07 FEB
6. Enter the time that the flight departs. On domestic tickets use A or AM, P or PM, and N for noon. EXAMPLE: 715A. On international tickets show the time in the 24-hour clock style. EXAMPLE: 2145
7. Enter the status of the reservation (OK) for confirmed, (WL) for waitlisted, or (RQ) for requested. EXAMPLE: WL
8. Enter the fare basis code. This code consists of three parts—the prime code, secondary code, and discount code. All tickets must have the prime code, which indicates the class of service. If applicable use the secondary and discount codes.

Example:

YLE 45 (Y) is the primary code, which shows that this is for coach seating (L) is the secondary code indicated the low season. (E 45) is the discount code which indicates the passenger is travelling on a 45-day excursion.

9. Enter the type of discount if it applies to the entire ticket. EXAMPLE: CH (child)
10. Enter the official tour code number if issuing the ticket for an international journey. On a domestic ticket involving a tour, use a tour ticket.
11. If the passenger is travelling on an excursion or restricted fare, enter the earliest return date for each segment.
12. Enter the date by which all travel must be completed.
13. On international travel only enter the free baggage weight allowance when applicable. Domestic travel and most of the major international routes are now using a per-piece allowance.
14. Complete the fare calculation box. This is required only for conjunction tickets, re-issued tickets, when a city not shown on the itinerary is used to construct the fare, to show a surcharge, a differential, a stop-over charge, or a mileage charge.
15. Enter the fare (without tax) and currency code if writing an international ticket.
16. Enter the amount of currency collected from the passenger and currency code. This box does not have to be completed when the passenger pays in U.S. dollars.
17. Enter the tax. If a ticket involves both international and domestic tax, show them separately.
18. Enter the sum of the fare and tax.
19. Enter the form of payment, when payment is other than cash or travellers check. When issuing an exchange ticket, enter form of payment shown on the original ticket. When a credit card sales is involved enter the 2-letter code of the credit card company and the credit card number.
20. Enter the city names in full showing where the transportation will commence and terminate.
21. When more than one ticket is needed to complete a passenger itinerary, you have to issue conjunction tickets. In this box enter the complete form and serial number of all other tickets being issued to complete the passenger's itinerary.
22. Complete this box when you are issuing a ticket in exchange

for another ticket. Enter the complete form and serial number of the original ticket.

23. Enter the number of the original tickets, the place and date of original issue, and the agents numeric code.
24. This box can be used to show any special restrictions or information or to show a requested or waitlisted flight.
25. This box is complete with the validator and shows the agency name, location and numeric code.
26. Enter the appropriate commission and tax. If these figures are a straight percentage such as 8% for domestic tax, put 8 in the tax box. If not a straight percentage, such as a $3.00 international tax, write in the actual dollar amount.
27. Enter the commission codes applicable to the ticket.

Example:

FT-8. This indicates an 8% commission based on family travel.

28. On domestic tickets use an (X) to indicate a connection, no stop-over permitted or a (O) to indicate a stop-over next to all cities except origin and destination.

UNIVERSAL CREDIT CARD CHARGE FORM

When a traveller uses a credit card to purchase an airline ticket, a Universal Credit Card Charge Form is issued to record the transaction. After signing the form, the client is given the blue copy of the charge form. The Contractor Invoice copy is stapled on top of the audition ticket coupon. When a ticket is purchased by a credit card, the credit card company pays the airline not the travel agency for the purchase. The agency still receives a commission on the ticket, whether it is purchased by credit card or cash.

When a passenger pays for an airline ticket by credit card, a Universal Credit Card Charge Form is filled out to record the sales transaction, as given in Figure 7.20.

The form is filled up as follows:

1. The three-digit airline number is entered in the carrier code box. In Figure 7.20. the passenger is someone other than the cardholder. The passenger name and connection of the passenger with the cardholder are noted on the form.

UNIVERSAL CREDIT CARD CHARGE FORM

I ACKNOWLEDGE RECEIPT OF THIS TICKET(S) AND FOR COUPONS FOR RELATED CHARGES DESCRIBED HERE ON. PAYMENT IN FULL TO BE MADE WHEN BILLED OR IN EXTENDED PAYMENTS IN ACCORDANCE WITH STANDARD POLICY OF COMPANY ISSUING CARD AND AS REFLECTED IN OFFICIAL TARIFFS. X PHONE ORDER / KM	UNIVERSAL CREDIT CARD CHARGE FORM CARRIER CODE 001 DATE OF ISSUE APR 17	3. CONTRACTOR'S INVOICE COPY IF EXTENDED PAYMENT APPLICABLE CIRCLE NO. OF MONTHS 3 6 9 12		DATE AND PLACE OF ISSUE
NAME OF PASSENGER IF OTHER THAN CARD HOLDER RAJAN / R.	QUOTA NO.	CONNECTION OF PASSENGER WITH SUBSCRIBER FAMILY	APPROVAL CODE 21	
COMPLETE ROUTING	RATE BASIS	CARRIER AIRLINE FORM 001 1227 421	SERIAL NO. 875	KM
CHI–PHX–CHI– BWE 147	AA	TICKETS NOT TRANSFERABLE NO CASH REFUND CREDIT CARD NAME/CODE AX		
FARE 30,000 TAX 3,000 EQUIV. AMOUNT PAID	TOTAL 33,000	ROUTE CODE		2316940004182000 9/94

Fig. 7.20: Specimen of Universal Credit Card Charge Form.

2. Obtain credit authorisation from the credit card company by telephone before the charge can be processed. If the credit card company approves the charge, an approval note is further furnished to the ticket agent or travel agent. The code is entered in the 'approval code' box on the charge form. The rating, validating carrier, and ticket number are also entered on the form. When the ticket number is entered, the three-digit airline number is written before the form number and special number. The base fare, tax and total fare are entered in the fare, tax and total boxes.

A credit card imprinter is used to make an imprint on the credit card on the charge form. When the imprint is made, the credit card account number, expiration date, and card holder's name are imprinted in the lower right hand portion of the form.

The passenger must sign the charge form to authorise the charge, unless the order was taken out by phone. In the case of phone order, a signature is not required, if the cardholder's signature is on file at the travel agency. The client's copy is given to the passenger. The contractor's invoice copy of the charge form is stapled to the auditor's ticket coupon. Eventually, both items are sent back to the airline for book-keeping purposes.

Table 7.1 indicates various Credit Cards and their codes.

Table 7.1: Credit Cards and their Codes

Credit Card	*Code*
Access Cards	XS
Air Canada	AC
Air Travel Card (UATP)	TP
Arwest Credit Card	RW
Alaska Airlines Credit Card	AS
Aloha Airlines Credit Card	TS
American Express	AX
American Airlines Vacation Credit Card	AA
Bank of Hawaii	BH
Barclay Card	BB
Branieff Fastcharge	BI
Canadian Pacific Credit Card	CP
Carte Blanche	CB

(Contd.)

(Contd.)

Credit Card	Code
China Airlines Dynasty Travel Card	DT
Citizen and Southern National Bank	CS
Club DES 200 Air France	AF
Connecticut Bank and Trust Co	CU
Continental Air System Travel Card	CO
Diamond Credit	MD
Diners Club/American Torch Club	DC
Eastern Airlines Charge-A-Trip Card	CA
Empire Card	MT
Federated Credit Card	FC
Hawaian Airlines Credit Card	HA
Master Charge	CA
Million Credit Service	MC
National Airlines Sun King Travel Card	NA
North Central Airlines On-Line Card	NC
North West Airlines Air Credit Card	NW
Ozark Airlines Tic-A-Trip Card	OZ
Pan American Airways Take Off Card	PA
Piedmont Airlines Air Travel Credit Card	PI
Select Credit	SR
Shoppers Charge	SC
Southern Airways Air Travel Credit Card	SO
Texas International Airlines On-Line Travel Card	TI
Trans World Airline Gateway Credit Card	TW
Trust Card	TC
United Airlines Personal Credit Card	UC
UNI-Serve (UNICARD)	US
Visa (Bank Americard)	BA
Western Airlines Travel Card	WA
Western International Hotels	WH

PREPAID TICKET ADVICE (PTA)

PTA authorises a ticket to be issued at different location than the point of purchase. For example, a passenger might purchase a ticket from a travel agency by telephone and arrange to have the ticket issued at the airline's ticket counter at the airport on the date of departure. In this case, the travel agency would sent a PTA to the airline, authorising a ticket to be issued at the airport ticket counter. PTA's can be used for either domestic or international itineraries, however some foreign carriers do not accept PTA's. The PTA could be used for different purposes:

1. Authorisation for a ticket to be issued at the airport ticket counter,
2. To arrange prepaid transportation. For example, a company might prepay a ticket for a contractor or an employee in a different city or a law firm,
3. Might repay a ticket for a witness who has been called to testify in a trial.

In most cases, a PTA cannot be used to ticket a passenger in the same city where the reservation is made, unless the reservation is booked less than 24 hours before the schedule of departure. Special ticket stock is used to document a PTA. A non-refundable processing fee is charged by the ticketing airline. Part of this fee may be added to the agency's commission. A PTA may be communicated to the ticketing airline either by telephone or by means of a computer reservation system.

When communicated by telephone, the following information is provided by the booking agent:

1. Name of the travel agency
2. PTA Number
3. Total base fare, tax, and total fare
4. Agency commission rate
5. Form of payment

Figure 7.21. is a specimen of a Prepaid Ticket Advice. The 'Remark' box is used to note endorsements, restrictions, or other information. The fee charged by the airline is entered in the 'SVC Charge' (Service Charge) box. If the PTA is charged to a credit card, the total charge, including both the airfare and the PTA Service Charge, should be entered on the Universal Credit Card Charge Form.

The fare, tax, cancellation penalty, and total refund are entered

PREPAID TICKET ADVICE (PTA)

Not Transferable	Prepaid Ticket Advice	Fare Rs. 39,630	8508:772:173
Issue to Passenger Name(s) MADAN / MR.	Auditor's Coupon Date of Issue 28 MAY 92	Tax Rs. 3,170	Date Place of Issue
Address 123 SOUTH MAIN STREET CHICAGO IL Phone No.: (1312) 565-1111	Tickets to be issued by CO	Other Tax	
		Other Funds	
		PTA Total Rs. 42,800	KM
		Equiv. Amount Paid Rs.	Currency USD / Rate of Exchange
Routing and Baggage Reservation Data		Service Charge Paid Rs. Rs. 2,500	Issued in exchange for
CO 25 Y 17 JUL ORD DEN	City / State / Country	Total Amount Paid Rs. Rs. 45,300	Date Place / Original Issue
CO 313 Y 18 JUL DEN PHX	CHI / IL / US	Comm. Rate 10	Form of Payment CHECK
Remark REFUND ABC CO ONLY / SVCCHG–NON REF		Issued by	
Tour Code	Commission 42 13 / Tax 31 70	VOID	
Purchaser's Name ABC COMPANY		For Training purpose only	
Address 4200 E. BROWN ST. Phone No. (602) 555-0120	CPN	A/L	Form / Serial No. / CK
PHOENIX, AZ	⊙		||"8508772173 6||" ⊙
			Do not mark or write in the white area above

Fig. 7.21: Specimen of a Prepaid Ticket Advice (PTA).

in the appropriate boxes. The ticket numbers of the flight coupons that are to be refunded are entered in the *refunded ticket number* block. On each line, the number of coupons, three-digit airline number, form number, and serial number are entered. The agency's ARC number is entered in the *agency code* block.

The agent's copy of the Refund/Exchange Notice is removed by the ticket agent. Under ARC guidelines, the notice must be kept on file a minimum of two years. The carrier's copy of the REN is attached to the invalidated flight coupons and sent to the ARC area bank with the weekly sales report.

REFUND/EXCHANGE NOTICE (REN)

This note is prepared to process the refund, in case a passenger returns a ticket to a travel agency. An entire ticket may be refunded, as if any flight coupons have been used, the unused portion of the ticket may be refunded, subject to any restrictions or cancellation penalties that may apply. If the ticket has a cancellation penalty, the amount of the penalty must be subtracted from the value of the unused portion of the ticket. If the ticket is non-refundable under the fare restrictions, the passenger must be denied a refund. Figure 7.22 is a specimen of Refund Exchange Notice.

When any portion of a ticket is refunded, the word 'Refund' is written by the ticket agent in large letters across the flight coupons to be refunded. The fare, tax, cancellation penalty, and total refund are entered on the appropriate boxes. The ticket numbers of the flight coupons that are to be refunded are entered in the 'refund ticket number' block. On each line, the number of coupons, three digit airline number, form number, and serial number are entered. The agency's ARC number is entered in the 'agency code' block.

The agenet's copy of the Refund/Exchange Notice is removed by the ticket agent. Under ARC guidelines, the notice must be kept on file a minimum of two years. The carrier's copy of the REN is attached to the invalidated flight coupons and send to the ARC area bank with the weekly sales report.

The Atlantic Coast stretches for miles of pure white sand and crystal sea for cruise line passengers.

Brochures give essentially general information on embarkation, travel documents, sightseeing tours and other passage contract information.

REFUND EXCHANGE NOTICE (REN)

COMPUTATION	
A Original fare paid	Rs. ...
B Less fare used	Rs. ...
C Fare value of unused ticket	Rs. ...
D Less fare value of new ticket	Rs....
Amount to be refunded/collected	
E Fare	Rs. ...
F Tax Rs. ...	Rs. ...
G Tax	
H Tax	
I Net Fare Paid Total	
J Penalty	Rs. ...
K Total	Rs. ...

REFUND/ EXCHANGE NOTICE **CARRIER'S COPY** **AGENCY CODE NO.** 8 8 | 9 6 4 3 | 2 1

Passenger's Name **SACHIN / Mr.**

Card holder/Corporate name

Form of payment/Account No. **CASH**

Today's Date: Month 03, Day 07, Year 2000

Check one Box

Refund Cash Credit
Unused ticket ☑ ☐

Exchange Cash Credit
Add Collect ☐ ☐
Even ☐ N/A
Refund ☐ ☐

Refund/Exchange Ticket Number: FLT CPNS, Carrier, Form/Sl.No.

New Ticket Number: Carrier, Form/ Serial No., CK

PFCs From Refunded/Exchanged Flight Coupons

Airport CD | Airport CD | Airport CD | Airport CD | Commission 3 | Tax 3

Fig. 7.22: Specimen of Refund Exchange Notice (REN).

Refund Exchange Notice

Ticket Surcharge Instructions	*Normal Cash/Credit Refund Instructions*
1. Invalidate all exchange transactions by making 'Exchange' across the exchanged coupon(s)	1. Invalidate all refund coupons by making 'Refund' across the refunded coupon(s)
2. Prepare only one notice per transaction, indicating the coupon numbers, carrier code and form/serial number from the exchange tickets, and the carrier code, form/serial number, and check digit from the new ticket	2. Prepare a separate notice for each transactions indicating coupon numbers, carrier code card form/serial numbers of the refunded ticket(s)
3. Check the applicable box: add collect, even, or refund under the appropriate column: cash or credit	3. Indicate whether a cash or credit refund by checking the appropriate box (to box only)
4. Complete boxes A through K for exchanges with refund; for all other exchanges, complete boxes E through K. Fill in the passenger name, card holder/corporate name, if applicable, form of payment, agency code number, date of exchange, commission and tax boxes	4. To compute convert fare to the refunded, complete boxes E through K only. Fill in the passenger name and card holder name, if applicable, form of payment, agency code number, and date of refund, commission and tax boxes

Do not try to sell the client one ship as the only one. As a good travel agent you should offer a couple of suggestions and explain differences between ships. You will have reports from your customers on their cruises; other agents in the office will make suggestions about ship travel; "Your own FAM (cruise) trips; trade publication reports on cruise travel will be of assistance in discussing the merits of a particular cruise with a customer.

TICKET EXCHANGES

A ticket exchange may be required for any of the following situations:

1. A change of fare
2. A change of itinerary or routing
3. A change of passenger name.

A fare change may require additional money to be collected from the passenger, or, if the new fare is less than the fare previously paid, a partial refund. A ticket could be exchanged either by refunding the original ticket and issuing a new ticket or by preparing a Refund/Exchange Notice. When a ticket is exchanged, the word 'exchange' is written by the ticket agent in large block letters across the face of the previously issued ticket.

TICKET EXCHANGE NOTICE

When a new ticket is to be issued to replace a ticket previously sold to a client, a ticket exchange may be required. A ticket could be exchanged in one of the two ways—by refunding the original ticket and issuing a new ticket by preparing a Ticket Exchange Notice, specimen of which is given in Figure 7.23.

CASH REFUND NOTICE

When a customer returns all or part of a ticket for a refund, a Cash Refund Notice is prepared. The word 'Refund' is written in large letters across all of the refunded ticket coupons. The agent's copy of the Cash Refund Notice is removed and retained in file. IATA requires the form to be kept on file for a minimum of two years. The carrier's copy of the Cash Refund Notice is attached to the invalidated coupons and sent to the IATA area bank with the weekly sales report. If the agency previously received a commission for the ticket, IATA will take the commission back. Specimen of Cash Refund Notice is given in Figure 7.24.

CREDIT CARD REFUND NOTICE

When a ticket that was originally purchased by credit card is returned for refund or exchange, a cash refund cannot be made. Instead, a Credit Card Refund Notice is prepared. The refund notice is validated with the appropriate airline's ID plate. For American Express, Carte Blanche or Diner's Club transactions, the contractor credit copy is sent to the credit card company. For Visa, Master Card, etc., the contractor credit copy is sent to the validating airline. The airline copy is sent with the weekly sales report to the IATA area bank. A specimen of credit card refund notice is given in Figure 7.25.

TICKET EXCHANGE NOTICE

Additional Collection or Refund Value

Fare

Tax

Other Tax

Exchange Penalty

Equivalent Amount Paid

Total

TICKET EXCHANGE NOTICE

Exchanged Ticket Number

FLT CPNS Carrier Form/Serial No.

Commision Tax

Original Agnet's Copy

BILL TO: NAME OF OPERATOR

New Ticket Number

Carrier Form/Serial No. CK

Check one Box Agency Code No.

☐ Add collect

☐ Even exchange

☐ Refund

Fig. 7.23: Specimen of a Ticket Exchange Notice.

CASH REFUND NOTICE

Staple here

CASH REFUND NOTICE

DUPLICATE CARRIER'S COPY

REFUND COMPUTATION

	Paid	Used	Refund
Fare			
Tax			
Less Cancellation Penalty			
Total Refund			

Refund Ticket Number

FLT	CPNS	Carrier	Form/Sl. No.

Agency Code Number

Date of Issue

Month	Day	Year

Passenger's Name

Commission	Tax

Fig. 7.24: Specimen of a Cash Refund Notice.

CREDIT CARD REFUND NOTICE

	Refund Computation	
A	Original Fare Paid	
B	Less Fare Used	(–)
C	Fare Value of Unused Ticket	(=)
D	Less Fare Value of New Ticket	(–)
E	Fare Refund	(=)
F	Tax Refund	(+)
G	Less Cancellation Penalty	(–)
H	Total Refund	(=)
	Credit Card Account Number	

CREDIT CARD REFUND NOTICE **6807:257:200**

Check one Box	Credit Card Contractor's Copy	
Normal Refund ☐	Date of Issue	Mail Today TO IATA Area Bank
Exchange with Refund ☐		

KM

Passenger's Name

Place of Issue/Agency

Card Holder/ Corporate Name

Refund Ticket Numbers

CPNS	Airline	Form/Serial No.

Credit Card name code	Date of original issue	
	Commission	Tax

Issued by

Subject to Applicable Tariffs

CPN	Airline code	Form	Serial No.	CK

6807:257:200

Fig. 7.25: Specimen of a Credit Card Refund Notice.

MISCELLANEOUS CHARGES ORDER

A miscellaneous charges order (MCO) (Ref. Figure 7.26) is a prepaid order form used when a client pays in advance for travel services and accommodations that are not included in a ticket. An MCO may include:

1. Air transportation (only when it cannot be included in a ticket). Note that if a carrier does not have a ticket agreement, it will not have an MCO agreement and will not accept an MCO for ticket payment.
2. Refundable balances.
3. Land arrangements (other than those included in a tour package)
4. Collection for PTAs (Prepaid Ticket Advices)
5. Surface transportation
6. Additional collections
7. Steamship transportation (air/sea tours, for example)
8. Deposits (initial payments with balance due)
9. Car rental or hotel accommodations (other than those included in a tour package)
10. Taxes (only when they cannot be included on a ticket–usually foreign)
11. Upgrading or under collections

An MCO has an auditor's coupon, an agent's coupon (Ref. Figure 7.27) and a passenger's coupon. The value of an MCO must not exceed certain limits. Specified transportation and land arrangements must not exceed the value of the MCO.

Staple the assembled documents together and submit in your next sales report, agent's, copies in your file for at least two years. Do not complete the PFC Boxes until instructed to do so by ARC.

When standard ticket stock cannot be used for a transaction, a Miscellaneous Charges Order (MCO) is prepared. The MCO may be used for any of the following types of transactions:

1. Air transportation
2. Surface transportation
3. Supplement charges
4. Land arrangements for inclusive tours
5. Car hire
6. Hotel accommodations

MISCELLANEOUS CHARGES ORDER—AUDITORS COUPON

NAME OF SERVICE FOR WHICH ISSUES		MISCELLANEOUS CHARGES ORDER AUDITOR'S COUPON	FORM OF PAYMENT CASH	8035:393:977
NAME OF PASSENGER NEGI / J. MR.		DATE OF ISSUE 29 MAR 79	DATE & TYPE OF CY	PLACE OF ISSUE - AGENCY VOID
TOUR NO.			AMOUNT IN FIGURES	
FOR VALUE	AMOUNT IN LETTERS: THREE HUNDRED TWENTY FOUR		COUPON VALUE 300.00	
TO	DELTA AIRLINES	MIAMI	TAX ON MCD 24.00	
MOTIVATION DATA	DL 1157 F MIA-BD2 31 MAR 79 - OPEN RETURN		TOTAL VALUE CY 324.00	ISSUED ON CONJUCTION WITH FORM & SERIAL NO.
MOTIVATION REFUNDABLE ONLY TO	PASSENGER Mrs. M. BIRON - PURCHASER		QUALITY AMT PAID	ISSUED ON EXCHANGE FOR FORM & SERIAL NO.
			TOTAL DATA 1	DATE & PLACE ORIGINAL ISSUE
	COMMISSION 7	TAX 8	ISSUED BY AIRLINE VALIDATION	
SUBJECT TO TERMS AND CONDITIONS ON BACK OF PASSENGERS COPY NOT TRANSFERABLE WORK IF MUTILATED OR ALTERED VALID ONE YEAR		FORM & SERIAL NUMBER || " 8035393977 2 ||"	CK	AIRLINE CODE

IT IS UNLAWFUL TO PURCHASE OR RESELL THIS TICKET FROM/TO ANY ENTITY OTHER THAN THE ISSUING CARRIER OR ITS AUTHORISED AGENTS.

Fig. 7.26: Specimen of a Miscellaneous Charges Order—Auditors Coupon.

MISCELLANEOUS CHARGES VOUCHER ORDER

MISCELLANEOUS CHARGES ORGER

Name of Passenger Not Transferable	Auditor's Coupon	Rate of Exchange		8520:770:004
Tour No.	Date of Issue	Equiv. Amount Paid Place of Issue Agency		It is unlawful to purchase or resell this ticket from/ to any other than the issuing carrier or its authorised agnets.
Type of service for which issued		Fare/Other (Rs.)		
		Tax		
	Valid for one year from the date of issue	Other Tax		
		Total Rs.	Comm. Rate	Void if mutilated or altered

Value for exchange	Amount in letters	Currency Rs.	Amount in figures	Issued in connection with
	To	AT		Form of Payment ....
	Reservation Data			
Remarks				
Endorsement Restrictions Coupon				Issued by
Issued in Exchange for		Commision	Tax	Subject to terms and conditions on back of passengr's coupon
Airline	Form Serial No.	ENC Code	CPN	
Original				
Issue Place Date	Agent's Numerical Code			8520:770:004

Fig. 7.27: Specimen of a Miscellaneous Charges Voucher Order.

7. Additional Collections
8. Deposit or down payments
9. Refundable balances.

The MCO form is validated with both the agency ID plate and airline ID plate. When it is validated, the MCO becomes a cash instrument, as valuable as an airline ticket.

MCO is a general purpose traffic document that may be issued for almost of any type of sale transaction, such as air or surface transportation, supplemental charges, car rental, tour or cruise deposits, and other transactions.

As given in Figure 7.27. a handwritten MCO must be validated with both any agency identification plate and an airline identification plate.

When a client pays in advance for a travel services and accommodation that are not included in a ticket, a prepaid order form is used which is known as Miscellaneous Charge Order. It includes the following:

1. *Air Transportation:* This is included when it cannot be included in the ticket. If a carrier does not have a ticket agreement, it will not have an MCO agreement and will not accept an MCO for ticket payment.
2. Refundable balances.
3. Land agreements (other than those included in a tour package).
4. Collections for Prepaid Ticket Advices (PTAs).
5. Surface transportation.
6. Additional collections.
7. Steamship transportation *e.g.* air/sea tours.
8. Deposits (initial payment with balance due).
9. Car rental or hotel accommodation (other than those included in a tour package).
10. Taxes (only when they cannot be included in a ticket usually foreign).
11. Up-grading under collections.

Each MCO has an auditors coupon, an agent's coupon and a passenger's coupon. The value of an MCO must not exceed certain limits. Specified transportation and land agreements must not exceed the value of MCO.

BOOKING A TOUR

The following information is required to book a tour:

1. Booking source
2. Tour identification
3. Departure date
4. Departure city
5. Passenger identification
6. Client preferences

The booking source is identified by the travel agency's name, address, telephone number, and ARC/IATA number. The tour is identified by the tour code or name. The departure date and city are required to determine availability and book air and hotel space. Departure for inland cities usually require air transportation to and from the gateway point. The passengers are identified by name, address, telephone number and form of payment. The number of travellers in the party and the number of adults per room are also required. If the party will include children, the age of each child may also be obtained.

When a tour is booked special client preferences should also be obtained, such as smoking or non-smoking accommodations, dietary restrictions, need for facilities for disabled travellers, optional activities, side tours and so forth. At the time a tour is booked, the fare is verified by the wholesalers, and a deposit is set, accompanied by an option date. The option date is the deadline by which the deposit must be received by the wholesaler. A confirmation may be given to the travel agency or to the client. Most wholesaler require payment in full 14 to 30 days before departure.

When all the costs of a tour have been paid in full the tour document vouchers are issued to the client. Typically, these document include the tickets for transportation and vouchers for transfers, accommodation and excursion tours. For example, if an air/land tour is booked, the tour documents usually include airline tickets, airport transfers and hotel vouchers.

HOW TO PROCURE TRAFFIC DOCUMENTS?

Rules and regulations for procuring traffic documents are given in IATA hand book. The usual method of obtaining supplies of traffic documents are detained by submitting a ticket requisition form. Standard ticket stock is ordered from the IATA Ticket Division. In general an agency's total ticket stock on hand should not exceed an average three month supply. In theory, the cost of ticket stock is included in the agency's annual fees to the IATA, regardless of actual usage. A handling charge is assessed to each shipment. Ticket stock is accompanied by a shipping order listing all issued items by serial number. On receiving the equipment, the travel agency must sign and return an acknowledgement. Until the acknowledgement is received by the IATA, additional ticket requisition will not be honoured.

TOUR ORDER

It is used in the sale of advertised air tours. When ticketing an air transportation package, a standard air ticket (air) and tour order (land portion) is required. The use of the tour order (Ref. Figure 7.28) assures the travel agent that non-ride air commissions are being claimed from IT-approved air tours. The standard tour order contains several coupons, *i.e.*, auditor's coupon, agent's coupon, ground transportation coupon, accommodation coupon and passenger's coupon. Each tour order contains the following information:

1. *Date of issue/issued by:* Validate with same carrier ID plate is used to issue passenger(s) air ticket(s), the agent's validation plate and the current date.
2. *Bill to tour operator:* Enter name of the tour operator.
3. *Tour code:* Enter tour code as shown in the manual.
4. *Tour name:* Enter name of tour.
5. *Passenger's name:* Enter passenger's first initials and last name.
6. *Party of:* Enter total members in the party.

Coupon No. 1

1. *Present to:* Enter name of airport transfer company or rental car company and name of the city where service will commence.
2. *Value:* Enter value of services rendered only when required by specific ticketing instruction.

A TOUR ORDER

NAME OF TOUR OPERATOR
PENROD PRODUCTIONS & TOURS

TOUR CODE
IT CATM-PPTBP3

AUDITOR'S COUPON

8053:093:115

OUR NAME
ROSE PARADE TOUR

DATE OF ISSUE
12 APR 79

TOTAL TOUR COST
445.00

PLACE OF ISSUE – AGENCY
VOID

IT IS UNLAWFUL TO PURCHASE OF RESELL THIS TICKET FROM/TO ANY ENTITY OTHER THAN THE ISSUING CARRIER OR ITS AUTHORISED AGENTS.

PASSENGER NAME
SUNITI NEGI

NOT TRANSFERABLE

FTP OF

LESS DEPOSIT
— 0 —

CODE	PRESENT TO	AT	VALUE
1	.... VOID		
2	PENROD PRADUCTIONS HOLLYWOOD, CA		....
3	.... VOID		445.00
4	.... VOID		....

FINAL PAYMENT
445.00

EQIV. AMOUNT PAID
— 0 —

AMOUNT TICKET NUMBER
001 86SD 323041

COMM. RATE
10

ISSUED ON EXCHANGE FOR

OUR FEATURES
HOTEL ACCOMMODATIONS — BEVERLY HILTON, RT TRANSFERS, RESERVED SEAT FOR THE ROSE PARADE, PLUS ALL OTHER TOUR FEATURES AS PER BROCHURE

FORM OF PAYMENT
CHECK

DATE AND PLACE OF O.R.G. ISSUE

SIGNATURE

NOTE DETAILS
☐ ☐ OTHERS
☐ OTHERS

COMMISSION
10

NET PERMITTANCE TAX
— 0 —

ISSUE BY
AIRLINE VALIDATION

SUBJECT TO TERMS AND CONDITIONS ON PASSENGERS COUPON

3

IN DATE 30 DEC. 78

OUT DATE 02 JAN 79

FORM

SERIAL NUMBER

CK

AIRLINE CODE

||"8053093115 4||"

Fig. 7.28: Specimen of a Tour Order.

Coupon No. 2

1. *Present to:* Enter name of tour operator or hotel as specified in ticketing instruction and name of city where tour commences.
2. *Enter value:* of services rendered only when required by specific ticketing instruction.

Coupon Nos. 3 and 4

1. *Present to:* Enter name and location of airport transfer company or additional services produced in the tour.
2. *Value:* Enter value of services rendered only when required by specific ticketing instructions.
3. *Tour Features:* Enter services included in the packages as specified in the tour.
4. *Hotel Details:* Check the type of hotel company purchased.
5. *Number of Nights:* Enter number of nights purchased at hotel.
6. *In/out Date:* Enter check in and check out date at hotel.
7. *Arrival Flight/Date:* Enter the arrival airline flight number and date.
8. *Departure Flight/Date*: Enter the departure airline flight member and date.
9. *Commission:* Enter applicable commission code (maximum) allowed commission is 10 per cent of final payment).
10. *Net Remittances:* Enter dollar amount to be remitted on travel agency sales reports.
11. *Total Tour Cost:* Enter total value of tour (this amount should equal total coupon valuer of coupon values are required by specified ticketing instructions).
12. *Less Deposit:* When prior deposit has been made, enter total amount of deposit and insert MCO member in Form of Payment 'box'.
13. *Final Payment:* Enter total value of tour (less deposit where applicable).
14. *Equivalent Amount Paid:* If payment is made with other than US dollars, enter equivalent amount of currency presented and the three letters, Alpha Currency Code.
15. *Form of Payment:* Enter form of payment used to purchase tour *e.g.* cash, cheque, credit card number etc. Also enter deposit MCO number if applicable.

16. *Air Ticket Issued:* Enter air ticket(s) issued in connection with tour order.
17. *Issued in Exchange For:* Enter appropriate member only when issued in exchange for another tour order or Miscellaneous Change Order (MCO).
18. *Date and Place of Original Issue:* Show date and place of original issue of tour order or MCO (used only when tour order is issued in exchange for another tour order or MCO).

Example:

Below is a blank Tour Order for travel agents with numbered column. You are to specify the required information to be filled therein.

A Standard Tour Order for Travel Agents (Ref. Figure 7.29).

Solution:

Item

1. A Date of Issue/Issued by – Validate with same carrier ID plate used to issue passenger(s) air ticket(s); the agent's validation plate; and the current date.
2. Bill to Tour Operator – Enter name of tour operator.
3. Tour Code – Enter approved tour code as shown in Manual.
4. Tour Name – Enter name of tour.
5. Passenger's Name – Enter passenger's first initial and last name.
6. Party of – Enter total number in party.

Coupon 1

7. Present to – Enter name of airport transfer company or rental car company and name of city where service will commence.
8. Value – Enter value of services rendered only when required by specific ticketing instructions

Coupon 2

9. Present to – Enter name of tour operator or hotel as specified in ticketing instructions and name of city where tour commences.
10. Value – Enter value of services rendered only when required by specific ticketing instructions.

STANDARD TOUR ORDER FOR TRAVEL AGENTS

BILL NO. 2	NAME OF TOUR OPERATOR		TOUR CODE IT 3	AUDITOR'S COUPON	8050:000:001
TOUR NAME 4			DATE OF ISSUE 12 APR 79	TOTAL TOUR COST 21	PLACE OF ISSUE—AGENCY 1 – A
PASSENGER NAME 5	NOT TRANSFERABLE	FTP OF 6		LESS DEPOSIT 22	
CPN	PRESENT TO	AT	VALUE	FINAL PAYMENT 23	
1	7		8	EQIV. AMOUNT PAID 24	AMOUNT TICKET NUMBER 26
2	9		10		
3	11		12	COMM. RATE 10	ISSUED ON EXCHANGE FOR 27
4	11		12	FORM OF PAYMENT 25	DATE AND PLACE OF O.R.G. ISSUE 28
TOUR FEATURES 13					ISSUE BY 1
HOTEL DETAILS: ☐ SINGLE ☐ DOUBLE 14 ☐ TWIN ☐ OTHERS...............		COMMISSION 19	NET PERMITTANCE TAX 20		
NUMBER OF FLIGHTS	IN DATE 16 / OUT DATE		O	||"8050000001 0||"	
ARRIVAL FLIGHT DATE 17	DEPARTURE FLIGHT DATE 18				

IT IS UNLAWFUL TO PURCHASE OR RESELL THIS TICKET FROM/TO ANY ENTITY OTHER THAN THE ISSUING CARRIER OR ITS AUTHORISED AGENTS.

Fig. 7.29: Specimen of a Standard Tour Order for Travel Agents.

Coupons 3 & 4

11. Present to – Enter name and location of airport transfer company or additional services provided in the tour.
12. Value – Enter value of services rendered only when required by specific ticketing instructions.
13. Tour Features – Enter services included in the package as specified in tour.
14. Hotel Details – Check the type of hotel occupancy purchased.
15. Number of nights – Enter number of nights purchased at hotel.
16. In/Out Date – Enter check-in and check-out dates at hotel.
17. Arrival Flight/Date – Enter the arrival airline flight number and date.
18. Departure Flight/Date – Enter the departure airline flight number and date.
19. Commission – Enter applicable commission code (maximum allowable commission is 10% of final payment).
20. Net Remittance – Enter dollar amount to be remitted on travel agency sales report.
21. Total Tour Cost – Enter total value of tour (this amount should equal total coupon values if coupon values are required by specific ticketing instructions).
22. Less Deposit – When prior deposit has been made, enter total amount of deposit, and insert MCO number in "Form of Payment" box (see item 25).
23. Final Payment – Enter total value of tour (less deposit when applicable).
24. Equivalent Amount Paid – If payment is made with other than U.S. dollars, enter equivalent amount of currency presented and the three-letter ALPHA currency code.
25. Form of Payment – Enter form of payment used to purchase tour, *e.g.*, cash, check, credit card number, etc. Also enter deposit MCO number if applicable.
26. Air Ticket(s) Issued – Enter air ticket(s) issued in connection with tour order.
27. Issued in Exchange for – Enter appropriate number only when issued in exchange for another tour order or miscellaneous charges order (MCO).

28. Date and Place of Original Issue – Show date and place of original issue of tour order or MCO. (Used only when tour order is issued in exchange for another tour order or MCO).

TICKET REVALIDATION

Sometimes due to the schedule change or an unexpected change in a client; travel plan may necessitate a flight change. If the ticket has already been issued, it may be possible to revalidate the ticket, instead of re-issuing on exchanging it. To revalidate a ticket, an adhesive level, called a revalidation sticker, is fixed to the flight coupon by a ticket agent or a travel agent. The label is applied so that it covers the segment to be modified. The carrier, flight class, date and time of the new segments are written on the label, a separate label is required for each segment to be changed. Revalidation labels can only be used if there is no change in routing, fare or class of service. A ticket with a domestic itinerary can sometimes be revalidated on a different carrier. However, an international ticket can only be revalidated on the same carrier.

CHARTERED AND GROUP TRAVEL

Revolutionary changes are taking place in the travel industry resulting in reducing air travel costs and making travel arrangements more convenient. Chartered and group travel are very common and are available to the general public. These travel enable clients to take advantage of the benefits of group travel at substantially reduced rates. Most of the important airlines like PANAMA, TWA, United American, Air France etc. have planes for charter. These airlines act as a wholesaler. They sell block of tickets on one flight to a charter operator. The chartered operators set their own price as such there is lot of competition among them. All schedule airlines have same prices/rates except when wholesaling a plainfull of tickets to charter operator. Most of the charter flight/programmes are offered by scheduled on supplemented airlines. Traditionally, chartered vacation are sold on a round trip basis and operate on fixed schedules. The dates are fixed and the departure itinerary not be known at the time of booking. Travellers are not allowed to extent their stays and must choose well in advance trip packages based on scheduled which are offered with deviations. One of the most important benefit of the chartered flight is that the client receives immediate confirmation of flights and hotel arrangements which otherwise might be difficult or impossible to secure. Transfers, porterage, gratuities and taxes are included in these package tours. Arrangements are made and confirmed in advance, usually with the large financial obligations by the tour operator. Reliability of departures of charters is similar to scheduled flights. As regards to assignment of hotel room it depends on the availability in the hotel at the time of arrival. It is not possible to designate specific location of rooms in advance. All ingredients and conditions of charter programme *i.e.,* booking procedures, cancellations and deviations are carefully stipulated in the brochures. All the travellers are encouraged to purchase the available low cost insurance coverage to guard against loss of baggage and unexpected health emergences, and purchase air fare protector insurance coverage provides protection against unexpected cancellations of postponement of trip due to medical reasons.

Travel industry is encouraged to simplify and lower cost. A first step in the mass travel age was the 'Advance Booking Charter' (ABC) regulation in October 1986. It permitted competition in the air travel market including the maximum charges.

Types of Charter Tours

Some of the most available types of flights or charter tours are as follows:

1. *Advance Booking Charter* (ABC): It refers to airline fare only but may include land arrangements.
2. *Affinity Group on Charter Flight* (AFF): It is available only to bonafide affinity groups with a maximum of 20-40 passengers.
3. *Apex or Super Apex or Advance Purchase Excursion* (APX): These are heavily discounted excursion fares which require booking and ticketing well in advance of departure. There is penalty for cancellation after tickets have been purchased. No land arrangements are required. Fares offered only on schedule carrier for trips includes restrictions *i.e.,* 14-15 days, full payment must be made in advance and there is cancellation penalty.

Group Travel

Group Inclusive Tour (GIT)

These are available through tour operators of airlines. Some group fares require purchase of land packages.

Inclusive Tour Charter (*ITC*)

It means a non-affinity charter with tour programme elements in a pre-planned itinerary including hotel accommodation: sight-seeing tours, meals, etc. It includes air fares, land package and minimum of three package destination per programme.

Inclusive Tour Excursion Fare (*ITX*)

This is available to schedule flights only. Price usually includes air fee and ground/hotel packages.

Non-affinity Group Fare (*NAG*)

It is operated on schedule services.

One Stop Inclusive Charter (*OTC*)

It includes air fare and land package to one destination. It may also include more than one destination.

Public Charters (*PUB*)

It refers to charter flights open to all with affinity or group size requirements. Advance purchase is not required. One way flight is usually available. Optional return dates may be offered by chartered operation.

Super Saver Fare (*SVR*)

It is a discounted fare on scheduled airline service. Advance booking and payments required.

QUESTIONS AND DISCUSSIONS

Objective Type

Q. 1. *Read each of the following statement. Write 'T' if the statement is true or 'F' if the statement is false:*

1. The code XF in a tax box indicates a custom user fee.
2. A PTA can only be used for domestic travel.
3. An MCO may be issued for an airport transfer, hotel accommodations, or a tour.
4. The code XU in a tax box indicates the transportation tax paid by the passenger.
5. NN is entered in the status box if a reservation has been requested but has not yet been confirmed.
6. On a hand ticket, a stop-over indicator must be written before each off point from which a continuing flight departs.

7. The auditor's coupon and agent's coupon are kept by the issuing agency for accounting purposes.
8. The name of the issuing carrier appears at the bottom of the ticket.
9. The ticket cannot be used for passage until it has been imprinted with the identification plate of the issuing airline.
10. If an itinerary requires six segments 2-multiple-part & ticket booklet would be used.

Q. 2. Below is sample ticket and answer the following questions:

1. What airline is the validating carrier?
2. What is the name of the issuing agency?
3. What is the fare bases?
4. What is the total fare, including tax?

Q. 3. In each of the following sentences, write the correct word or phrase that belong to each blank:

1. When a passenger pays for an air travel by credit card, a .... is filled out to record the transaction.
2. A .... is negotiable document which may be used for air or surface transportation, land arrangements, hotel accommodations, deposits, and other payments.
3. The ticket is validated with two identification plates, an identifying the .... and the other identifying. The ....
4. When a ticket that was originally purchased by credit card is returned for refund, a .... is prepared.
5. The .... of the origin city is entered in the form block on each itinerary line. For cities served by multiple airports, the .... is written in this block.
6. Tickets are issued on .... issued by the IATA.
7. A ticket is validated when the .... and .... are imprinted on the ticket with an identification plate supplied by the carrier.
8. The .... is located on the upper left corner of the ticket, immediately beneath the name of the validating carrier. Any important .... or cancellation penalties pertaining to the ticket appears in this box.
9. The .... box may be used to show any tariff restrictions, record or waited listed flight, endorse the ticket to a different carrier, or cross reference tickets under .... travel rules.

SAMPLE TICKET

Passenger Ticket and Baggage Check Issued by—
MURCURY TRAVEL

Subject to condition contained in the ticket

ORIGIN ....

7777:000:4564

Endorsement and Restriction

IATA Agent Coupon

VOID

Subject to Fee

Date of issue

Destination

For Training Purpose Only

Passenger Name GAURAV M/NEGI

Not Transferable

Issued in Exchanged

24 Feb

X/O	From		Carrier	Flight/ Class	Date	Time	Status	Fare Basis/ Ticket Designator	Not valid before	Not valid after	Allowance
O	To	**Washington**	A	**316 B**	**24 Feb**	**900 A**	OK	**BAP 3**			
O	To	**Dallas FT Worth**	A	**874 B**	**28 Feb**	**104 P**	OK	**BAP 3**			
O	To	**Richmond**	A	**95 B**	**4 Mar**	**103 P**	OK	**BAP 3**			
O	To	**Dallas FT Worth**	A	**813 B**	**4 Mar**	**410 P**	OK	**BAP 3**			
O	To	**Washington**									

Fare ....

Fare calculations ....

Equl. Amt. PD **Rs. 15,000**

24 Feb WAS AA–XDFW AA RIC 7500.00 AA–XDFW AA was 7500 TL 15,000

Tax ....

....

Tax **Rs. 1,500**

Total **Rs. 16,500**

Form of Payment

Check Approval Code Tour Code Airline CK Commission Tax Comm. Rate

A/L Agent No. ....

Control No. ....

005 7777:000:4564

Fig. 7.30: Specimen of a Sample Ticket.

Q. 4. From the following list of terms, write the letter of the word, phrase or name next to the concept/definition that best matches it below:

A Ticket Validator
B Airline Ticket
C Ticket Stock
D Endorsement Restriction Box
E Conjunction Tickets
F Passenger Receipt
G Refund/Exchange Notice (REN)
H Cash Refund/Exchange Notice (REN)
I Revalidation Sticker
J Flight Coupon
K Prepaid Ticket Advice
L Miscellaneous Charge Order (MCO).

1. A form that authorise a ticket to be issued at a different location than the location where the ticket is purchased.
2. A box on the face of a ticket that is to indicate if the ticket is non-refundable or if a penalty applies for cancellation or change.
3. A form that is prepared when a passenger returns a ticket to a travel agency for a cash refund.
4. A general purpose traffic document that may be issued for air or surface transportation, supplemental charges, a tour deposit, or a car rental.
5. A legal contract between an air carrier and a passenger, entitling the bearer, at a stated fare, to travel on one or more specified flights.
6. Multiple ticket booklets issued for one itinerary.
7. A term that refers to standard ticket form issued by IATA.
8. The portion of a ticket that lists all the flight segments for which flights coupons have been issued and serves as a proof that the passenger has paid for a fare, but is not valid for passage.
9. A form that is prepared when a ticket that was purchased by a credit card is returned for refund.
10. A portion of a ticket that entitles the passenger to board a flight.
11. An adhesive ticket that is affixed to a flight coupon by a ticket agent or travel agent to change an air segment.
12. A machine that is used to imprint the airline identification and agency identification in the proper places on the ticket.

Ans.: A-12; B-5; C-7; D-2; E-6; F-8; G-9; H-3; I-11; J-10; K-1; L-4.

Q. 5. *In each of the following sentences, write the correct word or phrase that belongs in each blank:*

1. The issuing information includes the name of the .... which applied the imprints plates used to validate the ticket. Other issuing information includes the .... and name and location of the travel agency that issued the ticket.
2. For domestic fares, the standard agency commission is .... per cent. The normal itinerary agency commission is .... per cent.
3. A standard ticket booklet has a maximum of .... flight coupon. For itineraries requiring more coupons multiple .... are used.
4. Each ticket is supplied in booklet form and consists of cover, a green .... coupon, a pink .... coupon, ... coupons and passenger receipt.
5. A ticket may be exchanged either by .... the original ticket and issuing a new ticket or by preparing a ....
6. The status code .... indicates a confirmed reservation. .... is entered if the reservation has been requested but not yet confirmed. The status code .... is used for an infant's ticket.
7. A separate .... is issued for each air segment in the itinerary.
8. When a passenger return all or part of a ticket for a refund, a .... is prepared

Q. 6. *In each of the following sentences, write the correct word or phrase that belongs in each blank:*

1. The 'Not Valid Before' and 'Not Valid After' blocks are used to indicate the .... or ....of a special fare.
2. The ticket numbers must be in .... order multiple ticket form used to ticket the same itinerary are referred to as .... tickets.
3. A .... is applied to a flight coupon to change an itinerary segment.
4. On a hand ticket, in the fare calculation, an open jaw is indicated by a .... in the city code block where the break occurs.
5. The fare ladder must be completed if .... tickets are

issued; if tickets are issued in exchange for portion of another ticket; if a .... applies; or if an .... itinerary is being ticketed.

6. The supply of unused ticket stock kept on the premises is normally limited to ....
7. The code .... before the originating city indicates a connecting city, and code .... indicates a stopover.
8. A .... is an authorization to a carrier permitting a ticket to be issued at places other than the issuing agency.
9. The agency validating information appears in the .... box.
10. A ticket is a .... between the carrier and the passenger, bearing a monetary value.

Q. 7. *Match each traffic document with the correct use or purpose.*

Card Ticket	1	Conjunction Ticket
Four Flight Booklet	2	Change Itinerary Segment
MCO	3	Issue Credit Card Ticket
Refund/Exchange Note	4	Computer Printed Ticket
Revalidation Label	5	Issue Ticket Elsewhere
PTA	6	Hotel Room Deposit
Two-flight booklet	7	Two Segment Itinerary
	8	Refund Ticket for Cash or Issue New Ticket for Old.

Q. 8. *Given here is a sample schedule:*

To SEATTLE, WASH B-BFI (BOEING FIELD) S-SEA (SEATTLE/ TACOMA)							PDT SEA
SEA							
14	0	MI	S	25 MIN		I	$2.00 RA
					BFI		
5	0	MI	S	25 MIN		I	$1.50 RA

(*a*) Looking at the "To Sea" listing above, how many miles is the airport (SEA) from the city and in what direction? ....

(*b*) What ground transportation is available, in addition to rental cars and Air Taxi? ....

(*c*) How much does it cost? ....

Ans.: (*a*) *14.0 miles south*

(*b*) *Limousine*

(*c*) *$2.00.*

Q. 9. *Read each of the following statements and write 'T' if the statement is true or 'F' if it is false:*

1. Cabin space is determined, in part, by whether a both or shower is provided.
2. A rate guarantee is a promise to refund the fare if the passenger finds a lower fare offered by another cruise line.
3. Cruise lines offer substantial discounts of reservations made and paid at least three months before the date of sailing.
4. Most add-on airfares are higher than the airline's published fares.
5. Lower decks experience more rocking motion at sea.
6. Luxury cruises offer the longest itineraries.
7. Speciality cruises account for about 60 per cent of all cruise revenues.

Q. 10. *Read each of the following statements and write 'T' if the statement is true or 'F' if it is false:*

1. Volume cruise lines emphasize short itineraries and show turn over.
2. The option date is the schedule sailing date.
3. Late summer and autumn are the low season for Caribbean cruises.
4. Inside cabins are the most expensive.
5. The terms cabin and state room both refer to sleeping rooms on a cruise ship.
6. The term turn over refers to the number of times that new passengers are brought on a board.
7. The destinations at which a ship docks are called port authorities.

Q. 11. *From the following list of terms write the letter of the world, phrase, or name next to the concept/definition that best matches it below:*

A Share Excursion
B Share basis
C Luxury cruises
D Queen Mary
E Deck Plan
F Early seating
G King Charles IV of Sweden

1. The European head of state who launched the first cruise ship in 1821.
2. A diagram of the layout of a cruise ship, showing the location of state rooms and public room on each deck.

3. A land-based tour that can be booked on board a cruise ship or in advance through a tour operator.
4. An arrangement by which a passenger travelling alone shares cabin fare with another single passenger.
5. The cruise category that provides passengers with highest level of luxury and service.
6. The first great 'floating hotel', which was modified to transport British troops during World War II.
7. The dinner seating referred on evenings with featured entertainment in the main lounge.

Q. 12. From the following list of terms write the letter of the world, phrase, or name next to the concept/definition that best matches it below:

A	Air/Sea package	E	Part of Call
B	Embarkation point	F	Volume cruises
C	Stateroom or Cabins Guide	G	OAG World of Shipline.
D	Volume or mass market cruises		

1. A printed reference for searching cruises.
2. A cruise package that includes airfare as well as passage
3. A port at which a cruise ship/ships along its itinerary.
4. The point from which a cruise ship departs.
5. The cruise category that includes both budget and standard cruise.
6. Sleeping room on a cruise ship.
7. The largest segment of the cruise industry.

Q. 13. In each of the following sentences, write the correct word or phrase that belongs in each blank:

1. The term refers to an arrangement whereby a single passenger pays half the double rate by sharing a cabin with another passenger.
2. Passengers who .... have priority are those who pay only a deposit.
3. After receiving verbal confirmation, a cruise passenger must pay a deposit within a some limited days. The dead line is referred to as ....
4. The most popular cruise destinations for North American Travellers include the Caribbean, Bermuda, the Bahamas, the Panama Canal, Mexico, Canada .... and ....

5. A .... includes air travel as well as cruise ship passage. With such a package the .... itinerary may not be known until 30 days prior to sailing.
6. The term .... refers to the city from which the cruise ship departs.
7. It is customary to tip the dining room steward Rs. .... and the bus boy Rs. ....
8. Although the price of a cruise includes almost all costs, some costs such as port taxes, liquor, shore .... tipping, laundry, and .... are usually not covered.

Q. 14. *In each of the following sentences, write the correct word or phrase that belongs in each blank:*

1. On most ships, public rooms, such as the dining rooms and recreational facilities, are located on ....
2. Whereas mass-market ships emphasize quick .... luxury lines feature long itineraries and exotic destination.
3. Cabins with bunk beds are suitable for .... and ....
4. Cabin selection depends on the client's budget, ... and ....
5. Sleeping rooms on a cruise ship are called .... or ....
6. Whereas mass-market ships emphasize quick .... luxury lines feature long itineraries and exotic destinations.
7. .... Cruises, which are also called Upscale Cruises, represent one of the largest segment of the cruise industry.

Q. 15. *Identify the person/word/phrase for each of the following concepts:*

1. A point from which a cruise ship departs.
2. An arrangement by which a passenger travelling alone shares cabin fares with another single passenger.
3. A port at which a cruise ship stops along its itinerary.
4. A land-based tour that could be booked on board a cruise ship or in advance through tour operator.
5. A diagram of the layout of a cruise ship, sharing the location of store rooms and public rooms on each deck.
6. The European head of the state who launched the first cruise ship in 1821.
7. The first great 'floating hotel' which was modified to transport British troops during World War II.

8. The cruise category that includes both budget and standard cruises.
9. The cruise category that provides passengers with the highest level of luxury and service.
10. The largest segment of the cruise industry.
11. Sleeping room on a cruise ship.

Ans.:

1. Embarkation point	*6. King Charles IV of Sweden*
2. Share basis	*7. Queen Mary*
3. Port of call	*8. Volume or Mass-market Cruises*
4. Share excursion	*9. Luxury Cruises*
5. Deck Plan	*10. Volume Cruises*
	11. State rooms or Cabins.

Q. 16. From the following list of terms, write the letter of the word, phrase or name next to the concept/definition that best matches it below:

A	Voucher	L	Airline space
B	Tariffs	M	Selling Airline Space
C	Itinerary	N	Prepaid Ticket Advice (PTA)
D	To quote a fare	O	Settlement Account
E	Conference	P	Inhouse Agency
F	Auxiliary segments	Q	American Society of Travel Agents (ASTA)
G	OAG		
H	Appointment on accreditation	R	Surety Bond
		S	Antitrust laws
I	Freebased pricing	T	Air Transport Conference (ATC)
J	Sales Agency Agreement		
K	Base fare	U	To request price information.

1. The number of seats reserved for a particular party.
2. A reference tool published bi-monthly that lists the schedules of all regularly scheduled airline flights.
3. To communicate the correct price for air travel based on the client's situation and needs.
4. In most cases, why does a prospective client first contact a travel agency?
5. A special bank account in which revenues from ticket sales are deposited for distribution to the airlines.
6. Printed references containing airfares.
7. The act of booking an airline reservation.
8. A list of point to point flights required to complete a trip.
9. A document issued to a travel vendor indicating that the client has prepaid for the vendor's service.

10. The organisation formed by domestic carriers to create industry-wide standards and account for revenues from ticket sales by travel agencies.
11. An association of travel agencies.
12. The practice of charging for consultation services, in addition to the cost of airline tickets and other travel products.
13. The total fare for air travel, excluding taxes or surcharge.
14. An agreement that requires a travel agency to maintain business, ethical and professional standards and to transact a sufficient amount of business.
15. Official approval to sell airline tickets.
16. A sum of money deposited in a bank account as a guarantee to fulfill certain financial obligation.
17. Laws aimed at assuring free competition in business and preventing the formation of monopolies.
18. A notification to an airline that a client has prepaid for a ticket.
19. A department or division of a company set up to handle the travel requirements of the company's employees.
20. Non-air reservations such as hotel reservations and car rentals.
21. An organisation formed by companies within the same industry to set up voluntary organisation.

Q. 17. *Identify the person/word/phrase for each of the following concepts:*

1. A legal contract between an air carrier and a passenger, entitling the bearer, at a stated fare, to travel on one or more specified flights.
2. A term that refer to standard ticket forms issued by IATA.
3. A machine that is used to imprint the airline identification and agency identification in the proper places on the ticket.
4. The portion of a ticket that entitles the passenger to board a flight.
5. The portion of a ticket that lists all the flight segments for which flight coupons have been issued and serves as a proof that the passenger has paid the fare, but is not valid for passage.
6. Multiple ticket booklets issued for one itinerary.
7. The box on the face of a ticket that is to indicate if the ticket is non-refundable or if a penalty applies for cancellation or a change.

8. A form that authorises a ticket to be issued at a different location than the location where the ticket is purchased.
9. A form that is prepared when a passenger returns a ticket to a travel agency for a cash refund.
10. A form that is prepared when ticket that was purchased by credit cards is returned for a refund.
11. A general purpose traffic document put may be issued for air or surface transportation, supplemental charges, a tour deposit or a car rental.
12. An adhesive label that is fixed to a flight coupon by a ticket agent or travel agent to change an air segment.

Ans.:
1. *Airline Ticket*
2. *Ticket Stock*
3. *Ticket Validator*
4. *Flight Coupon*
5. *Passenger Receipt*
6. *Conjunction Tickets*
7. *Endorsements/restrictions*
8. *Prepaid Ticket Advice (PTA)*
9. *Refund/Exchange Notice (REN)*
10. *Refund/Exchange Notice (REN)*
11. *Miscellaneous Charge Voucher (MCV)*
12. *Revalidation Sticker.*

Essay Type

Q. 18. If your trip includes destinations in the Caribbean, South Pacific, Mexico, or the Mediterranean, consider a cruise for a portion of the itinerary. Decide on a budget, time allowance, ship and type of accommodations. Selected several cruises, and select one for your FIT. Write down the following information for the cruise segment of the itinerary:

1. Cruise line
2. Departure city
3. Departure date
4. Type of accommodation
5. Cost.

Q. 19. What is the difference between the ship's crew and the hotel's crew?

Q. 20. Explain the four components of the cruise programme.

Q. 21. In what way do government promote and regulate the cruise industry?

Q. 22. Answer the following:

(*a*) After a crew has been booked, what happens on the option date?

(*b*) How would deck level affect cabin selection?

(*c*) Why did the big ships of the early twentieth century begin operating vacation cruises during winter months.

(*d*) Explain what is meant by the term share basis.

(*e*) What factor influence variable costs?

(*f*) What is the advantage to volume cruise lines of a high turn over rate?

(*g*) What information is required to book a crew?

(*h*) For what type of passengers is the late dinner seating recommended?

(*i*) What factors influence the 'personality' of a cruise ship?

Q. 23. Discuss the advantages and disadvantages of a cruise in comparison with a land-based vacation.

Q. 24. Discuss the advantages and disadvantages of a volume, luxury, and speciality cruises.

Index